Health and Social

for NVQ/SVQ level 4 and Foundation degrees

Frances Sussex   David Herne   Peter Scourfield

www.heinemann.co.uk

✓ Free online support
✓ Useful weblinks
✓ 24 hour online ordering

01865 888080

054845

Heinemann is an imprint of Pearson Education Limited, a company incorporated in England and Wales, having its registered office at Edinburgh Gate, Harlow, Essex, CM20 2JE. Registered company number: 872828

www.heinemann.co.uk

Heinemann is a registered trademark of Pearson Education Limited

Text copyright © Frances Sussex, Peter Scourfield and David Herne 2008

First published 2008
12 11 10 09 08
10 9 8 7 6 5 4 3 2 1

British Library Cataloguing in Publication Data is available
from the British Library on request.

ISBN: 978 0 435 500 07 8

Edited by Linda Mellor/Bruce Nicholson
Designed by Tony Richardson
Typeset by Saxon Graphics Limited, Derby
Original illustrations © Pearson Education Limited, 2008
Picture research by Caitlin Swain
Cover design by Pearson Education Limited, 2008
Cover photo by Pearson Education Limited, 2008
Printed by Ashford Colour Press Ltd, UK

Acknowledgements

Every effort has been made to contact copyright holders of material reproduced in this book. Any omissions will be rectified in subsequent printings if notice is given to the publishers.

Photo acknowledgements

The authors and publishers would like to thank the following for permission to reproduce photographs:

© Bill Bachmann/Alamy; © Bubbles Photolibrary/Alamy; © Dennis MacDonald/Alamy; ©Getty Images/Chris Baker; © GmbH & Co.KG/Alamy; © Javier Corripio/Alamy; © Jethro Collins/Alamy; © Mark Jordan/Alamy; © Mary Evans Picture Library/Alamy; © Pearson Education Ltd/Jules Selmes; © Pearson Education Ltd/Lord & Leverett; © Pearson Education Ltd/Mindstudio; © Photofusion Picture Library/Alamy; © Stock Food Creative/ Getty Images; © Stuart Clarke/Rex; © UpperCut Images/Alamy; © www.pictureline.co.uk/Alamy

Contents

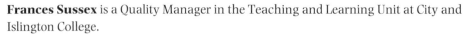

About the authors

Frances Sussex is a Quality Manager in the Teaching and Learning Unit at City and Islington College.

I have always had a commitment to care work, having worked in residential services for adults with learning disabilities for many years. After developing an interest in training I qualified as a teacher and have since worked with students of health and social care in Further Education and at University. I am now a Quality Manager in the Teaching & Learning Unit at City & Islington College and continue to learn a great deal from the diverse learners and innovative colleagues who I am privileged to work with. I also enjoy my role as External Examiner for the University of Essex Degrees in Health and Social Care at Colchester Institute. I am interested in developing teaching and learning strategies that benefit students and the service users that they support, and am currently undertaking research in this area. For six years my partner and I have enjoyed our role as respite carers for a young woman who is blind and has learning difficulties; she is a constant inspiration to us. Whilst I love living in London, I also enjoy escaping to the countryside for a long climb in the hills.

I am ever appreciative of the support and dedication shown to me by my wonderful partner Mike. With much thanks to Pen, Bruce, Juliet and Linda at Heinemann for their patience and continual support.

David Herne is a Consultant in Public Health currently working in the NHS in the Salford area. He has specialist experience working in the sexual health, alcohol and drugs fields as well as the school setting. He has previously managed a large health promotion service, working on a wide range of areas including nutrition and activity. Prior to this he worked within local government as a senior health policy lead in a unitary authority and before that as a health education officer in an environmental health team. He started life as a secondary school teacher in the biology and human and social biology subjects and has retained his interest in education through tutoring for the Open University on two courses, Understanding Health & Social Care and Promoting Health Skills Perspectives and Practice. A keen athlete he competes both in athletics and triathlons on a regular basis at home and abroad.

Peter Scourfield is a qualified social worker and currently works as Senior Lecturer in Social Policy, Institute of Health and Social Care at Anglia Ruskin University.

Introduction

These are exciting times for those who work in health and social care. Everyday there are news items that relate to our work; most people will come into contact with a health and social care worker at some point in their lives, either with their own need for support, or for that of a relative or friend.

Providing care services has never been straight forward. On 5th July 2008 it was the 60th anniversary of the National Health Service (NHS). Reports around the organisation and financing of health and care services are still prominent, alongside debates on whether individuals should be entitled to innovative interventions. Research and technology provides us with more options for improving the circumstances and support that individuals can receive through health and social care providers.

This momentum of change also ensures that the care workforce have continued challenges. *Options for Excellence: Building the Social Care Workforce of the Future* (Department of Health 2006) established a vision for all care workers for 2020. This commitment recognises the significance of the health and social care workforce now and in the future. We know that you are part of that future.

This book aims to contribute to that vision by being a key text for your professional and academic development. We have designed it so that it can be used in a number of ways:

- **As a study guide if you are doing a qualification:**
  to develop your understanding of subjects with structured activities and also to prompt your ability to produce evidence towards your NVQ, Foundation Degree or any other care related award
- **As a support for your own professional development in your health and social care career:**
  to improve your practice by being more knowledgeable and skilled in what you do
- **As a manual for the workplace:**
  as a useful resource to refer to when queries arise.

The Contents page provides an indication of what you will discover in the chapters. The book covers all aspects of health and social care and is especially useful for anyone working in mental health, learning disability services or with older people. You may decide to read these chapters in turn but they can also be a useful resource to refer to in any order, either when you are studying particular topics on your course, or when issues arise in your work that you need some guidance with. The Features guidance on the next page will help you in maximising your use of the book.

We hope you enjoy reading the book and wish you every success in both your qualification and in your career.

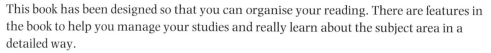

Features of this book

This book has been designed so that you can organise your reading. There are features in the book to help you manage your studies and really learn about the subject area in a detailed way.

You may want to read the **Appendix: Study skills** first to prepare you for study. If you are a confident learner familiar with study then this section may give you some useful tips to improve your study. **Chapter 11 Research methods** supports all the other chapters as it provides the foundation for your continued learning beyond this book. When you are working your way through other chapters research skills will enable you to respond.

Reflect

You will learn new things in each section of the book and the Reflect will help you to stop and think about the topic in a way that deepens your understanding. Having acquired new knowledge you need time to process your thoughts so that you can use this new information to good effect. Reflection in Action, Study Skills and Research sections will teach you about the importance of reflection and give you strategies to reflect.

Activity

These tasks will extend your knowledge of the subject. By completing the Activity you will be stretched a little further in the topic. Writing your responses to these may produce evidence for your portfolios. Sometimes they require you to investigate an aspect of health and social care yourself and this is where developing your own research skills will be useful.

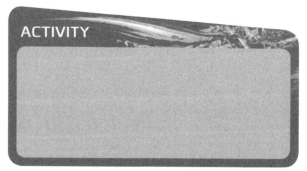

Case Study

Some Case Studies are scenarios to illustrate a theme or topic and to enable you to consider what you have been reading about. They give you the opportunity to think about what you have been reading and apply it to the care situation in a more meaningful way. Some case studies are of people, and the questions afterwards will develop your ability to manage similar scenarios when they arise in your own practice. Other case studies are of organisations; reading these will inform you more broadly of the organisation and delivery of care nationwide. After reading these case studies it will be useful for you to research your local organisations for similar information.

Knowledge Check

This book is a very enjoyable read but it is also a key resource for your development. The Knowledge Checks will ensure that you consolidate what you have been learning about it in each section before you rush on to read the next. They remind you of what each section has been about, and help you to link the topics together so that you are clearly informed and can apply this new knowledge to your own care practice.

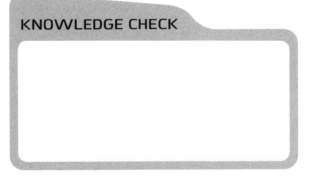

Mapping Framework

This book is invaluable for anyone undertaking a health and social care qualification. If you are doing an NVQ then there is a mapping framework for these two Occupational Standards at the back of the book:

- NVQ Health and Social Care level 4
- Leadership and Management

Writing up your responses to the features as you are progressing through the book will provide evidence for your portfolio against these awards.

If you are on a Foundation Degree the Features will be useful when you are undertaking some of your assignments. Reflecting on your work-related learning is a key feature of Foundation Degrees and writing up your responses will evidence your reflection for your portfolio. Many Foundation Degrees require you to maintain a journal of your work practice and learning from the work place and all these Features will enable you to do that in a more structured way.

We hope this helps you plan your use of the book. The aim is that you develop in all aspects of your care practice, your knowledge, your skills and your professional understanding.

CHAPTER 1

The context of health and social care

Introduction

This chapter introduces you to the context of care – the political, social and economic factors that influence the organisation and provision of these services.

It is important to acknowledge that all these influences are very fluid; they change all the time. As care workers we need to be aware of current issues and debates about care provision so that we are up to date. The nature of care-related activity is always being reviewed, as seen in the rest of this book; and because of this the structure of services is affected.

The legislation and policies in this chapter relate to England, as in recent years Wales and Scotland have developed more autonomy in decisions about care provision. In Wales the Welsh Assembly promotes policies within the boundaries of legislation passed in the Westminster Houses of Parliament. In Scotland devolution has facilitated the creation of law-making processes through the Scottish Parliament.

This chapter addresses the following areas:

- Factors influencing health and social care provision
- History of health and social care services
- Organisation of care services
- **Policy** making and implementation
- Provision of health and social care services
- Funding care provision
- **Regulation** and **enforcement** of quality in health and social care
- Issues in provision of care

After reading this chapter it is hoped you will be able to:

- understand the current organisation of care services
- consider issues relating to the provision of care services
- understand the range of factors that impact on care.

Factors influencing health and social care provision

Care relates to individual people, who, just like you and I, have numerous influences on their lives. In Chapter 4 we focus on individuals and what influences their lives and their experience of health and social care. In this section we focus more generally on the environment and social context that informs care provision.

Figure 1.1 Factors that impact on health and social care

Resources

Within central government the Treasury makes decisions about the allocation of resources to the health sector and to local authorities. They do this through:

- annual budget setting
- legislation regarding the transfer of funds between organisations
- legislation regarding the charges that health and social care organisations can charge for services.

The appropriateness and availability of facilities have a considerable impact on care. Some of the failings of the general policy of community care have been ascribed to the lack of facilities that were available to respond to this policy and the fact that the resources allocated were insufficient to compensate for the lack of already established facilities.

Professional skills

Staff are the most important resource in the care sector. The skills of professionals have an impact on the type of care that can be provided. The increased need for nursing care within the community has put pressure on district nursing services, and became an issue for domiciliary care services. This book explores what is required of the health and social care employee in terms of their skills and knowledge, and what policies have been developed to shape what we do in the professions. Skills for Care and Skills for Health have been researching what roles individuals should have in the health and social care sectors so that the changing needs and expectations of those who use services are met. The New Types of Worker project by Skills for Care provides some examples of innovative responses to care needs.

Existing organisation of services

The relationship of care services to other organisations has changed over the last decade as local authorities have organised service departments to suit local arrangements. The relationship between health services, social care services and other organisations is explored in Chapter 6 on collaborative working but brief mention here will help you to consider these when reading throughout this book.

Criminal justice system

The response of society and government to people who undertake illegal activity is often a balance between care and control, punishment and rehabilitation. Present approaches are placing a stronger emphasis on control, and this moves the criminal justice system away from other care services. Some people would benefit from a holistic approach to managing their re-integration into society through housing, education, benefits and employment. An example of an overlap of interests is in the use of illegal substances.

Financial welfare

Benefits sometimes provide a means for individuals accessing particular support.

There is a strong association between disability, older age and poverty. Many people do not claim the benefits that they are entitled to. This may be due to a number of factors including:

- stigma
- lack of understanding of the application process
- difficulty in completing forms because of problems with language, sight or cognitive ability
- inability to access information
- social iolation, which can mean that people are unaware of benefits to which they are entitled.

Children and Young People's Services

In some local authorities and Care **Trusts** the provision has been divided. The Special Educational Needs and Disability Act 2001 is the most recent legislation requiring children and adults to have their individual needs met in the education sector. This was supported by the *Valuing People* White Paper, which states that one aim is to 'help integrate disabled children into mainstream leisure and out of school services' (Department of Health, 2001, page 33).

Transitions from children services to adult services can be problematic. The Child and Adolescent Mental Health Service (CAMHS) was developed in response to gaps in the service for some adolescents with mental health needs.

> The Secretary for Health in January 2008 was Alan Johnson. He stated that the current reforms to re-organise health and social care were far-reaching:
>
> > Our success will no longer be measured by the synergy between Health and Social Care alone but the interchange between the NHS, housing, employment, education/training, leisure , transport and environmental service. (December, 2007)

Social environment

Demography

The age structure of the national and local population influences the numbers of people requiring care services compared to the potential income of national and local government from tax contributions by working age people. It can also affect how people perceive the need to support people and provide healthcare. We are often told of the 'age time bomb', as our population gets older and the public sometimes view increased longevity in a negative rather than a positive way.

> The Social Care Institute for Excellence (SCIE) has revealed obstacles to delivering social care in rural areas. It found that:
>
>> People in rural areas may be less well served by social care and health services. Social care services in rural areas generally don't provide the same level of service as those in towns and cities. Older people in rural areas are likely to be receiving lower levels of supportive services such as domiciliary care and meals on wheels than those in urban areas. (SCIE, 2007)

Many people who require care, or extra support in their lives, experience social exclusion. 'The poorest in society seem often not to have benefited greatly from government intervention in social and economic matters.' (Malin *et al*, 2002, page 44). Governments have a responsibility to make sure that people are provided with an environment that addresses these problems; the challenge for policy makers is in ensuring that the ideas and strategies that they come up with address what are known as the *determinants of ill-health and disability*.

The White Paper, *Modern Local Government: In touch with the People* made it clear that local authorities need to stop thinking that social care is separate from other activities in people's lives if they are to 'promote the economic, environmental and social well-being of all their citizens'. This reflects that a person's well-being cannot be secured through either housing or social services, but needs a more comprehensive and holistic approach.

Housing

There are several aspects to the relationship between housing and health and social care. People's circumstances are strongly influenced by their home situation. The ability to maintain good health and manage your own care is an important factor. In addition, care services are provided through the Supported Living agenda to promote appropriate housing solutions for people with mental health needs, or those who are learning disabled. Both the availability and the condition of housing have an influence on an individual's general health and ability to function well in managing everyday life. Someone in a rented damp bedsit, with neighbours who use drugs on the stairwell, has a completely different experience of 'home' from a person who has a choice over where they buy a new house.

Lifestyle

Lifestyle factors include behaviours that have a negative impact on the health of the population, such as smoking, alcohol and substance usage. People who use care or support services may find it difficult to manage areas of their lives, and this can develop into abuse or addiction to substances that are harmful to them.

Addiction can cause people to behave in ways that harm themselves or others. It can also have a negative impact on their physical or mental health, or lead them into illegal behaviour. The provision of services has sometimes been criticised for being judgemental about lifestyle. In the past, the use of vouchers to exchange for household provisions was interpreted as an indication of mistrust of some people's ability to choose appropriate purchases with money they would be receiving. Some Trusts have stated criteria for receiving services such as stopping smoking, or losing weight, before any intervention will commence. Society seems more approving of the use of these judgements in determining whether a person 'deserves' to receive support.

Legal framework

The delivery of care is affected by the laws that are in place to allow or require organisations to function in a certain way. The government introduces policy guidance and will ascertain whether they need to introduce a new Act of Parliament in order to implement the policy. Sometimes the legal framework, or indeed the use of it, is unclear to policy makers and their vision is not realised when organisations act; for example, the use of criteria by local authorities (discussed in Chapter 7 on assessment), or the exemption of private care homes from the human rights legislation (as discussed in Chapter 3).

Values and expectations of society

Communication methods have increased public awareness of what is happening in the national and local delivery of care services. As a nation we are no longer grateful recipients of whatever health and social care is available; we are generally proactive citizens who know our rights and entitlements and we actively pursue these. Discussions about whether someone can have life-saving heart treatment are replaced with debates on whether in-vitro fertilisation or cosmetic surgery should be free. Many people choose to pay for medical treatment without thinking twice about the efficacy of this in the context of national healthcare. One thing is clear; these debates are not going to be resolved easily as advances in health and social care intervention will raise the expectations of the public and create more dilemmas for governments and professionals

History of health and social care services

Nineteenth century

In the early part of the nineteenth century people were encouraged to support their own families, as structured provision outside family life was limited. Older people who were unable to look after themselves were cared for by their families, particularly their children. Those without appropriate family support were looked after in workhouses. These institutions provided accommodation and healthcare on the basis that the residents were still able to work; it was an early form of occupational welfare. It was a time when many charitable organisations were set up by philanthropists, who had the social position and wealth to help support the welfare of local people. Learning disabled people and

those with mental ill-health were ho[use]d [in] institutions known as asylums. Older p[eople were] gradually living longer during this perio[d and] older women were placed in the asylums b[ecause] there was nowhere else appropriate. Howeve[r a] rising infant mortality rate was an issue, so pu[blic] health gradually became a key issue in terms of housing, sanitation, etc.

The table below shows the numbers of people being cared for in asylums in the mid-nineteenth century.

People in asylums	1844	1860	1870
Total numbers of people in institutions	11, 272	23, 717	35, 163

The notion of the care that should be provided can be seen from the following quote about an institution for those with mental illness:

> It is a vast and straggling building… The gates are kept by an official who is attired in a garb as nearly as possible like that of a gaoler. All the male attendants are made to display the same forbidding uniform.
>
> (Mortimer Granville on Hanwell Asylum, London 1877, in Scull, 1979, page 195)

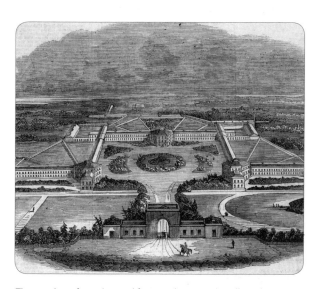

The number of people cared for in asylums rose rapidly in the nineteenth century

wentieth century

There was a growth in the development of hospitals at the end of the nineteenth century. In the twentieth century, after World War One, an opportunity to increase the use of local authority services by extending National Health Insurance was suggested but not taken up. In 1929 local authorities could take over the Poor Law 'infirmaries', as they were called, to create municipal hospitals; however, this only actually happened in London.

1900–1920

This period saw the origins of a structure to develop comprehensive social policies that covered a wide range of areas in people's lives. There had been an economic recession, which meant there was limited public provision of care; however this did not meet the demands of society. A concern for public health meant that housing and sanitation were given a priority as a means of improving the well-being of the population. A relationship was acknowledged between people's hygiene and cleanliness in their housing and public areas, and general health.

1920–1950

This period ended with the development of what was called the welfare state in Britain – the National Health Service (NHS) and the local authority structure for providing social care. World War Two had a huge impact on this country and the way in which succeeding governments approached welfare. The emergency medical services had been set up to respond to the many casualties of war. The idea of providing free healthcare was considered a good thing by all political parties. In 1942 the Beveridge Report on *Social Insurance and Allied Services* set out the aims of tackling the 'five giants' or 'social evils' of welfare. This was a comprehensive and holistic approach to developing the well-being of individuals.

A White Paper in 1944, *A National Health Service*, led to the 1946 National Health Service Act. Hospitals were nationalised under the control of the government, and a tripartite system of care was launched with:

- hospitals
- local authorities
- General Practitioners.

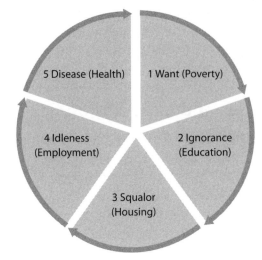

Figure 1.2 The five giants of welfare

The system focused on regional planning. Interestingly it had been envisaged that local authorities would play a leading role in co-ordinating the delivery of this structure, and that this would involve having responsibility for health centres, but for various reasons this did not happen. The focus of the government remained on the *acute* hospital sector; this was helped by developments at this time in both medical specialities and the availability of medicines. The NHS was also responsible for the *chronic* hospital sector where people with learning disabilities and mental ill-health lived separately from the rest of society and often since childhood. In these institutions there was a very different understanding of what support needs were, and individuals were managed rather than cared for; there was no notion of these individuals having rights.

1950s–1960s

Government spending on welfare increased during this period. This was encouraged by support from the public and by the need to care for those who had participated in the war.

1970s–1980s

The cost of delivering welfare under the NHS far exceeded the various estimates that were made between 1948 and 1974. After this time different governments sought to control these costs. During the 1980s the Conservative government decided to privatise welfare provision by introducing the idea of a *market approach* to delivering services, as they thought there were too many costs involved in local authorities directly providing care to people through the current system.

1990s

The Conservative government continued their marketisation policy to change the state monopoly of welfare. In addition to the majority of services being provided by the NHS and the local authority social services departments, the government encouraged private businesses to provide care. This has been continued by the subsequent Labour government.

1997 – present day

The Labour Party assumed power in 1997. Their political rhetoric was that they were introducing a 'third way' approach to care, balancing social provision for those in need whilst retaining and developing the market approach with private enterprise. Traditional socialist views promote the provision of support for those in need based on the redistribution of resources. These ideas are now contested. Political ideas may be based on the values of a political party but recent years have seen a changing emphasis.

REFLECT

When you thought about political issues earlier on you may have considered how these materialise into policy and the values that will influence both the overall idea of the policy and the detail. Questions may arise which will inform the development of policy such as:

a What responsibility should family members have for looking after their relatives?

b Should patients/service users have control over the support they receive?

c Who should pay for this service?

d Should this service be provided to everyone or just a few?

There is often a tension between central and local government as the former sets the agenda which establishes the framework and funding for local governments to deliver. Local governments obtain funds through local council taxes, or through central grants, and also (as recently exposed) through the collection of fines.

The Labour government (since 1997) has stated that it wants to promote a 'philosophy of devolution and earned autonomy' (Crown, 2002, page 32). It states that the government plans more local decision-making through local government, but there has also been accusations of more centralised presidential-type control.

REFLECT

How much did you know of the history of community care and asylums, for example? Did any of it surprise you?

CASE STUDY

Transition in community care

Freddie was born in 1942. At the time the doctors told his parents that he would not be able to do anything in his life as he was 'mentally retarded'. Freddie was placed in Willow Grange Hospital, a very large hospital in the countryside. He lived with other children and was cared for by nurses.

In 1992 Freddie moved from Willow Grange Hospital to a hostel, where he lived with 11 others; some of the people he had lived with at Willow Grange moved with him. Freddie attended a local day centre, he had a key worker and reviews, and this led him to identify that he wanted to move when an opportunity arose.

Freddie has now moved to a new home. He calls it his home as he helped to choose it. He lives just with two other men whom he gets on with most of the time. Although Freddie will always need support in his life, he has a very different experience from what he had in his early life.

Questions

1 Have improvements in the provision of health and social care really made a positive impact on Freddie's life?

2 Do you think that all the positive changes that have been made have had the intended impact on Freddie?

The development of community care

The development of community care was a particularly significant aspect of change in health and social care. Community care refers to the provision of support to people in the community rather than in hospitals or large institutions. The phrase 'in the community' can mean a number of things. It can mean people being cared for in their own homes and accessing the usual community-based care services, or living in accommodation set up for those who need care or support, sometimes known as residential services, or being cared for in homes which house groups of people who live together with support. In 1971 the Commission on Mental Illness recommended community care for 'people diagnosed as mentally ill and mentally handicapped' but this change never materialised and discussions about community care continued. There was limited provision of domiciliary care and meals on wheels by voluntary groups. Domiciliary care, now often known as home care, is central to community care if the aim is for individuals to live in their own homes with support. However, the policy in 1971, *Better Services for the Mentally Handicapped*, called for an expansion of residential homes, rather than discussing the planning of any new home-based services. This redefined community care to include residential care. The effect of this was that 39,000 new local authority homes were opened between 1948 and 1960,

predominantly for older people. This indicated a lack of a clear policy as to what community care was going to mean for individual service users. Discussions on community care ignored the role of informal carers and the need for a policy on how to support them in their role in providing community-based care.

A review of this policy came about due to public concern over the numbers of well-publicised scandals regarding treatment of individuals in large institutions, such as the exposure of bad practices at Ely Hospital in 1968.

The NHS was reluctant to close the long-stay mental health and learning disabled hospitals and it was only when Health Authorities were given a financial incentive by the Conservative government to close their large institutions and sell the land in the 1980s that the policy gathered momentum. However, the process has been much slower than was hoped. The *Valuing People* White Paper specified that learning disabled adults in institutions should be found alternative appropriate homes by April 2004, but this date had to be extended. Residential care is now mainly for older people and there are also alternatives provided, but these are often only available to those with geographical mobility, money and without any mental health considerations.

Not everyone has coped with transition so positively. For some people, the freedom of a large institution with open grounds has been exchanged for a small place with constant supervision due to the excessive number of risks that now surround them.

Although the idea of people living in the community is valued, there has been extensive criticism of the manner in which community care was introduced:

> Taken overall, the policy of care in the community failed because it left some people vulnerable, others a threat to themselves or a nuisance to others, with a small minority a danger to the public. With the dedication of staff it did, though, bring many beneficial changes to the care and treatment of people with mental illness. Sheltered employment and rehabilitation programmes were developed, and new drugs were discovered. During the past

thirty years, many people left the Victorian asylums for a better quality of life in their own neighbourhoods with support from community-based staff.

> (Department of Health, 1999, page 24)

Organisation of care services

Department of Health

The Department of Health is the central government department that has all responsibilities for health and social care. It devises an overall vision and strategy for how services should be organised in terms of national and local structure, funding arrangements, legal **powers** and **duties**. Most importantly, it determines priorities and shapes the relationship that you and I have with those organisations that deliver our health and social care.

ACTIVITY

1 Find out the names of the other departments in the Cabinet Office. Think about how the other departments might relate to the Department of Health in terms of their responsibilities.
2 Find out the name of your Member of Parliament (MP). Which political party do they represent?
3 Investigate local health and social care issues that your MP is currently engaged in (for example, closure of a department in the local hospital, the right of a local resident to access a particular service). What do you think are local political issues?

There is a contentious relationship between central government and the local organisations and authorities engaged in care. The organisation of services to deliver health and social care is subject to local variation and constant change so it is important for you to make effective use of live resources in order to check that your information is relevant and up to date.

In December 2007 the Health Secretary Alan Johnson made the following announcement about proposed changes to health and social care within the *Putting People First* agenda:

• Transfer of resources for Social Care for Adults with Learning Disabilities from Primary Care Trusts (PCTs) to local authorities from 2009/10. Local authorities will be expected to spend existing resources differently to ensure the health and well-being of their communities by working in a genuinely collaborative way with the third and private sector providers.
• NHS organisations to engage in 'authentic partnership' (not 'tick box') arrangements with other organisations on issues such as **commissioning**, local area agreements, co-located services, high-quality information and advice and personalised support packages including streamlined common assessments and workforce development.
• 'If we are to truly personalise public services we will have to finally make a reality of the long standing and often stated ambition to 'demolish the Berlin Wall between statutory agencies and their partners in the Third and Private Sectors.'

Next stage review

Alan Johnson stated that:

This concordat will demonstrate our determination to create a single health and well-being system in every community: a goal which can only be achieved through consistent national policy, effective local leadership and listening to the aspirations of those who use these services and their families.

There are five elements of the shared vision for transformation.

1 A new relationship between government, local authorities, the NHS, independent sector providers and the Regulator.
2 A major shift of resources and practice to prevention, early intervention and re-enablement.
3 High–quality accessible information and advice available to all irrespective of financial means.
4 A commitment to treating carers as partners, maximum power, control and choice in the hands of the people who use these services and their carers.
5 A major redistribution of power from the State to the citizen according with the fundamental human right to self-determination. This has the potential to be one of the most radical public service reforms for a generation: twenty-first century social justice with an active and empowering state, rather than one which is paternalistic and controlling.

Our Health, our Care, our Say White Paper

This introduces an important new stage in the reform programme with a vision to shift health and social care closer to people's homes. The White Paper expands the health reform programme to focus more on community services, with the aim of:

• better prevention services with earlier intervention
• more choice and involvement

- improved access to community services
- reduced inequalities
- more support for people with long-term needs.

The intention is a new direction for community services, as a central part of reform. It sets out fundamental changes for care outside hospitals, making sure care is not just more convenient but also more personalised, treating people as equal partners in their care and actively seeking their views. The government has stated the goal to be: **better, fairer health and social care for everyone.**

1 Patients and service users are given a greater say and more choice over where and when they receive their NHS care.
2 A wider range of high-quality, convenient and personalised services for patients to choose from.
3 Money to pay for treatment will follow each patient, so the best providers attract the most patients and the most money, while unresponsive or wasteful organisations are encouraged and supported to improve.
4 A clear set of rules and standards so patients are guaranteed safe, fair and high-quality NHS care, wherever they choose to receive it.

Statutory providers

Statutory providers are providers who have a statutory (legal) duty to manage care arrangements in their local area. Having this responsibility for ensuring that care is provided is not the same as actually delivering all the care services. Organisations can commission other care providers through a contract to deliver aspects of care that they are responsible for. Two key players in this arena have always been:

- local authority managed social services departments
- the NHS.

In the past the NHS has been responsible for healthcare, and Social Services have been responsible for social care. They have interacted where professionals have needed to work together in relation to particular service users. The Health Act 1999 and the Health and Social Care Act 2001 challenged the responsibilities of these organisations in relation to each other and, as discussed, there have been continuous legal and financial developments since

then, towards the government's vision of a more integrated system of care delivery.

In some areas the local health trust takes on work that has been carried out by the local authority. Where organisations commission other organisations to perform certain functions they may still retain the statutory responsibility for ensuring their suitability. In other areas, the local authority has merged its departments to form social care and housing departments. This area is still developing, and localities are restructuring based on local need and experience.

We will now look at the structure of a local authority organisation, which has within its remit the provision of social care services. All councils are also divided into departments as a way of organising the delivery of services that they are responsible for. The provision of adult social care used to come under the heading Social Services, which also had responsibility for children's services. City and County Councils have made their own decisions about what structure best fits their delivery strategy. Some councils have a separate children's department with responsibility for children's social care, health and education. Others have retained the type of profile that Social Services provided, with a department for adult, young people and children's social care.

The organisation of social care means that there is a difference between the organisations responsible for making sure that support services are provided, and the organisations that actually provide the services.

For each council area the local authority is responsible for ensuring that appropriate services are provided; each area will make its own decisions regarding the process for that delivery to actually happen:

- commission
- tendering
- **procurement**.

This chapter focuses on the provision of health and social care services but it is worth noting the other services that councils are responsible for which also have an impact on individual health and well-being. For example, councils manage neighbourhood problems such as littering, fly tipping, dog-fouling, pollution, pest control and drainage blockages. They carry out inspections to make sure that businesses

Birmingham City Council

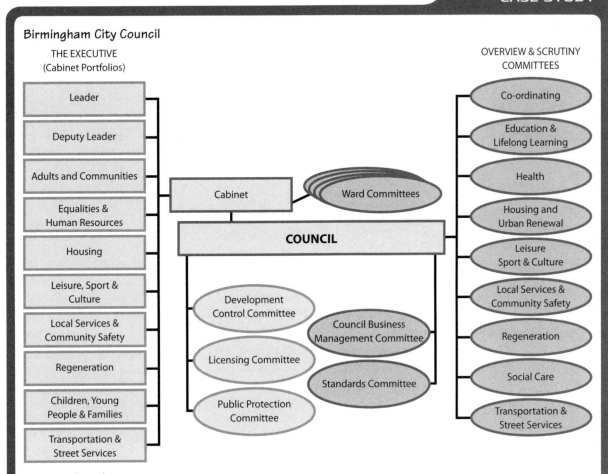

Figure 1.3 Council structure

The Adult and Communities Executive in the Council is responsible for adult social care and local authority provided health. It has devised seven outcomes for adults:

- improved health
- improved quality of life
- making a positive contribution
- choice and control
- freedom from discrimination
- economic well-being
- personal dignity.

Local authorities do have some responsibilities relating to local health. Various council committees set priorities, including the Public Protection Committee. Public Health is about making Birmingham a safe and pleasant city in which to live, work and visit and the Public Health Section of the City Council carries out work at a local level to promote and protect public health.

Questions

1 How do the local government arrangements for your area differ from those in Birmingham?
2 What different services provided by local authorities are of most concern to your service users?

know how to comply with the law and to check that they do.

Councils are legally responsible for enforcing a very wide range of legislation including:

- food hygiene and safety including food poisoning and infectious diseases
- heath and safety at work
- environmental protection
- nuisances such as noise, illegal littering and rubbish dumping.

NHS structure

The NHS comprises the following: Strategic Health Authorities, NHS Trusts and Primary Care Trusts (PCTs).

Strategic Health Authorities

These have been responsible for research into health needs of an area and the commissioning of organisations to deliver an appropriate response to these needs.

The Local Government and Public Involvement in Health Act 2007 stipulates that:

> Section 116: Health and social care: joint strategic needs assessments
>
> This introduces a requirement on responsible local authorities and Primary Care Trusts (PCTs) to undertake a joint strategic needs assessment of the health and social care needs for the area of the responsible local authority. This will determine what will be needed in terms of the discharge of health and social care functions in relation to the area of the local authority.

NHS Trusts

Many NHS Trusts manage hospitals. They function on business principles, and are subject to concerns if they are not generating the income needed to provide a good service. They make decisions regarding which clinical procedures they carry out. They have to function financially and are also subject to scrutiny clinically as the government publishes league tables on the performance of individual hospitals.

Homerton University Hospital, for example, has the following clinical departments: Cardiology, Clinical haematology, Dermatology, Ear, Nose and Throat, Endocrinology, Gastroenterology, General medicine, General surgery, Geriatric medicine, Gynaecology, Neurology, Ophthalmology, Oral surgery, Rheumatology, Thoracic medicine, Trauma and orthopaedics and Urology

Primary Care Trusts

These have been established to manage the community-based healthcare in local areas. They vary in size significantly according to not only geographical area and population, but also the responsibilities they have assumed regarding primary healthcare. Led by clinicians and local people, PCTs are the cornerstone of the local NHS, and are responsible for:

- assessing the health needs of their local community
- preparing plans for health improvement
- being the leading NHS organisation for partnership working with local authorities and other partners.

Primary Care Trusts are reviewing their remit for the social care needs of people and some trusts are employing more care workers as they co-ordinate the delivery of care to people in their localities.

Since the 1990 NHS and Community Care Act the role of local authorities in providing services has changed. They are now responsible for securing care services, but not to automatically provide them directly. This has enabled other care providers to become key providers in some localities, and even nationally.

Commissioning of care

Commissioning is the process of securing care services for a region or in a particular activity; where a local authority or NHS Trust identifies a care need and works out the best way for this to be delivered.

The key stages in commissioning are:

Analysis It is important to identify what services are needed in a local area. The devolved nature of this planning means that local initiatives can be developed to respond creatively to the specific requirements of a population.

Strategic planning This involves having a broad overview of a range of issues and being able to apply these to the short- and long-term.

Contract setting Contracts are legal agreements as to what services an organisation is going to provide and at what cost. A contract might be small, for one service to a small group of people in one geographical area, or it could be a larger contract dealing with a whole range of services across a wide locality.

Market management Authorities have needed to ensure that there are sufficient providers to meet the needs of individuals in a region. An example of where this is problematic is in home care services. In some geographical areas, domiciliary care agencies have had difficulty meeting the obligations of a number of care packages. Local authorities can enter into a contract with established or new care providers for them to provide services to the area and people that they are responsible for.

Contract monitoring Organisations which take up contracts will have different levels of experience regarding management of a contract and meeting the requirements of the purchasing authority. A further dimension to tendering has been the introduction of best value, as organisations have to demonstrate that they are securing the best services by investigating comparable alternatives.

ACTIVITY

Find out the main organisations that are responsible for managing care provision in your local area.

1 How is your local authority organised? What is the name of the department that is responsible for social care?

2 What is the name of any local NHS or Primary Care Trust in your local area? What are the areas of responsibility?

CASE STUDY

Commissioning care

ADVERT

Expressions of interest are sought to provide:

Out of Hours Community Mental Health Support Services

A contract for 3 years commencing 1 January 2009 will be awarded

Providers must be able to demonstrate their:

- ability to provide a quality mental health service
- financial viability and cost effectiveness
- inclusion of service users in managing and monitoring service delivery.

For a Tender Information Pack please contact: Jake at Heather County Council

Following the award of a contract the commissioning local authority will announce details.

Announcement of a new provider

The London Borough of Bexley commissioned the charitable Trust MCCH Society Ltd, as the new provider for its accommodation and day opportunity services through a 10-year contract. MCCH are responsible for provision and development of residential and short break services, supported living and day service opportunities, and the details of the standards of these services is set out in a Service Specifications. The organisation provides services across London and the South East of England. www.bexley.gov.uk (2007)

Questions

1 What services are currently being tendered local to you? Look in the back pages of Community Care or your local paper.

2 Is your organisation one that has been awarded a tender? If so, see if you can find out the details of how they were awarded the contract, and its content.

Policy making and implementation

Policy making includes all the legislation that government implements to frame how health and social care is to be provided, the policies that NHS Trusts and local authorities devise to facilitate the implementation of this legislation or other ideas they think are important. A White Paper is a policy statement that organisations are required to follow; if these can be implemented with the current legal framework a change in law may not be required. These statements are written as policy documents, guidelines or pieces of legislation, depending on whether the law needs to change to accommodate the new ideas. An example of a policy statement from the government outlining their plans for the future is the NHS Plan. This document provides a comprehensive framework for the development of smaller policies. Policies relating to health and well-being have since referred to the Plan.

Legislation

'The Department of Health works to define policy and guidance for delivering a social care system that provides care equally for all, whilst enabling people to retain their independence, control and dignity.'

Putting People First: A shared vision and commitment to the transformation of Adult Social Care; this Ministerial Concordat was launched in December 2007:

> This establishes the collaboration between central and local government, the sector's professional leadership, providers and the regulator. It sets out the shared aims and values, which will guide the transformation of adult social care and recognises that the sector will work across agendas with users and carers to transform people's experience of local support and services.

The Department of Health also issues Local Authority Circulars, for example *LAC (DH)(2008)1: Transforming social care*, published 17 January 2008.

This Local Authority Circular sets out information to support the transformation of social care. It includes a copy of the Social Care Reform Grant Determination and the details of the new ring-fenced grant to help councils to redesign and reshape their systems over the next three years.

Local Area Agreements

These determine the priorities and targets for a particular area, as agreed between central government, the relevant local authority, and other partners.

For a policy document to become law it has to progress through the Houses of Parliament, the Commons and the Lords, and receive Royal Assent. An Act is a legal document that provides:

- *Permissive powers*
  'An organisation may ...' This allows an organisation or person to carry out certain functions with the support of legislation.

- *Statutory duties*
  'An organisation shall ...' This specifies what individuals or organisations are required to do.

The Care Standards Act was a piece of legislation setting out the formal arrangements for the inspection of standards within care services. The legislation allows the government to make changes to the current organisation of regulation and inspection. It gives new organisations both duties and powers to undertake particular work activity.

Policy statements

A White Paper is a policy statement relating to a particular aspect of government. The objectives contained within a White Paper do not always require legislation; it may be possible to carry out their contents within the current framework of the law and so no further legislation is required. Whilst they are not legally binding documents, there is a strong expectation that the contents of a White Paper are taken on board by individual authorities. There is sometimes disappointment that a White Paper is not continued in development to become an Act of Parliament. This was true of the *Valuing People* White Paper. This very broad-ranging document on learning disability set out guidelines for how services should be organised, and what people with a learning disability should expect from care services.

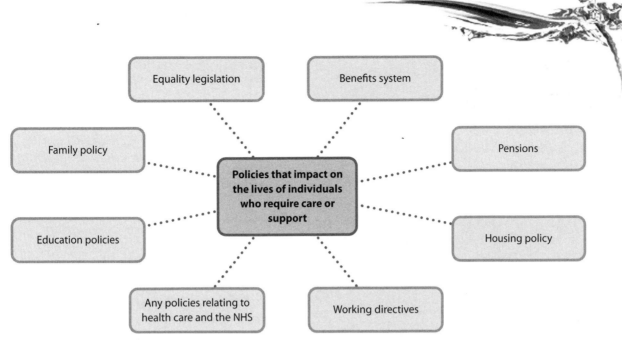

Figure 1.4 Areas of care influenced by legislation

Policies sometimes have a variety of agendas that they aim to address. They link in with each other. For example, all current policies should aim to:

- promote the involvement of service users in planning
- respond to human rights and equality legislation
- acknowledge the health and social services agenda
- develop partnership with the independent sector.

The context of care is influenced by legislation that applies to the areas detailed in Figure 1.4.

Since the Labour Party came to power in 1997 it has introduced a range of legislation that has enabled changes to the organisation and delivery of care. The NHS Plan was 'a plan for investment, a plan for reform' and it set out the expectations of change in the provision of care services. It is not specific to the acute healthcare sector and is therefore relevant to the social care sector as well.

NHS Plan

This 10-year policy proposal established the following principles:

- The NHS will provide a universal service for all based on clinical need, not ability to pay.
- The NHS will provide a comprehensive range of services.

- The NHS will shape its services around the needs and preferences of individual patients, their families and carers.
- The NHS will respond to different needs of different populations.
- The NHS will work continuously to improve quality services and to minimise errors.
- The NHS will support and value its staff.
- Public funds for healthcare will be devoted solely to NHS patients.
- The NHS will work together with others to ensure a seamless service for patients.
- The NHS will keep people healthy and work to reduce health inequalities.
- The NHS will respect the confidentiality of individual patients and provide open access to information about services, treatments and performance.

National Service Frameworks

National Service Framework for Older People

This is the key vehicle for ensuring that the needs of older people are at the heart of the reform programme for health and social services. (Department of Health, 2001, page 5)

Standards for older people must be assured and maintained

The principles of the National Service Framework (NSF) for Older People are to:

- assure standards of care
- extend access to services
- ensure fairer funding
- develop services which promote independence
- help older people to stay healthy
- develop more effective links between health and social services and other services such as housing, and partners in the voluntary and private sectors. (Department of Health, 2001, page 5)

An example of strategies to implement policy is provided with the National Service Framework for Older People. There are five underpinning programmes that will support local and national implementation:

- finance
- workforce development
- research and development
- clinical and practice decision support services
- information.

National Service Framework for Mental Health

The National Service Framework for Mental Health sets out priorities for this service users group, illustrating the importance of joint working with health services and social care services, and also significantly acknowledging the importance of support for carers.

Mental health promotion

Standard One:

Health and social services should:

- promote mental health for all, working with individuals and communities
- combat discrimination against individuals and groups with mental health problems, and promote their social inclusion.

Primary care and access to services

Standard Two:

Any service user who contacts their primary healthcare team with a common mental health problem should:

- have their mental health needs identified and assessed
- be offered effective treatments, including referral to specialist services for further assessment, treatment and care if they require it.

Standard Three:

Any individual with a common mental health problem should:

- be able to make contact round the clock with the local services necessary to meet their needs and receive adequate care
- be able to use NHS Direct as it develops for first level advice and referral on to specialist helplines or to local services.

Effective services for people with severe mental illness

Standard Four:

All mental health service users of Care Programme Approach (CPA) should:

- receive care which optimises engagement, anticipates or prevents a crisis, and reduces risk
- have a copy of a written care plan which includes the action to be taken in a crisis by the service user,

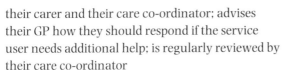

their carer and their care co-ordinator; advises their GP how they should respond if the service user needs additional help; is regularly reviewed by their care co-ordinator

● be able to access services 24 hours a day, 365 days a year.

Standard Five:

Each service user who is assessed as requiring a period of care away from their home should have:

● timely access to an appropriate hospital bed or alternative bed or place, which is in the least restrictive environment consistent with the need to protect them and the public, as close to home as possible

● a copy of a written after-care plan agreed on discharge, which sets out the care to be provided, identifies the care co-ordinator, and specifies the action to be taken in a crisis.

Caring about carers

Standard Six:

All individuals who provide regular and substantial care for a person on CPA should have:

● an assessment of their caring, physical and mental health needs, repeated on at least an annual basis

● their own written care plan which is given to them and implemented in discussion with them.

Preventing suicide

Standard Seven:

Local health and social care communities should prevent suicides by:

● promoting mental health for all, working with individuals and communities

● delivering high-quality primary mental healthcare

● ensuring that anyone with a mental health problem can contact local services via the primary care team, a helpline or an A&E department

● ensuring that individuals with severe and enduring mental illness have a care plan which meets their specific needs, including access to services around the clock

● providing safe hospital accommodation for individuals who need it

● enabling individuals caring for someone with severe mental illness to receive the support which they need to continue to care.

In addition they should:

● support local prison staff in preventing sui~~~~ among prisoners

● ensure that staff are competent to assess the risk of suicide among individuals at greatest risk

● develop local systems for suicide audit to learn lessons and take any necessary action.

Health and social care services

The NHS Plan identified that 'if patients are to receive the best care, then the old divisions between health and social care need to be overcome' (Section 7.1).

This section explores the legislation that has had a significant impact on the organisation of the care sector, especially in relation to the changing boundaries of health and social care. At a strategic level, four new posts were created as regional directors of health and social care. They are responsible for:

● overseeing the development of the NHS and social care

● assessing performance

● managing the appointment, development and succession planning of senior management staff, and supporting ministers and troubleshooting.

Key legislation relating to the merging of healthcare and social care includes the Health Act 1999 and the Health and Social Care Act 2001.

Health Act 1999

Partnership in Action proposed a new way of working together for health organisations and social care organisations. The Health Act provided the legislation to enable these more flexible ways of working together, especially in relation to the funding of services to people. Previously, funding has been an obstacle to joint working as it provides a complex dimension to organising projects. More opportunities for pooled funding and targeted resources for joint projects provide not only an incentive, but also the mechanism for the merging of health and social care services. The Act facilitates a more proactive approach to joint working so organisations can take on different responsibilities, which were previously delivered by others.

Care Standards Act 2000

The main purpose of the Act is to reform the regulatory system for care services in England and Wales.

(Crown, 2000, *Explanatory Notes to the Care Standards Act*, page 34)

This legislation provided a framework for the regulation of care services across a number of care settings and service user groups.

The main points relevant to adult social care are that the Act:

1 established the new regulatory body for care services (National Care Standards Commission). It should be noted that this body would become the Commission for Social Care Inspection with the Social Services Inspectorate and the social care responsibilities of the Audit Commission.
2 established the General Social Care Council for:
   - registration of social care workers
   - setting standards in care work
   - regulating the education and training of social workers.
3 requires the Secretary of State to maintain a list of individuals considered unsuitable for work with vulnerable adults:
   - care organisations must obtain clearance from the Criminal Records Bureau for new employees.

Health and Social Care Act 2001

This legislation established care trusts. Care Trusts are the new organisations that assume responsibility for a particular geographical area in relation to a particular area of care. They may operate with a particular remit for one group, as with mental health trusts, or they may assume more general responsibility across service user groups.

The benefits of Care Trusts are:

- the development of new approaches to the provision of services by a single body
- a consistent approach to quality improvement by bringing together existing systems to work more effectively
- a single strategic approach, with a single set of aims and targets
- the potential for financial flexibility and efficiency

- better and clearer working arrangements for staff, with more varied career opportunities
- a single management structure, multi-disciplinary teams managed from one point, co-location of staff, as well as single or streamlined cross-disciplinary assessments
- better communication between staff about packages of care. Care Trusts will be in an excellent position to develop a single information system.

The Health and Social Care Joint Unit was established in August 1998 to develop policy on joint working between health and social services. It has focused on issues relating to:

- continuing care
- NHS funded care
- delayed discharges.

Modernising Social Services (Department of Health, 1998) specified the use of pooled budgets to promote the potential for integration. Integrated provision was also a feature of the document *Delivering the NHS Plan: Next Steps on Investment, Next Steps on Reform* (Crown, 2002).

The Health and Social Care Change Agent Team was set up in January 2002 to:

- help reduce delayed transfers of care
- support aspects of the NSF that relate to transfers of care
- assist in developing a more integrated service, using the Health Act 1999.

It aims to support the issues arising through what are known as:

- *winter pressures* – the additional numbers of people who experience vulnerability over the winter period, and require care and support services at this time
- *bed blocking* – the rather derogatory term given to individuals who are in hospital but who no longer have medical needs and are therefore deemed fit for discharge. The reason for delay in their discharge is sometimes associated with the complexities of arranging care packages in the community where there are constraints on resources, or a lack of, or delay in, services that are available.

The Delayed Discharge Act 2003, which came into full effect in 2004, provided a financial penalty to local authorities for delaying the discharge of a person from hospital. 'If they cannot meet the agreed time limit they will be charged by the local hospital for the costs it incurs in keeping older people in hospital unnecessarily.' These include:

- costs of readmission
- lack of available carers in areas, especially rural areas
- lack of resources to supply equipment in preparation for a move home.

One direction in which all this could be leading is the shift of adult services out of local government into the NHS. While official statements deny this intention there is a distinct shift in this direction, perhaps enhanced by the development ... of separation of adult social care from child care in some local authorities.

(Hill, 2003, page 194)

The relationship of values to policy

As mentioned above, legislation is both permissive and restrictive. Some permissive laws are required to allow the NHS, local authority and partner organisations to deliver their services in a particular way. Other restrictive laws prevent activities or behaviour from people that is not considered to be appropriate.

This can create tensions. The courts have to decide any actions when someone has broken the law.

Avon and Wiltshire Mental Health Partnership

Our Trust is managed by a Trust Board. The Trust Board makes certain that affairs are conducted in a responsible, honest and open way so that taxpayers' – your – money is spent in an accountable way that provides the best possible service for local people.

All Trust Board meetings are held in public and we warmly invite people to attend to observe the Board make decisions about local healthcare.

The Trust Board is made up of:

- a non-executive chair plus six other non-executive directors, all of whom have voting rights
- eight directors, five of whom have voting rights.

The chair and the non-executive directors are appointed for fixed lengths of time by the Secretary of State for Health, usually for four years at a time up to a maximum of 10 years.

The chief executive and directors are appointed on permanent contracts, but can tender their resignation to the Trust Board at any time.

Mission statement

We aim to provide high-quality specialist services to people with serious mental health problems. We cover Bath and North East Somerset, Bristol, North Somerset, South Gloucestershire, Swindon and Wiltshire.

Vision

- Users and carers will be actively involved in all aspects of the Trust's work
- As a specialist provider, the Trust will provide a coherent range of services across its area
- Trust services will be delivered locally with maximum integration and sharing of resources between health and social services
- The Trust will work in partnership with others, to ensure that mental health services are part of, and not separate, from the community
- Trust services will be sensitive to culture and diverse needs
- Trust services will be designed and managed in line with best practice and research
- Trust staff will be appropriately trained, supported and involved in all aspects of the Trust's work.

Questions

1 How does the mission statement and the values of this agency compare to that of your organisation?
2 Do all your colleagues and all the service users have access to this statement?
3 How transparent are the activities of the senior management team or board?

> ### Husband who helped wife with multiple sclerosis (MS) to die is spared jail
>
> *'I carried out my wife's dying wish.'*
>
> A husband who helped his wife to kill herself to save her from suffering the degenerative effects of multiple sclerosis was spared jail yesterday. Robert Cook, who had been asked by his wife Vanessa to help her die, placed a plastic bag and pillow over her face after she had taken an overdose of pills. The 60-year-old admitted manslaughter on the grounds of diminished responsibility and aiding and abetting suicide and was given a 12-month prison sentence, suspended for two years, by a judge who described the case as 'tragic'. Lewes crown court heard that Cook told police after being arrested in October 2006: 'The only reason why I done what I done was through love and affection through 29 years. I carried out my wife's dying wish.'
>
> *The Guardian, Saturday 2 February, 2008*

Some people feel that the laws should be changed so that people who are unable to take their own life can be assisted to do so in a dignified manner. For others this is contrary to the most basic of care values and potentially puts professionals in difficult situations that are in opposition to the heart of their work.

The focus of care provision in both social care and in health is becoming underpinned by the idea of rights and entitlement. This has not always been the case and these are previous ideologies of care. These ideologies are not mutually exclusive and government policy reflects aspects of these.

The following is a summary of some ideas about welfare, as discussed by Deacon (2002):

> Each perspective has a different idea about the role and purpose of welfare, drawing upon a particular understanding of the relationship between welfare and human behaviour and motivation.
>
> Welfare as **an expression of altruism**. This assumes that a more equal and cohesive society will create mutual help to realise the moral potential of society. The task of welfare is to redistribute resources and opportunities, and thereby provide a framework for the encouragement and expression of **altruism**.
>
> Welfare as **a channel for the pursuit of self-interest**. This view feels that the majority of people who claim welfare act rationally to improve their circumstances. Welfare should provide a framework of incentives that channels this desire for self-improvement in ways conducive to the common good.
>
> Welfare as **the exercise of authority**. This assumes that a significant proportion of claimants lack the capacity to pursue their own self-interest. They do not respond to changes in the framework of incentives in the way that the previous perspective assumes. Welfare should compel people to act in ways that are conducive to their long-term betterment, and the good of society as a whole.
>
> Welfare as **a transition to work**. This developed in response to the previous two. It starts from the premise that cash benefits alone can never alleviate the problem of poverty. Generous benefits undermine work incentives and threaten the stability of the family. Welfare should be a transition to paid employment.
>
> Welfare as **a mechanism for moral regeneration**. This perspective starts from the assumption that people are also motivated by a sense of commitment, and by an acceptance that they have obligations to the communities in which they live. The task of welfare is to foster and enhance this sense of duty, and it should look to do so through persuasion and moral argument.
>
> (Deacon, 2002)

These views are important to consider and they are explored in more depth in sociology textbooks. An appreciation of them can help in considering new policies that are introduced.

Government

The government reviews its policies in response to:

- **the electorate** and the need to convince voters that they are delivering what was promised in their election mandate
- **campaigns** by organisations which are interested in health and social care

- **research** by organisations such as SCIE and GSCC who have a remit to inform the government of issues relating to their activities
- **issues and concerns** which are often highlighted by the media and which demand a response from government, for example hygiene in healthcare delivery and the costs of social care for older people.

The government is advised on ideas about policy by organisations which represent care services, as well as other departments. The new Commission for Social Care Inspection will advise ministers and policy makers on:

- the impact of policies on the ground
- how best to assess performance
- appropriate intervention when a council fails to provide an adequate service.

There are many factors that influence the development of policy, not just values that underpin the sector. Sometimes it is difficult to identify the principles that policy developers say they have when you consider the policies that they develop.

ACTIVITY

1 Find out in your place of work what policies have had an influence on how the service is provided and consider what the effects have been.
2 Did the values of the policy match with the values of the organisation?

You may already have strong views on care and how it should be provided. During your reading you will develop an understanding of the contemporary issues that inform the current development of policy; it is important that you are able to participate in any debates about this.

Policy making process

Policy has to take into account current legislation. If existing legislation does not enable new policy to be implemented then new legislation must be proposed.

All new policy needs to respond to and facilitate the spirit and letter of the Human Rights Act 1998. This marked 'a change in the constitutional relationship between citizens and the state' (Home Office

Communication Directive, 2000, page 1). 'One of the reasons for changing our mental health laws, which date largely from 1959, is to bring them more fully in line with the European Convention on Human Rights.' (Home Office 2002, page 19). Governments sometimes look abroad for inspiration when considering new policies.

It is important for government, local authorities, the NHS, and care organisations to consider how policies relate to each other in different environments. An illustration of this is the Human Rights Act 1998. This legislation has had a major impact on the implementation of other policies that were already established and has influenced the development of new policies.

Human rights legislation needs to be considered because:

- it is the law
- it can bring benefits to service users.

  Human rights legislation has been used innovatively as a framework to improve the equality and dignity of people with learning disabilities in their relationships with carers. (Audit Commission, 2003, discussing the Doughty Street HR Unit and LSE HR Centre Research, 2002)

Implementing policy

A policy is usually a written statement of what should happen in a document. Sometimes the government has to use incentives or 'a carrot or stick' approach to ensuring that relevant organisations respond to policy directives.

For example, in order to promote the discharge of people from hospital once their medical needs had been met, so that they could return to their own homes or into care homes, the government initiated payments of £100 each day for care (£120 in London and some parts of south east England). This prompted a change in the arrangements for delivery of care between the NHS and local authorities as there were many disputes between them that mitigated against effective care and support for individuals.

The requirements for smooth transfer of a person from hospital to home once their medical needs have been met and they are fit for discharge need to be worked out. The following are the questions that need to be asked in this regard.

Assessment of social care needs

Since the NHS and Community Care Act 1990, the process of care management has been developed to ensure that individuals are provided with an assessment of their needs prior to the delivery of care. Chapter 7 explores issues relating to the assessment process and the current organisation of assessment. In mental health services the care programme approach has provided a comparable assessment framework.

Section 46. (1) Each local authority:

(a) Shall ... prepare and publish a plan for the provision of community care services in their area

Section 47. (1) ... the authority:

(d) shall carry out an assessment of his needs for those services

(e) having regard to the results of that assessment, shall then decide whether his needs call for the provision by them of any such services.

This legislation also required that local authorities understand what the care needs are in their locality and plan for meeting these needs.

Provision of health and social care services

This section looks at the range of services that are provided to individuals and groups who need care or support.

Independent providers: the third sector

There have always been independent providers who have played a significant role in providing support for people. In the form of charities, these types of providers are no longer on the periphery of care service delivery. Since the NHS and Community Care Act 1990, the creation of the internal market has allowed and encouraged independent organisations to establish a niche in the care market. Some of these providers were established voluntary organisations, others were private businesses. These organisations might remain as small concerns with perhaps one home, or they may develop into large established businesses.

Whilst independent organisations are now mainstream providers of social care services there have been tensions about the provision of care by non-public agencies; some people would prefer services to remain funded by and provided by publicly managed and delivered organisations.

Not-for-profit organisations

These are companies established to provide a particular service. They act as independent businesses but all their profits are invested in the organisation to benefit the service they provide.

Private organisations

The care industry is big business and some organisations have developed their capacity to operate within the care sector by expanding the services that they provide, or the region that they provide to. These organisations assume responsibility for the delivery of care on the basis of contracts, either with local authorities, or directly with individuals who need care services.

Voluntary

A definition of the voluntary sector is that it

> ... covers formally constituted organisations, managed by unpaid committees, that are not part of the state or the market or the informal world of spontaneous or unstructured action. The term includes organisations with paid staff; they can trade, but not distribute profits. Their objectives are generally taken as being to enhance public benefit.
> (Alcock, 1998, page 162)

Charities

Charities are voluntary organisations that have been formally registered by the Charity Commission, which then regulates them. Some charities, but not all, operate to provide a service to the public; some of these provide care-related activities.

> Some charities operate as large businesses with a pressure group remit, that 'in modern times have played an increasingly influential and continuous

role in the political process ... they are not democratically accountable to the general public. It is the political parties which have to accept that form of responsibility and which are vulnerable to the verdict of the electorate at every General Election, and at other elections to a lesser extent as well.

(Forman and Baldwin, 1996)

CASE STUDY

Leeds City Council: neighbourhood community care schemes for older people

The 36 Schemes listed in the directory are voluntary organisations that provide a range of community care services for older people. They receive some of their core funding from Leeds Social Services, and an evaluation of the organisations in February 1998 revealed that together they were supporting 11,000 older people with their 80 staff and 850 volunteers.

The range of services provided is shown below. This is a comprehensive list and not all of the organisations provide all of these services. Some of the organisations focus on specific areas (for example, day care); 26 of the organisations focus on particular geographic areas in Leeds, and the remaining 6 have wider, and in some cases city-wide, remits:

- advice, information and newsletters
- **advocacy**
- annual needs assessment visits to individual older people
- bathing
- befriending and voluntary visiting.

Questions

Investigate a charity that relates to the service user group with whom you work. You may be able to research it on the Internet, contact the charity by phone for information, or visit them in person. Explore:

- how the charity originated
- who it aims to provide a service for, and what the role of the charity is in the development of policy.

Charities play a key role in the development of services for people. Some registered charities are service user groups managed by disabled people or those with mental health issues. They may respond to policy discussion documents – this activity has been made more accessible with new technology. Any individual can access recent documents via the Internet and can usually submit comments to the Minister about them.

Community groups

Community organisations have a valuable role to play in reaching people who need services. Sometimes statutory services have been found lacking in their ability to engage with some people in their locality, due to cultural perceptions, language or lack of appropriate access to the community communication network.

Volunteers

There are many different ways that volunteers provide a service to individuals and groups. They may work for voluntary organisations themselves or can work in local authority or NHS Trust organisations or in private companies. An individual may be formally contracted as a volunteer and be expected to undertake a certain number of hours or activities within that contract. Alternatively, a volunteer may provide support in a more flexible manner with no obligation to turn up at a particular time or perform any required tasks.

Some volunteers will receive expenses or 'pocket money' payment to carry out a certain role. Other volunteers do not access any funds for the work that they carry out. The National Minimum Wage and Working Time Directives have required some organisations to review their approach to having volunteers.

Informal care

This type of care refers to the care that is delivered to individuals by relatives, neighbours, or friends. The word informal is misleading, as this type of care is often substantial in terms of both time and type of activity; it can also be permanent and ongoing. A carer is someone who 'provides or intends to provide a substantial amount of care on a regular basis' (Carers (Recognition and Services) Act 1995).

Carers do not always recognise that they are entitled to support; the charity Carers UK estimate that £660 million of carers allowance is not claimed each year (Carers UK, 2003). Partly this relates to the fact that many people do not recognise themselves as a 'carer'.

Informal carers provide invaluable support

CASE STUDY

Informal carers

Grace is 23 years old. She moved here from Trinidad five years ago to live with her 83-year-old grandmother. Grace helps her grandmother to get up in the morning and makes sure that she has something ready for her lunch while Grace is at work. Grace was grateful that her grandmother wanted her to come and live with her so she does not mind helping her at home.

Mr and Mrs MacDonald are both in their 60s. They have three children, one of whom is Nicholas who is 34 and lives at home with them. He has a learning disability and needs support with many of his usual home and personal care activities.

Jack is 20 years old. He has been caring for his mum who was diagnosed with multiple sclerosis two years ago. His mother has not coped well with the deterioration in her capabilities and she is a regular drinker; this affects her mood and she gets angry with Jack if he refuses to buy her any alcohol. Jack has lost contact with many of his friends as they have gone to university. He works part-time at a local baker's so that he can spend a lot of time with his mum.

Questions

1. Identify what the needs of the following people might be in the above case studies:
   - the person with care/support needs
   - the carer/s.
2. What services and professionals are available to support these families?
3. Investigate the work of the Carers' National Association and Carers UK.

The census in 2000 recognised the need for the government to identify the extent of informal caring that was taking place in individuals' homes. Many people live with family members who need support; they do not even identify themselves as carers because they see the role that they are carrying out as an extension of the family relationship.

The nature of work undertaken by informal carers includes:

- personal care – washing, bathing, dressing, and general attention to physical needs and comforts
- domestic care – cooking, cleaning and laundering
- auxiliary care – baby-sitting, child-minding, shopping, transport, odd-jobbing, gardening, borrowing and lending
- social support – visiting and companionship
- surveillance – 'keeping an eye on' vulnerable people.

(Abbotts and Ackers, 1996, page 167)

The low benefit take-up has compounded the problems of social exclusion. 'If carers don't get the right support then their health suffers and it leads to poverty and isolation.' (Redmond, 2003).

The government's carers' strategy

Over the past decade the government has implemented several strategies to address the needs of carers through a Carers' Strategy. There are reservations about the success of this policy and its implementation. Carers' rights have been compromised by lack of funding; in some areas carers have been slow to be informed of their right to an assessment.

The Labour government's approach to supporting carers includes:

Information:
- charter outlining expectations and standards of long-term care
- consistency in charging of services
- health information
- NHS Direct helpline
- Internet information.

Support:
- carers' involvement in planning and providing services

- consultation with carers' organisations.

Care:
- right to have health needs met
- local authority powers to provide services to carers
- emphasis on carers' breaks, £140 million targeted funds
- financial support for working carers.

The carers' grant that is provided centrally has been used in different ways by local authorities. Great Britain has an estimated 5.7 million carers and one in six households (17 per cent) contains a carer. Of the estimated 5.7 million carers, 1.7 million devote at least 20 hours a week to caring. Of those, 855,000 care for 50 hours or more.

Carers' legislation

The Carers (Recognition and Services) Act 1995
- It gave carers new rights and a clear legal status. Individuals who provide a substantial amount of care on a regular basis are entitled to request an assessment of their ability to care and to continue caring.
- Local authorities are required to take into account the results of that assessment in making decisions about the type and level of community care services to be provided to the person receiving care. This applies to carers of all ages.

The Carers and Disabled Children Act 2000
- It gave local councils mandatory duties to support carers by providing services to carers directly.
- It gave carers the right to an assessment independent of the person they care for if they are over 16-years-old.
- It empowered local authorities to make direct payments to carers.
- It enabled councils to support flexibility in provision of short breaks through the short break voucher scheme.

The Carers (Equal Opportunities) Act 2004
- It placed a duty on councils to inform carers, in certain circumstances, of their right to an assessment of their needs.
- It provided that when assessing a carer's needs, councils must take into account whether the carer works or wishes to work, undertakes or wishes to undertake education, training or leisure activities.

- It facilitated co-operation between authorities in relation to the provision of services that are relevant to carers.

Young carers

There were 175,000 young carers identified through the census of 2001 and their average age is 12 years. Of these young carers, 13,000 spend more than 50 hours per week in a caring role; that is more than a full-time job! Over 30 per cent of young carers have a parent with mental health needs; 50 per cent of young carers live with one parent.

The *Every Child Matters* agenda aims to address the needs of this and other groups; young carers miss out on playing, socialising, education and their own health needs. Care organisations are expected to address any child's needs or ensure an organisation is in a position to help them.

Continuing care

This is care provided over an extended period of time to meet physical or mental health needs that have arisen as a result of either disability, an accident or an illness.

Respite care

Respite care is care provided on a temporary, although very often regular, basis. It may be provided in the person's own home or the person may go to a care home. Direct Payments has enabled individuals to target care as required. For example, a care user can employ short-term support to cover for their carer who needs to have a break, or they may move into a care home where they can have appropriate support. Many care homes have beds dedicated to respite care. The advantages are that the family carer is able to have a break knowing that their relative is in a

CASE STUDY

Caring for the carers

The charity Barnardo's does much work with young carers whose years growing up are affected by a commitment to caring for one or both parents. It provides support and outings and activities as many children are excluded from usual patterns of friendships and trips due to their family circumstances.

The Carers and Disabled Children Act 2000 enables local authorities to offer support to carers helping them to maintain their own health and well-being. Carers are entitled to an assessment independently of the person that they provide care for. As a result of this assessment they may be provided with the Carer's Allowance.

Questions

1 Think about how Grace, Mr and Mrs McDonald and Jack in the case study above (page 24) may feel about their role.
2 Why is it sometimes difficult for people to seek help in their own family situation?
3 What issues do professionals have to be aware of when assuming care/support responsibilities for someone who has previously received these from a family member?

CASE STUDY

Respite care

Leeds City Council family placement

This city-wide service provides breaks for older people, people who have a physical disability, people with a learning disability and people with dementia.

Staying with a family – this is when someone goes to stay with another family at their home. This could be on an occasional basis, or if there is an emergency (for example, when a carer has been taken into hospital). There is also a home-based service that provides a carer to stay in people's own homes, giving carers a break for a few hours, a day or even overnight. There is a small charge for these services. www.leeds.gov.uk (2007).

Questions

1 Does your local authority provide a respite care service such as the one in the case study?
2 How do you think a family may benefit from having the opportunity for respite care?

supportive care environment and they do not need to worry about them.

Respite care can be arranged through a local authority care manager or may be arranged directly with a respite care provider.

Care homes

Care homes vary in size and some have more than 50 older people living in them. There is a preference, especially in learning disabled accommodation, for smaller homes as this reflects ideas of 'normal' living.

The Care Standards Act 2000 specifies the term of care home but still attributes status of residential or nursing care through the registration process. Registered for residential or nursing provision, care homes are also provided with registration specific to a number of service users and service user groups category.

The aims of a care home are to meet the identified needs of individuals who live in that home. This is achieved through regular assessment of needs and the care planning process. Each care home has to produce a statement of purpose that specifies what it provides for people. The initial assessment of need can serve as a contract for the provision of care. An older person may live in a care home for years; for many it is their last home. Care homes may be able to provide for people until they die if the home is equipped with appropriate skilled care workers.

The Centre for Policy on Ageing discusses the inference that independence can only be maintained for older people if they stay in their own homes (Centre for Policy on Ageing, 2001).

The Care Standards Act 2000 provides a structured framework for the regulation of care homes as explained later in the chapter.

Supported living

Care homes are not the only type of accommodation services available to people. Housing associations have been providing supported tenancies for people in need of care or support, and there has been a growth in this with the supported living agenda of national government being applied locally.

Tenancy arrangements are provided where a housing association, or other organisations, manages the accommodation and obtains or delivers the support services for people who are learning disabled or with mental health needs. The idea of tenancy arrangements is that the support allocated can be more specific to individuals.

Individuals are benefiting financially from these living and support arrangements which can increase their independence.

Sheltered housing

Within older people's services, sheltered housing, either in the form of purpose-built complexes or apartment blocks, provide a good balance between independent living and security and well-being (including peace of mind that someone is available to talk and to help).

Very sheltered housing is a more recent solution to the care needs of people who want to retain their independence but who have a range of complex care needs. They may live in a sheltered housing scheme and receive additional support provided externally.

Care at home

People can receive services in their own home. Some learning disabled adults and people with mental health problems have continued to live with their parents, who may themselves be in need of support due to their age. For many people, the transition through adulthood requires that they have support in their home lives. Ideas about what form this support should take are under constant review.

Home care

Also known as *domiciliary care*, this refers to services that are provided to people in their own home, described by the Social Services Inspectorate as 'the mainstay for many older people living at home' (2002). Community-based care incorporates the idea that individuals may be best placed in their own homes. In order for some people to remain in the home that they live in they may need one or more of the following:

- adaptations to their accommodation

- aids to daily living tasks
- support with getting washed and dressed in the morning and at night
- assistance with using the toilet.

As early as 1958 the government of the time stated that: 'The underlying principle of our services for the old should be this: that the best place for old people is in their own homes, with help from the home services if need be.' (Townsend,1962, page 196)

Care support workers who support individuals in their own home provide a range of personal care and physical support services.

> Physical functioning was consistently associated with greater use of both statutory and private home care services, suggesting that efforts should continue to be made to improve older people's physical functioning, such as preventive home visits.
>
> (Stoddart *et al*, 2002, pages 348–360: 358)

Technological developments have meant that there are increasing innovations to enhance the capacity of people to stay in their own homes.

CASE STUDY

Telecare in Newham

In the London Borough of Newham, every household with someone over 75 can now get a free telecare package. The original pilot study showed real benefits for individuals and their carers. One carer said, 'I think it helps me more than my mum, I feel I can relax a bit more, and I am not so worried when the 'phone rings in the evening, that I might have to dash out to see my mum.'

Questions

1 Is telecare a valuable addition to the current range of services available to increase independence? Or, as some fear, is it a poor substitute for having a personal visit and just a way of cutting services and reducing costs?

2 Are there any examples of telecare in your area or any potential uses of it by your own organisation?

Intermediate care

This was introduced through the National Service Framework for Older People. The aim was to provide support to individuals in order to reduce the need to enter hospital for acute healthcare services. It also would provide support to people when they left hospital to reduce the need for re-admission. The principle behind it was prevention which, whilst being a valued concept in healthcare, has been missing from dialogue on social care. Some of the strategies for delivering intermediate care are:

- rapid response teams
- intensive rehabilitation services
- recuperation facilities
- one-stop older people's service
- integrated home care teams.

Primary Care Trusts have developed initiatives based around their district nursing services, with home care staff focusing on rehabilitation. Local authority home care teams are being provided with specific training on rehabilitation so that they can increase their role in developing the ability of older people in their own homes: 'They will have the freedom to decide the precise organisational arrangements for their area.' (National Service Framework for Older People, Section 7.5)

Any services which form part of a package of intermediate care as defined in the regulations must be provided free of charge for six weeks.

The aim of intermediate care was to:

1 provide services that would prevent a person needing hospital admission
2 ensure people did not need re-admission to hospital when they had left.

Day services

Older people may attend day centres or lunch clubs. At these centres activities may be provided in-house by the staff, or sometimes they are brought in from outside. The activities include:

- therapeutic activities, which may include aromatherapy, music and art activities
- physical activity in the form of gentle exercise
- day trips
- the provision of lunch at these centres, which gives some people the chance to have a hot meal.

Some centres are able to respond to the particular social needs of a cultural or religious group in a local area.

Learning disability

Historically, learning disabled adults have attended adult training centres where they take part in a range of activities including:

- sports
- crafts
- domestic skills
- personal hygiene
- relationships
- healthcare.

With care planning and reviews there has been a move away from group activity at the centre so that activities have been more focused around the needs of the individual. This prompted the name change to social education centres.

The purpose of day centres for adults with learning disabilities is partly affected by the level of discrimination against people in usual everyday activity and partly by the level of resourcing required to enable disabled people to access usual community facilities and activities.

A primary activity in usual life for many people is that of paid employment. Learning disabled people may need a different approach in terms of the support

Group activities for people with mental health needs

London Borough of Newham Mental Health Day Opportunities Service

This organisation provides group activities for people with severe and enduring mental health support needs. The Team comprises occupational therapists, support workers, specialist employment support workers, a nurse, a social worker, manager, deputy manager and an administrative officer. The activities take place at various locations in Newham, including community centres, church halls, leisure centres, health centres – plus some 'out and about' groups.

Activities include:

- classes on anxiety management, assertiveness and healthy eating
- supportive discussion groups
- sport and exercise activities such as crafts, music, horticulture and acting
- a number of women-only groups, as well as a young person's group.

There are employment activities including:

- a hospitality-related scheme run at a health centre via a café project
- an office work scheme focusing on building the confidence and skills to find work.

Anyone referred to the service must be on the Care Programme Approach Register, and involved with Newham's mental health services. Referral is made through Community Mental Health Teams, the Home Treatment Team, Assertive Outreach Team, the Rehabilitation and Recovery Team, Psychological Therapies Service, Newham Centre for Mental Health and the out-patients clinic.

An assessment is made and then individuals are offered a programme of group activities to suit their needs and interests. Each person has a 'named worker' in the team who keeps in touch with them regarding their progress, liaises with referrers and care co-ordinators and attends Care Programme Approach meetings.

www.newham.gov.uk (2007)

Questions

1 What is your view on services being organised locally by different organisations? Do you think this creates innovation and a close response to local needs, or does it create a divided country with too much variation in what people can access?
2 Are there any new organisations locally that have been set up specifically to manage services?

required to undertake work activity; they may need assistance in terms of appropriate work relations, pace and level of work. There is an emphasis on day services being a focal point for accessing supported employment.

The White Paper *Valuing People* stated that individuals should engage in more locally-based community activities in small groups, rather than minibus groups of people travelling to an allocated slot for disabled people at the sports centre. Many day centres have been closing and new arrangements for the provision of day activities have been sourced.

End of life care

This has also been known as palliative care and relates to the support of individuals towards the end of their life. It can take place in a person's own home, a care home, hospital or hospice. A formal review on end of life care is being led by local clinical pathway groups in each Strategic Health Authority during 2008 and the *End of Life Care Strategy* is due for publication in June 2008.

Hospices

These provide a holistic approach to nursing and social care needs in an environment appropriate to the last weeks of life. Due to pressures on rooms, a hospice may need confirmation that a person is in the

Helen & Douglas House

Helen & Douglas House is a registered charity providing respite and end of life care for children and young adults with life-shortening conditions, as well as support and friendship for the whole family. The two hospice houses are bright, vibrant and positive places, where the emphasis is on living life to the full, even when that life may be short.

There are many families in the UK who are caring for a child, or a young adult, who has a life-shortening condition. Caring for someone with such a condition, often for 24 hours a day, seven days a week, over many years, can put an immeasurable strain upon the family. And whilst families willingly invest love, energy and care, life becomes governed by the relentless timetable of nursing and medical needs. Relationships can suffer, careers may have to be abandoned, healthy brothers and sisters can feel left out and regular family activities and holidays can be rare. Families can often feel alone and afraid in their grief.

How Helen & Douglas House can help: Children can stay at Helen House and young adults can stay at Douglas House, along with their families, for short periods of time for rest and recuperation, treatment of distressing symptoms, end of life care and support. Helen & Douglas House aims to help the children and

young adults who stay at one of the two Houses to live life to the full as far as possible.

Sister Frances Dominica, founder of Helen House, the world's first children's hospice, which opened in Oxford in 1982

end stages of their life as they particularly cater for this group of people. People may move to a hospice from hospital. The pleasant environment is set up to support individuals and their families at a time when they need privacy, dignity and individual respect, at the same time as sometimes requiring continuous nursing support and substantial personal care. Some hospices provide respite care for those who have their needs met at home but whose family carers require a break.

NHS walk in centres

These are part of the local delivery of community-based healthcare and are seen as an essential way of preventing inappropriate admission to hospital or calls to the emergency medical services. They provide immediate advice, support and treatment, and are available at times when GPs may not be available.

NHS Direct and Care Direct

These have been designed to support individuals out of normal weekly hours. Although there are difficulties in delivering a service over the phone they have been used by many people. The aim has been to have continuity in contact with services out of hours and also to prevent people contacting emergency services when the health or social care needed can be managed until an appropriate time.

Care Direct was awarded £2 million of Department of Health grants in the first year, when 40 per cent of all callers to Care Direct were 70 years and over; this is a significant support to a potentially isolated group of people.

An example of a Care Direct scheme is Gloucestershire Care Direct. When this was set up it worked closely with Social Services and rapid response teams and established links with Age Concern to ensure that it was able to provide comprehensive support to older people in the area.

Funding care provision

Monitoring funding

The role of the Audit Commission is to improve the quality of financial management in the NHS and encourage continual improvement in all public services. They:

- audit NHS trusts, PCTs and strategic health authorities to review the quality of their financial systems and their work with foundation trusts
- publish independent reports which highlight risks and good practice to improve the quality of financial management in the health service
- encourage continual improvement in public services including in the field of public health and health inequalities.

CASE STUDY

Annual budgets

The annual budget for Bexley Care Trust, Kent 2004/05:

£236 million to spend on health services

£3.8 million to provide social care services

These resources were distributed between:

- Prescription services 12%
- General Practitioner Services 12%
- Learning Disabilities 2%
- Mental Illness 10%
- Maternity 3%
- General Hospital Services 44%
- Accident and Emergency 4%
- Community Health 11%
- Administration 2%

Questions

1 Obtain a copy of your local authority's annual budget and explore how funding is divided between services.

2 Think about this in relation to the profile of your local population. Are there any services that seem underfunded compared to others? Are there any areas of increased investment over the next few years that have been announced?

Individual funding

But shouldn't care be free?

There has been much public voice regarding the costs of services that individuals receive. Many people expect to receive services free of charge and are surprised when they either pay for them in full or are assessed to establish what level of payment they are responsible for. This is partly due to the fact that most people pay the following:

- National Insurance
- income tax
- local council tax
- taxes on goods and services.

The idea of free care sounds good and for years this has been the expectation for many people. In Scotland a decision was made to provide free personal care as well as health care. In January 2008 it was announced that this policy was under review as the Scottish government was unable to commit to this expenditure indefinitely.

Guidance on charging individuals for their residential care

Capital assets (property and savings in accounts) and current income are considered when an individual is assessed for charges for residential care.

People with less than £21,500 are entitled to apply for financial help from social services. The National Assistance Act 1948 stipulated that where a local authority pays towards the cost of a person's care in a care home, the authority must assess what a person can afford to pay for that care and then charge them accordingly.

Local authorities assess a person's ability to pay charges using the National Assistance (Assessment of Resources) Regulations 1992. The Department of Health *Social Care Guidance: Charging for Residential Accommodation Guide* provides guidance on this; it aims to encourage a consistent and fair approach.

Key factors in the assessment

Capital assets and income, including the former home, have always been taken into account in the assessment of fair charges. Residents of care homes with £13,000, or less, have this sum disregarded in the calculation of what they can afford to contribute towards the cost of their care.

There are times when the value of the resident's former home will be disregarded. For example:

- if the property continues to be the home of a spouse or certain relatives
- for the first 12 weeks after admission into a care home.
- local authorities may use their discretion to disregard the value of a resident's home if it continues to be the home of a former carer or other type of person. They also have discretionary powers to agree a deferred payment arrangement; this means that they can place a charge against the value of the property which is not collected until the end of the contract.

Elements funded by the government

Any nursing care that the individual requires is paid for by the NHS. Care home residents who are supported by local authorities contribute most of their income to fees but to ensure that they have money to spend on personal items, residents are guaranteed a weekly Personal Expenses Allowance (PEA).

Charging for services is controversial and this applies across all aspects of local authority provision, not just concerning health and social care.

Audit Commission: facts and figures for local authority charging

Research by the Audit Commission has shown the significant contribution that charging has on council income.

- In 2006/07, councils in England raised £10.8 billion from charges for services, not including housing rents. This was around 8 per cent of their total income and about half as much as they raised in council tax.

Campaigning for personal allowances

At the beginning of 2008, Age Concern was campaigning for the *Personal Expenses Allowance* (PEA) in Care Homes to be increased. The charity stated that:

> Many older people living in care homes are amongst the poorest and most vulnerable members of society. With the average weekly care home fee in England being £400, almost 260,000 people need financial support from the state to pay their fees. The vast majority of these people are 65 years old or over, most are aged over 85. Under national means-testing rules, these people part with their only source of income – their pensions – to pay towards their care home fees. Normally all they are left with is £20.45 Personal Expenses Allowance. £20.45 is expected to cover the cost of all personal items not covered by the care package agreed by the local authority, including clothes and toiletries. We believe that the Personal Expenses Allowance given to older people in care homes is symbolic of the way that older people are treated in society.

Age Concern is seeking the following response:

From the government:

- to increase the PEA to at least £40 for people living in care homes who are supported by local authorities

- to increase the PEA each year in line with any rise in earnings
- to ensure that funding for Adult Personal Social Services reflects this increase in the PEA.

From local authorities/ Primary Care Trusts and service providers:

- to ensure that older people living in care homes are aware of and have access to free NHS services, such as chiropody and physiotherapy
- to provide older people living in care homes with information, support and access to varied leisure and social activities that are stimulating and compatible with individual interests, needs and abilities.

Questions

1 Make a judgement about what level of personal allowance individuals should receive if they live in a residential service.

2 If you work in a care home, try to establish what views are evident in the home about the personal allowance. If you work in a different service, consider any elements of provision that people are expected to pay for. Do you think this is appropriate?

- County councils collect the most charging income, but it is for district councils that charges make the greatest contribution to service delivery; equal to nearly one-fifth of total service expenditure.
- Over a quarter of councils generate more income through charging than they do through council tax.

Councils also use charging to influence individuals' choices and behaviours, to bring other benefits to local communities:

- Charges can be set to encourage or discourage people to use services and, through concessions, to target services at particular groups.
- They can also be used to ration services and other resources where demand is high or where overuse is deemed undesirable.

- Councils have used charges and concessions to pursue local objectives, such as promoting participation in sports and leisure activities by target groups to reduce health inequalities.

In choosing how charges are used, councils and central government make an important political decision – which users should pay for which services and which services should be subsidised by taxpayers:

- They make very different decisions about which services to provide and whether, and at what level, to charge for and subsidise services.
- As a consequence, households in different council areas can pay different amounts for essentially the same services.
- There is no relationship between income from charging and levels of council tax, although many

councils use charging to minimise council tax increases.

- There is no clear relationship between councils' income from charging and either overall council performance or levels of local deprivation.

The flexibility to use charges to meet local challenges is limited by centrally imposed restrictions:

- Central government sets the level of some charges and restricts the extent of charging in other areas and is limited because of concerns about geographic variation in charges.

Councils' perceptions of local opposition to charges are not always backed up with robust evidence:

- The public is more receptive to charging for some services than is often assumed. People are more willing to pay charges where they can see what they are getting for their money and have a degree of choice.
- People believe they get value for money from almost all of the local authority services for which they pay charges.

The reasons for the growth over time in health spending have been examined in some detail and the following factors have been identified:

- Inflation in the health sector has tended to be slightly higher than in the economy as a whole.
- Demographic changes have created extra demands on the health system, particularly from a growing proportion of older people who make more use of healthcare.
- Intensity of use of health services has been increasing constantly, with each individual on average making more use of them: more consultations, more hospital admissions, more operations, and more prescriptions. In turn these are more expensive because of the advanced equipment, more and better paid registered nursing and medical staff, higher standards and so on. (Webster (ed.), 2001, page 308)

Private Finance Initiative (PFI)

The government has taken several approaches to introduce private finance into the care sector through first the Private Finance Initiative and then the public private partnerships. Media attention has been on the use of private monies to build new hospitals, but there

CASE STUDY

Paying for care

Mr Peck is 92-years-old and has finally decided to move into a care home. Whilst he is still very able mentally, his physical mobility has reduced over the recent months and he knows he cannot really manage. He owns his house, which he bought with his wife in 1963 for £2,600. He has been paying National Insurance through his salary all his working life and feels that he has worked hard to provide for his wife when she was alive and their family. Mr Peck is surprised that the care manager talks to him about his finances when he discusses moving to a care home, as he thought he would be looked after in his old age.

Questions

Should individuals pay for their own care if they can afford to?

1. Give the reasons why Mr Peck should be able to keep his house and any financial assets he has, and pass them to his children for them to benefit from.
2. Give the reasons why the sale of Mr Peck's house should be used to pay for his care in the foreseeable future, along with other assets that he has.
3. Consider your overall response, thinking as if you were a policy maker in the government and you are looking at the projected demography of the population.

are continuing contentious ideas about how to develop the role of private finances in the provision of both health and social care.

Funding organisations

Organisations obtain funding from local authorities to pay for the care services that they are providing. This payment is sometimes made directly to the individual, who then makes a payment to the service provider. The monies may also be paid directly to the organisation where a long-term contract has been negotiated. The independent sector has been more focused on the relationship of individual service users to the exchange of monies, but this model is now applied to local authority managed services as well.

In a care home the registered manager or accountant will obtain monies from the people who live in the home and this may be made by direct transfer from their own account.

Traditionally, nursing care, as with most NHS services, has been provided free of charge. There appears to be continued dispute over who has responsibility for paying for the care needs of people, whether they have nursing or personal care needs. The NHS has a responsibility for financing the continuation of care following transition to alternative accommodation after leaving hospital.

The Coughlan judgement of July 1999 ascertained that 'The nursing service must be provided by the NHS where the primary need of the person for nursing home accommodation is a health need' and if the secondary need for accommodation is nursing, then this can be provided by either the NHS or social services department.'

Funding individuals

Before the 1990s individuals were very removed from discussions about finances and who would pay for their care. The relationship between individuals and finances was not so tightly monitored. Groups were provided with care and monies were often pooled to accommodate the group needs rather than being attached to meet individual need. Currently, care services are provided to individuals on the basis of need. Once a person's needs have been established there are services to which an individual may be entitled free of charge, or services for which they will need to have a financial assessment in order to establish any level of contribution. There are also care services available to individuals who wish to purchase these separately.

There are some services to which an individual is entitled as a statutory entitlement, and they will be provided free of charge. These are:

- an assessment of need for an individual and any carers
- provision of accommodation and day services for learning disabled individuals
- accommodation for some individuals with mental health needs.

Some services are also an entitlement but the individual may need to undergo a financial assessment in order to establish whether they need to make a contribution. These are:

- moving into a care home
- home care (domiciliary) services.

There are also some care or support services which people can access that they may not have been assessed for, or for which they may have been assessed but not found to be entitled to. Some of these services individuals can access independently by making their own arrangements and paying directly themselves.

The changing relationship of individuals to the care that they receive in terms of money has meant that some people are able to be more assertive about the care that they receive, as evidenced in a social services report. 'Why am I charged for two half-hour visits per

---

CASE STUDY

Funding Maisie's care

Maisie is moving into Sherwood Lodge Care Home. She has assets of £73,000 as she sold her house when she moved. Maisie does not have any children and has been given advice from Age Concern about her finances. She will be paying for her care each week through a standing order that she has arranged. When the money that she has reduces to less than £13,000 she can have a financial assessment with a local authority care manager who will arrange a contract for the continuation of care, usually in the same home. Age Concern has also given Maisie some advice about having an advocate and the legal arrangements for managing her money in the future if she needs additional support.

Organisations are accountable for the monies that they spend. Maisie has an individual accounts book in the home and her money is not used to finance the care of other people.

Questions

1 If Maisie has any particular items that she wants, or particular activities that she wants to get involved in, how can she finance these?
2 What do you think might happen if Maisie's situation changes so that she needs nursing rather than residential care?

day when the carer is in such a hurry and stays for less than fifteen minutes each time?' (Social Services Inspectorate, 2002, Section 3.21)

Resource allocation is a tighter science than it used to be. Budgets have to be justified and then accounted for. The White Paper *Valuing People* stated that: 'decisions about resource allocation need to be evidence-based and take account of the likely increase in demand for services from people with learning disabilities'. (Department of Health, 2001, page 95). It also identified that quality assurance needed to be a feature of the budget. 'The application of best value principles will achieve better value for money.'

Legislation since the 1990s has progressed a change in the relationship of individuals to the state with respect to money. People with disabilities, and older people, are no longer viewed as having state handouts and are viewed as claiming what is rightfully theirs. The Direct Payments policy, as discussed in Chapter 7, is an example of this change, as are the changes associated with carers' legislation.

One of the first discussions in this chapter explored the relationship between poverty and individuals who have care or support needs that have been identified through research. Appropriate financial support can facilitate the participation of individuals in society and prevent them from developing additional needs associated with poverty. The Labour government has been developing its strategy for enabling disabled people to engage in employment whilst also obtaining support through additional income. Some people who require support of care services are financially self-sufficient due to either current income or past ability to earn and save. In recent years, more attention has been paid to the potential for providing support to individuals in need through the allocation of more funds directly to them. Benefits are one means of providing additional income to people in order for them to make decisions about the level and type of support that they want.

The benefit system provides an example of how complex individual's lives can be where they have to obtain income from different sources. Many authorities have care managers who have developed a level of expertise in this area in order to support individuals in maximising their incomes.

Financial arrangements

James has been struggling to continue working full-time following his diagnosis with multiple sclerosis. He really wants to work as he enjoys his job but he is concerned for his health and also needs to access more medical support on a regular basis.

Shona left her job following a prolonged period of depression. She felt unable to function and had returned to her parents' home. She now feels that she wants to regain her sense of independence as a step to regaining control and mental well-being. She is uncertain where to start as she has no money.

Questions

1 Investigate the financial arrangements for these two individuals. Make a note of how long it takes you to find out this information and how many people or places you had to source.

2 Consider how easy this process would be if you were actually at the point of needing this support.

Regulation and enforcement of quality in health and social care

Health and social care services are constantly undergoing change in order to achieve better and fairer health and social care services for everyone. It is important for government to ensure that local authority and health reforms work together in an integrated and coherent way.

The aim is that there should be locally driven health and social care services that:

- are more personalised and shaped around an individual's needs and preferences
- give everyone access to high-quality care
- get the best value for taxpayers' money

Performance judgements

The Audit Commission judged that one council provided a poor, zero star, service in carrying out its responsibilities for the planning and delivery of the Supporting People programme.

A rapid increase in services within one year has been driven by providers, rather than consultation with users. The council did not take control of the emerging service provision and exacerbated the rapid and uncoordinated development of services through its own actions in putting pressure on residential care service providers to seek de-registration for financial expediency rather than from strategic and needs-driven criteria.

The review programme is the key to understanding whether services are high-quality, delivering positive outcomes for users and represent value for money. It also needs to link to and inform wider commissioning strategies. Early reviews undertaken by the council have shown that a small minority of services are poor, do not comply with grant conditions and need urgent action. This is now underway, but value for money issues have not been fully addressed to date. The service review programme needs to be adjusted to ensure that the highest cost services are reviewed at an early stage and action taken so that resources can be refocused to meet the gaps in services that still exist.

The Audit Commission identified the need for the following response:

- ownership of problems and willingness to change
- a sustained focus on what matters
- the capacity and systems to deliver performance and improvement
- integration of continuous improvement into day-to-day management.

The council has responded well to the challenge of inspection and senior managers have shown commitment to respond in a positive manner. Partner organisations recognise that the core strategy group needs to increase its skills and focus on strategic direction.

Positives:

- A joint strategy for the development of older people's housing support is being written following guidance.

- The need to rebalance sheltered and extra care housing has been recognised and will be addressed by the strategy.
- Each district developing specific local plans which will give a clearer direction to planning across housing, health and social care.

Negatives:

- Neither the council nor the Supporting People team has provided effective leadership to ensure Supporting People is integrated with the council's wider priorities and planning frameworks and those of partners.
- There is no coherent strategy that articulates what the council and its partners wish to achieve. Uncertainty over the future funding of some learning disability services is stated to be causing a planning blight.
- Little action has been taken to move beyond this stance and the Supporting People team have been focused on implementation during the last year rather than on developing a strategy.

Summary

We consider that the Council has uncertain prospects for improvement in the planning and delivery of its Supporting People programme.

Good progress was made in the early planning stages for the Supporting People programme. A team was in place and working with service providers to identify gaps in service provision and develop new floating support services. There is also evidence of constructive partnership working through the core strategy group and commissioning body. However, since its implementation the team have struggled due to a massive, largely unplanned, late growth in services and staff turnover.

There has been a lack of corporate ownership and action to tackle the problems which were not clearly reported outside of the core strategy group and the commissioning body. The Supporting People team still appears isolated and line management arrangements are not effective. Performance monitoring of the Supporting People team is not robust and there are no agreed measures that are used as indicators of the team's performance.

- give staff the opportunity and flexibility to work in new ways and develop better ways of delivering services.

The government remains committed to delivering the 2000 NHS Plan which was a 10-year strategy for reform.

Health and Social Care Bill November 2007

This proposal contained a number of important measures to modernise and integrate health and social care. It was part of the Labour government's 'Governance of Britain: The Government's Draft Legislative Programme'.

It contains four key policy areas:

Care Quality Commission

The is the new integrated regulator for health and adult social care, bringing together existing health and social care regulators into one regulatory body, with tough new powers to ensure safe and high-quality services.

Professional regulation

This will enhance public and professional confidence in the system of professional regulation and strengthen clinical governance as part of the government's response to the Shipman Inquiry.

Public health protection measures

This provides a comprehensive set of public health measures to help prevent and control the spread of serious diseases caused by infection and contamination.

Health in pregnancy grant

This will be a one-off payment to expectant mothers ordinarily resident in the UK, to help with the costs of a healthy lifestyle, including diet, in the later stages of pregnancy.

The Bill included a number of smaller measures:

- powers to extend membership of NHS indemnity schemes
- the extension of direct payments
- changes to the National Assistance Act 1948
- the creation of a power for the Secretary of State to give financial assistance to social enterprises
- the creation of the National Information Governance Board for Health and Social Care.

Any service sector requires systems to ensure that the quality of delivery is being maintained and that established standards are being observed; this is particularly true of the care sector. In a sector where people's rights are being given more respect, it is important that the users of care services are provided with appropriate mechanisms for telling service providers what they think of the services that they are getting.

There are several strategies for applying standards to the provision of care to ensure that the quality of care services is appropriate and these operate on a national level managed through organisations established by central government. The origins of current regulations were established in the Care Standards Act 2000.

Commission for Social Care Inspection (CSCI)

The Commission for Social Care Inspection (CSCI) wants to know from service users if the services:

- promote their independence
- provide the opportunities they seek
- offer them protection when they need it
- support their rights and choices.

The Care Standards Act 2000 introduced a new body for the regulation of care services, the National Care Standards Commission. From April 2004 the CSCI took over this role. This independent body, created from the Health and Social Care (Community Health and Standards) Act 2003, took responsibility for the role that had previously been carried out by the National Care Standards Commission, the Social Services Inspectorate and the SSI/Audit Commission Joint Review team. These responsibilities will be assumed by the new Care Quality Commission during 2008.

It has responsibility to:

- promote improvement in social care
- inspect all social care – public, private and voluntary
- register services that meet national standards
- inspect council social services
- publish an annual report to Parliament on social care
- hold performance statistics on social care
- publish the star ratings for council social services.

The CSCI aims are to:

- put the people who use social care first
- improve services and stamp out bad practice
- be an expert voice on social care
- practise what we preach in our own organisation.

The CSCI will be able to track the service provided for a person from the point at which their needs are met,

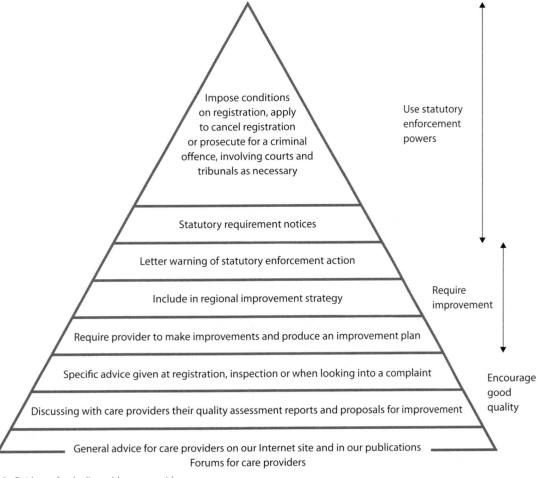

Figure 1.5 Guidance for dealing with care providers

through to the planning and delivery of the services they receive. It will work closely with other inspectorates, especially the Commission for Healthcare Audit and Inspection, which has a similar responsibility in healthcare services. Reports are provided from these regulatory bodies that are in the public domain. These include specific inspection reports based on individual visits.

The Health and Social Care Bill 2007 set in motion the creation of the Care Quality Commission which will be assuming responsibilities across both the social care and the health sectors. The CSCI:

- works with organisations that commission care services, such as councils and Primary Care Trusts, to identify ways they can encourage care services to improve
- publishes inspection reports that give information about the quality of care services; this helps people to choose the right service for them
- may use statutory enforcement powers if a care provider fails to abide by the law.

It will use enforcement if:

- the provider does not make the improvements needed within a reasonable time, or
- people using the service are at risk and there is a need to act straightaway to safeguard their interests.

The CSCI has legal powers to enforce improvement or cancel registration if care providers do not do what the law says they must when providing care services. There are different types of enforcement action that it can take, depending on how seriously the care service is failing to meet its legal obligations, what effect this is having on the people using the service and the care service provider's response. The CSCI will be replaced by the Care Quality Commission in 2008.

National Minimum Standards

Just as there are standards to which care workers should aspire, there are also standards that specify the quality of the care to be provided to individuals in a particular service setting. Checking on organisations that provide services involves requiring organisations to audit themselves and this has been facilitated through the creation of National Minimum Standards. National Minimum Standards originate from the Care Standards Act 2000. They are the

statements that are to be referred to in the inspection of particular care organisations.

National Service Frameworks

National Service Frameworks are policy statements that establish the priorities that need to be worked to, and the standards which need to be addressed generally, usually across a range of organisations. The National Service Framework for Older People is introduced by the Department of Health as '... this ambitious programme of change ...'. (Department of Health, 2001, page 14)

The themes are:

Respecting the individual
Standard 1: Rooting out age discrimination

CASE STUDY

Organisation of care services

Portsmouth Social Services

Reviewed by team: Audit Commission and Department of Health, January to March 2003

'The Council has an impressive record in tackling regeneration and has achieved beacon status for neighbourhood renewal.'

Some of the main findings are:

'Users and carers are very positive about the services they receive in Portsmouth.'

'Assessment and care planning is generally good.'

'Support for carers is good but more priority now needs to be given to carers' assessments.'

'Adult mental health services are of an exceptionally high standard.'

'Reviews and carers' assessments need to be prioritised and planning for people with physical disabilities needs to improve.'

Questions

1 Find out about the most recent report on your local authority.
2 What do you think is the local perception of how good the council is? What areas need to be improved?

Standard 2: Person centred care

Intermediate care
Standard 3: Intermediate care

Providing evidenced based specialist care
Standard 4: General hospital care
Standard 5: Stroke
Standard 6: Falls
Standard 7: Mental health in older people

Promoting an active, healthy life
Standard 8: The promotion of health and active life in older age

Issues in provision of care

Partnership with service users

Other chapters in this book focus on the relationships that care workers and organisations should have both with services users and other care providers. Working in partnership with service users and other care organisations empowers people and can give service users more control through facilitating their input into the policy making process.

The NHS has embarked on a consultation project to ascertain from local populations their view of how healthcare should be provided. London's 'Consulting the Capital' is an example of this.

The People's Parliament aims to provide a framework for the organisation of disabled people to have input into the way that services are organised and policies are introduced.

The Learning Disability Partnership Boards should ensure that:

- people with learning disabilities and carers contribute to the board
- local cultural diversity is reflected in its membership
- the local independent sector and voluntary sector are fully engaged.

They are responsible for:

- developing and implementing the joint investment plan for delivering the government's objectives
- overseeing inter-agency planning and commissioning of comprehensive, integrated and inclusive services that provide a genuine choice of service options to people in their local community
- ensuring that people are not denied their right to a local service because of a lack of competence or capacity amongst service providers
- using Health Act flexibilities
- ensuring arrangements are in place to achieve a smooth transition to adult life for learning disabled young people.

> **REFLECT**
>
> Identify and think about the key policies that have an impact on the work that you do. Make a list of how the policies affect:
> - the lives of the individuals that you support
> - the organisation that you work for
> - the role that you have.

Policy has a big impact on the quality of experience for individuals. The main advantage of direct payments is that the person can decide who will best meet their needs and when. Direct payments give the user a far greater amount of freedom and control than they would if receiving services directly from the local authority or other service provider (Luckhurst, 2002, page 19).

A lack of consultation means that services remain inappropriate and inflexible, service staff do not develop a sensitivity to the circumstances of minority ethnic groups or to the support needs which they themselves identify, and users feel undervalued (Butt and Mirza, 1996, in Department of Health, 2001, page 15).

An example would be withholding correspondence in the interests of the patient with, or sometimes without, their consent.

In the Mental Health Bill 2003: 'Decisions to apply compulsion will be made subject to overriding principles. The code of practice must set out the general principles and the circumstances in which they will apply.'

TATE

The TATE Project (Through **Assistive Technology** to Employment) has been helping people with learning disabilities to take up jobs by providing them with equipment, skills and training. It installs technology in the home to make everyday living easier for individuals and their carers.

Examples:

Ian does not enjoy showering. TATE installed a 'disco shower'. When he turns on the shower, his favourite music plays and lots of lights flash, making it an enjoyable experience.

Clare has trialled a smart microwave oven which reads bar codes from prepared meals. This enables Clare to prepare meals independently.

TATE also provides dedicated training and computer programmes to help people with managing budgets, health and safety at work and other important skills, so that they can take up jobs and live independent lives.

www.tateproject.org.uk

Questions

1 Be imaginative and think about an aspect of daily life that presents a challenge to those who you support. What item would really make an impact on their ability to be independent?
2 Find out more about TATE and consider how its assistive technologies could be used to help different service users.

The principles will require:

- patients to be involved when decisions are made about them
- the decision maker to demonstrate that the proposed treatment imposes the minimum level of intrusion consistent with the ability to address the person's disorder and its effects
- decisions to be taken in a fair and open way, so that the patient knows what is happening.

In the document *Nothing About Us Without Us: The Report from the Service Users Advisory Group* it was explained that the involvement of learning disabled people has helped government to understand what needs to change. (Department of Health, 2001, page 11)

Health and social care workers

Our understanding of what response the care sectors need to make to individuals who have health and social care needs is constantly adapting. It is therefore no surprise that the role of social care workers, their job descriptions and job titles change to accommodate new expectations.

The Care Standards Act 2000 established the General Social Care Council (GSCC) which has a role in developing and regulating the social care workforce. The registration of social care workers has begun, starting with social workers. The aim is to prevent people from continuing work in the sector by moving to a new employer when they are dismissed for poor practice. It also aims to monitor the progress of social care workers in terms of their qualifications and continuing professional development.

A further means of ensuring the appropriateness of care workers is through the checks undertaken by the Criminal Records Bureau when people first start employment with an organisation.

Sector Skills Councils are responsible for ensuring the raising of standards in the workforce through the development of appropriate qualifications and training.

REFLECT

1 Read through the statements on pages 43–44 and reflect on how your own care practice demonstrates that you adhere to these codes. If there are any statements that are challenging to you, you may need to consider how you can improve your practice against this standard.
2 Think also about the role of your organisation in ensuring that you can meet these requirements.
3 If you have management responsibility you will need to consider whether you are supporting your care staff in their requirements.

Skills for Health and Skills for Care work closely together so that the workforce is responsive to changes in the care needs of the population. They have developed induction and foundation standards that provide awards based on assessed criteria to which newly recruited care workers will work.

In this section we have looked at the regulatory context of care and how organisations have to respond to the requirements of the Care Standards Act 2000. We now look at how the legislation impacts on the individual care worker.

Care workers need to adhere to the following Code of Practice produced by the GSCC as part of their remit under the Care Standards Act 2000.

The General Social Care Council: Code of Practice for Social Care Workers

The General Social Care Council expects social care workers to meet this code and may take action if registered workers fail to do so.

Employers of social care workers are required to take account of this code in making any decisions about the conduct of their staff.

Social care workers must:

- protect the rights and promote the interests of service users and carers;
- strive to establish and maintain the trust and confidence of service users and carers;
- promote the independence of service users while protecting them as far as possible from danger or harm;
- respect the rights of service users whilst seeking to ensure that their behaviour does not harm themselves or other people;
- uphold public trust and confidence in social care services; and be accountable for the quality of their work and take responsibility for maintaining and improving their knowledge and skills.

1   As a social care worker, you must protect the rights and promote the interests of service users and carers

This includes:

1.1 treating each person as an individual;

1.2 respecting and, where appropriate, promoting the individual views and wishes of both service users and carers;

1.3 supporting service users' rights to control their lives and make informed choices about the services they receive;

1.4 respecting and maintaining the dignity and privacy of service users;

1.5 promoting equal opportunities for service users and carers; and

1.6 respecting diversity and different cultures and values.

2   As a social care worker, you must strive to establish and maintain the trust and confidence of service users and carers

This includes:

2.1 being honest and trustworthy;

2.2 communicating in an appropriate, open, accurate and straightforward way;

2.3 respecting confidential information and clearly explaining agency policies about confidentiality to service users and carers;

2.4 being reliable and dependable;

2.5 honouring work commitments, agreements and arrangements and, when it is not possible to do so, explaining why to service users and carers;

2.6 declaring issues that might create conflicts of interest and making sure that they do not influence your judgement or practice; and

2.7 adhering to policies and procedures about accepting gifts and money from service users and carers.

3   As a social care worker, you must promote the independence of service users while protecting them as far as possible from danger or harm

This includes:

3.1 promoting the independence of service users and assisting them to understand and exercise their rights;

3.2 using established processes and procedures to challenge and report dangerous, abusive, discriminatory or exploitative behaviour and practice;

3.3 following practice and procedures designed to keep you and other people safe from violent and abusive behaviour at work;

3.4 bringing to the attention of your employer or the appropriate authority resource or operational difficulties that might get in the way of the delivery of safe care;

3.5 informing your employer or an appropriate authority where the practice of colleagues may be unsafe or adversely affecting standards of care;

3.6 complying with employers' health and safety policies, including those relating to substance abuse;

3.7 helping service users and carers to make complaints, taking complaints seriously and responding to them or passing them to the appropriate person; and

3.8 recognising and using responsibly the power that comes from your work with service users and carers.

4   As a social care worker, you must respect the rights of service users while seeking to ensure that their behaviour does not harm themselves or other people

This includes:

4.1 recognising that service users have the right to take risks and helping them to identify and manage potential and actual risks to themselves and others;

4.2 following risk assessment policies and procedures to assess whether the behaviour of service users presents a risk of harm to themselves or others;

4.3 taking necessary steps to minimise the risks of service users from doing actual or potential harm to themselves or other people; and

4.4 ensuring that relevant colleagues and agencies are informed about the outcomes and implications of risk assessments.

5   As a social care worker, you must uphold public trust and confidence in social care services

In particular you must not:

5.1 abuse, neglect or harm service users, carers or colleagues;

5.2 exploit service users, carers or colleagues in any way;

5.3 abuse the trust of service users and carers or the access you have to personal information about them or to their property, home or workplace;

5.4 form inappropriate personal relationships with service users;

5.5 discriminate unlawfully or unjustifiably against service users, carers or colleagues;

5.6 condone any unlawful or unjustifiable discrimination by service users, carers or colleagues;

5.7 put yourself or other people at unnecessary risk; or

5.8 behave in a way, in work or outside work, which would call into question your suitability to work in social care services.

6   As a social care worker, you must be accountable for the quality of your work and take responsibility for maintaining and improving your knowledge and skills

This includes:

6.1 meeting relevant standards of practice and working in a lawful, safe and effective way;

6.2 maintaining clear and accurate records as required by procedures established for your work;

6.3 informing your employer or the appropriate authority about any personal difficulties that might affect your ability to do your job competently and safely;

6.4 seeking assistance from your employer or the appropriate authority if you do not feel able or adequately prepared to carry out any aspect of your work, or you are not sure about how to proceed in a work matter;

6.5 working openly and co-operatively with colleagues and treating them with respect;

6.6 recognising that you remain responsible for the work that you have delegated to other workers;

6.7 recognising and respecting the roles and expertise of workers from other agencies and working in partnership with them; and

6.8 undertaking relevant training to maintain and improve your knowledge and skills and contributing to the learning and development of others.

These standards influence the role of the care worker and also the approach that the care worker should take in carrying out their responsibilities. They are evident in all the chapters in this book and there is a grid at the back of the book referring to sections that relate to these.

ACTIVITY

Think about the way that your own organisation has changed in the time that you have been there and make a list of what these changes have been.

For each of these changes, explore the reasons behind them. Do they relate to:

- skills profile of the team, roles and job descriptions of care staff and others?
- the management and finances of the organisation?
- the relationship that service users have with how the organisation is run?

Think about the effects that these changes have had on:

- the service users and their relatives/other carers
- yourself and your colleagues
- your manager and the organisation.

It is good practice to be constantly aware of changes that take place as this helps us to be more adaptable to change, and more professional in the way that we manage this with service users.

The subjects covered in this chapter are constantly changing so you need to keep up to date. The Internet is a very useful way of keeping up with new legislation as well as providing guidelines relating to your role as a care worker. This form of communication has enabled the government to go some way in meeting its aim to be more open. Watching, reading or listening to the news is also a means of making sure that you know what changes are proposed, or taking place.

At the beginning of this chapter we considered the history of health and social care and it will be interesting to consider the potential changes over the next few decades. Some people are choosing to live in hotels to overcome the difficulties of managing shopping, cleaning and cooking without having to become a user of care services.

Shared Vision for Transformation of Health and Social Care Services

December 2007

It is worth revisiting the statements made by the Secretary of State for Health about the 'shared vision for transformation'.

1 A new relationship between government, local authorities, the NHS, independent sector providers and the regulator.
2 A major shift of resources and practice to prevention, early intervention and re-enablement.
3 High-quality accessible information and advice available to all irrespective of financial means.
4 A commitment to treating carers as partners and
5 Maximum power, control and choice in the hands of the people who use these services and their carers.
6 A major redistribution of power from the state to the citizen according to the fundamental human right to self-determination. This has the potential to be one of the most radical public service reforms for a generation: twenty-first century social justice with an active and empowering state, rather than one which is paternalistic and controlling.

KNOWLEDGE CHECK

1 Think about the potential for realising these goals and draw a diagram illustrating what care services may look like in the future.
2 What is happening in your local area that reflects this significant change?
3 What impact does this change have on your own organisation?
4 Think about the service users who you work with. What benefits does this new organisation of care services have on their lives? Are there any potentially negative outcomes for them?

Glossary

Advocacy: support for people who are thought likely to be disregarded or to have difficulty in gaining attention, so that their opinion is listened to.

Altruism: an attitude, or way of behaving, marked by unselfish concern for the welfare of others.

Assistive technology: any device that enables a person to improve their ability to communicate or carry out daily living skills.

Commissioning: statutory providers making arrangements for a health and social care provider to deliver services or facilities that they are responsible for.

Duties: the activities that an organisation is legally required to carry out.

Enforcement: management of compliance with legal requirements of organisations.

Policy: written guidance that informs or shapes practice can be a guideline or an actual law.

Powers: the activities that an organisation is allowed to carry out within its legal responsibilities.

Procurement: the process of identifying and securing an organisation to deliver an aspect of health and social care.

Regulation: the monitoring of quality and compliance with legal responsibilities.

Statutory Providers: government organisations with a legal responsibility to deliver an aspect of health or social care.

Trust: organisations with a Management Board set up to organise and deliver an aspect of health or social care to a geographical area.

References

Abbotts, P. and Ackers, L. (1996) *Social Policy for Nurses and the Caring Professions*, Oxford, Blackwell

Alcock, P. (ed.) (1998) *The Student's Companion to Social Policy*, Oxford, Blackwell

Audit Commission (2003), discussing the Doughty Street HR Unit and LSE HR Centre Research (2002)

Butt and Mirza (1996) in Department of Health (2001) *Valuing People*

Crown (2000) *Explanatory Notes to the Care Standards Act*, London, HMSO

Crown (2002) *Delivering the NHS Plan: Next Steps on Investment, Next Steps on Reform*, London, HMSO

Dalley, G. (2001) *Owning independence in retirement: the role and benefits of private sheltered housing*, London, Centre for Policy on Aging

Deacon, R. (2002) *Perspectives on Welfare*, Buckingham, Open University Press

Department of Health (1998) *Modernising Social Services*, London, HMSO

Department of Health (1999) *Modernising Mental Health: Safe, Sound and Supportive*, London, HMSO

Department of Health (2001) *Valuing People* White Paper, London, HMSO

Department of Health (2001) *National Service Framework for Older People*, London, HMSO

Department of Health (2001) *Nothing About Us Without Us: Report from the Service Users Advisory Group*, London, HMSO

Forman, F. and Baldwin, N. (1996) *Mastering British Politics*, Basingstoke, MacMillan

Granville, M. *in* Scull (1979) in Webster, C. (ed.) (2001), *Caring for Health: Ethnicity and Diversity*, Buckingham, Open University Press

Hill, M. (2003) *Understanding Social Policy*, Oxford, Blackwell

Home Office (2002:19) Human Rights Act: Home Office Communication Directive

Luckhurst (2002) 'Direct cash in the hand', *Mental Health Today*, June 2002

Malin, N., Wilmot, S. and Manthorpe, J. (2002) *Key Concepts and Debates in Health and Social Policy*, Buckingham, Open University Press

Pugh, R., Scharf, T., Williams, C. and Roberts, D. (2007) *SCIE Research briefing 22: Obstacles to using and providing rural social care*, Social Care Institute for Excellence

Redmond, I. Carers UK (2003) www.carersuk.org.uk

Stoddart, H., Whitley, E., Harvey, I. and Sharp, D. (2002) 'What determines the use of home care services by elderly people?', *Health and Social Care in the Community* 10 (5), 348–60:358

Townsend (1962) in Webster, C. (ed.) (2001) *Caring for Health: Ethnicity and Diversity*, Buckingham, Open University Press

Webster, C. (ed.) (2001) *Caring for Health: Ethnicity and Diversity*, Buckingham, Open University Press

Useful websites

Association of Directors of Social Services: www.adss.org.uk

Carers UK: www.carersuk.org

Department of Health publications are found at www.dh.gov.uk

Guardian Newspaper Society Section (in the newspaper on Wednesdays): www.guardian.co.uk/society

Joseph Rowntree Charitable Trust: www.jrct.org.uk

Kings Fund (for research and Government Commissioned Reports): www.kingsfund.org.uk

National Care Forum: www.nationalcareforum.org.uk

National Carers Network: www.carersuk.org.uk

Sector Skills Council: Skills for Care: www.skillsforcare.org.uk

Sector Skills Council: Skills for Health: www.skillsforhealth.org.uk

CHAPTER 2

Reflection in action

Introduction

Health and social care work requires a professional attitude and this chapter aims to support you in developing as a reflective practitioner. The chapter starts by looking at what reflective practice involves and why we should be interested in this. It will then introduce you to some theories about learning and give you an opportunity to explore the way that you learn as an individual. We will look at some models of reflection that you could use in order to explore and improve your own care practice. This chapter also links with Chapter 11 on research.

This chapter addresses the following areas:

- What is reflective practice?
- Aims of reflective practice
- Policy context
- Knowledge
- Skills
- Understanding
- Theories of learning
- Models of reflection
- Connecting learning with our care practice
- What to reflect on
- Frameworks for evaluation
- Evidence-based practice
- Integration of theory and practice
- SWOT analysis
- Use of research
- Who to reflect with
- Why reflect?
- Ethical issues in reflection
- When should I reflect?
- Supporting your peers and developing others

After reading this chapter it is hoped you will be able to:

- understand why reflective practice is important in care work
- understand theories of learning
- know how to use models of reflection
- know the range of resources that can be used to facilitate reflection.

What is reflective practice?

Reflection is a process of reviewing an experience of practice in order to describe, analyse, evaluate and so inform learning about practice.
(Reid, 1993, *in* Ghaye and Lillyman, 1997, page 6)

Reflection is a process of reviewing (describing, analysing and evaluating) and therefore learning about practice.

If you said you had thought about your work when you have finished at the end of a shift then we could say that you have reviewed it, that you have looked over it again. This may have been a very useful exercise for you and it may have led you to work differently in the future. If so, then you have probably analysed or evaluated your work. We shall look at what these words mean in this section, but before we look in depth at what reflective practice is, it would be useful to think about what it is that we do as care workers and why we do it.

Let us look at what care work entails. Thinking about your job as a whole, you could separate out your work role into what you know and what you do.

ACTIVITY

Read through the following task that is being carried out and identify the following:

1 What the care worker needs to *know* in order to carry out that task.
2 What the care worker needs to be able to *do* in order to carry out that task.
3 What *attitude* to their work would enable the care worker to perform the task appropriately.

This task involves assisting a person with their personal care first thing in the morning. Carrying out the task is described in the following way.

'I knock on the person's door and ask them if they would like to get up. I assist them in getting out of the bed, being careful to not take any of the weight of the person.'

You could do this when you start a job, or you could do it by looking at your job description. When you start a job, the job description will sometimes specify what experience you have, what knowledge you have, and also other factors to do with your approach to working with people. We can call these areas knowledge, skills and understanding. The relationship between them is set out below.

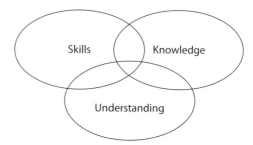

Figure 2.1 Dimensions of your care role

Knowledge, skills and understanding

What we have done here is to break this care task down into the knowledge, skills and the attitude or understanding that I would need in order to carry this task out well. By doing this we can explore what role these play in developing our ability to carry out this task effectively. Some aspects of my knowledge, skills or attitude may be a feature of general knowledge and not something restricted to care work, for example a manager would not have to give you a long induction showing you how to knock on the door; it may, however, be necessary to explain to you the reasons for, and importance of, knocking on the door. Depending on the particular task, there is sometimes more of an emphasis on knowledge, sometimes on skills, and sometimes on attitude.

To illustrate this, we will look at the same task as if I do not have any of the knowledge, skills or attitudes that we have identified as being important in the table above:

> I walk into the person's room and prop the door open, as it is then easier for me later to assist her to the bathroom. I don't ask her what she wants to do, as it is the same routine every day, so it is pointless to me to have a dialogue about it. I then assist the person out of bed; it hurts my back supporting them, but it is quicker than waiting for her to move herself.

The following table sets out these elements in more detail.

	What I do	The *knowledge* I have in order to do this	The *skills* I use	The *attitude* I have that affects my approach
1	I knock on the bedroom door	I *know* that this individual action shows respect		I *respect* the person I *value* the person's privacy
2	I ask the person if they want to get up	I *know* how to communicate with a person who has a hearing impairment I *know* how to communicate with someone when they are in bed	I can *communicate* with a person whose hearing is impaired	I *value* the person's sense of control I *understand* the importance of empowerment
3	I physically assist the person to get out of bed	I *know* how to provide appropriate physical assistance I *know* the guidelines for moving and handling	I can *assist* the person without putting them or myself at risk of physical injury	I *am sensitive* to how the individual may experience this action

As you can see, the way that I carry out this task now does not make use of any of the knowledge about communication or moving and handling. Also, I am not using my practical skills to support the person appropriately, and I do not have a good understanding of the need to respect the person's privacy or their independence, and this affects my attitude. The way I carry out this task has a direct influence on the person that I am supporting. Their experience of this task would be completely different if I carried it out in the way it was described earlier. This is just a very small task to illustrate the point. Imagine the impact that lack of knowledge, skills and a poor attitude would have on the lives of individuals across the whole of their day.

Reflecting on the function of the task

Of course, your role as a care worker is not just a grouping of tasks. You may wonder how appropriate it is to divide the work you do into such tasks, as care work is not a production line activity. In care work it is important to understand the actual purpose of the work activity, and how the individual tasks fit together in order to support a person *appropriately*.

For example, a 'task' may be to support Andrew, who is learning disabled, travelling from his home to the local college for a course. The easiest way to do this would be to drive him there – it is only ten minutes in the car. If this task is explored in more depth we may see that there are some important elements to it

which would not be addressed if we drove Andrew there.

The aims of the task should be that:

1 Andrew takes responsibility for attending the college
2 Andrew develops his ability to make his own way to the college by public transport so that he develops his independence.

These aims will influence the way that the original task is carried out. Instead of just driving Andrew to the college, his support workers would need to devise a plan with him for developing his ability to gradually undertake this journey independently. The purpose of the task is therefore very significant; it can be described as its 'function'.

ACTIVITY

Identify a task that you carry out regularly at work. Think about what the *function* of this task is for the person, how it supports their overall needs, and the development of their independence or general well-being.

In what ways could you improve how you carry out this task in order to enhance the role you are playing in the overall care/support needs of the person you are caring for?

Developing our care practice involves our knowledge, our skills and our understanding or attitude. Bloom

(1997) refers to a taxonomy of learning with the following 'domains':

1 The *cognitive* domain concerns our thinking and memory, and our capacity for understanding new knowledge.
2 The *psychomotor* domain deals with our abilities, the skills that we have, what we can physically do.
3 Our *affective* domain relates to our understanding, i.e. our approach, our attitude to what we do.

We do not always think about our work in relation to these three areas; we tend to just get on with our work. Hopefully, reading through this chapter will give you an opportunity to stop and think, to take stock of the kind of work that you are in and what impact you are making.

If we return to the case of Andrew (page 49), and think about how effectively he is being supported, we can see that the support workers need to make use of all three of these domains if they are going to promote his independence. All care work requires us to make good use of all of these domains. While we may sometimes be very conscious of our use of one domain, our best practice comes together when we know, understand and can actually perform a task.

The support workers may need to develop their knowledge of supporting Andrew in his learning about the journey and the different strategies that they could use. They may need to develop their skills in assisting him in a way that does not restrict his development of independence. They may need to apply their understanding of Andrew's rights, and the importance of developing his independence in the long-term, so that they do not choose the easy option in the short term.

Andrew's support workers may not actually be conscious of using all three domains in this activity; sometimes we are more aware of this than at other times. So, I may be very aware of my use of the cognitive domain if I have read about how to do something and then I try to remember what I read as I am doing the task. I may be very aware of my psychomotor domain if I have watched a colleague carrying out a task and then they assist me as I practise this skill. I may be very aware of using my affective domain if I am talking to relatives and I am aware of observing the confidentiality of the individual that I support.

Reflection is not just about looking back – it is about moving forward. Reflection in action is about developing knowledge, skills and understanding so as to maximise these for the benefit of the people with whom you work.

Aims of reflective practice

Care work is very pressurised; time is limited so we need to value the impact that reflective practice can make on us in the long-term. Who is responsible for making sure that we provide the best care at all times to the people that we support? Is it:

- our colleagues?
- our managers?
- the General Social Care Council?

Although all these do have a role which we will explore, it is important to remember that *you* have a key responsibility in both developing and then monitoring your own ability, and reflective practice can help.

Reflective practice can:

- expose poor practice
- identify issues that arise in care work
- assist in understanding what you do in work
- justify particular types of intervention
- increase accountability

Accountability, responsibility and autonomy

Nadia is a Care Director in a business that manages care homes for older people. We will look at these three key issues in the context of Nadia's work.

Accountability: In a direct way Nadia is accountable to:

- the older people who live in the care home
- the care home manager
- the staff team.

She is also accountable to:

- the Commission for Social Care Inspection/Care Quality Commission
- the Company Management Committee and the Chief Executive
- the relatives of the residents
- the public in their expectation of what support is provided in care homes.

Responsibility: Nadia is responsible for ensuring that care and support is provided effectively to all those who live in the homes that the business manages.

Autonomy: Nadia has control over making decisions about what time to undertake certain tasks. She has to respond in the best way to issues that arise in the night, as in the case of someone who is unwell. She needs to use her initiative in responding to phone calls from people who are phoning in sick.

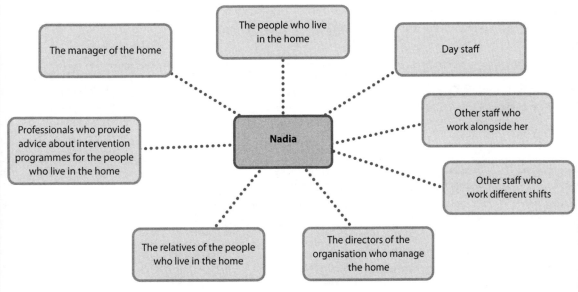

Figure 2.2 People who benefit from Nadia's work

Look at the different people who benefit from Nadia's work, and then identify the people or other agencies who benefit from your own work.

Think about what relationship you have to these other people or agencies in terms of your:

- accountability
- responsibility
- autonomy.

- highlight good practice
- promote good practice
- enhance good practice, and further improve what you do at work
- promote quality in your provision of care
- help to manage stress.

Of course there are other ways of achieving these desired outcomes; you could attend a training course, be supervised more closely or follow instructions whenever you undertake a task. Reflective practice does not replace these methods of learning and developing, it provides an additional tool for addressing all of the above, and also for enhancing your ability to maximise these other methods of improving your practice.

It can help by:

- bridging the gaps between what you learn on a course, or in training, and what actually happens when you are at work
- providing a framework for you to discuss your work with yourself. This is known as 'counter discourse' and is particularly useful if you work alone and do not have many opportunities to talk about your work with others.

Policy context

Evidence-based practice

As discussed in Chapter 1, the relationship of professionals to individuals who need care/support has changed. Service users are no longer expected to be grateful recipients of a paternalistic approach to care provision; the focus is more on rights and the empowerment of individuals. There is an increased emphasis on justifying why a certain course of action was taken, or why a particular type of intervention has been adopted. It relates to the 'why?' of care practice. There is more regulation in care work with the introduction of the Care Standards Act 2000, and from this the development of accountability. There now needs to be evidence that forms the basis of decision-making.

	Technical rationality	Personal/practice knowledge	Experiential knowledge	Ethical/moral knowledge
The context of care	Facts about government policy	That policies, funding and organisations change with time	Knowledge about how to ensure the organisation responds to new legislation	Valuing the important role I have in promoting the values of the organisation
Values in care practice	Legislation relating to discrimination	Some people have different values	Dilemmas arise in providing care	That these are important
Working with service users	Models of intervention with different service user groups	General communication skills	Strategies to support people that can be most effective	Valuing empowerment
Assessment	What assessment tools to use	Importance of first contact when meeting people	Different expectations of the assessment from service users	Knowledge of the importance of the individual owning their assessment
Planning care	Organisational policy and the care planning process	Knowledge that change can be difficult for people	Knowledge about the availability of services in the local area	Importance of service user control over the planning process
Collaborative working	Organisational expectations; theories of collaborative working	General awareness of the complex nature of communicating with different people	Knowledge of how best to work with a particular agency	Knowledge of the importance of collaborative working, even if at times there are tensions to overcome
Adult protection	No Secrets Knowing; my responsibility for protecting adults	Awareness of abuse as an issue in society	Knowledge of the difficulties in maintaining confidentiality	Knowing how important protection is

That evidence can come from your own experience, 'I did it before and it worked', or from the experience of others, 'Someone else did it before and it worked.'

Certain key words in the Care Standards Act 2000 need to be looked at here: *accountability, responsibility* and *autonomy*.

Accountability

This is defined as being 'responsible, required to account for one's own conduct.' (*Concise Oxford Dictionary*, 1991). As a care worker there will be people who you feel you have to 'report to' about your work. This may not mean checking in with them all the time, but it may be a line manager or supervisor who is responsible for the service as a whole.

Responsibility

This is having the 'authority, the ability to act independently and make decisions.' (*Concise Oxford Dictionary*, 1991). These are the responsibilities that you have in the role that you perform and the function of that role.

Autonomy

This is 'the right of self-government'. This relates both to accountability and responsibility. The autonomy that you have includes the decisions about your work that you are allowed to make, self-management, and the way you set priorities.

The idea of reflective practice must take account of the context of your care practice. This means that you need to consider not only who benefits from your work, but who is responsible for you knowing about what you need to do.

We will return to the three domains of learning that we looked at earlier and explore these in more detail.

Knowledge

Our knowledge about anything is built up over time; it is cumulative. Different types of knowledge are sometimes divided into the following four areas:

1 *Technical rationality* – knowledge of the facts.
2 *Personal/practice knowledge* – life experience and knowledge acquired through general work activity.
3 *Experiential knowledge* – acquired through your care work.
4 *Ethical/moral knowledge* – intuitive judgements.

We can consider these different types of knowledge in relation to the subject areas of this book, as in the table on page 52.

We can acquire knowledge in different ways. For example, you may not have read about collaborative working before, but feel you have quite a bit of knowledge about it based on your experience with professionals from other agencies. You may feel that your knowledge of values developed well before you started working in health and social care, as you have always had an awareness of issues to do with discrimination and confidentiality.

Using our knowledge

Bloom's cognitive hierarchy provides a way of exploring what we can do with our knowledge.

Stage in the processing of knowledge	Definition
Knowledge	Information, facts
Interpretation, understanding	Making sense of this knowledge
Application	Using this knowledge by connecting it to the work situation
Analysis	Thinking about the knowledge from different angles, asking yourself questions about it
Synthesis	Bringing together different areas of knowledge in order to understand a situation, or use a skill
Evaluation	Looking back on a situation using this knowledge and making a judgement about it

To identify valuable information you can draw on to inform your reflection, you need to be able to distinguish between different types of information; for example is the information fact or an opinion?

REFLECT

Lisa is thinking about how effective her care practice is in relation to ascertaining what service users think of the Supported Living scheme that she manages.

'I know exactly what people think of the scheme because the tenants complete questionnaires. The tenants know that they can complain about anything that they are not happy with. Staff inform me of any issues in supervision, and the tenants have regular meetings, at which they can say anything.'

From Lisa's account distinguish between what is fact and what is opinion.

The following table shows responses to this activity.

Lisa	Fact?
I know exactly what people think of the scheme	Lisa may only know part of what people think
I get staff to support the tenants in completing a questionnaire	Evidenced by signed questionnaires
The tenants know that they can complain about anything	Some tenants may not feel comfortable complaining
Staff inform me of any issues in supervision	Evidenced by supervision notes
The tenants have regular meetings	Evidenced by dates of meetings and minutes
The tenants can say anything at these meetings	Tenants may feel uncomfortable speaking up

Lisa's impression of what she knows is influenced by her expectations of what should be happening.

Interpretation of knowledge

When we focus on evidence we may emphasise what we saw as 'hard' data – that is, the paperwork and statistics that support statements. This may mean that we miss the point when it comes to valuing the opinions of individuals within the service. Initially we may think that facts are more important than opinions, but is this true? If a service user feels that

they do not go out as much as another service user, this may be untrue; however, it does not mean we can dismiss it as being of no significance. The service user's experience is valuable and important. The fact that they *feel* like that is the significant point, whether or not there is any truth underlying that feeling. It then becomes important to understand *why* the service user feels like that and to address this feeling. If we had ignored this comment and just looked at statistics that showed us it was not the case, then we would have been missing the point.

It is important to know how to interpret information and how to understand the value of individual pieces of information, and how to piece them together so that they make sense as a whole. It is much more common now for research to make explicit reference to anecdotes as a valuable contribution to the results of research. This represents a shift towards accepting qualitative knowledge as well as quantitative information.

Knowledge becomes a resource for us to use in our work. It can inform our understanding of how to perform certain tasks. It can help us to understand why a person might behave in a certain way. It can prevent us from intervening in a way that could be harmful. In order for us to utilise the knowledge that we have, we need to become more conscious of it.

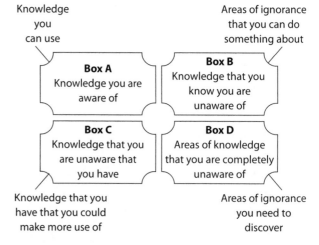

Figure 2.3 Types of knowledge

What do you know that you know?

The diagram above (Pedler *et al*, 2001, page 56) separates out four types of knowledge. These depend on being very aware of our knowledge (Box A), having knowledge that we do not realise we have (Box C), being aware that there are areas of knowledge we do not know about (Box B), or areas of knowledge that we do not even know exist (Box D).

The following illustrates what we should aim to do with these different areas of knowledge.

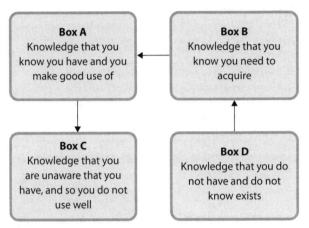

Figure 2.4 What we can do with different areas of knowledge

How does this process apply to Serena's situation (case study, page 56)? Her aim is to develop more of a command of the knowledge that she already has, and understand what she needs to find out about in order to develop as a support worker.

Serena wants to move all areas of her knowledge to Box A – knowledge that she is conscious of and can use effectively.

	Strategies that Serena could use
Box B	Request training. Obtain resources about this – books, Internet, library. Ask other professionals.
Box C	Reflect on all areas of her work and identify knowledge that she is not making good use of. Try to use this knowledge more in her daily care practice.
Box D	Think about her job in a very broad way to identify aspects of it that are underdeveloped. Consider what the experience of the service user is and develop a holistic approach to supporting them. Ask the service user, other professionals, family members etc. what they feel would make a difference to the individual. Access information from organisations that advocate for older people through telephoning them or through the Internet.

In order for any of these to happen, Serena needs to be proactive about her work, she needs to have that sense of accountability to the service user and her organisation and take responsibility for self-development. She needs to be motivated to address her own learning needs and to understand how she can change.

We have identified that knowledge, skills and understanding, while being discrete areas, are dependent on each other, and all interlink. We look now at skills.

ACTIVITY

Think about your work as a whole and identify an example of the four different types of knowledge.

A Knowledge that you are aware of
B Knowledge that you know you are aware of
C Knowledge that you are unaware you have
D Knowledge that you are completely unaware of

1 For each of these boxes (A–D) think about how you can move these areas of knowledge into Box A.
2 Develop a list of the strategies that you could use.
3 Set yourself some realistic targets for developing these areas.

Skills

Skills are what you can do; sometimes they are referred to as areas of competence.

While skills describe what you can do, rather than what you know, it is clear that the development of skills is dependent on your knowledge. Have you ever thought of a particular task that you have some knowledge about, but you just seem unable to do? With some activities it is not enough to know what you need to be able to do, you need to be able to perform the task too! Sometimes this gap between what we know and what we can do relates to:

● lack of opportunity to practise
● the need for further knowledge
● support or guidance about changing what we do
● development of confidence.

What do we know?

Serena has been a home support worker for a home care agency for six months now. She mainly supports older people, but also has provided care for people with physical mobility needs. The following is the knowledge that Serena has acquired.

Box A: Knowledge you are aware of	**Box B: Knowledge that you know you are unaware of**
Serena knows what the care needs are of older people and how to support them in their homes effectively. She is conscious of this knowledge and uses it all the time.	Serena knows that she needs to find out more information about how to communicate with older people with sensory impairments.
Box C: Knowledge that you are unaware you have	**Box D: Knowledge that you are completely unaware of**
Serena has developed a lot of knowledge about supporting people in rehabilitation through the work that she does with people in their own homes.	Serena doesn't know that she has a whole area of knowledge missing – knowledge relating to the mental health needs of older people. She does not realise that older people can have specific health needs.

If you have ever done an NVQ (National Vocational Qualification), you will be familiar with the idea of competence. It means that you are able to complete a task or action to the required standard.

A skills model

Dreyfus provides a model of skills acquisition which explores the different levels of ability that we may have with different skills (Tight, 1996, page 123).

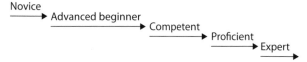

Figure 2.5 Dreyfus' model of skills acquisition

Novice This means that you undertake the task as if it is new to you. You may not have done it before, or only a few times.

Advanced beginner This means that you are able to do the task but are still learning about it, so you may still need to be supervised or to check out how to do it each time.

Competent This means that you are able to do something in the required way and to the required standard.

Proficient This implies that not only can you do the task above the required standard, you would feel confident in your ability to do it and would not need assistance or advice about it in order to undertake it well.

How skilful are you at caring?

Des has been a mental health Support Worker for four years and he feels that he has acquired a number of skills in this area of work. He has just joined a project that is focusing on supporting people with mental health problems who also have alcohol or substance dependency and this is new to Des.

We could say that Des has a general level of competence in the area of supporting people with mental health problems. There will be some aspects of this that he may be quite proficient in. However, he may feel that he is a novice in the area of supporting people with dependencies and addictions.

Questions

1 In your current job role think about an example of an area of practice that you are new to. How can you move from being a novice through to becoming competent in this task?
2 Also think of an aspect of your work that you feel competent in and identify how you can progress from competence through to becoming an expert. This can prove motivational, in striving to see if you can develop expertise in an area.

Expert This level of skill means that you have developed in this skill to such an extent that you can perform a task well above the required ability and standard. You would undertake a task in a way that others could learn from you.

REFLECT

Think about these levels in terms of your job as a whole, or in relation to particular tasks.

1 How long have you been doing your job and what level would you place yourself at generally?

2 Do you feel that you are a novice, competent or an expert in any specific tasks that are required of you?

Understanding

Your approach to your work is not only the combination of the knowledge and skills that you have, but also your understanding of the work.

Let us return to the example at the beginning of the chapter:

'I walk into the person's room and prop the door open, as it is then easier for me later to assist her to the bathroom. I don't ask her what she wants to do, as it is the same routine every day, so it is pointless to me to have a dialogue about it. I then assist the person out of bed; it hurts my back supporting them, but it is quicker than waiting for her to move herself.'

How does this care worker understand their work?

Obstacles to the way we work

There are different factors that prevent us adopting a professional approach to our work. These include

- dissatisfaction with aspects of employment, for example pay, hours, holiday entitlement
- problematic relationships with colleagues
- not getting on with managers
- not feeling valued ourselves.

There are ways to overcome these negative feelings and adopt a more positive approach. These include

- seeing the value of doing our job properly
- understanding our job in terms of the role that it serves, rather than just as a series of tasks
- having a sense of accountability to the service users
- focusing on the relationship with the service user as a key feature of our role
- being proactive about dealing with issues that are causing concern.

Together these amount to 'being professional'.

Theories of learning

Reflection is a process that can promote learning and support development. In this section we look at what learning actually is.

Jarvis provides five meanings for the idea of learning (Tight, 1997, page 23).

Learning may involve:

- a change in behaviour as a result of experience
- a change in behaviour as a result of practising (more deliberate than in the first bullet)
- the process whereby knowledge is created through the transformation of experience
- the processes of transforming experience into knowledge, skills and attitudes
- memorising information.

Think about the relevance of each of these to any care worker's experience of learning, as shown in the table at the top of the following page.

REFLECT

1 Think about what you know, and what you can do in your current job.

2 Think of an example of each of the above types of learning from your own care practice.

3 Work out how you can develop each way of learning so that you are more aware of new learning situations in your workplace.

Type of learning	Explanation
A change in behaviour as a result of experience.	What you do today in your care work will have been influenced by the experiences that you have had in the past, both in work and in your own life.
A change in behaviour as a result of practice (more deliberate than in the first type of learning above).	You try out a new task and it doesn't go to plan, so you try it out several times until you feel that you have got it right.
The process whereby knowledge is created through the transformation of experience through what happens when you do something.	The knowledge that you have has not only been acquired through training, reading, etc., you also acquire knowledge.
The processes of transforming experience into knowledge, skills and attitudes.	When you have an experience in the workplace it is useful to separate out the knowledge, skills and attitude that influenced that task in order to identify what needs to change.
Memorising information.	This is where you have to remember certain facts or situations.

Reflecting and evaluating as part of learning

To *reflect* is to think about, to reconsider, look back over what you have done; to *evaluate* is to make an assessment of, to judge what you have done. Thinking back over something is not necessarily going to improve what you do. Along with this thinking back there needs to be some evaluation of what you have done and then some learning about what could be done differently.

ACTIVITY

Before you look at theories relating to learning, think about your own experience of learning in the past.

1 Identify a positive learning experience you had and identify what made it positive. How could you make sure that you have more learning experiences like this in the future?
2 Identify a negative learning experience you have had, and think about what made it negative. What could you do to make sure that this type of experience is not repeated?
3 Think about something that you found easy to learn.
4 Think about something that you found difficult to learn.

When you reflect on these what are the differences you can identify from a variety of learning experiences?

We may ask what we mean by the word 'learning'. It can be seen as an *outcome*, as in 'I have learnt how to

use the new hoist' or as a process, as in 'I am learning how to communicate with people using British Sign Language'. If we do not reflect on our work, we are likely to do it in a routine way without thinking about what it is we do. The most important aspect of reflection is that you *learn from it*.

How do we learn?

Auditory (What we hear) Have you ever had the words to a song you have heard on the radio go round and round in your head even if you do not particularly like the song?

Visual (What we see) Have you ever described someone's appearance to a friend even if you can't remember that person's name?

Kinaesthetic (What we physically feel and actively do) Have you ever been surprised that you were able to complete a task, because you have previously done it once?

Written (What we read) Have you ever remembered what was written on an advert on a bus, or at a train station, even though you were not making an effort to read it?

What sort of learner are you?

Learning can mean different things to different people, and can mean different things according to different contexts. Your memories of learning to drive may be very different from your memories of learning history at school. Learning is usually affected by our interest in the subject, our motivation to learn and the way in which we are taught. Much research has been carried out to explore the different ways in which people learn.

There are some factors that prevent or disrupt learning. These include:

- emotions
- lack of motivation to learn
- time
- environment.

It has been suggested that learning takes place according to how our bodies and senses respond. It suggests that some people have a preference for whether they learn through seeing, hearing, doing or reading what they need to learn.

ACTIVITY

Answer the following questions that can help you to think about what type of learner you are.

1 When learning how something works do you:
- follow a diagram or picture (visual)
- need to be told how to put it together (auditory)
- try to fit the pieces together until it all fits (kinaesthetic)
- read the instructions (written)?
2 When cooking something new do you:
- try to make it by trial and error, tasting it as you do it (kinaesthetic)
- watch a DVD of TV chefs such as Delia or Jamie (visual)
- follow a recipe in a book (written)
- remember what a friend said you should do (auditory)?
3 If you are visiting somewhere new, do you prefer to:
- follow a map (visual)
- have written instructions (written)
- go there with someone else as a trial run (kinaesthetic)
- be told how to get there (auditory)?

These three types of questions are not intended to tell you which learning style you have, but they may help you to think about how you like to learn new things. Learning does not happen in isolation, however. We do not always get to choose what method of learning we use; it is usually imposed on us.

CASE STUDY

Learning styles

Think about the following scenario. What types of learning style are expected of Lucy on her second day as a Support Worker?

Lucy arrives at the Disability Resource Centre. As part of her learning she does the following:

- She **reads** the policies and practices folder to learn about health and safety issues.
- She **watches** how one of the other care workers assists one of the service users at mealtime.
- She **talks to** some of the service users, **adjusting** how she communicates in line with the feedback she is getting from them.
- She **listens** to how she should move the hoist, and then is expected to move it back to a person's bedroom.

REFLECT

1 If you need to learn something new at work do you prefer to
- sit in the office and read about it
- watch a colleague
- listen to someone telling you what to do
- practise it yourself?
2 Think of examples of each from your own experience. Consider how your choice relates to the four styles above.
3 In your present job, what are you usually expected to do when you need to learn something new?
4 What implications does this have for your learning in the workplace?

Even when Lucy (see case study above) has been in her job for days, weeks, months or years it is likely that she will carry on using all these methods of learning.

Enhancing your capacity for learning in all these styles will improve your overall performance. However, you may not be in a situation where you can choose the method of learning to use, as in the context of work or when you go on training courses; sometimes we don't get to choose which style of learning is being used. We have a preference to use one style but it is important that we can use all methods.

You may not have thought of work as a learning environment. We tend to think of learning as something we do on a training course or in reading a book. However, there are many opportunities to develop in our understanding, knowledge and skills through our experiences at work. The activity that you will carry out on Kolb's reflection (below) should enable you to do that.

> ## REFLECT
>
> Think about the following statements and which ones you most agree with.
>
> 1 'I take pride in doing a thorough, mechanical job.'
> 2 'The present is much more important than thinking about the past or the future.'
> 3 'The key factor in judging a proposed idea or solution is whether it works in practice or not.'
> 4 'I like to relate my actions to a general principle.'
> 5 'I tend to solve problems using a step-by-step approach, avoiding any fanciful ideas.'
> 6 'I do whatever seems necessary to get the job done.'
> 7 'I like to ponder many alternatives before making up my mind.'
> 8 'I enjoy the drama and excitement of a crisis.'

Honey and Mumford identified four different types of learning style: reflector, pragmatist, theorist, activist. According to this you might have chosen the following styles to match the statements in the exercise above.

1	Reflector	5	Theorist
2	Activist	6	Pragmatist
3	Pragmatist	7	Reflector
4	Theorist	8	Activist

The following are some of the general characteristics of the learning styles.

Learning style	Some general characteristics
Reflector	Cautious. Likes to collect information and think over the past before taking action.
Activist	Open-minded and will try anything once. Acts first and considers the consequences afterwards. Likes new challenges.
Pragmatist	Likes to try out new ideas and see if they work. Likes problem-solving and making practical decisions.
Theorist	Perfectionist. Likes to think about things in a logical way.

Once again it is not possible here to provide the full interpretation of these styles, but hopefully this snapshot allows you to think about your own approach.

Looking at the advantages and disadvantages of each of these learning styles, it becomes clear that it might be useful to draw on each of these – irrespective of what is your preferred style. You can adapt to using a different style to suit varied situations and this will be of benefit to you in your learning and your career.

Models of reflection

Kolb's model of reflection

We now explore some models of reflection that can be used as a framework for reflection. This is particularly useful when learning through work in order to develop your practice and also to facilitate the thinking required to write assignments and journal entries for your qualification. The Kolb cycle is a well respected theory of experiential learning that explores the stages through which a person progresses in order to complete what he calls a cycle of reflection.

Stages of the Kolb model

The stages are:

- *Stage 1 Concrete experience* This is the initial experience: what has happened, what you did, what the outcome was. It is the description of a work activity that you are looking back on.
- *Stage 2 Reflective observation* This takes place after the event or occurrence at work. This stage

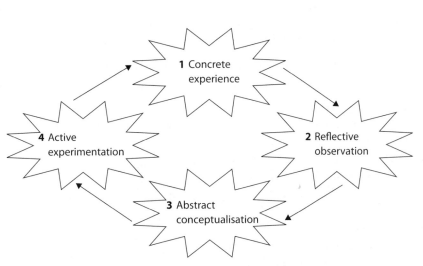

Figure 2.6 The Kolb learning cycle

involves thinking about the experience, trying to look at it from a number of perspectives.

- *Stage 3 Abstract conceptualisation* This stage involves analysing the experience, unpicking all the detail of what happened. It involves identifying theories that could relate to the experience and seeing the connection between what you did and what could have been done. It also includes making reference to relevant theories that explain this situation, or identifying models that could be used to structure your future work.

- *Stage 4 Active experimentation* This stage involves applying the theories that you have identified in Stage 3. It includes testing out the new ideas that you have thought about as a result of your thinking in Stages 2 and 3, and putting into practice the new way of undertaking a particular task.

After Stage 4 we revert back to Stage 1 so that a continuing cycle of experience and reflection emerges.

This process can become quite natural, but if you have never gone through this cycle in a formal way

Strategies for reflection

Stage 1 Concrete experience

- Being more aware of what is happening at the time that it is happening. Being conscious of what you are doing.
- Thinking about what you are doing, while you are doing it.

Stage 2 Reflective observation

- Making time to reflect when the experience is fresh in your mind.
- Making a few notes about what happened and how you feel about it.
- Being aware of how valuable this process can be will help you to allocate time to do this.
- Not dismissing an event as inconsequential.
- Not making too big a deal of it. If you think you have got to set aside two hours to reflect then you will probably never get round to it. Set

yourself ten minutes and then if necessary you can build on this. Not starting to reflect is the main stumbling block.

Stage 3 Abstract conceptualisation

- Making sure you have access to a range of theories and models that may relate to this experience.
- Keeping up to date with ideas about your work.
- Practising thinking about your work from different angles or viewpoints.

Stage 4 Active experimentation

- Being prepared to try out new things.
- Having a structured approach to applying these theories that will then provide the next learning opportunity.
- Having open and supportive discussions about trying new ways of working with your manager and colleagues.

then there are some ways of starting this process and making it more effective. Let us look at each stage and identify strategies to maximise what happens in each.

As with many aspects of care work, caution needs to be applied to certain aspects of this cycle of reflection:

- In Stage 1 a concrete experience for you would usually involve other people and you need to be aware of how others have experienced it; that experience does not become yours to reinvent.
- During Stage 2, reflecting on a situation can sometimes lead to negative feelings about your own ability to perform a task or role effectively. Inertia can then set in, and we spend a disproportionate amount of time reflecting instead of getting on with a new task. This approach can be overcome by focusing on the *aims* of reflection.
- While undertaking Stage 3 you need to remember that theories are *possible* ways of looking at a situation; they do not necessarily provide a factual account of why something happened. It may be inappropriate to adopt a theory wholesale and then pretend to be an expert on a particular situation. The same applies to models of working; these may have to be implemented with caution.
- In Stage 4 individuals you work with are not meant to be part of an experiment, so trying out new things needs to be done with consideration for the best interests of the patients or service users.

CASE STUDY

Cycle of reflection

Brenda is Deputy Manager at a day service for learning disabled adults.

At work one day she is disappointed in the way she handles a team meeting. She needed to discuss some important changes that are going to be taking place and wanted to involve everyone in the team. Once again two Support Workers on the team, who she has been trying to get more involved, created a situation beforehand that they said they needed to sort out, and therefore did not attend the meeting. Brenda feels frustrated that this has become a pattern, and feels annoyed with herself that she has 'allowed' this to happen.

How could Kolb's model help Brenda to deal with this situation?

Let us take Brenda through the stages in Kolb's model of reflection:

Stage 1 Brenda describes what has happened. She planned a meeting, two members of staff did not want to attend and they manufactured a problem to excuse themselves from the meeting.

Stage 2 Brenda reflects on this experience and identifies the key points:

1 Two members of staff did not want to come to the meeting – why?
2 Two members of staff were able to avoid the meeting – how?
3 The meeting went well as far as those who attended were concerned.
4 The people who Brenda feels will have issues with the changes were not part of the team discussion – this does not bode well for the future.

Stage 3 Brenda considers different ways of looking at this situation and tries to identify ideas or theories that may help her to understand what happened with more clarity. She explores possible reasons why the two support workers are not team players (for example, in supervision with individual staff Brenda discusses the person's approach to working with the team and finds out that they just do not like team meetings. One Support Worker says that she thinks they are a waste of time).

1 She looks for different views on how she could approach this situation.
2 She discusses it in supervision with her manager.
3 She asks her peers who manage other services.
4 She thinks about how she handles other situations and what she could learn from previous work settings and how she has observed other managers handle things in the past.
5 She gets a book from the library on managing meetings.

Stage 4 The big test: the next team meeting. Brenda takes the following action:

1 She anticipates possible problems and changes the time of the meeting.

ACTIVITY

Choose something that has happened in work recently that you are not happy with. It could be a disagreement with a colleague, or a discussion with a relative that did not go well, or an intervention with a service user that you think was not effective.

Work your way through Kolb's cycle of reflection.

1 Describe what happened.
2 Think about the reasons behind what happened. Make a note of any thoughts that come to mind.
3 Identify some theories that may be relevant to this situation. There may be examples in this book that you could use.
4 Work out a new way of dealing with this situation, think about what you would do differently and then try this out.

When you have tried this out think about what you have learned from this process so that you really consolidate this experience.

2 She posts an agenda on the staff notice board and encourages staff to put their own agenda items on the list. This way staff will feel that it is their meeting.

3 She plans a rota so that staff will take it in turns to be 'on call' during the meeting if any issues arise; in this way it is not the same person missing the meeting.

Of course we do need to be aware that sometimes we try new things and they do not work either. This can be de-motivating but should not prevent us from continuing through the cycle of reflection and developing new ways of looking at a situation and new strategies for handling it.

The benefits of this reflection impacted on the whole staff team and not just the staff member about whom Brenda had concerns. Brenda valued the process of reflection, and although it was painful to realise that she had not been handling things in the best way the outcome was very positive.

Johns' model of reflection

Core question: What information do I need access to, in order to learn through this experience?

Cue questions to help you identify this information are divided into five sections:

1 Description of experience
   1.1 Phenomenon – Describe the 'here and now' experience
   1.2 Causal – What essential factors contributed to this experience?
   1.3 Context – What are the significant background factors to this experience?
   1.4 Clarifying – What are the key processes (for reflection) in this experience?

2 Reflection
   2.1 What was I trying to achieve?
   2.2 Why did I intervene as I did?
   2.3 What were the consequences of my actions for:
       2.3.1 myself
       2.3.2 the service user/family
       2.3.3 the people I work with?
   2.4 How did I feel about this experience when it was happening?

   2.5 How did the service user feel about it?
   2.6 How do I know how the service user felt about it?

3 Influencing factors
   3.1 What internal factors influenced my decision-making?
   3.2 What external factors influenced my decision-making?
   3.3 What sources of knowledge did/should have influenced my decision-making?

4 Could I have dealt better with the situation?
   4.1 What other choices did I have?
   4.2 What would be the consequences of those choices?

5 Learning
   5.1 How do I now feel about this experience?
   5.2 How have I made sense of this experience in the light of past experiences and future practice?
   5.3 How has this experience changed my *ways of knowing*?

Note: The word 'patient' has been replaced with 'service user'.

Johns' model of reflection

Johns' model of reflection (Davies *et al*, 2000, page 85) provides a structured set of questions to help you explore what you think about a situation or event (see page 63). It focuses on the need to identify different aspects of information in order to learn from what happened. The questions provide a way of learning about an event.

> **REFLECT**
>
> 1 Think about a situation at work that you do not feel entirely happy with; it could be a one-off incident or something ongoing.
> 2 Go through the questions in the Johns' model of reflection.
> 3 Think about whether this process of reflection has been of any benefit to you.

Connecting learning with our care practice

This section looks at how we can make the connection between theories of learning and models of reflection. In order to do this, we draw on work developed in general care practice, nursing, education and social work.

> Professional exercise consists in instrumental problem solving made rigorous by the application of scientific theory and technique.
> (Schon, 1983, page 21, in Romer, 2003)

If we think about this statement in relation to care work, it is clear that we have to think about what we are doing and make decisions about how to act on the basis of our knowledge and skills that are useful to working with service users.

Reflection provides opportunities to:

● *acquire knowledge and understanding*. Experience in the workplace can provide new knowledge. We can learn new facts about the service user group that we work with through daily contact with them. We can understand how to communicate with a person through our knowledge of what has worked in our previous communication with them.
● *apply formal knowledge*. When we read something new or go on a training course and learn something new we are sometimes invited to put it into practice, to test it out. Have you ever read anything in a book and thought, 'Well that wouldn't work where I am'? Sometimes it can be challenging to think about trying new theories out.

Evidence-based practice

The inclusion of a chapter dedicated to research is testament to the importance of gaining a sound foundation of knowledge. When you search journal articles relating to your work you will discover the importance of researching health and social care activity in order to understand the best way for professionals to work with service users and patients. To produce evidence we need to obtain information. When we make judgements we must look at the evidence and form some conclusions based on that evidence. Caution is needed to make sure that all the evidence is interpreted in an unbiased, professional way. It is easy to overlook negative comments, or to dismiss them as the views of a minority rather than acknowledge their significance and do what we need to.

Research into performance

What does the word 'performance' mean to you? Care services and NHS Trusts have their performance measured and the results are published (see Chapters 1 and 5). League tables and star ratings may be focused on a particular aspect of care, but they will relate to the ideas of efficiency, effectiveness and economy.

How do we measure performance, and who are the judges of good practice? (Everitt and Hardiker, 1996, page 85) suggest the use of performance indicators as 'tin openers' to prompt questioning of good practice. This idea of using performance indicators as 'tin openers, not dials' emphasises the need for them to be less a comprehensive measure of what we do or a standard to be aimed at, but rather a means of suggesting changes to practice rather than explaining what good practice is. The use of triangulation, where

a variety of methods are used to find out information, can establish a comprehensive and accurate picture of a service. This is discussed on page 66. In care service delivery we could add to this the principle of equity.

The inspection process for care homes includes sending evaluations to professionals, relatives and residents. The comments made by service users are included in the overall assessment of the care home in meeting the National Minimum Standards.

Care work is very focused now on the needs and wishes of the 'customer' of care, i.e. the service user. Consumer-led care needs to be provided by workers who are committed in their delivery of a professional service, and responsive to the messages that they are getting about what is not working well.

Reflection 'is imbued with values' according to Everitt and Hardiker (1996). This means that care workers cannot necessarily evaluate in an isolated way, that is not influenced by other values. An organisation's emphasis on performance can give undue weighting to some types of information rather than others, sometimes to the detriment of the service users. It may, for instance, be linked to monitoring what is going on within the organisation.

Evaluation is a means of highlighting what is really happening, making decisions about this and making sure that future outcomes are managed. Evidence-based practice implies that there is research involved. The research will produce the evidence on which to base future practice. There is increasing recognition of the value and importance of involving people who

are involved in the delivery or receipt of the service in the research process; one method of this is known as action research.

> Action research is the study of a social situation carried out by those involved in that situation in order to improve both their practice and the quality of their understanding.
>
> (Winter and Munn-Giddings, 2001, page 8)

Care organisations now acknowledge the significance and importance of what is known as user-led research.

Information, or data, is sometimes referred to as 'hard', as in statistics, or 'soft', as in the views and opinions of the service users. Quantitative data is measurable, and is often presented in the form of figures, tables etc. Qualitative data may be more subjective, and may include comments and anecdotes. However, it should not be thought of as less valuable.

The care manager (above) would not need to be an expert in research in order to carry out this exercise. Winter and Munn-Giddings (2001) emphasise the importance of not seeing research as an activity

exclusive to professional researchers. You are doing research when you ask colleagues about what they do, or if you go on a course and ask someone from a different organisation what they do. This is referred to as research-mindedness.

Triangulation

Triangulation is the use of different types of information to ensure that our assessment is valid and reliable. For example, in making a judgement about whether the meals provided are nutritious you could look at:

- how healthy individuals are
- how the meals compare to Department of Health guidelines
- the views of a nutritionist.

Each type of information can either confirm or challenge the other. If each type of information we obtain confirmed the others then through triangulation we will have demonstrated our assessment to be a valid one.

What to reflect on

We all reflect on our work, often without realising it. Even if you have not been aware of the formal process of reflection you might have left work and wondered about something that has happened and ask yourself 'What did I do wrong?' or 'Why did that happen?'

Reflection can be based on the following:

- A single incident (for example, an uncomfortable encounter with a colleague). It can be important to think about something that happens in isolation, even if we anticipate never being in that situation again. The reason is that we may need to reconcile ourselves to what has happened so that we do not dwell on it to the detriment of our future actions.
- General performance about one aspect of my work (for example, how I relate to relatives of the individuals that I support). Having been doing a job for a while we may not think there is any room for development. We may be very proficient in an area of our work, but it is unlikely we are doing it to perfection. There is always the potential to develop our practice or to help others to do so.
- A series of repeated events (for example, whenever we have a team meeting I always leave it feeling that I haven't said what I want to). If you ever feel as though you make the same mistakes over and over again, then it may be useful to challenge why this is happening. We can be guilty of labelling ourselves in this way. Have you ever said, 'Oh I'm always like that. I can't help it – it's just me' or 'I'll never change, it's who I am? Well, for some things it may be best not to stick to the same behaviour

and passively accept the role we attribute to ourselves, but to identify what it is that we are regularly doing and why, and then to change our behaviour.

Problem solving

Reflection can also be issue based. The earlier quote by Schon (1983, in Romer, 2003) about professional exercise refers to problem solving as an activity that we need to engage in if we are to develop as practitioners. This is not a negative concept; we do not need to think of every situation we are presented with as being a problem in a negative way. This approach provides a framework for considering how to view new or difficult situations and a model of working our way through them to arrive at a successful conclusion. A first step in reaching new conclusions that are likely to be effective is to reflect on what has happened in the past, and prevent the same old mistakes, or the same old problems, arising.

Frameworks for evaluation

Whether we are reflecting on our own or with others there is literature around to facilitate our reflection. In this section we look at guidance to help us measure our performance, as a 'tin opener', to use Everitt and Hardiker's (1996) phrase.

There are lots of opportunities for Alex and Charlie (case study page 68) to be proactive in their reflection on how their performance is addressing the aims of the organisation and the needs of individuals. They do not need to wait until their managers direct them in change. Some of the many benefits for Alex and Charlie are that they:

- no longer feel like novices in their work and they develop in a particular area of expertise
- feel valued within the organisation
- develop more of an interest in their work
- apply their new knowledge and improve their skills in working with people.

Another method of ongoing reflection is to keep a diary or work journal.

Professional journals

A professional journal is a diary of work, containing a collection of entries about work events. Some people find it useful to reflect on what has happened in work each day, while others prefer to select significant events to write about at infrequent intervals.

A work journal may contain the following:

Anecdotes

These may be brief, or quite lengthy accounts of situations at work, for example; 'Had a successful meeting with ... It made a difference that I had written down my questions, as I felt more relaxed amongst the other professionals from the health service.'

Interpreted stories

The writer may discuss a series of events or an ongoing issue with their reflection on what is going on and why, for example; 'There is some tension amongst the staff team developing. I think this might relate to the changes I am making to the keyworker system. I think I need to have a meeting and bring some issues out into the open with the team, nip it all in the bud.'

Critical incidents

These are significant events which the worker thinks should be reflected on, for example; 'I made a mistake today by telling a relative about their (adult) son changing activities at the centre, which meant they had to explain to their father who was unhappy about the change. I know why it happened; the parent has always been so involved and the son is very close to them. I need to think before I speak to relatives and stop myself from disclosing information casually, it was careless of me.'

Interpretation of the significance of an event

The writer may put down in words their thoughts about why or how something happened in work and why it is important, for example; 'A new policy has been introduced which is likely to have an impact on our work by ... '

Reflection on performance

Alex works in a service for learning disabled adults.

1 He could go through the National Minimum Standards for Care Homes (Adults 18–65) and consider his role in addressing these. Achieving the NMS is the responsibility of everyone in the home, not just the registered manager, and Alex could reflect on what contribution he is making, and if there are any areas in which he is not very effective. For example, Alex looks at the standards in relation to care planning and asks to discuss these with the registered manager to identify any areas that he could look into more. He may then take responsibility for exploring a particular aspect to develop the practice of everyone in the care home. For example, he may visit another home in order to find out how they produce their care plans.

2 Alex could also look at the document *Valuing People* and reflect on whether his role and actions support the principles identified in that White Paper. He may consider what contribution he is making to the debate about the future of services, and whether there are any individuals in the home who would benefit from a move to a supported living environment.

3 Alex could look at the mission statement of his care home, as what this contains is pertinent to the role of everyone in the home. How is his practice ensuring that people are provided with what they are entitled to, and to the standards required?

4 If Alex was fairly new to his job he could reflect on whether his practice is meeting the requirements set out in the LDAF Induction and Foundation Awards.

5 Alex could also read through the General Social Care Council's Code of Practice for social care employees and identify whether he is complying with the statements in this.

6 The National Occupational Standards also provide a way of measuring performance. Alex could request to work towards achieving an NVQ so that he is assessed on his competence.

7 Within the organisation the individual service user care plans would provide statements relating to the care that individuals expect to receive. Alex could consider whether the way that he performs his role is effectively supporting the organisation in meeting the care objectives as specified in the care plan.

Charlie works at a day service for older people.

1 Charlie could look at the National Service Framework for Older People (see Chapter 1 for more discussion on National Service Frameworks). He could think about the standards that are relevant to the service he works for.

2 He could also look at research on care practice carried out by the organisation Age Concern, by going to their website.

3 Charlie asks the health professionals who come to the centre what he could do to support individuals more. He learns about the emphasis on rehabilitation, for example. Charlie then suggests a regular service user meeting in order to find out what changes the day service could make to more effectively support people.

4 Charlie could also read some information about care for older people by visiting his library or asking his supervisor for any resources that the day centre has.

Questions

1 Write a list of documents that could assist you in the process of reflection.

2 Make a commitment to follow this up by devising an action plan.

Methods of analysing incidents

The writer will discuss different approaches to analysing what has happened in work.

This method of reflective practice has a number of benefits for the care worker. If someone is keeping a journal then it means that they are setting time aside to reflect, which is valuable in certain ways:

- It can provide a skill for lifelong learning, which is currently a theme in all areas of life and in all work sectors.

- It can also be a necessary skill for effective learning in the context of work. As with any work situation there may be times when we feel that we are not

testing out new skills or acquiring new knowledge. Writing a professional journal can provide a way of making learning happen for you.

- It also has the potential to add value to formal learning. Have you ever been on a course and then a week after being back at work you have forgotten everything, or it all seems irrelevant outside the classroom? Well, if you were to write a journal you may develop a structure for applying your learning from the course or training event to the workplace.

Always remember to ensure privacy and confidentiality when producing any work that relates to your care practice. Never mention specific names and be aware that people and organisations should not be identifiable; anonymity of service users, colleagues and others need to be respected.

Your development through this chapter should enable you to make more effective use of knowledge and skills that you acquire through any work-based training, college or university care courses, your own research and reading. Learning how to learn is an important stage in anyone's development.

ACTIVITY

Keep a journal as a tool to help your development as a reflective practitioner.

Don't set yourself unrealistic targets; it would be easy to spend an hour writing your first entry and then on day five you are down to writing 'Nothing happened much at work today'.

Try this for at least a fortnight and then use it to reflect back and analyse your performance.

Evidence-based practice

Evidence relates to information about how things should be done, the best forms of working, and the types of intervention. It provides a reason for acting in a certain way and gives a justification for doing so. This justification is the available evidence that a proposed course of action is the best one.

Evidence-based practice has become an important dimension of care work and is being applied more systematically in nursing and social work. Muir Gray (2001, page 11), introduces evidence as a motivation for practice alongside values and resources. Gray argues that the three combine to inform practice, but that more emphasis should be placed on evidence as pressures to focus on resources often dictate opinion-based decision-making.

Your organisation may engage in systematic evaluation of service provision before it tries to understand the need for, or implements, change. This is because it is searching for evidence to identify what changes should occur, and to support the introduction of these changes.

Integration of theory and practice

Theories are ways of understanding; they attempt to provide an explanation of how and why something happens. Theory is sometimes removed from the context in which we need to apply that theory. Have you ever read anything in a book and thought 'But it is not like that where I work, that's not real life'? Eraut (2003) discusses the importance of seeking out the relationship between the theory and practice. This helps us in exploring the use of theory in the workplace so that we are not disillusioned when the reality of care practice does not appear to relate at all to what the theory is telling us.

SWOT analysis

SWOT analysis is another process for considering all the different aspects of a situation before you commence a task. It involves exploring the strengths, weaknesses, opportunities and threats associated with a situation.

- Strengths are the advantages that we identify for taking a particular action.

- Weaknesses are the disadvantages that we identify for taking a particular action, or the barriers that will prevent us from taking a particular action.
- Opportunities can include the resources or support that we have to support us in taking a particular action, and enabling us to overcome the barriers.
- Threats are the blocks to us making effective use of these opportunities; they might obstruct our progress.

If I do a SWOT analysis on reflecting on my care practice it may look like the following:

Strengths	I want to reflect.
	I am motivated.
Weaknesses	Not knowing how to reflect – what do I do?
	Not having time to reflect.
Opportunities	I can read this chapter to learn about it.
	To overcome the issue of time I can use my journey home each day to make a start.
Threats	I might give up if I find it difficult.
	I might lose interest.

The value of working through the negative aspects is that you can confront, challenge or address them. If we were to just focus on the positive side, we may be unable to realise our good intentions in the long-term because of the practical difficulties. Focusing on the negatives gives you a more realistic chance of being positive in the long-term.

Use of research

Research is the structured collection of information about an organisation or group of people, or about a situation, in order to come to some conclusions about it. Some organisations have their own research workers. You may have been involved in research yourself. For example, have you ever completed a questionnaire about how good or poor a service is? Do you use service user surveys in your organisation?

We mentioned earlier that the CSCI sends questionnaires to care homes for service users, relatives and other professionals in order to obtain information about what others think of the service provided.

Research can also be carried out by people outside the organisation. An organisation may invite another organisation to conduct research into a particular project or service. Research that has been carried out in one organisation can be useful to others. Research may be written up in the form of a report for an organisation. It is also often discussed in professional magazines such as *Community Care*, or in journals.

ACTIVITY

Obtain a journal/professional magazine that relates to your own area of care practice. Find an article that interests you, that is describing what happens in a different organisation. Make a list of what you could learn from this research.

Who to reflect with

Reflection need not be a solitary activity. Having a positive approach to reflective practice will enable you to incorporate feedback from people who are involved with your work (service users, informal carers, relatives, other workers, colleagues, managers). It could include all those you are accountable to, and it can make you feel more able to respond to the level of autonomy that you have.

Reflecting by yourself

The conversation that you have with yourself is sometimes referred to as a 'counter-discourse'. Just asking yourself 'Why did I do that?' is a good start to reflective practice.

Reflecting with your line manager/supervisor

This kind of reflection may take place in regular formal supervision and annual appraisals. The supervision session belongs to you, and you will get more out of it if you think about it beforehand. You will usually be provided with forms to complete prior to these meetings, but if not, a SWOT analysis provides a useful framework to think about your work. Structured formal supervision and appraisals can be made more effective if you prepare in advance and reflect on how well you are doing in your job, what areas could be developed and those that you feel you need more support with (see the section on supervision in Chapter 5).

You may also talk to your manager informally; perhaps they are completing a work activity with you, or working a shift with you. Feedback about your strengths and the areas you need to develop that is ad hoc can be as informative and relevant as more formal arrangements. Requesting more regular informal feedback and comments from your manager may just be a case of asking them now and again how they think you are doing when they are around or working alongside you.

Reflecting with your service user/s

Earlier we referred to the importance of 'soft' data. So don't dismiss the 'throw away' comments from service users as these can provide a valuable insight into what matters, what is working well, and what needs changing (Chapter 4 discusses listening effectively.) An organisation reviewing how well it is doing in its care practice would usually involve its customers in that process, so service users are key to discovering this.

There may be issues about how you obtain this type of information. Let us consider some of the ways your organisation may obtain feedback from the individuals that it provides a service to. Formal complaints procedures should be accessible to the individuals they are targeted at, with questionnaires and structured feedback, such as that obtained through service user meetings.

Informal carers

People who provide care to individuals, neighbours, friends and relatives can and should play a significant part in the evaluation of service provision. The perspective of the care professionals on the relationship that they have with relatives has changed. There are now more boundaries and issues of confidentiality to consider.

Reflecting with colleagues

Handovers to colleagues can sometimes be very task oriented; which can be understandable after a long shift. It may, however not actually take a lot more time to discuss service users in a more informed way and to question the way that support is provided, or to raise suggestions as to new approaches of working with people.

REFLECT

Think about the different outcomes of the following scenarios.

Jo is handing over to Errol, having just got back from a visit to the Resource Centre with Philip.

Jo: 'He wouldn't get out the car again when we got to the Resource Centre; it took ages and yet he loves it when he is in there.'

Errol: 'Everyone has that trouble, don't worry about it.'

Here is a different conversation between the same two workers:

Jo: 'Philip wouldn't get out the car again, it took ages. I don't know what I could do to make him feel more comfortable about getting out. Do you know what other staff do?'

Errol: 'I make sure he really understands where he is going by talking about it throughout the journey. I also always make sure I go the same route so that he can begin to understand where he is going. I then sit in the car with him for a few minutes when we get there while he gets used to being outside the Resource Centre. I reassure him about who he sees there so he feels familiar with it. We see other people going in who he knows which helps him. Try that next time and let me know how it goes.'

Jo: 'Thanks Errol, that's really helpful having that chat about it – I wish I had mentioned it sooner.'

The outcome of the second conversation, which took only a few seconds longer, is that Jo knows she is not on her own in making decisions and problem solving about appropriate support for Philip. Even if Errol's suggestion does not work, Jo may feel more able to ask again, now that she knows that someone else is taking an interest in the way that she does things with Philip. More communication between people who support Philip in the same activity is always going to be of benefit.

It is useful to discuss concerns with colleagues

Informal and formal meetings

The more you participate in meetings, the more you will get out of them. Chapter 5 discusses meetings in detail. Observing what others do, the way that they communicate with a person, or the way that they provide physical assistance can introduce you to new ways of working. Asking a colleague for feedback when they have observed you working can give you regular ongoing support. It can provide reassurance about what you are doing well, as well as suggestions as to what to do differently. It is important, but not always easy, to avoid being defensive when a peer makes suggestions about how we could change our practice. If someone seems to do something differently from you, ask them why they are doing it that way, and if they have tried other ways. Tell them how you do it and ask them what they think.

Discussing your work while you are doing it will have several benefits, it may:

- stimulate you, and those you are working with
- develop the relationship you have with colleagues
- ensure that you are learning from the working environment
- be a means of accessing support over difficulties
- make it easier to bring things up that are difficult
- help you cope more effectively with difficult or stressful situations.

Other organisations and professionals

Different professionals and agencies are working closely for the benefit of service users and patients, as discussed in Chapter 4 on supporting individuals. If professionals have identified a strategy of intervention that is effective for the individual then it makes sense for everyone to be making use of this strategy. We have much to learn from each other.

Why reflect?

There are many advantages to developing reflection.

1 We develop self-awareness.
2 It enhances our problem solving skills.
3 It supports our development as 'lifelong learners'.
4 We can attribute more value to our care role.
5 It can increase our self-esteem.
6 We are more able to handle responsibility in the workplace autonomously.

The impact of reflection on practice

Ghaye and Lillyman (1996) state that there are different effects of active reflection on care practice and they divide these into the following:

- *Technical aspects* Structured reflection can support the development of our potential as accountable and professional care workers.
- *Practical aspects* Reflection can increase our ability to make sound decisions based on competent and ethically informed judgements.
- *Emancipatory aspects* Reflecting on our own care practice can promote our ability to think about, question, and be critical of what we are required to do.

To provide further justification of our need to develop a reflective approach to our individual practice, we can consider the possible *implications of not reflecting.*

The health and social care worker may:

- stay at a minimum level of competence
- repeat mistakes
- never change what they do until they are instructed to
- become bored

- lose interest in their work
- be very task focused without fully appreciating the people aspects of the job.

The service user may:

- be supported by in a thoughtless manner
- feel that you have to get used to poor practice as nothing is going to change
- not feel valued, that those supporting do not care; you are just a task for them to complete
- not be given new opportunities or allowed to take risks.

Service users have the right to the best possible care outcomes. To ensure that this happens we need to be innovative in the way that we work with people. Innovation involves the ability to look at new ways of doing the same things, or sometimes new ways to avoid doing the same things. It is useful to be creative in our thinking.

As with all dimensions of care practice there are issues that have to be thought through regarding reflection.

Ethical issues in reflection

There is an emotional dimension to reflection. As you are an individual who cares about your work it is important to reflect in a way that does not dwell on negative issues as this can be debilitating. A more productive and positive approach to reflection will focus on what the outcome and purpose of reflection are. Negative emotions, such as guilt, anxiety, or a feeling of never achieving what you need to achieve, will not support your own development or the achievement of more positive outcomes for the service or its users.

There are also practical issues to the process of reflection. It is a means to an end and should therefore not become the focus of your care practice; it is not feasible to spend half the day reflecting on how to carry out your job, you need to actually be getting on with it. Your reflection as an individual employee is one means of supporting quality and improvements, but it does not replace the responsibilities of management.

When should I reflec

Here we will consider the advantages of reflecting at a number of different points and different periods of time that will suit us in different ways. There is a value to reflecting in all the following time periods.

Reflect before you act

This chapter has focused on reflecting, that is thinking back over what you have done with a view to improving your care practice. Have you ever advised someone to 'Look before you leap', or has someone advised you to 'Think before you speak'?

If you work your way through Kolb's cycle of reflection and continue to use this model in your care practice then you will be developing an approach that means you systematically reflect before you act.

Even if you are starting a completely new care task you can still reflect on what to do before you perform that task, as you can:

- reflect on the tasks that are in some way similar to the new one
- reflect on the skills that you have that might relate to this new task
- reflect on how you have observed others performing this new task.

Reflect as you act

Schon (1983) describes this as 'reflection in action'. Depending on what you are doing, you may be able to think about how you are carrying out a task and if it is working well as you are doing it. Have you ever said, 'Stop, let's start again'? If you have, this may be because in the middle of doing something you have realised that it is not the best way to do it and you want to try a better way.

You may get feedback from an individual about the appropriateness of support you are giving them at the time and as a result adapt what you are doing. You do not need to adopt a 'I've started so I'll finish' approach. Remember, changing mid-course can sometimes save time afterwards.

Reflect after you have completed a task

At different points after doing a task it can be valuable to reflect on what has happened.

- *Immediately after a task* It is fresh in our minds, so that our recollection of what happened will not be distorted by any changes in our perception of it. We need to incorporate reflection into our busy working and home lives in a fashion that is manageable and productive.
- *Shortly after a task* There may be periods in the day when you are carrying out practical tasks on your own which do not require full concentration, such as washing up, travelling to a different service user, and these could provide periods for reflecting on other tasks you have done. If this is not possible then you may be able to reflect on the way home or while you are getting ready for work the next day.
- *After a period of time* Sometimes we forget about a situation at work (unless we are keeping our professional journals!). We may be prompted to think about it again when the same situation arises again, or a colleague tells us they had the same experience. Reflection remains a valuable exercise even if there are limitations relating to the time delay.

ACTIVITY

You have already considered theories of learning in this chapter. Now identify a theory from one of the other chapters that you feel could be useful to your own care practice.

Read through the theory and think about it in relation to your own work. You may need to explore this theory in more depth by looking it up in a library or on the Internet. Reflect on how this theory could influence the way that you work with people, service users and colleagues.

Theories and models of care

A theory is a way of explaining something that happens. It provides a possible explanation or interpretation of a situation, event or condition. There are several theories discussed in this book in other chapters which could:

- influence your understanding of a situation and therefore help you to approach the situation in a new way
- provide you with a clear explanation of why something happened and so enable you to make sure it doesn't happen again.

A model is a framework for action. It provides a structure as to how you respond or intervene in a situation. If you like the idea of a model of working you can adopt it and use it to shape the way that you work.

REFLECT

You have already used models of reflection in this chapter. Now identify a model from one of the other chapters and think about how useful it could be in your development. You may need to discuss it with others at a team meeting before you introduce it as a framework for your own work.

It is important to feel positive about reflective practice. Reflecting on the work that you do can, however, also involve having to think about negative aspects – the things that are not going so well. But if you focus on the idea that you are doing this in order to improve your practice, then it will help you to feel positive about the overall experience. If you reflect on something and it becomes clear that you did not handle a situation well, or that you made a mistake in what you did, then the important thing is that you have identified this, which opens the door for changing what you do next time.

There are several ways of handling negative reflection. They are to:

- focus on the positive aspect of identifying a difficulty in your work – you don't have to wait until someone else points it out
- focus on the benefits that the people you work with will experience (both service users and colleagues) as a result of your reflection on your work and how to improve
- talk to your colleagues about what you have discovered – sharing your experience may encourage others to share what has not gone well for them, which is helpful
- talk to your line manager about it – you are not on your own in terms of your responsibility for doing a good job.

Supporting your peers and developing others

Reflective practice can be contagious! If you open up discussions and start talking about your own practice, you may find that your colleagues will appreciate the chance to start doing the same. This will create a healthier environment, and the service users should benefit. It can be a gentle process of initially just asking questions about the 'What, When, How and Why' of care tasks.

You can make a difference in developing a culture of reflection in your organisation just by asking:

'What do you think about the way we ... ?'

'I have difficulty doing ... how do you do it?'

'Has anyone got any better ideas on how we ... ?'

If you observe colleagues in areas of practice that you think are particularly good you could invite them to share this with you so that you can develop the way you do things. Adopting a reflective practice approach to your work will enable you to utilise more effectively the knowledge that you acquire. It will also enable you to transfer your learning from one situation to another with more ease and to better effect. It is important for you to think now about the difference your understanding of reflection can make to your role in care work.

What? Here you have learnt about the importance of reflection and some strategies to facilitate your own reflection.

So what? This is important as it could enable you to become a more effective care practitioner.

Now what? This is down to you. What are you going to do in order to put these ideas into practice?

KNOWLEDGE CHECK

1 Why is reflection important in health and social care work?
2 What strategies are available to facilitate productive reflection?

REFLECT

1 When you read another chapter in this book start by exploring your own understanding of the subject area. Think about 'What do I know already?'.
2 Then, when you are reading that chapter, become familiar with how you can apply that knowledge to your own work practice. The Reflect exercises within each chapter are designed to help you do this.

References

Bloom (1965) *Taxonomy of educational objects: The classification of educational goals*, New York, Langmans, Green

Eraut M. (1994) *Developing professional knowledge and competence*, London, Falmer

Everitt, A. and Hardiker, P. (1997) *Evaluating for Good Practice*, Basingstoke, Macmillan

Ghaye, T. and Lillyman, S. (1997) *Learning Journals and Critical Incidents: Reflective Practice for Health Care Professionals*, Salisbury, Mark Allen

Honey, P. and Mumford, A. (1992) The Manual of Learning styles in Britton, A. and Cousins, A. (1990) *Study Skills: A Guide for Lifelong Learners*, London, South Bank University

Muir Gray, J. A. (2001) *Evidence-Based Healthcare*, London, Churchill Livingstone

Pedler, M. *et al* (2001) *A Manager's Guide to Self-Development*, London, McGraw-Hill

Quinn, F. M. *in* Davies, C., Finlay, L. and Bullman, A. (eds) (2000), Blackwell *Encyclopaedia of Social Work*, Oxford, Blackwell

Schon, D. (1987) Educating the Reflective Practitioner, San Francisco, Jossey–Bass

Tight, M. (1996) *Key Concepts in Adult Education and Training*, London, Routledge

Winter, R. and Munn-Giddings, C. (2001) *A Handbook for Action Research in Health and Social Care*, London Routledge

CHAPTER 3

The value base of health and social care

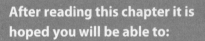

Introduction

This chapter focuses on the ethical principles and values that underpin good practice in health and social care. Values are important because they influence the way that we work with individuals; they inform our decision-making and our practical actions with people. This chapter starts by looking at what is meant by the terms 'values, ethics and rights'. We look at how individuals acquire values in their own lives, and how society's values influence us. We explore the relationship between government policy and values and investigate society in terms of an individual's identity, ethnicity, ability, gender, age etc. The chapter also looks at how specific values influence our care practice with individuals.

This chapter addresses the following areas:

- Definitions: values, ethics and rights
- Why values are important in care work
- Values in relation to individual identity
- Discrimination, oppression, stereotyping and prejudice
- Anti-oppressive practice, anti-bias practice and anti-discriminatory practice
- Care values and care standards

After reading this chapter it is hoped you will be able to:

- understand the terms 'values, ethics and rights'
- know what values underpin good care practice
- understand issues of identity in terms of people's race, ability, age, gender, sexuality, religion and other characteristics
- be able to work in an anti-discriminatory manner
- be able to practise confidentiality.

This chapter links very much with Chapter 4 (Supporting individuals and their families), as values are at the heart of your individual intervention with service users or patients.

Definitions: values, ethics and rights

Before we investigate what we mean by values, ethics and rights, we need to look at what we mean by 'care' as it is a value-laden term and is not always viewed positively. For some, the very term 'care' imposes a value on the nature of activities that support people. This is because 'care' emphasises the role that 'professionals' are engaged in when supporting people. It has associations of a parent–child relationship and can evoke ideas of dependency and power imbalances.

Health and social care organisations have traditionally been established on a 'them and us' relationship, but this has increasingly been questioned and resisted in recent decades. A Disability Rights Commission report in 2007 identified health and social care organisations as still being discriminatory in their lack of employment of disabled people; they attributed this to organisations regarding people as service users or patients, rather than peers. The language of care work – workers as professionals and those cared for as 'patients' 'service users', 'clients' or even 'consumers' – reflects a set of beliefs about what the care relationship is, or should be, and this needs to be regularly reviewed.

Values

Values are the ideas that influence the way we work; beliefs about the way that we should 'support or care' for others. Values guide our approach to those who we support and can provide the foundations underpinning good care practice. These values include the following:

1 Individuality and identity
2 Rights
3 Choice
4 Privacy
5 Independence
6 Dignity
7 Respect
8 Partnership

Ethics

Care work is a complex human activity that raises all kinds of moral dilemmas on a daily basis. Knowledge of different ethical positions can help us to approach dilemmas and decision-making in our work in an informed way.

Ethics is the branch of philosophy which concerns itself with questions about the morally right course of action to take in any given situation; how do we know what is right and what is wrong?

Allmark (Fulford *et al*, 2002) provides an interesting discussion on whether there can actually be an 'ethics of care', a right and wrong way of caring. The ethics of care says that we *should* care, that caring *is* a moral quality and that we should encourage conditions which create care. What it means is that we should care about the *right* things in the *right* way and encourage the required qualities. But, by focusing on care as a moral quality in itself, something it is not, the ethics of care can tell us nothing of what those right things are. (Fulford *et al*. 2002, page 68)

> **REFLECT**
>
> 1 How, as care workers, are we meant to know what the right things to care about are?
> 2 How are we to know how to care about them in the right way?

> **ACTIVITY**
>
> Think about the various factors that influence the way that you do your job and the approach you take to it.
>
> You may identify some of the following:
> - what your manager asks you to do
> - what you see colleagues doing
> - what the service user asks you to do
> - what you have read about, or learned on a course
> - what you think you would like if you were in need of that care.
>
> Out of the factors that you have identified, what do you think is the most important influence on how you carry out your caring role?

Rights

Rights are statements indicating what a person is entitled to. Most modern democracies accept that there are some basic rights and freedoms that are so important and so fundamental that everyone should enjoy them – just because they are a human being (Home Office, 1998, page 2).

Negative rights (*liberties*) relate to the freedom to do something without interference. An example of this would be having your privacy respected without someone invading your personal space.

Positive rights (*claim rights*) claim against someone to do something. An example of a positive right would be someone saying the care organisation had not provided appropriate support.

These themes are discussed in greater detail later on in the chapter.

Ethical theories

Deontology

Deontology is concerned with the nature of *moral duty* and the *rightness* of actions. Kant, the German philosopher, made the classic statement of the deontological position when he said 'Let justice be done even if the heavens fall.' In other words, if you can be sure that your decision is morally right then go ahead and do it – whatever the consequences may turn out to be. The key to this ethical position is the belief that, if what we are doing is right, it is our moral

Human rights in healthcare – a framework for local action

The British Institute of Human Rights and the Department of Health have devised a framework to assist NHS Trusts to develop and use a human rights based approach (HRBA). They realised that lack of respect for people's human rights is bad for their health.

The aim is for NHS Trusts to:

- put principles such as dignity, respect and equality into practice
- shape services and procedures that put the 'human' at the heart of healthcare
- effectively support their staff and commissioned providers to fulfil their specific duties under the Human Rights Act 1998, as well as progressing Healthcare Commission standards on human rights and patient treatment.

As public service providers, NHS Trusts have a legal duty to take steps to protect human rights. This is reflected in increased monitoring of human rights policy and practice by existing bodies such as the Healthcare Commission, and the Commission for

Equality and Human Rights (CEHR). Such monitoring helps to ensure that individuals get fair, dignified and equitable treatment within our healthcare system and that NHS Trusts contribute to building a wider culture of respect for human rights here in the UK.

The framework was developed with the support of NHS staff. It is not a legal requirement but the guidelines haves five key principles which are considered to be valuable:

1 Putting human rights principles and standards at the heart of policy and planning.
2 Empowering staff and patients with knowledge, skills and organisational leadership and commitment to achieve human rights based approaches.
3 Enabling meaningful involvement and participation of all key stakeholders.
4 Ensuring clear accountability throughout the organisation.
5 Non-discrimination and attention to vulnerable groups.

duty to do it. Worrying about negative or unfortunate consequences should not be part of the decision-making – we must 'grasp the nettle'. This approach sees moral decision-making as based on reason and on being able to argue that a particular course of action is self-evidently the right one.

Utilitarianism

A different position to this is proposed by a group of philosophers who are known as *utilitarians*, Jeremy Bentham being one such proponent of this idea. People with these ideas consider that a way through dilemmas and ethical decision-making is to consider that the best outcome is likely to be the result of the *greatest good occurring to the greatest number of people*. This idea focuses on the importance of the *consequences of actions*. Have you ever heard (or said) the phrase 'The end justifies the means'? If you have, you are working within a utilitarian framework of ethics. In our field of work it is important to think about the process of ethical decision-making; these are not just fancy ideas for the philosophers. As a

professional involved in the lives of individuals you may be required to make important decisions. Throughout this book there are case studies that reflect the situations which care workers come across; often with no clear solution, an appreciation of ethical theories can help our thinking on these dilemmas.

How can these theories benefit the care worker? Well they may not provide conclusions to how we should behave, but they can provide a framework for understanding the dilemmas that arise, and enable us to understand our motivations, as individuals, organisations and as a society as a whole. They can provide us with a new way of looking at complex issues relating to values. The health service has a strong foundation in ethics and the idea of addressing dilemmas.

When considering the case study on this page you may have suggested that the eight people should have their wishes respected as it is their home too and they are in the majority. Alternatively, you may have thought that Mrs George has as much right to stay in the communal area with the others – even if she experiences distress at times.

There seems to be no clear solution that will satisfy everyone, which is why we refer to it as a *dilemma*. People may approach this situation from different ethical positions that have an impact on their individual decision-making.

As mentioned in Chapter 2 (Reflection in action) it is important for care workers to utilise the tools available to them in order to maximise their effectiveness; as well as making use of values to inform their practice it is also important to make use of research, policy guidelines, evidence from own practice and self-reflection. Awareness of our own motivations in analysing situations and coming to conclusions can improve your effectiveness.

CASE STUDY

A moral dilemma

After many years of living on her own, Mrs George has just moved into a care home. She likes the idea of having more company, having been quite isolated in recent months due to spending a lot of time in bed. Mrs George frequently experiences considerable pain which causes her to cry out for periods of time. There are eight other residents who live in the home. They are upset by the noise, and have indicated that they would prefer Mrs George to spend time in her own room when she is making such a noise.

Questions

1 Thinking about the theories we discussed earlier, how can the ideas of Kant and Bentham guide us in deciding the correct course of action?
2 What would be your recommendation of a solution to this dilemma?
3 What is the balance of rights in this situation? Is it influenced by the numbers of people?

Why values are important in care work

Our individual value base is not something we are born with; neither is it coherent, well thought out or fixed at any particular stage in our lives. If we want to develop a set of *professional* care values then we must start by evaluating our own *personal* value base. There are several ways in which values become a part of our own lives. In our early development we are introduced to ideas from family, school education and friends by the process of socialisation. As we grow older we may acquire new values, as some of our earlier beliefs are challenged by new ideas that we are exposed to. If you have a strong sense of family support you need to be aware that you should not impose expectations on other family groups who do not share the same values. It is important to be aware of the impact our own values can have on others and how easy it is to articulate this in our dialogue with others. This will be discussed in more depth in Chapter 4 on Supporting Individuals and their Families, but for now consider what values are implicit in the following communication between a service user, or patient, and care worker.

> *Care worker*: 'Aren't you going to stay with your daughter for Christmas?'
>
> *Individual service user*: 'No'

If the person did not have a relationship with their daughter that meant they wanted to stay with them then they may feel guilty about this. If their daughter did not want to have them staying in their home the person may feel upset.

> *Care worker*: 'Isn't your father going to stay with you over Christmas?'
>
> *Relative*: 'No'

This dialogue is also making the assumption that an individual thinks of Christmas as a special period of time, as well as assuming that the son/daughter should take their father home.

It is tempting to believe that as long as we do not *intentionally* behave inappropriately towards someone in our care then this is good practice. However, as we have seen, if we don't stop and think about values and assumptions that we take for granted, we could easily offend others without even realising it; for example, asking someone who is Jewish or Muslim 'Can you tell me your Christian name?'. You need to be conscious of your own actions in order to be able to assess what impact your values have on others. We all have prejudices and beliefs that may influence our behaviour with others and it is important not to underestimate their impact.

Society's values

Our society is diverse; each group has its own beliefs and values, but we know these do not all carry the same weight. Sociologists refer to *dominant* cultures and *dominant* beliefs. These are the values and beliefs of certain majority groups that may ignore the views of others. Two examples of dominant beliefs within society that have an impact on the way people usually think and behave are ethnocentrism and heterosexism.

Ethnocentrism is where the values and practices of one ethnicity are considered to be the norm to such an extent that all other ethnicities are ignored or considered to be irrelevant. This may seem inevitable when social processes and the need for a society to develop norms is considered. This process does, however, need to be acknowledged and attempts made to expose the effects of this process. An example is where Christmas is recognised as a period of celebration, but it is difficult for an individual to take time off work to celebrate their own religious festivals.

Heterosexism is where the dominant values and practices in a society reflect a view that all people are heterosexual, ignoring the possibility that individuals may be homosexual. Society has not historically recognised, valued and included individuals who are homosexual. An example is where official forms ask for details of husband or wife. This places the onus on the person to state 'I am different' rather than just answering the question in the same way a heterosexual person might.

Celebrating diversity

Ethnocentricity and heterosexism are both based on, and perpetuate, stereotypes of minority groups. Difference is constructed negatively, creating a cycle of prejudice. Instead of disapproving of difference, 'celebrating diversity' is about recognising the significant and valuable contribution that all groups can make to society often because of their differences.

The policy context

When considering your own experience of values as a care worker we can look at three levels:

1 Legislation and policy.
2 Organisational procedures.
3 Your own individual practice.

In Chapter 1, on the context of health and social care, we look at the current legislative framework for the delivery of care, and the policies that are shaping care provision. How do values influence these policies and legislation?

The Care Standards Act 2000 provided a comprehensive review of standards within the care sector that were based on care values. The practices of a care organisation will then need to capture these values. Some organisations will try to be very transparent with their values, making sure that potential users of their services are clear about what they should expect. The challenge is to successfully translate these values into the everyday approach of all members of staff.

REFLECT

Look at the mission statement of your organisation and analyse what values are evident. Are these values clear to all those who use the service? What would their summary of the organisation's values be?

There are some areas of care practice where you need to acquire new knowledge to work more effectively with people. There is a much clearer framework now for discussing care values with more related written policy. The Care Standards Act 2000 provided the necessary legislation for some values to become more formalised as a requirement of care providers. The government placed the idea of standards within a legal framework and values are an intrinsic part of this. Health services and social care services have their foundations in different value bases and emphasise different dimensions of care practice as being most significant. The integration of these two providers of care, as discussed in Chapter 1 on the

context of health and social care, has led to a meeting of these value bases.

ACTIVITY

A useful starting point is for you to consider what values you have in your own life. Make a list of the things that you value in life, for example being respected by the people that you work with, having your own private space at home etc. Think about how important these values are to you, and what your life would be like if these values went unacknowledged by other people.

Chapter 2 (Reflection in action) shows you that it is important to keep up to date with government guidance and policies. Some policies provide a good indication of what values are important within the care sector; an example of this is the White Paper relating to learning disability.

There are four key principles at the heart of the government's proposals in *Valuing People* (Department of Health, 2001b)

1 Legal and civil rights.
2 Independence.
3 Choice.
4 Inclusion.

If you are working with service users with learning disabilities, this policy will have had an impact on changes in your organisation, as it contained strong recommendations relating to every aspect of service delivery.

The relevant Sector Skills Councils, Skills for Health and Skills for Care have a significant role in developing the care workforce. They encourage values to be learned through induction standards that state a range of values which should underpin the work of all care employees:

1.1 The values
1.1.1 Understand the importance of promoting the following values at all times:

Individuality and identity	Independence
Rights	Dignity
Choice	Respect
Privacy	Partnership

1.1.2 Understand the meaning of prejudice and equal opportunities in relation to the service users they will be supporting.

The last statement in the list refers to the important area of equality. Equality can be difficult to describe, and professionals need to be clear about whether they are focusing on equality in the *provision* of health and social care services, or equality of individuals in their *experience* of health and social well-being. The former statement emphasises that there should be equity in the way that care services are organised, funded and delivered – the process. The latter statement recognises that by focusing on the outcomes for individuals, the need for difference in the process of providing care may be required.

Diversity is a fact of modern life

Values in relation to individual identity

Diversity in the UK today

The term diversity refers to differences in the characteristics of individuals within the changing population in the countries of the UK. The population comprises a diverse range of individuals with a variety of races, abilities, religions and cultures etc. The reason for investigating this here is that care happens in a context and the care worker needs to understand the social context of care in order to understand the circumstances of individuals that they support.

The following table provides some idea of the diverse range of people who live in the UK today.

Total population: 60.2 million	Males	30.3 million
	Females	28.9 million
Ethnicity:	Asian or Asian British	2,329,000
	Black or Black British	1,148,000
	Chinese	243,000
Religion (77% of population)	Christian	71.7%
	Muslim	3.1%
	Hindu	1.1%
	Sikh	0.6%
	Jewish	0.3%
	Buddhist	0.3%

Source: National Statistics Online 2007

Of course, there is geographical variation in the percentage of individuals living in a particular area. For example, consider these two urban areas in different parts of the country.

Islington Borough, North London

Ethnicity:

White British: 57%

Mixed ethnicity: 4.1%

Asian: 5.4%

Black: 11.9%

Chinese: 1.7%

66% of the residents of Islington were born in England

13% of households were lone parent families

32% of households had at least one person with a limiting long-term illness

www.islington.gov.uk

Chester City, Cheshire

Ethnicity:

White British: 98%

5% of households were lone parent families

18% of residents have a limiting long-term illness

www.chester.gov.uk

REFLECT

1 Consider your own area, how do the statistics above compare to your local environment?
2 Where do you fit into the statistics above?
3 What characteristics do you have as an individual?
4 How would you represent yourself in terms of the characteristics that you have?

As individuals we do not always like to be categorised according to one aspect of our identity; in one context I may emphasise my nationality, in a different context I may emphasise my gender and see that characteristic as being of greater importance.

Issues relating to diversity

The way that services are usually organised is a response to a general identification of need; services are arranged around characteristics of *service user groups*. This may sound like common sense but the characteristics of one individual within a service user group could be very different from others within that group. Focusing on one aspect of a person's identity can lead to *labelling*. Individuals within a service user, or patient group, have similarities and also differences in terms of their life experiences and their care needs. Labels and grouping of individuals may better suit the delivery of services rather than the needs of the individual who requires a service.

When considering the context of care delivery the care worker must consider the inequality of social experience by members of the public and whether the response by welfare services condones or challenges this.

CASE STUDY

Diversity

Meadow Lane Community Centre is holding its Annual General Meeting. On the agenda is allocation of resources for the coming year, including costs of translating services. There is dissatisfaction amongst some long-standing members that resources have not been targeted at their needs due to new people moving into the local area. The local newspapers have labelled some of these people as 'bogus' asylum seekers and economic migrants who take local people's jobs. In addition, regular changes to immigration policy and uncertainty surrounding the government's attitude towards people is not helping.

Questions

1 How would you manage this negative communication about those seeking refugee status and economic migrants?
2 What measures can organisations put in place to prevent these negative feelings arising among those who feel sidelined?

Race

In the past, race was an accepted term for biological groupings of individuals. This concept has been challenged in recent years as research has evidenced that there is as much biological difference between individuals who share the same race as there is between individuals of different races. While debate about the use of the term 'race' continues it is important to recognise that categorising individuals into racial groups has historically been used as a means of oppression of groups.

Racism

Racism is an ideology, a set of beliefs. As an ideology it includes the following:

- the superiority of (usually) white members of the population
- the inferiority of specific black races due to biological difference
- a justification for different (unequal) experiences of society due to the above.

For some people racism serves the purpose of justifying the power they claim over other groups as being legitimate; they then benefit from the consequences. Racism can also mean that people from black and minority ethnic groups feel inferior and are powerless to oppose the oppressive actions towards them. Historically, racism has shaped societies; obvious examples include the period of apartheid in South Africa and the oppression of Aboriginal people in Australia where racism was used to justify the oppressive actions of whites over indigenous groups. In Britain there are local and national examples of people holding racist views and employing discriminatory practices. The significance of this historical experience can influence individual interactions between people in society today.

Ethnicity

Ethnicity is often the preferred term to describe the social grouping of individuals. In addition to 'race', factors such as culture, religion and nationality may account for a person's overall ethnicity. Smith (in Spybey, 1997, page 247) provides a list of characteristics of an ethnic community:

1 A collective and proper name.

2 A myth of common ancestry.
3 Shared historical memories.
4 One or more differentiating elements of common culture.
5 An association with a specific homeland.
6 A sense of solidarity for significant sectors of the population.

The use of the phrase *ethnic minority* can be unhelpful in encouraging equality of experience. In some localities people of a particular ethnic group may actually not be in a minority. Another factor is that if services are to be allocated according to needs then even being in a minority should not limit an individual's experience of care.

Culture

A person's culture may relate to the customary practices that they adopt distinguishing them from other groups. Culture can be acquired through family and local community influences; some may originate in religious beliefs, place of birth, family practices, nationality, contemporary influences etc. Care workers should respond to individual service users or patients about how important certain customs and practices are. For example, a dominant value in care practice today is that of informing the patient or service user of everything that is happening to them and engaging them in decision-making while keeping information confidential from family members. Some cultures do not value this process, preferring to involve the whole family in decision-making practices, especially around end of life. The health and social care professions have to consider whether they want to promote the cultural practices of the individual, or to interpret them as oppressive and impose western values on the family.

Nationality

Nationality usually relates to the country (geographical and political boundary) that an individual is connected to either from birth or because they have acquired this status by living there; many people have dual nationality where more than one country may feel like 'home'. In the last decade more countries have joined the European Economic Community and there are more freedoms to work and live across Europe; these people are known as economic migrants. Some people from the Eastern

European ascension states have come to live in England and are working in organisations, including the health and social care sector, where recruitment has been difficult.

Why do people seek asylum?

- **Political oppression:** In some countries people do not have the freedom to speak out against the political party that is in power. If a person opposes the government or leader of that country they may be persecuted. Some Zimbabwean people would be threatened if they return to their home as they have challenged the government.
- **Genocide and religious oppression:** Sometimes whole groups of people are attacked or made vulnerable because of their faith.
- **War:** If a country is at war it can leave the infrastructure devastated, populations can be homeless and without any means of supporting their families. A recent issue has been the right to remain in the UK for the Iraqi interpreters who worked for the British army.
- **Natural disasters:** Natural events such as famine or floods can cause whole populations of people to be left in an environment which can no longer support them.

Migration: 2006 (National Office of Statistics 2007)

An estimated 400,000 long-term migrants left the UK. This was the highest recorded level of emigration. Just over half of these emigrants (207,000) were British citizens.

An estimated 591,000 long-term migrants arrived to live in the UK. This was up from the previous highest figure of 586,000 in 2004. Just over 85 per cent of immigrants (510,000) were non-British citizens.

Creed

Creed refers to an individual's statement of beliefs. This of course may be associated with nationality, religion etc., but it can also be different within family groups as individuals acquire new ways of thinking.

ACTIVITY

Migration varies in different geographical areas. Look at the local statistics available for your area and identify trends in migration. Consider the following questions.

1 What is the local perception of migration?
2 How do the actual statistics compare to the local view of migration?
3 How is your local council responding to the changing demography of the area if it is changing?
4 Do the users of health and social care services locally reflect any changes to the population?

Language

There are many languages in the world; Chinese Mandarin is the most commonly used, followed by Spanish and then English. Within the countries of the UK other languages are spoken as first languages in addition to English. The effective use of language is a powerful tool for gaining access to socio-economic and political processes, as will be discussed in the chapter on supporting individuals and their families (Chapter 4). Language as a form of communication can promote a person's participation in society and enable him or her to gain access to the facilities and services that will empower them. In a similar way, not having access to language can disadvantage individuals and limit a person's ability.

British Sign Language (BSL) has until recently not been acknowledged as one of the languages of the UK, and yet it is the main form of communication of many deaf individuals; estimates suggest 50,000 people (Royal National Institute for the Deaf (RNID), 2007, www.rnid.org.uk, Information and Resources section). If we think about the idea of power and structural discrimination that we mentioned earlier, consider how liberated some deaf people would be if BSL was on the national curriculum and all schoolchildren were able to develop these skills and communicate with deaf children and adults. The Medical Research Council estimates that there are about 9 million deaf and hard of hearing people in the UK. This number is likely to increase as the percentage of people over 60 years increases.

The most common languages into which the National Literacy Trust translate written materials include: Arabic, Bengali, Chinese, French, Gujerati, Polish, Punjabi, Somali, Tamil, Turkish and Urdu.

ACTIVITY

Disability, discrimination and poverty

The Royal National Institute for the Deaf (2002) Survey on Employment found that there was an unemployment rate of 19 per cent of deaf and hard of hearing people; this is four times the national average for people who are not disabled. Almost a third of deaf people who were in full-time work earned under £10,000 per year compared to 11.8 per cent of the UK general population.

The Equality and Human Rights Commission (EHRC) was introduced on 1 October 2007. This organisation replaced the different bodies that previously advocated for equality and rights for different groups. The activities of the Disability Rights Commission (DRC), the Equal Opportunities Commission (EOC) and the Commission for Racial Equality have all been incorporated into the responsibilities of this organisation.

The Race Relations Act 1976 aimed to address the negative experiences of individuals from minority ethnic groups in society, especially in relation to employment. Employers had to consider their practices, such as requesting photographs for interviews and monitoring the characteristics of employers to ascertain how successful they are in counteracting discrimination.

The Commission for Racial Equality used to promote racial equality and ensure that there was appropriate representation for individuals within the Race Relations Act 1976 and the more recent Race Relations (Amendment) Act 2000. Other legislation has promoted the ability of individuals to have appropriate support; an example is the NHS and Community Care Act 1990, which allowed for the delivery of specific services through local authority

contracts with organisations who had the e... consider the needs of certain groups. This po... enabled the tailoring of services to meet more... needs and reach groups who had previously ha... their needs marginalised in 'mainstream' services. It stated that culture needed to be considered when assessing needs and allocating services.

Government initiated service standards such as the National Service Frameworks and National Minimum Standards policies now identify the significance of race and culture in determining people's experience of care.

Here is an extract from the Domiciliary Care National Minimum Standards:

> Service users have some choice of staff who work with them, such as staff from the same ethnic, religious or cultural background or the same gender.
>
> (Department of Health, 2000, page 34)

Sexuality

Sexuality is not a reason why individuals require care. So why is it important to consider the experiences and needs of service users in relation to their sexuality? The reason is that sexuality is part of an individual's identity, whether or not they are or have ever been engaged in any sexual activity. As part of individual identity it is an important dimension of individuality for the health and social care worker to be aware of.

The care profession has not necessarily promoted homosexuality in a good light. The medical profession has at times contributed to homophobia with its need to establish a cause of homosexuality. This has led in the past to its association with mental illness. The history of homosexuality in the UK has included it being classified as mental illness or a criminal activity. It was only as recently as 1992 that the World Health Organization declassified homosexuality as a mental illness. There is an absence of conclusive proof that homosexuality is completely biologically determined and the stance adopted by Stonewall, which is acknowledged as leading campaigners on gay rights issues, is that sexual orientation is likely to be the product of biological and environmental factors. In December 2005 the first civil partnerships took place in England. For some, this provided a welcome recognition of long-term homosexual relationships;

for others it fell short of giving equal marriage rights to couples who value their homosexual relationship in the same manner as heterosexuals.

An important dimension of promoting rights is that of sometimes treating people differently in order for them to enjoy equality of service. Dismissing individual needs as irrelevant to the care task is easier, and still in many instances the needs arising from sexuality are ignored; sometimes, individual service users dismiss their own needs themselves (Wilton, 2000, page 6).

A holistic approach to care requires that an individual's physical, social, emotional, intellectual and cultural needs are considered in any area of health and social care delivery. This necessitates respecting people's identity, including their sexual identity. The National Minimum Standards now acknowledge this dimension of individuality.

Remember that one of the Skills for Care induction values is that of privacy; sexuality is not part of the reason for care giving, and it therefore does not need to become the focus of attention when providing care to a lesbian or a gay man. However, the care worker needs to be aware of the heterosexist practices of both themselves and the organisation, and the potential needs of individuals who are homosexual, or bisexual.

Heterosexism can create mental and physical stress in individuals who feel pressurised into presenting a heterosexual identity.

Wilton (2000, page177) identified the following experiences within care services:

1 Professionals are ill-informed about health issues.
2 Many care professionals hold ill-informed and prejudicial views on lesbian and gay people's lifestyles.
3 A significant proportion of gay men and lesbians receive poor treatment, hostility or abuse by care providers.
4 Education for professionals is inadequate and tends to be focused on issues (e.g. HIV/AIDS).
5 Medical knowledge can perpetuate negative attitudes.
6 Statutory powers can be used to support discrimination.
7 A significant number of gay men and lesbians feel unsafe about revealing their sexuality to care

professionals and so remain without appropriate treatment.
8 A significant proportion of young homeless people are made homeless by their rejection by family members when their sexuality is made known
(Wilton, 2000, page105)

Stonewall conducted research on lesbian healthcare:

'A survey carried out by Stonewall in just one city has revealed serious gaps in the provision of healthcare for lesbians. The survey of almost 300 women in Brighton, carried out by Stonewall's policy team, covered a range of areas, including smear tests and screening, and asked lesbians about both positive or negative experiences they'd had with healthcare providers.'

Their findings included:

- Almost 20 per cent fewer respondents (64 per cent) had had a cervical smear in the last three years than the figure for women nationally (80 per cent).
- Over half had received no sexual health screening at all in the last three years, yet 69 per cent of respondents had had sex with men in the past.
- Over a third of respondents had not disclosed their sexuality to their GP.
- 78 per cent of respondents drank regularly, 28 per cent smoked and 12 per cent said they took recreational drugs.
- One respondent disclosed that, after she had revealed her sexual orientation to her GP, the GP had put on a pair of gloves. This was unconnected with any treatment being given.
- While one woman was undergoing a smear test, a nurse had insisted that a male doctor be present on discovering the patient's sexual orientation.
- One patient who sought GP help after her partner had died was asked if her partner had died of AIDS.
(Stonewall, 2007)

The Equality Act (Sexual Orientation) Regulations 2007 outlaws discrimination in the provision of businesses and services to lesbians, gay men, bisexuals and transsexuals. In January 2008 the House of Commons approved the Criminal Justice and Immigration Bill, including provisions to make it illegal to stir up hatred on grounds of sexual orientation.

This group experience some severe opposition to their rights presented under the banner of morality or religious beliefs. People sometimes feel morally justified in opposing equal rights for homosexuals on the basis of their religion, examples being in fostering and adoption practice.

Gender

When you considered your own values you may have identified that some of the origins of these are associated with your gender. Gender is the word used for the social grouping of people where the biological grouping is sex. Care workers need to develop a critical approach to the experience of gender, as with the focus on other equality issues it may be overlooked, or issues which have been on the agenda for years are assumed to have been dealt with. There is nothing wrong with differences originating in gender, but care workers should question what is commonplace and identify the sources of poor practice associated with gender.

Assumptions about gender assume femininity in women and masculinity in men. These assumptions can differ according to a person's culture, age and personal values. Expectations of roles associated with gender can be oppressive, and may serve to exclude individuals from certain roles, services, social networks or support. This is a further example where the importance of identifying need in partnership with service user or patients is important.

The Sex Discrimination Act 1975 and the Equal Pay Acts of 1970 and 1975 tackled unequal relations between males and females, especially in the workplace where it was recognised that there were examples of overt discrimination. This legislation was carried further in 1986 with an additional Sex Discrimination Act that outlawed discrimination on the basis of gender to even small organisations, and made the age of retirement and pensions equal. In 2007 there are still cases where employers adopt discriminatory practices in relation to employment, pay and promotion of women. Trevor Philips states that gender differences need consideration, given that the Equal Pay Act is almost 40 years old.

We have looked at theories and models previously to understand a particular issue. *Feminism* is a perspective, a way of looking at a social situation that focuses on the belief that structures in society serve to oppress women, and that these need to be taken into account in all interaction and dialogue. Feminist discussion has included the desire to politicise the personal and to personalise the political (Thompson, 2001, page 54). This means that individuals should see their own experience of discrimination in the context of wider society, and that society as a whole should acknowledge the significance of the very real experiences of individuals.

The Equal Opportunities Commission was the predecessor to the EHRC, focusing on gender discrimination. Research findings in *Women and Men in Britain: The Lifecycle of Inequality* highlight the significance of interrelated issues. An example of this is the subjects that are predominantly chosen by girls in schools, which then lead them into particular careers that are low paid due to the concentration of women in some jobs. In recent years 90 per cent of students taking GNVQ Foundation Health and Social Care were female, while 81 per cent of those taking GNVQ IT were male. The EOC recognises that the costs of gender stereotyping in occupational choice are:

- discrimination
- wasted talent
- skills gaps
- unequal pay
- disaffection.

The report *Women's Incomes Over The Lifetime* estimated that a well-qualified childless woman who had not had a break in employment to raise children will still face a loss of income of £143,000 over their life compared to a well-qualified man.

Ability

In this section we focus on how the ability of individuals affects their experience of life and participation in society. In the UK 15 per cent (8.5 million people) of the population are registered disabled. There have been several words associated with disability and it would be useful to clarify some of these.

Impairment: This word relates to the functioning of an individual in relation to a particular physical or cognitive feature. For example, a person with a hearing impairment would not have full capacity in their hearing ability.

Disability: A definition of disability provided by the Disability Discrimination Act 1995 is:

- a mental or physical impairment
- the impairment has an adverse effect on the ability of the individual to carry out normal day-to-day activities
- the adverse effects are substantial
- the adverse effects are long-term (having lasted, or likely to last, at least 12 months).

Disabled people: The phrase 'people with disabilities' is favoured by some as it emphasises the idea that individuals are people first. However, the phrase 'disabled people' is usually used as it identifies that the disability is not located within the individual, but that individuals are disabled by society and inaccessible environments. Some disabled people's groups use the phrase 'temporarily able' about members of society who are currently without an

impairment, in recognition of the fact that the majority of people will at some point experience a change in their ability.

Disability can be associated with physical, sensory or learning needs. It can have an effect on an individual's day-to-day activities through affecting the following areas of well-being:

- mobility
- manual dexterity
- physical co-ordination
- continence
- ability to lift or carry
- speech, hearing or eyesight
- memory, concentration, learning or understanding
- understanding of the risk of physical danger.

These aspects of a person's condition relate to the extent to which an individual has the physical, social and psychological ability to participate in their society. When considering this we could focus on the ability and inability of the individual, or we could focus on factors in the environment that affect the person's ability or inability.

Language has been a defining factor in the history of disabled people. Historically, this group has been labelled as 'imbeciles', 'invalids' and 'handicapped'. It is important for health and social care professions to respond both to the language that is preferred by disabled people's groups as a whole and by the individual with whom they are working.

Models of disability

In order to appreciate the experiences of individuals, and understand how society has responded to them previously, we will now look at models of disability. Models provide a way of explaining what is going on, a way of viewing the situation. There are three different models of disability:

- the personal tragedy model
- the medical model
- the social model.

The ***personal tragedy*** model starts with the individual situation of the disabled person. It focuses on the loss of ability in the individual, and emphasises the physiological reasons why an individual is unable to undertake certain tasks. A person is described in terms of what they cannot do. The response from others in society is therefore one of pity and sympathy.

> Poor Jenny, she has multiple sclerosis and can't look after herself any more. She can't get herself dressed and her legs are useless, she needs to use a wheelchair all the time.

The **medical model** emphasises the pathology of the individual. It focuses on what the body is capable of and how the physical reaction to the impairment can be improved by the care profession. Discussion on overcoming disability would focus on correcting the impairment. Comparisons would be made with what an able-bodied person is capable of, and providing feedback based on the 'norm'.

> 'Jenny has experienced a change in her condition, which means she is currently unable to walk or physically attend to her personal care needs. Her condition is degenerative so her ability to do things herself will decrease over time. There are new medical techniques that we could consider to reduce the effects of this change.'

The **social model** starts from the premise that the environment we live in restricts some individuals in what they can do, and limits some people's access to, and participation in, society. The focus is not on the individual who experiences disability, but on society, which has created barriers for some people. This model is further strengthened by the idea of rights; individuals who are disabled by the communities in which they live have the right to have their needs addressed. It values the individual with the impairment and aims to support them by changing the physical and social environment rather than changing the person's identity.

> Jenny has multiple sclerosis, which has affected her experience of society and her environment. Jenny will need her environment to respond to her changing needs, with more appropriate access to buildings and an increase in the practical support that is given to her. Jenny has a right to continue participating in the activities that she has always been involved in and will need advice and support to do this.

You may be wondering why models of disability are useful for care workers. Their significance is evident from the role that professionals take on when working with individuals. As with the example of Jenny,

models impact on both the individual and the response of those around her, including the provision of services by the care worker.

REFLECT

Having read through the models and how each one would interpret Jenny's circumstances, think about the impact that each model would have on the attitudes of the following:

- people in society
- care workers
- Jenny and her family.

Models of working with learning disabled individuals have focused on the ideas of:

- **normalisation** (ensuring that the life of a learning disabled person follows the usual patterns associated with age etc.)
- **social role valorisation** (where the role and status of a learning disabled person is valued by society)
- **ordinary life principles** (where people have access to normal daily living and the usual expectations on all of us are applied to learning disabled people).

The similarities of these have been that they aim to promote inclusion of individuals in society, and validate the status of learning disabled individuals.

Disability has often been associated with dependence and tragedy, which is a patronising way of viewing people.

Experiences of disabled people

People experience other unequal treatment as a result of their disability. In addition to employment, individual's social lives can be affected. Society imposes stereotypes about individuals with disabilities; these range from disabled individuals having no sexuality to being very promiscuous. Disabled people can also be treated as a homogeneous group, or they are arranged into a hierarchy of disability. It is important therefore for the care worker to acknowledge their responsibility in addressing inequality.

Disabled people are now not only claiming their rights as people but they are asserting their sense of identity as disabled people. Society disrespects this sometimes and tries to impose values on individuals in relation to their ability. For example, medical advances have enabled technology to overcome some causes of deafness. Within the deaf community there is a mixed response to cochlear implants as many feel that having corrective intervention negates the very positive experiences of deafness by individuals.

The DRC raised issues relating to innovations in medical practices. Genetic screening and medical treatment to correct disability are examples of where there are tensions between different views.

ACTIVITY

In some countries assisted suicide is legal and is considered by some to be the ultimate in empowering individuals to have control and choice over their lives, and their death. For other people it remains a real taboo and the health and social care sector is divided in opinions.

Research the positions of different countries with regard to this and make a list of points in favour and against euthanasia and assisted suicide.

Sport: Football

There are many examples of organisations that are promoting more access to competitive sports both in inclusive activities and also as separate activity. The English Football Association has developed the capacity of local disabled footballers to create the following international teams:

- England Amputee Football Team
- England Blind Team
- England Partially Sighted Team
- England Deaf and Hearing Impaired Team
- England Cerebal Palsy Team
- England Learning Disability Team

In 2012 London will be hosting the **Paralympic Games** (International Paralympic Committee). Athletes belong to six different disability groups in the Paralympic Movement: amputee, cerebral palsy, visual impairment, spinal cord injuries, intellectual disability and 'les autres', a group which includes all those who do not fit into the other groups. Athletes are grouped in classes defined by the degree of function presented by the disability. Classes are determined by a variety of processes that may include a physical and technical assessment and observation in and out of competition. The classes are defined by each sport and form part of the sport rules.

See www.abilityvsability.co.uk

Legislation and disability

The Disability Discrimination Act 1995 made it unlawful to discriminate against a disabled person in:

- employment
- the provision of goods, facilities and services
- education
- management, buying or renting of land or property.

Under this legislation, discrimination means:

- the disabled person is being treated less favourably
- the treatment is for a reason relating to the person's disability
- the treatment is not justified

or that:

- there has been a failure to make reasonable adjustments for the disabled person
- this failure is not justified.

The DRC advocated for rights following the Disability Rights Commission Act of 1999 until the inception of the Equality and Human Rights Commission in October 2007. The principles that the DRC proposed, that should underpin all policies and practice with disabled people, are choice, control, autonomy and participation.

Their statutory duties have all now been assumed by the CEHR who have within their remit to:

- work towards the elimination of discrimination of disabled people
- promote equalisation of opportunity for disabled people

- take steps as considered appropriate with a view to encouraging good practice in treatment of disabled people
- keep under review the workings of the Disability Discrimination Act 1995.

Sometimes services designed to meet the needs of disabled individuals do not get it right. There are some tensions in care practice relating to individuals' rights. The current legislative framework creates conflict between health and safety legislation and the principal aims of community care. The local authority's duty to their care staff overrides its duties towards an individual who requires assistance with mobility, for example. As a care worker it is difficult to work safely with individuals who need practical physical support with their personal mobility when you know they hate using the hoist. The Royal College of Nursing guidance indicates that employees lift manually only in 'exceptional or life threatening situations'. The Health and Safety Executive has devised a more positive solution for care workers aiming to promote the values inherent in community-based care.

Creating An Alternative Future was produced by the Disability Rights Commission in February 2007 as a legacy document.

Mental health

Research by Mind indicates that one in four of the population will experience mental ill-health at some point in their lives. It is a significant area of society and certainly not a 'them and us' situation. The following terms are important here:

Mental health – This phrase refers to well-being associated with thinking and emotions.

Mental disorder – This refers to a specific group of conditions that affect mental well-being.

CASE STUDY

Disability discrimination

Sharon Coleman, whose son Oliver was born with a rare condition affecting his breathing and was also deaf, brought a case claiming she was forced to resign from her job as a legal secretary after, she claims, being harassed by her employers and refused flexible working. She believes she was specifically targeted because she has a child with a disability, and was denied the flexible work arrangements offered to her colleagues without disabled children.

In January 2008 the employment rights of a mother of a child with a disability were challenged. The carer was supported by the Equality and Human Rights Commission. An Employment Tribunal referred it to the European Court of Justice (ECJ). The Advocate General (AG) of the ECJ said that treating employees less favourably because of their caring responsibilities for disabled relatives is unlawful. The AG stated that a European Directive regarding equal treatment in employment prohibits 'disability discrimination by association' and should apply to British law. Whilst this case of Sharon Coleman related to her son, this could also mean carers of other relatives could have the same legal protection. It was felt that this would potentially help the 6 million carers of disabled children and people.

The AG explained: 'One way of undermining the dignity and autonomy of people ... is to target not them, but third persons who are closely associated with them.'

The AG's opinion now needs to be ratified by the Court's judges who heard Ms Coleman's case, but it is highly likely they will follow the AG's lead.

Ms Coleman's victory will ensure that the UK's Disability Discrimination Act is interpreted to provide protection on the grounds of someone's association with, and caring responsibilities, for a family member with a disability. The ruling will also mean that those caring for elderly relatives are protected under age discrimination legislation.

Questions

1   What are your views on the Coleman case?
2   How can organisations ensure that they treat carers with respect without compromising the work of their organisations?
3   What policies are in place in your organisation to allow employees to provide appropriate support for family members in need of care?

Mental health problems – This refers to situations and conditions that have a negative effect on a person's mental well-being.

Mental distress – This refers to ill-health experienced as a consequence of disorders or problems.

Research presented by the Mental Health Foundation has concluded that:

- 'mixed anxiety & depression is the most common mental disorder in Britain'
- women are more likely to have been treated for a mental health problem than men
- about 10 per cent of children have a mental health problem at any one time
- depression affects one in five older people living in the community and two in five living in care homes
- British men are three times as likely as British women to die by suicide. In 2004, more than 5,500 people in the UK died by suicide. Suicide remains the most common cause of death in men under the age of 35
  (*National Service Framework For Mental Health – Five Years On*, Department of Health, 2005)

- depression affects one in five older people living in the community and two in five living in care homes
  (Mental Health Foundation quoting *Psychiatry in the Elderly* (3rd edition), Oxford University Press, 2002)
- dementia affects 5 per cent of people over the age of 65 and 20 per cent of those over 80. About 700,000 people in the UK have dementia (1.2 per cent of the population) at any one time
  (National Institute For Clinical Excellence, 2004).

For example, if we have total faith in the organic model we may see that supporting individuals with a mental health problem should remain the responsibility of the medical profession and psychiatrists, and that family, friends or individual support workers have little to offer. There is awareness that a very few individuals have a mental disorder which will necessitate much medical intervention, but the majority of people will benefit from a holistic approach to their support. Some people will experience mental health problems that are not associated with a disorder, and the need for medical intervention may be limited.

The values of the Mental Capacity Act 2005 were a concern as they could 'entrench discrimination' faced by this group of people. Entrenchment here means that discrimination of individuals with mental health problems can be condoned and furthered by legislation. With rights come responsibilities, and mental health campaigners are clear that both individuals with mental health issues and society in general have responsibilities. People with mental health problems sometimes face stigma from their own families, society, employers and colleagues. Mental health is sometimes viewed as embarrassing to discuss, or not something to bring into the open.

Even within service delivery there is discrimination about the capacity of individuals who use mental health services to retain control of their decisions. Discussing the low take-up of Direct Payments amongst this group of individuals, Carmichael discovered that professionals did not advocate the system with mental health service users due to the perceived ability of individuals to meet the 'willing and able' criteria for Direct Payments and the perception that service users or patients would involve carers in their delusions or obsessions. (Carmichael and Brown, 2002, page 804)

Language has played a significant role in the values associated with mental health. The words 'lunatic' and 'mad' are part of the history of mental health services and are still used to sensationalise media reports. Some groups prefer to refer to people experiencing mental health issues as being in an 'unresourceful state'; this term emphasises that mental health is a resource for living and changes to a person's mental health will affect this resource.

Age

In many ways society determines our behaviour by categorising us according to age. Issues arising from age occur throughout the life course. Stereotyping of young people creates expectations that they are 'trouble' and new language, such as the term 'hoodies', further alienates young people in society. Older people are considered to be a burden as demographics suggest there are too many to look after.

Some companies are embracing the benefits of capturing the 'silver surfers' market as wealthy actively retired people have time and money to spend on holidays and leisure products.

Young people have experienced lack of continuity in service delivery as they undertake transition from adolescence to adulthood, exampled in mental health and learning disability services. In mental health this is being addressed through CAMHS (Children and Adolescent Mental Health Services). Older age should not necessarily be a reason for coming into contact with care services; some people will go their whole lives not requiring any support from professionals, but many people do need some level of assistance in later life. Older people experience more poverty than other age groups. Political discussions about pensions do not seem real to us until we stop work and become dependent on a low income through our pension. The political weight of older people is weakened by their status in society. Discrimination is even evident within care service delivery as older people receive less mental health support than other age groups from specialist teams when individuals acquire dementias such as Alzheimer's.

Society perhaps feels justified in discriminating against people due to older age, perhaps because it is a characteristic that we may all share at some point. Many images of older people are negative and emphasise that it is the last stage or even the end of life. It may be that this group of people have been unsupported in advocating for themselves and therefore their issues remain on the fringe of society.

Let us look at the factors that influence our perception of older age.

In society the emphasis is usually on health and biological factors, so older people are often associated with what they *cannot* physically do any more. Age is frequently one of the criteria for being allowed or not allowed services: within the NHS you are labelled as being an 'older person' when you are 70 years, within local authorities this age is 65. Means testing legitimates some individuals' access to domestic care or mobility aids at home while others go without.

Just as we have looked at models of disability and mental health, let us explore theories of ageing. This should provide an opportunity for you to reflect on your own personal values associated with age.

Economic circumstances
Money gives us the means to
continue in some activities

Environment
How safe it is for individuals
to access their locality

Individual
Ability to maintain lifestyle
is linked to wealth

Family situation
Changes in role and
relationship with children

Society
Age of retirement is linked
to the economy

Biology
Physical ability of the body to
undertake different tasks

Psychological changes
Self-esteem may change with
change in circumstances

Culture
Expectations of what people do at different stages of life
Old = wise or old = out of touch and past it

Figure 3.1 Factors that influence how we perceive older age

Ageism

Some older people face poverty, isolation, poor care standards and ageism in general.

Ageism is also present in healthcare provision. One in six people over 65 have been discriminated against in healthcare or health insurance because of their age (Age Concern/ICM poll December 2001). One in 20 people over 65 has been refused treatment, while one in ten has been treated differently since the age of 50 (Age Concern/Gallup survey 1999). More than three-quarters (77 per cent) of GPs confirm that age-based rationing occurs. Many GPs say that they are aware of upper age limits in a range of services, including heart bypass operations (34 per cent) and kidney dialysis (35 per cent) (Age Concern).

REFLECT

Look at the factors that influence society's perception of age. Think about what your individual view is of age in relation to each of these.

1 What would be the view of age of the service users that you support?
2 In what way does the organisation that you work for influence the views of age held by the staff and service users?
3 Is this a positive or negative influence?

Theories of ageing

Chronological age refers to the timeline of birth to older age and looks at age as a progressive, and then degenerative, experience. There is an emphasis on how our biology changes with time, and how what we are capable of doing is affected by age.

The social construction theory of age recognises that society can dictate what expectations individuals have of what they can or can't do at certain times in their life. For example, when is the 'right age' to marry, have children, go to college or university, start and stop working? There are lots of pressures to conform to what society expects of us. There are ways that society controls what we do, there are laws that say when we can drink alcohol, consent to sex or leave full-time education.

Policies

The proposed new comprehensive legislation on discrimination will encompass age. There are current examples of where age discrimination is being addressed through government policy:

The *National Service Framework for Older People*

Standard One: Rooting Out Age Discrimination

Aim: To ensure that older people are never unfairly discriminated against in accessing NHS or social care services as a result of their age.

Standard NHS services will be provided, regardless of age, on the basis of clinical need alone. Social care services will not use age in their eligibility criteria or policies to restrict access to available services.

(Department of Health, 2001a)

ACTIVITY

Compare the National Minimum Standards for Older People and for Adults and identify the differences between what is required for the age groups 18–65 and 65.

This standard raises issues as many services are organised around criteria, which provide a rationale for providing services to an individual, as well as an excuse for not providing them to others. This links with the organisation of services and whether we do have a needs-led or service-led provision, as discussed in the chapter on the context of care (Chapter 1).

The government report *Fit for the Future* sought to provide a more positive view of this generation:

- The older population should not be viewed negatively but as a major achievement of the twentieth century.
- Old age should be seen as a distinct phase of life which brings new opportunities and developments for both individuals and society. Older people have considerable assets of time and experience contributing to inter-generational interactions, within families and wider communities.
- Social inclusion should be a goal for ensuring opportunities for all citizens to participate fully in society, regardless of age, gender, ethnicity or socio-economic group.
- Policies and practices should reflect the principle of age neutrality and should not use age as a basis for discrimination.
- Strategies must focus on maintaining and enhancing what older people are able to do, rather than what they cannot do.
- Promoting positive values and attitudes should be part of public policy and law.

Sexuality and older age

The impact of the process of social construction on individual perception of age is illustrated through society's attitude towards older people and sex. Bytheway (1995) discusses the negative impact of humour on older people as they evoke ridicule or disgust from others. Many individuals – including many care workers – tend to view older people as no longer having any aspect of sexuality.

CASE STUDY

Sex and older people

Babs and Donald have been married for 67 years. They have been caring for each other for the past 8 years, but a recent chest infection has meant that Donald is very weak and unable to support Babs any more. Babs and Donald have been assessed and they will be moving into a care home very soon. They are pleased that they can share and this has been arranged for them; they had not spent a night apart since the end of World War Two until Donald's recent spell in hospital.

Questions

1 What difficulties arise for services regarding respecting the individual wishes of individuals?
2 What is the difference between an individual's preference, and an individual's human right, and should the health and social care services respond differently to them?

Religion

Religion may relate to a person's:

- faith and spiritual beliefs
- customs and practices
- association with a religious community.

This aspect of life in society has come more to the fore in a very negative way recently with increased prejudice against Muslim groups, due to political events. Some people may think that religion is irrelevant today and holds no significance in their own life. However, religion may be a very important part of a person's identity and so the threat of intolerance, discrimination and abuse can be debilitating for an individual, even if actual discrimination is not experienced by that individual. Many Muslims reported that their perception of prejudice against themselves in the lead-up to the war in Iraq during 2003 arose as a result of negative media reporting against them as a group.

The care worker needs to acknowledge that their own religious beliefs can influence their interpretation of and response to an individual's circumstances. Religion can be an important part of an individual's life, and it should be up to the individual to determine the support they require to access religious practices.

This is also acknowledged in the National Minimum Standards for Care Homes, Older People and Adults.

Government proposals that we have previously mentioned will include making discrimination, on the basis of a person's religion, illegal. This area is a little more complex than others as issues are more subjective. There is no absolute definition of what constitutes a religion or faith by individuals in society. Some people would describe themselves as Christian or Muslim without being affiliated to a religious organisation, attending a church or mosque regularly. People who hold the same faith may have differences of opinion about what customary practices should be observed and how strict this observance should be.

Religion is an important part of life for many people

Should the UK secular legal system accommodate religious practices?

In 2008 the issue of whether religious beliefs should be formally instituted in the UK legal system was raised. For many it is of particular significance with regard to family and marital issues, banking practices and contract law.

Islam

Sharia Law derives from the teachings of the Islamic Holy Book, the Qur'an and the Haddith, the sayings of the prophet Muhammad which form the Sunna, a religious code of living for Muslims. There is an Islamic Sharia Council in Leyton, East London and when invited to do so they will make a religious judgement on disputes between Muslims who have agreed to resolve their issues within Sharia Law. The decisions have no legal status with UK law and they are not allowed to make decisions that would lead to the breaking of any UK laws. Their aim is to provide a framework for Muslims to resolve issues within the teaching of Sharia Law.

Judaism

The Beth Din is the rabbinical court that is presided over by rabbis. It has been established in the UK for over 100 years and although it does not have legal status it provides a means for Jews to resolve matters with the teachings of Judaism.

Another example of religious practices is the creation of the *eruv*. The *eruv* is an area that has been identified with appropriate boundaries to form an area for Jews to apply the restrictions of the Sabbath. An example is the area of North West London. This allows for the restrictions on Jews based on the family home on the Sabbath to be applied within the boundary area.

Religion is sometimes a criterion for access to schools or jobs as it is viewed practicable to segregate children whose families share the same beliefs. There are different views as to whether this self-segregation serves to perpetuate stereotyping and lack of awareness of different groups, or whether it is a sensible solution for families who share the same religion.

ACTIVITY

1 Investigate the religious profile of people who use the services of the organisation that you work for.
2 Find out more about these religions so that you can be more receptive to the care needs of people.
3 Think about how your own religious beliefs can potentially influence your ability to support others.

Health status

When we looked at disability we focused on examples where an individual's disability would be recognised by other people. There are also conditions which are not obvious to others, that can increase an individual's chances of being disabled by society, such as asthma and diabetes; these are often described as hidden disabilities. These conditions can make a negative impact on the lives of individuals, as there is generally a lack of understanding about how they affect people. Disability legislation prevents active discrimination on the basis of health but this does not stop discriminatory practices occurring.

Rayner (2002) discusses the issue of an emerging genetic underclass who experience discrimination by insurance companies when having to declare conditions that they have awareness of through genetic testing:

> The Human Genome Project promises a glorious future ... At some point the science should make us healthier, happier people ... For the time being diagnosis is far ahead of treatment and so long as this remains the case, thousands of people will find themselves discriminated against every year.
>
> (Rayner, 2002, page 96)

Criminal convictions

Care workers have a responsibility to provide a quality service to whoever is entrusted to their care, and this may include individuals who have criminal convictions. Personal values can be tested in such circumstances and need to be acknowledged when working with an individual who has contravened

society's values, and/or those of the care worker, in the past. When supporting an individual, is it realistic for the care worker to say that they are not affected by the history of the individual? It would be important for care workers in such situations to access support to recognise potential issues that may arise and to have an opportunity to discuss their feelings towards the service user so that they do not negatively impact on the task that the care worker is commissioned to carry out.

In employment practice applicants have to complete the Criminal Records Bureau documentation. The rehabilitation of offenders does not apply to most areas of employment in health and social care services.

REFLECT

Read the following descriptions of individuals and reflect on what you think about the person and how your own values could influence your ability to provide professional support for them.

Clarissa has a criminal record for possessing and supplying illegal drugs. She has been diagnosed with multiple sclerosis and needs some practical support.

Ten years ago **Terry** served a custodial sentence for sexual abuse of a child. He is now 73 years old and needs an assessment of his needs due to a change in his physical mobility.

Class

Some people feel that we live in a classless society, and that values associated with being working, middle or upper class are no longer relevant. Class is often associated with the economic circumstances of an individual, both in terms of the income and assets that an individual has, and also the lifestyle choices they make on how to spend it. We may have the ability to present ourselves to others as we choose, and can create an impression of our lifestyle, values and status in society. Many service users experience intrusion into their lives so that they cannot do this; and it would be easy to make judgements about them based on what we find.

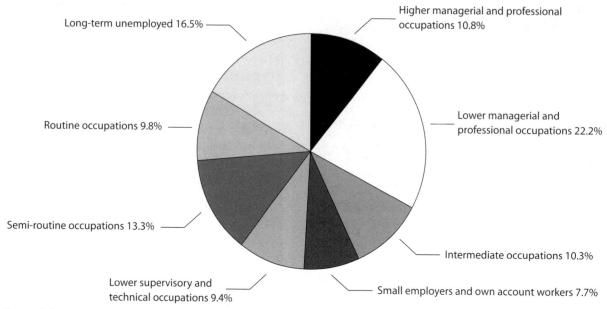

Long-term unemployed 16.5%

Higher managerial and professional occupations 10.8%

Lower managerial and professional occupations 22.2%

Routine occupations 9.8%

Intermediate occupations 10.3%

Semi-routine occupations 13.3%

Small employers and own account workers 7.7%

Lower supervisory and technical occupations 9.4%

Figure 3.2 Socio-economic categories 2008

Characteristics usually associated with class are economic circumstances, employment activity and education.

Economic circumstances

An example of government policy that does acknowledge different characteristics and experiences of individuals is the White Paper *Saving Lives: Our Healthier Nation*. This identified that in improving the health of the population they needed to focus on the worst-off groups in society and reduce the imbalance in health, known as the health gap (Department of Health, July 1999). This represents recognition of the causal relationship between poverty and ill-health. If poverty makes such a significant contribution to the experience of inequality then how does this affect the users of care services?

Care work is not necessarily about working with individuals who experience poverty, and just because a person requires support in some aspect of their lives does not necessarily mean that they experience disadvantage; however, many users of care services do find themselves in circumstances of economic disadvantage. We need to have an understanding of the characteristics that can contribute towards poverty, as these include some of the characteristics shared by users of care services – older age, physical disability, mental health.

Still in the twenty-first century the wealthiest 1 per cent of the population own 22 per cent of total wealth, while 50 per cent own just 6 per cent of total wealth. This unequal distribution of wealth has a significant impact on the life experiences of people. Poverty can affect an individual's ability to participate effectively in the education system, in the work sector and to have equal experience of healthcare.

So how do economic circumstances affect care today? People's entitlement to an assessment of need does not mean that all those needs will be met. A person's financial assessment will identify their ability to pay for some of the services that they require and depending on how much disposable income they have this will influence whether they choose to take up that care.

An individual's employment status can have an impact on other people's perception of them and on their ability to participate effectively in their local community and society. For many, a job brings with it a sense of personal satisfaction, financial stability and financial credibility in terms of accessing other funds (for example a mortgage to buy property). The self-esteem of individuals is closely related to their sense of achievement and validation by those around them, and this can be linked to employment. The government has created many schemes to increase the employability of individuals so that they can gain economic independence. Discrimination in the workplace has in the past prevented those with physical or learning disabilities from participating in the workforce and there have been campaigns to challenge employers' perception of mental health in employees. Recent age discrimination legislation has given people who want to work in later life more opportunity.

Education

The educational background of individuals is often associated with their class. A sound education can provide individuals with a good start in life, and give them the resources to look for the career that they want. Education can also inspire confidence in people and enable them to represent their views more articulately when dealing with other professionals. Of course, service user groups are representative of the population as a whole but there are reasons why people who need care services may have been disadvantaged by the education system:

- children sometimes miss school due to ill-health
- disabled people may not have been provided with an appropriate curriculum in the past when they were children

- mental health problems can mean children are labelled as odd at school and they are excluded from social activities; this may reduce their confidence in class.

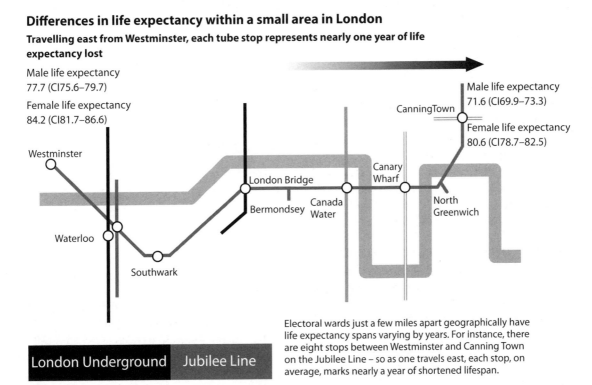

Differences in life expectancy within a small area in London

Travelling east from Westminster, each tube stop represents nearly one year of life expectancy lost

Male life expectancy
77.7 (CI75.6–79.7)

Female life expectancy
84.2 (CI81.7–86.6)

Male life expectancy
71.6 (CI69.9–73.3)

Female life expectancy
80.6 (CI78.7–82.5)

Westminster

CanningTown

Waterloo

London Bridge

Canary Wharf

Southwark

Bermondsey

Canada Water

North Greenwich

London Underground   Jubilee Line

Electoral wards just a few miles apart geographically have life expectancy spans varying by years. For instance, there are eight stops between Westminster and Canning Town on the Jubilee Line – so as one travels east, each stop, on average, marks nearly a year of shortened lifespan.

Source: Analysis by London Health Observatory using Office for National Statistics data.

Figure 3.3 The 'postcode lottery' affects your life chances

Geographical location

The government has been criticised for what is described as the 'postcode lottery' associated with geographical location. Choice and access to services is affected by:

- the resources of an area, which affect the professional support available or buildings and facilities
- the priorities of a Primary Care Trust or local authority
- the level of eligibility criteria set within the authority's region.

London Health Observatory/Department of Health 2008

The Department of Health's Health Inequalities Intervention Tool was produced by the Association of Public Health Observatories and the Department of Health. It is designed to aid Spearhead PCTs and partner local authorities in ensuring local planning and commissioning will narrow local inequalities, in support of Local Delivery Plans and Local Area Agreements.

Health inequalities start early in life and persist not only into old age but subsequent generations. Tackling health inequalities is focused on narrowing the health gap between disadvantaged groups, communities and the rest of the country, and on improving health overall.

The Health Inequalities Unit (HIU) is a small team in the Department of Health with a cross government focus. The work of the unit is shaped by a Public Service Agreement (PSA) target to reduce inequalities in health outcomes by 10 per cent by 2010, as measured by infant mortality and life expectancy at birth.

Health inequalities are the result of a complex and wide-ranging network of factors. People who experience material disadvantage, poor housing, lower educational attainment, insecure employment or homelessness are among those more likely to suffer poorer health outcomes and an earlier death compared with the rest of the population.

(Department of Health, 2008)

Discrimination, oppression, stereotyping and prejudice

Now that we have looked broadly at the identity of individuals in society, we will consider what happens when individuals are affected negatively or disadvantaged due to their characteristics.

Discrimination

Discrimination is the term used to describe what happens when individuals are treated differently.

Positive discrimination

Before we consider negative experiences of discrimination, let us focus on positive discrimination. Positive discrimination is used in the policy of 'affirmative action' in the USA where, for example, in the job application process individuals from disadvantaged groups have been given favourable treatment. Some job application processes in the UK will try to increase the number of applicants from disabled people by guaranteeing interviews to applicants with disabilities who meet the criteria.

What is the purpose of positive discrimination?

- It aims to counterbalance the disadvantage that individuals from minority groups are likely to have experienced in education and previous employment.
- It requires organisations to consider their institutionally discriminatory practices.

It is sometimes thought to counteract the intended outcomes as some people are labelled as the 'token' disabled/black/female employee. People from minority groups state that they do not want to jump the queue, they just want to be given fair opportunity in the same queue.

Forms of discrimination

Indirect discrimination

If everyone is treated the same but some individuals experience inequality as a result, then this is an instance of indirect discrimination. It is covert behaviour but it can have a detrimental impact. For example, if in an organisation staff training is always provided 9–5pm, it means that part-time employees who have childcare responsibilities are unable to participate. The employer may say that the same thing is on offer to everyone, so what is the problem?

Direct discrimination

If a person or group are treated differently from others then this can result in them experiencing inequality. Using the same example, it would mean that training is only offered to full-time employees.

The outcome for the person who is part-time or has childcare responsibilities is the same. In any issue of discrimination it is what the individuals or group experience that matters, not whether the actions were intentional or not. The important point to remember is that sometimes you need to treat individuals differently in order for them to have the same access or opportunities as others.

Levels of discrimination

These relate to the origins of activities or circumstances that cause discrimination.

Individual discrimination

This is where a person's actions can cause disadvantage to an individual or group of people. This can affect psychological, social, physical, cultural or economic well-being.

An example of individual gender discrimination would be the manager of Bailey Lodge Care Home recruiting for new care staff, but not short-listing any male applicants as she thinks they wouldn't fit in with the female staff group.

Institutional discrimination

This is where an organisation has policies and procedures that condone or perpetuate unequal treatment. It does not mean that everyone employed in the organisation acts in a discriminatory way, but that systems allow discrimination and are not proactive in addressing inequality. The Macpherson Report (Crown 1999) was produced as a result of the Stephen Lawrence Inquiry. It exposed the extent to which institutional racism had impacted on the work of the police force, and its findings were applied to all areas of society, especially public sector organisations.

Continuing with our example of Bailey Lodge Care Home: it is always the younger members of the care team who are given any interesting new tasks to undertake, and the older staff are not sent on any training sessions. Everyone seems to agree that it makes sense as the younger staff are more motivated and the older staff are very set in their ways.

Structural discrimination

This type of discrimination recognises that society has an infrastructure which favours some groups. If you consider the disadvantage that some people experience then it is clearly not just the product of one person acting in a discriminatory way. Society can make discrimination the norm.

A deaf person is disabled by a society that excludes them from local schools as a child and then does not promote the development of BSL skills amongst hearing people in society. Society creates an environment that depends on being able to hear and disadvantages those who cannot. A child's experience is then continued into adulthood when the person has to access public transport, public facilities and employment which are not prepared for people without hearing.

Oppression

Oppression is linked to discrimination, as it refers to the use of power to make a group or individual feel inferior. A contentious issue is the relationship that disabled people have to formal charities. In a society where an emphasis is now placed on rights, questions are raised about the values still attributed to individuals who are offered charity, and whether this reinforces the lower status of individuals with disabilities in society.

Stereotyping

Stereotyping is the process where we automatically attribute the same characteristics of one person to others who share similar characteristics. It is a complex dimension of human behaviour; it is convenient for us to group people together in a positive and negative way. However, this process then creates an expectation of how a person is then going to behave. For example, the media has demonised young people who wear their hoods up – 'hoodies' – and so many people will think that all young people who wear their hoods up are drug-dealing gang members with knives or guns. There is very selective reporting of news items concerning health and social care so the public have a distorted view of people based on stereotyping. Concerning mental health, people often only hear about incidents where a mental health service user has acted violently and killed another person. Because general news about mental health does not make 'news', it seems that mental health is associated with violence. People feel justified in stereotyping and this leads to discriminatory behaviour.

Prejudice

Prejudice is where an individual pre-judges another person and develops an attitude towards them (positive or negative) that assumes what characteristics they have or what behaviour they are likely to display. Prejudice is a natural human process that it is important for us to acknowledge. It would be a mistake for care workers to claim that they have no prejudices; we need to deal with inappropriate attitudes rather than pretending they do not exist.

Explanations of prejudice

The **biological explanation** proposes that prejudice results from conflict between groups and it is an inevitable consequence of human nature and differences in our genetic make-up. Critics of this perspective argue that we cannot excuse social behaviour by blaming our genes as it assumes that individuals have no control themselves.

The **psychoanalytical group of explanations** suggest that prejudice is the result of deep-seated motives, either as a result of personality formation (Adorno *et al*, 1950) or as a result of innate energies and instincts (Freud, 1920). These theories lack recognition of the complexities and impact of social relationships. Individuals do not operate in isolation and we are influenced by others in society.

A Stonewall report, *Profiles of Prejudice*, **revealed:**

- Almost two thirds of people (64 per cent) can name at least one minority group towards whom they feel less positive – representing 25 million adults across England.
- The most frequently cited groups are travellers/gypsies (35 per cent), refugees and asylum seekers (34 per cent), people from a different ethnic group (18 per cent) and gay or lesbian people (17 per cent).
- Prejudice against one group tends to go hand-in-hand with prejudice against others. People who are prejudiced against any ethnic group are twice as likely as the population as a whole to be prejudiced against gay and lesbian people. They are four times as likely to be prejudiced against disabled people.
- Knowing someone who is gay or lesbian reduces by half the likelihood of being prejudiced against gay or lesbian people as a group. Similarly, knowing someone from a different ethnic group reduces by half the likelihood of being prejudiced against people from different ethnic groups.

The **cultural explanation** explores the way prejudices change with time and location contexts. This theory takes into account prejudice and the relationship of one group to another as a significant factor. Political debate is distorted against some groups as they are blamed by others who also experience economic disadvantage, 'They have taken our jobs and our housing'.

The **socio-cognitive explanation**, such as that proposed by Tajfel (in Hayes, 1998) is based on mechanisms of prejudice, commencing with the *categorisation* of people into groups and then the *accentuation* of difference. This exaggeration of the difference between people then leads to *intergroup conflict*; *group membership* then affects individual self-esteem due to differences in power and status.

While it is useful to gain an understanding of why people may be prejudiced, this does not justify why people remain prejudiced and act on their prejudices to cause harm to others.

Discrimination can occur when people who have power exert this power on the basis of their prejudice in order to disadvantage another individual or group. An issue for the health and social care sector is that the combination of prejudicial attitudes and power has consequences for individuals and groups.

Effects of prejudice

Prejudice can manifest itself in different ways. Allport (1954) identified these strategies that remain evident in the world today:

1 *Antilocution* Verbal denigration of groups and hostile talk about groups

2 *Avoidance* Segregation of groups in society to keep some groups at a distance from society as a whole

CASE STUDY

Discrimination

Amrullah is a doctor from Afghanistan, who has been given refugee status in the UK.

Some examples of the effects of discrimination on Amrullah may include:

- Social:
  Isolation from society, social exclusion, due to his lack of confidence and limited English skills. Unable to work as a doctor due to prejudice in the employment system.
- Physical:
  Injury from physical assault by neighbours.
- Emotional:
  Fear of verbal or physical abuse, effects on self-esteem and confidence. His awareness of his changed status in British society compared to the value he had as a practising doctor in his own country.
- Intellectual:
  Lack of access to professional educational experience, suppression of potential.

- Cultural:
  Denying one's own culture, inability to observe important cultural practices for fear of standing out and being picked on.
- Sexual:
  Denying one's own sexuality, lack of fulfilment, fear of consequences of expressing sexuality.

The discrimination that Amrullah may be subjected to may affect him in every area of his life.

Questions

1 What can be done at these different levels in order for Amrullah to have a more appropriate experience as a professional health worker coming to the UK?
   - By the NHS and other health organisations?
   - By potential colleagues of Amrullah's?
   - By Amrullah?
   - By the Government?
   - By the Equality and Human Rights Commission?

3 *Discrimination*	Either through government policies or the experience of minority groups
4 *Physical attack*	Violence against property and people
5 *Extermination*	Violence against entire groups, wiping out whole groups in society

Earlier we looked at the experience of different groups in relation to inequality. Now we will consider some general ways in which discrimination can affect people whatever the origins of the discrimination.

Thompson (2002) summarises the effects of oppression as:

- alienation, isolation and marginalisation
- economic position and life chances
- confidence and self-esteem
- social expectations, career opportunities.

REFLECT

1 Consider your own life experience and think about any oppression that you have experienced.
   a How did this affect you at the time?
   b How can you use this experience to improve your awareness of oppression with the people that you work with?
2 What oppression might the individuals that you work with have experienced previously, or be vulnerable to?

Power

The relationship between power and discrimination allows some groups to assume a higher status of themselves as a social group in relation to the status of other groups. Some groups have experienced oppression where a dominant group, which has more power, creates structures in society to maintain their own status and experiences by individuals and groups. This means that they set up education, laws and policing etc. in a way that elevates their own importance over others. This can lead to marginalisation of particular groups and the exclusion of some individuals and groups from participating in society fully.

While service users have a diverse range of individual characteristics, their life experiences often share an element of inequality and discrimination. There is no reason why requiring support as a service user should mean that you experience social exclusion, but this is frequently the case. Society seems to be accepting that for many, for example, poverty is a consequence of older age.

Anti-oppressive practice, anti-bias practice and anti-discriminatory practice

These refer to our strategies to eradicate discrimination and oppression from our own practice, challenge them in the practice of others and also in the institutional structures in which we operate. It provides a framework for working with individuals so that we do not perpetuate the discrimination that individuals face in their lives. As care workers we need to be conscious that we can unknowingly contribute to the oppression that some individuals experience.

Thompson (2001) discusses what he calls 'PCS' analysis. This involves:

- **P Personal**
  Individuals have their own values, and some of these form prejudices. These influence their actions towards others.
- **C Cultural**
  Earlier in the chapter we looked at ethnocentrism and heterosexism, as examples of the cultural level of oppression. Values and beliefs can be reinforced by groups sharing these values.
- **S Structural**
  Society has structures and systems which create an environment of discrimination and oppression; for example there is evidence that the education system disadvantages African-Caribbean children, and legislation has not recognised same-sex relationships. This level refers to the social, political and economic framework of society.

Discrimination and anti-discrimination

At Ashbridge Day Resource Centre, the manager feels that the service users benefit from an efficient service. Activities are structured so that the men do sports and the women do craft work. Individuals with complex needs spend more time at the centre than those who are more independent and mobile. A dietician advises the centre on meals, and everyone eats the same so that they have a balanced diet. One of the service users, who the staff call 'Art' (as they cannot pronounce his name), does not speak much English. The staff are confident that they have got used to what he needs based on the little communication that they have with him.

Question

Identify the different levels of oppression and where anti-discriminatory practice should be happening.

- Personal: The manager's values and actions.
- Cultural: The everyday activities and relationships.
- Structural: Political, economic and social systems in society that condone the way the centre is being managed.

In the case study, we can see that oppressive practices include:

- activities being very gender-based
- everyone having the same meals
- Art not being provided with an interpreter (the staff cannot even say his name)
- individuals with complex needs staying in the centre.

Working with individuals in a care setting, whether this is the individual's own home, a day resource, or a care home, often means that as an individual you are charged with a certain amount of autonomy and responsibility for what it is that you as an individual do with service users. You are responsible for addressing your own practice, but also for challenging the practices of an organisation that you understand to be oppressive.

Social position

A first stage in anti-discriminatory practice is recognising the social position of the individuals who you work with, and the relative power that they have in society and in relation to yourself as a worker. Understanding the experiences of individuals will also enable you to adopt sensitivity in your approach with people.

For example, if you are working with a refugee who had their life uprooted during ethnic cleansing in their home country, the experience of discrimination that they now have here needs to be considered in this context. The social position of such an individual has been influenced by:

- the individual's experience of discrimination (extermination of friends/family) in their own country
- media reporting of the 'masses of bogus asylum seekers'
- UK government policies that denigrate individuals and confirm this group's low status in comparison to others (i.e. voucher systems)
- complexities in accessing appropriate support.

Ignoring the different social positions and assuming everyone is the same will not provide you with a sound attitude for making progress with an individual. When working in an anti-discriminatory way it is also important to be aware of the actions of others. You should not be content with getting your own house in order; you should be actively questioning what is going on around you. If you are not part of the solution then you are a part of the problem. It is not always easy to challenge the practice of others, and there may have been times when you have wanted to speak up but have had difficulty doing so. Recognising the consequences of not speaking up can empower you to do so. There are legal frameworks to support you in this.

Remember that sometimes people can commit oppressive actions without deliberate maliciousness. For example, adult children may assume control of an older parent's finances, and start making decisions for them because they think it is in everyone's best interests. The social position of older people in society does not encourage adult children to challenge this assumption, but in supporting the older person you may be able to facilitate a different perspective from the older person and their family members.

We should not just focus on the here and now when we are working with people; we should acknowledge an individual's life history and the experiences that have shaped their current identity.

As we discussed earlier, an understanding of prejudice can be useful to us in understanding ourselves and dealing with inappropriate feelings, and also in supporting other people to confront their own values. A service user or patient may still be able to accept responsibility for their own actions and behaviour if they behave inappropriately. Being a patient or service user does not excuse us from such behaviour, and just because it is a patient or service user that you observe being racist, you are not excused from challenging them. We should not make excuses for service users or patients because they are older or disabled. This is not empowering them as individuals. Individuals that we support should be empowered to accept their responsibilities in supporting other people's rights, as well as enjoying their own rights.

Discrimination against workers

Discussion on discrimination within the care sector should not only focus on the experiences of the people the sector is set up to serve. Employees within organisations can also experience discrimination.

There is a lack of disabled individuals working within the care professions. Where people have gained access to employment and training they are often working with individuals who share the same disability and are faced with difficulty when attempting to work with a different service user or patient group. A young care worker may be labelled as being inexperienced,

or if they demonstrate particular skills in an area may be described as a young upstart. This may lead to discrimination by a senior worker who feels threatened. An older person may be excluded from training or bypassed for particular projects. They may be labelled as 'out of touch' or 'set in their old ways' rather than being attributed with being experienced.

Research into the lives of 120 people in the North West found that older people with learning disabilities (50 years plus) are offered fewer opportunities than younger people to develop personal skills and take part in community activities or develop social networks. Older people with learning disabilities also fall between services for older people and services for people with learning disabilities as they are 'too difficult', disabled or too young for the former or too old for the latter (Walker, Ryan and Walker, 1995, Joseph Rowntree Foundation).

The health and social care profession is a female-dominated profession, so it is important to consider the experience of male colleagues. The reason why care work is low paid compared to other professions is often cited as being its association with the assumed natural care-giving ability of females. Some care workers who do not have the same ethnic or cultural characteristics of those they work with may experience more intrusion into their personal lives, as there is a focus on them as a novelty.

It is also important not to be naive about racism. Discrimination does not just occur when people make an oversight, or fail to see the significance of something; there are people in society who are actively racist, and they feel very comfortable about this. Care work happens in this context, our service users are not immune to what is going on in society, and neither should we be.

Care values and care standards

At the beginning of this chapter we mentioned a list of values identified as being important for all workers in health and social care services. We will now explore these in more depth.

You are unique; even if you have very similar siblings or an identical twin you are an individual in your own right and there is only one of you. That is a very special fact about being a human being. What makes you unique are the characteristics that shape your personality and your appearance; some of these you may have been aware of throughout your life, while others may be characteristics that you have acquired. Life experiences influence your development as a person. Look back to the exercise where you described who you were (page 000). If you had to place these characteristics in order of importance to you then you may find that some of them have a higher priority. Some of these characteristics may become more prominent depending on who is asking you, or when you are asked.

This chapter has explored the diversity of individuals that we work with. Each person that you come across is also unique. Individuals who use care services are frequently grouped together for the convenience of arranging care delivery. This may not seem problematic, and would be viewed as a sensible stage in the process of organising support. However, an individual may find themselves labelled as a 'learning disabled person' or an 'older person'. Other characteristics may be seen as secondary, and will therefore not be prominent in shaping the care professional's response.

The National Minimum Standards for Domiciliary Care states that, 'Service users are addressed by their preferred name at all times.' (Department of Health, 2000, page 16)

Of course, we may say there are instances where individuals do not have their individuality respected and this may affect a person's spirit and sense of self. If a person feels that they do not matter as an individual and they are just one of a group then they may feel devalued and insignificant.

Labelling

We mentioned earlier that individuals are grouped together and given a label that then becomes their defining characteristic. This process is considered by some professionals to be necessary in order for individuals to access the services that are categorised in the same way. But a different view proposes that it is often very unhelpful to attribute a label to an individual that then shapes all the services, intervention and professional relationships that they engage in.

Labelling can reinforce characteristics that may be assumed. For example, if you are an agency member of staff working a new shift at a place and you are told about a service user who is 'difficult', then you may influence their interaction and create a type of response that confirms what you have been told. In the past labelling has served a purpose in grouping individuals together for the purposes of service delivery. The aim now should be for services to be shaped around the identified need of individuals, not just focusing on the category of service user or patient group that they come under.

Recognising the variety and different needs of individuals will enable you to respond to individuals in a more appropriate way. Individual identity has a strong association with a person's self-worth. If an individual has elements of their personality or character affronted this can have an impact on their overall self-esteem. Historically, individuals who lived in large institutions may not have considered themselves as individuals. The values in the profession at that time did not facilitate what we now would consider to be appropriate staff support; an example of this would be the sharing of clothing by people who were the same size. The idea of personhood, which relates to the importance of individuals having value as individual people, was not a feature of care work at that time.

Ways of encouraging individuality will be different; for one person it may be supporting them to bring their own possessions into a new care setting, for another person it may be enabling them to develop self-awareness about what they like as an individual so they don't always feel they just do things as a group. Being able to represent yourself is an important aspect of this.

In health and social care work rights are significant because we work in a social and legal context and there are many grey areas concerning the idea of rights. Individuals may feel that they have rights in respect to something and it is important to take this into account. In your own practice, think about what difference it makes to assume a paternalistic caring role for individuals based on the idea that they need care support and you sympathise with them in providing it, to adopting a more rights-based approach.

Legislation and rights

There is increasing reference to the idea of rights within legislation. Some policies are designed to provide a framework of rights for particular service user groups, such as the National Minimum Standards or National Service Frameworks. The implementation of the National Minimum Standards in Care Homes for Older People was reviewed due to

the awareness that individual residents were losing the right to decide whether they were content with the provision they received.

In 1998 the countries of the UK introduced the 1998 Human Rights Act in order to bring our legislation in line with European law. This would enable UK courts to deal with issues of human rights rather than cases being referred to the European Court of Human Rights. The European Court of Human Rights was established to provide a legal framework of rights with member states.

The main purposes of the European Convention for the Protection of Human Rights and Fundamental Freedoms are to:

- be an instrument for the protection of individual human beings
- promote the ideals and values of a democratic society
- promote and guarantee rights that are practical and effective
- ensure that in its interpretation courts reflect the sensitivity of the public to the fair administration of justice
- expect courts to give the words of the Convention their ordinary meaning.

The Human Rights Act 1998 requires all legislation to be interpreted and given effect as far as compatible with the Convention rights. These rights must be taken into account by the UK courts in all cases brought before them and in the development of common law (developed through individual cases and the setting of precedents.). The Act also makes it unlawful for a public authority to act incompatibly with the Convention rights and cases may be brought before the UK courts if they do.

Much consideration is now given to the impact of human rights legislation on care practice and there are often tensions. You may already be aware of the potential impact that the Human Rights Act 1998 has had on your individual work, or that of the organisation and service users. If you look at the list of articles it is clear that some relate to key aspects of care delivery. Within the countries of the UK many of the articles were already provided for in our legislation, but some of the articles are new and potentially have an impact on care work. An example would be Article 5 and the right not to be deprived of your liberty. Care organisations have to be more explicit now about any

European Convention of Rights and Freedoms

The Convention rights are described as articles and protocols:

Article 1 Obligation to respect human rights

Article 2 The right to life

Article 3 Freedom from torture or inhuman or degrading treatment

Article 4 Freedom from slavery or forced labour

Article 5 Personal freedom, the right not to be deprived of liberty

Article 6 Right to a fair trial

Article 7 No punishment without law

Article 8 Right to respect for private and family life

Article 9 Freedom of thought, conscience and religion

Article 10 Freedom of expression

Article 11 Freedom of assembly and association

Article 12 Right to marry

Article 14 Prohibition of discrimination

Protocol 1 Article 1 Peaceful possession of property

Protocol 1 Article 2 Children's right to education and parents' right for their beliefs to be respected in the education of their children

Protocol 1 Article 3 Free and fair elections

Protocol 6 Abolishes the death penalty

Articles 17 and 18 These relate to appropriate interpretation of individual articles so as not to limit any of the other rights.

reasons for depriving an individual of their liberty with clear risk assessments and written documentation of safety being the reason for not allowing someone free access. This is discussed in Chapter 4 (Supporting individuals and their families).

A further example is in relation to Article 8 and the emphasis on privacy. Care homes would need to provide the means for individuals to have individual security in their rooms and for others not to have free access or opportunities to take possessions. The EHRC are the national organisation to ensure that the

Human rights for all? Private care homes

Katie Ghose is director of the British Institute of Human Rights and she is concerned about the exemption of private care homes from the requirements of the Human Rights Act

'Two-thirds of middle-aged people in a recent Guardian poll said that the prospect of living in a care home 'frightened' them. (3 December 2007)

When a person lives away from their own home and in the care of the state, they become particularly vulnerable ... To take just one example: at the British Institute of Human Rights, we often hear of cases of privacy abuse, with people being left naked or in view of others when receiving help with washing and dressing.

So it is surprising that the Human Rights Act – brought in to ensure that people are treated with dignity, respect and fairness – does not apply to many people in dire need of its protection.'

She explains that this is due to an unintentional legal loophole. She feels strongly that this should be addressed legally so that:

1. All providers of public care services directly accountable for respecting the human rights contained in the Human Rights Act would provide a clear 'chain of command'.

2. Providers are given direct responsibility which would help to shift the culture of care provision away from thinking about needs to focusing on entitlements. This fits with our modern understanding of care services as emphasising empowerment and independence.

'There is an important relationship between directly enforceable legal remedies – ultimately the right to pursue a case in court – and the creation of a wider human rights culture, which would see all care providers embracing human rights as a means of providing the very best and tailored care to everyone who walks through their doors.'

Her hope is that the Health and Social Care Bill 2007 will achieve change now.

provisions of Equality and Human Rights legislation are delivered.

Choice

'For choice and control to be meaningful, service users and carers must have clear information.' (Department of Health, 2001a) This may seem like a very simple value but it has its foundations in a number of other values such as respect and rights. The value choice was recognised by O'Brien (1981) as one of his 'accomplishments' for learning disabled people. It may seem like a trivial aspect of life, or a very simple one, but actually supporting individuals to access proper choice can be a complex but empowering process.

> ### REFLECT
>
> Think about how many decisions about your own life you make in one single day. Take today for instance, did you decide:
>
> - what time to get up? (maybe not if you started your shift at 7am!)
> - whether to have a bath, shower, or quick wash?
> - whether to have breakfast? (fruit and cereal or a big fry up in café).
>
> If I continued this list of the decisions you make about your activities in one day it would be a long list. These individual decisions may not seem so important but if I was to tell you what you were going to do, what time you were going to do it, and how you were going to do it, then this may have a big effect on how your day goes. Your sense of control and responsibility for yourself would very quickly become eroded.

Choice is a complex concept partly because it is necessary for us to include the ability for an individual to make inappropriate choices and to take risks. Choice enables an individual to retain ownership of their lives through decision-making and control. Choices do, however, need to be real. Asking someone if they want A or B may make the organisation feel that they are giving choices to a person, but it still means that the care organisation is keeping control of those choices. One of the main benefits of the Direct Payments system has been the choice and control it

has given to individuals. You may work with individuals who present you with the challenge of providing access to choice in a meaningful way.

> People with learning disabilities with more complex needs had a more difficult time getting choice and control over their lives than those with less complex needs, who in general were able to participate more easily in assessments and reviews.
>
> (Social Services Inspectorate, 2003, page 22)

In Chapter 4 on supporting individuals and their families we will explore strategies that promote choice with individuals and we discuss Direct Payments in Chapter 8 on care planning.

Privacy

Is there anything that you don't want other people to know about you? Have you ever been fined for not paying your television licence, or caught speeding, or is your home a mess unless you have people coming around? The Big Brother approach to entertainment has become popular with the general public viewing people on television for entertainment or documentaries. People who use care services sometimes have their whole lives exposed to others whether they choose to or not; every success or achievement, every failure and mistake may be discussed at meetings, written about in reports, and reminded of at a later date.

This is not usual in life; we all have an element of control over whether we make the same mistakes, what information about our past we share with new people we meet, how we represent ourselves to others etc. Imagine what new social situations would be like if every person you met had been briefed about your good points and bad points.

It is therefore important to retain an individual's privacy wherever possible, and this does not just concern material privacy, it relates to both the physical and social aspects of their care. A frequently used example is that of leaving a bedroom door open so that others can look, or go in. Less obvious examples of privacy relate to information about the person, i.e. not telling the neighbours that the service user is going to a home for respite care next weekend. Individuals should own their personal information, and a care worker should encourage the person to manage the information that relates to them where this is possible. This links with empowerment, as will be discussed in Chapter 4.

A difficulty with this value is that people have different expectations of the idea of privacy. Have you ever thought a person to be withdrawn or unsociable if they prefer to have long periods of time on their own?

As you saw under the section on rights, privacy is acknowledged as an important dimension in life as it is contained within one of the Human Rights Convention articles. UK government policy has also recognised its significance, as evidenced for example in the National Minimum Standards for Domiciliary Care:

Standard 8

Personal care and support is provided in a way which maintains and respects the privacy, dignity and lifestyle of the person receiving care at all times with particular regard to assisting with:

- dressing and undressing
- bathing, washing, shaving, oral hygiene
- toilet and continence arrangements
- health and medication requirements
- manual handling
- eating and meals
- handling personal possessions and documents
- entering the home, room, bathroom or toilet.

ACTIVITY

Think about the following physical environments in which care may be provided. Identify ways in which you could create more privacy for individuals who use this space:

- an individual's own home
- a day centre for people with a learning disability
- a hospice.

Confidentiality

Confidentiality relates to the need to make sure information is not accessed inappropriately. As care workers we are privy to much information about individuals and managing this information can present difficulties for an organisation.

Article 8 Human Rights Act 3.70 Study Guide states:

> Your right to private life can also include the right to have information about you, such as official records, photographs, letters, diaries and medical information, kept private and confidential. Unless there is very good reason, public bodies should not collect or use information like this.

You may already be familiar with issues of confidentiality, it forms part of the induction standards and there are statements in policy:

National Minimum Standards for Domiciliary Care:

Confidentiality

Outcome: Service users and their carers or representatives know that their personal information is handled appropriately and that their personal confidences are respected.

As a care worker it is helpful to remind yourself of why you are privy to some information. You work on

---

CASE STUDY

Discrimination against disability

In 2007 a married disabled woman offered to pay the extra so that she could have a double bed for her and her husband. She needed a new profile bed so that carers could provide her personal care in bed. Supported by the British Institute of Human Rights she successfully invoked the Human Rights Act to challenge a decision made by the occupational therapy department that she could only have a single bed. (British Institute of Human Rights, Case Study 2007)

Questions

1 How can care organisations prevent situations where those who use their services feel their human rights are being infringed?
2 To what extent do those who use the services of your own agency understand how the human rights framework can support them in accessing the level of service to which they are entitled?
3 How can you as an individual promote this awareness?

Principles	Explanation
Purpose of the information	This principle asks why the information exists and suggests that each piece of information should have a clear purpose.
Use of identifiable information	There should be justifiable reasons why named information is used.
Reduction of identifiable information	The less information available the easier it is to manage confidentiality. This principle suggests that organisations reduce the amount of named information that they produce.
Accessibility to information	Within an organisation there should be a rationale for why each person has access to information. Some information should be kept locked away with limited access. This includes information held on computer files.
Responsibilities	Each individual should be aware of their responsibilities with information and the need to keep information confidential. There should be identified people to monitor issues of confidentiality within an organisation.
Compliance with legislation	All care organisations are required to adhere not only to care legislation and policies such as the National Minimum Standards but also the Data Protection Act 1998.

behalf of an organisation and the information that a service user or patient shares with you is communicated because of your role in that organisation.

The Caldicott Principles were developed for use within the NHS but have also been applied to social care practice.

ACTIVITY

1 Make a list of the types of information that are generated within your work in a typical week (for example, notes on care plans, diary entries, letters written/received, emails etc.).
2 Consider your own use of information and how you could limit the amount of information that is generated for service users without compromising the quality of care delivery.

The **Data Protection Act 1998** relates to both written and electronic information. It requires that individuals have access to data that is held on them, and where appropriate a request should be made to view this information so that reference to other people can be removed from documents before they see it. It relates to all forms of information, paperwork and files on the computer.

The **Public Interest Disclosure Act 1998** provides an important framework for individuals to disclose information, which would otherwise be confidential, where there are concerns regarding well-being of individuals or groups. It facilitates whistle-blowing, where an employee may require protection as a

consequence of their actions to inform authorities of poor practice.

Your organisation should have policies and procedures that enable you to work responsibly with the information that you are privy to.

The issue of confidentiality is complex. Within the care sector it is recognised that good communication between both professionals and organisations can lead to sound continuity of care and consistency in service delivery. It is sometimes difficult to balance this with not wanting to share information that is not relevant.

Once information is obtained it attracts a legal duty of confidence. This information can only be used in a manner that breaches confidentiality if:

● there is a statutory requirement
● there is a court order
● there is a robust public interest justification.

Under Department of Health guidelines there are three types of consent for using information:

1 It is important to establish trust in your relationship with an individual. To this end it is therefore important that the individual is aware of your requirements regarding information that is shared.
2 There may be some secrets that it is appropriate to keep in the spirit of the relationship that you have with the service user, for example if they have bought a present for someone as a surprise etc.
3 A care worker should never make indiscriminate promises to keep a secret as this could compromise their position in the future.

	Explanation	Some issues
Consent	Agreement either expressed or implied based on knowledge of the likely consequences.	Does an individual really understand the consequences? How is consent implied?
Express consent	Consent which is expressed orally, in writing or through other forms of communication.	Evidence of consent if provided orally? Communication ability of the individual consenting?
Implied consent	Consent which is inferred from a person's behaviour.	Potential for misinterpretation of an individual's behaviour?

Adapted from Crown Copyright (2001)

Independence

Think back to the last time that you learned a new skill. How did this make you feel? Did you have a sense of achievement? A feeling of pride? A sense of your own capability? Did it give you motivation for learning something else new? Increased self-esteem and sense of value to self and others?

These are all feelings associated with achievement of skills.

At the beginning of the chapter we mentioned the dialogue around the use of the word 'care'.

> Indeed, the term 'care' perpetuates the view of disabled people as separate and dependent beings, reinforcing their exclusion from mainstream society.
>
> (Carmichael and Brown, 2002, page 806)

What is care work? Doing things for people, caring for people, supporting individuals, enabling people to do things for themselves? Care work has changed from an exercise where care workers were doing things for people who society felt could not do things themselves, to enabling individuals to maximise their own abilities and retain their own independence with appropriate levels of support.

Independence is sometimes given differing levels of value according to the service user or patient group and care setting. With older people there is a tension between whether support at this stage of life involves hotel-type facilities in a care home or being encouraged to continue the use of their skills in care home settings. With people under 65 the emphasis is usually on continuing the use of established skills, and developing new ones. There is an emphasis on the development of personal living and social skills with people who are learning disabled, whatever the care setting. This value may apply to older people who live in their own home, but for some reason it alters

CASE STUDY

The importance of independence

Consider the life of Elisabeth, who was born 57 years ago. Her parents were told that she would not be able to do anything due to her disabilities and that it was best for everyone if she stayed in a hospital. She lived in Mapledene Hospital with other children who had disabilities and was adequately looked after, but not given much opportunity to develop her own skills. When the hospital closed ten years ago she moved to a smaller home in the community and has been given different support from her care workers so that she can develop new skills. If Elisabeth was born today she would be given a different start in life that would aim to promote her ability to gain independence in her personal care, mobility, home management; she may always still need support but every chance would be provided for her to gain some independence.

Questions

1 How can older people with learning disabilities be supported so that they do not lose the opportunity to gain skills in later life?
2 What is your understanding of the difference between an individual being 'cared for' and 'being supported'?
3 What do you think your feelings would be if, when you were 47, the place that you called home closed and you moved to a much smaller place?
4 How can care workers support individuals going through transitions such as this?

where group living arises in a care home; perhaps this is partly because it is more difficult to manage the environment and ensure individuals have the potential to develop their own skills on such an individual basis.

Another dimension of independence is that of **self-determination**. This also links with the value of choice, as a principle of ensuring that individuals have control over their lives. As stated in the Human Rights guidance, 'Your Article 8 Rights include matters of self-determination.' (Home Office, 2000, page 18):

> Care workers should question the extent to which their actions promote dependency in service users, dependency that includes decision-making as well as practical dependency.

Dignity

Just as service users are exposed to more intrusion into their lives they experience more situations that others would find humiliating, but as service users they may be conditioned to accept that behaviour. The care process may lead to situations which expose individuals to potentially degrading situations, and care workers need to be aware of this. A sense of self-worth is accompanied by inner respect and self-esteem. If you have assaults on your dignity that indicate a lack of respect from others, this can lead you to doubt your own worth. Think back to the exercise where you identified the characteristics that made you who you are (see page 000).

Promoting someone's dignity means that care workers do not engage in any intervention that is demeaning or that devalues the individual. The amount of intrusion into an individual's life increases the opportunity for this. The social status of individuals who require our support may also make them more vulnerable to assaults on their dignity.

The following are examples of not respecting dignity with different service user groups.

- **A learning disabled person:** Clothing that is not age appropriate.
- **A person who is registered blind:** Doing things in front of them that you would not do if they had sight.

- **A person who uses a wheelchair:** Leaving the door open when you are assisting them in the bathroom.
- **A person with mental health problems:** Talking to the individual as though they have lost the capacity to use any skills and make any decisions.
- **An older person:** Dismissing the fact that the individual's life story and history are important or valued.

CASE STUDY

Protection of human dignity

This is from the British Institute of Human Rights, (reported in *Disability Now*, June 2006, page 14).

Protecting human dignity when staff refuse to clean up a man's bodily waste:

- A man detained in a maximum security mental health hospital was placed in seclusion where he repeatedly soiled himself.
- Staff declined to clean up the faeces and urine or to move the man to another room, claiming that he would simply make the same mess again, and any intervention was therefore pointless.
- The man's advocate, having attended a BIHR training session, invoked human rights arguments to challenge this practice. He argued that this treatment breached the man's right not to be treated in an inhuman and degrading way, and his right to respect for private life.
- These arguments were successful and the next time he soiled himself, the man was cleaned and moved to a new room.

Questions

1 How do care organisations balance the rights of individuals who use their services with the rights of those who provide this service?
2 Many service users challenge organisations due to their behaviour. How can organisations ensure that all practices within an organisation are underpinned by the appropriate values?

Respect

> All staff are instructed during induction on how to treat service users with respect at all times.
>
> (NMS Care Homes (Older People) Standard 10.5)

The word *respect* is much used amongst young people and generally there is now more awareness of its significance in life. Many believe that respect needs to be earned from individuals – so how can it be an automatic value for the care worker? Respect gives people positive self-esteem and validates their life as an individual. Actions that indicate lack of respect may include not acknowledging an individual when you walk into their personal space and carrying out care tasks without involving the person. The potential effect on the individual may be that they feel like an object being moved around.

Having respect for individuals can benefit the care worker by enabling them to perform their tasks appropriately; it can create a professional disposition. It will inspire the need to be honest with service users or patients, and to develop trust within the relationship. Respect will enable affirming the person's values and taking into consideration the individual's account of what they want to happen.

It is important to have respect for the people you work with

Respecting an individual will lead to supporting them in their choices, recognising what dignity means to that particular individual.

Dignity also relates to confidentiality with regard to aspects of personal care. An older person may not want all their relatives knowing that you are concerned about their incontinence. This information should only be shared with others if the individual so chooses.

Partnership

Working in partnership with service users should be a main feature of any work with service users or patients, and a goal of care workers whatever their role. This involves communicating with service users or patients and enabling them to communicate effectively with yourself and others, so that they are instrumental in identifying their own needs and strategies to meet their needs. At the beginning of this chapter we raised issues related to the role of the professional as the 'expert', which needs to be questioned as service users are involved in defining their own care delivery. The idea of partnership is at the heart of this challenge.

CASE STUDY

Promoting a care user's values

Mr Dakshy is an 82-year-old man who has been living in his own home, and has recently been assessed as needing to move into a care home. Mr Dakshy is a private man who doesn't always share what is going on with him with his family, although he would say he was close to them. He is Hindu, following certain beliefs and practices, although he hasn't participated in the local Hindu community for a long while due to his restricted mobility. Mr Dakshy can communicate very well verbally, but is disappointed he cannot read and write well any more due to his sight, as he cannot keep in touch with family members abroad.

Questions

Bearing in mind what you have just read in this case study, think about one person who you work with and answer the following questions:

1 How do you know what values are important to this individual?
2 What issues arise when supporting this person relating to the promotion of their rights and values?
3 What can you do as an individual care worker in order to ensure that their values are respected?

This value is not dealt with in great depth here as it is a significant feature of the chapter on working with individuals (Chapter 4). Partnership can operate on a large scale, as with the introduction of Learning Disability Partnership Boards, or on an individual level where professionals aim to empower individuals in their communication rather than assuming the role of expert. The NHS has undertaken a large consultation with patients to decide potential changes to the organisation of healthcare (*Consulting the Capital*, NHS, 2008).

Care Standards Act 2000

This landmark piece of legislation was the first real attempt to enshrine values in a legal framework. It initiated the General Social Care Council (GSCC), which has responsibility for regulating the workforce. It has devised a set of standards for employees and employers of care:

ACTIVITY

The General Social Care Council's Code of Practice for Social Care Workers

1 As a social care worker, you must protect the rights and promote the interests of service users and carers

  1.1 Treating each person as an individual

  1.2 Respecting and where appropriate promoting the individual views and wishes of both service users and carers

  1.3 Supporting service users' rights to control their lives and make informed choices about the services that they receive

  1.4 Respecting and maintaining dignity and privacy of service users

  1.5 Promoting equal opportunities for service users and their carers

  1.6 Respecting diversity and different cultures and values

We have been looking at the values that are important in care work and you have completed some activities to give you a chance to think about how these apply to care work. We are now going to focus on your own relationship to these values.

CASE STUDY

Supporting the values of a care user

'My name is Dave. I am a 28-year-old man who has cerebral palsy. I love living on my own, having moved out of my parents' home six months ago. I need a lot of assistance in personal care and daily living tasks, and use a wheelchair at home as well as when I go out. I have an advocate who, with my care manager, has supported me in using Direct Payments to employ my own personal support worker. I am vegetarian, love watching football, and like going down the pub for some real ale.'

Values that are important to me:

  'Being able to live in my own home.'

  'Having a say in who comes into my home and works with me.'

  'Being able to make bad decisions and do the wrong thing on occasions!'

  'Having areas of my life that I can control.'

  'Not everyone knowing all my business all the time.'

  'Not being told I'm a fire risk when I go to new places, and having a toilet around that I can actually get into.'

Questions

1 How does the personalisation agenda enable services to be appropriately planned for an individual such as Dave?

2 Thinking about the New Types of Worker programme promoted by Skills for Care, describe a job role that would suit Dave and his support needs.

Some activities that would enable a care worker to support any individuals in promoting their values include:

- finding out relevant facts about the individual
- considering your own values in respect to this person, so that these do not impact negatively on the care process
- ensuring that the individual is engaged in their own care
- increasing your knowledge base about the individual's care needs and practical ways of supporting him or her

- making sure you let relevant people know about what values need to be observed
- not making assumptions about what the individual would want or what could enable the individual (such as 'He's too old for glasses' etc.).

Chapter 4 (Supporting individuals and their families) explores many of these themes in more depth as it focuses on practical skills when working with individuals. If you take responsibility for developing good practice, recognising gaps in your own experience and the service you provide, then acquiring new knowledge about diversity and rights should lead you to more productive and effective practice. Learning from the experiences of service users and other professionals will make a key contribution to this. It is important not to underestimate the impact you can make as an individual.

KNOWLEDGE CHECK

1   What is the difference between a prejudice and an act of discrimination?
2   Should care workers have a different response to care standards, values and Human Rights?
3   How has the local demographic profile of your area changed in the past five years and how does this impact on the provision of health and social care services?
4   What organisations are currently prominent in addressing equality and human rights issues, and ensuring that the values of the profession are embedded in standards?

References

Adorno,T., Frenkel-Brunswik, E., Levinson, D. and Sanford, N. (1950) *The Authoritarian Personality, Studies in Prejudice Series, Volume 1*, New York: Harper & Row

Age Concern (2007) *Older People in the United Kingdom: Key Facts and Statistics*

Allport, *The Nature of Prejudice*. (1954;1979) Reading, MA: Addison-Wesley Publishing Company

Banks, S. (2001) *Ethics and Social Work*, Basingstoke, Macmillan

British Sign Language courses http://www. sign.co.uk/

Bytheway, B., Bacigalupo, V., Bornat, J., Joh Spurr, S. (1995) *Ageism*, Buckingham, Open University Press

Carmichael, A. and Brown, L. (2002) 'The future challenge of Direct Payments' *Disability and Society*, Vol 17, pages 797–808

Commission for Equality and Human Rights www. cehr.org.uk, www.equalityhumanrights.com

Crown (1999), *The Stephen Lawrence Inquiry: Report Of An Inquiry by Sir William Macpherson Of Cluny* advised by Tom Cook, the Right Reverend Dr John Sentamu and Dr Richard Stone

Department of Health documents can be accessed via www.dh.gov.uk

Department of Health (1999) *Saving Lives: Our Healthier Nation*, London, HMSO

Department of Health (2000) *National Minimum Standards for Domiciliary Care*, London, HMSO

Department of Health (2001a) *National Service Framework for Older People*, London, HMSO

Department of Health (2001b) *Valuing People: A New Strategy for Learning Disability for the 21st Century*, London, HMSO

Department Of Health (2005) *The National Service Framework For Mental Health – Five Years On* London, HMSO

Disability Rights Commission (2007) *Creating An Alternative Future*

Fulford *et al* (eds.) (2002) *Healthcare and Human Values: An Introductory Text with Readings and Case Studies*, Oxford, Blackwell

GSCC (2002) *Code of Practice for Social Care Workers*, London, HMSO

Guardian Online Newspaper www.guardian.co.uk

Home Office (1998) *Study Guide to the Human Rights Act*, London, HMSO

Home Office Guidance on Human Rights Act 2000

Hunt, R. and Cowan, K. (2008) *Harassment and sexual orientation in the health sector* (From Stonewall website 2008 www.stonewall.org.uk)

Mental Health Foundation quoting *Psychiatry in the Elderly* (3rd edition) Oxford University Press, 2002: 29

NHS (2008) *Consulting the Capital* London, HMSO

National Institute For Clinical Excellence, 2004

O'Brien J. (1981) 'Framework for accomplishments', quoted in Tyne A, *Five Values for Every Care Package, Care Plan*, (1981), Positive Publications

Rayner, J. (2002) in Fulford *et al* (eds.) *Healthcare and Human Values: An Introductory Text with Readings and Case Studies*, Oxford, Blackwell

Sigmund, F. (1986) *The Essentials of Psycho-Analysis.* London: Hogarth and the Institute of Psycho-Analysis

Skills for Care www.skillsforcare.org.uk

Skills for Health www.skillsforhealth.org.uk

Social Services Inspectorate (2003) *Fulfilling Lives: Inspection of Social Care Services for People with Learning Disabilities*, London, HMSO

Spybey, T. (1997) *Britain in Europe: An Introduction to Sociology*, London, Routledge

Tajfel, H. *in* Hayes, N (1998) *Foundations of Psychology: An Introductory Text*, Surrey, Nelson

Thompson, N. (2001) *Anti-Discriminatory Practice*, Basingstoke, Palgrave Macmillan

Thompson, N. (2002) *Understanding Social Care*, London, Russell House

Thompson, N. (2003) *Promoting Equality*, Basingstoke, Macmillan

Walker, C., Ryan, T. and Walker, A. (1995) *Disparities in Service Provision for People with Learning Disabilities Living in the Community*, Joseph Rowntree Foundation Research 75

Wilton T. (2000) *Sexualities in Health and Social Care*, Buckingham, Open University Press

Useful websites

Age Concern: www.ageconcern.org.uk

British Institute for Human Rights: www.bihr.org (BIHR ref. p.119)

National Office of Statistics: www.statistics.gov.uk

Royal National Institute for the Deaf: www.rnid.org.uk

Skills for Care: www.skillsforcare.org.uk

CHAPTER 4

Supporting individuals and their families

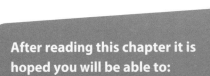

Introduction

This chapter focuses on the relationships that you are engaged in with individuals and looks at the tasks that you carry out with them in your care worker role. We will be looking at the purpose of these relationships, what influences them and how care workers can develop skills to make relationships effective for the people that they **support**. What will become evident is that whilst we can discuss approaches that care workers can adopt when working with people, it is more difficult to describe in detail the range of practice that is necessary in order for care workers to successfully fulfil their roles. However, this chapter introduces some care activities and explores some of the issues for a care worker to consider; it also offers some practical advice regarding appropriate support (emotional, social, physical and intellectual) to individuals in their lives. This chapter links particularly with both Chapter 2 on reflection in action and Chapter 3 on the value base of health and social care.

This chapter addresses the following areas:

- Factors that influence care relationships
- Reasons why individuals have support needs
- How policy influences practice
- Understanding people
- Relationships
- Supporting individuals through change
- Communication
- Empowerment
- Advocacy
- Working with significant others
- Supporting people
- Managing yourself in a relationship

After reading this chapter it is hoped you will be able to:

- know some of the reasons why individuals need care or support
- understand the nature of the professional care relationship
- communicate effectively with individuals in a care context
- support individuals in physical, social, emotional and intellectual well-being.

Factors that influence care relationships

Care work involves working with people, and whatever the actual job role it is necessary to have a relationship with them. This relationship will be very different depending on several factors, which we shall now consider.

There are differences between our usual relationships and those that we have with people who use care and support services:

- There is a specific role that shapes the relationship.
- The relationship exists for the purposes of the service user.
- The service user and care worker do not always have a choice in the relationship.
- The relationship may be time limited.
- There are boundaries to the relationship.

As illustrated in the box on the next page, these values influence the way that the organisation is managed and what is expected of work with the service users.

Reasons why individuals have support needs

Before we start looking at individual ways of working with people, we will consider the reasons why individuals require support. Whilst there are many additional reasons why individuals require support we will focus on learning disability, mental health, physical ability and older age.

Learning disability

Learning disability is a label applied to individuals who experience a **cognitive** impairment before reaching adulthood that has a sustained impact on them throughout their lives. However, there are problems associated with the label 'learning disability'. People may be able to function perfectly well if society did not present barriers, or if they were provided with appropriate support to enable them to overcome these barriers.

There is a range of causes of learning disability:

1 *Biological determinants* of learning disability include:
   - genetic influences, such as those related to Down's Syndrome

CASE STUDY

MCCH is a charitable trust that provides services in London and South East England; its purpose is to support people to live full and valued lives.

'Our vision is:

A home, a job and a social life for everyone

For people with learning disabilities, autism or mental health needs.

Our mission aspires to:

- Support you to live as independently as possible in the home of your choice
- Support you to choose activities that could lead to volunteering, training or holding down a paid job
- Support you to have fun and try new things in your social life so that you can choose and access the things you want to do.

We do this through our values:

m eaningful lives: a home, a job and a social life

c hoice: your choice matters

c ollaboration with partners and communities

h onesty, openess and transparency in our work

v alue for money through quality services

a ccountability and local decision-making

l eadership through management and governance

u ser focus in all we do

e nvironmental awareness and management

s taff are valued as our key to success.'

Influences on relationships

Kevin works in a day centre for people with learning disabilities. He has particular responsibility for recreation, sports and leisure activities. His job has developed over recent years; he used to set up whole group activities in the centre, but there is now an emphasis on smaller groups and individuals participating in community-based activities rather than providing whole group sports events at the centre. Kevin makes sure that an activity plan and risk assessment has been devised for each individual involved; he also supports staff to ensure that they can undertake activities well and that they observe health and safety guidelines.

Factors currently influencing the relationship Kevin has with the people who use the day service include the following:

Kevin's role with the individual as defined through:

- his job description
- the service user's care plan
- supervision
- policies of the organisation.

The service user's characteristics, personality, expectations and needs:

- gender
- age
- ethnicity
- culture
- religion
- personality traits, e.g. patience
- physical ability
- communication skills.

Policy guidance:

- government guidelines and legislation
- current thinking and research
- organisational policy and procedures.

Questions

Having considered Kevin's working relationships with service users, think about your own.

1 What are the characteristics of the relationship that you have with people?
2 What aspects of your role impact on this relationship?
3 Draw an image similar to the one below, noting all characteristics of this relationship. How do the tasks that you carry out affect relationships with individuals?

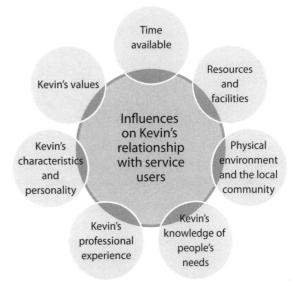

Figure 4.1 Kevin's relationship with others in the centre, the manager and colleagues, and with other professionals is affected by different factors

- non-genetic prenatal factors such as those that cause learning disability with cerebral palsy
- trauma during birth that then affects the cognitive development in the child.

2 *Social factors* that can affect the learning and development of a child may include the experience of significant events in childhood, such as illness or accidents, abuse or neglect. Oppression and discrimination can also impact negatively on a child's development.

3 *Environmental factors*, such as poverty and deprivation, can contribute to the development of a child and introduce a delay in ability and skills that become associated with cognitive ability.

It is important to acknowledge that a person's ability to participate in society is associated with the way that society is set up. Learning disabled individuals may have jobs, drive cars, gain academic qualifications and establish successful personal relationships, including being parents.

Autism

There are probably 300,000 adults in England who have autism. The National Autistic Society (NAS) believes a government-funded prevalence study is what is needed. It says numbers of people with autism – not just those receiving services – should be counted locally, and autism training for staff who carry out care needs assessments is also required.

> **Anne's story**
>
> Anne Wheeler wasn't diagnosed with high functioning autism until she was 30. Now 44, she lives independently in a housing association flat provided by the mental health team. She has support from a consultant psychiatrist, a GP, a community support organisation and the NAS employment agency Prospects. But she has a history of depression and mental health problems and partly attributes this to a lack of support for her autism. She struggled to be diagnosed because she had a degree and seemed relatively independent.
>
> 7 February 2008 *Community Care* 'I don't look ill enough'

According to *I Exist*, a report by the NAS, 45 per cent of councils do not manage how autistic adults receive support if they do not fulfil the criteria for either learning disability or mental health services.

> Oldham Council has invested in multi-agency autism training so that, whether a service user needs a speech and language therapist, a psychologist, a health professional or a drama therapist, it can understand the needs of people with autism.
>
> The council was also a pilot for the 'In Control' scheme, and several autistic adults have been helped to use their budgets to buy support services and employ a PA. It also provides supported housing. Those with Asperger's or higher functioning autism are supported by the vulnerable adults team.
>
> 7 February 2008 *Community Care* 'I don't look ill enough'

Mental health

There are also changing approaches to understanding what 'mental health' might mean in today's world. Mental illness is a contentious term. It is often used to describe a situation where a person has a severe and enduring mental health problem, which adversely affects their ability to function in daily life.

Mental illnesses are often categorised as:

- *Psychoses* These are distortions in the perception of reality. An example of a psychotic mental illness would be schizophrenia. The person may experience delusions or hallucinations and lack insight into their illness.
- *Neuroses* These are severe forms of experiences which are considered to be part of normal life. An example would be a phobia, anxiety attacks or compulsive behaviours.
- *Organic* These cause conditions like dementia, caused by physical deterioration in the brain.

People may experience mental health problems as temporary features of their life. Mental health is not a static condition; anyone of us can experience mental health problems at some time in our lives.

Causes of mental ill-health

There are several ways of viewing the causes of mental ill-health.

- **The disease model**
  This explains mental illness in terms of identifiable disorders. Mental illnesses are classified as disorders and there are identifiable treatments, including prescribed medication, associated with each of these.
- **The functional model**
  Psychodynamic This explanation of mental ill-health states that emotions, often from early life, have not been expressed or resolved. Childhood experiences often have a deep impact on our emotions and behaviour in adult life, although as individuals we may not be aware of their influence, or understand why.
  Behavioural/Cognitive This explanation states that mental ill-health can be understood through looking at the symptoms and behaviour of individuals. It explores the reasons for that behaviour or those thoughts.

- **The social model**

  This model includes attributing the cause of mental ill-health to life events that we are presented with. Relationship problems, poverty, loss, and other situations can present stress or conflict to people.

- **The political model**

  This model acknowledges that the organisation of society contributes to the mental well-being of individuals, and can therefore also have a negative impact on people's mental health. The experience of oppression and discrimination can affect a person's psychological well-being and provide feelings of depression, or despair.

Dementias

Common types of dementia are Alzheimer's disease and vascular dementia.

Alzheimer's disease is linked to changes in the structure of the brain causing brain cells to die. This may progress gradually.

Vascular dementia happens when small strokes cut off the supply of blood and oxygen to the brain. It can develop in sudden stages as each of these strokes happen.

Other, less common, types of dementia include:

Lewy body disease, which is similar to Alzheimer's, with additional experience of hallucinations or sensing things that do not exist, and also physical difficulties of tremors and falls.

Pick's disease is also known as frontal lobe dementia.

Huntingdon's disease or *chorea* is rare and usually develops in younger people.

Creutzfeld Jakob disease has become known as the human form of 'mad cow disease' (BSE) due to its suspected association with eating infected beef.

Dementia can also happen as a result of *Parkinson's disease, AIDS*, a *brain tumour, head injuries* or *alcohol misuse*.

Our understanding of mental health is more influenced now by the experiences of individuals and their narrative of what influences their experience. For example, people who hear voices were often labelled as having schizophrenia, whereas now there is recognition that some people may hear voices without having an associated mental illness.

Physical ability

A person's ability to function effectively in their environment depends on how responsive that society is to adapting to their needs and how empowered individuals feel to overcome the remaining barriers to their participation. Some people have physical characteristics that initiate this need for particular support.

A person's physical ability may be affected by:

1 **Genetics**

  There are some conditions that are determined before birth when the foetus is developing, which may or may not be hereditary. These may be evident from birth, or develop in later life.

2 **Problems occurring that affect oxygen to the brain**

  Our ability to function physically is related to the functioning of our nervous system, including our brains. If our brains experience any damage then this potentially can have an impact, temporarily or permanently, on our physical ability. For example, this might happen if there are problems during birth or if an adult has a stroke.

3 **A condition may be acquired during a person's lifetime**

  - Some illnesses and poor health can affect our body's ability to undertake usual tasks. For example, a person who has Acquired Immune Deficiency Syndrome (AIDS) may experience changes in their physical functioning as the condition develops, and their general health and mobility is affected.

  - An accident may cause physical damage to part of the body, or affect the nervous system. For example, a person may suffer damage to the brain, which then affects physical functioning, or they may acquire a physical injury to part of their body which then affects functioning and mobility.

  - Lifestyle and behaviour can create physical problems for a person. A common condition that affects many people is that of backache. There may be a gradual deterioration in the strength or condition of the spine, sometimes

Cerebral palsy

This is the result of damage to the brain or poor development of the brain:

Around one in ten cases of cerebral palsy are caused by problems during labour and birth, due to lack of oxygen.

In 1 in 50 cases, the cause is a defective gene.

Cerebral palsy can also be caused by infections that affect the brain when the child is very young and the brain is still developing. Examples are meningitis and encephalitis. They cause part of the brain to swell, again resulting in a lack of oxygen getting through, and the death of brain tissues.

Other factors increase the risk of cerebral palsy, including smoking or drinking excess alcohol during pregnancy, infections caught during pregnancy, complications during childbirth, and premature birth.

Cerebral palsy cannot be cured because it is not possible to repair damage to the *brain*. However, much can be done to help children control their muscular action and to prevent deformities from forming.

- Physiotherapy develops posture and movement and can prevent deterioration in ability.
- Prescribed muscle relaxants can control spasms or hyperactivity in the muscles. Botulinum Toxin is a type of bacteria that is injected into muscles, making them less stiff and enabling joints to move more freely.
- Dorsal rhizotomy cuts nerves in the spine that cause abnormal tightening of muscles.
- Braces can strap up joints and help with movements such as walking.

Additional support where required:

- Seizures may be controlled with anticonvulsants.
- Speech and language therapy helps with speech but also eating, drinking and swallowing.
- Hearing aids and glasses.
- Individuals benefit most now when they get special help from an early age. For many adults this was not available during their childhood.

due to continuous inappropriate lifting. This can then limit an individual's capacity to undertake certain tasks.

4 Life stages

Our bodies change as we progress through the life stages. This happens at a different rate with people, and contributing factors such as health and lifestyle can affect this change, some of which may affect a person's mobility. It is only the reluctance of society to adapt the environment to suit the needs of older people that means that people are disabled by these changes.

5 Cognitive ability

Physical ability may also be affected by a person's level of awareness and understanding. For example, a learning disabled person may need continued support to promote their independence at mealtimes, even though physical functioning in their limbs is fine. An example of how mental health can affect someone's physical ability is that of dementia. The person may forget how to perform certain tasks or not remember to undertake them.

It is these circumstances that initiate the needs of the individual and prompt the level and type of support that is required from us as care workers. Some service users require physical support in order to undertake certain activities; others may need assistance with the development of new skills through **rehabilitation** with the aim of one day performing these tasks independently.

REFLECT

Think about the care activities of:

- supporting an individual in making their own lunch
- assisting a person with their personal care in the bathroom
- listening to a person describing how distressed they are feeling.

1 Identify the reasons why these individuals might need support.
2 How might a care worker provide support to these people?

How policy influences practice

It was mentioned in the introduction that the nature of relationships with service users has changed over the years, and part of this change has been the policy framework of care provision. Chapter 1 on the context of health and social care describes the history of care services and the provision of 'care' in large institutions. It also explores the current context of care and the policies which currently shape the way that we work with people. This section in this chapter provides a few examples of these as a way of illustrating how policy influences the way that we work with people.

The Community Care (Direct Payments) Act 1995 provided the means for local authorities to give cash payments to individuals for them to purchase their own care. This has enabled individuals to set out the specific requirements they have for the support that they receive.

The possible effects of this are:

- the service user sees themselves as the employer
- a more direct relationship between the person requiring care or support and the care worker
- the service user has more influence in what role the care worker has, and the tasks that they perform
- the service user is able to dismiss a care worker if they are dissatisfied with the standard of their work or unhappy with any aspects of the relationship.

The Care Standards Act 2000 provided a comprehensive base recognising the importance of standards in care provision. Through National Service Frameworks and National Minimum Standards there are specific statements about the way that care should be provided; this in turn can shape the relationship that the professional has with the service user. It embedded the idea of entitlement and the importance of standards as a foundation for the provision of care and support services; people do not have to feel grateful and accepting of what is provided for them.

The Data Protection Act 1998 influences the care profession's observation of confidentiality and has changed the ownership of patient/service user information. People have more access and control over the use of information about them.

ACTIVITY

Make a list of national policies that have an impact on the working relationships that you have with those you support.

Include documents from within your organisation, as well as national policies. If you are unsure where to start, think about the policies mentioned above.

Supported Living arrangements have altered the identity of learning disabled people or individuals with mental health problems in supported tenancies. The organisation that provides their accommodation may differ from the organisation that provides a care/support service. This is a different arrangement from other care home or hostel arrangements for living.

Human Rights policies supported by the Equality and Human Rights Commission (EHRC) have enshrined in law the expectation of fair treatment. Individuals are now able to contest issues of unfair treatment.

Understanding people

Developments in the way that care workers are expected to work with people are due to changes in how we understand human behaviour, disability, illness, psychology and the role of professionals. Chapter 3 describes the changing perception of disability from one of sympathy for incapable people to one of challenging society's ability to discriminate against some groups and empowering individuals in order to participate.

Theories can provide us with a way of explaining why people behave in a certain way, or why their circumstances are affecting them in a particular way. In the past the predominance of theories was based on the idea that the professionals knew best. Now, recognition is given to an individual's perception and own interpretation of their behaviour. Whilst we still have a long way to go in this area, it has helped to shape current discourse on some areas of individual experience. An example of this is the situation of people who 'hear voices'; they have challenged the clinical diagnosis of people who hear voices as having schizophrenia; their account of their experience is that they are voice hearers without an associated mental illness, so it should not be labelled as a symptom of schizophrenia.

The table on page 129 gives a summary of approaches to understanding people.

So why are these theories of interest in health and social care work?

Obviously, caution has to be displayed in applying a little knowledge that is usually used by specialist professions. These theories may help in opening up our understanding of people, but not in providing a strategy for working with people; for that you would need to investigate these in more depth than can be provided for in this book.

Power imbalances are not always straightforward. There are other factors to consider in the dynamics of this interaction – gender and race. If you want to explore how these may impact on the dialogue between them, you could go to the relevant sections in the chapter on ethics and values.

The case study opposite illustrates the importance of distinguishing the person from the behaviour, and the behaviour from the feelings. In doing this we can seek to support people more appropriately.

Relationships

We will now look at what relationships with service users are all about. We start with a focus on the stages that these relationships may progress through. We all experience the development of relationships in different ways and your own feelings about each of these stages may have an influence on your relationship with service users.

For each stage we will look at your relationship with the people whom you support, and also how you can support individuals in the relationships that they have with other people.

At the beginning of this chapter we identified that relationships with service users are different from the other relationships that we have, and this affects the progression through these stages.

Approach	Explanation	What it means
Behaviourist	Emphasis on the relationship that individuals have with their environment, behaviour being related to the responses that individuals have to stimulus	A behaviourist approach to understanding a person would focus on their learning. It emphasises the role that conditioning can have on people, where you learn how to behave due to the responses you have previously received when you either behaved like that, or differently. It focuses on the relationship that humans have with stimuli (what happens to you) and responses (how you react).

There are variations of this theory. As responses can be learned and therefore unlearned, we can be trained to manage our response to certain stimuli which are unfavourable. The context of a situation can be a significant factor in shaping our response. |
| Humanistic | Emphasis on the self-concept and the individual's understanding of themselves | These theories emphasise the individual's self-concept and the importance of the psychological well-being of a person that then influences their behaviour. The idea of the 'self-actualising' person is characterised by:

- realistic perception
- personal responsibility
- capacity for good personal relations
- ethical living
- rationality
- self-regard

Again there are various approaches within this broad grouping:

Person-centred approaches.

Transactional analysis explores the relationship between the parent, child and adult that is present in all of us, with reference to early experiences.

Reality and rational emotive therapy explores the individual's perception of what the situation is and seeks to manage their thoughts. |
| Psychoanalytical | Emphasis on the significance of stages in early development | This set of approaches to understanding people explores the relationship between early experiences and how people then respond in adult life.

Freud identified three areas of a person's consciousness:

1 The id relates to an individual's impulses and biological instincts.
2 The ego acts as the mediator between the id and the external environment, it manages reason and common sense.
3 The super-ego contains the demands of the id through moral influence on the ego.

People's behaviour is sometimes influenced by defensive mechanisms, which continue to operate after they have fulfilled their initial usefulness. People then have different responses to new situations. Earlier experience may influence this:

Repression: information in the mind is not allowed to enter the conscious thoughts of the individual.

Information is pushed into the unconscious.

Sublimation: displacing impulses into more socially acceptable behaviour.

Reaction formation: the person feels strong impulses which are opposite to the existing ones.

Denial: the person ignores or disregards information that would be painful to acknowledge.

Fixation: a person fails to move on to the next stage of development due to anxiety or insecurity.

Regression: an individual returns to an earlier phase of development.

Projection: in order to avoid acknowledging feelings within oneself a person externalises these feelings, and their awareness of such characteristics in other people becomes heightened. |
| | | |

Compare the following scenarios.

Mrs Galloway has a care worker visit her in the morning to assist her with getting up, she then spends most of the day in her front room until another care worker assists her in the evening.

Care worker A: 'Hello Mrs Galloway, I am Jo, what do you prefer me to call you?'... 'I'm an agency member of staff so this might be my only visit to you but make sure I do things how you like them, tell me if I get it wrong won't you'... 'Can I read your notes in your care plan to check what you need me to do?'... 'I see that the nurse visited the other day, is everything all right to do with...'

Care worker B describes her work: 'I let myself into the house, I let Mrs Galloway know that I was there and then I read the care plan and got on with the tasks that I was required to do. I didn't chat to the service user as I was only going to visit her the once. It was pointless getting to know her.'

The service user's experience of these encounters would be very different, and this is significant; care tasks can be very personal activities, and the care was taking place in Mrs Galloway's own home. Something else to consider is that on this particular day the contact with the care workers was the only social contact that Mrs Galloway had.

Reflect on your own relationships with service users.

1 How do your relationships with service users progress through different stages?
2 What are the characteristics of these stages, and how are they influenced by your role?

As care workers it is easy to view the relationships that we have with individuals simply in terms of our role and the approaches that we use. It is, however, very important to consider the experience of the service user.

To return to Mrs Galloway, her account of the two separate mornings are as follows:

About *care worker A*, she said, 'Another new care worker this morning. Still, she was very pleasant and cheered me up first thing. Made me feel very safe and wanted, I felt like we began to know each other a bit. She even asked me if she was doing everything right – never been asked that before! I hope she comes back another time.'

About *care worker B*, she said, 'I was woken up this morning by a person, don't know her name, I suppose she knew mine though as she read my notes. I wanted to ask her what the weather was like outside as I had not slept well due to the heavy rain, but she didn't seem interested in chatting so I didn't like to bother her.'

Relationships with service users

What was your first contact with the people who you support? You may work in an environment where the people who use the service are very constant, such as in a care home, or it may be that you are a care manager in a hospital and you are introduced to new service users on a regular basis. Can you remember the first time that you met your best friend, your partner or your manager? How important was the first contact? It may have shaped the beginning of the relationship, and may have continued to influence it.

Starting relationships

It is Douglas' first day at the Valley Road Resource Centre. It was suggested that he try it to see how he gets on. Douglas is 73, he has cerebral palsy and has a personal support worker but it was felt that he would benefit from some social contact through the Centre.

1 Think about what feelings Douglas is likely to have that will have an impact on the way the relationship starts.
2 What thoughts are likely to be going through Douglas' mind as he waits outside?
3 What can the support worker do to ensure that Douglas feels positive about this new situation, and the new relationships that may develop?

Think about the various ways you can start to establish a relationship with the people you have to care for.

In starting relationships with service users it is very important that the care worker does not trivialise the feelings that the individual may have about the circumstances of the relationship.

Do:

- make it clear what the aims of the relationship are, and what role you as an individual have with that person
- make it clear what the potential duration of the relationship might be – this will range from supporting someone for a couple of hours to a life-long commitment
- remember that being a service user doesn't make it easier to cope with new situations
- remember that you are there for them – they are not there for you
- support the person to assert their own expectations on the relationship. This may range from 'I'd like to be called Mr Bain' and 'Call me Douglas' to 'I want support with dressing, but I shall choose what I wear myself.'

Don't:

- make promises about the relationship that are not within your role and that you will be unable to honour
- negate the experience of the individual prior to their relationship with you and your organisation.

Supporting individuals in relationships

The people that you support may not have the same motivation, confidence or opportunities to initiate relationships in the same way that we do. The more intense the level of support required to attend to a person's physical well-being, the easier it is to overlook their social needs and relationships.

The care plan will guide your relationship with each person. The development of your role with the person will also be affected by the impact of other relationships that the person has, both professional and otherwise. All relationships need nurturing. As we saw at the beginning of the chapter, relationships are affected by the amount of time spent on them; of

course, mostly this time is limited and outside the control of the individual care worker.

It may be that individuals can be encouraged to be:

- more confident
- more in control
- more assertive

in the relationship that they have with you, other **carers**, family, and socially.

The purpose of the relationship should be regularly reviewed to ensure that it is meeting the needs of the individual. Are the skills of the service user being developed, as they become more confident in their independence?

When we think about the relationships that the service user develops with other people we can consider these features:

- **Content:** What activities the people in the relationship do together.
- **Diversity:** The range of different activities the people in the relationship undertake.
- **Quality:** How people in the relationship approach interaction.
- **Patterns:** What type of interaction takes place, and its frequency.
- **Reciprocal or complementary:** Whether the roles adopted by people in the relationship are similar or very different.
- **Intimacy:** Self-disclosure and revelations.
- **Interpersonal perception**: The way that the individuals in the relationship view the other person.
- **Commitment:** How each person sees the relationship in terms of its duration.

Insights into the relationships between clients and others can create dilemmas for workers. On the one hand, it is not appropriate to make a judgement about a person's family or friendships and the worth of these, and yet, on the other hand it may be important to identify potential situations where a person is being taken advantage of in a way that needs addressing.

In the case study on page 132 this is not untypical in a sibling relationship; lots of sisters argue and there may be one sister who tries to dominate the other. On just this information it would be wrong to come to conclusions that there is anything wrong in the relationship. Service users are as entitled to problems in relationships as the rest of us! If the upset that was caused by one argument developed into continuous distress caused by constant harassment then this would be cause for alarm.

Sibling relationship

Geraldine has always had a close relationship with her sister Philippa, and Geraldine talks of her with affection; she always asks her advice and looks to her for guidance. As a home support worker you visit Geraldine to assist with personal care in the morning and evening. One evening you arrive and Philippa is just leaving; the sisters have been arguing and Geraldine tells you that Philippa is telling her what to do.

Questions

1 Do you feel concerned about this news?
2 Is it necessary for you to do anything as a result?

As relationships develop, they also change. Within the care worker/service user relationship it is useful to consider who has control over any changes. It may be that the role you have alters due to changes in the person's development of skills, or the health of the individual; sometimes tasks that you carried out regularly may no longer be required and you need to have a different approach.

An example of change associated with loss is where an injury has occurred affecting a person's cognitive and physical capacity. Severe acquired brain injury can happen to anyone through road accidents, strokes, neurological disease, respiratory failure and assault.

Supporting people through conflict and difficult relationships

Relationships do not always go to plan, and the care worker/service user relationship may experience similar tensions and issues that arise in your own life.

The diagram below illustrates some of the relationships that service users have.

REFLECT

What potential is there for conflict in the following relationships?

Daughter: 'Mother never accepts that I know what is best for her.'

Person living in a care home: 'Coral always gets more attention because her hearing is better than mine, the staff don't get fed up with talking to her.'

The cause of conflict may be:

- in the past, recent or a current situation
- real or imagined
- temporary or permanent
- with the service user or with the other person/ people.

The chart on page 133 illustrates that there is no single way of responding to conflict. It focuses on extremes in the assertiveness of each person in pursuing their own goals, and how co-operative each person is in pursuing the goals of the other person.

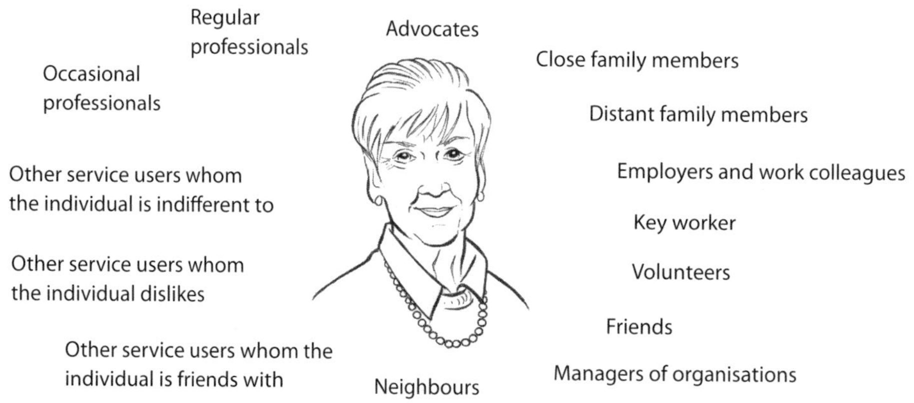

Regular professionals
Occasional professionals
Advocates
Close family members
Distant family members
Other service users whom the individual is indifferent to
Employers and work colleagues
Key worker
Other service users whom the individual dislikes
Volunteers
Other service users whom the individual is friends with
Friends
Neighbours
Managers of organisations

Figure 4.2 *Relationships that service users will have*

Strategy	Description	Issues for service users
Exit	This can involve leaving the relationship physically or just mentally	Do people have a choice? ● Is a person physically able to leave a relationship? ● Are people supported in articulating their desire to end relationships? ● Are decisions made by the service user, acted upon?
Voice	Discussing the issues	● Experience of the person in communicating dissatisfaction? ● Is the person's view taken seriously? ● Are changes going to be made?
Loyalty	Waiting and hoping for improvements in the relationship	● Is the service user able to establish a point when they will wait no more, or is this a constant situation?
Neglect	Allowing the relationship to dissolve gradually, making no attempt to address issues	● Does neglect of relationships happen because the service user needs support in actively maintaining relationships? ● Is this related to self-esteem?

(Hayes, 1998)

The ability of an individual to respond to conflict in an appropriate way will be influenced by:

● the relationship that they have with that person
● their sense of self
● their communication skills.

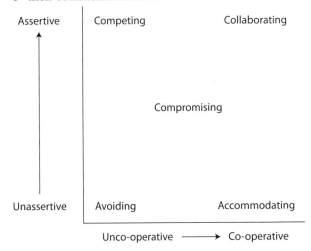

Figure 4.3 Ways of handling conflict (Pedler et al, 2001, page 152)

If difficulties in relationships remain, there are several strategies we can use to manage problems.

Loneliness

Many people who use care services experience physical isolation, possibly due to changes in physical mobility. Some people experience emotional isolation, perhaps being isolated at home through withdrawing from their usual activities, or through changes in mental health. Situational loneliness is due to changes in circumstances, as a geographical move can create temporary isolation until a person becomes more established and more confident in an area. A change in mobility can cause practical difficulties in continuing usual social contacts. Situational loneliness needs to be recognised, acknowledged, and the individual needs to be supported in self-managing so that they can overcome their loneliness. (Hayes, 1998, page 356)

Chronic loneliness is more related to long-term emotional well-being. This type of loneliness is not necessarily associated with lack of social contact and may need more specialist intervention.

CASE STUDY

Loneliness

Mr Bahrami moved into Maple Green Care Home three months ago. He is feeling very cared for in terms of the personal care that he receives, but has a deep-seated loneliness that has made him very withdrawn. His move was associated with the death of his wife, who had been his main carer. She also was the main person that he communicated with in Farsi. Although he moved to Britain from Iran ten years ago and can speak some English, his dialogue is very limited.

Questions

1 What are the causes of Mr Bahrami's current emotional well-being?
2 How could this potentially affect him in the long-term?
3 What could be done to prevent Mr Bahrami's current loneliness becoming chronic?

Supporting individuals through change

During life a person can experience many different changes. These include those shown in the diagram below.

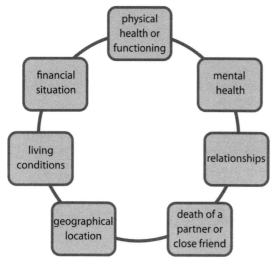

Figure 4.4 Life changes

Some of these life changes may be positive or negative experiences. A negative change can produce some positive effects. A very positive, welcomed change can also lead to some negative effects. Change is associated with 'push and pull' factors – when what we may try to do is to establish some level of equilibrium. Change is described as transition, in recognition that it is a process that people are involved in. The reason why some individuals become users of care services is because they experience negative change in their lives.

REFLECT

Make a list of all the changes that take place for the people you support. Consider how effective you are at supporting people to:

- recognise the transition that they are experiencing
- deal with the emotional and physical response to this change
- manage the change.

People react differently when facing change.

CASE STUDY

Facing change

Marjorie is an 84-year-old woman whose husband died three weeks ago; they had been married for 61 years. He supported her with some aspects of her personal care as her mobility changed when she had a fall 18 months ago. Marjorie relied on her husband to keep her in touch with all the news; he would read the newspaper to her each day and tell her what he had chatted to family about on the phone.

Questions

1 What changes will Marjorie face now she is a widow?
2 What kind of support do you think she will need?

The changes that Marjorie has experienced recently may have affected her in the following ways.

Change	Effects
Marjorie's husband dying	Loss of ● life-long partner ● living companion ● practical support in the home ● emotional support ● social company ● stimulation – discussing the past, family, current affairs.
Previous change in mobility	Loss of ● health ● physical mobility ● confidence. Changes in ● social activities ● dependence on husband.

Loss and bereavement

It has long been recognised that loss is not just associated with the death of family or friends; it is also associated with other changes that occur in our lives. Grief is the emotional process associated with loss.

A care worker who is supporting someone through the grieving process may need to consider:

- the need for both physical and emotional space and privacy
- the effects of changes to routines and patterns of behaviour that have been disrupted
- the desire or ability of the person to express their feelings when in the company of others; as service users people can be frequently in the company of people who they may not feel close to
- not making assumptions about the worth of any relationship – people may feel a variety of emotions about a person when they die
- supporting family members who you come into contact with, accepting their feelings or behaviour without being judgemental
- not fussing over individuals or feeling the need to interpret every aspect of the person's behaviour as a symptom of the grieving process.

Relationships can develop in a natural way, usually as a result of spending more time with a person. In some care roles this is not always possible and the care worker needs to be more focused on how they can influence the development of the relationship.

Ending relationships

There are many reasons why relationships with service users come to an end; some are related to the care worker, and some to the circumstances of the service user.

The service user:

- is no longer eligible for a service
- has a change in needs that require a different job role
- has a change in financial status so that they are not entitled to the services of the organisation or they can no longer purchase the care provided
- moves to another area outside of the geographical area that the organisation covers
- dies.

The care worker:

- moves to a different job
- changes job in the same organisation.

The organisation:

- loses its contract to provide a service to that person
- changes its focus or budgeting priorities.

People respond differently to change, including changes in relationships.

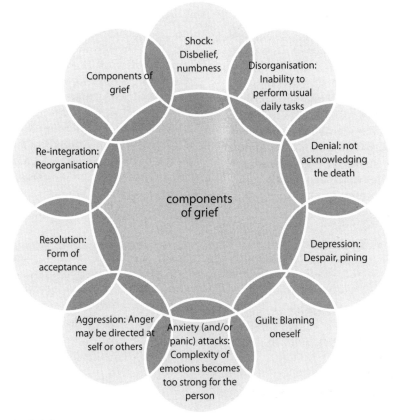

Figure 4.5 Different aspects of grief

Neurological Rehabilitation

The Brain Injury Rehabilitation Trust (BIRT) and the Northern Lincolnshire and Goole Hospitals NHS Foundation Trust (NLAG) have established a new neurological rehabilitation service based at Goole and District Hospital.

The model of clinical assessment and rehabilitation is designed to meet the needs of people who require post-acute rehabilitation, where service users are admitted directly from neurosurgical or acute medical/surgical services, and also of those people seeking community integration rehabilitation. The aim is to provide a continuous link for each individual through their pathway of care from in-patient services through to re-integration into the community.

- 14 bed spaces
- ground floor access, with its own dedicated entrance
- easy access to a range of key NHS services, for example psychiatry, diagnostics and dietetics
- additional accommodation for therapy activities and practising daily living skills, as well as for recreational purposes
- a number of small lounges.

The neuro-behavioural model they use ensures that each client has an individual rehabilitation plan, including a structured learning programme, **daily living skills**, community access skills, behavioural management techniques, social skills training and vocational training and support. The focus is on rehabilitation carried out in real-life settings, such as going to the shops, travelling on public transport or going to work placements. This method has been shown to be much more successful than concentrating on doing exercises in a rehabilitation centre.

The goal of rehabilitation is to help people re-learn skills lost as a result of their injury, so as to minimise the effects of the brain injury. Longer term effects can be divided into:

- physical effects (problems with movement and sensory abilities such as vision, touch or taste)
- cognitive problems (thinking processes such as memory, concentration, etc)
- behaviour (self-control, motivation, etc).

As well as physical changes a person may experience:

- Cognitive problems

The most common cognitive problems following brain injury are certain types of memory problems, concentration difficulties and finding it harder to process incoming information. Another common type of cognitive problem following brain injury is known as an executive problem. The frontal lobe is the part of the brain responsible for planning, integrating and organising other parts of the brain. These problems become obvious to those living with someone with a brain injury or to the person him or herself.

- Behaviour issues

As well as confusion, difficulties such as initiating, monitoring and regulating behaviour may become apparent. The person may become much more impulsive than usual and fail to think before they speak or act. They may become irritable and aggressive or they may become very placid. Sometimes the person acts on impulses that they previously would have controlled. Sudden changes of mood are also common and some people have great difficulty experiencing emotions.

(Disabilities Trust, 2007)

REFLECT

1 Reflect on the relationships that you have had in your life which have come to an end. Some of these may have come to a natural end and both parties felt OK about this, however there are others you may not have felt so comfortable about.
2 Identify what is important for you in the way that a relationship ends.
3 How do you support service users in managing the endings to relationships?

Sometimes it is important to feel OK about the end of a relationship. The idea of closure relates to the ability to resolve in our own minds the end of a relationship, so that feelings related to it do not re-surface later. Being able to say goodbye to people is a step in addressing this issue. Not saying goodbye to people, and ending the relationship inappropriately, may affect people in the long-term if they do not have the opportunity to explore this.

It is important to acknowledge each person as an individual, and to recognise that service users have a variety of expectations about relationships, just as you or I do. An individual may want to end a relationship because they feel that the relationship is no longer progressing. The phases in relationship breakdown are shown below.

The importance of relationships can be underestimated by professionals, as we often make assumptions about the significance of people to those we work with based on our observations.

Intra-psychic phase: Dissatisfaction in the relationship, the relationship is questioned

↓

Dyadic phase: Expressions of uncertainty and indecision about the relationship continuing

↓

Social phase: Practical implications are worked out

↓

Grave-dressing phase: Individual accounts of the break-up are developed

Figure 4.6 Different stages in the breakdown of a relationship

Loss of a friend

Bill and George, who attend the same luncheon club, are always arguing over who sits where, and what activities should be happening. When Bill dies, George actually misses him more than anyone else; he always valued the banter that they shared, and he felt the arguments were a reflection of the respect they had for each other. He misses the stimulation he got when Bill was alive.

Relationships with service users may last for a couple of hours, or they can last for years. You have a responsibility to make sure the relationship is effective for the purpose that it is meant to serve, however long it lasts. It is important to be sensitive to the way the service user experiences the relationship. For example, it would be easy to think that as you are only covering a shift as a one-off it would not be worthwhile to invest in a relationship with a service user during that time. From their experience, the service user may believe that every service worker has that attitude, and they may easily feel as though they are an inconvenience. Your individual approach will influence this person's experience.

Now that we have considered what factors influence the relationship that care workers have with individuals we shall think about the **principles** that are required to support people effectively. A person's values influence their attitude to others and the approach they have to working with people. Attitude can influence the way you work on a one-to-one basis, and this will have the biggest influence on the welfare of the person receiving care.

Principles underpinning the professional relationship

Having explored some of the reasons why individuals might need support and the approach to understanding people, we now turn to consider some of the underpinning principles that should inform the practice of the care worker.

Power

How do you think that power affects the relationships that you develop with service users? The care worker should always consider the position of power within the relationship. In Chapter 3 we looked at the significance of power in the status of individuals in society. Now we shall look at the impact of power on the relationship that you have with individuals.

There are different types of power:

- reward
- coercive
- legitimate
- referent
- expert
- informative.

Power is about control. Care workers can have considerable control over the nature of the interventions they provide. Recognition of this power can lead us to address the power imbalance and work with people in a manner that develops their control in the relationship. These are fundamental aspects of a person's life.

REFLECT

Think about your own work and identify situations where you potentially exert power over individuals.

1 Which of the above types of power are implicit in the relationships that you have with service users?
2 What factors are influencing the power balance between you and the people that you support?
3 What steps could (a) you and (b) your organisation take to address this power balance?

Values

Underpinning the care relationship should be the values that are discussed in Chapter 3. They are:

respect
dignity
confidentiality
partnership
promoting independence.

Other dimensions to the relationship include *trust* and *honesty*. The relationship should also encourage a feeling of being relaxed as this creates the best situation for communication to take place. This can be a difficult area, as although it is important to be open and honest with people there may be situations where issues arise. Individuals and their families need to know that any aspects of care intervention are implemented for very positive reasons for the service user.

CASE STUDY

Trust and honesty

Mrs Buxton's granddaughter has recently had an accident. Mrs Buxton's children do not think it is appropriate to tell their mother the full extent of her granddaughter's condition, as it will cause great distress. They inform you, but say that they do not want their mother to know. Mrs Buxton often asks the staff if her granddaughter has called, as she was used to her popping in sometimes on her own. The staff understand the reasons for the family's wishes, but are feeling very unsettled by not telling the truth. They feel that Mrs Buxton is anxious about not seeing her granddaughter.

Questions

1 Identify the issues for the following in their relationship with Mrs Buxton:
   - relatives
   - manager of the care home
   - care workers.
2 What could be done to address this dilemma so that the relationships with Mrs Buxton are not compromised?

The importance of applying values to care practice can be seen when past practice is considered. The use of sanctions used to be an accepted part of behaviour modification programmes used to develop people's skills; any sanctions are now unacceptable. For example the use of seclusion is no longer condoned as a useful strategy.

Skills in relationships

There are a range of skills that care workers can use in order to meet the requirements of the relationships that they are involved in. The skills that we shall look at are: communication, empowerment, advocacy, practical support skills.

Communication

Communication skills can enhance the ability of any person to do their job well, irrespective of the kind of work they are involved in. Such skills are also a resource for living in that all of us use communication to function in our own lives.

Communication is important in care work as we need to:

- understand what specific communication needs the people we work with have
- utilise the skills that we have to maximise the support we are providing for people
- develop our skills.

Communication is about giving and receiving messages and there are numerous reasons for conveying messages to other people; they may be expressions of feelings or giving or requesting information. Sometimes we convey messages without wanting to, or without realising it; others can pick up the subtle signals that our words or body language convey.

Human behaviour comprises many codes and communication is laden with values. It is also influenced by the context in which communication is taking place. If a friend says to you, 'I don't think that you should do that' when you are out socialising with them, it has a different meaning from if your manager says exactly the same words in the place where you work.

You can usually tell from people's faces and body language whether individuals are unhappy or angry about something. You can identify this even though you cannot hear the words they are saying. It is a non-verbal message, i.e. the body language. The verbal and non-verbal messages need to be considered together, but we will explore them separately in this section.

Figure 4.7 *Body language may convey a different message from the one the person is conveying verbally*

The balance in the importance of the verbal and non-verbal message will be influenced by the communication needs and skills of the persons giving and receiving the message. You should consider how relevant the points being made in this section are to the people that you support.

Verbal communication

This relates to the content of what is said. There are various reasons for communicating orally. It is usually the most immediate and efficient way of communicating with another person. Where possible it can also be the most effective way to establish a relationship with that person.

There are several categories of verbal behaviour:

- **Seeking ideas:** 'What can we do about the medication issue?'
- **Proposing:** 'I think it would be a good idea if Joan became Adam's key worker when Susan leaves.'
- **Suggesting:** 'Why don't we try it this way?'
- **Building:** 'Good idea, we could also ask relatives to join in.'
- **Disagreeing:** 'I don't think we should.'
- **Supporting:** 'I think that would be a good idea.'

Communication issues

1 Steve

Steve has just arrived at work in a care home and has been told by his manager to change his weekend shift. He is angry about this. When he goes into the lounge to support one of the people who live there he doesn't really listen to what they are saying because he is thinking about the change to his shift and the plans he is going to have to alter.

2 Cecil

Cecil has an acquired language disorder (dysphasia) as a result of a stroke. This affects his choice of words and his ability to structure sentences. He has a new care worker who finds it difficult to understand what he is saying.

In the first of these scenarios, Steve's communication is being affected by his emotions. His anger is stopping him from paying attention. In the second, Cecil's communication is being affected by the awareness and skills of the other person. He is clear in what he is saying, but the other person is unable to receive that message.

The diagram shows how messages and feedback flow

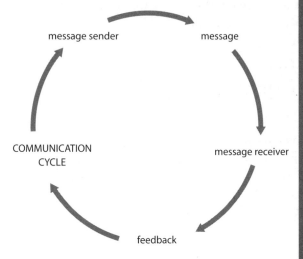

Figure 4.8 The communication cycle

Questions

1 What are the communication issues in each of these scenarios?
2 What would improve the communication in the above scenarios of Steve and Cecil?

- **Difficulty stating**: 'I'm not sure that we can manage without them.'
- **Seeking clarification/information**: 'Could you point to where it is most painful?'
- **Clarifying/explaining/informing**: 'I'm just letting you know that the GP is visiting you later this morning, after her surgery has finished.'

Questioning

The nature of questioning in care work has changed over the years along with other aspects of the relationship between professionals and individuals who require care services. The nature of questioning in the caring professions used to consist of narrow, closed, biomedical and technical questions; this approach has now been replaced with broader, open questions relating to psychosocial and lifestyle issues. There is a new emphasis on the importance of the service user's narrative, their own account and story of their situation, as reflected in the emergence of the Expert Patient in the NHS. We now value what an

individual has to say about themselves rather than just focusing on a professional's (the 'expert') point of view. We challenge that idea of the care worker as the expert in Chapter 3, and this approach to communicating with individuals reinforces this debate.

There are different types of questions that can be used.

- *Open:* This invites a response from the person without suggesting what that response might be, 'What do you want to do this afternoon?' The person being asked is free to come up with any answer.
- *Closed:* This question implies an answer, which can potentially affect the decision-making of the person. 'I don't think you'll like going to the sports centre, do you really want to go?' This question is inviting just a yes or no answer, and the person asking the question has made it clear what response might be best. It might be difficult for the person to say 'Yes I do want to go.'

- *Clarifying:* Involves checking what the person has said. There are various ways of doing this. You can simply ask 'Can I check what you meant ... ?'
- *Reflecting:* This is a way of clarifying, where you say back to the person what they have just said. It gives them an opportunity to think about what they said and to potentially change anything if they were not able to accurately articulate what they meant.
- *Paraphrasing:* By summarising what has been said to you and saying it back to the person in your own words. Not only does this act as a buffer between listening and responding, but it will also enable you to clarify or confirm what has been said to you. It helps the person continue thinking about what they have said.

You may think you have put your message across clearly, but it is always useful to reflect on how well you have communicated.

REFLECT

'I thought that you were assisting Alan this morning.'

What is the key point that someone is making here? Read through the statement again (out loud if possible), emphasising each word in turn (words in **bold italics**). Consider how an emphasis on different words actually changes the meaning of the sentence. The differences in the message are indicated by the paralanguage, for example the tone and pace of communication. These form part of the non-verbal communication.

'I thought that you were assisting Alan **this morning**.' (not this afternoon)

'I thought that you were assisting **Alan** this morning.' (not Jimmy)

'I thought that you were **assisting** Alan this morning.' (not doing something for him or instead of him)

'I thought that **you** were assisting Alan this morning.' (not me)

'**I thought** that you were assisting Alan this morning.' (the manager thought differently)

We all have different styles of communication. If communication is at least a two-way interaction then the communication is influenced by not only the style of the person giving the message but the communication needs of the other person. For some people their ability to communicate is affected by impairment – sensory or physical ability.

Staunton (2003) describes the six Cs of communication – as shown in the diagram below.

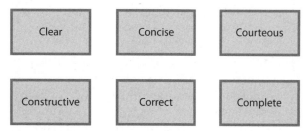

Figure 4.9 The six Cs of communication

You need to find the most effective way of conveying your message to the person or people who are going to be receiving that message.

Speaking to someone should convey

- clarity
- accuracy
- empathy
- sincerity
- warmth.

Ways of encouraging the above can be through creating a relaxed dialogue, and being aware of your presentation. We have all felt tense in situations and this can affect our ability to communicate effectively. Being relaxed does not mean being laid back or slovenly; it means being aware of encouraging the other person to be relaxed through your careful use of language and non-verbal cues.

In order to use these speaking skills, you may need to consider the following:

- Think about what you are going to say before you say it.
- Be aware of your feelings towards the person and their situation, and the context of the communication. Manage these feelings to facilitate the communication. We do not need to like everyone we work with in order to be able to work effectively with or for them.
- Be aware that you are communicating through more than the spoken word; there are subtle clues in the tone and pace of your words, and your whole body will be transmitting a message.

This exercise will help you to reflect on your best use of language.

1 Try to rephrase these sentences using more effective use of language:

'We have a multidisciplinary conference for all stakeholders in the service that we would like service user representation at.'

'We need professional support in identifying a more appropriate package of care that addresses your current mobility requirements.'

2 Think about the phrases that are used in the organisation that you work for, either in meetings or in documentation. Are you confident that all the language used is clear to the service users?

- Don't fancy things up or use jargon – use the best words for what you want to communicate; these are usually the simplest words.
- Be sensitive to the individual's expectation of language because of the differences in generation, culture, sensory abilities.
- Be aware of how what you are saying is interpreted by others. A message is only clear if the other person receives and interprets it in the way you wanted.

Developing appropriate vocabulary can provide you with a tool for more effective communication. It will also make you more able to control the potential problems associated with communication.

Listening

How good are you at listening? Listening draws on a number of skills – cognitive and interpersonal ones. A first step to becoming a good listener is actually valuing what the other person is saying. A positive attitude and appropriate values are essential if you are going to listen to someone else.

Listening can be improved by:

1 *Preparation*: Knowing some background to the person or situation can help you in understanding new information they give you. Listening involves the use of schema; by interlocking knowledge that we utilise in everyday conversations we can accommodate new information. Think about why you are listening to the person and the overview of what they are saying.

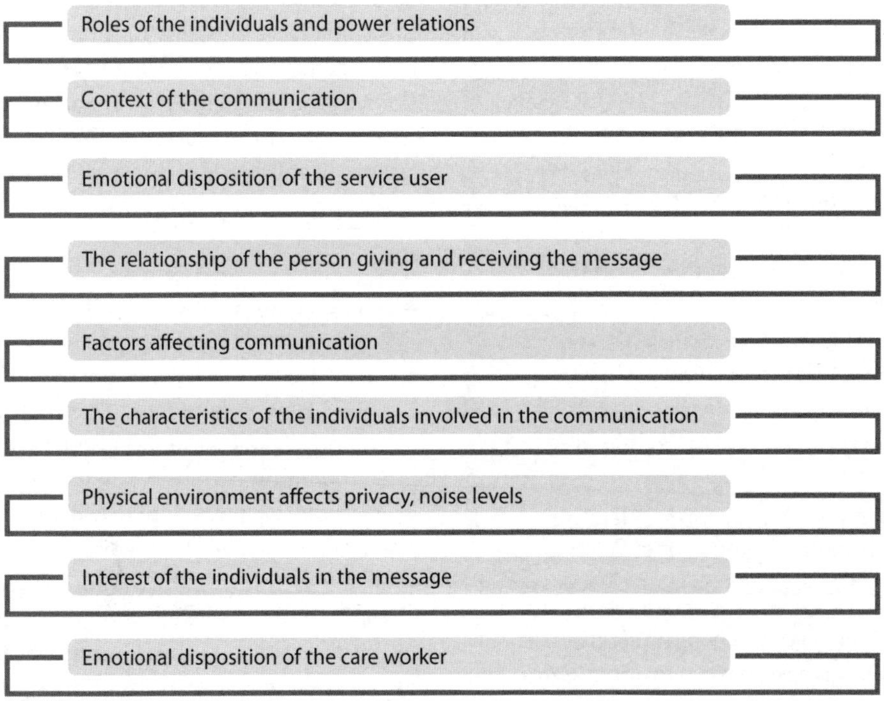

Roles of the individuals and power relations

Context of the communication

Emotional disposition of the service user

The relationship of the person giving and receiving the message

Factors affecting communication

The characteristics of the individuals involved in the communication

Physical environment affects privacy, noise levels

Interest of the individuals in the message

Emotional disposition of the care worker

Figure 4.10 Factors affecting communication

2 *Being interested*: Be proactive about learning about the needs of the people that you work with, or the views of the colleagues in your team.

3 *Being open-minded*: If you are closed about what you think, then you will be reluctant to actually hear what someone is saying to you. Don't anticipate what they are about to say.

4 *Identifying the main ideas*: Identify the main points the person is making, as it is not always appropriate or possible to have a notebook with you to write these down.

5 *Being critical*: This doesn't mean being negative, it means thinking about, questioning and analysing what is being said as a way of understanding and coming to know it.

6 *Avoiding distractions*: Try to overcome internal distraction, such as being preoccupied, and external ones, such as feeling you need to answer the telephone.

7 *Taking notes*: Record what someone says. In care work this is an essential way of maintaining continuity and ensuring that individuals are supported in the best way.

8 *Helping the speaker*: You can do this through the questioning and use of body language that are discussed in this chapter.

9 *Holding back*: Resist jumping in with your own views or interpretation of what the person is saying. This will disrupt their thinking and also make them think that you are not interested in them.

Small talk

Small talk can provide a way of identifying common ground or avoiding having to talk about intimate personal things straight away. It can be used as a tool in situations where initial contact is problematic. It should not be used in a careless way, but as a way of building a relationship with a person, enabling them to relax into the conversation perhaps, rather than feeling pressurised from the first contact.

It can be useful for individuals to be able to continue conversations that you have had with them previously so that it:

- establishes a bond
- makes them feel valued as you demonstrate your interest in what they have been doing
- provides more depth to the small talk that the person engages in

- is less likely to be repetitive of conversations they are having with others.

Humour

Use of humour can improve communication, but before you consider it as a communication tool in your work you may need to reflect on your ability to use it in your personal life.

Humour can be used:

- as a stimulus, to initiate dialogue
- as a response
- as a disposition, an approach to communication.
  (Chapman and Foot in Hargie, 1997, page 260)

Humour can be appropriate to reduce tension in a situation or to distract a person's focus on the negative side of a situation. It needs to be used only when the relationship and the context suit the use of humour. Where used inappropriately it can be interpreted as disrespectful. Being a care worker is about being a professional person who thinks about what they do, and how they do it. Never think, 'Oh that's just how I am, they will have to get used to me.' It may be you who needs to adapt.

Self-disclosure

Some service users may be seeking mutual self-disclosure. If you work in a care home or day service where you see the individuals on a daily basis and know what they are involved in, they may feel that it is part of usual conversation to ask, 'What are you up to at the weekend?' It may appear rude if you do not engage in conversation with someone about this. Talking about yourself can serve a useful purpose in helping to develop the rapport that you have with individuals. However, you do need to consider whose needs you are meeting when disclosing information about yourself to a service user. You have to be cautious, because discussing your own life can potentially affect the relationship in a negative way, if it:

- dominates the conversation
- affects the relationship with the service user
- becomes a distraction to the core tasks.

It is also important to remember that if you invite a person to be interested in what you are doing in your personal life then it may be difficult to withdraw this offer when it doesn't suit you for them to know.

Using a person's name will depend on your role with the individual. It is always best to ask the person how they would like to be referred to, as some people prefer to commence relationships more formally and then may invite you to call them by a different name. Differences in people's ideas about this may be influenced by their culture, age, and their perception of the relationship they have with you.

Metacommunication

Metacommunication refers to all the non-verbal behaviour which contributes to communication. We established at the beginning of this section that non-verbal communication plays the most significant part in the communication process. There are different ways of viewing this, either as a feature of personal characteristics or as a set of skills that individuals can develop and use. Whatever the origins of non-verbal communication, it is important to acknowledge that it is also a tool that can be used with people. The care worker's knowledge of a person's non-verbal communication will increase their ability to observe the subtleties of communication and to pick up significant messages.

Skilful use of non-verbal communication can also control the signals that you give to support your own communication. It can:

- assist speech, give emphasis to the attitude or emotions that we are expressing through speech; for example, saying 'I'm so pleased to see you', with a smile and a big hug
- replace speech, for example looking very displeased without saying anything. For some people speech is not an option in communication, either due to physical or cognitive impairment, or perhaps temporarily due to current emotions.

Paralanguage

This refers to all the communication that takes place other than the content of what is said or written. The physical and sensory ability of individuals needs to be taken into account when thinking about non-verbal communication. For example, a person who uses a wheelchair may be restricted in their control over proximity and the ability to use their posture to encourage warmth in the development of a relationship. They may need to rely on the verbal message more. A person who is deaf and uses British Sign Language may not pick up on the subtle emphasis of words that hearing people do. A person who has not lived in the UK all their life may not understand the historical references that are made in conversation, and the context of conversations that take place.

Body language

You are confronted by someone with their hands on hips or arms folded. What messages do these two images convey? As we have seen, only a small percentage of a message is actually conveyed through the spoken word. As we walk around, meet people and talk to them we are not always aware of our body language, we don't usually have to be.

Why do you think an understanding of body language is important to the work you do?

Care workers need to develop their awareness of body language for two reasons:

1 We need to understand how our own body language supports our ability to communicate with others.
2 We need to be able to interpret the body language of others.

Proxemics

This refers to the distance that we maintain when interacting with another person. Individuals have personal preferences about proximity that will be based on their culture, experience, and the relationship that they have with the person. There are social norms relating to how close we stand to people with whom we want to communicate according to:

● what our relationship is to them
● the context of the communication
● what the message is.

Some people may not be able to influence the distance that they have with other people during communication due to their physical mobility, or others may need support in identifying what is appropriate space due to learning needs.

Proximity is also a feature of different types of care. If you are involved in providing personal care then the people that you work with may have to accept very intimate physical contact and proximity with a range of people, which is untypical. Some service users have little personal control over proxemics; they may not like it when a new care worker stands physically close to them to introduce themselves, but because of their physical mobility they may not be able to move away or indicate unease with their body language.

Always:

● be sensitive to an individual's expectations of proximity that relates to cultural, generational or gender differences
● encourage service users to assume control over proximity, for example walking into a person's house and then asking, 'Where would you like me to sit?', rather than just assuming a position.

Posture

Posture is not something that we are always aware of, and people naturally have different ways of holding themselves. Be respectful when working with individuals, as your posture will be interpreted as part of the message. For example, some people would consider it insulting if you lounged in front of them rather than adopting a more formal posture.

Be aware of the posture of those that you work with. Changes in mobility or the commencement of pain can change the posture of a person, and it may be that some assistance or advice would prevent long-term posture issues.

Gestures

Gestures are very context specific; there are geographical variations as well as cultural.

With some people who have multiple communication needs, gestures may be a part of their intentional or unintentional communication. It is important for care workers to be receptive to gestures and to recognise communication in others, and not to dismiss messages.

Always:

● use gestures to reinforce what you want to say, and make sure they are not contradicting what you want to say
● use gestures that are familiar to the individual

- use gestures that are appropriate, especially if the person may choose to use them with other people.

Facial expressions

Have you ever been told 'It's written all over your face' when your verbal message is clearly at odds with how you are feeling? Some people are less able to control their facial expressions but may still be able to communicate. Have you ever smiled when you are not happy or pleased, or laughed when you really don't find the joke funny? We have learnt how to manipulate our facial expressions to convey the message that we want.

For people who communicate a range of emotions and needs through their facial expressions, continuity of care is very important. You need to keep accurate records so that the person's needs are met consistently. It is important not to diminish the significance of this.

Eye contact

People can sometimes avoid eye contact because they find it difficult to not betray how they are feeling with their eyes. People who have multiple communication needs may rely on eye contact to communicate. Eye contact can be a very personal aspect of communication – too little and you can appear rude or uninterested, too much and you can be accused of glaring. Eye contact can encourage communication in others, as it is a way of inviting a person to continue speaking.

Mirroring non-verbal behaviours

Copying the body language of the person that you are talking with can be used to establish rapport with an individual. It may also be possible to test whether rapport with an individual has been established by ceasing to copy them, and then seeing if the person starts mirroring your own behaviour. There can be a certain element of unease about this as you may feel that this is manipulative, and an abuse of your knowledge over the other person.

Appearance

You may work in an environment where you wear a uniform which means you have less to think about in terms of your appearance. Society tends to judge

people and make assumptions about them based on their appearance. You may need to consider the balance between expressing your own individuality, promoting an image consistent with the values of the organisation that you work for, and respecting the feelings of the person you are working with.

Dress and appearance are dependent on the context. Very formal dress may be impractical in a care environment where close personal care is provided. Appearance is influenced by and is a reflection of culture. Individuals you support may have their appearance affected by their current circumstances. For example, some clothes are easier to put on and take off, so the decision by the individual to wear a particular item may influence this. It is important to ensure that it is not the organisation or care worker selecting attire that the person does not like but that is easier for them to manage.

Having an awareness of these aspects of body language will enable you to:

- adjust your body language to support your communication more
- pick up on the subtle meanings in the communication of others.

> **REFLECT**
>
> Think about your current approach in each of the above areas and consider the needs of the individuals that you support in terms of the way that you should be communicating with them. Make a note of your strengths, and think about if there is anything you need to adjust.

Barriers to communication

At the beginning of this section (page 140) we looked at two scenarios where communication had been affected by internal factors relating to the communicator (the person receiving the message), or external factors outside either person's apparent control. Of course, communicating can be difficult. All of us will have had encounters with people where we feel that communication has not really taken place, either because we don't understand the other person, or the person has not understood us.

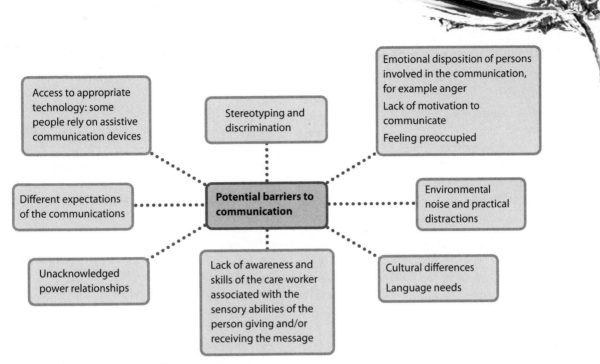

Figure 4.11 Some of the barriers that can affect communication

Distractions that impact on effective communication will include:

- Noise: it may be possible to reduce distracting noise by closing a door or window, or suggesting the communication takes place at a later time or in a different place.
- Thinking about something else: this will probably show in your body language! It usually means that the communication is going to be wasted, as you will not receive the full or even part of the message.
- Lack of interest in communicating: possibly due to personality differences or preoccupation with other issues.

Being proactive and acknowledging that there is a communication difficulty does not need to sound rude. Consider the following:

- 'I'm a little preoccupied with something else I have to sort out at the moment, could we talk about this later? You suggest a time.'
- 'I don't know about you but I can't concentrate in here. Shall we go somewhere else where there is less distraction?'
- 'I'm too anxious to discuss this now; can we talk about it tomorrow?'

In the last example it is the emotional state of the person that is potentially going to affect the communication; it is much better that the dialogue occurs at a later time.

Communication needs of individuals

The following is not a comprehensive list, but it outlines some suggestions regarding communication relating to individual needs.

1 Communication needs associated with English language skills

Don't:

- assume the person has little to say just because they can only say very little
- interrupt when the person is pausing to think of how to say what they are thinking or feeling
- rely on family members to interpret, as this is usually not appropriate
- avoid communicating with the person.

Do:

- access an interpreter
- access information in the person's own language
- make use of all messages that are being communicated to you: non-verbal communication etc.
- ensure your body language is encouraging for the person to communicate at the pace that they need to.

2 People who have a hearing impairment or who are deaf

Don't:

- all speak at once
- shout at the person
- make assumptions about how the person will be communicating or will need you to communicate
- talk loudly to the person about personal or confidential information when others are around.

Do:

- learn British Sign Language
- ensure that others who are communicating with the person are aware of the individual's needs
- be aware of lighting and the position of yourself in relation to windows – the individual will advise you about the best position
- face the person consistently
- speak a little slower than usual
- think before you speak – it is easier if you don't change your mind halfway through a sentence
- learn appropriate communication skills, and/or access interpreters
- access professional advice so that you can maximise communication opportunities.

3 People with visual impairments or who are blind

Don't:

- use body language (gestures etc.) that the person will not be able to access
- make reference to visual objects without using description that is meaningful.

Do:

- check with the person what you need to do to support communication with them
- introduce yourself and others as people enter/leave the room
- state names at the beginning of each communication until the person is familiar with everyone's voices.

4 People who have dual sensory impairment

Don't:

- assume that someone is not communicating just because you don't understand them
- exclude people from conversation

- talk about people without including them through your body language and use of language, be respectful.

Do:

- be aware of only using communication that is meaningful to the person
- use a total communication approach.

5 People whose behaviour is described as challenging

Don't:

- label the person as difficult to work with as this may contribute towards the problem
- contribute to the problem by being complacent about your own communication and behaviour
- ignore positive aspects of the person and their skills
- assume that all behaviour is part of the 'challenging behaviour'; some behaviour may be an indication of abuse, discomfort, unhappiness, being physically unwell or in pain.

Do:

- take responsibility for your role in the behaviour and review your communication methods and skills
- teach relaxation and a positive mental attitude through your own approach with the person
- encourage social skills
- communicate with others to ascertain patterns of behaviour
- communicate with the person to enable them to identify the causes of their feelings and behaviour
- access appropriate support for the individual.

REFLECT

What are the particular communication needs of the people that you support? Think about all aspects of communication and whether there are any areas of your own communication skills that you could improve.

Assistive technologies

'**Assistive technology** is any item, piece of equipment or system that is used to increase, maintain and improve the functional capabilities and independence of people with cognitive, physical or communication difficulties' (Audit Commission, 2004)

- Traditional examples, such as long-handled reachers, jar openers and bath seats, can make a task easier to perform. They are low tech, relatively cheap and low maintenance.
- Electronic devices provide a higher level of assistance, for example a stairlift for getting up and down stairs or a communication device to replace speech. Home automation falls within this category, with adaptations to programme lights on and off and to control other electrical devices such as the TV or use of the phone.
- Telecare is an example of modern assistive technology that increases the potential for independence. It uses the telephone network to provide a remote means of supervising and monitoring a person at home. This technology can give a person the confidence to live alone with the re-assurance that should things go wrong a system is in place that will initiate help, support and action.

(*Assistive Technology*, February 2004, from the Disabled Living Foundation)

Empowerment

Earlier we looked at the significance of power on relationships with service users. In this section we shall be looking at the tool of empowerment, and how care workers can support individuals to regain control in their own lives.

Empowerment is a broad concept that encompasses a range of ideas. It focuses on the idea that individuals who need support can frequently lack power and control over their lives. Care workers can develop skills to ensure that they are competent in working with the service users that they support in an empowering way.

Self-determinism

An empowerment model of working with people can lead them to self-determinism, whereby they have control over their own decisions and feel that they are shaping the course of their own lives in the same way that you and I are. Of course, we all have limitations on our freedom and our ability to control everything we do. Many people would not want to get ready to go to work on a Saturday night; but responsibilities to the care home, and the need to be paid at the end of the month dictate that they do.

Developing power and control in your life is not an easy process. People who come under the broad umbrella term of 'service users' may need to be supported in developing these skills and becoming more assertive, due to both their individual and their collective life history of not having access to such control and responsibilities. In an empowerment model of working with an individual, it is their definition of their needs that is significant.

The aims of empowerment can be achieved in different ways according to the setting and the needs of service users. You will need to consider the most effective techniques for ensuring that the people you support feel empowered. It is therefore useful to consider practices that potentially disempower. These might include the following:

- Asking for service users' opinions on existing services rather than encouraging innovative proposals for new provision.
- Use of a professional's agendas and professional jargon.
- Ignoring or minimising comments that individuals make about their care.
- Only allowing one person to represent others.
- Making individuals or groups an addition to the main agenda of a meeting, as any other business.

The positive ways you can help empower your clients might include these:

- Enable the service user to see themselves as an agent of change. You are not doing this for them; they are the pivotal part of this process.
- Help the service user to use the knowledge and skills that they already have.
- Help the service user to access professionals and to use their knowledge and skills.

- Help the service user to change the power dimension of the relationships that they are in through effective communication, assertiveness and so on.
- Involve service users in the evaluation of their experience of the service.

In supporting individuals in the self-empowering process it is necessary for professionals not to patronise service users and act as though they should remain dependent on them. Some disability rights organisations are critical of disability organisations that are not led by disabled people themselves. They want to challenge the assumption that change has to be led by professionals, and they can only be participants in this process. Individuals do not need to be rescued by professionals, and professionals need to acknowledge whether they are one of the obstacles that individuals face in assuming responsibility and control.

Solomon (1976, in Payne, 1991) discusses the idea that powerlessness is created through negative valuations. People become negatively valued through their membership of a stigmatised group and being labelled along with that group. Empowerment should therefore focus on working with an individual to reduce the powerlessness that is experienced.

Aims of empowerment

These are the aims of empowering service users:

- It is important for service users/patients to be active in the process of addressing their needs, not passive recipients of care services.
- Professionals should be seen as a resource for the service user to access.
- Professionals should be viewed as peers, adopting a partnership approach to working with service users.
- Service users should be able to acknowledge the power structure, but see that it can be influenced.

Principles of empowerment

The following four principles were identified by Solomon (1985) for Black empowerment, but they can be applied to other groups who are disempowered.

Enabling: Making sure the service user recognises what strengths and resources they have that are useful.

Linking: A professional may support a service user/patient in accessing support networks and making connections. This assumes that collective power can be gained by joining with others.

Catalysing: The resources and strengths that a service user or patient has may need an additional resource before they can become useful.

Priming: This principle aims to promote more positive relationships and interactions with organisations by individuals or professionals informing others of potential difficulties before they arise.

Figure 4.12 Principles of empowerment

Models of empowerment

Consumer model

This approach to empowerment sees people as consumers. Empowerment is developed through expanding the choices available to people. Dissatisfaction with services can be encouraged and acknowledged through complaints procedures.

Democratic model

This approach includes the role that individuals have in the development and organisation of services for them, rather than just a choice between services established by professionals. Information needs to be provided to people.

Neither of these **models** acknowledges the power issues that people who use care services face. Care service users experience substantial social exclusion and limited opportunities to participate in decisions that affect them. Sharkey stresses 'the desirability of collective empowerment strategies through involvement in self-help groups and community development'. (Sharkey *et al*, 2000, page 124) Although it is not just to do with individual activity, empowerment must be seen as *including* individual activity so that we as professionals take responsibility for our individual action to support empowerment. The idea that if you are not part of the solution then you are part of the problem seems pertinent.

The following is a cycle of empowerment.

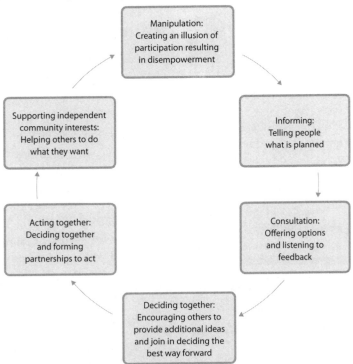

Figure 4.13 A cycle of empowerment (Barr et al, 1997, in Sharkey 2000, page 120)

This illustrates that sometimes we can think that we are empowering individuals when in fact our actions serve to perpetuate their circumstances.

O'Brien (1981) suggested that empowerment can come from the following sources:

- **Choice** Individuals need to have access to alternatives and real choices, not just options from a predetermined list. Acting on individual choice leads to a sense of control.
- **Competence** This relates to the development of skills that support an individual in their independence. Being able to do something reduces your need for others to be constantly supporting you. The development of skills should influence the role that professionals have with people.
- **Presence** We have discussed in other chapters that people who require support have often been excluded from society. Today children who are learning or physically disabled may attend schools alongside other children. Their presence is valuable in many ways, including that they feel part of society.
- **Participation** People who require the support of care/support services are often marginalised in their participation in society and sometimes excluded from active involvement.

REFLECT

Consider how each of the above aspects of empowerment relates to your place of work. Identify some of the issues, for example you may think that presence is affected by the mobility needs of a person. It would be important to acknowledge that legislation places the onus on organisations to address access issues and, by withdrawing service users from the physical environment, care workers may be colluding with society.

What steps can you take as an individual worker to ensure that you are promoting these principles?

- **Status** Society comprises different individuals who have a different level of power, control and respect from others. These influence their status in society. Older people, mental health service users and disabled people are not always respected by society or considered by others as being of any importance.

Assertiveness

This is a skill that is useful for you as a care worker and also for the individuals that you support.

The table below outlines the distinctions between being passive, assertive and aggressive.

Advocacy

Advocacy can facilitate empowerment of individuals and groups. The Alleged Lunatics Friends Society was set up in 1845. This might be considered one of the first examples of an advocacy group. Advocacy is a process that supports individuals in managing their lives and the decision-making process around them. It involves accessing information, negotiating decisions and protecting people from being exploited.

Principles of advocacy

There are different views on advocacy. Southgate (1995) identifies five activities within the process:

- **Nurturing** Supporting the person in their development, encouraging them.
- **Witnessing** Acknowledging what a person's experience is, recognising their circumstances.
- **Protesting** Registering dissatisfaction with a situation, making it clear that you or they are not happy with a set of circumstances.
- **Translating** Interpreting what is going on.
- **Supporting** Working alongside the person to achieve positive outcomes.

Passive	Assertive	Aggressive
Valuing others more than yourself	Valuing both yourself and others	Not recognising the importance of others
This leads to: accepting others' interpretation of a situation and others not knowing what you want	This leads to: discussion regarding an appropriate solution to differences	This leads to: only valuing your own interpretation of a situation

The skills required for advocacy include the following:

- **Listening** This means really hearing and accepting the other person's account of the situation, not adding your own view.
- **Informing** This may be just stating the facts about a situation, but in a manner and language that are meaningful to the person.
- **Encouraging** This involves developing the confidence of a person, motivating them to continue in a particular course of action.
- **Liaising** Identifying who is going to be a key to accessing the support the individual needs and then setting up situations for communication to take place.
- **Mediating** If communication does not happen in an effective way then it can mean that the advocate needs to identify strategies to enable communication to continue, by identifying common areas of discussion or possible routes to resolve a situation.
- **Negotiating** Some people have negotiation skills that are well-developed, perhaps because it is part of their job.

CASE STUDY

Using advocacy to support a service user

Nigel is an advocate for Julian. Julian has bi-polar affective disorder. His anxiety is exacerbated by situations in which he feels under pressure. Julian meets with Nigel in a local café, which he feels is neutral and relaxed. He does not like attending the day centre and wants to get back into employment. Julian has a formal review coming up where he will meet with a number of professionals. At the last meeting he felt overwhelmed and was unable to articulate what he wanted to say.

Questions

1 Identify how Nigel might support Julian by using the five tasks stated on page 152.
2 After you have considered these tasks think about how they may have an impact in your care work. Think about the skills that you have, or would need to develop in order to effectively engage in the process of advocacy with an individual.

- **Representing**: This should be working alongside the person, representing with rather than acting on behalf of.

Types of advocacy

The aim of advocacy is to develop the ability of a person to represent themselves effectively in any situation. This is a tall order for many of us, as different situations present different challenges. All of us sometimes depend on others for support and guidance. There are targets for the creation of more effective local authority partnerships with User Led Organisations (ULOs) to encourage more systematic involvement of service users. The English Advocacy Grant Scheme and local groups aim to help young people with a learning disability/difficulty who feel they do not have a voice. Advocacy comes in a number of forms, including:

Self-advocacy

An individual is able to represent themselves. This requires a number of skills. Self-advocacy should be the aim of people.

Self-advocacy may be carried out by one individual or by a collective of people who share some common characteristics, circumstances or aim.

Collective advocacy

People can provide support to each other in a group and convey the sense of feeling about an issue. This may enable a person to feel part of the norm.

A political or organisational framework may act against an unstructured system, i.e. a body of people that does not have a structure. There is dissatisfaction sometimes at the idea of two or three representatives attending larger meetings where the balance would remain with the organisation.

In theory the aims of all other forms of advocacy could be to promote advocacy by self as the main objective, however long-term that might be in reality.

People First and Mind are examples of organisations which represent individuals; the former is a learning disabled organisation and the latter is for mental health. A group approach can be a means of developing the self-advocacy skills of individuals; such groups can provide positive role models and motivation to aspire to.

Advocacy by relatives or friends

An individual is represented by a relative or friend. There may be a need to consider the extent to which a relative or friend can be objective about an individual service user and disregard their own interpretation of what that person needs or wants.

Peer advocacy

An individual who has shared a similar experience or is in similar circumstances may be a useful resource as an advocate. As well as the immediate practical support they can provide, they also can facilitate the development of skills to enable self-advocacy.

Citizen advocacy

This involves a one-to-one relationship, the development of a partnership. The advocate needs to be aware of the dynamics of power in the relationship and would need to acquire appropriate skills and to have access to the legal framework to ensure successful outcomes.

Professional advocacy

These are paid individuals, usually employed by an organisation to be an advocate for a person. They should always be independent of the relationships and organisations that are involved in providing care, so as to avoid a conflict of interest and ensure that the person is being provided with the most effective advocacy.

Cause advocacy

This type of advocacy may focus on a particular issue. It can draw people together who have different circumstances but who want to focus on a particular concern.

Legal advocacy

This may be a solicitor, barrister or advice worker who can focus on knowledge associated with, for example, benefits or discrimination. Such individuals have specialist knowledge of the law and the legal system in order to support and negotiate a person

through the complications of this. Some service providers such as social services or NHS Care Trusts may pay advocacy schemes to provide this type of advocacy on a contract basis. They may also pay independent consultants.

Advocacy for a sister

Faith lives with her sister and brother-in-law. Her sister is a carer for Faith, and has had an individual carer's assessment.

Marcia is an advocate for Faith. Marcia feels that being a Black British woman with a Caribbean background she is able to recognise some of the issues that Faith has, as they share a similar cultural heritage. Her aim is that Faith may not need an advocate in the future, that Faith will develop her ability to articulate her own needs, and handle disputes over decision-making in the home that could affect her detrimentally. Faith has benefited from Marcia's support as she now understands more the options that are available to her, including potentially moving out of her sister's home; previously she had not even considered this.

Formal advocates can be provided by organisations to support people. This can create tensions with staff who feel their position with the person is undermined. Advocacy is not about setting up power issues, but may expose existing ones that professionals may overlook.

REFLECT

1. If the individuals that you support have advocates consider the benefits that this brings to them.
2. In what ways could you promote this amongst other service users?
3. What are the benefits or advantages of each type of advocacy, and the potential limitations?
4. How could the service users that you support benefit from access to advocacy?

Bateman (2000) identifies some useful principles, which are described as a 'code of ethics for advocates in health and social care':

- Always act in the client's best interests.
- Always act in accordance with the client's wishes and instructions.
- Keep the client properly informed.
- Carry out instructions with diligence and competence.
- Act impartially and offer frank, independent advice.
- Maintain confidentiality.

(Bateman, 2000, page 63)

He also identifies that formal advocacy will involve:

- putting things in writing
- viewing an individual's problems as symptomatic of a wider malaise
- regarding it as positive to complain
- considering the role of publicity to change matters
- having a good understanding of the facts
- having a good understanding of any relevant technical, procedural or legal aspects.

(Bateman, 2000, page 107)

As with many features of care work, there are issues relating to advocacy. In the absence of formal advocates, care professionals may consider that they have an advocacy role. For example, in a care home a key worker may see that they support the particular interests of an individual in whole home decisions. Of course, care workers do welcome the employment of independent advocates and the consequent distancing of the advocacy role from the organisation. Decisions are taken in a context and care workers, despite the best of intentions, may find it difficult to think beyond what are the issues for the organisation as a whole. It can allow for broader thinking and discussions that are not limited by obstacles and foregone conclusions. A further caution is in ensuring that the growth of formal advocacy does not preclude the development of self-advocacy.

ACTIVITY

Investigate how you can access more resources to support the individuals with whom you work. If you have not worked with an advocacy service before, access a local one to identify how they could support individuals.

Working with significant others

Service users may have varied contacts with people; some of these relationships will overlap with the relationship that you establish with a service user. Service users may be involved in a variety of relationships with:

- parents
- children
- siblings
- friends
- neighbours
- volunteers/befrienders
- informal carers.

As well as those listed above, there are all the formal relationships that those you support have with all of your colleagues and other professionals in other organisations.

Recent policies have helped bring about a shift in the dynamics between parents and their adult children. For example, some parents of learning disabled people have had to get used to not being involved in decision-making about their son or daughter, or not having automatic access to information about them. This can be difficult for the parent to adapt to; they may have had years of feeling unsupported and feeling that they have had to make all the decisions for their child. Changes should be managed sensitively, by explaining in plain language the new requirements of policy and the aims of this in that it values their son or daughter's right to privacy.

Tensions can arise in this aspect of care work as some people may be used to having control over a relative. People may feel that they are acting in the best interests of the service user by trying to make decisions for them; but as the care worker you need to focus on the rights of the individual that you are commissioned to support.

Your relationships with individuals may be very task-focused, and we will now look at how focusing on relationships can facilitate the fulfilment of the care tasks that are required.

> **Caring for Carers**
>
> The Learning Disability Foundation investigated the experience of carers. Of parents who are caring for sons or daughters with learning disabilities:
>
> - 76 per cent suffer depression
> - 72 per cent lose sleep
> - 51 per cent have financial difficulties
> - 32 per cent experience trouble at work
> - 22 per cent have housing problems
> - 10 per cent suffer domestic violence.
>
> The study of 2,000 parents says nearly a quarter suffer four or more of the problems.

Ben Gray *et al* investigated tensions that arise in the application of confidentiality with their research with *Crossroads Caring for Carers*.

The protection and use of information in mental health is firmly rooted in ethics and professional codes, law and policy, as well as values and professional practice. While government initiatives have attempted to augment the role and rights of carers, policy guidance involving information sharing between professionals and carers has failed to deal with the practical dilemmas of patient confidentiality.

- Professional codes and training do not consider moral and ethical ground that stands between the service user's need for privacy and the carer's need for information.
- Policy and training guidance on confidentiality is scattered, ambiguous, confusing for professionals and inconsistent.

- There is uncertainty in practice about the information that professionals may share, and many professionals do not take into account carers' rights to basic information to help them care for service users.
- 'Confidentiality smokescreens' may sometimes lead to information being withheld from carers.
- Professionals sometimes find it easier and safer to say nothing.

Findings highlighted confidentiality 'smokescreens'. These created barriers that limited the effective use of information. For example, the inappropriate use of confidentiality reduced good risk management, did not help carers who were in crisis and also prevented the sharing of good practice across services. The research identifies the need for the training of professionals on confidentiality issues and the rights of carers.

- erect barriers that limit effective information sharing; issues involving confidentiality, risk management and carers in crisis
- examples of good practice
- need for the training of professionals on confidentiality issues and the rights of carers.

Supporting people

Having looked at some features of relationships with service users we turn now to the specific aspect of care that you provide. When you described the tasks that you carry out with service users you may have focused on one of the following areas: physical, emotional, intellectual or social support. Whichever

	Example of care tasks	**Other dimensions to these care tasks**
Physical	Assisting an older person with their mobility	Providing personal care in a way that supports the person's emotional well-being Communicating with the person to stimulate their interest
Social	Supporting a mental health service user to access community facilities	Empowering Providing practical support in new situations
Intellectual	Enabling a person with learning disabilities to manage their home budget	Facilitating the development of numeracy skills Coaching them to develop confidence
Emotional	Listening to a physically disabled person express their disappointment with recent news	Emotional support Encouraging contact with others for social support

service-user group you work with, people may need support across all these areas. A physically disabled person will have intellectual needs; a person with mental health problems will have social needs, etc.

In this section we focus on each of these areas. This chapter cannot provide a comprehensive guide to working with individuals in every aspect of care; however, it will raise some key points to consider and introduce some guidance on suitable approaches to fulfilling a range of care tasks with different service-user groups.

> ### West London Mental Health Trust SAGE
>
> A community arts group called SAGE was awarded a grant from the trust's charitable fund to enable paid posts in addition to the volunteers. The aim is to support the development of creative and talented individuals whose potential has been overshadowed by lack of opportunity due to ill-health and life's hardships. The project is structured to support an individual's potential and skills, many of whom may be isolated or displaced in society.
>
> The group meets each week on Saturdays at the ARK studio – an artist's space in Ealing.
>
> As well as exhibiting work SAGE runs a programme of events in partnership with the ARK.
>
> West London Mental Health Trust, *Mental Health Matters* 2008

Providing physical support

Sometimes people need physical support to undertake what we would describe as the usual daily tasks, such as getting up and dressed in the morning. This may be due to their

- physical strength
- mobility due to impairment
- manual dexterity
- hand–eye co-ordination.

Physical mobility

People may need support with their gross motor movements (large body movements by their limbs) or with manual dexterity (finer movements, such as

with the hands). There are a number of issues for us to keep in mind when supporting people in a practical physical way.

Touch

Providing physical care often means that you will need to touch people. Touch is a very personal dimension in any relationship and it has different purposes in different contexts. Think about the role that touch plays in the care relationship, and the amount and type of touch that you may experience in a usual day. For most people touch is controlled and appropriate to the amount that is desired, and it is provided only from those that it is wanted from. For example, you may hug a friend you have not seen for a while, but just greet other work colleagues politely after a break from seeing them. As we saw in the section on communication skills, touch may be used to express emotional connectedness. It can convey:

- support
- love
- sexual feelings
- anger.

In care work touch can be necessary for the care worker to support the person. It may be an essential component of the care task to physically touch or handle someone. If so, it is important to do this in a way that conveys respect for the person's personal space, to facilitate a sense of dignity and to ensure the person feels safe and secure, both physically and psychologically.

Pain and comfort

An individual's experience of pain cannot be measured accurately by someone else. Some people's mobility is affected negatively by pain. Pain management is a complex area and one where the care worker may need to access support from others. The role of the care worker can be to ensure the individual has access to professional help. There may be structured interventions and advice concerning posture or movement that can reduce a person's pain. Medication may not be the first choice of the individual, or the professional, but can be an option.

Care plans can ensure that an individual does not experience additional problems as a result of their current circumstances. It ensures that all people involved with the person are aware of what is important. An example is if the person's mobility has affected their movement in bed or when they are sitting still. The potential for developing pressure sores is great if care plans are not monitored and adhered to.

Individuals may suffer from acute pain due to localised trauma and chronic pain, which is long-term and may have an unidentifiable cause

Assisting with mobility and handling

As with the other physical care tasks it is important to empathise with the individual regarding how it feels to be physically moved around and to be limited in how you can adjust your position. The principles of moving and handling have developed as guidance regarding the safety of staff and the needs of people who require support has changed. Local authorities and independent providers are employers of care staff. As such they have the complex task of balancing service user care and support needs with preserving staff from injury. (Mandelstam, 2002, page 203)

Care staff should always adhere to organisational guidelines, as these will be based on legislation. The principles of moving and handling change according to legislation and good practice guidance regarding safe techniques. You need to communicate with the team and managers about potential issues in meeting the guidelines.

Mandelstam (2002) discusses the need for accurate and consistent interpretation of guidelines to ensure that risk is managed appropriately and that the person's rehabilitation and mobility needs are not compromised. As an employee it is important that any risk assessment with regard to manual handling involves you so that any limitations on you providing support due to your own health can be considered. You should always inform your manager if there is any reason why you are unable to carry out the tasks required of you. The phrase 'reasonably practicable' refers to the balancing of risk against the cost necessary to remove or reduce that risk.

Physiotherapists can provide sound advice and support for both the individual and care staff to ensure that a person is supported safely and in a manner which maximises opportunities for rehabilitation.

Using hoists is now a requirement to move individuals who are unable to manoeuvre in a safe way. Any piece of equipment can be a hazard if used inappropriately, so it is important to have proper training and to feel confident that you can use equipment. When using equipment it can be difficult to manage the safety of the service user whilst at the same time respecting and securing their dignity, but this should always be the aim.

The accountability of the care worker to a number of other parties can influence their relationship to the service user. It can be difficult if an individual prefers you not to use the hoist when you are required to, and you know that it is in your own and the service user's best interests to do so. The introduction of Direct Payments has implied that the employment of the care worker is the responsibility of the disabled or older individual. However, test cases have confirmed that the local authority is ultimately responsible as they are the initiating body in terms of assessment of need. If they are not satisfied that the monies from the Direct Payments system are being used in a way which meets the requirements of legislation then they can stop the payments (Mandelstam, 2002, page 100).

There has been criticism that the rigid interpretation of health and safety legislation has meant a negative impact on disabled people's lives. There remain unresolved tensions in this area.

Negligence is referred to where:

- there was a duty of care with the alleged perpetrator
- the duty was breached through carelessness or lack of reasonable competence
- the harm was directly caused by this breach of duty.

You can follow this basic guidance that requires you to:

- empathise with the individual; it is not always pleasant being handled by other people
- be clear about your responsibilities and follow care plans
- plan through the whole action before you start so that problems do not arise
- look after yourself
- use the equipment that is provided
- inform people when you anticipate difficulties

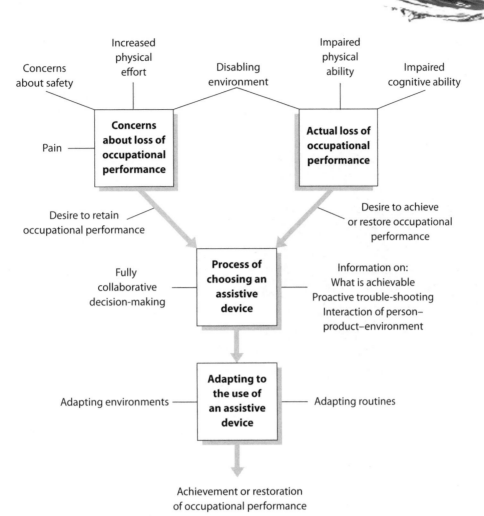

Figure 4.14 *Pathway to introducing an assistive device*

- keep up to date with guidance on techniques; these are what are referred to in court decisions.

Assisting people with daily living skills

The care task may involve supporting an individual in developing the capacity to manage independently in ordinary daily living skills. There is additional support for people in this area: occupational therapists provide expertise in identifying the skills a person could develop and provide strategies or assistive devices to support this development.

The pathway to introducing an assistive device is shown in Figure 4.14. (Pain *et al*, 2003, page 203)

The occupational therapist can work with the individual in order to maintain a person's occupational performance, or to rehabilitate a person to return to a previous level of functioning.

Many people need assistance if they have had a change in their ability due to ill-health or an accident.

Through the assessment of a care manager they can access the additional support of other professionals. If you work in home care you may be familiar with this process. It enables some people to stay in, or return to their own home. It is important that all care workers involved with the person know their role in supporting the rehabilitation of the person; the major changes over months cannot happen without the small daily progress.

Personal care

You may have had experience of someone looking after your personal care if you have had an accident or illness that has reduced your ability to self-manage. If you have not, then it would be worthwhile to think about what it would be like to need support in the areas of your life that are usually the most private.

It is important to understand what routine the individual desires with regard to their personal care. Individuals who are supported in the community may find that they are provided with care support at times not of their choosing; there is often little that the individual care worker can do to overcome this except to inform their managers, and to enable the person to manage the time as best they can.

It is essential to maintain an individual's sense of dignity and personal privacy

Some general principles would include:

- Encourage a sense of dignity in the person. An individual may say, 'Oh don't worry about closing the door', because they are either used to other staff members not worrying, or because they don't want to cause you too much trouble. We should encourage or re-instil self-respect in individuals. Only expose areas of the body as necessary.
- Prepare yourself properly – plan tasks all the way through to avoid any unnecessary interruptions to the task.
- Always encourage independence and responsibility, on whatever scale the individual can manage. If the person needs total physical support then this may be through asking them to make decisions about what they are going to wear etc.
- Communicate with the person throughout the task; make sure that it is clear that you are focused on them.
- Be aware of how the individual will be experiencing the situation, don't become complacent.
- Enable the person to take as much responsibility themselves as possible, position them so that they can see their clothes, or take out some clothes from the wardrobe for the person to decide, as it is often

difficult to choose without seeing. Let the person consider what they will be doing that day, and let them look out the window to see what the weather is like in case they want to go out.

- Think about whether there might be some aids to assist the individual in dressing independently.
- Consider how the environment supports or restricts the person's independence.
- Small physical adjustments to a person's physical environment and space can promote their independence.

Be aware that the person may need support in their personal care at other times during the day. If they have guests coming to see them, or they are doing a completely different activity, such as sports, then it may be appropriate for them to change their clothing.

Promoting continence

Continence is described as 'being able to pass urine or faeces voluntarily in a socially acceptable place.' (White in Swiatczak and Benson, 1995, page 67). For some people this is not possible, either as a temporary or chronic condition. There are various causes of incontinence, among them:

- changes in the physiology of the person that may affect their muscle control
- ill-health or infection that can affect the urinary tract or bladder
- emotions that can influence continence, for example anxiety or as a symptom of abuse.

The types of incontinence are:

- *Stress incontinence* This is where there is a leakage when the body exerts itself. The muscles and bladder can usually be strengthened through exercises.
- *Urge incontinence* Developing a pattern of rushing to the toilet and emptying the bladder frequently can soon become a habit, and then a problem. Such a pattern of behaviour can usually be adjusted through a programme of help.
- *Overflow incontinence* Continuous leakage, which could lead to infection and embarrassment. There may be a physical cause, which will require treatment.
- *Reflex incontinence* If the nervous system is damaged for any reason then it may stop monitoring the need to use the toilet and so the bladder empties without any warning message

passing to the brain. The timings of this may be monitored so that the person becomes more aware of when it is likely to occur, or continence aids may be required temporarily.

- *Functional incontinence* This is where there is no physiological cause of incontinence, but the capacity of the person to respond to the need to use the toilet is affected. It can help to make sure that the person is near to a toilet and that they are able to undo clothing easily.

Identifying the reasons for incontinence is vital to providing the correct intervention and support.

Incontinence can cause:

- embarrassment
- a feeling of unease or disgust
- an unwillingness to take part in social activities.

Support with continence is available from professionals. Continence advisers can provide valuable expertise in care homes or day services, with advice to other professionals as well as the individuals who are affected. Assurances about the availability of toilet facilities can encourage a person to resume social activities. Whenever you assist the person in visiting somewhere new make sure that they know exactly where the toilet is. Being able to talk about their feelings can help some people, whereas others simply do not want to talk about it. A person's age should not preclude them from developing skills to manage their own incontinence.

Hygiene and infection control

Hygiene and infection control are the responsibility of everyone involved in the care profession. The first point to consider is that we should respect the service user's own hygiene routine and how it is influenced by culture, religion or just personal preference. The care plan should indicate the approach that is required.

Your organisation will have specific guidelines it requires you to follow, depending on the care setting. These should be adhered to and you should inform your manager if there are issues to do with your ability to adhere to policy. The organisation is responsible for providing appropriate equipment such as gloves, aprons and hand-cleansing products, and you are responsible for making sure that you use them. Make sure that the people you support are

aware of the reasons for you doing things so that you are not compromised in your actions. This can be particularly true if you work in a person's own home. It is also important that you understand why you are required to do certain things. Knowing 'why' can enable you to fulfil the task appropriately. For example, putting on some disposable gloves at the beginning of the shift may be appropriate if you are about to support someone in their personal care. However, wandering around the care home providing personal care for four individuals, opening doors and cupboards before you take them off an hour later, is not addressing the hygiene issues, and you would be contributing to an infection problem.

Never underestimate the importance of hand washing. Hands are the primary transmitters of infection in any environment, and thorough hand washing can make a big contribution to improving the hygiene issue. Support the individuals that you work with in taking responsibility for hand washing as well.

CASE STUDY

The need for physical and personal care

Maureen has Parkinson's disease. She experiences difficulty in her physical construction of language due to dysarthria. This means she understands exactly what she wants to say but has difficulty in physically producing the words. She also needs support in many aspects of her physical and personal care, due to her lack of self-awareness and physical mobility. She lives on her own and support workers visit her three times each day.

Questions

1 Identify all the support needs that Maureen has.
2 What feelings might the individual have in relation to all aspects of their needs and abilities?
3 What skills would the care worker need in order to work effectively with Maureen?

Health Care Associated Infections that are acquired in hospitals and other care settings are known as nosocomial infections. They may originate due to their natural presence in a person's body. MRSA and

Clostridium Difficile are two examples that have been much publicised.

There are a number of strategies to deal with the management of infection control in a group care environment. Issues for hospitals are the high turnover of people entering and leaving the hospital and the varied range of health and infectious conditions that patients have. In a social care setting the issue is that it is less acceptable to maintain a clinically hygienic environment, for example in a setting that people want to call home.

- **Barrier infection control** This protects the environment and therefore other patients – not possible in a group care environment.
- **Personal Protective Equipment** – a generic name that is used to describe any equipment that aims to protect people in their working environment.
- **Cleaning** – is the process to eradicate a place of dirt whilst the disinfecting process aims to cleanse an area of any pathogenic micro-organisms and to protect it from their re-emergence. Budgets were set aside at the end of 2007 for the 'Deep Cleansing' of hospital wards so that the problem of antibiotic-resistant viruses was contained.

Hand washing and drying techniques are the key to maintaining a clean environment:

- use an alcohol gel
- rub palm to palm
- palms over back of other hands
- palm to palm fingers interlaced
- interlocked fingers together
- thumbs and wrists
- finger tips into palms of other hand

(ICNA, 2002, Adams, page 213)

This process becomes a waste of time if a commonly shared towel is used to dry hands! Dry hands are less prone to transmitting micro-organisms.

Meals

Supporting an individual with mealtimes may involve developing a working knowledge of the particular choices that they would make in respect of their culture. Eating a meal is often part of a social situation, and the aim should be that it is a pleasant experience, and should not be rushed or viewed as an obstacle in the day. The emphasis should be on promoting independence, making sure people have access to the cutlery and crockery that is going to

Thorough hand washing is essential to maintain hygiene and infection control

enable them to self-manage. This support and encouragement to develop skills needs to be consistent.

Where people need total physical assistance then they should be focused on and involved in the meal, by talking to them about what the meal is and other conversation that relates to them. It can be disrespectful to turn around, and get up and leave the table halfway through supporting a person with their meal.

If the consistency or texture of the food needs to be altered the individual may still want the different foods to be kept separate so that they can still taste the different ones rather than have a mixed-up meal.

People should be supported to have meals where they would like to, and to move to a different area, such as a dining room, if they choose. Decisions about where people eat should be made with the person involved, based on their choice, not the convenience of the organisation or individual care staff. If the food drips onto an individual's clothing this should be dealt with immediately rather than leaving the person with dirty clothes for the rest of the day. Some people may choose to wear an apron; these should be used appropriately and not left on throughout the day.

The cultural needs of an individual may dictate their choice of food, and when they eat. It should be recognised that a textbook guide to a religion may not represent each individual's preference. For example, in the Hindu faith some people will not eat meat or fish at all, whereas others do eat lamb, chicken or white fish. It is unusual for Hindus to eat pork or beef and some Hindus fast for one day each week. In the Islam faith pork or products of carnivorous animals are not usually eaten, and alcohol is not usually allowed. During the 30 days of Ramadan there may be a period of fasting for healthy adults.

CASE STUDY

Managing to entertain

Frank is a 57-year-old man who had a stroke 12 months ago. He lives at home with his wife who has been assessed as his carer. He used to enjoy entertaining people at home before his stroke, and it has taken him a while to develop his skills so that he can invite people to his home again without feeling embarrassed. He still doesn't like to eat in front of other people; he finds that he makes a mess when he eats and it doesn't do much for his self-image. He has always prided himself on his appearance and likes to look smart.

Questions

Imagine what feelings Frank has about his current situation.

1 If you were going to support him in his care needs what factors would be important to consider?
2 How do you think the changes in Frank's ability might have affected his wife?

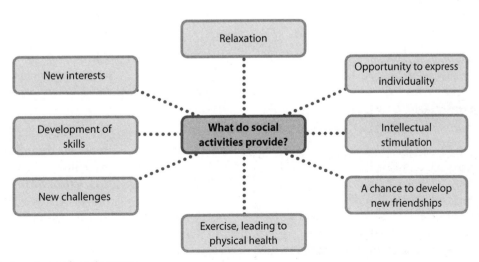

Figure 4.15 The importance of social activities

Providing social support

Social activities are usually an important part of life. For some people their dependence on others limits their potential for actively participating in a full range of social activities.

> 'Supporting and enabling friendships requires consistency, creativity and persistence, but can make a real contribution to personal quality of life and general well-being.'

This quote from the Foundation for People with Learning Disabilities can be applied to other service-user groups. It is clear that relationships and social activities are important in all of our lives.

Some people find they engage more in social contact with care workers or the people that they live with than they do with other people; they may have quite a closed circle of friendships. Some people also feel that whilst they participate in social activities that are the norm, or visit the same recreational facilities as others, they always do so in a segregated way, at a time allocated to them as a group. Leisure opportunities for people with learning disabilities are often segregated from usual activities that other members of the public engage in, but it is now recognised that they should:

- be responsive to the interests and wishes of the person and support real choice
- be available to all, including those individuals with high support needs
- offer practical help to enjoy the activities
- enable use of facilities in the same way as others
- be available evenings and weekends as well as day time as appropriate
- allow a choice of people to spend time with.

The emphasis is on individuals accessing community facilities in the same way that you or I may choose to.

REFLECT

Consider the social experiences of the people that you support. Identify how the social activities they engage in develop their skills or promote their well-being. Identify whether these could be extended, or whether you could improve the support you give people.

Social activities can provide us with valuable shared experiences and memories. Some of these may need to be recorded, so that a person's history is represented through photographs and other media that are meaningful to the person. The person should have control over these, and ultimately be able to destroy memories if they choose to. New hobbies can be a way of developing relationships between people, and widening the contacts that an individual has.

The National Minimum Standards for Older People and 18–65-year-olds specify the need for people to have access to a range of social activities in recognition of its importance as part of the function of care providers.

A sense of belonging

Suzanne is 28-years-old and has just started a cookery class at her local college. She likes attending the class because no one there knows that she has recently spent some time in hospital following a period of severe depression. She likes the conversations that she has there as they focus on how people are getting on with their cooking; she feels no pressure to talk to people about herself, and she has a sense of belonging. She has developed a friendship with Andy who attends the class. She feels relaxed in that environment with him but secretly hopes that she will develop the confidence to see him when the classes stop in six months.

Supporting people in sexual relationships

It is clear that many people with learning difficulties are not being supported to develop friendships and relationships, and even fewer are being supported to exercise their sexual rights. (Carson and Docherty in Race, 2002, page 151)

When it comes to supporting people in relationships, there needs to be an appropriate balance between the assessment of risk and the empowerment of individuals to take control of their own circumstances. Care workers need to work within legislation and be aware of the limitations of their own role. Ordinary life means that people sometimes make poor judgements and decisions that they later regret. Individuals have the right to make mistakes in their own lives, and care workers should not impose their own values, assumptions and judgements on others. People have a right to develop relationships whether they are an older person, have a cognitive impairment, mental health concerns or are physically disabled. The idea of risk is discussed in more detail in Chapter 7 on assessment. The role of the care worker is usually to ensure that people have access to appropriate advice, whether this is in the form of literature or professional health or counselling support. As a care worker you should not take on responsibilities that are outside your area of expertise.

Providing intellectual support

This chapter has emphasised the need to support people in a way that promotes their independence and ability to self-manage. This usually entails supporting them in learning how to do something or practising a new skill. Chapter 2 on reflective practice provides some guidance on the process of learning that we can consider in relation to supporting service users.

This section provides some additional factors to consider.

- The context of learning is important. Acquiring new skills may be required due to the sudden loss of ability, so it would be important to be aware of the emotional dimension to learning when the person is coming to terms with their loss of ability.
- Motivation can be a real driver to an individual's learning; this may influence the sequencing of learning that you initiate. Sometimes it may be useful for the person to independently finish the task that you have started with them, to give them a sense of achievement, and then to gradually withdraw the support earlier on in the task.
- The practice of over-learning produces reinforcement of a sense of achievement before moving on to the next stage, and it can enable a person to move towards independence in a particular skill.
- The principles of feedback include beginning and ending with positive comments. Any suggestions for development that focus on negative aspects of the skills should be included in the middle. The reason for this is that learning is closely associated with self-esteem and motivation.

Supporting an individual in their learning of skills should be based on the following.

- Plan interesting tasks that are meaningful and appropriate for the person. Break down the whole exercise into individual actions that need to be carried out. Identify the skills required to undertake each task.
- Provide short sessions at a length and pace to suit the individual. Think about the ability of the person, the skills that they currently have, and their ability to learn the new skills that are required.
- Access specialist support from psychologists, physiotherapists or occupational therapists to enable you and the person to develop an action plan.
- Set short-term targets that can be achieved and take small steps that provide early achievement and are rewarding and motivating. It sometimes works best for a person if they develop their independence in completing rather than starting the task, and then on the next occasion the support is gradually withdrawn at an earlier stage.
- Provide regular encouragement in a manner which suits the situation and is meaningful to the person. Learning often provides intrinsic rewards; a person may feel a deep sense of achievement when completing a new task.

Providing psychological and emotional support

We have already explored that there is an emotional dimension to most of the other areas of support. We will now focus on what emotional support entails and how we should provide it.

Psychological support requires an understanding of the needs of the individual and acknowledgement of the value of the person who is to receive appropriate support. Support should be tailored to the particular needs of the individual. At the beginning of the chapter we looked at some of the reasons why people need support, one of which was due to dementia. The table on page 169, describes some of the behaviours associated with dementia and suggested responses from care workers.

End of Life Care

Young *et al* investigated the quality and adequacy of care received at home in the last three months of life by people who died following a stroke; they used the Views of Informal Carers Evaluation of Services questionnaire to obtain their information.

Strokes are the third leading cause of death in the UK. The research explored the role of informal carers and the provision of community-based care in the last three months of life.

Family and friends helped:

- 82 per cent of deceased with household tasks
- 68 per cent with personal care
- 66 per cent with taking medication
- 54 per cent with night-time care.

Health and Social Services helped:

- 30 per cent with household tasks
- 54 per cent with personal care
- 20 per cent with taking medication
- 6 per cent with night-time care.

- Two-fifths (43 per cent) of informants had to give up work or make major life changes to care for the deceased.
- 26 per cent of informants found looking after them 'rewarding'.
- 51 per cent reported that help and support from health services were excellent or good compared to 38 per cent for social services.

The National Sentinel Stroke Audit (2007) has recommended increased community provision for stroke patients. The Gold Standards Framework's Prognostic Indicator Guidance is a tool currently advocated as part of the UK **End of Life Care** Strategy. It can assist GPs in identifying patients who are likely to die over the forthcoming 6–12 months. The criteria given for patients with stroke or dementia include:

- Urinary and faecal incontinence
- Barthel Activities of Daily Living (ADL) Index of less than three
- Reduced ability to perform ADL
- Cognitive impairment.

Sargent *et al* researched patient and carer perceptions of case management for long-term conditions, following the introduction of the 'community matron' role by the Department of Health, to provide case management to patients with highly complex long-term conditions.

Five categories of case management tasks emerged from the data:

- clinical care
- co-ordination of care
- education
- advocacy
- psychosocial support.

Psychosocial support was emphasised by both patients and carers, and was viewed as equally important to clinical care. The findings emphasise the importance of seeking patient and carer input when designing new case management programmes.

Mental health self-management

There are many different ways that people experiencing mental health problems can manage their own mental health. Self-management has another, more specific, meaning when it describes the way that people can learn to control long-term health problems. Increasing numbers of people with a physical health problem use self-management, many of them following the NHS Expert Patient Programme.

Similarly, service users can use the strategy to control serious mental health problems such as bipolar disorder or schizophrenia. Through self-management, many service users gain the confidence, skills and knowledge to better manage their mental health and gain more control of their lives at a time when they may feel they have lost control.

Self-management can have as positive an impact on mental health as medical treatment, enabling people to lead fuller, more active lives. Research has shown that it can help boost the self-esteem of people with bipolar disorder and lower the risk that they will contemplate suicide. It can help them to:

- recognise what triggers a crisis in their own mental health
- read the warning signs of a possible crisis
- identify if any particular actions can prevent a crisis developing
- figure out which coping strategies work best for them in a crisis
- tap into other sources of support like local groups for people experiencing similar distress
- build ongoing coping strategies into a mentally healthy lifestyle
- compile an action plan
- draw up an advance directive setting out how they would like to be treated if they ever lack the capacity to make decisions about their treatment in the future.

Arts therapies

The importance of creative expression to healthy human development and recovery from mental distress is well established across cultures. For people who have mental health problems, the arts therapies have specifically been developed to allow people to tap into their inner, creative resources while exploring personal issues in a safe, contained space with a trained arts therapist and a view to psychological change.

The Arts Therapies – (Art, Dance Movement, Drama and Music Therapy) – have their origins in early twentieth century psychiatry and its discovery of the unconscious. Some psychiatrists perceived that art tapped into unconscious processes and began to use it as a tool in their work. Arts Therapists in the UK work in a variety of settings and across the age and need spectrum. Work settings include: hospitals, mental health teams, social work, prisons, the voluntary and private sectors, and schools.

Electro-Convulsant Therapy (ECT)

This may be used with people with severe depression who have not responded to other forms of treatment. It may be used for those with a diagnosis of bipolar affective disorder (manic depression) or schizophrenia. The effects are based on theories rather than evidence, and there remain many controversies about its use:

- **Neurotransmitter theory:** changing the way brain receptors receive important mood-related chemicals as with anti-depressant medication.
- **Anti-convulsant theory:** inducing seizures teaches the brain to resist future seizures. This reduces abnormally active brain circuits and stabilises moods.
- **Neuroendocrine theory:** seizures cause the hypothalamus to release chemicals, such as neuropeptide, that create changes throughout the body.
- **Brain damage theory:** the shock damages the brain, causing memory loss and disorientation, creating a more positive illusion for the person
- **Psychological theory:**
  - depressed people often feel guilty, and the shock is accepted as punishment, which the person finds helpful.
  - ECT and the nursing care afterwards ensures that patients feel they are being taken seriously.

Complementary therapies

These may also be helpful and include the following:

- homeopathy
- aromatherapy
- reflexology
- herbal medicine
- nutritional therapy
- massage
- Ayurvedic medicine.

Medication

Drugs may be helpful as a short-term solution to enable individuals to overcome a crisis. Others may need ongoing, long-term treatment, enabling them to manage severe and persistent problems with their mental health. Some people are reluctant to take medication at all, and individual doctors also vary in how often they prescribe it.

Medication is categorised with:

- A **generic** name of a drug, for example nitrazepam. This describes the particular chemical family to which the drug belongs. Nitrazepam is the generic name for a drug used to treat insomnia. It is sold under trade names.
- A **trade** name, for example Mogadon. This is the brand name given to the drug by the company which manufactures it. Each company will have a different name for the same drug.

- The **chemical** group name, for example benzodiazepines. This describes the larger chemical family to which the drug belongs. For example, nitrazepam belongs to the family benzodiazepines which are used to treat insomnia and anxiety.

Most drugs used in the treatment of mental health problems fall into four main categories:

- anti-anxiety drugs
- anti-depressants
- anti-psychotics
- mood stabilisers.

Prescribing of medication is influenced by:

- Symptoms: most drugs are designed to treat particular problems or symptoms, for example anxiety or depression.
- Reaction to and sensitivity to a particular drug or class of drugs. Some drugs work better for some people than others and it may take some time to find the right medication and the right dose for you. Your doctor should monitor and review the drugs s/he prescribes for you, checking their usefulness in controlling symptoms and their side-effects.
- The side-effects or risks associated with a particular drug.
- Familiarity with or preference for the drug.
- Cost effectiveness of the drug.
- What the drug is designed to do.
- How long it will be before it takes effect.
- How long the drug needs to be taken for.
- If there are any precautions.
- Consideration of alternative interventions.

The purpose of the medication needs to be very clear to both the individual and those who care about them or formally advocate for them. Historically there has been much use of medication in health and social care settings as a means of managing the behaviour of a person; this is known as *chemical restraint* and it is considered unacceptable unless as part of a recognised and agreed care plan where a person may cause harm to themselves or others.

Skills related to counselling

Being a care worker does not entail taking on a counselling role with people; counselling is a specialised field of work that requires substantial training and the development of skills. However, parts of this knowledge and skill base can be useful for all care workers in their care or support role.

An important dimension of supporting individuals in their emotional well-being is to acknowledge and accept them as an individual. On page 259 we look at Maslow's hierarchy of need and the idea of 'self-actualisation', i.e. when people reach their potential in terms of their psychological identity. Individual interaction can go a long way in promoting this. By empowering an individual who is feeling very unworthy and unskilled it can inspire confidence and a sense of control.

Rogers (1961) identified that there is a difference between who a person is known as, i.e. their 'self', and their 'self-concept', or their perception of self. He proposed that relationships should have the following features:

1 *Unconditional positive regard* This is where a person is respected without any conditions or expectations on their behaviour. A person feels valued because of who they are rather than what they do, or what role they perform to others.
2 *Genuineness and congruence* The messages that a person with mental health concerns receives should confirm to them the support that you are providing in a way that is sincere.
3 *Empathy* provides a tool for supporting people in any situation. It can be particularly relevant to supporting a person's emotional well-being. Tilbury (2002) identifies the following 'axioms' of empathy in relation to supporting people experiencing mental ill-health:
   (a) Empathise with the sufferer's reality and the responses it generates. This means that you do not dismiss what the person says is their experience or how they are feeling.
   (b) Help the person to keep in touch with reality by focusing on general well-being, management of symptoms or creative self-expression. In order to promote well-being and an ability to self-manage it is important to support the person to focus on real situations and the practical issues in life that need to be managed.
   (c) Relate to the person not the symptoms. The symptoms of mental illness can sometimes distract others from who the person is, and the

Behaviour	Possible reasons	Suggested responses
Repetitive questioning	Short-term memory loss Anxiety or insecurity about ability to cope	Answer in a tactful way Distract with an exercise Leave the room for a while
Repetitive phrases or movements	Discomfort, due to thirst, hunger, heat or cold, constipation	Check that the person is not in discomfort Try to alleviate any boredom through stimulating activities Reassure the person
Repetitive behaviour	Behaviour may relate to previous occupation	Try to ascertain what the exercise relates to as a prompt for conversation Try to provide an exercise that will relieve any boredom that is similar to the behaviour the person is carrying out and uses the skills that they have
Trailing and checking	Memory loss means that a few moments may seem like hours Only feeling safe when in company of others	Don't be sharp with the person If you need to get on with a task away from the individual then keep talking to the person or sing as reassurance that you are still around Be aware of how draining this can be on you, the care worker
Shouting and screaming	Physical illness or pain Hallucinations Lonely or distressed Anxiety about failing memory	A night light Talk to the person about their past Stimulating occupation and engaging in activities together
Laughing and crying	Hallucinations Delusions Brain damage due to dementia	Reassuring the person Some people may prefer these episodes to be ignored
Lack of inhibition	Failing memory General confusion May be due to specific brain damage	Remain calm and respond in a reassuring way Take them somewhere private and ask about the need for the toilet Distract the person, provide something for them to be involved in with their hands
Pacing up and down	Discomfort, pain, hunger, thirst, constipation Wanting to use the toilet Feeling ill Side-effects of medication Boredom or excess energy	Find appropriate activities and exercise that the person can engage in They may like a quieter room Ensure that the person, and others, are safe if the pacing continues Offer snacks and drinks to encourage regular rest from pacing Offer different environments to pace in (garden?)
Fidgeting	Need for more exercise Discomfort Boredom Damage to a person's brain	Try to find the reason for feeling upset Distract with an interesting exercise Provide some objects for the person to fidget with
Hiding objects or losing them	Insecurity may lead the person to hide objects so that they are safe, or can be found later (for example, food)	Make sure important objects/documents are not accessible for the person to hide/lose Have spare keys Make a note of hiding places that the person uses so that you can support them in future to find things Be aware of food that may be hidden
Suspicion	Fear and insecurity Inability to recognise people Failing memory The person trying to make sense of what has been happening	Try to avoid arguing or distressful conversation State what you know to be true in a calm manner Be aware that there may be some truth in the person's statements, and do not dismiss them automatically

Suggested Appropriate Responses to Individuals (taken from The Alzheimer's Society website) hope that at some point the symptoms will no longer exist.

(d) Promote the person's skills to manage themselves and their lives so as to:

(i) prevent any loss of skills

(ii) reinforce skills that could diminish

(iii) compensate for lost skills by reviving others

(iv) renew skills that promote self-sufficiency.

It is not always appropriate or necessary to medicalise some mental health conditions; all of us can experience changes in our mental health. Where a person is receiving structured intervention through care management or the care programme approach, it would be important for the support worker to ascertain exactly what their individual role is and how they can promote the mental health of the individual through the tasks that they perform with that person. In Chapter 2 we look at the function of care tasks.

An important step would be to understand the treatment that a person is receiving. Interventions that are available to support people include:

- **Talking treatments** This group of interventions includes both short-term counselling and long-term psychotherapy. The emphasis is on exploring the cause of the current mental health problem with the individual in order to promote change and an ability to cope. There are different models of therapy based on the schools of thought that the therapist is working to.
- **Physical or physiological treatments** These include:

1 *Medical intervention* Whilst not commonly used, electro-convulsive therapy is still a recognised form of treatment by the medical profession. It produces an electrical stimulus through the nervous system, which can induce an epileptic seizure and create a desired change in the individual.

2 *Medication* Some drugs are prescribed in order to affect the chemical balances in the brain. They may induce sedation, or act as a stimulant, depending on the diagnosed need of the individual.

An emphasis in supporting people with mental health problems today involves recognition of self-management techniques, so that the support people are provided with does not take away any independence that they could develop. Mental ill-health creates an unresourceful state for the person; any intervention should aim to facilitate a return to resourcefulness rather than creating dependency on any intervention regimes.

Care workers need to ascertain the role they play in supporting individuals to manage change. They will need to acknowledge that people may experience transitions themselves as intervention progresses through different stages. Information about the type of intervention can enable the care worker to be more understanding of changes and developments.

Managing yourself in a relationship

Boundaries

Remember that whether you are a volunteer or salaried employee, you are part of an organisation. Your role with the service user provides a function that has been identified, usually through an assessment.

If you ever feel that your relationship with a service user is compromising your role, either due to its closeness or negative feelings, then it is important that you seek advice from a line manager immediately.

Stress

Any job that involves working with people can be stressful, and care work is no exception. Even if the environment is pleasant and working relations are good, there can be an emotional cost to supporting people if we do not access support ourselves.

Stress can be evident through physical symptoms such as:

- backache
- other muscular strains
- tiredness
- regular ill-health.

Other symptoms include:

- inability to concentrate or listen to others
- making regular mistakes
- snapping at people uncharacteristically.

We are all individuals and need to find our own ways of managing stress at work. Some suggestions include:

- anticipating tricky situations and planning support
- recognising stress in yourself, both physical and psychological symptoms
- not bottling things up – be prepared to talk to others
- reflecting on work in a constructive way.

ACTIVITY

Think about a typical day that you have at work. Write down the areas of work that you find most challenging. It may be work with a particular individual, or it may be a routine activity that you do with everyone. Think about strategies to develop this area of work so that it becomes less of a challenge and you feel more capable in undertaking this task effectively.

Glossary

Carers: broadly describes all those involved in supporting individuals but is mostly used for the diverse group of people who provide unpaid practical support to family members.

Daily living skills: the tasks that we all need to carry out in a typical day.

Cognitive: intellectual aspects including memory, concentration, knowledge, learning.

Empowerment: the process of a person, or group, claiming control over their lives and the factors that affect them.

KNOWLEDGE CHECK

1 What are some of the causes of the following:
   a Learning Disability
   b Mental Health Issues
   c Physical Disability
2 What are the key features of empowerment and advocacy and how can you utilise them in your own practice?
3 What are the barriers to effective communication and how can you improve your own strategies to communicate with people?
4 What role do assistive technologies have in addressing the practical support needs of individuals?
5 What role do you have in infection control and ensuring good practice in relation to all aspects of hygiene?

End of Life Care: also known as palliative care. This is the specialist range of support provided to individuals and families when a person's prognosis suggests that they will die in the foreseeable future.

Healthcare Associated Infections: conditions that developed during a period in hospital (e.g. a patient having surgery developing MRSA during their stay).

Models: in academic and professional life a model is a way of looking at a particular aspect of practice; they can inform the way that we work but giving us a strategy for interacting with people.

Principles: these are a combination of ideas, often relating to thoughts and emotions. These ideas will underpin the activities that an organisation or its employees carry out.

Rehabilitation: the process of overcoming a change in circumstances or adapting in order to manage a new situation.

Support: this word is used as an umbrella term to cover all the roles and activities that happen in health and social care work.

References

Barr, A., Drysdale, J. and Henderson, P. (1997) in Sharkey, P. (2000) *The Essentials of Community Care: A Guide for Practitioners*, Basingstoke, Macmillan

Bateman, N. (2000) *Advocacy Skills for Health and Social Care Professionals*, London, Jessica Kingsley

Braye, S. and Preston-Shoot, M. (1995) *Empowering Practice in Health and Social Care*, Buckingham, Open University Press

Disabled Living Foundation (2008) *Choosing Equipment to Maintain Safety and Independence at Home (introducing telecare) Fact Sheet 2008* (Audit Commission quote 2004 is from page 5 of this fact sheet)

Gray, B. *et al* (1981) *Crossroads Caring for Carers*

Hargie, O. (ed.) (1997) *A Handbook of Communication Skills*, New York, Routledge

Hayes, N. (1998) *Foundation of Psychology: an Introductory Text*, Surrey, Nelson

Infection Control Nurses Association, Morris, R., Hand Hygiene in Infection Prevention and Control in Adams, R. (ed.) (2007) *Foundations of Health and Social Care*, Basingstoke: Palgrave Macmillan

Mandelstam, M. (2002) *Manual Handling in Health and Social Care*, London, Jessica Kingsley

O'Brien, J. (1981) *Learning from Citizen Advocacy Programmes*, Georgia Advocacy Office, Georgia, USA

Payne, M. (1991) *Modern Social Work Theory*, Basingstoke, Macmillan

Pedler, M. *et al* (2001) *A Manager's Guide to Self-Development*, Maidenhead, McGraw-Hill

Poindexter, C. *et al* (1998) *Essential Skills for Human Services*, Brooks Cole

Race, D. (ed.) (2002) *Learning Disability: A Social Approach*, London, Routledge

Rogers, C. (1961) *On Becoming A Person*, Boston, Houghton Mifflin

Solomon, B. (1985) *How do we really empower families? New strategies for social work practitioners*, Family Resource Coalition report

Southgate, J. (1995) quoted in Brandon, D. (1995) *Advocacy: Power to People with Disabilities*, Venture Press

Staunton, N. (2003) *Mastering Communication*, Basingstoke, Macmillan

Tilbury. (2002) *Working with Mental Illness: A Community Approach*, Basingstoke, Macmillan

White, H. in Swiatczak, L. and Benson, S. (1995) *The Handbook for Hospital Care Assistants and Support Workers*, London, Hawker Publications

Useful websites

Disabilities Trust: www.disabilities-trust.org.uk

Kings Fund (for research and Government Commissioned Reports): www.kingsfund.org.uk

National Care Forum: www.nationalcareforum.org.uk

National Carers Network: www.carersuk.org.uk

CHAPTER 5

Managing for quality

Introduction

Management activity has always been important in health and social care work as organisations deliver care and support services as businesses. Increasingly, management ethos that is valued in other business areas has been applied to the public sector. This chapter is not just for those with the title 'manager' or 'supervisor' in their job description, it will also be of interest in considering how organisations are managed and how you manage yourself and your working relationships. If you are studying towards a Level 4 NVQ, the Registered Managers' Award or a Foundation Degree there is likely to be an element of learning relating to management in your qualification, and this chapter aims to broaden your knowledge on this.

So, what is management?

Strategic management refers to the setting up of organisational structures, establishing policies and securing finances.

Operational management relates to the everyday procedures and practices that deliver the business of the organisation, and this includes daily care activities.

Drucker summarises the activities that a manager engages in:

- setting **objectives**
- organisation of daily activities
- **motivation** and communication in order to create a team
- measurement of performance of individuals and the organisation
- development of people in the organisation.

This chapter takes you through the following:

- reflection on current skills
- managing yourself
- managing people
- managing communication and information
- managing other resources
- managing health and social care activities
- managing quality
- managing change.

Reflection on current skills

Management skills do not all come naturally to people and there is a great value in trying things out and practising skills. As with any other skill, management skills can be learnt and developed. Whatever level of management or supervision you are involved in, it is useful to think about the existing skills that you have; the importance of reflecting and adapting your practice should never be underestimated. This sets a standard as a role model that your own performance is reflected upon and you can change according to the organisation and team's needs. Being reflective also allows you to change your behaviour and not fall into a pattern of responding to situations in the same way.

It will be a useful reflection activity to re-consider each of these areas at different points in your career.

There are ideas about how it is best to manage organisations and the people employed by them, and we draw on advice from health and social care organisations as well as management theory generally throughout this chapter.

Managing yourself

Sometimes the most difficult person to manage may be yourself; it is too easy to adopt patterns of behaviour which we simply accept and then we do not try to change. Learning to understand yourself as a manager can help you to become a reflective person, who is capable of adapting and improving their own performance. With all the people and activities that you need to manage it may seem odd to have a section on managing yourself; but as a reflective practitioner it is important to consider to what extent you are making your management role harder and how you could help yourself more. Management activity is based on a set of skills, some of which will need developing more than others.

Think back to how and indeed why you became a manager. Not many people dream of becoming a manager when they first start to think about a career; maybe you have focused on career progression since you first started work in care work or maybe you feel that you have become a manager by accident as you have been given new opportunities. Expectations of managers to be able to deliver consistently are usually high. In order to do this, you may need to accept at

ACTIVITY

Before you start this chapter, read and think about the statements in the table below then make your own assessment of how well you undertake each aspect of management activity.

For each activity is it:

1 A great strength
2 More a strength than a weakness
3 Neither a strength nor a weakness
4 More a weakness than a strength
5 A real weakness?

	1	2	3	4	5
1. Excellent organisational skills					
Prioritises work effectively					
Sets clear targets for self and staff					
Effective at managing projects					
Keeps good records					
Able to use information effectively					
Delegates work effectively					
Keeps a clear desk					
Manages routine communication effectively					
Completes tasks consistently					
Meets deadlines consistently					

2. Inspired leadership					
Able to create a shared vision among staff					
Keeps team focused					
Motivates staff					
Encourages initiative in staff					
Leads by example					
An effective decision maker					
Always accountable for actions					
3. Effective forward planning					
Meets strategic and operational targets consistently					
Has effective processes and procedures to ensure actions are implemented					
Is effective at devising individual work plans for staff to meet operational and strategic targets					
Is effective at monitoring progress and evaluating and reviewing targets					
4. Clear, consistent and supportive approach to managing people					
Has a clear , consistent and supportive approach to staff					
Is effective at developing staff					
Treats staff fairly and equitably					
Supports individuals					
Sets a good example to others					
Carries out effective support and supervision					
5. Meaningful and effective communication					
Has sensitive inter-personal skills					
Involves staff in decision-making					
Has good negotiating skills					
Listens to groups and individuals					
Communicates clearly and in a jargon-free manner					
Is accessible to staff					
6. Clear understanding of funding with effective management of budgets and resources					
Sets and keeps to budget effectively					
Maintains good financial control					
Maximises the use of available resources					
Understands funding mechanisms					
Gains value for money					
Has a good understanding of financial systems					
7. Building, maintaining and supporting effective teams					
Is skilled at team building					
Encourages team spirit and commitment					
Sets clear targets for the team					
Encourages the sharing of experience and expertise					
Encourages involvement and initiative					
Is a good team member					
8. Personal qualities					
Maintains high standards of honesty and fairness					
Manages time effectively					
Is efficient at work					
Knows own limits					

times that the way you are currently working may not be the best way and that you need to change your approach. Letting your colleagues or team realise that you are prepared to review your style of working to suit different people and different situations shows that you are a thinking person and reflective about your work.

Creativity is the key to success as a manager; Mullins describes it as 'the application of imaginative thought which results in innovative solutions to many problems' (Mullins, 2002, page 372)

Let us return to the themes of management that Drucker identified and apply this to practice:

- setting objectives
- organisation of daily activities
- motivation and communication in order to create a team
- measurement of performance of individuals and the organisation
- development of people in the organisation.

Managing time

Many people cite time management as an area which they would like to improve. There may be different issues involved here, including the following:

- **Taking too long to complete a task**. Why is it that you spend too long on things? Is it because you have a sense of aspiring to perfection, which is usually unrealised or does not actually exist for that task? If you have a tendency to spend too long on some tasks then set yourself a time limit for these and stick to it.

CASE STUDY

Inspection for Jenny

Jenny manages a care home for eight older people, with one new person moving in tomorrow. Most of the staff are part-time; she has 16 care staff, two cooks, three cleaners and a gardener. The new person is blind; no one in the team has worked with someone who is blind before. One member of the team is returning from a long period of sickness absence this afternoon. Jenny arrives at the care home on Monday morning and the first letter she opens informs her of an announced inspection in three weeks.

Let us think about Jenny's role and what activities she is going to be engaged in during her day.

Jenny's activities	Setting objectives	
	Management tasks	
Jenny thinks about how to communicate news of the inspection to the whole team and how she will encourage everyone to work effectively in preparation for it	Motivation and communication in order to create a team	
Jenny meets with the member of staff returning to work and sets her objectives for the first week back in a supportive way	Measurement of performance of individuals and the organisation	
Jenny ensures that preparations have been made for the new person arriving. She has allocated a keyworker who has had substantial specialist training on working with someone who is blind, and made sure all staff have had other training.	Development of people in the organisation	

- **Procrastination** 'Don't put off to tomorrow what you can leave until the day after.' If this is your way of organising your time then you are definitely guilty of procrastination! What you should be saying to yourself is, 'Don't put off until tomorrow what you can do today.' It is not easy to change our patterns of behaviour and controlling procrastination requires a combination of both attitude and technique.

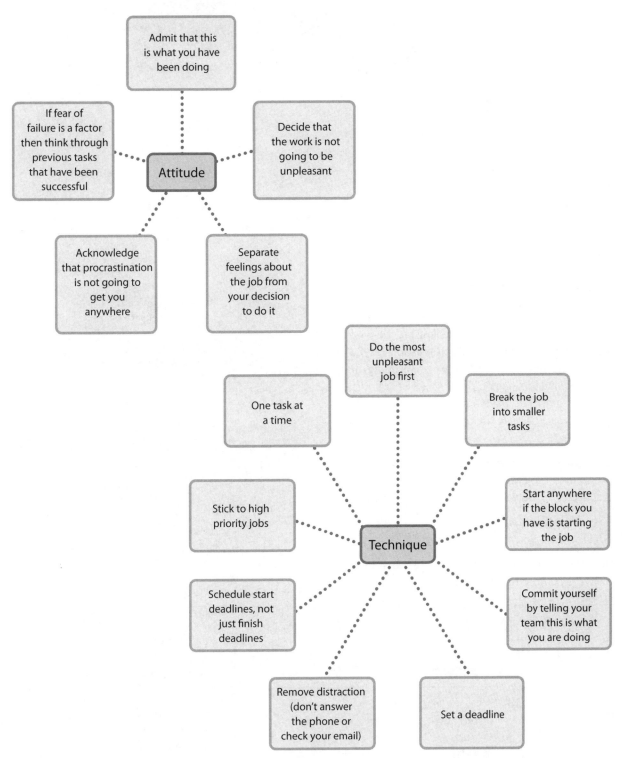

Figure 5.1 Attitude and technique are both important to change behaviour

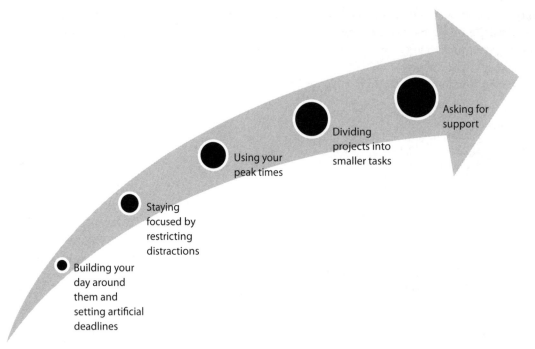

Figure 5.2 *Stay focused to keep on top of important tasks*

Prioritising tasks

This can help in the management of your own time. The key to prioritising lies in recognising the significance of individual tasks. It is all too easy to respond promptly to tasks that we enjoy doing, and then to spend too long on them. Ways of organising your day more effectively include dealing with activities according to the impact they will have on your role.

High pay-off activities: Make a conscious commitment to dealing with your time and activities. Then reward yourself when the tasks are complete.

Low pay-off activities: These must be dealt with but not always by you or straight away.

Other people will want you to prioritise their tasks, of course. You need to feel confident about

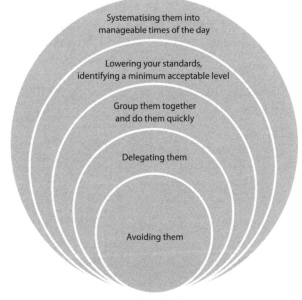

Figure 5.3 *Dealing with less important tasks*

1st Task - Do this first **Urgent** **and** **important**	2nd task - Then do this **Urgent** **but** **not important**
3rd task - This one can wait a bit **Important** **but** **not urgent**	4th task - Leave this one until last **Neither** **urgent nor important**

communicating your own priorities while accommodating the demands of others when appropriate. Communicate your own priorities to those around you who do make demands that in your judgement can wait. If a member of the nightstaff phones in unwell then your priority is to ensure that this is covered – other things have to wait.

If you are working on something that is both important and urgent then make it clear to your team so that they leave you to get on with it. Use your body language to indicate that you cannot give them your full time if they do interrupt, and make your first response, 'Can these wait until later?', 'Is there a colleague who can support you with this?' or 'Can you deal with this yourself?' If your team always relies on you as a first point of call it is not functioning effectively and is too dependent on you.

Delegation

This is where a task is passed on to a colleague. Remember that it does not necessarily need to be to someone that you manage – it can be passed to another colleague or your own manager. Sometimes we find it difficult to delegate:

- It is important to understand why you may have difficulties in allowing members of the team to carry out tasks. Perhaps you do not think other people can do the job as well as you. But they will not have a chance to try if you do not give them opportunities to develop new skills.
- Maybe there is concern about taking a risk or not being able to measure the impact. Ensure that you provide full instruction and information to equip the person with the best possible chance of being able to carry out the task well. Be available for support or set up someone else as a support. Prepare to be surprised – your team may do things differently from and better than you.
- For some activities it may seem quicker to do it yourself. This may be true on this occasion but the idea is that a team member will assume responsibility for the task and do it quicker (if quicker is better!) next time. Think of time you spend explaining as an investment.
- Finally, your role is to develop your team and **delegation** is a key strategy for this. Your job is to support them to develop. You could be depriving people of their job role and de-skilling them. Team members like to be challenged and find it stimulating to try new tasks that initially are a bit out of their reach.

ACTIVITY

Decide whether the following tasks are urgent and important and place them in order of priority.

Task	Urgent	Important	Estimated time	Order?
1 Setting a date so that letters for the next relatives' meeting can be sent			10 minutes	
2 Nicole has been late on the last three mornings and has asked her colleagues to let her leave early every day			45 minutes	
3 Seeing Claudia (93-year-old resident) who returned from hospital this morning			5 minutes	

Task 1: Once you have set the date with others, could the rest of the task be completely delegated?

Task 2: Not dealing with this issue will send a poor message to both Nicole and the rest of the team. It is creating frustrations that she is taking advantage of them.

Task 3: You know your team is taking care of Claudia but how will she and the staff feel if you show no interest in her welfare?

Remember that the idea is that all the tasks get completed. If a date for the relatives' meeting is not set and letters do not go out then this will eventually become urgent, or issues will arise that take up more time because there has not been that level of communication.

A further column should also be added which considers the extent to which a task must be completed by you or whether it can be delegated.

Managing your emotions

Being a manager means that you have a responsibility to your team to manage your own emotions, which is not the same as denying that you have any emotions. Understanding how and why you respond to individuals in your team in a particular way can help you to communicate more effectively with them. Some team members will prompt certain emotions in you and understanding this will enable you to manage to good effect. Communicate with her or him about what aspects of your working relationship work really well, and also what aspects are not **effective**. Every member of your team will have a different personality, different drives and motivations, and different personal issues that they may find difficult to leave at home.

You need to find a way of bringing out the best in each person. Do not see difficulties as an obstacle; try to think of them as a chance to develop your management skills further. There is much literature on emotional intelligence (Goleman, 1995) and how this can make a difference in the workplace. Personality has an influence on your own management style and also on the individuals within your team. One dimension to this is what motivates individuals in their job.

Goleman, with the Hay Group, developed the following model of competencies:

Personal competence: these competencies determine how we manage ourselves.

1 **Self-awareness**: knowing one's internal states, preferences, resources and intuitions.
2 **Emotional self-awareness**: recognising one's emotions and their effects.
3 **Accurate self-assessment**: knowing one's strengths and limits.
4 **Self-confidence**: a strong sense of one's self-worth and capabilities.
5 **Self-management**: managing one's internal states, impulses and resources.
6 **Self-control**: keeping disruptive emotions and impulses in check.
7 **Trustworthiness**: maintaining standards of honesty and integrity.
8 **Conscientiousness**: taking responsibility for personal performance.
9 **Adaptability**: flexibility in handling change.

10 **Achievement-orientation**: striving to improve or meeting a standard of excellence.
11 **Initiative**: readiness to act on opportunities.

Social competence: these competencies determine how we handle relationships.

1 **Social awareness**: awareness of the feelings, needs and concerns of others.
2 **Empathy**: sensing others' feelings and perspectives, and taking an active interest in their concerns.
3 **Organisational awareness**: reading a group's emotional currents and power relationships.
4 **Service orientation**: anticipating, recognising and meeting customers' needs.
5 **Social skills**: adeptness at inducing desirable responses in others.
6 **Developing others**: sensing others' developmental needs and bolstering their abilities.
7 **Leadership**: inspiring and guiding individuals and groups.
8 **Influence**: wielding effective tactics for persuasion.
9 **Communication**: listening openly and sending convincing messages.
10 **Change catalyst**: initiating or managing change.
11 **Conflict management**: negotiating and resolving disagreements.
12 **Building bonds**: nurturing instrumental relationships.
13 **Teamwork and collaboration**: working with others toward shared goals. Creating group synergy in pursuing collective goals.

Understanding yourself will enable you to understand better the individuals with whom you work. If you are in a management role then thinking about the motivations of those who you work with may increase your knowledge of how to support them.

Motivation theory suggests that the link between motivation and performance is usually a positive one but that there are varied reasons behind people's motivation; it is useful for us to understand these.

The table below shows some different motivational drives.

Motivational drive	
Achievement	When accomplishment is important, the need to finish a task well
Affiliation	Social interests are important, loyalty to the organisation and the team
Competence	A person has a drive to be good at what they do
Power	If a person is motivated by an interest in changing things and influencing others

Knowing how to manage your own emotions can equip you with the personal skills to manage your role better. Being a manager can at times be a lonely job and you need to find out what internal resources you can draw on at times when you need them most.

Managing your manager

Just as you are not perfect, neither will your manager be; this does not mean that you are *not* a good manager and neither does this mean that they are not a good manager. It will help you if you communicate well with your manager, respect the pressures that they have on their time while also being clear about the aspects of the job that you need most support with. There are likely to be differences in the styles of working that you have and this has the potential to create unnecessary conflict.

Stress

Most management activity involves some aspects of **stress** and developing strategies to manage this in yourself will enable you to recognise and manage it in other people. Stress is often described in a negative way but it need not be like this. Being in a stressful situation can prompt the most creative of responses and for some people pressure adds to their ability to meet deadlines and manage situations.

Cooper identified the following major sources of stress at work (Mullins 2002, page 318)

Source of stress	Related to
Intrinsic to the job	Limited resources, shift work
Role in the organisation	Too much or too little to do
Relationships at work	Especially with line manager
Career development	Concern regarding future

Source of stress	Related to
Organisational structure and climate	Any constraints due to rules and regulations
Home-work interface	Pressures and conflicting demands

As a manager you need to recognise when you are feeling stressed as others certainly will do and it is important that you manage your stress or use it to good effect so that you minimise any negative impact it may have on your colleagues. It is interesting to note that a Skills for Care survey in 2007 discovered that social care workers were generally happy at work despite low pay relative to other jobs.

Managing your absence

Health and social care work is typically 24 hours a day, seven days a week and 52 weeks a year. The paid working week is usually 35 hours. This means that if you work full-time it is still only possible for you to be there for a total of about 20 per cent of the time across an average year. It is therefore necessary for you to consider how you manage the large amount of time when you are not physically present. Focusing on this can also enable you to free up time when you are at work as your team will not be dependent on you. Systematically planning ahead is the key to organising this.

If you are not at work and get phoned at home, or on your mobile, then conduct the conversation in a way that respects the fact that a member of the team has felt the need to call you, but at the same time talk to them in a way that empowers them to know what to do next time so that they feel confident and able to manage the situation themselves. Do not assume total responsibility for what they have told you. Keep them involved and accountable; don't let staff call you as a way of absolving themselves of any responsibility for what is going on at work. If you have a mobile phone make sure your team understand what sorts of activities are appropriate to call you about. Creating dependency may seem to help in the short term but it does not mean that you are a good manager or that your team is functioning effectively.

A good aim is to make your team better than you and in order for this to happen you need to be confident about your role and not defensive about the way you work. You are a manager and your job is to develop individuals to become the best team. Your team should not be dependent on you; this will be easier if you feel secure about your own skills and abilities. Managing your scheduled absences well will also pay off when there are unexpected work or non-work absences.

Be efficient

Some people are at their most efficient just before they go on two weeks' leave; this is because they stay focused on the task (time is running out), they delegate (they have to – they are not going to be here this time next week) and they have a clear sense of what matters in the job (priorities have to be met before going away – the rest can wait). Group tasks together and aim to minimise the time spent on those that are less significant. A manager's absence can provide a good opportunity for the skills of individual team members to be stretched and developed.

Be effective

Management activity sometimes focuses on processes; i.e. the systems that are in place for the smooth running of the organisation. Systems are important but these can only be judged to be effective if the desired outcome is achieved. If you are someone who seeks perfection then you may need to accept that when there are time pressures, and you have to prioritise, you will need to decide which tasks need not be completed in a perfect manner. If the correct outcome can be achieved with less investment in time and effort, then this would be an acceptable measure of whether a task has been carried out to a required standard.

Managing people

Managing people is a key part of managing health and social care services; in social care the workforce accounts for 80 per cent of expenditure. In your organisation you may have access to income and expenditure and know how much is spent on human resources. The *Options for Excellence: Building the Social Care Workforce of the Future* document provides a commitment to developing the social care workforce, (Skills for Care, 2006).

There are many theories of understanding people that can be useful to you as a manager but you need to maintain a focus on your role as a manager and be aware of boundaries in that role and also the limitations of your skills.

The Code of Practice for Employers of Social Care Workers was written by the General Social Care Council (GSCC), it is detailed in the chapter Supporting individuals and their families. All social care workers should have a copy of this and it is a useful outline of expectations that any organisation can refer to.

CASE STUDY

Clare as manager

Clare has recently become deputy manager of Ashburton Home Care Agency. She has worked there for four years and this was promotion for her. She now manages some of the team who she used to work alongside.

Clare knows that this is a tricky time of adjustment for both her and her colleagues; so what may help Clare?

- Acknowledging that her role requires her to have a different relationship with her colleagues as she now has a responsibility for line managing them.
- Taking a lead and setting some boundaries.
- Talking to her friends to explain how she wants to remain friends but that she needs to respect the experience of other people in the team of this scenario.
- She may need to distance herself from them socially. Some managers are able to maintain friendships and social networks with a few members of a team but this is difficult to do while still ensuring fairness across the team and not creating issues.

Questions

1 What else would help Clare in managing her role as a manager and also managing her relationships at work?
2 How do you manage your social relationships at work? What is your colleagues' experience of this?

Management style

Managers are all different and you could probably list a number of ways in which you have been managed. Some of these may have been very effective in bringing out the best in you; others may have not done anything to improve or develop the way that you work.

You may have a natural preference for adopting a particular **leadership** style, but this does not prevent you from using the other styles when appropriate.

Leadership styles

Throughout this chapter reference is made to the different approaches that managers can take in situations. Some of this decision-making will relate to the leadership style of a person. Leadership style is a combination of the natural qualities and manner in which a person carries out their role as a manager, along with the way they have consciously decided to perform this role.

Leadership can be described as the balance between supporting and directing team members. An effective manager will be able to adapt their leadership approach to suit the needs of individual team members and the situation.

A very coercive approach where the manager is authoritative is not valued as being most effective in bringing out the best in people. A more democratic approach, where the manager focuses their attention on developing team members and encouraging them to share in decision-making, is more valued.

The key to success is knowing how to use management skills to best effect with individuals.

Some common characteristics of leadership have been described as shown in the diagram opposite.

Figure 5.4 *Characteristics of leadership: Sewell–Rutter (page 262)*

Supporting your own managers in your team

Supervising staff who also have a management or supervisory role provides an added dimension to your responsibilities. Some of your team may have good skills and it would be wise to let them develop their own style of management. You must accept that they do things differently from you and that sometimes they do things better than you. If they do, then be pleased that you have a good manager to delegate to.

You should entrust people with management skills whatever their level of responsibility. Communicate thoroughly and in a way that ensures you develop a trusting relationship, as there will be times when others want to test this for their own benefit. Train them to bring you solutions not problems.

You need to be aware of the relationship that those you are managing have with their colleagues and with the organisation. The night staff in a care home have responsibility for decision-making and they have

Leadership style	Potential limitations	Possible benefits
Autocratic Directive autonomous decision making, tells others what has been decided	Under-utilisation of people's skills, team members do not feel valued	Developments can take place quickly
Democratic Involvement of all the team in decision making	Actions can take longer	Everyone feels valued and involved in the organisation
Laissez-faire Allows the team to shape its own direction and limits direct management of activity	Lack of direction, limited accountability	Team members can develop skills

Good communication with co-workers is essential to develop trusting relationships

Students and volunteers

Students and volunteers can be a valuable addition to any team. It is good to encourage new people to the profession and local colleges and training companies are frequently in need of work experience placements. Course co-ordinators should inform you of the learning that they want students to gain during their time with you. Be conscious of the experience that service users and patients have with students as their needs are paramount.

It is important to supervise people closely and in a developmental way and to adhere to restrictions regarding age and responsibility. Encourage the team to work with the person as they can often have much to offer your organisation. You will need to feel assured that individuals are safe and in a position to both contribute and develop. What volunteers and students need is:

- direction on activities that they can get on with
- clear boundaries regarding tasks that they must not undertake
- health and safety training and ongoing support
- all the team to know what the expectations of the person are
- instruction on what they need to do if they are anxious, uncertain or unhappy.

You should ensure that your insurance and liability covers the activities of non-pay team members. If the student or volunteer comes to you via an agency or college, their host organisation should also make sure that they are covered.

to work more autonomously and often in isolation. Some supervisory roles involve responsibility for the tasks that people in the team carry out without having line management responsibility for them. This arrangement has its limitations but also provides you with some opportunities to focus on tasks and outcomes.

Managers often feel more confident managing people who are doing a job role that they have carried out. This can make it difficult to manage non-care jobs such as domestic staff, cooks, administrators and caretakers. In some organisations, managing agency staff may be a significant aspect of your role and not just related to times of staff shortage. Your investment in that person relates to the necessity for them to be fully informed about what is required in order for them to do their job well. A key feature of this involves information they need and you need to balance the time you spend with them or in preparing information that any new staff can have to immediately bring them up to speed on what they need to know. A comprehensive induction pack can promote this.

Supporting learning

The Learning Resource Network is the vehicle through which Skills for Care and Development work with partners to deliver the policies of workforce development such as Options for Excellence.

Some people need specific instruction in order for them to carry out a particular task successfully; there is more on this in Chapter 2. Learning occurs differently in individuals and people often need a range of activities in order to learn.

Coaching skills entail working alongside a person and giving smaller chunks of encouragement, guidance and information to enable them to improve their work in a gradual way.

Performance management includes a more directive approach to support and supervision. Setting targets and monitoring progress towards these is a key feature of the modern managerial culture.

Basic principles of competency frameworks

'Competencies are a signal from the organisation to the individual of the expected areas and levels of performance. They provide the individual with a map or indication of the behaviours that will be valued, recognised and in some organisations rewarded. Competencies can be understood to represent the language of performance in an organisation, articulating both the expected outcomes of an individual's efforts and the manner in which these activities are carried out.'

CIPD.co.uk

According to the Chartered Institute of Personnel Development 2007 survey, the most popular skills found in employer competency frameworks are, in order:

- communication skills
- people management
- team skills
- customer service skills
- results orientation
- problem solving.

Aims of supervision

Targets should be set on the following basis, that they are **SMART**:

Specific
Measurable
Achievable
Realistic
Time-limited

These allow a standard to be set for how the role is performed.

Expect your team to reflect on whether they are meeting these targets and make sure that you always return to them so that both you and the person you are supervising find them to be meaningful. Encourage creativity from your team members so that they come up with targets for self-development for themselves and for the benefit of the team.

Management by objectives

This focuses the supervision of people on the organisational tasks that need to be achieved. You should apply the same requirements to yourself that you do to others. A useful way of looking at the manager's role is to consider what the manager needs to do in order to ensure that the people they are responsible for are able to do their job effectively.

Development and supervision

The Social Care Institute for Excellence (SCIE) makes reference to five features of what they describe as a 'learning organisation' (SCIE, 2004), an accolade that all health and social care organisations could aspire to.

- The *organisational structure* empowers all employees, carers and service users to make decisions. Strong lateral relations internally and externally are encouraged.
- The *culture of the organisation* is based on openness, creativity and experimentation. All members have freedom to nurture innovation and to learn from mistakes by taking risks.
- There is effective knowledge management in these organisations as *information systems* facilitate rapid acquisition, processing and sharing of rich and complex information.

- *Human resource* management focuses on provision and support of individual learning concerned with long-term performance.
- *Leadership* provides empathy, support and personal advocacy in order to communicate learning, change and development.
- In addition the setting should challenge through one-off activities/projects and identify any Continuous Professional Development (CPD) activities (see below). This also involves:
  - formal meetings to review work activities and the performance of individuals in a private meeting with their manager
  - any discussion on performance should be supported by examples as evidence (both positive aspects and areas to develop). It is more meaningful for your team if they hear you specifying what they do well and it reminds them that you know what is going on.

It is useful for any organisation to have a supervision policy so that all staff are clear about the purpose and practice of supervision:

- statement of intent
- contract, recording and confidentiality
- supervision contract
- accountability
- concerns and complaints
- endorsement of activities that the person has been actively involved in.

REFLECT

Think back to an occasion when you were supported in a way that made a big impact on your work; this need not necessarily be a formal meeting. What stands out for you as the reason that this meeting made such a difference for you?

Individual supervision should take place in a private place without interruptions; it is an opportunity for you as a manager to show that you value that member of staff through the attention you are paying them.

Supervision should be a two-way discussion around the following areas:

- discussion of work activities and priorities

- reviewing performance on tasks, both positive aspects and areas to develop/improve
- setting new targets and discussing expectations
- support with any concerns regarding service users/patients
- reflection on experience of the work, any emotional responses that need reflecting on.

Appraisal

This is usually an annual meeting that allows both a review of performance over the past year and also the setting of targets for the coming year. It will focus on performance and development issues, looking at current job role and opportunities for taking on new responsibilities. It is a good time to praise a person for their hard work, as well as a time to set formal targets for those who are not doing their job in the expected way.

There are many theories of understanding people that can be useful to you as a manager but you need to maintain a focus on your role as a manager and be aware of boundaries in that role and also the limitations of your skills.

The Code of Practice for Employers of Social Care Workers was written by the GSCC, it is detailed in Chapter 4 (Supporting individuals and their families). All social care workers should have a copy of this and it is a useful outline of expectations that any organisation can refer to.

Recruitment

Managing people starts with recruitment – getting the right people into the organisation. Successful recruitment is essential for the right personnel to be employed and for new members to provide continuity to your organisation.

As in other work sectors, recruitment from overseas has helped some care organisations in some localities to fill workforce gaps. Monitored by the Trades Union Council's Commission on Vulnerable Employment, social care falls outside the remit of the Gangmasters' Licensing Authority that was set up in 2005. In August 2007 the Home Office stated that senior care worker posts do not meet its minimum skills criteria for individuals to be granted business and commercial work permits for staff from outside the European Economic Area. In order for these posts to meet the

Appraisal

Siobhan is Deputy Care Director of Churchwood Home Care Agency. She is having her appraisal with her own manager.

Form HCA 4
Churchwood Home Care Agency
Staff Support and Development Programme
Appraisal
Name: Siobhan Cooper
Line Manager: Alison Barnes
Date: 5th July 2008　　　　　　　　　　　**Date of previous appraisal**: 7th July 2007

Key Areas of Responsibility:
- Co-ordinating operational arrangements: rotas, new service user assessments and allocation of key workers
- Training of team
- Deputising for manager in absence

Strengths:
- Organisational skills are excellent
- Ability to identify potential issues before they become a concern and to manage these well
- Focus on needs of service users
- Understanding of individual team members

Areas for development:
- Managing individual poor performance so that it improves
- Assuming management responsibility in areas of concern, reducing need for intervention from own manager

Continuing Professional Development

Activities undertaken during last year:
- Worked closely shadowing manager during inspection – May
- Infection Management – February
- Completed NVQ level 4 in Health and Social Care

Areas for development:
- Would like management training on managing poor performance
- Adult protection
- Wants to start a Foundation Degree in Health and Social Care

Actions for next 3 months	Work with Manager on expansion of the Home Care Agency Devise action plans for care workers who are under-performing Investigate Foundation Degree options
Actions for next 6 months	Deliver training on PoVA and Infection Control to all team members where required Undertake appraisals with Team Leaders Undertake management training on dealing with poor performance
Actions for next 12 months	Train Team Leaders in assessments of service users Continue development of management role by deputising for manager

Questions

1　How does this appraisal compare with any that you have undertaken?
2　Copy out this form and fill it in as if it for were your appraisal.

criteria then the vacant post must require 3 years experience in a level S/NVQ 3 job. Where the Home Office's Borders and Immigration Agency will issue work permits to senior care staff, they state that their minimum wage must be £7.02 per hour (2007). From 2008 a points-based system for entry into the UK means that overseas recruitment may be affected.

In tackling poverty the National Minimum Wage is reducing exploitation of people in the labour market. It does mean that care organisations are competing with other work sectors in recruitment. There are, however, funding projects to facilitate more recruitment to the sector. The European Social Fund has facilitated recruitment and training packages for individuals who are unemployed and wanting to progress into work in the care sector; a pan-London Skills & Jobs for Health, and Carelink (a Black Country Partnership of seven organisations) are examples of these.

Retaining staff

Once an organisation has employed the right people it is important to retain them both because this is more cost-effective and also because continuity is better for the experience of those who use care and support services. Research suggests that people do not leave their jobs – they leave their managers, so there is a responsibility on anyone with a role in supervising or managing other people to get this right. The National Care Forum's Annual Survey reported that staff turnover in older people's residential care fell from 25 per cent in 2006 to 21 per cent. At the same time, staff qualified to NVQ Level 2 rose from 59 per cent to 67 per cent; it is likely that these statistics are connected. In any work sector, investing in staff should be a key management activity – trained staff offer more benefits to service users who value continuity.

Sandwell Community Caring Trust (SCCT) came second in the 2007 *Sunday Times* survey into the 'Top 100 companies to work for'. Described as having progressive management practices, it was excellent to have a care organisation represented; the staff manage their own rotas, having worked out with service users what they want. (See *Community Care*, 30 August 2007.)

The Trust provides services throughout the Black Country including supported living, residential, respite and day care for adults and children with physical and learning disabilities, as well as residential and day care for older people. Chief Executive Geoff Walker believes the Trust's passionate approach to making sure people feel valued reaps financial dividends and leads to high-quality services.

- Treating staff and service users with dignity and respect is the central tenet at SCCT. Staff know their work contributes towards the organisation making a positive difference to the world (85 per cent positive in our employee survey, ranking it third).
- Employees think the experience they gain from their job is valuable for their future, rating this question 85 per cent positive (third highest score).
- They find the training they receive beneficial to them personally (84 per cent, the highest score of any organisation).
- Staff are more content with what they earn than most, giving the question that asks if they are happy with their pay and benefits a 79 per cent positive score, the fourth best in the survey.
- Stress levels are low and people are happy with their work/life balance. Work not interfering with responsibilities at home rated an 85 per cent positive response, another top score.
- What is clear from the *Sunday Times* survey is that employees are proud to work for the organisation (85 per cent), would strongly recommend working for it to others (88 per cent) and would not leave for another job (84 per cent)

(See the *Sunday Times*, 11 March 2007)

Legislation and policy context

The organisation and development of agencies and employees is influenced by what is happening nationally in policy, and the legal framework in which health and social care organisations are set up.

Skills for Care have undertaken a New Types of Worker project to help ensure that the workforce develops in a way which reflects the changing needs of those who use health and social care services.

The New Type of Worker & Working national programme is managed by Skills for Care in order to:

- investigate and re-design roles for workers in social care
- enable employers to develop and implement new roles
- bring about new types of working.

The idea is that the support needs of individuals are met by appropriately designed job descriptions and organisational roles so the personalisation agenda is delivered. For too long many people have either disorganised or poor quality of support and care because those who work with them have unrealistic restrictions on the activities that they carry out, or outdated job roles that do not meet the person's needs.

Skills for Care identify the following examples of new roles:

'Hybrid roles' – social care workers doing tasks that have traditionally been done by other professionals such as workers from health, housing, justice, leisure, employment or other professions.

'Person-centred working' – working in such a way that people who use services have as much control of their own lives as other people.

'Experts by experience' – people who have experience of using social care services or caring for people and who contribute to the 'business' of social care such as recruiting and training social care workers, assessing quality, commissioning services, planning changes to service delivery or regulation of services.

'Prevention/early intervention' – services which help people early enough or in the right way so that they don't need more intensive services.

'Changes to services' – to make them more effective or efficient such as enabling workers to get their qualifications more quickly, working in partnership with other organisations and professions or commissioning differently.

'Community Support' – supporting community networks so that people can be independent from services.

Some of the job titles or 'roles' that have been tried so far are called:

- personal assistants
- community enabler
- WRAP coordinator (wellness, recovery, action plan)
- advocate/navigator
- S.T.O.P. worker (Support To Older People).

Skills for Care are working on the training and qualification requirements of workers to support this sea change in roles.

The National Minimum Data Set (NMDS) was established to enable more informed management of workforce development. Funded by the Department for Health, through Skills for Care, the NMDS aims to collate detailed information about the social care workforce with data on the organisation and individual employees.

The Direct Payments scheme has allowed individuals who require support to employ people directly and for many it has facilitated a new level of control in their lives. However, some people have expressed concern regarding the suitability of and checks on individuals employed directly by service users through direct payments. For some disabled people this indicates mistrust in disabled people's expertise and capability as employers. (See *Community Care*, 2–8 Nov 2006.)

Equality and human rights legislation is discussed fully in Chapter 3 in the section on ethics and values, but brief consideration is given to its role in recruitment practices in health and social care from an employer's perspective.

The Disability Rights Commission (DRC) concluded that regulations in the recruitment of health and social care professionals requiring people to prove 'good health' were discriminatory. Leeds Employment Tribunal found the GSCC to have unlawfully discriminated against a man with HIV-positive status when they delayed his registration.

Key legislation to be aware of:

Sex Discrimination Act 1976

Race Relations Act 1976

Disability Discrimination Act 1995

Data Protection Act 1998

Employment Equality (Sexual Orientation) Regulations Act 2003

Employment Equality (Religion or Belief) Regulations Act 2003

Employment Equality (Age) Regulations Act 2006

Criminal Records Bureau

The rehabilitation of offenders is important for government and while health and social care services do not aim to discriminate it is important that service users have confidence in recruitment practices.

Continuing Professional Development (CPD)

Staff development will include the activities that all staff are required to undertake as part of the legislative framework for the health and social care workforce. This starts with a good induction.

Induction

Corporate induction should include the knowledge skills and values that relate to the following areas:

- legal aspects of the job
- organisational context
- vocational relating to the role
- occupational relating to the sector.

Other required training will depend on what services your organisation provides and includes:

- health and safety legislation
- food handling and hygiene
- manual handling
- infection control
- first aid.

REFLECT

Focusing on the experience of the service users with the staff, write a list of the information that is essential for individuals starting work at your organisation.

When you have a new addition to the team who may need ongoing support beyond the initial guidance, it is a good idea to enlist the support of a mentor; as well as helping the individual this also provides an opportunity for one of the team to take on some supervisory tasks. Sharing out the responsibilities of induction allows the new employee to develop relationships with several of their new colleagues, rather than developing a dependency on one. Where possible involve service users so that a new employee learns quickly about the values of the organisation and the role the services have in shaping the service. Maintain support and identify tasks that should not be carried out if the person is unconfident or if they need specific training (for example, use of a hoist).

In addition:

- Provide an induction checklist to the new member of staff so that they share responsibility for ensuring all topics are covered.
- Try to avoid overloading a person on day one and then not providing continued support over the next months.
- Keep written records of induction activity, especially those pertaining to health and safety.

- Make sure that induction introduces the new employee to the values and ethos of the organisation and focuses on the experience that the service users need to have from them.

Some organisations refer to *talent management* where they focus development on employees who are excelling in the current role and identify new challenging roles for them. In health and social care organisations the fairness of this has to be considered so that all employees feel their potential is realised in their current job and can be given new challenges.

Funding

Skills for Care distributed the Training Strategy Implementation Fund: Social Care Fund targeting NVQ Common Induction Standards and LDAF Induction.

National Vocational Qualifications are competency-based qualifications that can be delivered by training organisations, colleges or care organisations. The government commitment to raising the skills levels of the workforce are reflected in its 'Train To Gain' strategy. All adults are currently funded if they are working towards their first full level 2 qualifications, with most health and social care NVQs counting as full awards. In 2007, adults aged 19–24 who are working towards their first full level 3 award are also entitled to their fees being paid.

A new qualification launched in 2008, the *Diploma in Society, Health & Development*, is aimed at improving the progression of young people to this work sector while also providing a nationally valued qualification. Development of this award was led by Skills for Health in collaboration with other Sector Skills Councils – Skills for Care, the Children's Workforce Development Council and Skills for Justice.

Skills for Care

Sector Skills Agreements are designed to improve the delivery of services through developing the workforce. Comprehensive funding, planning and delivery of staff development activity across sectors aims to improve the workforce planning of the future.

Learning Resource Networks

Social Care Institute for Excellence research reveals that social care staff do not have access to training through e-learning opportunities; 75 per cent of employers thought only 10 per cent of their training utilised this method.

Good practice is essential:

> A better trained workforce benefits employees by giving them the skills to care for others to the very highest standards ...
> ('Skills for care accolades', *Community Care*, 1 November 2007)

There are various methods and models of workforce development. Any new staff development should be based on a Training Needs Analysis. This is a thorough review of how the organisation is functioning and what the skills gaps are in terms of delivering the service.

Commissioning training through consultants can be useful for providing bespoke learning and skills development that is focused on your own organisation; training providers will usually come to the workplace to deliver this.

It is important to consider the following design features so that you know what you are paying for:

- schedule and terms/conditions
- training design (times and days to suit your staff work patterns)
- delivery (monitoring and evaluation)
- assessment and qualification
- monitoring and evaluation
- follow-up and review.

Skills for life assessments are useful to identify any ESOL (English for Speakers of Other Languages) numeracy and literacy needs. These are all-important workforce skills that are required in order for service users to receive appropriate support; communication misunderstandings can frustrate service users and patients, and potentially cause serious errors, such as with medication.

Coaching

It may be necessary to adopt coaching skills with some staff in relation to particular activities. This is usually a more informal approach that is more regular and continuous than other types of staff development activity. It should be planned and monitored to ensure that it is having the desired effect.

Coaching is about:

- being a good role model
- trust between the manager and individual
- the manager knowing exactly what an individual has to do in a particular task
- encouragement: feedback being advice and guidance about how to carry out specific tasks
- understanding the individual's behaviour and learning needs
- long-term development of an individual.

'Investors in People' provide a Kitemark for organisations which demonstrate that they are developing their employees and valuing staff development activities. Looking at innovative new ways to do this is important. Their framework is based on the following three key principles:

- *Plan* – developing strategies to improve the performance of the organisation
- *Do* – taking action to improve the performance of the organisation
- *Review* – evaluating the impact on the performance of the organisation.

The Investors in People website has a number of diagnostic tools for organisations to use to manage support and develop their staff to achieve the standards.

Courses

Foundation Degrees

This is a level 5 qualification that is usually studied part-time at a university or college of further and/or higher Education. A key feature of the **Foundation Degree** is that learning is based on both study and work related learning, learning through work activity.

National Vocational Qualifications: NVQs

In Chapter 2 we looked at the relationship between knowledge, skills and attitude/values. National Vocational Qualifications (NVQs) are the assessment of skills in the workplace; confirmation that an employee is competent in all the tasks that they carry out. There are NVQs relating to health and social care and also management.

Vocationally Related Qualifications: VRQs

The Learning Disability Awards Framework and Certificate in Community Mental Health Work are examples of VRQs that are usually assessed by formal reflection on work activity.

Managing difficult situations

Mediation

Bringing employees together in order to resolve conflict is known as mediation. Some principles of mediation include the desire to:

- intervene early
- prepare all those involved
- expose all aspects of the issue
- encourage parties to generate solutions
- reach an agreement
- follow up.

If you are a manager then you may do this informally – or maybe more formally – with members of the team who are not relating well to each other for various reasons. You may feel that someone less involved in the situation may be able to provide a better basis for mediation, for example a manager from a different service within the same organisation.

More formal mediation can be obtained through the Advisory Conciliation and Arbitration Service (ACAS).

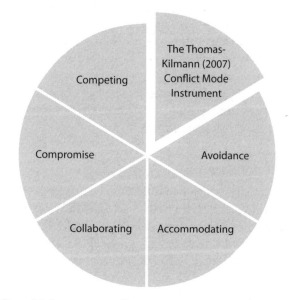

Figure 5.5 Responses to conflict

There are reasons why conflict can arise and it often relates to normal patterns in an individual's way of thinking and working that do not quite match with a colleague's approach to these factors and communication about them. The Thomas-Kilmann (2007) Conflict Mode Instrument looks at normal differences in people's behaviour in relation to assertiveness and co-operation and explores how these can lead to conflict. It suggests that there are several responses.

Dealing with poor performance

Managing poor performance involves identifying what the source of the problem is. It can be helpful to distinguish between the person and the performance. For example, if someone appears to be lazy then trying to understand what would prompt an employee to behave like this and avoid new responsibilities can stop you from diving in critically with little positive effect.

It is worth re-reading Chapter 2 so that you understand processes of learning. Your team members will learn in different ways and will have different interests in learning.

So why do some people not do their job properly?

Setting clear targets may encourage an individual to focus on the aspects of their work that they are struggling with. Reviewing these targets will enable you to identify the reasons why the person is under-performing and to put support in place to address this. Make notes of all support and meetings as these may be required if you are going to address someone's incompetence.

Figure 5.6 Reasons people give for poor performance

Disciplining

Managing a team should be an enjoyable activity and if any team members are under-performing support and development should usually set things back on track. There are, however, times when an individual is not performing and you need to consider a different approach to supporting their work and helping them to manage their behaviour.

Hopefully, most of your activity with staff is based on people wanting to work hard and well for the good of the service users that they are supporting. But there are times when staff can under-perform and you need to establish the reasons for that.

Misconduct

This relates to specific incidents or series of activities where an employee has clearly acted inappropriately. The misconduct is usually investigated by someone other than the line manager and then a case is presented. The outcome must be communicated to the employee in writing.

In social care, any misconduct is dealt with internally unless the police are involved. This is changing with the GSCC which is providing more regulation of the workforce. At the end of 2007 there were 14 people who had been struck off the Social Care Register General Social Care Council. Any investigations that result in admonishment mean that a caution is given and a public record of the offence may be placed on the care worker's record.

Balancing the rights of employees and service users can create dilemmas. In 2007 judges ruled that care workers were entitled to a fair hearing before being suspended; the previous PoVA (protection of vulnerable adults) process violated the human rights of employees. Service user organisations have stated their dismay at this new guidance as they feel that on balance the rights and welfare of the vulnerable people should be prioritised. The Care Standards Act 2000 is to be rewritten to accommodate these changes.

If the performance of an individual fails to improve then this needs to be challenged, either through a

---

CASE STUDY

Dealing with Donna

Sonia is responsible for line managing a number of health care assistants. She is concerned about the under-performance of one of the team, Donna. This member of staff is frequently late, her absence rate is high and there are complaints from other staff that 'she does not pull her weight' when they are on a shift with her. But there have been no complaints from service users as she is very personable and pleasant with them and she spends a lot of time talking to them.

Sonia needs to ascertain whether the nature of the poor practice relates to Donna's:

- skills and what she is capable of doing
- knowledge, what she knows
- values and how Donna feels about the service users
- attitude towards the job and her colleagues.

Sonia adopts the following attitudes when she meets with Donna:

- she communicates her own high expectations
- she is accurate and specific in her feedback and gives Donna examples of poor practice

- she relates Donna's performance to that of the team
- she is encouraging about the potential of the member of staff to change while making it clear that this change has got to happen by setting targets and a date for these to be reviewed
- she involves Donna in identifying changes that she can make to facilitate this
- Sonia ensures that Donna has a copy of the targets and then ensures that the next Support and Supervision takes place as scheduled
- Sonia considers the consequences of Donna not meeting the targets so that action can be taken if required
- Sonia makes sure that Donna gets the required support to meet the targets and also praises her promptly for any progress made.

Questions

1 What might be the reason for Donna's behaviour in these aspects of her work?
2 What would you do differently and why?
3 What should Sonia do if there is no observable change in Donna's performance over the next week?

disciplinary procedure or through a competency or capability framework. The organisation should offer clear written guidance to staff about how poor performance is managed. An action plan should be put into place, with clear steps as to how the person can improve and dates for when this will be reviewed. The staff member will have some actions that they are responsible for but there may also be some activities that the manager is to action.

Employment legislation requires that the organisation's procedures have been followed before a tribunal application can be applied for.

Managing a team

What makes a team and how is it created?

One answer to this is: forming, norming, storming and performing. In 1965 Tuckman divided the process of creating a team into these four stages, as outlined in the diagram below.

Discussion on teams can relate both to the activities that the team are designed to carry out – the *task* functions of the team – and also to the relationships within the team and how these are managed – the *maintenance* functions.

Dr Meredith Belbin devised some team roles that are useful to consider. These roles are: 'a tendency to behave, contribute and interrelate with others in a particular way.' They are outlined in the table at the top of the following page.

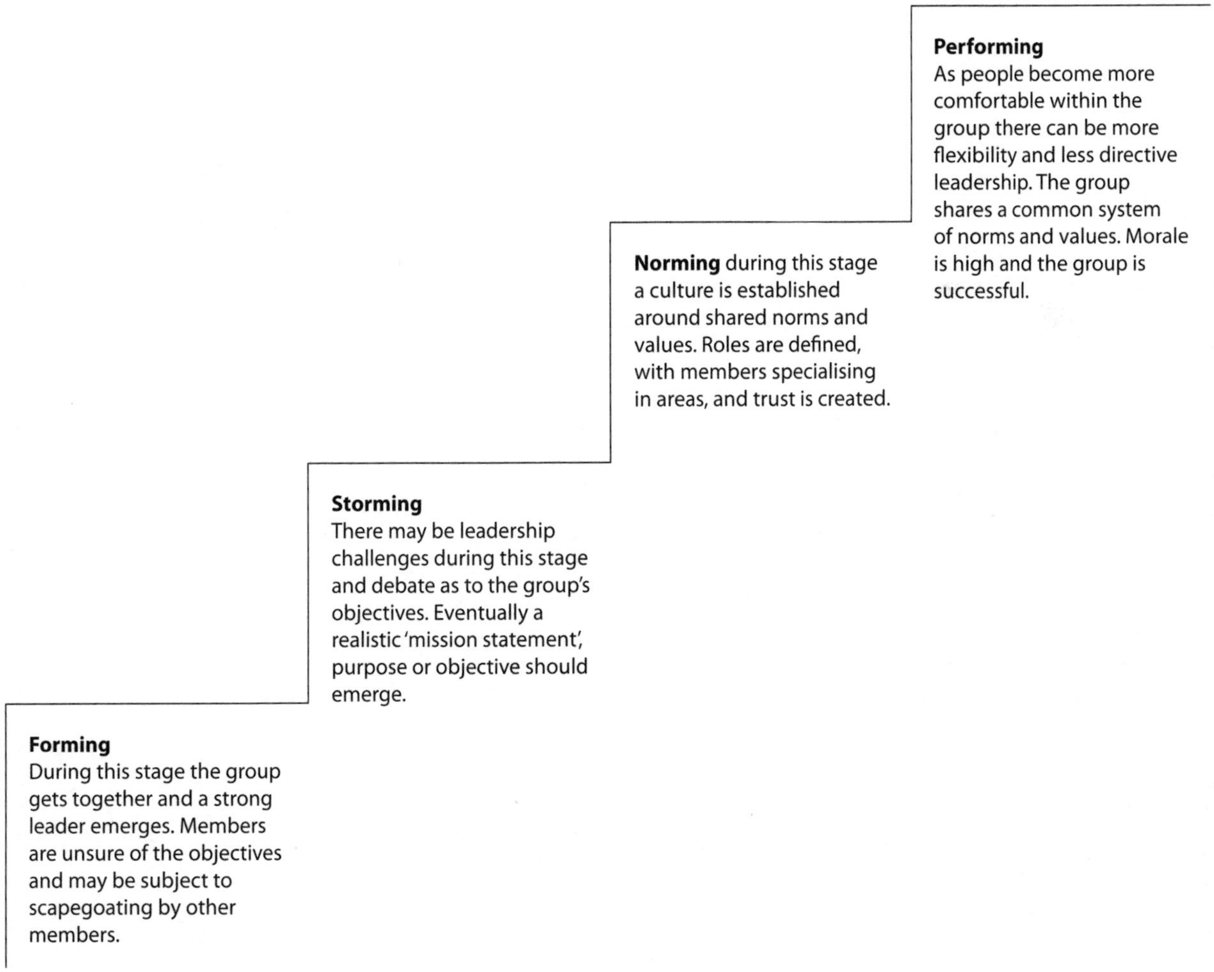

Performing
As people become more comfortable within the group there can be more flexibility and less directive leadership. The group shares a common system of norms and values. Morale is high and the group is successful.

Norming during this stage a culture is established around shared norms and values. Roles are defined, with members specialising in areas, and trust is created.

Storming
There may be leadership challenges during this stage and debate as to the group's objectives. Eventually a realistic 'mission statement', purpose or objective should emerge.

Forming
During this stage the group gets together and a strong leader emerges. Members are unsure of the objectives and may be subject to scapegoating by other members.

Figure 5.7 Tuckman suggested that groups go through a process of maturing before they function efficiently (Tuckman in Mullins, L., 2002, page 475).

Type	Team–role contribution	Allowable weaknesses
Plant	Creative, imaginative, unorthodox, solves difficult problems.	Ignores details. Too preoccupied to communicate effectively.
Resource investigator	Extrovert, enthusiastic, communicative. Explores opportunities. Develops contacts.	Over-optimistic. Loses interest once initial enthusiasm has passed.
Co-ordinator	Mature, confident, a good chairperson. Clarifies goals, promotes decision- making. Delegates well.	Can be seen as manipulative. Delegates personal work.
Shaper	Challenging, dynamic, thrives on pressure. Has the drive and courage to overcome obstacles.	Can provoke others, hurts people's feelings.
Monitor-evaluator	Sober, strategic and discerning. Sees all options. Judges accurately.	Lacks drive and ability to inspire others. Overly critical.
Team worker	Co-operative, mild, perceptive and diplomatic. Listens, builds, averts friction, calms the waters.	Indecisiveness in crunch situations. Can be easily influenced.
Implementer	Disciplined, reliable, conservative and efficient. Turns ideas into practical actions.	Somewhat inflexible. Slow to respond to new possibilities.
Completer	Painstaking, conscientious, anxious. Searches out errors, delivers on time.	Inclined to worry unduly, reluctant to delegate. Can be a nit-picker.
Specialist	Single-minded, self-sharing, dedicated. Provides knowledge and skills in rare supply.	Contributes on only a narrow front. Dwells on technicalities. Overlooks the big picture.

Belbin's Revised Team Roles (Mullins, L., 2002, page 498).

Negative features

Features and activities in your team that you will want to eliminate include:

- *A culture of blame*: it is necessary for your team to be able to own up to mistakes and to feel supported to improve their practice.
- *The development of cliques*: it is good for all your team members to feel comfortable about working with anyone else in the team.
- *Silences*: if something is not working correctly then it is best for this to be discussed openly rather than there being an unhelpful silence about it.
- *Complaining*: it is much better to talk about things that are not right and all aim to resolve them.
- *Gossip*: any communication that does not promote good teamwork can potentially damage your team, even if the communication is on the surface seen as casual and harmless.
- *Workplace bullying*: be aware of how your colleagues treat each other and tackle behaviours between staff that do not contribute well to the overall effectiveness of the team.

CASE STUDY

Dean's team

Dean manages a team of seven care managers in a rural area. Due to the nature of the work the team is quite dispersed and each person spends much of their time working in isolation. Some members of the team are very conscientious and able to manage their own workloads well, others are not so experienced and Dean is concerned about some poor practice that is developing.

Questions

1. Think of all the activities that Dean could implement in order to address this issue and prevent long-term problems.
2. How should he focus on the task functions of the team?
3. What are the maintenance functions of the team and how can Dean manage these as well?
4. Devise a management action plan for Dean so that he implements a changed approach by individuals in the team. What are the potential difficulties he might comer across?

Managing communication and information

The management of communication and information can greatly influence the success or otherwise of a health and social care service. As with other modern-day organisations, there is a need to improve the use of information for service users and patients. New technologies are providing new Management Information Systems (MIS) and care organisations, whatever their size, have new ways of ensuring efficient access to information while also ensuring the security of personal information.

Some larger organisations are able to employ administration staff who manage much of the written and computer-based information. Databases and spreadsheets are now routinely used in care services and have helped to save time and promote more efficient use of information.

Whatever your job role, and whatever the organisation that you work in, it is likely that you have an overload of information. It was hoped that computers would reduce the amount of paper that we use and store but not all organisations have been successful in this. There is no doubt that most people receive an overload of information each day at work and an important feature is how to manage this.

Dealing with information

Organisation diaries

This type of diary is used to manage communication between shifts about practical situations and appointments.

Communication about service users

Shola, Joe and Martha are learning disabled adults who live together.

2008	AUGUST

	THURSDAY 14
Shola wouldn't do anything today	

	FRIDAY 15
Joe – bowels opened twice	
Martha ate all her dinner (took ages)	

	SATURDAY 16

This is an example of very poor communication. Not only does it provide very little information for the other staff but it also indicates poor values towards the people who are being written about. Hopefully Shola, Joe and Martha's memories of the day are different from those that have been reported!

Factual statements need to be clear but must be written in a manner that is respectful of the person being written about. There is a place for opinions in written documentation but only when it is stated as such.

For example: 'Shola has had 2 full glasses of juice today. Please keep a record of the amount of drink that Shola has during the next few days as I don't think she is drinking enough.'

As well as formal acknowledgement that individuals are entitled to read any information about them, it is also useful to think about the person as a diary entry is being written and include them in what is being written. It helps staff to write more respectfully.

Prioritising information

In a management role information will come to you constantly and you will need to be discerning about the information that you act on. You also need to maintain a balance in the communication that you respond to. If information is from a service user then it should carry weight. If an individual has experienced something in a negative way then this makes it significant, even if the evidence suggests that circumstances have been different.

The value of information should be based on whether it is:

● comprehensive; is it complete, does it cover everything?
● accurate; is it full of errors?
● current; is it recent enough?
● relevant; does it relate to the issue or task in hand?
● clear; can it be understood clearly?

Obtaining information is important in management as you will be making decisions based on this information. Do not just depend on information that casually comes your way; make sure your access to information is systematic and that you are proactive in seeking information.

Documentation products

Some organisations will purchase documentation products; there are companies that produce templates of documentation and policies that can be purchased, for example Doc-u-care. This saves time spent on creating own record templates and they are usually tried and tested so will be useful as soon as you purchase them.

Patterns of communication

There can be a centralised pattern of communication with everything centred on the manager, as shown below.

Figure 5.8 Centralised pattern of communication

Alternatively, communication may be more centred on service users/patients.

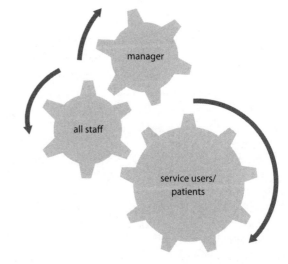

Figure 5.9 Alternative pattern of communication

Record keeping

Written communication between staff about service users needs to be of a high standard. It is always useful to write about people in such a way that you would feel comfortable if they read the information; this helps in writing respectfully and with clarity.

You should expect written information to be clear and accurate without errors. If any member of your team needs support with literacy then you may be able to obtain this through a local college.

The Electronic Social Care Record (ESCR) was due to be set up by October 2006 but the extent of cultural change within individual organisations away from paper-based records has prevented its inception. (See *Community Care*, 12–18 April 2007.)

Expectations of people are different now. Older people can expect access to their own telephones, or to have a mobile phone, rather than one phone to a house of residents. The Department of Health has set aside £80m for preventative technology grants to local councils to facilitate the development of more independent living for people. There is sensory equipment to ensure that the bath doesn't overflow and lights are available that switch on when a person enters the room or gets out of bed.

West Lothian Council have found that people are happy to accept the intrusion of sensors and monitoring if it means that they can stay in their own home rather than move into larger group living. (*Care Management Matters*, March 2007, page 31)

Computer-based support for those with mental health issues is being met with varied reception as some professionals have concern about the suitability of individuals accessing information without support. It does, however, give access to people. Beating the Blues by Ultrasis aimed at people with depression and anxiety, and FearFighter by ST Solutions for phobic, panic and anxiety disorders are examples of Computerised Cognitive Behaviour Therapy (CBT).

Data protection

Safety and security of information is vital whether it is paper-based or recorded on a computer. Large organisations need an information management system that can balance the need for accessible details with the requirement to observe privacy and security issues.

Confidentiality

Records are a valuable resource because of the information they contain. High-quality information underpins the delivery of high-quality evidence-based healthcare.

Information has most value when it is accurate, up to date and accessible when it is needed. An effective records management service ensures that information is properly managed and is available whenever and wherever there is a justified need for that information, and in whatever media it is required. Information may be needed to:

- meet legal requirements, including requests from patients under subject access provisions of the Data Protection Act 1998/2000 or the Freedom of Information Act
- assist clinical and other types of audits
- support patient choice and control over treatment and services designed around patients.

NHS organisations need robust record management procedures to meet the requirements set out under the Data Protection Act 1998 and the Freedom of Information Act 2000.

The Data Protection Act 1998 followed on from the Data Protection Act 1984 and the Access to Health Records Act 1990. Its aim is to ensure appropriate protection and use of patient/service user information, including appropriate access to information from individual service users/patients. The Act covers certain types of manual records (including all health records) as well as electronic records. There were transitional arrangements concerning manual records until 2007.

The key statutory requirement for compliance with records management principles is the Data Protection Act 1998. It provides a broad framework of general standards that have to be met and considered in conjunction with other legal obligations. The Act regulates the processing of personal data, held both manually and on computer. It applies to personal information generally, not just to health records, therefore the same principles apply to records of employees held by employers, for example in finance, personnel and occupational health departments.

Personal data is defined as data relating to a living individual that enables him/her to be identified, either from that data alone or from that data in conjunction with other information in the data controller's possession. It therefore includes such items of information as an individual's name, address, age, race, religion, gender and physical, mental or sexual health.

Care records must meet stringent legislation to ensure security and patient confidentiality

All individuals who work for an NHS organisation are responsible for any records which they create or use in the performance of their duties. Furthermore, any record that an individual creates becomes a public record.

'Processing' relates to holding, obtaining, recording, using, disclosing and sharing the information. It also includes disposal of the information, i.e. closure of a record by transferring it to an archive or destruction of the record. Organisations need to manage secure storage of information and appropriate disposal through shredding of documentation.

Senior managers of all NHS organisations are personally accountable for records management within their organisation. The Healthcare

Commission monitors a core governance standard relating to broad records management as part of its annual assessment of performance; this responsibility will be assumed by the Care Quality Commission. The NHS Litigation Authority also undertakes a risk assessment survey as an integral part of the Clinical Negligence Scheme for Trusts (CNST). The Health Service Ombudsman may also comment on data management when investigating a complaint.

NHS Connecting for Health (NHS CFH)

The NHS Care Records Service (NHS CRS) and the establishment of care trusts have transformed the way both health and social care information is managed.

NHS Connecting for Health (NHS CFH) is working to ensure that all NHS patient records will be kept in electronic format in the mixed economy of paper and electronic records which will exist as the NHS CRS is developed. It is essential that paper and electronic records are managed consistently to ensure that a complete health record is available at the point of need. This transitional period, during which the balance of paper and electronic records will change, will generate significant challenges; for example before patient data is migrated to the national data spine the data must be validated to ensure that duplicate registrations are eliminated and measures put in place in local systems to ensure that duplicate registrations are not created in the future.

Social care records

Social care records management is outside the scope of the NHS Code of Practice; good practice is, however, applicable to all organisations and colleagues from social care organisations are encouraged to adopt similar standards of practice.

National Information Governance Board for Health and Social Care

The creation of such an organisation was discussed in 2007. Its aim will be to ensure the ethical and appropriate use of records and documentation for the benefit of individuals and the public good by monitoring the structures, policies and practices which are used to ensure the confidentiality and security of records relating to the delivery of services.

It is likely to incorporate the functions of the existing statutory body, the Patient Information Advisory Group (PIAG).

All organisations which use NHS and social care information will have a statutory obligation to take account of advice provided by the National Information Governance Board and also to provide it with any information that it requests from them. It will report to the Secretary of State for Health.

Managing meetings

Time is a precious commodity in care work and you need to ensure that you maximise the opportunity to make the meetings that you have as constructive as possible.

An important starting point is to ensure that all those who are invited to attend have the chance to do so without worrying about service users. In residential services, or dispersed support teams, it is difficult to allocate an appropriate time for a meeting, but once you have ascertained a suitable time then consider how many people will be present at the meeting and whether it is likely to be productive for everyone.

An important point to consider is why the meeting is taking place and also the *aim* of the meeting. Be confident as the manager and expect all team members to be committed to the meeting.

SCIE Best Practice Guides suggest the following:

- start meetings on time, don't wait for anyone who is late
- expect all team members to attend
- expect all team members to be prepared through their knowledge of the agenda and by bringing any relevant documentation
- expect all team members to participate.

Service user/patient meetings

Look for opportunities for these meetings to be managed by the service users with any support that individuals require in order to facilitate total inclusion.

Managing other resources

Financial resources

You may be in a position where you have responsibility for a vast budget or just for smaller amounts; the principles of budget management can be useful for either scenario.

If you can forecast what money is coming into the organisation (income) and also anticipate the amount of money your organisation is going to spend (expenditure) then this is a good starting point.

You may have been set a budget by a more senior manager or need to set your own budgets.

Cost benefit analysis

Remember, when you undertake cost benefit analysis (CBA) you need to consider the non-financial aspects of the expenditure. In health and social care it is unusual for cheapest to mean best. CBA should start with the experience of the service users or patients as this will influence all stages of decision-making. Many organisations are more able now to involve service users in decisions about use of budget, from choice of carpet to contracting catering services. This is good practice and can help service users in feeling a sense of ownership; after all it is usually their money, or money allocated to them that is being spent. For one service there may be a reason to invest in a more expensive piece of furniture that is likely to last. However, for a different service it may make more sense to buy a cheaper item with a view to replacing it more frequently.

Budget setting and negotiation allow for the controlling of costs through people in the organisation. Involving all members of staff in managing a budget can really develop a sense of organisational responsibility. For example, the ordering of cleaning materials for use by the cleaners could be delegated to the cleaners. Identifying expected expenditure based on past activity will give an indication of how much should be allocated. If there is much variation to this then you can look into it further. If you suspect there is careless use of materials then devising an incentive plan can correct this. Even something simple like, 'If we save £100 in the cleaning materials budget over the next four months, we can buy a new vacuum', can include staff in managing budgets. It also stops you and everyone else in the organisation acting as if it is only the manager who manages the budget.

Fixed and variable costs

There will be a baseline of human resources as fixed costs but it is likely that there is also some variability to the expenditure as the needs of service users change.

Capital expenditure involves the purchase of larger products, furniture or changes to buildings that are non-routine; for example, this would include the purchase of table tennis facilities for a lunch club. A facility to purchase unexpected items needs to be allowable when budgets are drawn up. These are usually items that once purchased will be in use for a while.

Revenue expenditure could be defined as costs that are more routine or consumable, and it is likely the same items appear regularly.

Some costs are variable, even though the nature of the cost is consistent; for example staffing and utility bills. As an organisation there may be a year when there has been particularly high absence due to sickness, or the price of gas may have temporarily

risen. Although you may not have predicted these factors, financial planning will mean that the possibility of these happening will have been included in the budget for that year.

There are different options for expenditure which include:

- hire purchase
- leasing
- loans.

When considering how to manage purchases a manger needs to weigh up the potential financial risks. This is another reason for not making decisions on your own; you can be better informed and share responsibility as others will have differing views.

Some aspects of service delivery may be unavoidable. For example, the delivery of home care services in rural areas is more costly than that in densely populated cities. Travel equals time equals more costs, especially as domiciliary care agencies now have to specify time with service users rather than include time for travel. The burden of costs still falls on service users.

> ## KNOWLEDGE CHECK
>
> 1 What are the principles of cost benefit analysis and how can you apply them to your organisation?
> 2 How can a manager balance the financial long-term stability of the organisation with the daily comfort of service users?

Managing the environment

The first consideration in managing the environment should focus on the aims of the service and the needs of the people who use it. For some organisations that have been delivering care services for a long time this can be a challenge, as the available space might have been created in a time when the values and purpose of the service were very different.

A starting point is to consider the essence of the environment. Is it home? Is it a sociable place or a learning environment? Will people want a lot of privacy? What sort of access should there be from outside?

The design principles of a setting should consider the cognitive and sensory skills of those who will be using it:

- sight
- hearing
- memory
- learning needs
- housing and support needs
- domestic appliances with clear visual instructions
- internal design.

For example, open-plan arrangements that let residents see bedrooms from the communal area are invaluable for people with an impaired memory. However, this may not suit people who want a higher level of privacy.

In August 2007, Help the Aged published a report showing that of their respondents in their research:

- 12 per cent had difficulty with a bath or shower
- 19 per cent had difficulty with stairs
- 26 per cent had difficulty doing the garden.

However, there is now more new equipment available to enable more people to remain in their own homes and have adaptations to ensure that their mobility needs are managed well.

Managing health and social care activities

This section briefly discusses management issues in the delivery of care services. It should be read in conjunction with Chapters 4, 7 and 8.

Project management

Project management involves focusing on a particular objective and devising strategies to deliver outcomes. It usually includes setting targets and devising work plans that sit alongside or are separate from typical daily work activity.

There are varied situations where you may find that project management skills are useful; for example, for occasional activity that is time-defined (preparation for inspection, implementation of a new policy/

procedure). It is also useful to enable you and your organisation to focus on the improvement of a particular activity. With the best will in the world it is not possible to put 100 per cent into all areas of your work at all times.

Defining an aspect of your work as a project gives you the opportunity to:

- undertake an evaluation of the work
- develop individuals in new tasks
- feel a sense of accomplishment as an organisation that you are really addressing an issue
- focus with purpose.

This gives an opportunity to make all staff part of the management team and can add variety to individuals' work.

Managing health and safety

We often hear about a climate of litigation that is affecting organisations' management of health and safety but much of the current legislation is valuable. Working with people always creates its own challenges and there are risks inherent in many activities that are routinely carried out, particularly with vulnerable people.

Infection control is an essential part of health and safety management

In the early 2000s there were a number of high-profile cases where large organisations were held to account for the death of their employees or members of the public. Concern that no one person was held accountable has led to the Corporate Manslaughter Act 2007. This allows for the conviction of a person or people in an organisation, usually in a senior role, as being held accountable for the death of a person.

Managing health and safety can be difficult; in health care hygiene issues have been very publicly debated. In a period of ten years the rate of infection for Methycillin Resistant Staphylococcus Aureus (MRSA) had risen from 2 per cent to 40 per cent; and in 2007 this rate dropped by 10 per cent. The rate of increase in the infection of Clostridium Difficile has also slowed.

In care services, managing health and safety can cause tensions between ensuring people are safe and also ensuring that people's right to live as they wish is respected.

The Healthcare Commission inspect standards in hospitals and in 2007 the government gave directives regarding deep cleaning and the introduction of infection control nurses and anti-microbial pharmacists. The Health Protection Agency reports on standards of infection.

Risk assessment

Managing risk does not, however, mean avoiding it. Risk assessment is detailed in Chapter 7. There you will see that the choice and control from service users or patients remains an important of health and safety.

Research shows that professionals take into account the following when considering risks:

- identifying and meeting needs
- minimising situational hazards
- protecting this individual and others
- balancing benefits and harms
- accounting for resources and priorities
- wariness of lurking conflicts.

(See *Community Care*, 16 August, 2007)

Management activity needs to take account of different service user needs and an example is that of managing behaviours that challenge services and professionals.

The Health and Safety Executive describes workplace violence as 'any incident in which an employee is abused, threatened or assaulted by a member of the public in circumstances arising out of the course of his or her employment.'

The GSCC requires organisations to:

- make it clear to service users and carers that violence, threats or abuse to staff are not tolerated
- produce and publicise policies for preventing violence
- produce and publicise policies and procedures for how to manage violent situations.

CASE STUDY

Health and safety breach

A care organisation was fined £23,000 and ordered to pay £12,600 in costs following the death of a resident who became trapped in bed rails. The Health and Safety Executive Inspector said 'This prosecution should send a clear message to all care home owners about the risks associated with their everyday equipment. Bed rails might look harmless but if they are incorrectly fitted or if unsuitable rails are used or if staff are inadequately trained – particularly in the case of elderly and frail residents – then they could pose a real danger.'

(From *Care Management Matters*, March 2007, page 7)

Questions

1 In your organisation think of an issue, such as bed rails, that raises the most controversy amongst staff and those who use the service. What are the strategies that you and the organisation have used to manage this to date?
2 What could be done differently?

Following the Health Act 2006, the Department of Health issued the Acts, Code of Practice for the Prevention and Control of Health Care Associated Infections (Department of Health, October 2007).

Statements include:

The Environment:

An NHS body must ensure that:

a there are policies for the environment which make provision for liaison between the members of any infection control team ('the ICT') and the persons with overall responsibility for facilities management.

b it designates lead managers for cleaning and decontamination of equipment used for treatment.

c all parts of the premises in which it provides healthcare are suitable for the purpose, are kept clean and are maintained in good physical repair and condition.

d the cleaning arrangements detail the standards of cleanliness required in each part of its premises and that a schedule of cleaning frequencies is publicly available.

e there is adequate provision of suitable hand wash facilities and antibacterial hand rubs.

f there are effective arrangements for the appropriate decontamination of instruments and equipment.

g the provision of linen and laundry supplies reflects Health Service Guidance HSG (95)18, Hospital Laundry Arrangements for Used and Infected Linen.

h staff clothing (including uniforms) is clean and fit for purpose.

Clinical Care:

An NHS body must have in place core policies concerning:

a standard (universal) infection control precautions.

b aseptic technique.

c major outbreaks of communicable infection.

d isolation of patients.

e safe handling and disposal of sharps.

f prevention of occupational exposure to blood-borne viruses (BBVs), including prevention of sharps injuries.

g management of occupational exposure to BBVs and post-exposure prophylaxis

h closure of wards, departments and premises to new admissions.

i disinfection policy.

j anti-microbial prescribing.

k reporting Healthcare Associated Infections (HCAI) to the Health Protection Agency (HPA) as directed by the Department of Health.

l Control of infections with specific alert organisms taking account of local epidemiology and risk assessment. These must include, as a minimum, MRSA, Clostridium Difficile infection and Transmissible Spongiform Encephalopathies (TSE).
(Department of Health, October 2007)

KNOWLEDGE CHECK

1 What strategies are taking place to manage the HCAI?

2 What are the principles of project management and how can they be applied to effectively manage activities in health and social care?

Managing quality

We have already mentioned standards when discussing how you can measure the performance of individuals in your team. Managing quality should involve continuously evaluating the service that you deliver and addressing any aspects of it that need to improve.

Standards are indicated through expectations of what service users and patients experience through the National Minimum Standards for different services. Quality is also managed through the expectations of health and social care workers in the National Occupational Standards.

Regulation and inspection of care services

Until 2008 the regulation of health and adult social care was carried out by:

● the Commission for Healthcare, Audit and Inspection, known as the Healthcare Commission, (including PCTs and NHS Trusts)

● the Commission for Social Care Inspection (all adult social care services in local authority, private and independent care organisations)

● the Mental Health Act Commission (checks the functions of the Mental Health Act 1983).

Care Quality Commission

From 2008 it is expected that an integrated regulator for health and adult social care will replace these three organisations with the Care Quality Commission (CQC).

The Health and Social Care Bill in November 2007 described the new Commission's functions as:

- assuring safety and quality
- performance assessment of commissioners and providers
- monitoring the operation of the Mental Health Act
- ensuring that regulation and inspection activity across health and adult social care is co-ordinated and managed.

Its aim is to ensure better outcomes for the people who use services by managing compliance with registration requirements.

Health and social care providers will be required to register with the new regulator in order to provide services. The registration requirements that all providers must meet will be consistent across both health and adult social care. For staff working in provider organisations, the new regulatory system will provide a much clearer system of exactly which requirements they must meet in order to provide services. The risk-based approach means that regulation activity will be targeted where action is required. Managers and teams in social care organisations will demonstrate that they are complying with all the requirements of registration and addressing any actions that are identified during inspection visits.

The revised regulatory system will provide more clarity on the requirements that a health and social care organisation must meet. It will work on a risk-based approach which means that regulation activity will be targeted on organisations where action to improve standards is required.

The CQC is likely to have a wider range of enforcement powers and more decision-making authority about how to use these. The Commission will be able to apply specific conditions to respond to specific risks; for example it could require a ward in a hospital, or an organisation in the community, to close until safety requirements have been met if there has been an issue of infection control. Potentially it

will be able to suspend or de-register services where the CQC considers this to be necessary. The CQC will be able to use sanctions in order to maintain standards. These include fining service providers, issuing early warning notices and eventually closing services down.

The CQC will assume responsibilities of the Mental Health Act Commission by monitoring the use of the Mental Health Act, and oversee the treatment of individuals who have been detained using its functions.

The process of inspections may alter during 2008 with the new CQC, but they may continue with some of the activities of their predecessor organisations. For example this may include key inspections.

Key inspections

Relevant information is collated prior to the inspection visit by contacting service users and other stakeholders who are connected to the service. Requests for surveys may be sent out and people who use services are spoken to.

These inspections take into account such issues as complaints, allegations, incidents and other concerns. Previous inspection reports are considered and also required actions.

Star ratings		Frequency of key inspections
3 stars	Excellent	One key inspection every 3 years
2 stars	Good	One key inspection every 2 years
1 star	Adequate	One key inspection each year
0 stars	Poor	Two key inspections each year

Random inspections

Random inspections usually follow up progress in addressing actions from a key inspection or to follow up a complaint about the service. If there have been changes to the service, such as a new manager, then a random inspection may also take place.

Thematic inspections

These were introduced in 2006 to allow a regulatory body to report nationally on the quality of care provision. These focus on a particular aspect of service delivery and in order to inform their report they investigate what is happening in individual services or organisations, as an example.

Annual service reviews

Introduced in 2007, the aim of this process is to regulate the quality of services that have been previously assessed at Excellent or Good. Relevant information about the service is obtained through the collation of evidence and then a judgement is made about whether the timescale of the next key inspection is appropriate or whether it needs to be brought forward. If there are considered to be risks to people using the service then the key inspection may be brought forward or there may be a random inspection.

What do inspectors do?

The activities that inspectors carry out in order to monitor the quality of the service that you provide are useful activities for you to carry out as part of continuous quality monitoring.

Figure 5.10 Inspectors carry out a variety of activities to make their judgements

In order that the experiences of service users make a significant dimension to the inspection, the inspectors will track the experiences of an individual or group from when they commenced use of the service to their current experience. *Experts by Experience* assist the inspectors in making judgements, as people who have experience of using services are often well informed about expectations. Findings from all these activities are used as evidence to inform their judgement as to what extent the service is addressing the statements in the National Minimum Standards appropriate to that organisation.

The findings of the inspector(s) are discussed with the manager before they leave and the inspectors write a publicly available report that is published on their website so that existing or potential users of that service can view their findings.

National Minimum Standards

In evaluating whether you are addressing quality issues a good measure is whether you feel there is evidence that suggests you are not meeting that standard. If you are having difficulty finding evidence in support of a standard then you may need to adopt a project management approach to explore that aspect of service delivery. If you are unable to find evidence to demonstrate that you are meeting that standard then how will an inspector?

Managing outcomes

Management activity is a *process* and is considered a worthy activity in itself. Demonstrating that systems are in place is important but what is more significant is the measurement of what impact these systems are having on the service and lives of those who use it. In other words, managing the *outcomes* is also important.

The outcome relates to the *impact* of an action, what actually happens as a result of any task. The most important dimension to this is the experience of the patients or service users.

Total Quality Management

A Total Quality Management (TQM) approach to managing the service involves all those involved in delivering the service to be involved in the quality issues that need managing. When you have to provide evidence to external regulators about the quality of the organisation against the relevant standards then written data is important.

'Our health, our care, our say'

This government White Paper was published in January 2006. It set a new direction for the whole health and social care system, confirming the vision set out in the Department of Health Green Paper, *Independence, Well-being and Choice*. There will be a radical and sustained shift in the way in which services are delivered, ensuring that they are more personalised and that they fit into people's busy lives. The aim is to give people a stronger voice so that they are the major drivers of service improvement, as outlined in the table below.

Outcome heading	Description	Relationship to regulation of social care
Quality of life	Access to leisure, social activities and lifelong learning and to universal, public and commercial services	• People who use the service have their independence actively promoted • Are supported to live a fulfilled life making the most of their capacity and potential • Are encouraged to try new and different experiences and will be supported to do so if they so wish
Exercising control and choice	Through maximum independence and access to information Being able to choose and control services and helped to manage risk in personal life	• People who use services • Have access with their carers to a service they think will be responsive to their individual needs and preferences • Feel well informed as to their options, rights and responsibilities to help them make their decisions • Have choices within the service they receive and feel able to express preferences that might be different from others receiving the service
Making a positive contribution	Maintaining involvement in local activities and being involved in policy development and decision-making	• People are seen as full members of their community • Are helped to be as involved in their community as they wish and their contribution is valued equally with other people
Personal dignity and respect	Not being subject to abuse Keeping clean and comfortable Enjoying a clean and orderly environment Availability of appropriate personal care	• People are treated in a way that helps them feel confident and secure • Privacy and dignity is valued and respected • People are free from abuse and neglect and their human rights are protected • Respect for individuals is a priority in every part of the service • The environment is good • The processes and procedures support respect • The way people are treated shows respect • The uniqueness of each individual is acknowledged and appreciated
Freedom from discrimination and harassment	Equality of access to services for all who need them	• People who use services have fair access regardless of their faith, beliefs, colour, sexuality, ethnicity or disability • People are not excluded or marginalised from services for any discriminatory reason. People feel safe and are safeguarded from harm • The service has clear, open and transparent ways for people to express concerns and anxieties and these are acted upon and addressed • People are able to say 'no' without fear of reprisal • Services welcome feedback which is acted upon for the benefit of those who use the service or make other choices
Improved health and emotional well-being	Enjoying good physical and mental health Access to appropriate treatment and support in managing long-term conditions independently There are opportunities for physical activity	• People's health and well-being needs are appropriately addressed so that the best possible quality of health is maintained for as long as possible • Improvement of health is encouraged and actively addressed • Emotional and mental health needs are responded to even where the person has other primary needs • People have a right to exercise choice and control and where necessary this involves their advocates being involved on their behalf • People have a right to refuse invasive treatment • End of life care is managed in a sensitive way, taking into account the person's needs and preferences • The service actively engages with a range of health care professionals so that people have access to a range of health options

Outcome heading	Description	Relationship to regulation of social care
Economic well-being	Access to income and resources sufficient for a good diet, accommodation and participation in family and community life Ability to meet costs arising from specific individual needs	• People have access to services that meet their needs • People feel well-informed and supported through access to advice and support as their circumstances and needs change • People should feel in control of their resources so that they can make choices on a daily basis • People receiving social care services are facilitated to contribute to their community by carrying out paid and/or unpaid employment appropriate to their preferences and skills

Added by the Commission for Social Care Inspection		
Leadership and management		• People experience services that are well led • Providers and staff understand what makes a high-quality social care service and how to make it happen • They plan what they do around the needs of people using the service • They know how to make the service better and are able to do so • People receiving the service know their views and opinions are regarded as important • They feel listened to and can see changes come about because their feedback is treated seriously • Where people are less capable of participating in how the service is delivered, or of expressing their views and opinions, the service finds ways of establishing their preferences so that they are supported to participate as much as they are able to • The service promotes high-quality outcomes and high-quality care for each individual • Staff are well trained and competent to provide people with the service that they need. • Staff are supported by their managers to give a good service to people and to treat everyone involved in the service with respect

CASE STUDY

Maintaining standards

Chris is the Registered Manager of The Ridges Care Home. They have just had a successful inspection but Chris is anxious that the excellent work of the highly motivated team in preparation for the inspection does not now ease off to the detriment of those who live in the home.

Questions

1 Devise an action plan for Chris that would enable him to address the actions that were identified in the report.
2 How could he maintain the high standards of quality that the team are delivering at the moment?

KNOWLEDGE CHECK

1 What is the difference between managing the process and managing for outcomes?
2 What aspects of quality are most important for those who use health and social care services?

Managing change

Any literature on management needs to consider the influence of change and management issues in delivering change. Our attitudes to change will be very different:

- some people have a total commitment to change and will be proactive about engaging with change processes to make change happen
- others will comply with necessary activities and help change to happen
- others will let change happen with grudging compliance
- some people demonstrate non-compliance as they oppose any changes.

(Seden and Reynolds, 2003, page 101)

The level of stress that a particular event incurs depends on how the person involved views that event and how well they are able to absorb or manage stress. (Chamber *et al*, 2002)

Some people will have a physical, social, intellectual or emotional response to change. A useful model of change is that of seeing change as being progress along a journey.

A manager should not underestimate the effects of change on people.

The prospect of change can lead to the following feelings in individuals:

- insecurity
- anguish
- loss
- confusion
- reduced competency.

At such times it is helpful to allow individuals to express negative feelings and to reduce anxiety by involving people in both the *stages* and the *pace* of change. Transition will be experienced differently by individuals in the team, and an appreciation of this will make sure that you steer them through change positively. Any emotions that your team experience may also be experienced by the service users, as changes affecting the team will almost certainly affect the people who use your service.

Reactions to change involve pushing forces and restraining forces. Trying to maintain an equilibrium throughout the course of change can help some individuals. Some people thrive on change and relish an opportunity to do things in a different way, whereas others struggle with anything that feels unfamiliar and new. As a manager you will need to accommodate the experiences of all members of the team in the development of new practices.

CASE STUDY

Dealing with change for Fatima

Fatima manages a Supported Living Mental Health service for those with substance abuse issues. The organisation has a new policy/procedure to be implemented across a dispersed and diverse workforce. Some aspects of the policy are going to be unpopular as they involve changes to weekend working patterns and the schedule of team meetings.

Question

1 What do you think is the best way to communicate the change? Remember it does not have to just be one way!

KNOWLEDGE CHECK

1 Why is change a difficult experience for some people?
2 How do you experience change?
3 How would someone who experiences change in an opposite way to you feel?

ACTIVITY

Now you are at the end of this chapter, look through the summary of management activities at the beginning again. Ask yourself the following questions:

- Do I feel more aware of how I work as a manager?
- What are my strengths?
- How can I maximise my use of these strengths?
- Where do my weaknesses lie?
- Am I honest about these and how can I work on improving these?

Now set yourself some SMART targets in order to address these. Plan to review them in three months' time. Remember that for you to manage yourself, your team and your organisation effectively, you need to maintain your own Continuing Professional Development.

Glossary

Competence: the ability to carry out a task to a specified standard

Delegation: handing over the responsibility for a task to a member of the team.

Effective: successful in producing the right outcome or making the right impact.

Emotional intelligence: personal attributes that enable people to succeed in life, including self-awareness, empathy, self-confidence, and self-control.

Leadership: the ability to guide, direct, or influence people; can be seen as a particular dimension of management or a particular approach/style of management.

Motivation: a feeling of enthusiasm, interest, or commitment that makes somebody want to do something, or something that causes such a feeling.

Objectives: the purpose or target of the care/support activity; what is being aimed for.

Stress: mental, emotional, or physical strain caused, for example by anxiety or overwork. It may cause such symptoms as raised blood pressure or depression.

References

Belbin, R.M,., Revised Team Roles in Mullins, L. 1985 (2002:28) *Management and Organisational Behaviour*, 6th edition, Harlow, Pearson Education Ltd

Department of Health (2007) Act

Drucker, P.F., in Mullins, 1985 (2002:28) *Management and Organisational Behaviour*, 6th edition, Harlow, Pearson Education Ltd

Goleman, D. (1995) *Emotional Intelligence: why it can matter more than IQ*

Learning Resource Network 2006, National Plan for the Learning Resource Network 2006–2009

Mullins, L. (2002) *Management and Organisational Behaviour*, 6th edition, Harlow, Pearson Education Ltd

Seden, J., and Reynolds, J., (eds.) (2003) *Managing Care in Practice*, London, Routledge

Skills for Care (2006) *Options for Excellence*

Skills for Care (2006) *Organisational Change and Workforce Development*

Social Care Institute for Excellence (2004) *Learning Organisations: A Self-Assessment Resource Pack*

Thomas, K., and Kilmann, R., (1974) *Thomas-Kilmann Conflict Mode* Instrument 2007 (This is not a published document and has to be purchased from CPP. Inc, California, USA for licensed use.)

Tuckman, B. (1965) Development sequence in small groups in *Psychological Bulletin*, LCII (6)

Useful websites

Care Quality Commission
New organisation established by Government in 2008 in order to manage the inspection and regulation of care services and organisations.

Commission for Social Care Inspection: www.csci.org.uk
Inspect and report on care services and councils.

General Social Care Council: www.gscc.org.uk
Register social care workers and regulate their conduct and training.

Healthcare Commission: www.healthcarecommission.org.uk
The independent watchdog for healthcare in England promoting continuous improvement in the services provided by the NHS and independent healthcare organisations.

National Audit Office: www.nao.org.uk

National Care Forum: www.nationalcareforum.org.uk

Sector Skills Council: Skills for Health: www.skillsforhealth.org.uk

Skills for Care: www.skillsforcare.org.uk
Working in consultation with carers, employers and service users, Skills for Care aims to modernise adult social care in England, by ensuring qualifications and standards adapt to meet the changing needs of people who use care services.

CHAPTER 6
Collaborative working

Introduction

The focus of this chapter is collaborative working between organisations, teams and individuals. The **integration** of health and social care is a clear theme at this time and this impacts on how organisations are structured and managed. We start by looking at how 'working in partnership' has become such a strong and recurrent theme in all aspects of health and social care over many years. We identify key policy guidance in the area and examine the reasons behind the adoption of this philosophy.

The chapter considers some of the various overlapping terminology used and asks whether, in essence, the same principle is at stake whatever the language. We follow this by taking a detailed look at the kinds of problems that occur when agencies do not work together effectively. Reflecting on and understanding these difficulties leads us on to an in-depth discussion of what lessons we can learn from research in this area. We then focus down to 'worker level' in more detail. We investigate the various reasons why, despite the strong messages from above, working in collaboration doesn't always work 'on the ground'.

To conclude the chapter there is a detailed section which considers both useful methods and the specific skills needed to ensure that the policies of working collaboratively can be put more meaningfully into practice.

This chapter addresses the following areas:

- Why work collaboratively?
- Issues
- Why collaborative working doesn't take place
- Effective collaboration

After reading this chapter it is hoped that you will be able to:

1 understand the reasons why collaborative working has been placed on top of the care agenda in recent years
2 be aware of the various reasons why collaborative working between agencies has not always happened
3 appreciate the difficulties that can occur when effective collaborative working does not take place
4 examine ways for workers to facilitate successful collaborative working.

Why work collaboratively?

Within the field of social care, the theme of working collaboratively has a long history, particularly when it comes to bridging the divide between health and social care.

Commissioning Framework for Health and Well-being (Department of Health, 2007)

Commissioners do not necessarily share between them information that could help improve outcomes for individuals or the population as a whole, and there is often a lack of understanding about what is legally permissible. We need to work towards an environment of trust and partnership, which gives people reassurance that the confidential nature of information will be respected while enabling commissioners to make appropriate use of it for them and the wider public interest within existing legal and ethical constraints.

The White Paper *Our health, our care, our say* has set objectives for integrated health and social care records by 2010 and, while this is a challenging target, some useful initial work has been done. NHS Connecting for Health has established an electronic social care record board (ESCRB) with responsibility for overseeing national implementation of the electronic social care record, ensuring consistency of its implementation by local authorities with social services responsibilities and integration with other information systems.

The effective sharing of appropriate information about individuals is crucial to more integrated **commissioning** and care, but it is also a complex challenge. The role of the Patient Information Advisory Group and local Caldicott Guardians are important in this context and the National Information Governance Board will strengthen arrangements. A scoping study of closer integration between health and social care systems, covering all client groups, is due to be completed by May 2007. This will address issues about information-sharing between health and social care and will take account of the recently published NHS Care Record Guarantee, which emphasises the rights of individuals to consent to information about them being shared. This study is also looking into how the technical architecture recommended in the SAP project can be implemented.

*'The White Paper **Our health, our care, our say**, promised to help people stay healthy and independent, to give people choice in their care services, to deliver services closer to home and to tackle inequalities. This framework is about action, with a particular focus on partnership. It is for everyone who can contribute to promoting physical and mental health and well-being, including the business community, government regional offices and the third sector.'*

This framework identifies eight steps to more effective commissioning:

1. Putting people at the centre of commissioning
This involves giving people greater choice and control over services and treatments (including self-care), and access to good information and advice to support these choices. Mechanisms will be developed to help the public get involved in shaping these services, with advocacy to support groups who find it hard to express views.

2. Understanding the needs of populations and individuals
Joint strategic needs assessment by councils, Primary Care Trusts (PCTs) and practice-based commissioners will help them to better understand the needs of individuals, by using recognised assessment and care planning processes appropriately, and mitigating risks to the health and well-being of individuals.

3. Sharing and using information more effectively
In order to make effective decisions for individuals and groups, we need to use and share information in an effective way. This includes clarifying what information can be shared under what circumstances, joining up the IT systems of frontline practitioners and encouraging individuals and communities to be co-producers of information.

4. Assuring high-quality providers for all services
Commissioners should develop effective, strong partnerships with providers and engage them in needs assessments. Procurement should be transparent and fair. Commissioning will be focused on outcomes, leading to more innovative provision, tailored to the needs of individuals and supplied by a wider range of providers.

5. Recognising the interdependence between work, health and well-being
Commissioners can facilitate collaborative approaches with businesses to improve advice and support for individuals. Additionally, all providers of NHS care will be incentivised to support and promote the health and well-being of their employees.

6. Developing incentives for commissioning for health and well-being
Bringing together local partners using Local Area Agreements will help to promote health, well-being and independence, by using contracts, pooling budgets and using the flexibilities of direct payments and practice-based commissioning.

7. Making it happen – local accountability
The Department of Health and the Department for Communities and Local Government will develop a single health and social care vision and outcomes framework, including a set of outcomes metrics aligned with the framework.

8. Making it happen – capability and leadership
The Department of Health and other national stakeholders will provide support to all local commissioners to address their capability gaps, where these national organisations can add real value.

1 What do you understand by the phrase 'commissioning' and does your own organisation get involved in any aspects of the commissioning process?
2 What do you think are key factors in the way that agencies work together?
3 What model of partnership does your organisation work to and what is your role in supporting this?

Given the diversity of welfare services in terms of different professions, different departments, different training, changing roles and functions, it is little wonder that, despite the best efforts of many, effective collaboration between different agencies has been hard to achieve. Much of the time different agencies have been pulling away from each other rather than pulling together. The government made this blunt observation in its 1998 document *Modernising Social Services*.

> Sometimes various agencies put more effort into arguing with one another than into looking after people in need.

Next, we will look at how, since the late 1990s, New Labour governments have been determined to ensure 'joined up' government and 'joined up' ways of working and have made certain policy statements to back up the need for agencies to work in partnership. However, first you should be aware of where your own workplace fits into this agenda.

Collaboration: definitions and debates

A theme throughout this whole book is the need to be mindful of the language we use. We need to ensure clarity when we are communicating with others but we have seen that different words convey different nuances of meaning to different people. The temptation in this chapter is to talk in terms of 'other professionals'. We prefer not to use this term but instead use the more general term 'worker' because it is less exclusive and more accurately describes the full range of workers who get involved with our clients. For the purpose of this chapter, 'worker' refers not only to paid workers but also to unpaid workers, such as an advocate or volunteer.

Using phrases to clients such as 'we've had a meeting of professionals' may sound impressive but it is potentially belittling and disempowering to them and their families. It also calls into question who exactly is a professional anyway. There is too much 'us' and 'them' in this phrase. Such use of the word 'professional' may possibly exacerbate tensions between, say, a senior residential care worker and an occupational therapist – both of whom play an equally valuable role but have had different training.

This is obviously quite a subjective area. However, for the purposes of this chapter the chosen term to denote anyone with a formal role with the client is 'worker'. It is currently quite fashionable in social care discourse to refer to 'stakeholders' in the context of working together. Use of this word will mainly be avoided in this chapter for the reason that 'stakeholder' usually refers to both formal and informal involvement, and the main focus of the chapter is collaborative working between formal workers – that is, workers who work for some form of organisation – not families, neighbours or friends.

Mostly, the organisations that those other workers work for will be referred to as 'agencies'. This is an unfamiliar term for some people and can be difficult to get to grips with. Clients can mistake what you mean because they may associate the term with other types of agencies they are more familiar with, such as travel agencies or estate agencies. The term also has its limitations when referring to where, say, GPs or district nurses work. We might prefer to use the term surgery, practice or even primary healthcare team. However, when we talk about 'inter-agency', collaboration between, say, health and social care or social care and housing, we mean all those workers who work in that area of service provision.

What do we mean by collaborative working?

Literature in this area abounds with different words and phrases for what is essentially the same thing. We could talk about collaborative working, joint working, co-operation, working in partnership, working together, inter-agency working, multi-disciplinary working, networking, coalition, integrated working,

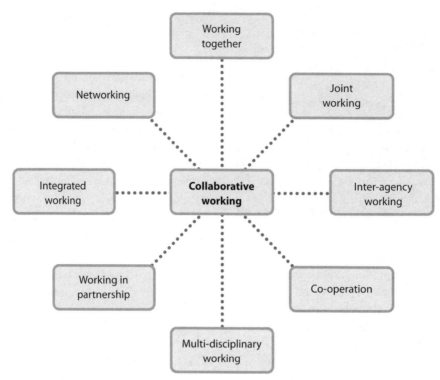

Figure 6.1 Types of collaborative working

or even consultation. Each of these terms could be said to have its own particular shade of meaning and, in certain contexts, there may be significant differences. Nevertheless, in the context of this chapter, we are essentially using the terms interchangeably. Our basic idea is that they are all used to refer to the notion of collective actions by individuals or their organisations which produce more benefit for clients than each could accomplish as an individual player.

If anything, collaborative working has been chosen mainly because this is a book primarily written for frontline workers. Other terms like joint working or working in partnership are often more associated – at least in some people's minds – with working together at a higher organisational level, such as joint investment, joint commissioning, pooling of budgets

and so on. We will, however, return later to discuss the different levels on which collaborative working can take place even between frontline workers.

What guidance have you had about the need to work collaboratively? You will need to locate your own organisation's mission statement or statement of purpose and find out what it says about working collaboratively. What about other manuals, practice guidance or operating instructions? Read them through – especially the introductory sections. What evidence can you find that there are moves to ensure more effective collaborative working?

It would be surprising if your research did not inform you that the requirement to work collaboratively is embedded in all kinds of policy documents. As indicated earlier, *Modernising Social Services* is the original New Labour blueprint for working collaboratively. However, before that, the need for health and local authorities to prepare Joint Investment Plans had already been established resulting from the *Better Services for Vulnerable People* guidance issued in 1997. In 1998, two significant developments took place. The government set up the Health and Social Care Joint Unit, whose job it is to develop policy on joint working between health and social services. It also published a discussion document called *Partnership in Action*. In the foreword Ministers for Health explain:

> All too often when people have complex needs spanning both health and social care, good quality services are sacrificed for sterile arguments about boundaries. When this happens people ... and those who care for them, find themselves in the no-man's land between health and social care services. This is not what people want or need. It places the needs of the organisation above the needs of the people they are there to serve. It is

poor organisation, poor practice, poor use of taxpayer's money – it is unacceptable.

Although the document goes on to say that 'major structural change is not the answer', subsequent legislation has paved the way for far-reaching structural and organisational change. For example, the Health Act 1999 gave both health and social care agencies powers to pool budgets and delegate functions to enable provision and lead commissioning. This impacted more at management level. The Health and Social Care Act 2001 introduced changes that would affect workers at all levels. This Act created a new body – the 'Care Trust'. The aim of this radical step was to achieve integration of health and social services for vulnerable people. Instead of persisting with the line that two separate agencies must work more closely together, the creation of Care Trusts meant the dissolving of existing organisational boundaries and creating new integrated organisations. To some extent, the way had been paved by the earlier phasing in of Mental Health Trusts which operate on a similar integrated principle. However, the tradition of multi-disciplinary working through the Community Mental Health Team made this change less of a culture shock.

It should not be assumed that the concept of partnership working is simply about health and social care, important as these two elements are. The National Service Framework for Older People, for example, set up Local Strategic Partnerships, whose role is to 'bring together the public, private, voluntary and community sectors' into a single 'overarching framework'. The document assumes that the various standards it sets can only be met by all relevant services working together. Therefore, issues of housing, transport and a range of other services have to be co-ordinated at a strategic level.

As far as actual working practices at the frontline level are concerned, collaborative working has been signalled in just about every policy document concerned with health and social care. For example, *Valuing People*, the government's major policy document for people with learning disabilities, under the heading 'Integrated Professional Working', makes this statement:

> (Learning Disability) Partnership boards should review the role and function of community learning disability teams in order to ensure that:

all professional staff become a resource for the local implementation of the White Paper and to help achieve social inclusion for people with learning disabilities

organisational structures encourage and promote inclusive working with staff from the fields of housing, education, primary care, employment and leisure.

(Department of Health, 2001, page 110)

It is clear that the principles of *Valuing People* can only be achieved if staff work collaboratively.

Standard 2 of the National Service Framework for Older People is about 'Person-centred care'. Its stated aim is that:

NHS and social care services treat older people as individuals and enable them to make choices about their care. This is achieved through the single assessment process, integrated commissioning arrangements and integrated provision of services, including community equipment and continence services.

(Department of Health, 2001, page 23)

Both managers and 'professionals' are told that they must 'provide co-ordinated and integrated service responses'. We have to remember that an important reason that the National Service Framework was introduced in the first place was to eradicate unnecessary delay and duplication of effort – this implies a commitment to working collaboratively. In a similar vein, the National Service Framework for Mental Health embodies the same principles. It states that people with mental health problems can expect that services will 'be well co-ordinated between all staff and agencies'.

Therefore, we can see quite clearly that in all areas of care the need to work collaboratively is clearly stated in official documentation. Over and above this, we have seen that in the field of health and social care, the government has been prepared to make radical changes to organisations to try to ensure that the old barriers to collaborative working practices might be dismantled.

Department of Health Private Finance Initiative: Criteria for bids approval

There are four Department of Health criteria for adult social care PFI. These are consistent with the White Paper *Our Health, Our Care, Our Say*. The emphasis is on using capital investment to integrate people rather than isolate them; and to provide them with choices and opportunities for getting better and getting back to independent living where possible.

One of the criteria is that of joint planning and joint working:

We expect projects to demonstrate close cooperation and joint working between health and social care in a way that supports social inclusion and is relevant to the client group needs that are being addressed.

The case for collaboration

We have seen how successive governments have set out the case for working collaboratively. This wisdom is handed down from 'on high'. There is no reason to accept this view uncritically. Many writers have commented on the dearth of hard evidence that

---

CASE STUDY

Integrating services

Barnsley is pursuing integration via its commissioning activity. Commissioning and provider functions are formally separated, there are pooled health and social care budgets, and services are commissioned from the provider arm. Barnsley's focus is on the practical implementation of individual budgets for routine care, rather than selection of an off-the shelf governance structure.

Questions

1 What is your local authority's approach to the organisation of health and social care and the commissioning process?
2 To what extent does your local authority encourage independent providers of health and social care?
3 What benefits does the commissioning process have to the organisation and delivery of care for local people?

supports this view. In fact, some have challenged the idea that collaborative working is inherently a good thing. Concerns have been raised about blurred accountability as well as questioning whether claims of comprehensiveness and seamlessness are justified (Leathard (1994), Loxley (1997), Hudson (2000)).

Therefore, we need to proceed positively but with a degree of healthy scepticism. If we reflect on our own experiences in social care, these can almost certainly provide many reasons to work collaboratively. We should ask ourselves what working in care would be like if we were compelled to work completely on our own. How successful or effective would we be if we were denied the advice, knowledge, opinion or any other type of input from other workers? How are our clients benefiting from workers working in isolation from each other?

It is perfectly possible that some workers do not think there would be any problems. They presumably enjoy the freedom from the interference of others, content in the knowledge that they are capable of sorting out all aspects of their client's care on their own. Sometimes we work with people assuming that we are the only worker who matters in their lives. This raises a key question – are we always aware of who else is involved in our service users' lives and what they do?

Completing this exercise should have brought out how many different workers may be involved with our clients. Some clients have many involvements, for others you may be the only worker. The exercise probably showed we work more closely and more frequently with some workers than others. There also might have been other observations, such as frequent contact with certain workers doesn't always mean that you have a good working relationship with them. You may even have started wondering more about what exactly it is that those other workers do! The basic premise of this chapter is that client care improves if there are good working relationships between all workers involved. Have any of your thoughts or discussions so far suggested otherwise?

Partnerships in practice

So far, we have established that, ordinarily in social care, several workers from different agencies work with vulnerable people. We have also seen that over a long period successive governments have urged that to promote better, person-centred care the various agencies – and the disciplines within them – need to work a lot more closely together. Government has also backed this up with key policy changes.

Whilst understanding the reasoning behind these exhortations, frontline workers, in their various workplaces, should be asking themselves what it actually means for them. Does it, for example, mean that we should team up with colleagues from other agencies and approach our work as a kind of double act, a kind of care version of Dalziel and Pascoe? It is one thing to extol the virtues of working

REFLECT

1 Think about your own work. With the clients who you work with, make a list of all the other workers, of any description, who have in some way had some input or influence in those clients' lives. Remember you don't have to see or speak with these workers personally; communication could be through referral or report, letter, fax or email. You may even be aware of their existence but have never communicated with them.
2 Group these other workers under main headings such as health, education, social care, housing, benefits, other.
3 Compare your list with someone else from another area of work, if possible. Either on your own or with another, go through the workers under each heading and identify:
   a Who do you have most contact with?
   b Who do you enjoy the best working relationships with?
   c Who the least?
   d Who have you got on your 'other' list? Are they from statutory agencies such as the police, voluntary organisations or private agencies such service providers?

REFLECT

When you see statements urging you to work more in partnership, work collaboratively or work in a 'multi-disciplinary' fashion, what does it actually conjure up in your mind that you should be doing? Write down how you understand this term.

collaboratively, it is another thing to put this into meaning for people.

If you had been undertaking that activity 'collaboratively' with another worker, it would be interesting to share your views and compare your different responses. This in itself would be an example of one form of collaboration. We are sure you have found that there are many meanings that can be attached to this whole area. If we were to arrange the various ways of what working collaboratively could mean in some sort of order or hierarchy, it might look like the following.

7 As below, but in addition different agency staff are invited to each other's team meetings, other means of communication are used such as group emailing, newsletters, study days etc. The purpose of this being to move forward together in terms of information sharing, raising of issues, giving access to certain resources, breaking down of any boundaries.
6 As below, but also routinely meeting with other key workers (either in professional groups or on the basis of locality or both), so that as well as specific cases, more general issues in common can be raised, discussed and sorted out.
5 As below, but, where relevant, setting up joint visits with another key worker, such as a district nurse, CPN, or housing worker, so that issues in common can be agreed and worked on jointly. Also, with client's permission, sharing case information with other agencies.
4 As for level 3 but also discussing your client's needs more fully with them and their carer(s) – referring on to other relevant agencies, explaining what your involvement is and what you would like them to do.
3 Making a point of finding out who is currently involved. Clarifying exactly what their role is and establishing contact with them, also explaining what your involvement is.
2 Being aware of the existence of other workers, having a clear idea of their role. Making a point of letting them know you have a client in common – where it's relevant.
1 Being aware of the existence of other workers, having a rough idea of their job role. Referring to them and communicating when it is obvious that the occasion calls for it.

Figure 6.2 A ladder of collaboration

The hierarchy can be drawn in many different ways with plenty of other stages built in. It is not definitive by any means. However, the point we are trying to make is that there is a spectrum where at the least collaborative end a worker will be mainly independent, reacting to the roles of others only where it is clearly obvious and usually just on the specifics of one case. At the other end, the approach is more proactive and thinking outside of the details of a particular case; here the worker is consciously seeing themselves as part of a wider network.

CASE STUDY

Working together

Gavin Chadwick is a 29-year-old man with cerebral palsy who is keen on all types of sports. He lives on his own and has a 24-hour carer paid for by social services. He has read about Direct Payments and would like to take this further.

You go and see Gavin to discuss things in more detail. It becomes apparent that there are other issues in his life. He is bored on his own with nothing to do, his main contact being with his family. He is also fed up with the bland diet that 'the medics' originally recommended he follow. He doesn't say so but you think he is depressed. His car is off the road and he is having problems with the Motability scheme so he can't get it replaced to go anywhere.

You are not very experienced in how Direct Payments work. You are also put off by the paperwork.

Questions

1 From the details you have, what would be the least collaborative working response to Gavin?

2 How might working more collaboratively benefit not only Gavin, but other people in similar positions and other workers as well? Give specific suggestions and explain your reasoning.

ACTIVITY

Identify recent government initiatives that urge closer working between health and social care.

Investigate your own organisation's approach to working with other organisations.

Issues

Although our focus in this chapter is primarily adult social care, there are nevertheless key lessons that can be learnt from the reports published in respect of child abuse tragedies.

We are probably all too aware of the number of inquests and enquiries that have been held when child abuse tragedies have occurred. One of the most high profile ones was the investigation into the death of Maria Colwell in 1973. The findings showed that a major contributory factor in Maria Colwell's death was the lack of inter-professional co-operation. On the back of the Report major changes were made to the UK's child protection system, and inter-agency working was built into the system. However, the new system could not prevent the death of Jasmine Beckford in 1985 and the huge problems in Cleveland in 1987 when the authorities overreacted in response to concerns about widespread sexual abuse. A new major set of guidelines was produced in 1988 called *Working Together* which was followed by the Children Act 1989. In 1995, the Department of Health published *Child Protection: Messages from Research*.

Unfortunately, the various initiatives to improve inter-agency working have not been able to prevent the deaths of children known to the authorities, the most high profile case in recent years being that of Victoria Climbie. Lord Laming produced the findings from his inquiry in 2003 and the progress against these has been regularly reviewed. He stated in 2007 his dismay at the lack of change in what he viewed as manageable actions.

REFLECT

Investigate the findings from the Laming Inquiry 2003 and consider to what extent your own organisation has adopted the principles that it suggests.

There is one striking feature of the vast majority of the inquiries that have been reported which stands out above all others – it is each committee's conclusion that inter-agency communication was flawed. Typically, there were crucial mistakes identified where agencies did not pass on or share information with each other. These reports show that tragedies occur not only when a single piece of information of major importance is not passed on properly, but when the passing of any information doesn't take place – however seemingly insignificant; this prevents workers in various agencies from building up a full picture of what is going on. The same 'small' thing happening many times is as important to know about as a 'big' thing happening once. This was evidently a problem in child protection, but can equally be a

CASE STUDY

The need for information to be passed on

Arthur Robins is an 80-year-old diabetic who also has Alzheimer's disease. He has domiciliary care at home but his 81-year-old wife Ada tends to keep an overall eye on him. Ada is rushed into hospital with suspected angina. The request is made by the GP to social services that Mr Robins must be found emergency respite because he has Alzheimer's and cannot be left on his own. The GP also says that with Mr Robins there is often a risk of hypoglycaemia.

Mr Robins is quickly assessed and taken to a nearby residential home for a two week stay while his wife undergoes investigations and treatment. The day after his admission Mr Robins becomes quite ill. Social services are also telephoned several times by his daughter wanting to know why he had been admitted to a home when her own daughter would have been able to stay in the house for at least a week. Both the district nurses and the daughter make a strong complaint that the home were not informed about Mr Robins' diabetes, saying that he could have been kept at home given the amount of distress it has caused him.

Questions

Think over these details.

1 What information is not passed on and why?
2 Why do you think this is?
3 How do you think the whole situation could have been improved – paying particular attention to the communication of information between different workers?

problem in work with vulnerable adults. The outcomes might not always have such seriously tragic consequences but could be very distressing or harmful nevertheless. The significance of one 'small' piece of information may not be appreciated until it has been collated with other 'small' pieces of information.

The pooling and sharing of case information is vital if collaborative working is going to take place effectively. There are reasons why this doesn't always take place as we will examine in more detail later on in the chapter. Failure to share information effectively can often lead to problems. However, equally important is the need to make sure that the other worker or agency understands the significance of any information given to them.

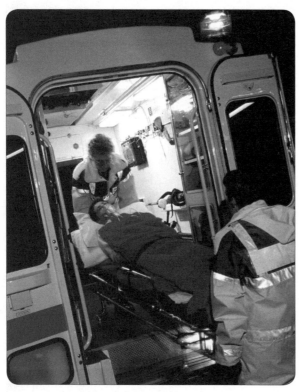

In an emergency vital information may not be passed on to all who need it

Key lessons to be learnt from the kind of case described above include these.

- Time taken to build up more information about Mr Robins' situation would have led to better decision-making. The impulse to do something quickly should be avoided.
- Workers from social services did not feel able to further interrogate the opinion of the GP. Is this a

sign of professional power imbalance? In any event, the GP and social services have not collaborated very well.

- Information about Mr Robins' health and how best to manage it was not fully made clear.
- Too much is taken for granted and insufficiently clarified to all concerned.
- Information about Mr Robins' family network was not fully investigated and shared.
- The views of Mr Robins, his wife and his regular carers don't seem to have been explored in any great detail.

There are other points that you could make about this kind of case but it shows the peril of making decisions and embarking on courses of action with too little information, and the problem of incorrectly using information that is known. The case study suggests some 'remoteness' between the workers involved. It does not seem that they have developed any real trust or mutual understanding – as a result, client care has suffered badly. If care is increasingly about the assessment and management of risk, then not only must this process be informed by an adequate flow of information between concerned parties but workers should make others clearly aware about what they consider the risk factors to be. As discussed in Chapter 7 on assessment, for all kinds of reasons not everyone has the same perception of risk – it should not be taken for granted that if, say, you use the term 'hypoglycaemia' in a discussion the other will know what the significance is. On the other hand, the person hearing the term 'hypoglycaemia' needs to clarify its significance and what to do about it.

What lessons can be learned?

How might the different workers react to the situation in the case study? Here is one scenario:

- The GP becomes exasperated by what has happened and makes this clear in discussion with their colleagues at the medical practice. They regret the lack of basic health care knowledge possessed by social care staff.
- The social services workers lament the autocratic style of the GP blaming them for passing on partial information.
- The residential home staff feel a mixture of guilt and anger about the way Mr Robins' admission to their home was managed. They have been

presented with a man who they weren't able to look after properly. They blame both the GP and the social services.

It would be nice to think that such defensive and blaming reactions would not take place. However, we all know that in reality they often do. We would suggest that the whole process could have gone better, and there would have been less cause for recrimination, if all parties concerned knew each others' ways of working and were familiar with and trusted each other *before* the incident takes place. A key lesson is that it is hard to work effectively with people who you don't know or are not sure about.

Therefore, while it is not hard to demonstrate that client care suffers when workers don't work collaboratively, it needs to be recognised that another more insidious problem is that each failure, like the one seen in the case study, can quite easily lead to a more entrenched view of one set of workers about another. Less trust and more suspicion are likely to further inhibit the good working relations needed to work collaboratively.

REFLECT

Reflect on your own work. Think about occasions where collaborative working did not take place effectively. What sorts of problems emerged? Who were they a problem for and why?

CASE STUDY

Confusion

Danny Miles is 25 and has Down's Syndrome; his learning disability is categorised as mild to moderate. He lives in a group home run by a housing association and staffed by an independent care agency. He has a keyworker at the group home. He also has a care manager employed by the local Learning Disability Partnership. Five days a week, he attends a life skills course at his local FE college. There he has a personal tutor, Mike. Danny's parents live about 15 miles away and see him at least once a month.

At lunch time, Danny has got into the habit of occasionally augmenting his lunch money by leaving the college, walking into town and telling passers-by that he has lost his lunch money. Sometimes he goes to the nearby pub and offers to buy drinks for others at the bar. Mike knows from first-hand experience that Danny has a very low tolerance of alcohol. The local pub has an arrangement with Mike that should they see this happening they will let him know. Mike then goes over informally to the pub to collect Danny. He reminds him that there are risks and 'morality' problems with what he's doing. The behaviour then usually stops for a while.

The college tutor has never passed this information on to anybody outside the college. This is mainly because he doesn't know who exactly is involved with Danny and also because he regards it as 'college business'. In any event, he thinks that the existing arrangement works fine. Every year Mike is invited to a case review held at the group home. Mike couldn't get to the last one because he was teaching.

Unbeknown to Mike, Danny also frequents the pub at the weekend when he goes with a small group of residents under the supervision of a group home worker. They mainly go for bar games and only order soft drinks.

On one occasion, however, a new member of the bar staff serves Danny and his new 'friends' at lunch time. He then continues serving other customers. After half an hour Danny is drunk and involved in a brawl with two other men. Danny ends up being violently sick. The member of staff calls the police who, in turn, call the social services. Danny's care manager is baffled by what's happened and takes Danny round to his GP for a medical examination. Eventually, after many phone calls the situation is sorted out and Danny is taken home. The following day, Danny's parents insist on talking to the group home manager – wanting to know how such an incident could take place.

Questions

1 Who is responsible for this episode – are Danny's parents talking to the right person?
2 If you were the care manager, how would you ensure that similar misunderstandings did not occur?

Your reflections might have thrown up several different kinds of problem. The next one we shall look at is confusion.

It would seem that a key factor in the scenario above was not only the lack of information passed on, or the failure to do a proper risk assessment, but the general confusion about who has responsibility for Danny's welfare, and what that responsibility entails. As a result, Danny found himself in a very vulnerable situation. It would be tempting to simply blame Mike, the college tutor, but it is more than that, it's more of a system failure. The overall network around Danny had broken down – or, as it appears, never been properly established. Working collaboratively would have entailed interested parties meeting, talking through what Danny is like and what he likes to do, the risks involved and, more importantly, discussing how to manage the situation collectively. This could have forestalled a very unfortunate incident.

Duplication of effort

The final problem we are going to focus on when people don't work collectively is that of duplication of effort. The introduction of the Single Assessment Process recognised that vulnerable adults usually have several social and healthcare workers attending to them. Also, when more than one worker becomes involved with an individual, that person can often face several assessments – all asking for a lot of the same information. This is a waste of time for all concerned and is potentially both tiring and irritating for the person concerned.

The Single Assessment Process may have gone some way in cutting down on duplication at the assessment stage, although this has yet to be fully researched. However, the initial assessment is only one area where, because of unco-ordinated inputs, duplication of effort can take place. It doesn't include all areas of involvement – just those from the statutory health and social fields. Unnecessary duplication can take place at every stage of care involvement. The result is always wasteful but often there are other negative consequences – confusion and alarm for example. If we go back to Danny's case, if all of the people involved with him had decided, for one reason or another, to contact his parents, the parents could have easily felt overwhelmed and much more concerned.

Information gathering and contact with clients and their families are two areas identified where duplication of effort takes place.

REFLECT

From your own practice, identify areas of work or procedure that are often unnecessarily duplicated by more than one worker. Consider these questions.

1 What are these areas?
2 How much is the duplication you have identified to do with individual work practices and how much is a consequence of organisational procedures?
3 In both cases, how could such duplications be avoided?

On the level of the individual worker, we would suggest that there are reasons why work is duplicated. Firstly, it may be that one worker isn't aware that another is involved. Secondly, they might not trust the other workers to do the task properly. Thirdly, agency working practices may not permit the sharing of information. In each case, the development of better collaborative working relationships could help deal with each of these problems – to the benefit of all concerned. There are clearly limits to what extent frontline workers can change agency procedures, but that doesn't mean there aren't many areas where improvements could be made.

KNOWLEDGE CHECK

1 Identify three major problems that can occur when workers don't work together effectively.
2 Explain why, sometimes, simply passing on information to another agency isn't always going to promote client care.
3 How would you put the vicious circle of suspicion and the virtuous circle of trust in your own words?
4 What types of confusion might occur in a case where several workers are involved?
5 Describe three reasons why work with clients can be unnecessarily duplicated.

Why collaborative working doesn't take place

Several studies have investigated the many barriers to effective collaboration that exist. Nearly all of them point to factors that run much deeper than the practices of individual workers – such as different organisational cultures or professional philosophies. Each of these factors will be examined in more detail later on. However, because this is a text written primarily with frontline workers in mind, we acknowledge that at day-to-day level there are obvious limitations as to how much the individual worker can influence organisational structures or cultures. Nevertheless, this should not be an excuse to shrug our shoulders, fail to take responsibility and put it down to being a 'management thing'.

We would argue that in many cases, collaborative working doesn't succeed because of a combination of factors – involving organisational, cultural, philosophical and personal factors. There is usually an interrelationship between one or more of these factors. The justification for saying this is that often, even when relationships are poor between agencies, there are some workers who still manage to establish good working relationships with others despite the barriers they face. Conversely, there are situations where two agencies might be committed to joint working. They could have many systems in place to ensure that this happens but there are still problems at the interpersonal level. Consequently, the situation is a complex one and needs to be tackled on many fronts and at many levels.

REFLECT

1 In no particular order, write down all the various ways you see your job role.

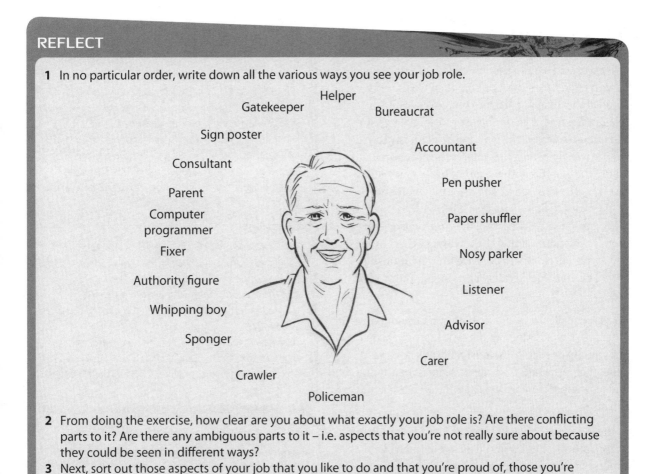

Helper
Gatekeeper
Bureaucrat
Sign poster
Accountant
Consultant
Pen pusher
Parent
Computer programmer
Paper shuffler
Fixer
Nosy parker
Authority figure
Listener
Whipping boy
Advisor
Sponger
Carer
Crawler
Policeman

2 From doing the exercise, how clear are you about what exactly your job role is? Are there conflicting parts to it? Are there any ambiguous parts to it – i.e. aspects that you're not really sure about because they could be seen in different ways?

3 Next, sort out those aspects of your job that you like to do and that you're proud of, those you're neutral about and those you actually dislike doing and that make you feel bad about yourself.

Personal factors

As will be discussed in Chapter 7 we all bring our own personalities, backgrounds and values to our work – this is called our personal context. We also argued that we should try to develop a degree of self-awareness about our personal context in order to ensure that it didn't interfere with the goal of being focused on our clients' needs. It is worth considering this as we seek to explore why sometimes problems emerge when we try to work collaboratively.

Clearly, depending on our jobs and personalities, we will all have different responses. It would be odd, however, if there were no ambiguities, conflicts or aspects of our role with which we were uncomfortable. There are several 'faces' we need to present to our clients and their carers. There are several aspects of our job roles with which we feel more comfortable than others. Sometimes, it is very tempting to try to pass the more difficult or uncomfortable sides of our role onto others. That way we have less role conflict, less ambiguity, less inner tension and more peace of mind. When working with other workers we can sometimes fall into this trap. If we can make them the 'bad cop' then we (having shuffled the difficult part onto our colleague) can relax in the role of 'good cop'. For example, we can present ourselves as the genuine helper, only too willing to help, whilst the other is the bureaucrat telling the client that they cannot have a particular service. There are many scenarios in which one worker tries to find a way of dealing with the perceived negative aspects of the case by projecting them onto or associating them with another. In this way, workers can try to improve their relationship with a client by deliberately disparaging the work of others.

This type of displacement activity can take place in any area of work. Much of the time it is not carried out wilfully or even consciously. In stressful and difficult circumstances, it can be seen as an attempt to find a personal comfort zone at another worker's expense.

In the case study above, there are likely to be personal factors at work but these can be put in the wider context of scarce resources and different organisational cultures. This is a good opportunity to look at some of the research which has tried to understand why inter-agency collaboration has not always worked particularly successfully.

University of Birmingham, Health Services Management Centre (Dr Tim Freeman and Professor Edward Peck) have produced a report, *Provision of*

CASE STUDY

Failure to work together

Joe Simpkins is a care manager. He has a case where the client is 88-years-old, barely being maintained at home and desperately in need of a permanent nursing placement. The client's family are putting Joe under constant pressure to get it sorted out as soon as possible. Joe has done his assessment and completed all the necessary paperwork, funding has been approved.

The problem is there are no nursing beds in social services contracted homes within a 40-mile radius. There is a private nursing home but their fees far exceed the social services benchmark figure. The family take every opportunity to lobby whoever is involved, to 'get the thing moving'. Joe has explained on several occasions that the private bed cannot be used unless the family want to top up the fees, but they are unable to do this.

District nurses visit regularly; they are also feeling the pressure. The district nurses understand the situation perfectly well but when confronted by the increasingly distressed family members they occasionally lapse into saying things like 'If only social services pulled their finger out', or on one occasion 'I'm not sure whether Mr Simpkins quite understands just how risky the situation is.'

Questions

1. Do you think Joe and the district nurses are working together effectively? Give reasons.
2. What effect do you think the nurses' statements have for Joe, the client, the family?
3. What effect do you think the comments have for the nurses?
4. How could collaborative working be improved in this case?

Model	Issue(s)
Care Trust	• Possible political difficulties as may be seen as an 'NHS solution' by local authority partners. • Not clear whether Care Trust is now a commissioner or provider model and to what extent it still has Department of Health support.
Community Foundation Trust	• Some Department of Health ambivalence perceived out in the field, presumably due to its potential monopoly provider status and creation of additional (and elaborate) formal governance structures. However, governance model promises community engagement. • Fears over PbR (possible loss of local provision). • Scope of Monitor's regulatory influence.
Social Enterprises	• Concerns over transfer of NHS and LA pensions. • Asset locks of some models may be attractive to staff who value a community ethos, but risk potential investment by private sector partners and reification of current patterns of provision. • Application of EU procurement rules and need for market testing could lead to uncertainty and loss of contracts.
Mental Health Partnership Trusts	• Concern over loss of 'local' emphasis (especially if expansion into area by adjacent existing Partnership trust). • Concern this is an NHS model not engaging local authorities. • Return to monolithic Mental Health Institutions of the past.
Arms Length Management Organisation (ALMO)	• Transferability of model from Social Housing and legal framework (not-for-profit company limited by guarantee).

Summary table: provider models and associated issues

adult services in partnership between health and social care: Considering the options, based on a closed seminar held on 23 May 2007 at the King's Fund.

The four geographical areas that they studied are similar to the extent that they are:

• unitary authorities, and already have co-terminous boundaries across local authorities and primary care trusts;
• actively pursuing service integration across health and social care;

CASE STUDY

Pursuing integration

Wolverhampton has been pursuing integration in service provision for some time. Their vision is for mental health services to be provided by local integrated community-based NHS and social care teams. They expressed concerned about the development of large mental health trusts which have the potential to lose local focus.

They currently have:

• joint governance arrangements for health and social care, with separate provider and commissioner structures, pooled commissioning budgets and integrated service budgets;
• jointly provided and managed services;
• an overarching Framework Partnership Agreement between the organisations and staff (agreed with Trade Unions) to cover all partnership arrangements.

In the context of ten years of joint commissioning and service integration, **Milton Keynes** is pursuing

a social enterprise joint venture between health and social care. They are keen to ensure continued local provision anticipating single-access and joined up services focused on well-being. The Milton Keynes pilot is the largest of the Department of Health social enterprise 'pathfinder' sites, and the choice of a social enterprise model (non-profit with social purpose) is intended to ensure continued staff support.

Questions

1 How does your local authority differ from Wolverhampton?
2 Investigate the models above and consider which one your organisation most closely resembles
2 What factors influence the success of partnership agreements?
3 What social enterprise is taking place locally to you?

- 'mainstreaming' mental health services provision within their organisation of adult primary, community and social care services;
- outcome focused;
- pursuing a shared NHS and local authority vision for service development, based on the individual needs of citizens.

Philosophical and professional barriers to collaboration

Van Eyk and Baum (2002) encapsulated many of these difficulties. They found that:

1 Staff normally feel loyalty and commitment to the agency in which they work. However, this can make it more difficult for them to think or work at an inter-agency level, which could potentially involve shifting resources or services between agencies. The addition of institutional and professional politics (both within and between agencies) can contribute to this difficulty. The research showed that there can be a 'them and us' attitude both *within* and between *different* professional groups, which can work against inter-agency collaboration.
2 In some cases, 'them and us' attitudes can be attributed to a response to new and threatening experiences and approaches. In other cases, they can arise from pre-existing views about other professional groups or approaches.
3 Tensions between professional groups and between agencies are accentuated at times of budgetary difficulties, when services are overstretched and under-resourced, and when staff feel that they are under threat because of the possible transfer of their responsibilities or services to another professional group or agency.

(Van Eyk and Baum, 2000, pages 262–5)

It would appear that because agencies have not been convinced of the possibility of 'collaborative advantage', they have tended to adopt a defensive posture towards inter-agency collaboration and have not fully committed themselves to joint working. In addition, developing and maintaining relationships with others requires the investment of energy, time and other resources such as training. In order to commit themselves to this, individual workers need to be freed up. If this does not happen then the worker's other commitments will suffer as a result and the whole experience will be stressful and will more than likely undermine collaborative working rather than support it.

REFLECT

1 What are the expectations from within your agency that you, as a worker, will invest energy, time and other resources in developing and maintaining relationships?
2 If the answer is that there are clear expectations, how much have you been freed up to properly commit to this task?
3 If you haven't got enough time, energy or other resources, how could you improve your situation?

Doubtless, different workers will have their own individual responses to the activity. However, some general points can be made.

1 If agencies commit themselves to collaborative working at the top level and back this commitment up with the training, time and other support necessary for their workforce to make it happen, then the chances of this being successful should be relatively good – assuming that the other agencies are similarly committed.
2 If, on the other hand, agencies commit themselves to collaborative working at the top level and *don't* back this commitment up with the training, time and other support necessary for their workforce to make it happen, then the chances of this being successful must remain doubtful. The reality will not live up to the rhetoric.
3 We have already hinted at a third possibility, which can probably best be summed up by the phrase 'it takes two to tango'. If one agency is fully committed to collaboration, with all the necessary support, but the other agency isn't ready or willing to collaborate – or is, but only on a rhetorical level – then the chances of successful collaborative working are slim.

Earlier, we acknowledged the difficulty faced by individual workers because they have to work within an organisational structure and fit into a certain work culture. Where there is a strong 'top-down' management style, the power of individuals lower down the hierarchy to effect change is limited.

Barriers to collaboration

A social services team is contacted by a senior district nurse from one of the local surgeries. The district nurse wants to speak to the team manager. However he is busy and asks the duty social worker to pick it up. The district nurse explains that with two new staff starting soon, they would like, as part of their induction programme, to spend some time with the local social services team. The duty social worker takes down the request and passes it on to the assistant team manager to attend to. Amongst all the new referrals to sort out, the assistant team manager doesn't manage to get back to the district nurse until the following week. The district nurse repeats her request. The assistant team manager says he's sorry but it might have to wait because things are so stretched at the moment, no one's really got the space. The district nurse decides to leave it. Things move on and the two new district nurses never make their visit.

Questions

1 How does this kind of scenario make collaborative working harder to achieve? What messages or lessons will the local district nurses take from this?
2 In the circumstances, what could the social services have done to at least have made some sort of positive gesture? Could, for example, the duty social worker have made their own positive response without passing it on? What reasons might there be for this not happening?

However, whatever the management culture of the organisation we work in, it is what occurs at the level of interpersonal relationships that still matters.

Stereotypes

Different professional groups often hold negative stereotypes about each other. The more entrenched the stereotypes – particularly if they are negative – the harder it will be to develop joint working.

It is worth reflecting on why the urge to stereotype is so powerful. Stereotyping 'fixes' and homogenises people. Stereotypes also tend to distort by oversimplification – which is part of their power. These days, to talk of stereotyping is to imply a narrow-minded, inflexible and prejudiced way of thinking. All of us do, however, stereotype all of the time.

To relate stereotyping to this chapter's theme, we should remind ourselves that through stereotyping people lose their individuality. We can see stereotyping people as an attempt to control or have power over them. Placing people in 'a box' and attributing certain general characteristics to individuals merely because they have a certain look, accent, title, job or role helps us deal with fears, anxiety or uncertainty. It establishes our position in relation to 'the Other'. By saying, for example, 'that's typical of a doctor!' we are communicating to others (but also to ourselves!) how familiar with and unthreatened we are by them. It helps us to think we 'know' them and what they are about. We have put 'the Other' in a box. Stereotyping is a both a functional and dysfunctional activity because whilst it helps us feel less threatened by a complex and potentially overwhelming world, at the same time it also locks us into a rigid and distorted way of looking at things.

REFLECT

1 Do you agree that to stereotype is put 'the Other' in a box? What other reasons might explain our need to stereotype?
2 Write a list of all the other workers who you come across or work with.
3 For each of them write down what the stereotyped view is of their role – this can be positive or negative.
4 Which workers are most stereotyped?
5 In your workplace, how strong do you think the stereotyping of others is and what effect, if any, do you think it has on collaborative working?

To conclude this exploration of how different groups of workers stereotype one another, we must recognise that if we are stereotyping others, then the chances are that they are stereotyping us. We are not immune. In which case we need to be able to break out of our box and assert our individuality. If we can do this, we greatly improve our chances of developing productive professional relationships.

REFLECT

Think about your job. In what ways do you think it might be stereotyped in the eyes of others? Do you think the stereotype varies according to which type of other worker is doing the stereotyping?

It is not enough just to feel aggrieved by being stereotyped by others – irritating as it might be. All this will probably lead to is more stereotyping! We need to be able to take steps to ensure that others find it difficult to lapse into a stereotyped picture of who we are and what we do.

The first point to realise is that if we are suffering from a stereotyped image, it's nothing personal. Blaming the other is not helpful either because, as we've seen, everyone stereotypes at one time or another. It's therefore usually not malicious. The most effective way of combating others' stereotyping of us is to ensure that they get to know us as an individual. This means that we have to think of strategies to have more contact, and preferably contact that is not always linked to specific cases. We discuss various ways of improving relationships in the next section.

Working in partnership at organisational level

Cultural differences

In addition to stereotypes, there are real and very important cultural differences between professional groups in terms of how they understand and respond to need. The same could be said for different organisational cultures. It is important to be aware of such cultural forces because the pressures to conform for individuals who are subject to them are very strong. In reality, it is unlikely that an individual worker could operate freely from the pressures and constraints of the work culture they are in. Therefore, a worker wishing to work collaboratively with others, but who works within a culture where this isn't valued or supported, would experience serious problems. These cultural differences include the use of jargon particular to each profession. In terms of joint working between health and social care professionals, tensions can also arise from differences in the dominant model of care each worker works to. The medical model and the social care model, for example, differ over how best to respond to the needs of service users and how clients should be treated.

We discuss the implications of workers within a medical or social model in Chapter 7 on assessment. Having earlier discussed the dangers of stereotyping it is worth reminding ourselves that not all health workers approach their work according to a strict medical model. Neither, for that matter, do all social care workers understand and fully embrace the social model. It would be too easy to caricature the work of others in this way. Medical and social models are not the only agency cultures that we need to consider. For example, the statutory social care sector, with its local government traditions, together with its tradition of means testing and charging for services, is a strongly bureaucratic culture. Care providers in the private sector have more of a commercial/business orientated culture. Voluntary agencies have their own culture,

ACTIVITY

1 Have a go at describing your own professional/organisational culture. Use any of the terms from the list given plus any others that you think are appropriate.

client-focused, caring, bureaucratic, organic, mechanistic, medical model, social model, innovative, entrepreneurial, creative, siege mentality, defensive, cost-conscious, oriented to customer satisfaction, hierarchical, rigid, flexible, open, closed, dynamic, undynamic, responsive, warm, impersonal, businesslike, efficient, wasteful, client knows best, worker knows best, empowering.

2 Because our theme is collaborative working, take a look at your list and identify those aspects of your professional/organisational culture that help collaborative working and those that don't.

often more flexible and less profit-minded than the others we have mentioned. Over and above these broad sectoral organisational cultural differences, all workplaces and agencies are bound to develop their own 'micro cultures' depending on factors such as the individual management style, the make-up of the workforce, location, availability of resources, type of agency and so on.

The value of this exercise is that it can help to know the obstacles we face in forming effective collaborative relationships. We shouldn't, for example, accept or attribute personal blame for what are larger, cultural factors. Trying to understand the points of friction between your professional or organisational culture and that of those you need to collaborate with can make it easier to develop links. This is because you can not only understand better the other worker's ways of working but you will be aware of the controls and constraints they face. If the overall cultural differences are too strong then, as we have argued, the individual faces a very difficult task.

Jargon

A key aspect of organisational and professional cultural differences is that different work groups develop and speak their own jargon. Jargon is a kind of specialist language that groups use. Using jargon has the effect of excluding those outside the group because they don't know what the specialist terms mean. As such it is disempowering and a definite barrier to communication.

When people enter residential care it is good practice for their GP to send in a medical report outlining the patient's physical and mental state of health, any medication and any specialist involvements. Quite often these reports are peppered with medical jargon such as 'suffered several TIAs over last two years', 'ca lung in remission', 'recovering from ARF', 'sups to be given PR'. It is not uncommon for the care home staff to have to phone the surgery for a translation; either that or they discuss it amongst themselves and proceed on the basis of informed guesswork. This is not only to save the time in having to call the surgery but often to avoid the embarrassment of revealing ignorance to a fellow worker. It is also not uncommon for residential care staff to ring the social services care manager to find out what a certain piece of medical jargon meant. Usually they cannot help but it is more time wasted.

It is not just health workers who use jargon unthinkingly. An occupational therapist, following up a referral to her local social services, was told crossly 'If it doesn't come in on a Soc 358 it won't get looked at.' There are plenty of these examples and the effects vary. However, to summarise, the use of jargon can:

- lead to people's needs not being met properly
- exclude other workers, the client and their carers
- disempower other workers, the client and their carers
- create unnecessary barriers to communication
- waste time
- cause unnecessary irritation
- lead to misunderstandings with injurious consequences
- lead to a hardening of professional boundaries.

REFLECT

1 Think about your own agency or place of work. Are you a jargon-free zone or do you use jargon at times? What is it?
2 What about workers from other agencies? Do they use jargon? If so, what is it and what effect does it have?
3 If you do face jargon from others, think of constructive ways in which you could ensure that colleagues in other agencies could be educated out of it.

Roles and responsibilities

If professionals disagree over their respective roles, responsibilities and competences, then this is likely to be an obstacle to effective joint working at the local level.

We have already talked about the importance of workers being clear about their own job role. However, the principle of close collaborative working raises some important issues around roles and responsibilities. Individual workers might well be clear about their own role but that can still leave 'territorial' disputes about 'who does what' when there is potential for more than one worker to perform a particular task. The experience of different types of multi-disciplinary team is often that, while workers retain certain key specialisms, there is also some blurring of professional boundaries. Many of the tasks carried out for clients are 'generic' – they do not require a particular professional specialism and can be performed by any member of the team. How these so-called 'generic' tasks are allocated can be the source of friction. The blurring of professional boundaries around generic tasks suits some workers better than others. Workers are reluctant to give up high status work for something which might be considered lower status.

What are high and low status tasks? Clearly, there is some room for discussion here. However, under high status work we might include:

- tasks that require specific professional expertise
- tasks that allow the worker to use their professional discretion and judgement
- tasks that can be carried out autonomously or with a high level of autonomy
- tasks that can further our career (good CV material!).

Under lower status tasks we might include:

- routine form filling and paperwork
- tasks that have a low skill content and permit no professional discretion
- tasks that allow little or no autonomy
- tasks that add nothing to one's CV.

Multi-disciplinary working can sometimes end up as an exercise in the 'cherry picking' of the high status tasks and its corollary – the avoidance of as many low status tasks as possible. Many collaborative working situations in care involve a lot of valuable but nevertheless, low status tasks – these are the 'bread and butter' of care work. This can provoke friction and disagreement amongst workers when it comes to negotiating who takes on this work. Often, the worker with the weakest professional identity loses out. When we use the term 'professional identity' here, we mean the sense workers have of what their professional skills and knowledge are. This would also apply to how clear workers are about their professional roles and responsibilities. A strong professional identity is where the worker is clear and confident about their particular skills and knowledge base. The opposite would be the case when the professional identity is weak. This discussion raises questions:

- How is it decided and agreed which tasks are generic?
- How are boundaries drawn around each worker's role and responsibilities?
- Who decides who is competent to perform certain tasks?
- How should the low status tasks be shared out?

Ironically, successful collaborative working can often stall over the 'bread and butter' matters – or the question of who does the donkey work. This is because the obvious specialisms are taken care of, but the mass of generic tasks are not so clearly allocated.

CASE STUDY

Working out roles and responsibilities

The newly formed management of a Mental Health Trust have embraced the principle of collaborative working and has urged the team members to work as generically as they can. The team is made up of community psychiatric nurses (CPNs), occupational therapists, a psychologist and social workers. 'Territorial disputes' arise in the team when it is explained to the CPNs that when they feel one of their clients would benefit from home care or day care, they must commission it themselves and complete all the necessary paperwork. The CPNs make it clear that they resent having to undertake a task they expect the social workers to do. They claim they are 'not bureaucrats' and it is a waste of their time and expertise. When things come to a head, they argue that because the social workers are not sufficiently well trained to do the CPNs' job (for example check medication and other clinical issues) they don't see why they should do what was traditionally a social work task.

Questions

1 How can this dispute be seen in terms of high status and low status tasks, strong and weak professional identities?
2 How do you think the social workers should respond to this dispute?

In attempting to answer the second question in this scenario, and at the same time promote the cause of collaborative working, the social workers could make several responses. An understandable but ultimately unhelpful response would be for the social workers to take umbrage and embark on a frosty relationship with their fellow team members. What they really need to do above all is to speak to each and clarify in their own minds what their role and responsibilities are and to be clear about what their specialisms are. If the social workers can work on strengthening their professional identity, for example by establishing their assessment and interpersonal skills, their values and identifying what their particular areas of expertise are – for example, dealing with adult abuse or complex legal matters – then the subsequent discussions can be more of a negotiation between equals. The trading can take place with more equanimity if each party can respect the professionalism and expertise of the other. It would help with the process of sorting out who does their share of the mundane tasks. To be uncertain and unconfident about one's job role and responsibilities is no position to bargain from.

Misunderstandings

Workers often have only limited knowledge about other professional groups or other organisations with which they wish to liaise and work. They simply misunderstand the priorities, organisational structures, cultures and working practices of fellow professionals. There is a lack of 'network awareness'.

This point returns to the discussion at the very beginning of the chapter, where we asked 'Do we know who else is working with our clients?'

From this we have to acknowledge that:

- in the first place, there are times when we simply don't know who else is involved
- on other occasions, we have a vague idea of who is involved but are not clear about the nature of their roles and responsibilities.

REFLECT

What reasons might there be for not knowing who else is involved in work with our clients?

One obvious reason probably springs to mind: the client and/or their carers do not communicate this information to us. This might be because they are unwilling, unable or they simply don't think it's relevant. For many people, it suits them to compartmentalise their lives. It might be easier for them to deal with different workers in isolation. To some extent, if this is a preference we shouldn't simply ignore it. Quite often people complain about workers coming along 'poking their noses into our business'. If this is their attitude, they might well withhold information about other involvements. This desire to protect one's privacy is not an uncommon feeling amongst service users. We should accept that it poses dilemmas for workers. We need to think seriously about whether and in what circumstances we need to seek someone's permission in order to share information about them. What is collaborative working for us may feel like 'plotting behind their back' to clients.

CASE STUDY

Finding out the facts

The care manager goes to assess Albert Jackson. He is an older man whose wife has recently died. The neighbours are concerned and think he needs opportunities to get out and meet more people. When the care manager gets there Albert admits to being lonely and missing his wife but turns down the offer of day care. The care manager tries to get as full a picture of health and social care needs as possible but Albert says that mainly he is OK and he'll be in touch if he needs anything. The care manager is on the point of 'closing the case' the following week when the district nurse rings up. She didn't know that the care manager had visited but wanted an assessment to be carried out for personal care as much as anything. This, she explained, was because she visits regularly to assist with Mr Jackson's colostomy bag. His personal hygiene has become noticeably worse since Mrs Jackson died; in addition, laundry is just piling up in the bedroom.

Questions

1. Why do you think Mr Jackson failed to mention such an obvious involvement to the care manager?
2. What lessons does this teach us about relying on the person concerned, their carer or even the referrer to inform us about other involvements?

This links us to the second point about being aware of involvements but not being very clear about what they are. If we rely on clients and/or carers to inform us precisely about the involvement of others, the information we get may be very limited. People can be less than forthcoming for the kinds of reasons set out above. Apart from problems with memory and confusion, or communication problems, they may choose to be deliberately vague. This, almost certainly, is not out of a mischievous desire to play games; it is more likely an attempt to retain some sort of control or power over the situation when they are feeling at their most vulnerable.

People in crisis or distress have to 'lay themselves bare' to strangers. It can be a humiliating and exposing experience. It is often something they want to remain silent about, particularly when they are faced with yet another stranger.

We have established that discovering the make-up of someone's care network is not always straightforward. It might require not only time and effort checking various sources, but also having to deal with dilemmas about respecting privacy. However, even when we are aware of various involvements, the second point we need to address is that workers can often possess limited knowledge about other professional groups or other organisations. For example, even if we are aware that, say, an occupational therapist, a member of the 'Rapid Response' team, or a day services support worker is involved with one of our clients, this does not mean that we are always entirely clear about what they do and what they are responsible for. This clearly poses problems for effective collaborative working. One obvious problem is how to ensure that the expectations we have of other workers is realistic and vice versa. There are many reasons why we aren't clear about the roles and responsibilities of others and this suggests that we should ask how we discover such knowledge.

It would be entirely reasonable to have a range of scores. Hopefully, there are no zeros! It is interesting to reflect on how we know what we know about each other's roles and responsibilities. Those whom we actually meet regularly and work with the most frequently probably score the highest. However, we might also acquire our knowledge of, say, a GP's role from our own personal contact as patients – that wouldn't be unreasonable.

What about those workers to whom you gave a low score? You might, with some justification, expect a textbook such as this to be able to fill in the missing details. That, after all, is what we expect from books. If you think about it, is this the best way to familiarise yourself with the specific roles and responsibilities of those working in your locality? For example, across the country there are groups of workers with names like 'Community Support Team', 'Crisis Intervention Team', 'Community Resource Team', or even 'Assertive Outreach Team'. They all are working in the field of social care for vulnerable adults. However, depending on the locality they could be doing completely different things for different client groups. There are workers with job titles such as GP Liaison Worker and Assistive Technology Officer. What one does in one area may not apply in another. In some areas the NHS might have a Falls Coordinator in others they might be called the Falls Prevention Officer, each with slightly different responsibilities. No single textbook, however well researched, is going to adequately cover this plethora of different roles. This means that workers need to gain the necessary information in ways that are appropriate to them and where they work. Workers need to take responsibility for finding out this information on the ground for themselves; there is no better alternative.

With your lists from the previous exercise, think about how you personally could get a clearer picture of what those workers do. We discuss some methods for doing this in the next section.

Lastly, a further complicating factor is that whilst certain individual workers have a particular talent for networking, others have the capacity to undermine joint working through the way they think and behave. This is to say that some people are simply not 'clubbable'; their overall approach to other workers is to annoy them with a bureaucratic, officious, often pedantic manner. They may lecture others on what their responsibilities should be, talk at length about why doing their job is 'not as easy as you think', and generally maintain a 'yes but' attitude to approaches to work collaboratively. When you encounter such people, if all else fails it can be simpler to work around them rather than waste further time and energy.

Organisational boundaries

In recent years, particularly to advance the cause of 'joined up' government, attempts have been made to make the various health authority and local authority boundaries coterminous – that is to say, the boundaries of responsibility for health authorities and local authorities have been redrawn to match the same geographical area, whether this is a town, region or county. There are unfortunately still quite a few exceptions. This means that a health authority can have responsibility over, say, the whole of one county, the southern part of another, and the western part of another. A single health authority is therefore dealing with three different local authorities, or maybe more if there is a unitary authority embedded in a larger county authority. A local authority might have two or more health authorities with responsibilities in different parts of its area of responsibility. This can cause problems at the level of strategic planning. These need not be insuperable but it does mean more people to meet with, negotiate with and to agree plans with – and more chance of confusion.

At a more local level, it is usually the case that several GP surgeries operate within the boundaries of a single local authority. However, the way that a local authority divides up its area, for example in East, West, North and Central divisions, can often mean that one surgery has half its patients in the East division whilst the other half are in the West division. Here, the problems involve having two different managers and two sets of workers – each with their own subtly different ways of working; there are twice as many links to make and maintain.

At ground level, care practitioners are not always sure whether a person living in a particular street is the responsibility of Dr Smith's or Dr Jones' surgery. Health workers refer to one locality social services team when they should be referring to another

because they are not entirely sure where the boundaries are drawn. The possibilities for confusion and the wasting of time are made more complex again once the different catchment areas of housing and education authorities are factored in.

REFLECT

Think about the various agencies involved in your area. As far as you know, are they working 'coterminously' or do they straddle one or more areas? Are there any problems?

CASE STUDY

The importance of localism

Portsmouth has separated its provider and commissioning functions. It maintains a wide range of directly provided services and has a history of good relationships between health and social care including integrated mental health provision. The PCT attained the second highest score in the national Fitness for Purpose process, and has a very strong vision for the provision of services for local people within the local authority. Localism and geographical community are considered to be of paramount importance, and agencies are keen to promote integrated local service provision – the fear is that an emphasis on **contestability/competition** may distract attention from risk and patient safety, and threaten local provision.

Questions

1 What do you understand by Portsmouth's commitment to 'localism and geographical community'?
2 Do you think that competition between service providers improves quality and value for money for those who purchase and use services?

As we have seen, the government is in favour of a seamless service and PCTs are meant to be an important step towards this. In addition, other initiatives such as NHS Direct and Care Direct are meant to create one-stop 'portals', whereby the person needing help only has one door to go through.

It is too early to say whether these initiatives have solved the problems caused by lack of coterminosity.

Data protection and confidentiality issues

All workers should be legitimately concerned about data protection and confidentiality issues. However, an eagerness to keep information safe can lead to an unwarranted withholding of information. Timely and effective interventions can sometimes be badly stalled by an overprotective mentality towards information sharing. The way in which different professional workers share information between themselves is far from settled. Different agencies are still reluctant to share information electronically for example, because there are concerns about security. Proper 'firewalls', passwords, and other access arrangements need to be put in place before one agency is prepared to pass its case information across a computer network to another. However, IT security concerns are not the only problem.

KNOWLEDGE CHECK

1 Track down your agency's policy on data protection and guidance on confidentiality. Thoroughly familiarise yourself with the contents.
2 List factors that can prevent effective working in partnership.
3 Why might stereotyping pose problems in professional relationships?
4 Give two examples of how different professional or organisational cultures may get in the way of successful joint working.
5 Explain why, in multi-disciplinary teams, disagreement over roles and responsibilities can lead to friction.
6 Explain why workers don't always know why others are involved.
7 How can having only a vague idea of other workers' roles and responsibilities impede working together effectively?
8 What does 'coterminous' mean and what effect can a lack of 'coterminosity' have?
9 What does data protection legislation tell us about the way information on clients is recorded, stored and managed?

Effective collaboration

In the previous section we discussed a range of problems that can create obstacles to successful collaborative working. Some of the solutions are beyond the powers of the individual worker and are more appropriately the responsibility of politicians, policy makers and senior managers.

The practical conditions for integration appear to require the following.

- Formal validation from above – often lack of central or management support for integration make the task of integration challenging.
- High level of local control – when resources, like Supporting People, are under local authority control they can be integrated, but where control lies elsewhere then integration seems to fail.
- Incentive to integrate – where resources are treated as belonging to a different part of the system then there is no incentive to make integration happen.
- Aligned local leadership – where management systems for different funding streams are aligned under one leader then integration is easier.
- Clarity of process – where the local leadership has one clear template for the final organisation of Self-Directed Support then integration is easier and more coherent.
- Strong sense of mission – where local leaders have a strong sense of purpose and are eager to bring about change integration is easier.
- No strong restrictions on process – where there is little flexibility in how processes can be re-engineered then integration becomes impossible.

(Waters and Duffy, 2007)

Improving community safety for older people

In March 2005, Barnsley Metropolitan Council Local Area Agreement committed local health, social care and housing agencies to share objectives within their Local Area Agreement, to improve community safety for older people. Their intention is 'to decrease the number of older people requiring hospital admissions as a result of a fall and achieve a reduction in the number of admissions to residential or nursing care as a result of a fall.'

However, there are clear messages and lessons to be learned for workers at every level. Collaborative working is most likely to be effective if certain key principles are followed:

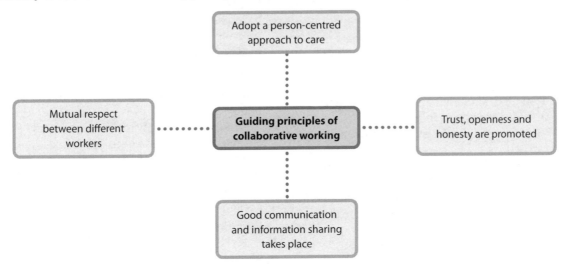

Figure 6.3 Principles for effective collaborative working

Skills for collaborative working

If we can work to the spirit of these basic guiding principles then it should be easier to overcome some of the obstacles we have identified. Our effort to work collaboratively will benefit both from acquiring and practising certain skills and adopting certain methods and strategies.

> **ACTIVITY**
>
> Given all the possible issues we have uncovered, make a list of all the skills and qualities you think are needed to ensure that we can establish good working relationships with other workers.

Your list is probably very similar to a list that you would make if asked what skills and ways of behaving you need to work in care. This would typically contain the following:

- being a good communicator
- having good interpersonal skills
- being non-judgemental
- being genuine.

Therefore, this does not necessarily involve the acquisition of specific new skills. However, in the light of some of the potential difficulties we have discussed in earlier sections, the following skills and ways of behaving are going to be particularly important.

Assertiveness

Assertiveness is a vital ingredient to working in social care and particularly when it comes to being effective in partnership working. The non-assertive worker denies their own rights and will forever find themselves in a subordinate (inferior) role with others, accommodating their interests, needs and wishes to the detriment of their own.

Assertiveness is a state of mind which requires you to know who you are and what you want. It is a way of behaving that enables you to communicate this knowledge clearly and effectively to others. It runs wider than just the ability to say 'no'. Assertiveness is often confused with selfishness or aggression, with putting our own needs before those of other people,

> **REFLECT**
>
> Which approach(es) do you have: aggressive, manipulative, passive or assertive?
>
> Basing your decisions on what is described above, reflect on which approach you adopt in your day-to-day dealings with other workers. Which approach most characterises the way you work? Does it vary according to who the other worker is? Explain.
>
> What do you need to do to become more assertive?

Assertiveness:

- Recognising our needs and asking openly and directly for what we want.
- Recognising and respecting the rights and needs of other people.
- Relating to people in personal and working situations in an open and honest way.
- Feeling responsible for and in control of our own actions.
- Not seeing situations in terms of win or lose, but being prepared to compromise.
- Being able to resolve difficulties and disputes in a way that feels comfortable and just to those involved.
- Expressing views coherently while being prepared to listen.

Aggressiveness:

- Expressing feelings and opinions in a way that punishes, threatens or puts the other person down.
- Disregarding the rights and needs of others.
- Aiming to get our own way no matter what.
- Views made forcefully to the point of rudeness.

- If we 'win' and get what we want aggressively it probably leaves someone else with bad feelings, making it difficult to relate to them in future.

Passivity:

- Not standing up for our rights. Allowing others to take advantage of us.
- Avoiding responsibility for making choices – leaving others to make decisions for us.
- Not being in control of our lives. Seeing ourselves as helpless victims of unfairness and injustice.
- Feeling that our view is less important or valid – backing down even when we think we are right.
- Avoidance of conflict at all costs.

Being manipulative:

- Unable to ask directly for what we want.
- Trying to get what we want indirectly, by playing games or trying to make people feel guilty.
- Expressing views in a covert manner. Often using snide remarks, gestures and facial expressions.

and pursuing them regardless of the effect on others. This is *not* assertiveness. Let us look at what assertiveness really is and compare it to other ways of relating to people's aggressiveness, passivity and being manipulative.

In becoming more assertive we develop awareness both of what we say and how we express ourselves.

Becoming more assertive

If you found that you were able to be properly assertive with other workers, whichever agency they are from, that is fine. If, on the other hand, in some situations you find this difficult, you need to do some work.

Some basic guidelines to becoming more assertive

Verbal aspects in becoming more assertive:

- *Aim to personalise pronouns* Use 'I' statements rather than 'You', 'It', 'We', 'One'. Using the personal pronoun 'I' acknowledges that the statement is true of our experience and that it may be different for other people.
- *Changing verbs* Change 'can't' to 'won't' where 'can't' is not an appropriate restriction. This change of verb encourages us to take responsibility and to be aware of what we can and cannot realistically do, and that we can

make a positive choice when we decide whether or not to do something.
Change 'need' to 'want' and differentiate between the two. This change of verb encourages us to be realistic and responsible about what we need and want.
Change 'have to' to 'choose to'. These changes in verbs acknowledge that we make a choice about what we do and are therefore responsible for the choice. This realisation that we have choices is an important part of becoming more assertive.
Change 'know' to 'imagine' when a fact is a

fantasy. Often we state we know something about someone when in fact we base this 'knowledge' on fantasy. It is important to differentiate between what we know, imagine, feel and think when making clear and assertive statements.

- *Changing passive into active* We put ourselves in a passive role when we talk about something happening to us. Part of becoming more assertive is recognising that we are responsible for things that happen to us. For example, 'I allow people to take advantage of me and often feel angry' is very different from 'Things keep happening to me that make me feel angry', in which we blame things/others for how we feel.
- *Changing questions into statements* Questions such as 'Don't you think?' are often indirect ways of stating 'What I think ... ' When we are clear and direct in our communication we are more assertive with ourselves and others.

There are non-verbal aspects to becoming assertive:

- *Eye contact* How a person looks at someone conveys how they feel about themselves and what they are saying.
  It is a powerful form of self-assertion to look someone directly in the eye. A person will often give their power away by looking away. When a person looks directly at who they are talking to they communicate that they are alert and present in themselves.
- *Posture* How a person stands or sits also communicates how they feel about themselves and what they are saying.
  When a person is standing talking to someone or addressing a group of people it is important that they stand with both feet firmly on the ground. This means that they are both centred and balanced in themselves.

You can assert yourself by saying no to whatever you dislike or disagree with. But why do we find saying 'no' difficult? There are many possible reasons but some common ones are:

- We don't want others to think us unkind.
- We want to be popular.
- We think we should be all things to all people.
- We think our refusal might devastate the other person.
- We may have been brought up to think saying no is impolite.

Hints for saying 'no':

- Get the word 'no' out early in your response, if possible make it the first word.
- Give reasons if you need to, but don't make excuses; others will see through them.
- Don't apologise unnecessarily.
- Keep your non-verbal message assertive; maintain good eye contact and don't smile inappropriately.
- When you've finished making your point, find a way to close the conversation such as 'OK?', 'Thank you for being so understanding' etc., or just change the subject.

Remember, you are turning down a request not rejecting a person – you have the right to say no!

How to criticise or challenge someone assertively:

- Before you start, work out a sound inner dialogue to make sure the criticism is specific and not a personal attack.
- As you criticise, introduce a topic and (if appropriate) say why you are raising it.
- Specify what the problem is.
- Get a response to your criticism.
- Ask for suggestions to rectify the problem.
- Summarise suggestions agreed.

How to respond assertively to criticism or a challenge from someone:

- Listen to the criticism carefully, rather than rejecting it or arguing with the person.
- Ask yourself whether the challenge is valid/invalid and/or whether it is in the form of a put-down.

If the criticism or challenge is valid:

- Acknowledge that it is true.
- If it is generalised then ask for more specific information.
- Ask other people for information, whether or not they experience you in a similar way.
- Decide whether or not you are going to change your behaviour as a consequence of the criticism.
- Thank the other person for their challenge/criticism.

If the criticism or challenge is invalid:

- Say so and assert yourself positively, for example:
  'You have made a mistake in your assessment.'
  'No, that isn't true. I am usually very careful.'

- When criticisms are made that are invalid, affirm yourself.

If the criticism is valid and in the form of a put-down:

- Acknowledge that it is true! Challenge the put-down and assert yourself positively.

It is important with put-downs to respond assertively and to confront the put-down, for example:

> 'Typical of you – you never return my emails.'

> 'Yes, I have not yet responded to the last two. However, I usually respond to all my emails as soon as I can and I don't like your put-downs!'

If the criticism is invalid and in the form of a put-down:

- Say so. Challenge the put-down and assert yourself positively, for example:

> 'No, that isn't true, I have answered all my emails and I don't like your put-down!'

Our discussion on assertiveness has probably made you realise just how important our use of self is in conducting effective relationships with other workers. It should also have reinforced how important it is to possess a clear professional identity. Low professional self-esteem and successful working in partnership are incompatible.

Clear sense of own role

We have seen how difficult it is to be assertive and therefore work effectively in collaboration with others if we have self-doubt about our own worth, our own competence and our job role. It is therefore of paramount importance that, as workers, we clarify what our job role is and what responsibilities it carries with it. This question will have been raised many times and we want to be sure that the lessons have been learned.

REFLECT

Imagine you have been asked to give a talk to a group of service users, your colleagues and other workers. You have fifteen minutes to make it absolutely clear to all of them what you do, what you are responsible for and what you are *not* responsible for; in other words you need to make clear the function of the organisation you work for and your role within it.

How would you structure your talk? Write down your headings together with what you would say. Make a point of identifying areas where you specialise.

If you found that exercise difficult it might suggest that you would benefit from doing some research. Look out your agency's mission statement and any other relevant documents that could help you summarise what business you are in exactly. What does the agency's literature say it is about? Look out your contract and job description. What are your core tasks and key responsibilities? What leaflets or other publicity does your agency have for the public? What do they say about the agency purpose and your role within it? If you are still unclear because, for example, you do not recognise what you do on a day-to-day basis from the official job description, then you should raise this at a staff meeting or some other appropriate forum. There is no shortage of people who are happy to tell us what social care or social work is or should be. Unless we want our roles limited and defined by others we need to have a clear idea of what the purpose of what we do is.

Then we can assert ourselves effectively.

Negotiating skills

To negotiate is to try to reach a mutually acceptable agreement with another party (or parties), usually through discussion. Negotiating is at the heart of social care work. We need to reach agreements with others on a range of matters – some relatively trivial, others more serious. These could be times of meetings, dates when care starts, where to have a meeting, when to have the next review, who is going to take key responsibility or even who is going to give someone the bad news! What we're trying to do is achieve a 'fit' which all those involved are reasonably comfortable with. Because most of these decisions are reached with little or no dissent, we can often take what we're doing for granted.

But clearly even the most straightforward of decisions do not happen automatically. Somebody needs to take the lead, identify what needs to be done, offer suggestions and then make an appropriate response, even if the minimum amount of negotiation is required.

From time to time, we will find that it is hard to obtain a 'fit' or a happy medium and that is when the ability to negotiate becomes very important.

What happens if someone has poor negotiating skills? We've probably all been on the wrong end of situations or 'agreements' that have been badly negotiated. This can leave us with feelings of anger, injustice, being cheated, put upon, outmanoeuvred, or even bullied. This is because the so-called 'agreement' has been settled on the other party's terms. Goodwill soon disappears in such circumstances. It is also equally true that if we impose our decisions on others without the possibility of negotiation, then they too will feel a similar sense of grievance. Collaborative working can only work properly if agreements are negotiated on terms that everybody is happy with.

In your responses you should have been able to link this situation to points we have made previously about power imbalances, professional identity, assertiveness and the need to have a clear job role.

Outcomes which would not promote effective joint working would be for Janet, the social worker, simply to:

- withdraw
- go straight to the team manager, or
- continue but vow never to help that particular CPN again.

Another approach could be for Janet to refer Joyce to the psychiatrist for a case review, and use this as an opportunity to disengage from the situation. However, this would not really be negotiating with Damien, it would be working round him. This could be considered manipulative even if it is in Joyce's best interest. Going straight to the manager would be a later option if negotiation proved unsuccessful. Working collaboratively is about trying to forge reasonable working relationships with colleagues, not trying to outsmart them.

Situations like the one outlined opposite should be resolved by negotiation wherever possible. In order to negotiate successfully in any situation we need to know what we want – it is no good simply grumbling, we must have our own clear proposals. We need to think about what our ideal solution would be; i.e. what would be the best possible result to come out of the negotiation? We then need to be realistic and prepared to concede some ground. This involves having a 'fall-back' option; i.e. what is the least satisfactory solution we would give our agreement to? We need to be clear that we will not go over this line. If someone tries to force us beyond our fall-back position then we need to be clear what we will do. This might involve taking things higher or simply refusing to co-operate further; it depends on the situation. In any event, it is no good having a fall-back position if it is ignored.

CASE STUDY

Negotiating a care plan

A care plan has been drawn up for Joyce McCullough, a 41-year-old with schizophrenia. When Joyce, who lives on her own, goes through occasional periods of instability, members of the Community Mental Health team make a point of visiting twice a day to ensure that any risk is managed. The key worker is Damien, a CPN, and he has asked Janet, one of his social work colleagues, to share the task. In the spirit of working collaboratively, Janet agrees. Damien then draws up a rota for visiting which requires Janet to visit at 6.00 pm each day whilst Damien visits Joyce at 9.00 am on his way to work.

Janet would have preferred the earlier visit because the 6.00 pm visit conflicts with a range of other tasks she wants to do – including going home! Initially, no comment is made as Damien says it will only be for a few days. After a week, Joyce is still unstable, and it is clear that Damien has no intention of offering to share the 6.00 pm call. When Janet half raises the issue of changing times, Damien says that the earlier call is more important for him to do because he checks medication – something Janet wouldn't be able to do. Janet feels trapped.

Questions

1 What options are open to Janet?
2 Can a more suitable agreement be negotiated? If so, how?

Having clearly set the parameters of what is acceptable in our head, we need to be able to argue successfully for what we want. We need to be able to show that our proposals are fair, reasonable and rational. We need to have arguments that reflect coherent care values. They cannot be arguments that can be attacked for being selfish or overlooking clients' needs.

The way we negotiate is as important as the quality of the arguments we use to negotiate with. This inevitably brings us back to assertiveness. If we try to negotiate in a way that is aggressive, angry, manipulative or passive we will greatly reduce the chances of success. If we aim to negotiate in a way that shows us to be open, flexible and reasonable then this will be more conducive to effective collaborative working.

Successful negotiation checklist

1 Am I clear about what I am trying to achieve?
2 Am I clear what my fall-back position is?
3 What will I do if I am pushed beyond my fall-back position?
4 How will I conduct my negotiation – what arguments will I use?
5 Have I got a case which can clearly be seen to promote client care?
6 How will I negotiate in a way that is assertive and not aggressive, manipulate or passive?
7 Am I being open, flexible and reasonable?

KNOWLEDGE CHECK

1 What does it mean to 'be assertive'?
2 How can assertiveness contribute to collaborative working?
3 Make a list of four skills or ways of behaving that will facilitate collaborative working.
4 Have you got a clear sense of your job role? Briefly explain what it is. What are your specialisms?
5 Give examples of negative effects if we possess poor negotiating skills.
6 Identify six pointers from the successful negotiation checklist.

Networking skills

Here we see networking as an umbrella term which includes a range of activities, all of which have 'contact' as an important feature. They include the activities shown in the diagram opposite.

Networking is not a precise science, in many ways it is more of an art. A common way of describing networking is to compare it to a bee busily buzzing around picking up pollen from one flower and depositing it on another. In their research, Means and Smith (1998) found that good networkers:

> ... tend to feel comfortable working above their hierarchical position, and they are willing to operate in a way not bounded by narrow organisational self-interest.
>
> (Means and Smith, 1998, page 143)

How to network

Good networking might be as much a product of personality as a set of skills we can learn. It requires a certain mindset. At a basic level, good networkers are 'chancers' and opportunists, they exploit situations for all their 'contact potential'. They are both active and proactive in their approach.

Therefore, to be able to network effectively, we need to see the value in making contacts.

REFLECT

Reflect on a job that you have done for a long period and in which you have built up a series of personal contacts. How often did you solve problems by drawing on personal contacts that you made or by using a specific agency and organisation that you learned about by someone telling you about them? Contrast this to a job where you have just started in a new locality and where you have little or no knowledge of what networks there are.

Networking is about building up contacts and sharing ideas and information. The more knowledge we have of what is available and who is out there to help, the more our clients have to gain.

In order to exploit situations, we need to have a raised awareness to the possibility of making contacts and be able to seize possible opportunities. We also need to actively create openings and not just wait for them to come to us.

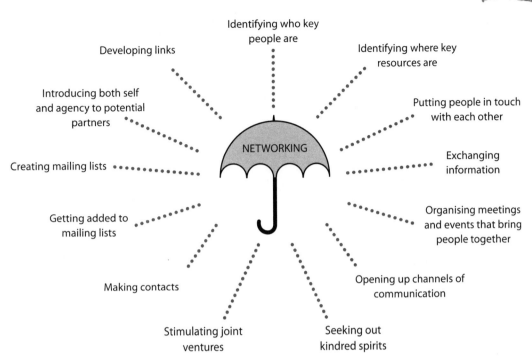

Figure 6.4 Networking skills

Networking

David is a new care manager for a locality team. He keeps hearing from his colleagues how the rapid response team are always moaning about how slow the locality team is in picking up the work which they want to hand over. There is quite a backlog of unallocated work. David is a bit unclear about what the rapid response team does, but knows that the two teams have quite a strained relationship. Whenever a member of the rapid response team rings up David feels defensive and apologetic even though he personally has done nothing wrong. When a district nurse rings about a client, David decides to ask whether there is any feeling among the district nurses that social services aren't picking up work quickly enough. The nurse starts to talk about certain cases, some of which David also knows the rapid response team are involved with. David decides that he needs to go and meet with the rapid response team and contacts their team leader. They welcome the opportunity for a 'clear the air' talk.

Questions

1. What are your comments on David's action? Is he networking? Give reasons.
2. If David wanted to take his networking further, what should he do?

Just about any situation can be used as the basis for networking. David could involve both the district nurses and rapid response team in regular meetings. Meeting together could help to foster a better understanding of each other's roles, work pressures and organisational cultures. This in turn could promote trust and facilitate problem solving. The network can also be enlarged, as other interested parties such as GPs and home care providers might have some useful input. The case study illustrates that by dealing with the problem directly, being proactive and making personal contacts you can increase the chances of making collaborative working run more smoothly.

Promoting collaborative working

In social care work there are several formal methods which bring different workers together to discuss cases and wider practice issues. Some common methods are now discussed below.

Case conferences/meetings

Case conferences are used widely in all aspects of social work and health and social care. In certain contexts, case conferences have a clearly laid down name, purpose and set of procedures that govern them. An example of this type of case conference would be the Initial Child Protection case conference. Official guidance covers all aspects of such a conference: when it should be called, who should be invited, what agenda should be followed and so on. However, in other settings the term is used in a very general way to mean a gathering of relevant workers involved in a case coming together to discuss details of the case. In the spirit of fostering user involvement, it is expected that the client, their carer and/or any other representative or advocate will be invited to attend part or all of the conference. Therefore, as a worker, if you felt that a case would benefit from a formally constituted meeting of those involved, you must invite the service user or their representatives. If you do not, you should have a very good reason why this would not be appropriate.

and call it a case meeting instead. This will stop people being confused about its status. Case meeting sounds slightly less formal and official than case conference. Nevertheless, if a case meeting is going to promote collaborative working it should still be conducted in a proper manner.

These questions raise several interesting issues for working collaboratively. The chairing and agenda setting inevitably raises questions of power, for example who decides what can be discussed; the recording question raises issues of confidentiality, for example will minutes be produced; how will they be disseminated and where will they be kept? Even thornier, could be the questions of how or, indeed, whether Danny is invited. Does he require an advocate? What about his parents? This raises further issues of accessibility and transport. All meetings have their own dynamics and this is where professional territorial disputes can emerge. This makes it all the more important to establish an agreed set of ground rules and to make sure that everybody observes them. Sending out a rationale and proposed agenda in advance to all parties should help settle the meeting down quicker than if the meeting is convened with a completely open agenda.

ACTIVITY

Earlier (see page 223), we looked at the case of Danny and his lunchtime visits to the pub. Imagine you were the care manager; explain how you would organise a case meeting so that the various issues could be sorted out. Key decisions that you will need to make in such a case would include:

- Who to invite?
- Where to have the meeting?
- When to have the meeting?
- Who will chair the meeting?
- How will the agenda be settled?
- How to record the meeting?
- What accountability, if any, will there be in any decisions taken?

Meetings must be planned in advance and the time used effectively

If your meeting is not a conference called as the result of official guidelines or procedures, but simply because a sharing of views and information would be a good idea, it might be better to drop the term 'conference'

These are some of the issues that practitioners must be aware of when thinking about calling case meetings. The last point to make is that just having a meeting is not necessarily a sign of working collaboratively. We have all been to meetings that have descended into a free-for-all or have merely been an excuse to let off steam. Some people are expert at sabotaging or hijacking meetings. Therefore, for a case meeting to be an effective collaborative working tool we need to think clearly about what we are hoping to achieve and how it will improve care; in short, what the meeting's aims and objectives are. No one likes their time being wasted through attending meetings that are not relevant or useful. We cannot simply call a meeting in the hope that answers to difficult questions will spontaneously appear. We need to express our views and ideas and be prepared to amend them if needs be.

Liaison meetings

Liaison meetings differ from case meetings in that they are not called to discuss a specific case but are regular meetings between workers from different agencies. The purpose of such meetings can vary but usually the overall aim is to improve links between agencies. There could be some case discussion but there might be other items on the agenda, such as one group explaining about a new service or procedure to the other. Key features of liaison meetings are information sharing, breaking down professional barriers and ensuring that the agencies work collaboratively to promote better care.

> ### REFLECT
>
> 1 At your place of work are there any liaison meetings with other agencies or other workers?
> 2 If there are, explain how they are arranged, venues, timing and so on. How effective are they in promoting collaborative working? How would you like to see them improved?
> 3 Which other agencies or workers don't you have liaison meetings with? What would it take to set them up?

As with case meetings, participants need to have a sense that attending the meeting is worth their while.

Liaison meetings can sometimes become 'ritualistic' in that people meet just because they have the date in their diary. Signs that liaison meetings are not working effectively are usually when absenteeism increases, when meetings are often cancelled or postponed or when participants merely 'go through the motions' – covering old themes and topics. The shame is that when these meetings are originally set up it is probably with a great sense of purpose and commitment. Workers often cite work pressures or lack of time for withdrawing from liaison meetings but this is often because they no longer see the value of meeting.

If you see the signs that liaison meetings are flagging, this does not mean that they should be allowed to simply wither away. Every section of this chapter has provided arguments for working collaboratively. To retreat into isolation, however tempting, raises the chances of client care suffering.

> ### How to revive the flagging liaison meeting
> - Acknowledge the problem and renegotiate the terms for meeting – change the interval, venue, anything to bring a fresher feel to the meeting.
> - Invite 'new blood' to the meetings. This can either be new members from the agencies or another agency altogether.
> - Consider guest speakers for joint training purposes.
> - Introduce treats such as cake or even more exotic fare.
> - Invite senior managers from time to time. Let them see the initiatives you are undertaking; they can also hear first hand your joint concerns.
> - Set yourself a project, for example develop a new joint system in some area of working. You could even write it up and get it published!

Joint visits

The joint visiting of clients is a very obvious sign of working collaboratively and can have benefits. However, it can also create problems, so this all needs a fuller discussion. The benefits of visiting a client together with another worker are many. For the client it means that they avoid the duplication of two separate visits and have the benefit of two sources of knowledge being available at the same time. Joint visiting improves the likelihood that everything the client says will be better remembered and recorded. One worker can also observe whilst the other conducts the interview. Workers are less likely to take shortcuts in the company of workers from other agencies, and they are also less likely to slip into a narrow service-led approach.

When it comes to broaching difficult or sensitive matters workers can be emboldened by the presence of a fellow worker. Consequently, important but difficult issues which may normally be minimised by the lone worker can get a fuller airing. During the visit, if one worker wants the other's opinion from their specialist perspective it can be offered straight away rather than waiting for a referral to take place and all the time that this may take. After the visit both workers will be in a position to compare their impressions and bounce ideas off each other because they will have both been there. The assessment will be all the more rounded as a consequence.

On the negative side, two people visiting might be overwhelming for an individual. They can be inhibited in participating fully if they are confronted by two strangers in their house. We should always seek permission to visit jointly because it can increase the feeling of invasion into someone's home, however well-meaning the 'invaders' are. Joint visiting obviously takes up twice as much worker time, so the addition of another worker needs to actually add something to the visit to make it cost-effective, they can't simply be 'there for the ride'.

Also, joint visiting won't be successful if the workers act out any differences of opinion in front of the client. Sometimes people deliberately try to play one worker off against the other often in an attempt to equalise the power difference. However, on occasions joint workers can be drawn into a competitive game with each other about who is the most helpful or who gets on best with the client. Never underestimate the powerful dynamics of the three-way meeting. If joint visits are to be successful, the visits must be:

- well planned
- on the basis of a shared philosophy of care
- consensual
- an effective use of two workers' time.

REFLECT

Identify a recent example from your practice where it would have been useful to have made a joint visit. Explain clearly what the advantages would be and explain any possible disadvantages.

Joint training

Joint training can mean different things. It can mean workers from different agencies attending a course together on a particular topic; for example 'Managing Risk with Frail Older People'. In this type of event it could be that issues are being raised and messages given to a range of people from different professional backgrounds. In other words, the audience is a 'joint' audience. However, the trainers might be coming from a single perspective, for example physiotherapy. Alternatively, the trainers themselves could be from different perspectives (joint trainers) and the audience from one professional background.

It could be that the training is both jointly organised and jointly attended. In colleges and universities there are often modules which can be shared between students on different professional pathways. For example, health professionals and social work students may come together for a module entitled 'Policies and Practices for Community Care', but go their separate ways for other parts of their qualification. Joint training opportunities have been institutionalised in areas like child protection – all events are multi-disciplinary – but this is less the case in adult social care. Joint training can be a positive step towards effective collaborative working not only because of the knowledge and skills gained from the training, but also because of the opportunities for different workers from different backgrounds to meet informally, share experiences and generally get to know each other as people. Such opportunities must be approached with an open mind, because professional rivalries and mistrust can easily be brought into the training situation. This diminishes the whole experience if joint training only serves to reinforce stereotypes and confirm prejudices.

Work shadowing

In many people's minds, work shadowing tends be associated with new and inexperienced workers accompanying a more experienced worker in order to learn the job. This is a useful technique to help inexperienced workers to learn, but there are other possibilities for work shadowing that contribute towards working collaboratively.

Work shadowing is useful in itself, and it need not simply be seen as an activity for new workers. It is an excellent way of learning about other job roles, organisational cultures and how other agencies operate. All of this information is valuable in taking forward collaborative working. Therefore, we should seek to work shadow others and be receptive to others' request to work shadow us. To be done properly it needs to be set up with attention to detail. You need to be work shadowing someone over enough time to get a representative and valid picture of their work. You also need to consider the issue of permissions and the perennial social researcher's problem – what effect will your presence have on the person being shadowed? Finding sufficient time is always going to be an issue but it can genuinely be treated as staff development and will make the chances of collaborative working much more likely to happen and to be effective when it does.

considerably from 94 at the end of September 2006 to 148 at the end of September 2007. There has also been substantial growth in the uptake of Direct Payments amongst people with learning disabilities and people with mental health problems, empowering them to have choice and control over their services.

- A 'Well read Scheme' set up between Adult Social Care, Cumbria Partnership Foundation NHS Trust and Cumbria Public Library Service has issued self-help material on more than 1,000 occasions to people experiencing mental health problems.
- During 2006/07, 91 per cent of equipment was delivered within seven days of an individual's need assessment, placing Cumbria's performance in this field in the top UK performance quartile.

Improved independence increases well-being through choice and control

- Cumbria Adult Social care is a leading Council in the national In Control Total pilot scheme for developing a system of self-directed support to enable people to exercise choice and control over the services they use to improve the quality of their lives. Over 600 people have an individual budget.
- The 'Prevention Works' programme has been developed with the Third Sector to support older people with long-term health conditions and assist in maintaining their independence as long as possible.

'What the County Council does and achieves as an organisation has to be set within its wider partnership context. Increasingly, the Council is playing a key role in shaping shared countywide objectives, coordinating shared resources and delivering shared outcomes to improve the quality of life of residents and communities.

The Local Area Agreement is the delivery plan for a more strategic document, the Community Strategy for Cumbria. The Council (through the Cumbria Strategic Partnership) has led the work to develop both the Community Strategy and the Local Area Agreement.

The Third Sector is a key partner for the Council, and Cumbria is fortunate in having a wide range of enthusiastic and active voluntary organisations. The County Council is committed to supporting the sector to increase its capacity to engage in partnership working and help deliver excellent and innovative services to local communities and communities of interest.

The Council also works with a range of commercial partners to deliver specific services. This has contributed to efficiency savings for which the Council has been nationally recognised. Partners such as Amey, Capita and Agilisys are also instrumental in achieving the outcomes set out in this Plan.'

(www.cumbria.gov.uk, 2008)

Questions

1 How do you think that Local Area Agreements influence the strategic direction of care services in an area?
2 Cumbria mentions both public and private providers, do you think that this should always be the case? Do local areas need a balance of private/public partnerships?
3 What aspects of partnership do your local authority seem most proud of in their public documentation?

REFLECT

Identify a worker who you would like to shadow. Explain why you chose that particular worker. Think about what you expect to learn from that person and explain what steps you need to take to put into practice what you learn.

1 Make a list of four skills or ways of behaving that will facilitate collaborative working.
2 In your own words, explain what it is to be assertive.
3 Explain why it helps to be assertive if working collaboratively.
4 Have you got a clear sense of your job role? Briefly explain what it is. What are your specialisms?
5 Give examples of the negative effects of poor negotiating skills.
6 Identify six pointers from the successful negotiation checklist.
7 Describe some of the activities which could be placed under the umbrella of 'networking'.
8 Give three reasons why networking helps promote collaborative working.
9 Explain two methods that promote collaborative working.
10 What questions does a worker need to consider when deciding to call a case conference?
11 What is the difference between a case meeting and a liaison meeting?
12 Describe two advantages and two disadvantages of joint visiting.
13 What factors will ensure that joint visits are successful?
14 Explain how work shadowing can help with collaborative working.

Glossary

Commissioning: the process of finding organisations to deliver services, by advertising, testing suitability and securing a contract.

Competition: where organisations are judged about their suitability to provide a service in comparison to other agencies.

Contestability: the process of considering different providers, with the potential for changing providers.

Integration: the joining of organisations for the delivery of services.

Governance: strategic management of an organisation; the systems and processes concerned with ensuring the overall direction, effectiveness, supervision and accountability of an organisation.

Pooled commissioning budgets: where organisations put their separate monies into a single pot in order to focus on delivering an aspect of a service together.

Social enterprise: profit-making business set up to tackle a social or environmental need.

References

Barclay Report (1982) *Social Workers, their Role and Tasks*, London, NISW

Burns, T. and Stalker, G. M. (1961) *The Management of Innovation*, London, Tavistock

Department of Health (1995) *Child Protection: Messages from Research*, London, HMSO

Department of Health (1997) *Better Services for Vulnerable People*, London, HMSO

Department of Health (1998) *Modernising Social Services*, London, HMSO

Department of Health (2001) *Valuing People*, London, HMSO

Department of Health (2001) *National Service Framework for Older People*, London, HMSO

Department of Health (2006) *Our health, our care, our say: a new direction for community services*, London, HMSO

Hudson, B. (1987) 'Collaboration in social welfare: a framework for analysis' in *Policy and Politics*, vol 15, no. 3, pages 175–82

Hudson, B. (2000) 'Inter-agency collaboration – a sceptical view' in Brechin A. *et al*, *Critical Practice in Health and Social Care*, London, Sage

Kings Fund (2007) *Provision of adults services in partnership between health and social care: Considering the options*, Birmingham, University of Birmingham, Health Services Management Centre

Leathard A. (1994) *Going Inter-Professional, Working Together for Health and Welfare*, London, Routledge

Loxley, A. (1997) *Collaboration in Health and Welfare*, London, JKP

Means, R. and Smith, R. (1998) *Community Care Policy and Practice*, 2nd edition, Basingstoke, Macmillan

Townroe, C. and Yates, G. (1999), *Sociology*, Harlow, Longman

Van Eyk, H. and Baum, F. (2002) 'Learning about interagency collaboration' in *Health and Social Care in the Community*, 10 (4) pp 262–9

Webb, A. (1991) *in* Means, R. and Smith, R. (1998) *Community Care Policy and Practice*, Basingstoke, Macmillan

Waters, A. and Duffy, S. (2007) 'Individual Budget Integration: An exploration of the possible scope of Individual Budgets', for *In Control*, for the Department of Health

CHAPTER 7

Assessment

Introduction

This chapter focuses on the knowledge and skills required to assess competently. We begin by reflecting on the various meanings and assumptions attached to the concept of 'assessment'. This raises interesting issues and questions that will help inform subsequent discussions in the chapter. From there, we consider the reasons why assessment has become so important in all forms of health and social care work. In short, we ask the question, why assess? We then aim to provoke both thought and discussion around the equally key but often difficult concepts of **need** and **risk**. Practitioners need to reflect on how the ambiguities and complexities of these concepts can affect practice, particularly in power relations. All assessments take place within different contexts and we consider how the various contexts in which assessment takes place can influence, guide or constrain practice. There are different views on how to assess and we discuss the strengths and weaknesses of different models of assessment. We address issues of empowerment and anti-discriminatory practice and relate these to assessment practices. Finally, we conclude by pulling together the various issues we have discussed as we aim to identify the elements of a competent assessment.

This chapter addresses the following areas:

- What is assessment?
- Why assess?
- Assessment of need
- Assessment of risk
- The context of assessment
- Models of assessment and assessment **tools**
- Assessment, empowerment and anti-discriminatory practice
- Elements of a competent assessment

After reading this chapter it is hoped that you will be able to:

- appreciate the importance of clarifying the scope and purpose of the assessment you are undertaking with all those involved
- understand the concepts of **intersubjectivity** and reflective practice and their relevance to assessment
- be aware of the importance of the way language is used throughout the assessment process
- have a clearer understanding of the key but ambiguous concepts of need and risk
- locate a particular assessment in its various contexts and understand how the context(s) of assessment influence assessment
- recognise the importance of how power operates in the assessment relationship
- identify and evaluate different models of assessment
- be aware of what assessment tools are and how they can be used to improve practice
- make links between assessment, empowerment and anti-discriminatory practice
- identify the elements of a competent assessment.

What is assessment?

Assessment is an important activity and core concept within all areas of health and social care practice. The requirement to assess can be found in a range of key documents.

The following extracts are all from either legislation or guidance on health and social care. As you read through them, reflect on whether it is clear what the activity of assessment actually is.

> We aim to carry out an assessment of your needs in partnership with you and with other people you would like to have included.
>
> Wherever possible we aim to cut out unhelpful duplication and delay by working together with colleagues from health agencies and other council departments. We may ask, when it is appropriate, for your permission to share information about you with colleagues from health agencies.
>
> (London Borough of Newham, 2007)

> ... local authorities, in accordance with directions by the Secretary of State, will assess the care needs of any person who appears to them to need community care and decide in the light of the **assessment** whether they should provide any services.
>
> (S. 47 National Health Service and Community Care Act 1990)

A domiciliary care needs assessment regarding new service users is undertaken, prior to the provision of a domiciliary care service by people who are trained to do so, using appropriate methods of communication so that the service user and their representatives, are fully involved. (Standard 2, Domiciliary care – National Minimum Standards, Care Standards Act 2000)

'In any case where the individual ('the carer') provides or intends to provide a substantial amount of care on a regular basis for the relevant person, the carer may request the local authority, before they make their decision as to whether the needs of the relevant person call for the provision of any services, to carry out an assessment of his ability to provide and to continue to provide care for the relevant person; and if he makes such a request, the local authority shall carry out such an assessment and shall take into account the results of that assessment in making that decision.' (Carers (Recognition and Services) Act 1995 1 (1))

As the extracts above indicate, the concept of assessment lies at the heart of much of the writing and thinking about health and social care. The frequency and location of where we find the term signals that it is an important activity. This raises important questions for us to consider at the outset:

1 What does it mean?
2 Does it have one clear, single meaning?

Consider the following extract from Smale and Tuson:

> Imagine turning up at the supermarket to be met by an 'assessor', or 'gatekeeper of resources', perhaps called a 'shopping manager'. On entering the shop to acquire your package of goods, or perhaps the shopping manager visits you because somebody has told them you need some groceries but cannot go out, this person explains that their job is to work with you to identify your needs, and to form an opinion of what kind of package of goods you need and what resources can be called upon to obtain them. The shopping manager also explains that this particular supermarket no longer provides many 'goods' themselves but the manager will contract with a supplier who does.
>
> (Smale and Tuson, 1993, page 4)

What meanings do the authors attach to assessment? Would you share their views?

Smale and Tuson interchange assessor with gatekeeper; they create the image of the assessor as

> ### ACTIVITY
>
> Think of as many meanings as you can of the word assessment. Explain how the meaning might change depending on the context. In your mind what image does the word 'assessor' bring to mind?
>
> If you are now saying to yourself, 'Isn't it obvious what a care assessor does and what a care assessment is?' we would suggest not, not even amongst people working in the same team. In any event, what happens when you make an appointment to 'assess' somebody – do they necessarily share your set of meanings?

an opinion-former, someone who will sort things out for you. Where else do we encounter the concept of assessment? National Vocational Qualification (NVQ) candidates require assessors. Are these 'gatekeepers', 'opinion-formers', or whatever you call them, people who you have to please in some way perhaps or present a certain side of yourself to?

Assessment is an 'intersubjective' activity

Because each assessment is about two or more human beings coming together, no two assessments are ever the same. Both the assessor and the person they are assessing bring their own individual ideas, interpretations and meanings to that particular social interaction. 'Intersubjectivity' is a difficult word but it sums up well what happens in the assessment situation. Assessments are about people meeting and getting to know each other. Each brings their own individual views, thoughts and perceptions to the meeting, and, by the end, what emerges is unique. It is a coming together of each person's way of looking at things. Two different realities have collided, producing a new reality. Even if there is a sharp disagreement, we are still changed through the experience.

The concept of intersubjectivity was introduced by a sociologist called Alfred Schütz. According to Schütz, when two or more individual people meet and share time and space with each other they become engaged in a process of communication and negotiation whereby they begin to discover and understand each other's thoughts and feelings. Intersubjectivity describes how people begin to inhabit each other's worlds. Social care is about trying to establish other people's wants and needs, their views – in short what their situation in the world is. It is also about those people understanding what we are about. This cannot happen in a mechanical way; it involves joining with each other in order to see the world through each other's eyes.

Intersubjectivity and reflective practice

If we accept Schütz's view, assessment is more than a simple question and answer session. It is a complex social interaction where the meanings given to it are the product of an often unacknowledged negotiation between the two or more people involved. These meanings cannot be automatically assumed. The 'reality' of the assessment will be informed by each participant's 'taken for granted' assumptions and preconceptions about what they believe 'goes on' in an assessment, what it is for and so on. As practitioners, we should always acknowledge the ambiguous and fluid nature of assessment. Those we are involved with will not necessarily share our viewpoint or our meanings. If we accept this then we should adopt an approach to assessment that is both self-aware and reflective.

Reflective practice means that assessors should be looking at themselves and asking themselves questions such as:

- What values and assumptions am I taking to this interaction?
- What part am I playing in constructing this particular assessment the way it is?
- Is the purpose of the assessment clearly understood by both parties?
- What effect am I having on this person – and what effect are they having on me?

Reflective practice means assessors putting themselves in the picture by thinking and acting with the people they are serving, so that their understandings and actions are changed by the experiences with others. At the same time as this is going on, assessors are influencing and changing others and their social worlds. It's a two-way process.

> **REFLECT**
>
> 1 Think about occasions when you have assessed someone and when you yourself have been assessed.
> 2 Write a list of all the activities that went on – put them under the headings of behaviours, thoughts, and feelings.
> 3 Does it make any difference whether you are the assessor or the 'assessed'?

Assessment and change

The activity of assessment itself can bring about change. As practitioners it is likely that, from the beginning of the initial process of gathering information, we are instrumental in bringing about change. This is by the nature of the questions asked, by the fact we are listening to the person concerned and, sometimes, the members of their family. It is by paying attention to and therefore validating that person and/or their family's difficulties or concerns, and also by the fact of providing information and advice. This underlines both the dynamic and interactive relationship between those assessing and those being assessed.

REFLECT

Reflect on a recent assessment in which you were involved.

1 What messages do you think you gave by the questions you asked, your response to what the individuals said, any advice or information that you gave, even the fact of turning up when you did?

2 From the beginning of the assessment to its finish, what do you think changed for them? What changed for you?

The importance of language in assessment

So far we have suggested that far from being a straightforward, clear-cut, bureaucratic or clinical process, assessments are always dynamic, 'intersubjective', complex social interactions. This is because assessments are about human beings coming together within a particular social context and constructing something unique. Each of the actors involved in an assessment brings their own set of meanings and assumptions based, to some extent, on past experiences. What they are there for, what is going on, the language used by each participant, in other words the 'reality' of each assessment is open to different interpretations.

In one of the original documents on assessment practice, *Getting the Message Across*, the Social Services Inspectorate stated:

Assessment is a participative process. It necessarily involves establishing mutual trust and understanding if meaningful information is to be obtained. The most effective way of achieving understanding may be to enable people to describe their situation in their own words, using their preferred language and at their own pace. Assessment should be a process of working alongside people.

(Department of Health/Social Services Inspectorate, 1991, page14)

In the same set of guidelines, the Social Services Inspectorate (SSI) provided revealing evidence of how the language frequently used by professionals led those they were assessing to misinterpret what was going on.

The following are some examples of what users thought words meant:

Voluntary agencies	people with no experience, volunteers
Sensitive	tender and sore
Agencies	second-hand clothes shops
Eligibility	a good marriage catch
Allocation process	being offered re-housing
Function	wedding (party), funeral
Gender	most did not know this word
Criteria	most did not know this word
Networks	no one knew this word
Advocacy	some users thought this word meant that if they did not agree with the assessment they would have to go to court – they wondered who would pay the bill

(Department of Health/Social Services Inspectorate, 1991, page 20)

This point is underlined by Smale and Tuson (1993) who stress that the assessor should possess the ability to 'join with people' and 'create a collaborative working relationship'. In other words, the assessor needs to enter the world of the assessed and ensure that the person being assessed understands the world of the assessor. Being aware of the problems of language is an important part of this.

The core of assessment is about understanding. This requires the assessor to listen, observe and relate both to what is being said and to the feeling with which this information is given. Whatever forms or templates we may need to fill in at some later stage it is always better to enable a person to tell their own story about their situation in their own way, in their own words, at their own pace. This approach allows somebody to convey what issues, events and questions they think are important.

Assessment as a form of story telling

Carrying out an assessment could be regarded as establishing someone's story. As a story requires at least one author, this raises questions such as 'If you were being assessed who would you want to be the author of your story, bringing you to life and constructing your identity?' We continue this theme in the section on assessment models.

Some of these ideas about the negotiated and dynamic nature of the assessor/client relationship might appear to be overly 'philosophical' at first. But we must recognise that assessment in social care or social work is a complex human activity and not simply a completed form or a checklist of questions. The importance of acknowledging the 'constructed' nature of assessment from the beginning will help inform discussions on all aspects of the assessment process and particularly those issues surrounding anti-discriminatory practices and 'power relationships' covered later in the chapter and elsewhere in the book.

KNOWLEDGE CHECK

1 What policies do you have where assessment is specifically mentioned?
2 What does intersubjectivity mean, and how does it apply to assessments in the care context?
3 Why is it important to think carefully about the language used in assessments?
4 What are the important features of an assessment as identified so far?

Why assess?

We have established that assessment is a complex process and that what people understand is going on when an assessment is carried out should therefore not be taken for granted. We have also seen that, whatever the service user group, assessment is a key part of health and social care practice. Whilst the extracts set out above indicate that the requirement to carry out an assessment is embedded in several pieces of legislation and official guidance, we should also recognise that assessments take place in a variety

Josephine and Connie

Josephine Henry is 89-years-old. She was admitted to hospital four weeks ago following a fall at home. She had a **full medical assessment on admission** to hospital and was found to also have severe respiratory problems. The medical team have now **assessed her following her treatment** and have said that she is ready to be discharged as all her medical needs have been addressed. The care manager in the hospital **assesses her regarding her discharge from hospital** but does not feel that Josephine can return to her own home as she is still vulnerable to falls. A care manager from her local authority has visited Josephine and **assesses options** with her and her family regarding moving into a care home. Two days later the Manager of Rosebank care home visits Josephine and her son in the hospital. She **assesses Josephine's care needs** to make a decision whether Rosebank would be able to provide for her support needs.

Connie is a 38-year-old learning disabled adult who lives with her parents, Mr and Mrs Maber. Her father has recently been diagnosed with multiple sclerosis. The home has been **assessed** and adaptations are taking place so that he can stay at home for the foreseeable future; carers will be coming in to support him and Mrs Maber in caring for him. For the first time Mr and Mrs Maber have thought that perhaps Connie would be better living away from home as they are concerned about their ability to support her in the future. A care manager visits to spend time with Connie and **assess** what alternative living accommodation would be most appropriate.

Questions

1 What issues can arise when family members need an assessment?
2 What feelings might an individual have when they are being assessed?
3 How can organisations make the process of assessment more manageable for people like Josephine and Connie?

of settings for a variety of reasons. Service providers, whether in residential, day or domiciliary settings, also carry out assessments. This raises questions of why assessing people is so central to health and social care work.

So when does assessment take place?

Chapter 1 on the context of health and social care details the legislation that underpins the organisation and provision of care. The main piece of legislation which guides the work of local authority social services departments for adults is the NHS and Community Care Act 1990. This Act and accompanying guidance should be available in all local authority offices. Legislation that also relates to the assessment process for adults includes:

- Chronically Sick and Disabled Act 1970
- Mental Health Act 1983
- Disabled Persons (Services, Consultation and Representation) Act 1986
- Carers (Recognition and Services) Act 1995
- Crime and Disorder Act 1998
- Health and Social Care Act 2001
- Mental Capacity Act 2005

Other Guidelines include:

- Care Programme Approach
- Single Assessment Process
- Safeguarding Vulnerable Adults
- Fair Access to Care
- Multi-Agency Public Protection Arrangements
- Independence, Choice and Well-being

This legislation has a different impact on your work, depending on your role and the organisation that you work for. If you have never actually read the official guidelines you should make the effort to read those sections (for example Section 47 of the NHS and Community Care Act 1990) that apply to your job role. That assessment is required by law is one obvious reason to assess, but this itself raises the further question of why assessment is made a legal requirement in the first place.

The extract from *Caring for People* provides one very clear answer:

'The aim of assessment should be to arrive at a decision on whether services should be provided and in what form. Assessments will therefore have to be made against a background of stated objectives and priorities determined by the local authority.' (Department of Health, 1989)

These priorities are determined through collaboration between the NHS and local authority, as explained in Chapter 1. They are then determined relating to assessment and eligibility by the local authority; an example is given later in the chapter.

Tensions and pressures

For statutory organisations, a key function of assessment is a gatekeeping one. For assessors this inevitably creates tensions. On the one hand they are pulled by the idea of the full 'needs-led' assessment with its underlying values of holism and humanism, and on the other hand they are constrained by the (often tightly drawn) criteria for eligibility and priorities laid down by their agency. Research has shown that care managers experience stress when trying to reconcile the competing demands placed upon them by the sort of contradictions in their role (Postle, 2002). These include the following:

Legal requirements	Needs-led
Managerial and bureaucratic	Person-centred
Eligibility criteria	Humanism
Budgets	Holistic approach
Service availability	'Consumer' expectations

The working out of these tensions in a way that doesn't leave the assessor or the subject of the assessment negatively affected by the experience is difficult. We will address the issue of what skills, values and knowledge are required in more detail later.

A key reason for assessing is because the law requires it but it is obviously not the only one, particularly for those people who work in non-statutory settings. Other reasons to assess include:

- ensuring the suitability of provision. Will the person actually benefit from using or having it? Will they fit in? Is it the right match?
- exchanging information. Is it really what the person needs or wants? Could some more appropriate course of action be taken?

- establishing the level of need, thus helping to prioritise response
- fine-tuning – establishing which particular provision will be most effective; how much of the service is needed and when
- profiling – does the person being assessed fit the profile for which a particular service was designed, for example are they the 'right' age, gender, category of need etc.
- analysing what the situation is so that planning can take place
- finding out what the person is like as an individual.

Who knows best – the patient/ service user or the assessor?

To return to the supermarket scenario provided by Smale and Tuson, we might ask why people cannot make their own decisions about whether they have care and what form these services should take; after all the principle of client choice is at the heart of much social care literature. Those with sufficient funds can buy what they like. However, even if you purchased all your own care it would not necessarily mean you were getting the most appropriate services. For example, some people, either because they have an exaggerated perception of risk or are simply unaware of how the care system can work, might choose to employ a 24-hour, live-in carer when they could almost certainly be helped to maintain their independence by having carers come in to attend them at several critical stages during the day with no greater risk and a lot less expenditure and intrusion into their lives. This raises difficult questions of when is choice informed choice? Whose 'solution' is the best?

Assessment can help address these issues, as long as potential ambiguities, complexities and conflicts are acknowledged at the outset. Assessment can be effective in determining:

- someone's ability to exercise informed freedom of choice
- whether a particular service provision is likely to be adequate and effective
- that all aspects of a client's situation are identified, their strengths as well as their problems. It helps us 'round' a person rather than just identify them with a minus.

Knowledge gained from assessment – fact or opinion?

You might have suggested that one reason to assess is to collect knowledge about somebody, their needs and their circumstances; in other words, to get at the 'true facts of the matter' – the unadorned truth. This is not as simple as it may seem.

During an assessment, some of the information gathered will certainly be factual: the person's name, address and age for example. Other items of knowledge about the person that assessors usually seek, such as an individual's ethnic group or religion, may also seem factual. A lot of assessment paperwork reflects this view because a series of pre-coded options are given and it involves the 'straightforward' completion of boxes.

These coded categories are often based on official administrative categories such as 'white British' or 'black African' and it is not too difficult to see how a certain approach to assessment can 'create' rather than 'reflect' the person being assessed. Skellington cautions:

> 'Race', racial groups and categories ... are not things that are given – objective facts waiting to be used – but concepts that have to be constructed. This construction involves a number of stages: differences of a certain kind between people have to be discerned; these differences have to be considered consequential; and these perceived shared attributes, such as skin colour, nationality, or regional or ethnic origins, have to become the basis for defining groups or categories of people.
>
> (Skellington, 1996, pages 18–19)

Most of the data gathered in assessment is *qualitative* – it is information which describes what the person is like, their preferences, how they are feeling, how they are coping, their degree of mental capability and so on. Here, once again, it becomes apparent that assessment is not so much about 'discovering the facts' about someone's circumstances but 'creating a picture' based on the participation of those involved. Assessment places the assessor in the position of 'agent of knowledge'. The assessor has the power to construct someone's identity on paper and thereafter for the purposes of official business.

This raises more questions for assessors, for example:

- Who should be involved in assessment?
- Should the views and opinions of each participant in an assessment carry equal weight?
- How do we ensure that the picture is a valid and authentic one?
- What kinds of language and terminology do we use to record the findings?
- Is there always going to be a power imbalance between the assessor and the person being assessed because it is actually embedded in the structure of the relationship between the two parties?
- How do we ensure that the assessor – 'the agent of knowledge' – doesn't either consciously or unconsciously abuse their power?

We will return to these issues later in the chapter but you might want to reflect on what your response would be and maybe raise further questions for yourself.

KNOWLEDGE CHECK

1 What are the main responsibilities, in terms of powers and duties, of your agency?
2 Give four reasons why assessment is an important activity.
3 What does it mean to say that data gathered in an assessment is *qualitative*?
4 What do we mean when we say that an assessor is an *'agent of knowledge'*?

Assessment of need

Definitions and categories of need

We know from our look at the policy guidance earlier in the chapter that a major purpose of assessment is to establish what someone's 'needs' are. The problem is that there is no overall agreement on what the concept of need means – different people use 'need' in different ways. Consequently, in academic circles 'need' is described as a 'contested' concept. Middleton (1997) observed:

'It is a pity that 'needs-led' has been set at the heart of community care, since it is fraught with the possibilities of misunderstanding. Hopes, wishes, aspirations, dreams and the barriers that prevent their realisation would have been so much easier to work with.'

We have discussed how assessment is a complex, and far from straightforward concept. 'Need' is just as culturally situated and probably that much more complex again. As with assessment it is open to interpretation. This is acknowledged in official guidance:

Need is a complex concept which has been analysed in a variety of different ways. In this guidance, the term is used as shorthand for the requirements of individuals to enable them to achieve, maintain or restore an acceptable level of social independence or quality of life, as defined by the care agency or authority.

(Department of Health/Social Services Inspectorate, 1991b, page 10)

However, need is also a personal concept. No two individuals will perceive or define their needs in the same way.

Those advocating a holistic approach to assessment sometimes place needs under a range of headings such as:

- physical
- spiritual
- intellectual
- emotional
- social
- cultural.

Other typologies categorise needs in terms of the services or resources available, for example:

- medical
- nursing
- social care
- home care
- mobility.

Texts on human growth and development frequently utilise the humanist psychologist Abraham Maslow's 'hierarchy' of needs.

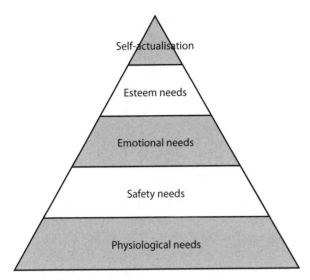

Figure 7.1 Maslow's hierarchy of needs

The basic premise of Maslow's idea was that people have an in-built tendency to develop themselves or 'self-actualise' as they progress through life. However, our basic physiological needs for food and drink, clothing, warmth and shelter – at the bottom of the triangle – have to be met before we can move up the 'hierarchy of needs' and start meeting other requirements for a fulfilling life. Although this view has been criticised as an oversimplified account of human development it is a useful way of distinguishing between different types of needs.

Needs/wants

It is often said that care practitioners should be careful to distinguish between 'needs' and 'wants' as if this was a clear-cut exercise – the separation of the essential 'needs' from the 'less than necessary' wants. In day-to-day situations, people commonly interchange the two words. They do not necessarily adopt the language of PISCES (physical, intellectual, social, cultural, emotional and spiritual) or Maslow. This can make it difficult for assessors not to create an artificial picture by reinterpreting the comments of those they assess.

In academic circles, needs are often seen in terms of being 'relative' or 'comparative'. In deciding about what we need we compare ourselves to what others have. What this means is that material things like plasma televisions, DVD players, mobile phones, certain types of clothing and shoes and so on have symbolic values that are often more important than

their material value. Deborah Stone cites the philosopher Michael Walzer, who says:

> People don't just have needs, they have ideas about their needs. (Walzer, 1983, in Stone, 1997)

For example, food is more than just nutrition – it has cultural and ritual aspects to it. Eating the same food as others can be a mark of belonging or membership. Think about why so many children come back from school with much of the contents of their lunch boxes untouched. You are in need if you cannot partake in the day-to-day activities of the culture in which you live. People from different cultures, histories, social groups will have different needs. So when we say need is relational or comparative we mean that need is specific to both place and time. If we accept that the symbolic aspect of need is important, then meeting

CASE STUDY

Needs

Charles Robins is 67-years-old. He lives alone in his own house. He used to live with his mother until she died 18 months ago. He has a son and a daughter who barely contact him. The house is very dirty and smelly; in fact it is squalid. Mr Robins has a state and a civil service pension. He usually lives on snacks and other convenience foods. Mr Robins hardly ever washes or changes his clothes. He uses a bucket to urinate in and empties it out of the front door. There is rubbish throughout the house and piled up in the garden. Recently he tripped and sprained his ankle which meant he could hardly get around. He is unable to climb the stairs to bed or go out shopping.

Think about this dialogue.

Assessor: 'You seem very isolated. Do you get lonely on your own?'

Mr Robins: 'I need to get a new TV. The old one died on me.'

Assessor: 'So you need social contact, would you like the company of others?'

Mr Robins: 'No, I'm not saying that.'

Questions

1 Do you keep going until Mr Robins admits that he wants to get out and meet people?
2 Do you record that Mr Robins 'needs a new TV'? If not, why not?

people's needs means protecting their identities as well as keeping them alive.

REFLECT

1 How would you define need?
2 What types of needs do you believe human beings have?
3 Look at the case study on page 259; what needs would you identify Mr Robins as having?
4 Which of those needs would you say are the responsibility of health and social care agencies?
5 Once a need is identified, does the assessor have a responsibility to meet it?

Bradshaw's 'taxonomy of need'

In 1972, a researcher, Jonathan Bradshaw, argued that there were four different ways of defining social need. Briefly they are:

- **Normative** need: this is what the professional or the agency defines as a 'need' in any given situation.
- **Felt** need: this is equated with 'want'.
- **Expressed** need: this represents a further stage and is 'felt need turned into action'. Therefore, this is more of a demand.
- **Comparative** need: this is where planners or researchers look at the characteristics of those already receiving a service and 'if people with similar characteristics are not in receipt of a service then they are in need.' For example, if there are elderly, lonely depressed people in one area able to access a day care service and others in another who aren't, then they would have 'comparative need'.

Need – living with ambiguity

You will have probably found that the activities will have raised many points about a wide range of issues, such as personal standards, choice, risk, how much you listen to what the other person wants, and maybe even issues about mental health.

We need to have some sort of rules or framework to guide us through the conflicts and **dilemmas** which situations like the case study above raise. Of course, we need to be aware of the relevant legislation which

guides our work, but that will not always help us with the types of issues raised above. It should be clear from the discussion so far that there can be no single text or authoritative set of guidelines which can answer all the questions raised in an unambiguous and straightforward way. We have to accept that 'need' is a contested concept. Parton and O'Byrne (2000) on the subject of assessment in general state 'that to pretend that there is certainty where there is little, is not good practice' (page 135).

Nevertheless, as we shall discuss in more depth later on in the chapter, assessment always takes place within a particular set of contexts. Assessors work within an agency or institutional context. Having a clear idea of their agency's function, the purpose of assessment within that agency and how that particular agency defines need, will at least ensure that ambiguities and differences of interpretation are brought out in the open, discussed and even recorded. Ironically, to be upfront and honest about areas of uncertainty, possible misinterpretations and clashes of opinion – in other words acknowledging that you are not sure and do not know everything – is a more professional approach than ploughing on, trying to convince yourself and others that all is crystal clear. Assessors can sometimes believe that it is a sign of their 'professionalism' that they can walk in and establish someone's needs single-handedly. In fact, usually the reverse is true. Letting go of this idea can only be beneficial for all concerned. Being honest about what you are uncertain of and what needs to be clarified, should either trigger a more specialist assessment, further discussion with the person themselves, or their carer. If you are not specifically trained in, say, mental health, sensory impairments or physiotherapy, then you won't properly be able to establish someone's needs in those areas.

In 1991, anticipating the introduction of the NHS and Community Care Act, the Department of Health produced the following guidelines for staff involved in assessing need.

In order to undertake an assessment of need, staff have to know:

- the needs for which the agency accepts responsibility
- the needs for which other care agencies accept responsibility
- the needs of carers which qualify for assistance

- the agency's priorities in responding to needs
- the financial assessment criteria for determining users' contributions
- the agency's policy on risk to the user and to community
- the legal requirements.

(Department of Health, 1991a, page 46)

REFLECT

Using the guidance above, how clear are you on each of the points outlined as far as your organisation is concerned? Which ones require further investigation and clarity?

KNOWLEDGE CHECK

Using material such as operational instructions, manuals, leaflets etc., collected from your workplace, make sure you can answer the following questions.

1 How does your agency define 'need' for the purposes of assessment?
2 What categories or types of need are specified? What language and terminology are these needs couched in?
3 What needs are your agency obliged to meet?
4 What efforts are made to ensure that those being assessed understand the points made above?

Barriers to a 'needs-led' assessment

Finally, we look at the research of Allison Worth. In 2002, she published her research into how both district nurses and care managers carried out assessments. Her observations showed that:

Practitioners had considerable difficulty in conducting client-led assessments. Clients are unaware of what is available, therefore practitioners have to suggest services ....

One difficulty in incorporating the client's views was very apparent ... Many clients were unable to define their needs due to mental impairment, and others wanted to pursue their expressed needs (for example not to have help at home) in

circumstances which practitioners, family and neighbours felt would mean an unacceptable level of risk. Another factor for some clients was an inability to express their views due to severe hearing loss or speech problems following a stroke. (Worth, 2002, in Bytheway *et al* (eds), page 326)

Worth's research underlines the sheer range of issues practitioners have to grapple with when trying to adopt a needs-led approach to assessment. The key point is that despite the difficulties, it is a principle worth adopting. It would be easy to become cynical. However, being aware and honest about the possible pitfalls and complexities is a sign of professionalism. The worst thing would be for assessors to delude themselves and others that they are taking a needs-led approach when they are not.

KNOWLEDGE CHECK

1 How does the Department of Health define need in its policy guidance?
2 What categories of need does PISCES stand for? Give an example of each.
3 What is the basic idea in Maslow's hierarchy of needs?
4 What are Bradshaw's four ways of defining need?
5 According to Department of Health guidance, what do staff need to know in order to undertake an assessment of need?
6 What barriers did Worth identify in her research into needs-led assessment?

Assessment of risk

It is very common in care work to talk about the need to do a 'risk assessment'. This can be for a multitude of reasons. For example, a person may be considered to be dangerous or aggressive; there might be moving and handling issues; there might be other health and safety issues; a person may be perceived to be at risk from falling, wandering, dehydrating, burglary or being abused by a stressed carer. It could be a combination of several or all of these factors, or something else completely.

Risk assessment is a term that, for many, has a reassuringly clinical, professional, clear-cut, even scientific feel about it. Whether such feelings are justified is another matter. Several writers on social policy have commented that 'risk' is gradually replacing 'need' as the guiding principle behind the assessment and delivery of services.

REFLECT

Think about your own job.

1 Do you regard your assessments as 'assessments of need' or 'risk assessments'? Maybe it's both, in which case what would you consider to be the difference between the two?

2 In your own organisation, what relationship does risk have to any discussions on needs?

Meanings of risk

Just as with 'need' we find that 'risk' can be every bit as slippery and ambiguous a concept. People attach different meanings to it, often depending on the context in which it arises.

What is risk?

Your discussion probably led you to question what 'at risk' means. Much of the time it is seen negatively and used interchangeably with 'danger'. Alaszewski (1998) observed that like many concepts used in everyday language and in more technical settings, ''risk' has a variety of different meanings and can be used in different ways' (page 9).

Alaszewski talks about 'a narrow commonsense definition of risk' where risk is equated with danger and negative outcomes. He also says there are broader definitions in which 'negative outcomes are balanced against positive outcomes'. This might well describe the gambler's attitude to risk.

He goes on:

Risk forms the tip of an iceberg of related words and terms. Some of these words tend to amplify the restricted meaning of risk in terms of the negative consequences of events; for example, hazard or harm. Other terms are linked to specific aspects of risk and tend to take the form of risk plus a

CASE STUDY

Mrs Prince and risk

Mrs Prince is 71-years-old and lives alone in a three-bedroom semi-detached house. She has Parkinson's disease which has impaired her mobility and created difficulty for Mrs Prince in looking after herself. She falls occasionally – often when trying to get up and down stairs or transferring from her bed or chair to her walking frame. Mrs Prince's daughter is very keen for her to move to a sheltered housing scheme and to accept carers to come and assist her with the activities of daily living. Mrs Prince is determined that she is going to stay put and manage on her own. She likes her house and her neighbours and says that she can cope with the odd fall as long as she's near enough to a piece of stout furniture where she can haul herself up. An occupational therapist has fitted grab rails and other aids in the past. Mrs Prince is an intelligent woman and prides herself in not being a bother to others. She claims that she's a great fatalist and her attitude to life is 'what will be will be'.

Questions

1 Do you consider Mrs Prince to be 'at risk' – if so what are the risks?

2 Do you consider the risk of Mrs Prince staying at home without care an acceptable one? What would your preferred course of action be? Give reasons.

3 Has considering these points led you to formulate a working definition of risk?

qualifying term, relating to either a more specialist or technical use, such as risk assessment, or to an everyday use, such as risk taking. (page 10)

The 'risk iceberg' (overleaf) illustrates the different associations and meanings attached to risk. Two of the associated issues highlighted in the iceberg are risk perception and risk taking. It is clear that two people, when confronted by the same set of conditions, can often have completely different perceptions of whether there is any risk and what it might be. In addition, the behaviour of smokers, for example, shows us that even when 'experts' spell out a risk and back it up with evidence (in this case the greater chance of developing lung cancer, heart

Figure 7.2 The risk iceberg

disease and so on) people choose to take the 'risk'. Both of these points are important to understand for those involved in assessment.

A culture of managing risk in partnership with service users is more appropriate to an environment where there is a complete avoidance of risk, what is known as being 'risk averse.' It takes confidence and a focus on the role of a professional in relation to supporting the individual for this to become second nature; it is usually easier for the professionals and organisations to avoid risks, rather than manage them. As the Department of Health (2007) states:

> Avoiding risks altogether would constrain their choices and opportunities.

Whose risk?

Assessors need to recognise that differences in opinion over risk are not simply a question of who is right or wrong, or who is seeing things most clearly. If we return to the theme of intersubjectivity, it becomes evident that a key part of risk assessment is establishing both the other person's perception of risk and their attitude towards it. It should not be the imposition of one's own 'expert' interpretation. This is important because as Lupton observes:

> People's perceptions and understandings of risk are established over a lifetime of personal experiences.
> (Lupton, 1999, page 112)

She goes on to make the point that the risk position someone takes may also be important to his or her

---

CASE STUDY

Mrs Prince again

Mrs Prince had another fall and suffered some grazing on her leg. She managed to get herself to her feet after about 20 minutes. The daughter was most concerned to learn about this and called the family GP. Mrs Prince was embarrassed to be the centre of such attention and said that it might be an idea to get a portable alarm system. The daughter explained to the GP that the risks were becoming more and more worrying and persuaded both her mother and the GP to refer to the social services. The talk, once again, is of a home care package and a possible move to sheltered accommodation.

Questions

1. Return to your answers from the first case study about Mrs Prince (see page 262). When you were forming your ideas about Mrs Prince's situation, to what extent did you take the points Lupton makes into account?

2. In Mrs Prince's situation, for whose benefit might an assessor emphasise the risks in order for a 'safe' option to be pursued? How does this link to issues of power, client choice and professional accountability?

3. In your job, are risk assessments undertaken in order to protect the worker or the client? Give examples.

sense of self-identity. For example, it may be an important part of someone's self-concept that they see themselves as a 'survivor', a 'battler' or simply 'no trouble to anyone'. Worth (2002) found that in her research a woman with a serious visual impairment had to be strongly persuaded to accept a home help and a community alarm against her will. The woman is quoted as saying 'I'm not the sort of person to have a home help.' Worth concludes that:

> ... by accepting help, an older person has to face that they have become a different sort of person, the sort of person who needs help to manage. Such situations occurred in half of the observed assessments and were all associated with practitioners' perceptions of risks not being acknowledged by clients. (page 327)

Research carried out in this area by Lindow and Morris (1995) concluded that:

> Community care workers face pressures to minimise risks to those with whom they work ... Such pressures can get in the way of the person's own preferences being acted upon and may lead to action being taken which inhibits their ability to make choices. (pages 31–2)

We have argued that, in recent years, risk has moved to the foreground of care practice. We have also argued that it is a complex, subjective and 'slippery' concept. The sources of risk are many and varied; it is not always easy to establish them in a clear, unambiguous way. Having identified risk, what to do next is not always straightforward either. This does not mean to say that risk should not be uppermost in the assessor's mind. However, careful consideration needs to be given to certain questions. These are:

- What is the nature of the risk(s) being assessed?
- Who is saying it is a risk?
- Who is it a risk for?
- What tools, methods or other specialist opinion is available for the assessor to analyse or quantify the risk?
- If a risk is established, what do official guidance or agency operational instructions say about what steps should be taken? Is there, for example, a legal power or duty to act?
- Whose responsibility is it to manage the risk?
- Should someone with mental capacity be free to live with any risks they choose to, however

harmful or dangerous this may seem to those around them?
- How should the risks identified in the case of someone without mental capacity be managed?
- If there is no overall consensus about either the extent or nature of a risk or the best way of managing it, what legal, practice or moral framework will inform decision-making?

The way forward

A realistic approach to this complex area can best be summed up by Alaszewski (2002). He is referring to an article that Hazel Kemshall published in 2000 when he concludes:

> There is great merit in Kemshall's approach. She both recognises differences in assessment of risk and argues that effective risk management requires mutual respect and negotiation. While public and service users have become cynical about expert assessment of risk and are less willing to take them 'for granted', they are still willing to accept and trust these assessments if their own perceptions are acknowledged, and if they are involved in the process of decision-making and risk management.
>
> (Alaszewski, 2002, in Bytheway et al)

ACTIVITY

1 Explain why it is hard to come to one, agreed definition of risk.
2 Give an example where an assessor and a client might not share the same perception of risk.
3 How does your agency define risk?
4 What guidelines do you have for managing risk?

Department of Health: *Guidance on Assessment of Risk*:

> Making choices about health and social care inevitably means balancing benefits and risks in order to make informed decisions.

The Department of Health aims to support people in making decisions that are right for their personal requirements and situation.

> Most of the choices that people make in life naturally involve some element of risk, and the decisions made by people using health and social care are no different.

Risk is a concept that tends to have negative connotations but people take considered risks all of the time and gain many positive benefits. As new health and social care choices and opportunities arise, they are likely to involve the consideration of taking risks.

People want choice and control for themselves and those they care for, but sometimes it is difficult to weigh the benefits of an option against the potential risks.

Independence, choice and risk: a guide to best practice in supported decision making (Department of Health, May 2007) This document provided a risk framework for everyone involved in supporting decision making. The White Paper *Our health, our care, our say*, set out plans for the future of health and social care in the twenty-first century, in which choice and control are critical components. This gave a commitment to develop a national approach to risk management.

The Care Services Improvement Partnership has also produced risk framework resources in recognition of this area being crucial to empowerment and independence for individual patients and service users, but also a tricky area for professionals.

The context of assessment

We discussed earlier that assessment always takes place within a context. In reality, there are several interrelated contexts. We know that assessments do not happen 'spontaneously' or in 'a vacuum'; there is always a history, a reason and a purpose. The assessor themselves operates within a variety of different contexts. Apart from the legal context, the activity of assessment can be 'situated' in several overlapping contexts. The assessor needs to have a clear idea of how they are situated in order to make proper sense of what they are doing and to perform their role as professionally as they can.

Understanding the context as fully as possible helps promote assessment practices that are:

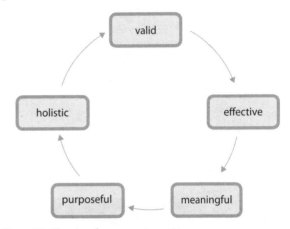

Figure 7.3 The aim of assessment practice

It prevents assessment becoming:

● superficial
● vague
● partial
● ritualistic
● over-bureaucratic.

Historical context

How does a person become a 'patient or service user'? Usually, either the person themselves or someone professionally or personally close to them makes their situation known to a responsible agency. This can be through a variety of ways and methods. We need to consider how, on occasions, the method and circumstances of referral 'set up' or at least colour certain aspects of the assessment to follow.

An agency makes a decision whether to assess following someone else's decision to 'make a referral for an assessment'. However, not everyone is familiar enough with the system to put it in those terms. Often the starting point is a situation being described with some course of action implied; a story starts to be told.

What happens thereafter is a matter of interpretation, judgement and decision-making. The course of an assessment is never pre-ordained. It is difficult to say when an assessment actually starts but it would be fair to say by the time the assessor and 'assessee' first meet it has already started.

It might have become apparent that assessments are not of an individual but of a situation. What is going on 'around' the person – the context – is all relevant in some way. We would suggest that it is seldom the case that an assessor embarks on an assessment with a completely open mind. Smale and Tuson (1993) advocate developing a 'neutral perspective', one 'outside the network' under assessment. Whilst it is easy to understand the rationale behind this point of view we would argue that complete neutrality is unattainable. The assessor, like the person referred, is also situated in a context. They are not a free agent, neither are they insulated from a range of contextual factors – some of their own and some of the person being assessed.

REFLECT

As a worker in social care, who decides whether you should do a particular assessment? Who collects the details and writes the referral? Is it prioritised how quickly you should do it? How much of how you approach an assessment is already 'laid out' for you? Do you feel you are able to take a 'neutral perspective' in these circumstances? Identify factors that make it difficult to be neutral.

Other contexts

It will have become apparent that it is important to be able to situate an assessment in its rightful context. Learning more about the different background factors allows you to learn how the events have unfolded, what decisions have led to referral, who the interested parties are, whose agenda is being pursued and so on. There are, however, other important contextual factors that we want to highlight here. This is because there are features about each assessment that can create tensions, problems and dilemmas for assessors. Being aware of them helps you prevent them from

distorting or invalidating both the process and outcome of an assessment.

Personal context

In many official texts on assessment the assessor is largely anonymous or invisible. It is the person on whom the assessment is carried out who is the focus of interest and the object of analysis. However, an assessor is more than a robotic 'putter into practice' of guidelines, each is a human being and a social actor with their own unique identity, values, views and feelings. It is neither possible nor desirable to completely divorce the 'professional' self from the 'personal' self. Too much 'role playing' by the assessor can lead to a lack of authenticity and genuineness.

If those carrying out assessments and subsequent care management are to relate to their fellow citizens as 'partners' rather than as 'clients' then it is important that care managers do not fall into the trap of 'role-playing' their part in the relationship. It is essential that workers do not approach these relationships as a faceless representative of their agency but as a genuine human being. (Smale and Tuson, 1993, page 48)

Each assessor inevitably brings something of themselves to assessments they are involved in. Exactly what that is cannot be stated simply here. It is for each individual to reflect on. The primary role of this section is to raise awareness rather than give instruction.

In Chapter 3 we discussed the values that inform policy and practice. There are many interrelated factors that shape us and make us who we are. Our perspective on life – work included – is influenced by a complex interplay of factors such as our background, our gender, our age, our ethnicity, sexual orientation, religious beliefs and life events, such as death and divorce.

If we return to the idea of intersubjectivity then we are back to assessment as a negotiated process, a coming together of different perspectives. A story is told, heard, interpreted, retold again, reformulated, written down. The assessor can never be neutral in this process.

One's own personal context is important for a variety of reasons. It will affect how we feel about the assessment, for example:

- whether we are confident, anxious, fearful, complacent, distracted or over-involved
- how patient we are
- how tolerant we are
- how focused on the other person as an individual we are
- what we are 'projecting' on to their situation
- what judgements we are making about the person and their situation based on things that we have personal experience of.

ACTIVITY

Write down brief notes on what your reaction (feelings and thoughts) would be were you to be required to assess a situation which involves:

- dementia
- cancer
- domestic violence
- deafness
- a Muslim woman
- a Hindu man
- a female Jehovah's Witness
- alcohol abuse
- a personality disorder
- a former prisoner
- two older gay men.

If possible exchange your comments with a colleague. It would be surprising if your reactions were exactly the same. We are bound to be more relaxed and comfortable about some issues and more anxious and apprehensive about others. The important thing is to be aware that our 'personal' context is as important as the other contexts we work within, knowing the case history, the agency setting we work in and so on.

Organisational context

As discussed earlier, your role and responsibilities as an assessor are determined by the particular agency you work for. We can only emphasise again the importance of workers having as clear as possible an idea of what the roles and responsibilities of their particular agency are. Be clear why you are assessing,

what the agency policies are, and on what basis the agency operates. You need to be aware of the framework of official and legislative guidance within which you are working. Being clear on these points can make you aware that legislative and other policy directives can create their own conflicts and tensions. These need to be looked at and worked out professionally.

Dilemmas and conflicts

An example of such conflicts is the emergence since the mid-1990s of a range of policies that stress the need for social care agencies to take the needs of carers into account. 'Caring for the carer' has found expression in several ways: the National Carers Strategy, carer's assessments, Direct Payments for carers and so on. Workers have discovered that carers, and the people they care for, are not 'an item' whose needs, views and opinions are identical; in fact it is more likely that the opposite is the case. This can present problems for agencies. For example, if a worker carrying out an assessment with someone offers their carer a carer's assessment, should it be the same assessor who carries out both assessments? Clearly, this could easily place the assessor in an uncomfortable and confusing position.

Another potential conflict for workers can be in situations where some form of 'abuse' could be said to be taking place. Official guidance on protecting vulnerable adults is covered by the Department of Health publication *No Secrets*. This is covered more fully in Chapter 9 on safeguarding adults. These guidelines identify six main forms of abuse. Two are defined as follows:

- *Psychological abuse*, including emotional abuse, threats of harm or abandonment, deprivation of contact, humiliation, blaming, controlling, intimidation, coercion, harassment, verbal abuse, isolation or withdrawal from services or supportive networks.
- *Neglect* and *acts of omission*, including ignoring medical or physical care needs, failure to provide access to appropriate health, social care or educational services, the withholding of the necessities of life, such as medication, adequate nutrition and heating.

Sometimes the 'abuser' is themselves vulnerable and in need of care. The case study below raises some of these difficult issues.

A dilemma

Roger Macintosh is a 76-year-old man with Parkinson's disease. He lives with his 75-year-old wife Dawn. Mr Macintosh's condition has progressed to the point where he now needs help with all his daily living activities. His wife is his only carer. Mr Macintosh falls frequently and the latest fall led to the couple being referred for assessment by their GP. As an assessor you establish that Mr Macintosh doesn't want any services. He describes himself as a 'private man' and says that he is happy for his wife to continue looking after his care needs at home. Mrs Macintosh is clearly stressed and bitter about having to devote so much time and energy to her husband. She says 'I have no life of my own now.' However, she too is reluctant to have 'strangers in the house'. She wonders whether her husband might have to go into a home but clearly is in two minds about this saying 'When you get married it is for better and for worse.' She describes her situation as 'Whereas before I was a wife, now I am just a skivvy.' She finds it hard to help her husband up after his falls. She already had a heart problem and now has persistent backache. Mrs Macintosh is also on tranquillisers prescribed for her 'bad nerves'.

She takes you to one side and tells you that now she routinely leaves her husband on the floor – sometimes for days when he falls. She only referred to the GP on this occasion because her daughter strongly urged her to. His bedroom floor reeks of urine. She knows it's wrong but can't see why she should 'bust a gut hauling him up all the time'. It is clear that there is an obvious punitive side to her behaviour.

Questions

1 As the assessor, who is your customer in this situation?
2 Do you take the comments of Mr and Mrs Macintosh at face value?
3 Do you believe there is abuse going on and what, if anything, should you do about it?
4 What guidance would you refer to, to help you make progress with this situation?

The multi-disciplinary context

As we have seen, much of the focus of recent policy on health and social care has emphasised the need for 'professionals' to work in partnership. A great deal of evidence has been generated to show the benefits of joint working, but much less discussion has been devoted to why such partnerships are not always successful. Simply instructing people to 'work together' won't necessarily make it happen effectively. Problems can occur at either a personal or institutional level. If we concentrate on the personal level, there are several ways in which 'professional partners' can both regard and relate to one another. Importantly, each 'partner' is not a 'professional' in exactly the same way, with all that this means in terms of their professional autonomy, status, knowledge and training. Few GPs, for instance, see social care workers as their professional peers. Partnerships can be weakened or distorted by lack of trust, lack of respect, jealousy, rivalry, deference, and a lack of clarity about the other's role, powers and responsibilities. Some of the difficulties with partnership working come about from the confusion within the field of social work and social care itself, about such basic questions as what the core tasks are, who should carry out the tasks, how the tasks should be carried out and several others. This is not the time to go deeply into this long-running issue but it is relevant to the discussion on assessment. Historically, the low emphasis on training in social care, shorter qualification periods, and lower pay have led to the professional self-concept of social care workers being generally less clearly defined and 'weaker' than those in healthcare.

REFLECT

1 Think about and identify the other main health and social care professionals who you might involve in your assessment of clients.
2 Write down in no more than two or three sentences what their particular skills and expertise are. Do the same for your job role.

Cultural differences when health and social care work together

The work of each 'profession' is founded on its own body of knowledge, value base and discourses (language and practices). Traditionally, the medical model of care has informed the approach of health workers whereas social care has adopted the social model.

The *medical model* involves the understanding of a person's problem, behaviour or condition in terms of illness, diagnosis and treatment.

The term 'medical model' is often referred to critically, to summarise what is considered to be the narrow, even oppressive, interpretation that medical practitioners and other health professionals sometimes apply to a client's condition. To put it simply, in the medical model the man in bed three with a ruptured spleen becomes just that – a ruptured spleen. His feelings, his opinions, what the effect is of his illness on his job and family are all ignored. The medical model concentrates on repairing that spleen.

ACTIVITY

We have briefly summarised the medical and social models.

1 What for you are the chief differences? Write down the differences under the following headings.
   ● Medical model
   ● Social model
   ● Attitude to the person
   ● Type of language used
   ● Factors that cause disability
   ● Issues that the professional should attend to
2 Which model more informs the work of your organisation? Give examples.

The *social model* of care not only situates people in their social context but it also emphasises the importance of social factors in preventing people with physical impairments participating in normal, everyday activities rather than simply focusing on the illness or disability to the exclusion of all else.

It is therefore important to recognise that while the argument for multi-disciplinary working is a strong one – not least on the grounds of person-centredness – there are potential difficulties and conflicts within multi-disciplinary working that can, at times, seep into and affect the assessment process. The assessor needs to be aware of these. See Chapter 6 for a fuller discussion of these issues and many more that are relevant to the whole issue of collaborative working.

KNOWLEDGE CHECK

1 Explain why assessors should make themselves aware of the historical context of any assessment they are involved in.
2 Why should assessors be aware of falling into the trap of 'role-playing' their part in the relationship?
3 Give two ways in which our personal context can influence our assessment.
4 Discuss an example of how an assessor might find themselves facing 'role conflict'.
5 Explain how there may be cultural differences between a social care worker and a health professional.

Models of assessment and assessment tools

In the health sector, continuity in observation of patients is considered to be an important key to successful assessment of needs, even if other clinically obtained information is also used, such as data from monitoring systems. The health sector has a number of assessment tools that are used in different contexts in hospitals and the community to ascertain health needs; their aim includes determining levels of:

● physiological functioning
● pain
● cognitive ability
● sensory awareness.

Within social care, assessment relates more to the ability of an individual to carry out their everyday activities and to ascertain if there are any support needs apparent.

Deficit model

Throughout most of the history of social care the approach taken by workers to assessment, either implicitly or explicitly, has been to concentrate on what the individual being assessed could not do, the abilities they lacked, their moral and practical failings, i.e. people's deficits.

The casework approach dominant throughout the twentieth century had its origins in the nineteenth century philanthropic tradition, whereby voluntary visitors would visit poor families and dispense aid based on the principle of their being 'deserving' or 'non-deserving'. The visitor would make careful investigation into the habits and lifestyle of those seeking help. If the individual was considered to be of bad character, e.g. a drunkard, lazy or immoral, then they would be deemed 'undeserving' and denied charitable aid. If the individual accepted the error of their ways and was prepared to be reformed, then they would be considered 'deserving' and help would be offered. This approach essentially regarded the problem as located in the defective make-up of the individual (individual pathology); it took little account of wider cultural, social and economic factors. Moral judgements about people's lifestyles were at the heart of early social work assessment. For example, to 'allow' oneself to become a single parent and slip into poverty was regarded as sinful, immoral and, basically, undeserving. It was the source of much social condemnation and stigma.

Attitudes have changed since those times. Social care in the latter decades of the twentieth century, has consciously adopted a 'non-judgemental' stance towards most lifestyle issues. Nevertheless, the traditional casework assessment continued to focus almost exclusively on an individual's deficits or 'lacks'. The tradition of much assessment in social care work has been 'hunting out the negative'.

Milner and O'Byrne (2002) writing about the influence of clinical psychology on social work with children and families observe:

> ... the identification of deficit of one sort or another became a central thrust of assessments, which set out to study problems in great depth, seeking explanations and remedies. Much of the discussion with service users was/is problem focused and service users came to learn to talk knowledgeably

about problems and identify with them, such as 'I am an alcoholic'. The main engagement was with the problem rather than the person and often the pictures that emerged were unbalanced, failing to bring to life the strengths and coping abilities of people. Guidelines and formats for assessments were also biased towards the negatives and may have strengthened the pathologising tendency further.

> (Milner and O'Byrne, 2002, page 263)

As health and social care has developed and moved on, this 'pathologising tendency' has been acknowledged and conscious attempts have been made to correct the tendency to focus on the individual's weaknesses, faults and failings to the exclusion of all else. However, we have to accept that our cultural heritage in this respect is hard to throw off completely and we can easily slip into an unconscious deficit model.

This next section draws extensively on the research and writing of Smale and Tuson (1993). They distinguished between three broad approaches to assessment – **exchange**, **questioning** and **procedural**. Their book was published by HMSO in 1993.

The questioning model

This model assumes that the worker is 'an expert in people' (page16). The skilled worker working within this approach adopts an orientation towards their 'subject' which is attentive, respectful and aims to be empathetic. The worker forms an assessment on the information provided, using their professional knowledge and expertise. The assessor's role in this model has been likened to that of Sherlock Holmes, meaning that the expertise is all with the 'skilled professional' in forming an accurate assessment and taking the appropriate action.

The questioning model is a traditional approach in that it places the assessor in the expert role and concentrates on the 'dependency needs of the individual' (page 17).

Apart from the assumption of expert knowledge about somebody else's life, there are other problems with this approach. One obvious source of difficulty can be a technical one – with the very questions used:

- questions may be limited to the worker's agenda

- the language in which the questions are couched may not be fully understandable to the people being interviewed
- too much closed questioning can limit the information received
- questions may be inappropriately eurocentric or ethnocentric
- questions can too easily predetermine a way of looking at things. For example, 'What is wrong with you that prevents you going upstairs to the toilet?' creates a bias towards a medical model whereas, 'What change/adaptation to your property is required in order for you to get to the toilet?' implies a social model
- it is not always easy for all those involved to establish which questions are the really important ones and which others less so.

The procedural model

The questioning model assumes a degree of professional expertise and autonomy on behalf of the assessor. That is to say, the questions asked can largely be of the assessor's own choosing. In the procedural model, the assessor is very much seen as an agency functionary. As Smale and Tuson say:

> ... many workers will operate within given agency guidelines and criteria for the allocation of scarce resources and will be expected to gather specific information as a basis for judgements .... In this the goal of the assessment is to gather information to see if the client 'fits', or meets, certain criteria that will 'make them eligible for services'. Those defining the criteria for eligibility, in effect pre-allocating services for generally identified need, make the judgement as to what sort of person should get which resources. The worker's task is to identify the specific people who match the appropriate degree of need defined within the categories of service available and to exclude those not eligible.
>
> (Smale and Tuson, 1993, page 19)

Many assessors working in statutory agencies have observed that the 'care management process' can tend easily towards the procedural model. They would argue that it has 'deskilled' the assessment process with its pre-coded forms, checklists, eligibility criteria and narrow scope. In its defence, if conducted properly, assessment within this model can be:

- more cost-effective
- a more equitable allocation of resources – everything is standardised
- a more efficient use of worker time – it asks the minimum number of questions necessary to determine eligibility
- relatively unobtrusive into people's lives – the obvious bureaucratic nature of the assessment can mean that people feel less threatened by it. There is no 'unnecessary' probing.

Other advocates of the procedural model claim that it is more 'honest' and doesn't raise false hopes. Basically, they ask why 'talk the talk' of a full 'needs-led' assessment if the assessment will, in reality, not only lead to one or two of those needs being seriously considered but also a limited service response. What tends to make the procedural model unsatisfactory for many practitioners is that the emphasis on bureaucratic procedures is at odds with notions of person-centredness, holism, choice, and user participation. It is too agency-centred. People at the point of needing any kind of social care assessment are generally vulnerable for some reason or another, their lives have become disrupted, but they are not given any freedom in the procedural model to express themselves or tell their story. If they try to, it is likely to be regarded as 'irrelevant information'.

What the models described so far also seem to have in common is that they all assume it is possible, by using the correct form of questioning, to get to the 'facts of the situation' and that there is an underlying 'truth' to be uncovered. Milner and O'Byrne (2002) make this observation:

> In line with the medical model, these assessments are usually made before any intervention takes place, are based on past performance and past reports, and perhaps presented as once-and-for-all judgements, lacking an appropriate uncertainty.

> A further worrying aspect of such assessments is the suggestion that people are fixed in their problem identities, with a resultant lack of self-determination, and people are often categorised and denied the individualisation with which earlier social workers credited them. (page 53)

The exchange model

This model assumes that services users are expert in themselves and assumes that the assessor:

- has expertise in the process of problem solving with others
- understands and shares perceptions of problems and their management
- gets agreement about who will do what to support whom
- takes responsibility for arriving at the optimum resolution of problems within the constraints of available resources and the willingness of participants to contribute. (Smale and Tuson, 1993, page 18)

This approach 'typically includes more people and takes longer'. It recognises professional expertise in the assessor but sees an important part of that expertise in 'establishing partnerships' and facilitating participation. The agenda is neither strictly prescribed by the assessor nor an agency's guidelines. Others' views are taken into account and this widening out of participation can help in mobilising all potential resources.

If pursued properly, the exchange model of assessment is more likely to lead to attainment of key goals laid down in official guidance (Department of Health, 1989). They are goals that see people:

- living as normal a life as possible
- achieving maximum possible independence
- having a greater say in how they live their lives and the services they need to help them do so.

The exchange model does have its negative aspects. As mentioned, it is likely to be more time-consuming than the other models discussed so far. It is also argued by critics that the notions of mutual respect and equal status between assessor and client embodied in this model are illusory, a myth cherished by workers who are uncomfortable with the authority invested in them. Critics say that a model that puts so much emphasis on listening to others' views can blur issues of accountability. They argue that vulnerable people and their carers want and expect professionals to take a lead. If people could sort their own problems out then they wouldn't need a professional assessment in the first place. These are the potential difficulties and complexities with the exchange model. Dependency, leadership and power issues are clearly part of that. For this reason, it is important not to take too simplistic a view of this model of assessment, especially around issues of participation and self-determination. Although someone does not clearly articulate their views or express their needs in a conventional way, it does not necessarily mean that they are perfectly satisfied and at no risk to themselves or others.

The constructive model of assessment

Parton and O'Byrne outlined what they called 'constructive' assessment. It links to several of the themes discussed earlier in this chapter, i.e. assessment is essentially seen as an intersubjective exercise. It acknowledges that even the most 'basic' assessment is a potentially complex and ambiguous process. 'Facts' may be slippery; what is said one day may be different the next. The assessor is not some kind of all-knowing expert scientifically completing his or her 'diagnosis' before drawing up his or her 'treatment' plan. Rather, the assessor is helping the patient or service user to tell their story. There is a conversational, 'two-way' feel to the experience. Parton and O'Byrne claim that the quality of assessments would actually improve if those doing the assessing gave up searching for 'false certainty' and instead, gave an honest account of how they were struggling for understanding (page 135). The assessor should try to shed the idea that they are some kind of expert analyst – putting their client in a 'box' – instead they should aim to be experts in drawing people out and gaining their trust. Nothing should be 'closed down'; all parties' perceptions of the problem should be sought in an ongoing process.

It would be a gross misunderstanding of this approach to believe that it virtually leaves the practitioner out of the process and simply lets the client get on with it. Such a misunderstanding – deliberate or otherwise – deskills and deprofessionalises assessment.

The assessor's skills lie more in their ability to develop solutions with the person they are assessing. It is not claiming that the practitioner isn't any kind of expert. It is saying that the worker is not the *only* expert. Clients and their families are often more expert than us in the problem. However, we may be more expert in thinking about solution-development. We use our skills to draw people out, get them to look at the problems in different ways, offer some possibilities and then build solutions with people.

We can see then that the constructive approach to assessment seeks for a 'balance of strengths and deficits'. It also wants to get more closely to the particular meanings people attach to their situations.

You are your dominant story

For any individual's situation in life, there will not only be different strands to their story; there will be different stories. The assessor must not be content with taking the dominant story about someone as the 'narrative truth'. The Department of Health emphasises this very point:

> A weakness of many assessments was that they failed to present an overall, holistic picture of users and their needs.
>
> (Department of Health/Social Services Inspectorate, 2000, page 30)

'You are your dominant story' – those you support must be allowed to tell you theirs whenever possible

In health and social care, an individual's 'narrative' can too easily become reduced to a set of well-established and oft repeated 'facts'. Individual service users inevitably become situated in different discourses; particularly those of their informal networks and those of the professionals. 'Facts' about people inevitably become bandied about and shared by those who are involved around them. Sometimes these 'facts' are written in official files, but often they remain at the level of what people say and think about that person. Often, the individual will come to accept – even 'author' – his or her own dominant narrative. This can be for a range of reasons. It may be for a 'quiet life', or because they genuinely feel that

others know best; it may be even that they have come to believe that that is all there is to their lives. All too often, people become summed up in a few well-polished and often repeated phrases. A typical example might be as follows:

> Mr Paterson, 86, a charming man, mildly confused, fiercely independent, never really got over the death of his wife, likes the occasional drink. Never been one to be overly concerned about personal hygiene. Daughter does all his housework and shopping. Yes, that's Mr Paterson.

We often slip into this mode of thinking about clients and it can make them seem very one-dimensional.

REFLECT

Think about a family member. Write about them in a maximum of ten sentences. How does your writing reflect them as a person, their personality, background, likes, dislikes and so on?

It is salutary to think that for many clients to have a ten-sentence story circulating about them would be an indulgence. For much of the time people are often reduced to the kind of three-sentence characters like Mr Paterson in our 'box'.

Parton and O'Byrne argue that:

> … the dominant story always has important 'lived experiences' missing. A sense of 'persons engaged in action' may be missing and exceptional behaviours that contradict the dominant story are unnoticed if we listen only to the dominant story. Without a belief in exceptions and a search for exceptions, data will be misleading. (page 141)

This approach aims to challenge the dominant story. It is suggested that a broader, rounded, picture of our client will emerge if we:

- come from a position of 'not knowing'
- are able to listen, and
- as part of our discussion, engage them in 'problem-free' talk.

A useful way of taking this approach further is for assessors to use 'scale sheets' to enable people to tell their story in such a way that it picks up on the nuances, contradictions and complexities that might be missed. We discuss the use of scale sheets in more detail in the next section on assessment tools.

Finally, we are advocating an assessment style that actually gives the client their voice and allows them to tell their own story in their own words.

KNOWLEDGE CHECK

1 What model of assessment most resembles that of your own organisation?
2 Write a summary of the assessment models, listing positive aspects and also their limitations.
3 How would an individual being assessed experience each of these models?

Assessment tools

Ask most people to say what a tool is and they are likely to mention implements such as hammers, saws and drills. The common meaning of the term 'tool' is associated with manual or mechanical work.

It is worth acknowledging this because many workers in health and social care don't always regard themselves as 'tool users'. They struggle with the idea of using a tool because it appears to be transplanted from another type of work. However, we have to accept that nowadays the term 'tool' has taken on a broader meaning, and in this context refers to a range of devices designed to improve the assessment process. It should not be regarded as just another example of unnecessary paperwork. Appropriate use of assessment tools can be very helpful for the person being assessed, by getting a more accurate picture of their overall situation. They can be of use in assisting with risk analysis for example.

In guidance issued by the Department of Health in 2002 an assessment tool is defined as:

> ... a collection of scales, questions and other information, to provide a rounded picture of an individual's needs and related circumstances.

The Social Care Institute of Excellence (SCIE) Best Practice Guide (www.elsc.org.uk) explained that:

> Assessment tools are standardised systems that help to provide an equitable and fair approach. They can be the means whereby individual and particular assessments contribute to the overall picture ...

> Tools include scales, checklists and interview schedules. They must be culturally sensitive, reliable and valid if they are to inform professional judgement.

ACTIVITY

Think about your own agency. What 'tools' do you use to help complete assessments? Are there checklists, scales and interview schedules? Do you use other systems?

If possible, compare your findings with someone with another agency. Are there any differences?

It is highly probable that you would have identified that your agency uses a particular form in order to record its assessments. In some people's minds, the assessment begins and ends with the form. This reflects a very narrow and limited approach to the assessment process.

As the SCIE Best Practice Guide states:

> The standardised systems used within social work departments are usually not tools in the accepted sense, that are tested in terms of the quality or effectiveness of the information they provide about an individual's state. They are more often an administrative record, more likely to measure output and workload than outcome for an individual service user.

Scales

Department of Health (2002) guidance on the single assessment process describes an assessment scale as:

> ... a means of identifying, and possibly gauging the extent of, a specific health or care condition such as ability for personal care, mobility, tissue viability, depression, and cognitive impairment.

Scales can have application across all service user groups. Parton and O'Byrne (2000) include several in their book (an example is set out on page 333). They acknowledge that:

> ... many service users say that the scale questions are the most encouraging part of the process; yet, they feel odd and mechanical to workers when they start to use them. (page 105)

If a scale is valid, reliable and culturally sensitive, it can ensure that all parties involved can be more confident about the assessment having a beneficial outcome. It also acknowledges that people's situations are seldom 'black or white' but are often subtle and complex 'shades of grey'. It is important to see the use of scales as something that can enrich the assessment process and not simply the sum total of the assessment. The Department of Health cautions that a literal and narrow interpretation of scales should be avoided. Assessors should see the use of scales that broaden the discussion rather than narrow it.

Policy

The Labour government set out its 'modernisation agenda' for social services in 1998. This applied across all service user groups. Good assessment practices feature in all official guidance.

Single assessment process

Those working with older people need to be aware of the single assessment process. This major initiative was outlined in the National Service Framework for Older People. The Department of Health explains that:

> The single assessment process applies to health and social services ... It recognises that many older people have health and social care needs, and that agencies need to work together so that assessment and subsequent care planning are person-centred, effective and co-ordinated.

The aim is that:

- the scale and depth of assessment is kept in proportion to an older person's needs
- agencies do not duplicate each other's assessments
- professionals contribute to assessments in the most effective way.

Local authorities were encouraged to 'explore and adopt' different assessment tools in producing their own overall single assessment process. However, guidance stresses that 'older people's views, strengths and abilities should be to the fore throughout assessment and that the contribution older people make to their assessment should be made explicit by the tool'.

As mentioned earlier the Department of Health launched *Independence, Choice and Risk: a Guide to Best Practice in Supported Decision Making* in May 2007.

This provides a risk framework for professionals who support adults using social care within any setting, whether community or residential, in the public, independent or voluntary sectors. It is for use by those in health sectors and social care, including all NHS staff working in multi-disciplinary or joint teams.

This best practice guidance aims to:

- outline a common set of principles to encourage people and their organisations to use as the basis for supporting people in making decisions about their own lives and managing any risk in relation to those choices
- support the principle of empowerment through managing choice and risk transparently in order to enable a fair appraisal of the decision process, if required
- provide a common approach to risk as the basis for working practices, and encourage practitioners and organisations to embed this guidance into their policies, their agreements with other agencies, and their own cultures and working practices
- highlight how to balance necessary levels of protection and preserve reasonable levels of choice and control, in order to help people achieve their potential without their safety being compromised.

The aim of this is to provide a common approach to risk for use across health and social care systems, complementing professional codes or clinical practice guidelines.

Fair Access to Care

This was another important initiative originating from *Modernising Social Services* (1998). It changed how assessments are carried out in statutory agencies. Fair Access to Care (FAC) has been implemented since April 2003. The purpose of this change was to ensure that local authorities had:

- consistency in the way people's needs are assessed
- clear objectives, based on the overriding need to promote independence, which should apply to all stages in the process
- a common understanding of risk assessment on which to base decisions about services

- regular reviews to make sure the services continue to meet objectives.

The framework is based on individuals' needs and associated risks to independence, and includes four eligibility bands – **critical**, **substantial**, **moderate** and **low**. When individuals are placed in these bands, the guidance stresses that councils should not only identify immediate needs but also needs that would worsen for the lack of timely help.

The guidance stresses that:

Assessment should be carried out in such a way, and be sufficiently transparent, for individuals to:

- gain a better understanding of their situation

Fair Access to Care and eligibility for services in Newham

In the London Borough of Newham, eligibility for adult social care services (for services of the carer and the person cared for) will be determined according to Fair Access to Care (FAC) eligibility criteria (see table on pages 278–280).

Fair Access to Care and the NHS

The FAC eligibility framework applies to functions/ services which the Council has delegated to the NHS, or pooled with, or provided alongside, NHS services.

So long as it is a social services function which is being performed or service provided for which the council has a statutory responsibility, FAC eligibility criteria apply. This would apply equally when the service/function has been delegated to the independent sector.

Delayed transfers of care – it is permissible to prioritise help to adults waiting in hospital for discharge.

Continuing care – the council will use the FAC criteria to determine eligibility for services for which it has accepted responsibility.

Section 117 Mental Health Act 1983 – councils are still expected to carry out assessments of individuals subject to section 117.

Which adults are eligible for social care services?

The Council has a legal responsibility to consider the social care needs of adults who are:

- over 18 years of age
- normally resident in the borough or a homeless person or a patient in a hospital in the borough for whom no other council has responsibility.

and who need help because they:

- are an older person, or
- have a physical disability, including sensory and visual impairments, or
- have a learning disability, or
- have mental health problems, or
- have a long term illness, or
- have alcohol or drug related problems, or
- are a carer of someone in one of the above groups.

The financial circumstances of an adult seeking social care help are irrelevant in deciding whether to carry out an assessment of need.

Questions

1 How appropriate is it that local authorities ascertain what level of need they are committed to meeting?
2 Why do you think that central government has set up the eligibility criteria in this way?
3 What eligibility framework does *your* organisation have and how suitable do you think this is for those who need the service that you provide?

- identify the options that are available for managing their own lives
- understand the basis on which decisions are reached.

Priorities for help

The Government requires councils to use the FAC eligibility framework to specify which adults are eligible for help. There are four bands of risk:

- critical
- substantial
- moderate
- low.

Councils are expected to prioritise adults with Critical needs ahead of Substantial needs, and so on. A council's eligibility criteria consists of those bands of need it has the resources to meet. Councils are expected to operate the same eligibility criteria across all the adult care groups.

Many councils have decided that they only have the resources to meet the needs of adults with Critical or Substantial needs. Adults with Moderate or Low needs are therefore not eligible for social care services.

Preventing Critical or Substantial needs developing

The FAC eligibility framework seeks to take account of both immediate and longer-term needs. Longer-term has been defined by some councils as needs which are likely to arise in the next six months. If it is likely that an adult with Moderate or Low needs will develop Critical or Substantial needs within six months if social care services are not provided, appropriate services can begin immediately.

This means that if risks are likely to become Critical or Substantial, but there is no effective action that can be taken to prevent this deterioration, services will not be provided until such time as the risks have become Critical or Substantial.

Department of Health (January 2008): Government orders review of social care eligibility rules

The eligibility criteria, which governs all older and disabled people's right to receive care services, is to be fundamentally reviewed.

Care Services Minister, Ivan Lewis, has asked the Commission for Social Care Inspection (CSCI) to undertake the review and report back to him with recommendations in the Autumn.

The review will focus on national definitions of need and their application at a local level by councils.

Ivan Lewis, Care Services Minister, stated:

This year the Government will consult extensively on a new long term funding system for social care, begin a radical programme of change through personal care budgets and announce a new deal for carers.

However, today's State of Social Care report highlights major inconsistencies in the way that eligibility criteria is being applied within and between local authorities; as well as a growing failure to support self-funders to make difficult choices about care for themselves or a family member.

I want to see an end to the 'no help here' culture, which is now creeping into parts of the care system.

There will always be a need for a national social care framework, but the existing system is leaving too many families on their own and runs the risk of damaging our commitment to support older and disabled people to live independently.

Dame Denise Platt, Chair of the Commission for Social Care Inspection, said:

Our State of Social Care report paints a stark picture of a sharp divide between people who do and do not qualify for social care from their local council. We are undertaking this review at the request of the Government as a contribution to the longer-term review of the funding of the care system. Our report will be published later this year and we will involve all interested parties, particularly the people who use care services. Our aim is to make the care they rely on more responsive to their needs.

Department of Health website,
29 January 2008

London Borough of Newham Eligibility Criteria 2007				
Risk	**Critical** risk to the independence of the person	**Substantial** risk to the independence of the person	**Moderate** risk to the independence of the person	**Low** risk to the independence of the person
Threat to life	Life is or will be threatened.			
Health	Significant health problems have or will develop.			
Abuse and Neglect	Serious abuse or neglect has or will occur.	Abuse or neglect has or will occur.		
Autonomy and Freedom to make choices	There is or will be little or no choice and control over vital aspects of the immediate environment.	There is or will be partial choice and control over the immediate environment.		
Personal Care and Domestic Routines	There is or will be an inability to carry out vital personal care or domestic routine.	There is or will be an inability to carry out the majority of personal care or domestic routines.	There is or will be an inability to carry out several personal care or domestic routines.	There is or will be an inability to carry out one or two personal care or domestic routines.
Family and Social Roles	Vital family and other social roles and responsibilities cannot or will not be undertaken.	The majority of family and other social roles and responsibilities cannot or will not be undertaken.	Several family and other social roles and responsibilities cannot or will not be undertaken.	One or two family and other social roles and responsibilities cannot or will not be undertaken.
Social Inclusion	Vital involvement in work, education or learning cannot or will not be sustained.	Involvement in many aspects of work, education or learning cannot or will not be sustained.	Involvement in several aspects of work, education or learning cannot or will not be sustained.	Involvement in one or two aspects of work, education or learning cannot or will not be sustained.
Social Support and Interaction	Vital social support systems and relationships cannot or will not be sustained.	The majority of social support systems and relationships cannot or will not be sustained.	Several social support systems and relationships cannot or will not be sustained.	One or two social support systems and relationships cannot or will not be sustained.

Your social care needs will be assessed as CRITICAL when

- There is or will be an immediate life threatening risk to you.
- You have or will develop significant health problems, putting you or others at immediate serious risk.
- You have or will experience serious abuse or neglect.
- You have or will have little or no choice and control over vital aspects of your immediate environment, putting you or others at immediate serious risk.
- You cannot or will not be able to carry out vital personal care or domestic routines, putting you or others at immediate serious risk.
- You cannot or will not be able to undertake vital family and other social roles and responsibilities without support.
- Your involvement in vital aspects of work, learning or education cannot or will not be sustained without support.

We will use the following indicators to assess whether your needs fall in the CRITICAL band

- Those needing support to avoid life threatening risks to their or others' life or safety.
- Those unable to carry out vital personal care or domestic routines, placing themselves or others' health and safety at immediate life threatening risk.
- Those whose care arrangements are breaking down, placing them or others' health and safety at immediate life threatening risk.
- Those requiring immediate permanent accommodation in residential or nursing homes.
- Those requiring immediate admission to residential or nursing care if services were not provided.
- Those requiring 24 hour live-in care.
- Those requiring overnight care.
- Those requiring temporary placements.

Your social care needs will be assessed as CRITICAL when

- You cannot or will not be able to sustain vital social support systems and key relationships without support.

Eligible for social care services.

Make an immediate response if this is necessary to stabilise the situation. In all cases, respond and start an assessment within 24 hours.

We will use the following indicators to assess whether your needs fall in the CRITICAL band

- Those requiring emergency or regular respite care.
- Those who have suffered or are at risk of serious abuse or neglect and need immediate support.
- Those experiencing or who will experience sudden sight or hearing loss and need immediate support.
- Those needing equipment or adaptations to avoid placing their or others' health or safety at immediate serious risk.
- Those with health problems with a poor prognosis or are likely to rapidly deteriorate within six months.
- Those experiencing a mental health crisis requiring immediate hospital admission or residential care or a community alternative.
- Those with severe and enduring mental health needs and who are eligible for the Enhanced Level Care Programme Approach.
- Those with a life-threatening substance misuse problem.
- Those who cannot participate in vital family, education, work or community life without support which is not otherwise available.

Your social care needs will be assessed as SUBSTANTIAL when

You have or will develop health problems, putting you or others at significant risk.

You have or will experience abuse or neglect putting you or others at significant risk.

You have or will have partial choice and control over your immediate environment, putting you or others at significant risk.

You cannot or will not be able to carry out the majority of personal care or domestic routines, putting you or others at significant risk.

You cannot or will not be able to undertake the majority of family and other social roles and responsibilities without support.

Your involvement in many aspects of work, learning or education cannot or will not be sustained without support.

You cannot or will not be able to sustain the majority of your social support systems and key relationships without support.

We will use the following indicators to assess whether your needs fall in the SUBSTANTIAL band

Those needing urgent but not immediate support to avoid significant risks to their or others' life or safety.

Those unable to carry out the majority of personal care or domestic routines, placing them or others' health and safety at significant risk.

Those whose care arrangements are breaking down, placing them or others' health and safety at significant risk.

Those requiring occasional respite care.

Those who have suffered or are at risk of abuse or neglect.

Those needing equipment or adaptations (or have them but they need attention) to reduce the significant risks arising from essential daily living tasks.

Those who have a neurological condition which will inevitably deteriorate and will need equipment or adaptations.

Those experiencing a mental health crisis or have severe and enduring mental health needs and who are eligible for the Standard Level Care Programme Approach.

Those with a history of substantial and dependant substance misuse who are motivated towards abstinence.

Your social care needs will be assessed as SUBSTANTIAL when

We will use the following indicators to assess whether your needs fall in the SUBSTANTIAL band

Those who cannot participate in many aspects of family, education, work or community life without support which is not otherwise available.

Eligible for social care services.
Take immediate action to help or assist if the service user is likely to become worse quickly without intervention. In all cases, respond within two working days, followed by an assessment.

Your social care needs will be assessed as MODERATE when

We will use the following indicators to assess whether your needs fall in the MODERATE band

You have or will develop health problems which indicate some risks to you and/or intermittent distress.

Those unable to carry out several personal care or domestic routines placing them at some risk.

You cannot or will not be able to carry out several personal care or domestic routines which indicate some risks to you.

Those whose carers have difficulty undertaking several aspects of their caring role placing them or others at some risk.

You cannot or will not be able to undertake several family and other social roles and responsibilities without support.

Those who cannot participate in several aspects of family, education, work or community life without support which is not otherwise available.

Your involvement in several aspects of work, learning or education cannot or will not be sustained without support.

Those with mental health support needs who are not eligible for the Standard Level Care Programme Approach.

You cannot or will not be able to sustain several of your social support systems and key relationships without support.

Ineligible for social care services
Provide information on alternative services, if any. Advise to make contact again if needs change.

Your social care needs will be assessed as LOW when

We will use the following indicators to assess whether your needs fall in the LOW band

You have or will develop health problems which indicate low risks to you.

Those unable to carry out one or two personal care or domestic routines placing them at low risk.

You cannot or will not be able to carry out one or two personal care or domestic routines which indicate low risks you.

Those whose carers have difficulty undertaking one or two aspects of their caring role placing them or others at low risk.

You cannot or will not be able to undertake one or two family and other social roles and responsibilities without support.

Those who cannot participate in one or two aspects of family, education, work or community life without support which is not otherwise available.

Your involvement in one or two aspects of work, learning or education cannot or will not be sustained without support.

You cannot or will not be able to sustain one or two of your social support systems and key relationships without support.

Ineligible for social care services.
Provide information on alternative services, if any. Advise to make contact again if needs change.

Adults ineligible for social care services

Adults assessed as ineligible for social care services after an assessment or a review can ask for the decision to be reviewed. They can also ask for an assessment if their needs change.

Councils usually provide information and advice on alternative services.

Asylum seekers

A council may provide community care services for adult asylum seekers who have assessed care needs, whether or not these care needs fall within the council's eligibility criteria if the person is considered to be destitute. These needs can be met under section 21 of the National Assistance Act 1948, as confirmed by the Law Lords judgement in the case of Westminster City Council v NASS in 2002.

Postcode lottery

The issues of the NHS postcode lottery have been discussed for a number of years as local Primary Care Trusts make very local decisions regarding the provision of particular prescription medication, and NHS Trusts decide what medical and surgical treatments are within their hospital's remit. There has recently been growing public awareness of the use of the eligibility criteria in determining local access to social care services and the government had to make a response in January 2008.

The 'modernising agenda' launched by the government in 1998 is based around certain key principles: person-centredness, fair access, national consistency and promoting independence being some of the most important. Workers in statutory organisations will have had the national guidelines interpreted for them and placed into operational guidelines by their employing organisations. Forms may have changed and practices may have been revised. Hopefully, training will have been given to ensure that practitioners understand the principles underlying changes in policy and practice. In any event, workers should always try to understand the policy context in which changes take place; this is important, not least because it helps when explaining the process to people being assessed. Lastly, it is worth restating an important point. This is that whatever the policy context, whatever new framework for

assessment is introduced, whatever assessment tools and scales are incorporated in the assessment process, the key part of the process is two (or more) human beings coming together attempting to communicate with each other and to gain a common understanding of what the issues are.

KNOWLEDGE CHECK

1 Give a brief summary of the deficit model.
2 Write a few notes which outline the main points of the questioning and procedural exchange models. Write down advantages and disadvantages of each.
3 Why is it important not simply to accept the 'dominant story' about somebody?
4 Identify three key aspects of the 'constructive approach' to assessment.
5 How do both the Department of Health and SCIE define an assessment tool?
6 What, according to the Department of Health, is an assessment scale?
7 What is the rationale behind the single assessment process?
8 What is the official purpose behind Fair Access to Care?

Assessment, empowerment and anti-discriminatory practice

As we have seen, the 'values climate' in which care takes place today emphasises several important principles. These would include person-centredness, respect, user-involvement, and promoting independence. In more recent years much has been spoken of the 'empowerment' of the service user. At the same time, the principle of anti-discriminatory practice has both been promoted by successive governments and embraced by organisations and agencies within the social work and care fields. It is tempting to assume that, because these principles are much talked and written about in social care, it can be taken for granted that they now occur 'naturally' and that we can take such practices for granted.

Empowerment

Empowerment has become a fashionable 'buzz word' in many areas of life over the last decade or so. It has certainly become a term that is frequently used in the field of health and social care.

REFLECT

1 What is your understanding of the term empowerment?
2 Give examples of what you consider to be empowering practice.
3 If possible, compare your ideas with another person.

Empowerment is very much a 'contested' term. That is to say, what it means exactly is the subject of debate and disagreement. As such, it has to be acknowledged that there is no single agreement on what exactly is empowering practice. Some writers regard the word 'empower' to be a much over-used term, arguing that it is often used when we actually mean to 'help' or 'enable' someone to do something. Others would even argue that it is wrong to think that social care practitioners can actually 'empower' anyone in any meaningful sense. Sometimes we use the term 'empower' when all we are doing is providing a limited choice of options to someone to enable them to make up their own mind.

Despite these reservations, the goal of empowerment is considered to be a stated objective for many care organisations and therefore we need to reflect on how assessment practices may or may not impact on this goal.

In *Empowerment in Community Care*, Ray Jack (1995) argues that power cannot simply be given by social workers to powerless members of the community – it is they who have to take it. This is a theme taken up by Milner and O'Byrne (1998) who state that:

> Social workers are not in a position to give people power, and their aim to help reduce the powerlessness that individuals and groups experience is likely to be limited by other individuals' and groups' investment in power

positions and in the complex nature of power.
(page 62)

Taking a slightly more optimistic view, Thompson (1997) states that empowerment:

> ... involves seeking to maximise the power of clients and give them as much control as possible over their circumstances. It is the opposite of creating dependency and subjecting clients to agency power. (page 83)

It is clear that the issues of empowerment and disempowerment are complex and go far beyond the field of social care. There are wider structural issues such as poverty, age, gender, race and so on that need to be taken into consideration when understanding how power operates in society. Milner and O'Byrne (1998) claim, 'it is naïve to underestimate the difficulties in operationalising empowering strategies'. Nevertheless, however simplistic and naïve it may be to believe that a worker in a care setting can easily 'empower' someone through their practice, this doesn't mean that we should completely ignore the issue of power imbalance in our relationships with those we assess.

Whilst it might be difficult to genuinely 'empower' someone through our practice in the broader sense of the term, that is not to say we should not be aware of the likelihood that bad practices can actually further disempower already vulnerable people.

Avoidance of disempowering practices is as important as the adoption of empowering practices. In his description of the 'disabling relationship', Jack (1995) cautions that in this form of professional relationship:

> Professionals use their power to protect their own interests by exaggerating the value of their skills and knowledge and restricting access to them. Their power is founded on expertise in assessing and defining problems – offering solutions which require the skills only they possess. (page 14)

Talking about those on the 'receiving end' of assessment, Jack claims that:

> ... it is simply right and proper that their views be given an airing and then taken seriously. No romantic view that clients and patients 'know best' is offered, but we do share the belief that the insights of the least powerful actors in social behaviour are as important as those of the most

powerful. And if left unchecked, the voices of managers and professionals soon drown those of their clients. (page 52)

Significantly, Jack argues that 'participation is a better term than empowerment or partnership'. Maybe aiming for participation is more realistic and therefore achievable than striving for the more grand and lofty goal of 'empowerment'.

Like a supermarket marketing all its products as 'new', 'improved', or 'farm fresh', indiscriminate use of the term 'empowerment' can easily mean the whole idea becomes 'debased currency' and loses all meaning. This can provoke cynicism in practitioner and client alike, and in doing so obscure the very real issue that assessors, as we have argued earlier, do have more power. They have the power to set the agenda, to define, to limit choice, to restrict access to resources and so on. This power can easily be abused without realising it.

ACTIVITY

Critically reflect on one or two of your recent assessments.

1 What factors, if any, made the person you were assessing relatively powerless?
2 Identify the points of the process where you used power.
3 What opportunities were given for the people involved in the assessment to do things another way, in a way of their choosing?
4 To what extent do you think they had 'control' over the situation?
5 How did you handle the imbalance in power between you, if there was one?
6 Would you agree that it is more realistic to aim for participation rather empowerment? If so, where do you see the difference?

Mental Capacity Act 2005

This Act came into effect in October 2007. It provides a legal framework for people who lack the mental capacity to make decisions about matters that affect them, including decisions about the provision of health and social care services during an assessment.

The ladder of participation

Jack (1995) adapts Arnstein's concept of a 'ladder of participation' to represent the different levels of participation and involvement that a client can have in the assessor/client relationship.

- Rung 8   Citizen control
- Rung 7   Delegated power
- Rung 6   Partnership
- Rung 5   Consultation
- Rung 4   Involvement
- Rung 3   Keeping fully informed
- Rung 2   Placation
- Rung 1   Manipulation
            (From Arnstein, 1969, in Jack, 1995)

Arnstein's 'ladder' was originally about local community politics. However, it provides a useful way of representing the differing degrees of power exercised by people in matters that concern them. We can adapt this idea to reflect the various types of power relationship that a social care worker can have with those they assess.

The following is an example.

Rung 1 – Manipulation This is where the assessor ensures that their agenda is followed and their interpretation of the situation is the one recorded. However, the client is nevertheless invited to sign the necessary paperwork and give their consent as if they had a say in the process.

Rung 2 – Placation This is essentially the same process as outlined above but the client is given the time to 'read through' their assessment and told they are free to raise any queries or make any amendments they want to. It is then signed.

Rung 3 – Keeping fully informed The client is given a full written and verbal explanation of what the assessment and care planning process consists of, including the right to state their preferences and to complain if not happy at any stage.

Rung 4 – Involvement At each stage of the process the client is given information about what is involved, their rights, and what the various options are on what can be done. Their views (and the views of those around them) are actively encouraged and recorded using their own words.

Rung 5 – What comes next? Can the 'client' ever be fully in control of the process? At this level the limits to and tensions around 'empowerment' become more evident. To some extent, how much more control a person has over the process at this stage depends on the purpose and the context of the assessment. Some agencies promote varying degrees of self-assessment. However, the question remains whether this still has to conform to a format and set of criteria laid down by the assessing organisation.

We have argued throughout that the assessment relationship is both a complex and dynamic one. We have also argued that for a variety of reasons, the assessor is always the more powerful person in the assessment process. The question remains, can assessment 'empower'? The answer must, to a great extent, be that it depends on what we mean by 'empower'. It could be argued that an assessment that enables a vulnerable person to live at home with a high degree of independence was an example of empowerment. However, this would omit the important issue of how that assessment was carried out. If decisions were made for and about that person with little or no participation by them along the way, then, in a sense, this only confirms and reinforces their powerlessness. Someone else has 'sorted them out' – however favourably.

Assessors should always be aware of power issues and, wherever possible, ensure that their practices do not disable those they assess. This requires a certain amount of openness and honesty with oneself. A starting point in the 'empowering' assessment is that the client should have as much control over the process as possible. There should be full sharing of information and a commitment to involvement and participation. Without these the person would almost certainly be disempowered; whether with them they are positively empowered, is a matter for debate.

Anti-discriminatory practice

Anti-discriminatory practice has ... been featuring as a regular and high priority item on the social work agenda for some time now, although there sadly continues to be a great deal of misunderstanding and oversimplification of the issues.

> (Thompson, 2001, pages 1–2)

This statement by Neil Thompson sounds a necessary note of caution to begin with. It would be impossible to do full justice to this key area in such a limited space. However, at the same time it would be wrong to conclude a chapter on assessment and not make some attempt to 'flag up' some key issues in this area, if only to give pointers for further development. Whereas the discussion around empowerment is sometimes ambiguous on such matters, there is no doubt that anti-discriminatory practice acknowledges political, cultural, social, and economic dimensions.

Anti-discriminatory practice (ADP) is an approach to social work which emphasises the various ways in which particular individuals and groups tend to be discriminated against and the need for professional practice to counter such discrimination.

The basis of discrimination

Discrimination can occur on the basis of differences arising from:

- ethnicity (racism)
- gender (sexism)
- class (classism)
- age (ageism)
- disability (disablism)
- sexual identity (heterosexism)
- mental health (mentalism)
- language (linguistic oppression)

and various other less formally codified or documented forms of unfair or oppressive differentiation.

All such forms of discrimination can be seen to occur at a personal, cultural or structural level as discussed in Chapter 3.

As the box above indicates, anti-discriminatory practice aims to combat the various 'isms'. Milner and O'Byrne (1998) observe that:

> The very real difficulties in operating anti-oppressive practice are most clearly seen when we examine the inter-relatedness and complexities of the various 'isms'. (page 63)

Problems with ADP

There are many potential difficulties and complexities for workers getting to grips with ADP. This is partly because it involves looking at oneself critically on a personal, professional and political level. One must be prepared to both reflect on and challenge what might often be long-held views and feelings – part of what makes us 'us'! ADP training is probably most effectively carried out by experienced trainers, with other work colleagues and in a safe environment. Quite often, the mere mention of ADP can induce feelings of defensiveness, cynicism or hostility in workers. This is because people feel they are being lectured, 'got at', blamed or made to feel guilty. All of this is counterproductive and the result can often be what Thompson (2001) calls 'colluding with the rhetoric':

> What this means is that some people may use the right language and may make the right gestures but without any underlying commitment to the values and principles of anti-discriminatory practice. They are just 'going through the motions', perhaps through confusion, ignorance, or insecurity about how to practise in a genuinely anti-discriminatory way.
>
> (Thompson, 2001, page 168)

The way forward

Our aim in this section is both modest and realistic. ADP cannot be covered in a few paragraphs. However, we can say that practitioners involved in assessment should, at the very least, aim to:

- **be open-minded** – the purpose of ADP is to make others' lives easier not yours harder
- **think seriously** whether those they are assessing fall into a group that faces discrimination. There can be more than one form of discrimination obviously, and those different forms of discrimination can overlay and interact with each other
- **take responsibility** for raising your own awareness of ADP matters. Use opportunities to go on proper ADP training, attend workshops, keep up with current debates on the subject
- **avoid stereotyping.** Stereotyping is the process by which people lose their individuality. Someone who has been stereotyped will have a range of feelings, behaviours, impulses and other

characteristics attributed to them because they happen to belong to a particular group. Stereotypes are simplifications and distortions. Stereotyped thinking leads to pre-judgements and assumptions being made about someone on the basis of a label or category rather than what they are really like as an individual.

Stereotyping can lead to harmful and inaccurate assumptions

Practitioners can stereotype on the basis of medical categories, whether age is a factor or not. Descriptions such as 'dementia sufferer', 'wheelchair user', 'Parkinson's sufferer' can often lead to inaccurate but powerful assumptions about an individual's abilities. The stereotype of the 'dementia sufferer' is someone who is confused, wanders and cannot safely be left on his or her own. If a practitioner takes this mindset into an assessment then this almost predetermines the outcomes. Misconceptions often persist even once the person has been met and the assessment underway – such is the power of the label!

Ahmed (1990) argues that black people are especially prone to stereotyping. They tend to be more readily 'pathologised' and constructed as having 'special' rather than individual needs. According to Ahmed:

> Consequently ... Black clients' 'special needs' can only be effectively catered for by 'special' provision, which was outside the general or mainstream social work policy and practice. (page 7)

Any discrimination black people experience in wider society is compounded because workers become preoccupied with the 'difference' and 'otherness' of the black person. Imagine the difficulties with stereotyping that a black person with dementia might experience!

Watch your language

We return to this key theme. Thompson (2001) writes that:

> ... it is not simply a matter of distinguishing between 'taboo' words and 'OK' words, as in the sense of political correctness. What is needed is not a simple list of proscribed words but, rather, an awareness of, and sensitivity to, the oppressive and discriminatory potential of language. (page 31)

In recent years, we have become sensitive to the depersonalising and dehumanising effect of words such as 'handicapped', 'crippled', or 'the elderly'. Nevertheless, to take up Thompson's point, if we write in an assessment that a young woman with severe mobility problems 'needs to be toileted after each meal', then the language used not only shows a lack of respect but constructs that woman less as a human being and more as an object of care or, at best, someone in an infantile state. Language actively constructs and changes reality.

We have emphasised the need for assessors to embrace ADP although we acknowledge that we have done no more than 'skimmed the surface' of the changing and contested field of ADP in this section.

Although it may not always feel like it, as an assessor one is a powerful person in the life of another. If your client is experiencing any form of discrimination then your intervention can add to it, maintain it, or help to reduce it in some way. There is really no choice on what basis to proceed.

KNOWLEDGE CHECK

1 What does it mean to say that empowerment is a 'contested' concept?
2 What is Thompson's definition of empowerment?
3 How does Jack describe the 'disempowering' relationship?
4 Explain how stereotyping people can lead to discriminatory practice.
5 Give examples of how the language we use can depersonalise or dehumanise the people we work with.

Elements of a competent assessment

This chapter has covered many different aspects of assessment and highlighted several factors for practitioners to consider when they assess. There is no such thing as the perfect assessment. Nevertheless, if we try to put it all together, what should the competent assessor be aiming for? In reading the list below, you will see that inevitably many of the elements overlap and combine with each other.

Elements of assessment

Person-centred Practically all official guidance makes this a priority. Start from where the person is. Make them the prime focus of your assessment. Be guided by that person's particular situation; don't be governed by a set format.

Ensure participation A competent assessment should always aim to seek the active participation of those involved.

Establish trust You will establish trust by being clear, open and genuine.

Valid An assessment should be 'true to life' and present a genuine and authentic account of that individual's situation.

Reliable No two practitioners work in exactly the same way. However, a reliable assessment would be one where different assessors would produce a broadly similar set of findings whichever style or format they used. The assessor should therefore not be too idiosyncratic in the way they work.

Culturally sensitive The assessor should acknowledge and respect cultural difference and not impose their own cultural values. Be aware of cultural stereotyping.

Clarify the purpose and scope Don't assume that the various parties involved in an assessment understand what the point, purpose and scope of it is. The word 'assessment' can have different meanings to different people, so can 'professional' names in health and social care. Ensure that you clarify what the other parties' understanding of what your role is, what is expected of them, what the assessment is about and, just as pertinently, what it is not about.

Assessment is not a one-off, static event Situations are dynamic, fluid and changing all the time. An assessment should reflect this. Your assessment will change the situation whatever else happens. The very fact of assessing somebody will change the situation. How you are, what questions you ask and how you ask them will produce change in itself.

Be sensitive to the language you use This is important at each stage of the process. How does the language used construct that person, that situation, tell that person's story? Would the person recognise himself or herself? Would they use the same words? Are you using jargon or somehow medicalising the problem?

Complexities, contradictions and tensions are acknowledged They are going to be there – don't gloss over them. This would particularly apply to issues around 'need' and 'risk'; these are easy to take for granted when, in reality, they are difficult concepts.

Don't assume that any one person has to be the expert It would be a rare occasion if the assessor had all the answers and unlikely that the person themselves knew everything they needed know.

Aim to be inclusive Seek the views of others – especially carers. However, no single view should predominate to the exclusion and detriment of others.

Think holistically An individual needs to be assessed 'as a whole'. People are more than the sum of their parts. Avoid a narrow, medical, pathologising or medical model.

Distinguish between needs, wants and preferences This is easy to say but a lot harder to do in reality – at least be aware of the differences though.

Comply with policies and guidance Be consistent with agency function and ensure your assessment conforms to any national and local guidelines and any relevant legislation. If you are tempted to play the 'maverick' and do your own thing, it could well be your client who pays the price either by having unfairly raised expectations, services withdrawn or having the inconvenience of a reassessment by somebody else.

Draw on best practice by using properly tried and tested assessment scales and tools. This is particularly useful in respect of risk assessment. A good assessment tool can help with risk analysis. However, we must recognise that not everybody shares the same perception of risk. We must also remember that a form – whatever headings or boxes it may contain – is not an assessment. A care assessment is a dynamic human process, drawing on interpersonal skills, judgement and interpretation.

Avoid repetition, duplication and ritualistic behaviour Research consistently shows that this is high on people's lists of hates. Amongst other things, this means spending time doing some research before the assessment.

Free yourself from unnecessary baggage, preconceptions and presumptions

Acknowledge power dynamics This is most important. An assessment can be manipulated the assessor's way – even without them realising it.

Anti-discriminatory practice This is of paramount importance. Be aware of how discrimination can be present in many forms and extend beyond the main areas of race and gender to include many other areas – age, disability, sexual orientation and so on.

1   What aspects of assessment can be improved by your organisation and how are you going to take responsibility for this?
2   What happens when needs are identified that aren't considered the responsibility of your agency?
3   What happens if there is a dispute about whether someone has a need or not?
4   List 4 factors that can contribute towards a positive assessment experience for a service user.

References

Ahmed, B. (1990) *Black Perspectives in Social Work*, Birmingham, Venture Press

Alaszewski, A. *et al* (eds) (1998) *Risk Health and Welfare Policies, Strategies and Practice*, Buckingham, Open University Press

Alaszewski, A. (2002) 'Risk and dangerous' in Bytheway (eds) *Understanding Care, Welfare and Community*, London, Routledge

Department of Health (1989) *Caring for People: Community Care in the Next Decade and Beyond*, London, HMSO

Department of Health (1991a) *Care Management and Assessment: Manager's Guide*, London, HMSO

Department of Health/SSI (1991b) *Getting the Message Across*, London, HMSO

Department of Health (1998) *Modernising Social Services*, London, HMSO

Department of Health (1999) *Working Together to Safeguard Children*, London, HMSO

Department of Health/SSI (2000) *New Directions for Independent Living*, London, HMSO

Department of Health (2000) *The Framework for the Assessment of Children in Need and their Families*, London, HMSO

Department of Health (2007) *Independence, choice and risk: a guide to best practice in supported decision making*, London, HMSO

Jack, R. (ed.) (1995) *Empowerment in Community Care*, London, Chapman and Hall

Kemshall, H. (2002) *Risk, Social Policy and Practice*, Buckingham, Open University Press

Lindow, V. and Morris, J. (1995) *Service User Involvement*, York, JRF

Lupton D. (1999) *Risk*, New York, Routledge

Middleton, L. (1997) *The Art of Assessment*, Birmingham, Venture Press

Milner, J. and O'Byrne, P. (1998) *Assessment in Social Work*, Basingstoke, Macmillan

Milner, J. and O'Byrne, P. (2002) *Assessment in Social Work Practice*, Basingstoke, Macmillan

Parton, N. and O'Byrne, P. (2000) *Constructive Social Work Towards a New Practice*, Basingstoke, Macmillan

Postle, K. (2002) 'Between the idea and the reality: ambiguities and tensions in care managers', in *British Journal of Social Work*, 32 (3), Oxford, Oxford University Press

Skellington, R. (1996) *Race in Britain Today*, London, Sage

Smale, G. and Tuson G. (1993) *Empowerment, Assessment, Care Management and the Skilled Worker*, London, HMSO

Thompson, N. (1997) in Davies, M. (ed.) (2000), *Blackwell Encyclopaedia of Social Work (2000)*, Oxford, Blackwell

Thompson, N. (2001) *Anti-Discriminatory Practice*, Basingstoke, Macmillan

Walzer, M. (1983) in Stone, D. (ed.) (1997) *Policy Paradox: The Art of Political Decision Making*, London, Norton

Worth, A. (2002) 'Health and social care assessment in action' in Bytheway, B. *et al* (eds.) (2002) *Understanding Care, Welfare and Community*, London, Routledge

CHAPTER 8

Planning and reviewing services

Introduction

This chapter takes an in-depth look at **planning** the delivery of health and social care, focusing on community-based delivery of services. We start with a discussion on definitions and meanings. From there, we look at what legislation and official guidance has to say about the purpose and practices of **person-centred** care planning. We look at models of care planning and the framework for delivery of more personalised care through current initiatives. The chapter then explores how practitioners can create choice in their care planning. One theme of this book has been the need for practitioners to ensure that care practice is person-centred and culturally sensitive. In the latter sections of the chapter, we turn the focus on two very important but sometimes undervalued elements of care planning: **monitoring** and review. We explain why these activities are important, offering suggestions for good practice.

This chapter addresses the following areas:
- Definitions and meanings
- Policies on care planning
- Features of effective care planning
- Models of care planning
- Strategies for care planning
- Care planning, care outcomes and care objectives
- Care planning as a holistic and culturally sensitive activity
- Monitoring care plans
- Reviewing care plans

After reading this chapter it is hoped you will be able to:

- explain what care planning means
- identify key features of effective care planning
- know about models of care planning
- understand government initiatives on care planning
- understand the process and purpose of monitoring and reviewing care plans.

Definitions and meanings

As was evident when we looked at assessment in Chapter 7, it is useful to consider the various possible meanings and interpretations that people can attach to a particular term. It means we can anticipate and, hopefully, deal with any possible misunderstandings, ambiguities and uncertainties that may occur. Although professionals might have a clear idea of what they are talking about (and this cannot be taken for granted!), it does not mean that those they work with will share that understanding.

Integrated Care Network

The Integrated Care Network aims to promote policy and practice in the delivery of personalised health and social care with more effective partnership working and integration of relevant service providers.

Self-directed support

Self-directed support is the name given to a way of redesigning the social care system so that the people who get services can take much greater control over them.

> The underlying principle for the development of self-directed support is the desire to move to a system where adults have the ability to take greater control of their lives and the social care that they receive, enabling them to make the decisions and manage their own risks.

Self-directed support puts people at the centre of assessing their own needs, deciding how best those needs can be met, and tailoring care to meet these individual needs.

Self-directed support is intended to develop a culture and the tools to enable individual clients and their carers to be involved in their assessments and to allow them to make the decisions as to how support of this is provided, within available resources. The professional should be the facilitator supporting the client/carer to achieve this principle.

This approach, along with Individual Budgets and the use of the Direct Payments system has promoted service user control over the services that affect their lives. In addition to this, the government has been developing Integrated Care Pathways that aim to maximise partnership working capacity for the benefit of individuals who need health and social care support.

REFLECT

What comes to mind when you see or hear the phrase *care plan* or *care planning*?

The term 'care plan' crops up in different contexts and has different meanings in each. Hospitals have care plans for their patients. In many of these contexts, the customer signs up to a scheme or a service which has been formulated, worded and arranged by the company. The terms and conditions naturally vary, depending on the situation. Often the customer's input is minimal – it is something they are given.

There is a new emphasis on personalisation in all aspects of public service provision. It is clear that in the situations we have outlined, meanings differ and, as a result, it is unreasonable to expect someone who is a stranger to the care system to know exactly what care planning and a care plan are. In the absence of any detailed explanation, people are likely to construct what for them is a plausible explanation. In many spheres of life, plans are seen as courses of action or documents drawn up by 'experts'. Often people take this assumption into social care situations as well.

In health and social care, it is worth noting that people interested in services hardly ever request a care plan. They might ask for a particular service, 'some help' or even an assessment but seldom will somebody specifically ask for a 'care plan'. Most people's tacit expectations are that once a need has been identified or a problem highlighted, the route to meeting that need or solving that problem will be left in the hands of you, the 'professional'. Expectations about being involved in the planning of care are often very low or even non-existent. Traditionally, social care workers also have left such assumptions unchallenged.

Clearly, these are generalisations but it is always a good idea never to take for granted knowledge of what care planning is. It is also worth reflecting on the forms of language we use and the different shades of meaning that can emerge often without us realising it. *What* a care plan is, *what* it is for, *what* it should include, *who* should be involved and even *what* a care plan should look like are all areas where interpretations can diverge. As we observed with Chapter 7 on assessment, it would be easy to assume that everybody automatically has the same understanding of what is going on, what processes are being followed – basically what should be happening. To help put this discussion into a context, we shall see how official guidelines explain what care planning means.

Policies on care planning

In Control project

Policy documents and initiatives concerning the delivery of social care emerging over recent years have supported the idea that people will get better outcomes from the social care support they need in their life, if it is more personalised. In 2003, six local authorities, through the In Control project, took on the challenge of redesigning the way the social care system worked, to give all people who used it the optimum amount of control over their support.

Influenced by the learning from the In Control project, *Improving the Life Chances of Disabled People* (Cabinet Office, 2005) introduced the concept of an 'individual budget', closely followed by *Opportunity Age* (DWP 2005) and *Independence, Well-being and Choice* (DH 2005). The Prime Minister then requested that the Department of Health lead the development of an Individual Budget Pilot Programme, working alongside the Department of Work and Pensions and former Office of the Deputy Prime Minister (now the Department of Communities and Local Government – DCLG).

Our health, our care, our say: a new direction in community services (DH 2006) set out the government's intentions to change how community services are planned and delivered. In order to ensure that these commitments are delivered, the document identified a number of mechanisms that needed to be put in place. A key element was individual budgets –

a means by which people could exercise control over the way social care resources were used and including some income streams that did not come under the Local Authority's control (e.g. Independent Living Fund (ILF)).

In Control is a multi-agency programme, supported by a range of partners, including Mencap and DH/Care Services Improvement Partnership; it works with local authorities to develop individualised budgets.

The following two extracts adapted from Mandelstam (1999) set out the legal basis of care plans within the sphere of community care.

Provision of services: care plans
Care plans are not demanded by legislation, but are referred to in both policy guidance (*Community Care in the Next Decade and Beyond*, Department of Health, 1990) and practice guidance (*Care Management and Assessment: Practitioners' Guide*, Department of Health, 1991). Failure, in respect of care plans and their content, to follow the former type of guidance without good reason, and to have regard to the latter, is unlawful. (page 63)

Care plans: scrutiny by the law courts
When scrutinising closely the actions and decisions of local authorities, the courts have been prepared to examine how closely authorities follow the guidance about care plans – and to declare that substantial divergence from it without good reasons is unlawful ... The court in the Rixon case also pointed out that 'a care plan is the means by which the local authority assembles the relevant information and applies it to the statutory ends, and hence affords good evidence to any inquirer of the due discharge of its statutory duties.

In practice, reports have continued to suggest that service users do not receive care plans as envisaged by guidance, with actions not carried forward (Joseph Rowntree Foundation, 2006, page 6).

While there is no specified duty in law for local authorities to produce care plans, there is an official expectation that such plans will be not only be drawn up but also shared with those for whom the care is intended. The requirement for care plans is also emphasised in official guidance resulting from Care Standards legislation such as the regulations for National Minimum Standards in Residential Care and

Domiciliary Care. In the *Care Management and Assessment* guidance issued to practitioners by the Department of Health in 1991, it is stated:

> A copy of the assessment of needs should normally be shared with the potential user, any representative of that user and all the people who have agreed to provide a service. Except where no intervention is deemed necessary, this record will normally be combined with a written care plan setting out how the needs are to be addressed. Where other agencies are involved, they should also have a copy of these plans.
>
> (Department of Health, 1991, page 56)

Recording the care plan

Care plans should be set out in concise written form, linked with the assessment of need. The document should be accessible to the user, for example, in Braille or translated into the user's own language. A copy should be given to the user but it should also, subject to constraints of confidentiality, be shared with other contributors to the plan. The compilation and distribution of such records has implications for the necessary levels of administrative support.

A care plan should contain:

- the overall objectives
- the specific objectives of
  - users
  - carers
  - service providers
- the criteria for measuring the achievement of these objectives
- the services to be provided by which personnel/agency
- the cost to the user and the contributing agencies
- the other options considered
- any point of difference between the user, carer, care planning practitioner or other agency
- any unmet needs with reasons – to be separately notified to the service planning system
- the named person(s) responsible for implementing, monitoring and reviewing the care plan
- the date of the first planned review.

(Department of Health, 1991, page 67)

CASE STUDY

Care plan for Mr Rees

Below is a typical care plan for an older man prior to discharge from hospital.

South London Social Services Community Care Division

Care Plan for:

Name: William Rees
Address: 17 Addison Road, London SW
DOB: 09.08.1921
Age: 87

Objectives of care plan (How are identified needs to be met?)
Mr Rees has a history of Parkinson's disease, which has now impaired all aspects of his life. Mr Rees will require a nursing home placement on discharge from hospital to meet both his physical and mental health care needs.

Planned start date: As soon as possible.

Services to be provided:

Service	Frequency/Manner of provision	Provided by	Financial arrangement
The provision of all nursing care needs	Every day	The Grove Nursing Home	Client, and when Mr Rees's finances fall below the threshold, Social Services Department
To monitor and treat appropriately all pressure points, to prevent sacral pressure sores	Every day	The Grove Nursing Home	

Service	Frequency/Manner of provision	Provided by	Financial arrangement
Assistance with all transfers	As and when required	Nursing care staff	
Assistance with nutrition, i.e. feeding and drinking	As and when required	Nursing care staff	
Assistance with toileting	As and when required	Nursing care staff	
Administering of medication	As per discharge instructions	Nursing care staff	
Assistance with all personal care tasks, i.e. washing, dressing, chiropody, fingernail care and any other personal care tasks required	7 days per week	Nursing care staff	
Finance/Personal allowance	On a monthly basis	Private, Mrs Rees and her daughter Mrs Dawes	Client and family

Monitoring and review

Who is responsible for putting the Care Plan into effect?

Name: Sarah Horne – Care Manager
Discharge Planning Team: South London Hospital, Candlewick Grove, London SE
Telephone: 020 7 777 7777

Who is responsible for monitoring the Care Plan?

Name: Sarah Horne
Address: As above.

Arrangements for review:

When? 6 weeks after placement
Where? The Grove Nursing Home
How? To be arranged by allocated care manager

What would trigger an early review? Home failing to keep to conditions of Care Plan

(Assessor) **Sarah Horne**   (Manager) **Tom Shore**

Questions

1 The care plan above is based on a real-life example but with the names changed. Evaluate the format. What do you think of the headings? Do they conform to the official guidance? What do you think of the language used? Comment on the style. What picture do you get of Mr Rees? What changes, if any, would you make?

2 Consider the care plans produced in your own agency. How far do they follow the points outlined in the official guidance? If possible, compare your findings with another.

In most texts, assessment and care planning go 'hand in hand'. In the care management guidance the seven stages involved in arranging care for someone in need are:

1 publication of information
2 determining the level of assessment
3 assessing need
4 care planning
5 implementing the care plan
6 monitoring
7 reviewing.

Stages 3–7 are regarded as part of the care planning cycle and this raises an important question. Are assessment and care planning two discrete and separate activities or are they two stages of what is fundamentally the same activity? To some extent, this depends on what we define as care planning. On the question of the care planning process, the guidance cited says that:

Wherever possible, the practitioner responsible for assessing needs should carry on to relate those needs to the available resources. This will help to ensure that assessment does not become a theoretical exercise but is firmly rooted in practical reality. As with the assessment of need, it is helpful if practitioners approach care planning as a series of linked activities.

- Determine the type of plan
- Set priorities
- Complete definition of service requirements
- Explore the resources of users and carers
- Review existing services
- Consider alternatives
- Discuss options
- Establish preferences
- Cost care plan
- Assess financial means
- Reconcile preferences and resources
- Agree service objectives
- Co-ordinate plan
- Fix review
- Identify unmet need
- Record the care plan.

(Department of Health, 1991, page 61)

We will return to this later on, to discuss how many of these linked activities work out in practice.

ACTIVITY

For a fuller official explanation of what is suggested for each of the linked activities listed it would be best to go to the source text: *Care Management and Assessment: Practitioners' Guide*. All statutory departments should have one. If not, a good academic library will have one in stock. Locate the guidelines in question and ensure that you have a clear picture of what the Department of Health's own guidelines envisaged the care planning process to involve.

If your role in social care involves working for a domiciliary or residential service provider you should find and acquaint yourself with:

Department of Health (2002), *Care Homes For Older People National Minimum Standards Care Homes Regulations*, London, HMSO

Department of Health (2003), *Domiciliary Care National Minimum Standards Regulations*, available from Department of Health website.

As mentioned at the beginning of the chapter, a person-centred approach is considered to be a key to the success of the care planning process.

British Institute for Learning Disabilities

Extract from: *Guidance on Person-Centred Planning*

The person-centred planning guidance describes five key features that help distinguish it from other forms of planning.

1 The person is at the centre: Person-centred planning is rooted in the principles of rights, independence and choice. It requires careful listening to the person and results in informed choice about how a person wants to live and what supports best suit the individual.

2 Family members and friends are full partners: Person-centred planning puts people in context of their family and communities. The contributions that friends and families can make are recognised and valued and give a forum for creatively negotiating conflicts about what is safe, possible or desirable to improve a person's life.

3 Person-centred planning reflects a person's capacities, what is important to a person (now and for the future) and specifies the support they require to make a valued contribution to their community. Services are delivered in the context of the life a person chooses and are not about slotting people into 'gaps'.

4 Person-centred planning builds a shared commitment to action that recognises a person's rights. It is an ongoing process of working together to make changes that the person and those close to them agree will improve a person's quality of life.

5 Person-centred planning leads to continual listening, learning and action, and helps the person get what they want out of life. Learning from planning can not only inform individuals but can affect service delivery as a whole and inform and inspire others to achieve greater things.

(BILD 2007)

Models of care planning

There are various tools that organisations can draw on to inform their approach to care planning. For many organisations it involves a change in organisational culture so that service user support is at the heart of care planning rather than individuals having to fit their needs around the services available.

> **Integrated Care Pathway for neurological conditions**
>
> In Derby there have been meetings between the PCT, Acute Trust, Social Services, GPs, Motor Neurone Disease, Macmillan Nurse specialists etc. to discuss how to ensure a smooth care pathway for people with motor neurone disease. They are focusing on the Community Matron as the key professional to work through the pathway with the individual.

Examples of approaches to care planning that were found to be most commonly used (Joseph Rowntree Foundation, 2006) are described below.

MAPS: The McGill Action Planning System

This focuses on the talents and needs of service users, negotiating changes in routines based on aspirations and desires. Everyone involved with the individual service user would take part in discussing the following questions:

1 What is the individual's history?
2 What is the individual's dream?
   This is a question of 'vision' and, therefore, all those answering should not focus on present-day realities.
3 What are the fears?
   If members of the group can verbalise their fears, they will have taken an important step in becoming committed to making sure that these are overcome.
4 Who is the person?
   Everyone takes a turn at the description; then, the people continue taking this idea around the circle until no one has anything else to add.
5 What are the individual's strengths?
   The MAPS group members are asked to focus on what they believe the person can do.
6 What are the individual's needs?
   When the list has been completed, the group then decides which of the needs are 'top priority' or demand immediate attention.
7 What would an ideal day be like for the person?
   The aim is to have a positive approach to considering changes to a person's life.

ELP: Essential Lifestyle Planning

BILD describe this as 'a very detailed planning style that focuses on a person's life now and how that can be improved. It helps people find out what is important to a person and what support they need to have a good quality of life from their perspective.' (BILD, 2007)

ELP is a way to discover and describe:

- what is important to a person in everyday life
- what others need to know and do, so that what is important to each person is present while any issues of health and safety are addressed.

An essential lifestyle plan is the document that comes from those efforts.

Personal Futures Planning

This approach focuses less on services and more on the development of building relationships with family, friends and community. It 'involves a committed group of people to describe a person's life now and look at what they would like in the future; it is useful to help people learn more about a person's life (unlike PATH, which assumes this knowledge) and create a vision for the future.' (BILD, 2007)

Personal Futures Planning was developed by Beth Mount and John O'Brien. It involves:

- getting to know the person and what their life is like now
- developing ideas about what they would like in the future
- taking action to move towards this, which involves exploring possibilities within the community and looking at what needs to change within services.

The process is colourfully recorded in words and pictures using different 'maps' as illustrations of different areas of the person's life, focusing on what is important to the person, and the five accomplishments (as described in Chapter 4 on supporting individuals).

The personal profile represented in the maps can be created through:

- a facilitator summarising what has been learned on the maps from different people
- the individual inviting people to a personal profile meeting where the information will be gathered directly on to the maps
- the person spending time recording her own life in a booklet similar to 'My Life, My Meeting' and putting this information on to maps.

Maps can include:

- dreams, hopes and fears
- places
- preferences
- relationships
- background
- health
- choices.

PATHS: Planning Alternative Tomorrows and Hope

These are individual action plans that focus 'strongly on a desirable future or dream and what it would take to move closer to that. It is a way of planning direct and immediate action.' (BILD, 2007)

Person-centred planning is a process of life planning for individuals, based around the principles of inclusion and the social model of disability.

Different agency approaches to the care planning cycle

We have seen what the guidelines say. Different agencies have evolved their own practices depending on their interpretation of how the assessment and care planning process should be undertaken. In some it is expected that the same practitioner will carry out all of the assessment, care planning and review activities in respect of their client. In others, one practitioner might do the assessment, another draw up the care plan and yet another carry out the review. It is therefore important that practitioners are aware of their own agency's operating instructions and how the different activities relate to each other.

Features of effective care planning

Creating choice

As discussed in Chapter 3 on values, offering choice to clients is a key value underpinning care activity. Good care practice is built around the important values of user participation, the rights of the individual to take risks and the individual's right to exercise choice and state their preferences about the way they are cared for. The spirit of the NHS and Community Care Act 1990 was that there should be a shift away from 'off the peg' service-led care planning and a move towards a more 'needs-led' individualised care planning process. This required a considerable shift in culture and the vision has continued to develop further.

It is debatable as to what extent the service-led model has been abandoned. Critics argue that the fact that most local authorities block-purchase much of their domiciliary, day and residential care from a small number of providers makes the possibility of a fully 'tailor-made' care system unrealistic. Budgetary constraints also tend to limit the choice of options available. This means that the practitioner, service users and carers therefore have to make choices within a framework of constraints.

We will cover many of the issues and difficulties in ensuring choice. We begin our discussion by looking at one of the most significant steps forward in this respect. In an attempt to give more control over options to 'the consumer', in recent years governments have introduced and steadily expanded the concept of Direct Payments. This means that instead of having care services arranged for them, people considered eligible will be offered a sum of money with which they can purchase their own services.

Individual funding

In order for care planning to be able to be more focused on the needs of individuals, a financial framework needs to be in place to suit any arrangements that are decided.

There are several examples of what are known as Conditional Resource Enhancements, which is described as 'not a "benefit" nor is it a direct service – instead it is a way of giving citizens control of resources within a managed framework of support and conditionality'. (Waters and Duffy, 2007)

These include:

- Wheelchair Vouchers – restricted to one form of equipment
- Local Housing Allowance – restricted to private sector renting
- Individual Learning Accounts – restricted to certain educational providers
- Direct Payments – restricted to certain forms of support
- Disability Parking Permits – providing improved access to resources
- Concessionary Travel Passes – reducing the cost of travel for people with eligible needs
- Independent Living Funds – funding which must be spent on personal care
- Direct Payments – funding for social care, regulated through a local authority care plan.

Funding sources currently committed to enhance Individual Funding include:

- Supporting People (SP) – £1.69 billion on housing-related support
- Independent Living Fund (ILF) – £0.22 billion on personal care
- Disabled Facilities Grant (DFG) – £0.121 billion on housing adaptations
- Access to Work (AtW) – £0.06 billion on adaptations in the workplace

- Integrated Community Equipment Service (ICES) – £0.052 billion on equipment.

Individual Budgets need to be:

- transparent
- flexible
- fair
- easy to use
- outcome-focused.

Individual budget integration

Adapted from the *Executive Summary: An exploration of the possible scope of Individual Budgets* (John Waters & Simon Duffy, 19 July 2007)

1 An Individual Budget is an innovation in the delivery of Social Care, enabling people who currently use Social Care services to become active participants in the design of their own support by telling them, upfront, how much money will be available to meet their needs.
2 They bring significant benefits to people who need support, and are affordable.
3 They are one element within a universal system of Self-Directed Support which could be used to transform the current Social Care system.
4 Increasing numbers of people are using Individual Budgets
5 An Individual Budget is just one example of a Conditional Resource Enhancement (CRE).
6 There are two distinct options: to extend the scope of the Individual Budget concept by including other funding streams within its scope or to develop other forms of CRE that are similar to, but distinct from, the Individual Budget.
7 Individual Budgets do appear to offer a very useful way of integrating some of the diverse funding streams that have evolved to meet overlapping objectives.
8 Integration of funding streams is not essential to the success of Individual Budgets and there is a danger that too much focus on integration will over-complicate the already complex task of implementing Self-Directed Support.

> **9** Currently progress towards Self-Directed Support and to funding integration is being led by Local Authorities and there are areas of funding that can be integrated without undue difficulty (e.g. Disabled Facilities Grant).
>
> **10** However, other streams lack flexibility to be integrated (e.g. the Independent Living Fund).
>
> **11** Other streams of funding could be integrated within an Individual Budget or developed into a distinct CRE.
>
> **12** There are a range of policy issues that will need addressing in the short-, medium- and long-term in order to support the shift to Self-Directed Support.
>
> (John Waters & Simon Duffy, July 2007)

Integrated Care Network

Self-directed support planning

The In Control project has identified seven key steps to the introduction of a self-directed support approach. The emerging tools and framework of self-directed support are discussed under these steps:

1 Set the budget

A simple assessment of need leads to the identification of an indicative budget sum, with a variety of funding streams (e.g. social care services; Independent Living Fund/Supporting People; Disabled Facilities Grant; integrated equipment services; Access to Work). Knowing the size of the budget is vital for an individual to begin to determine the design of that support to suit their own requirements. In Control has developed a best practice model (Resource Allocation System), which is under constant improvement, adaptation and iteration as it is applied in different local authorities.

2 Plan the support

Once people are aware of the level of funding they need to work out how best to use it to meet their support needs. The Support Plan will describe what the individual wants to change or maintain in their lives. Support planning encourages people to build on the natural resources already in their life, such as their own gifts and interests, what is available in their community, and the roles family and friends may want to play in their lives, as well as what they will need to buy in from outside these networks. To allow the plan to be signed off and funds to be released it must be costed and meet clear criteria established from the outset.

3 Agree the plan

The proposed plan, once defined, would require agreement from the local authority. If the plan could not be brought in within the individual budget level allocated, this would need to be addressed.

4 Manage the individual budget and organise support

There are a number of different ways that the individual budget can be deployed, giving individuals real choice over the day-to-day involvement they have in managing the support. One approach is by using Direct Payments – a cash payment in lieu of social care provision to the individual, or an indirect payment may be spent on behalf of someone, by an agent (e.g. a family member) or someone paid to undertake this role (for example, in a local voluntary sector organisation), or via a care manager.

5 Live life

The individual lives their life using the resources allocated.

7 Review and learn

This reviews how well the outcomes have been achieved.

Direct Payments

A Direct Payment is a payment made to people who would normally receive a service from social services if they have been assessed as needing one, so that they can arrange their own services instead. Direct Payments can be used only to buy services that you are assessed by social services as needing. You cannot buy health, housing or any other services with your Direct Payment. Residential care (respite) can be purchased with the Direct Payment but only for short breaks.

The DP may be used to employ a personal assistant or to employ a personal assistant through an agency.

The passing of the Community Care (Direct Payments) Act 1996 represented a significant change in the way local authorities provided for those deemed eligible for care services. The National Assistance Act 1948, which largely mapped out the post-war social care landscape, actually forbade local authorities from giving out money – it was for the bureau-professionals to arrange welfare services in kind for their clients. The 1996 Act enabled local authorities to make cash payments in lieu of services. Direct Payments represent a shift from the 'welfarist' tradition to 'consumerism'. Glasby and Littlechild (2002) argued that one of the original barriers to Direct Payments being fully implemented was the following:

> By involving social workers in cash payments to individual service users, direct payments will have to overturn more than fifty years of social work practice if they are to become a mainstream feature of social service provision.
>
> (Glasby and Littlechild, 2002, page 63)

Much of social workers' uneasiness in promoting Direct Payments could be explained by their reluctance to return to something that had echoes of social work's previous function as reliever of poverty in the days of the Poor Law. This might assume a stronger grasp of social work history than perhaps many of today's care managers actually possess, but it is another attempt to explain the less than full backing they seem to have received from many workers within the caring services.

In the first instance, only physically disabled people under the age of 65 were eligible. This has subsequently been extended to people over 65, people with learning disabilities and the parents of disabled children to receive Direct Payments.

In their key document *Modernising Social Services* (1998), the Labour government stated:

> One way to give people control over their lives is to give them the money and make them make their decisions about how their care is delivered.

> Direct Payments are giving service users new freedom and independence in running their own lives and we want more people to benefit from them.

The process

People still need to be assessed and meet the eligibility criteria at the level set by the local authority. If the eligibility criteria are met, and the person is willing and able to use the money to buy services themselves, then payments will be made to an equivalent value of the level of care decided in the assessment.

Usually the person on Direct Payments effectively becomes an employer of their own staff or 'personal assistants'. The money must be used to buy support which meets their identified needs. This can also include financing short breaks away from the home, or services out of the home such as educational and recreational activities.

Most authorities have developed means by which independent agencies can give advice, assistance and support to people who need help with the employment and financial management aspects.

Obstacles to successful implementation

Hasler (2003) cites a study which revealed concerns amongst potential older applicants which include:

- difficulty in being able to find a suitable person as a personal assistant
- a lack of knowledge about what a personal assistant is or can do
- no designated Direct Payments support worker to help them
- some care managers' uncertainty or confusion about the 'willing and able' criteria for eligibility to Direct Payments
- lack of time for care managers to explain the scheme properly
- concerns over protecting users from risk
- confusion over the role of informal carers.

(Hasler, 2003)

A major issue which has been found from many different studies is that in its initial implementation, people could not employ their own relatives as personal assistants. The Department of Health in 2003 decreed that, in appropriate cases, local authorities could approve the use of relatives (*Community Care, Services for Carers and Children's Services (Direct Payments) Guidance*, England, 2003).

ACTIVITY

1 How much do you know about Direct Payments in your area?
2 What is the level of take-up?
3 Do you know any service users on Direct Payments?
4 What are the advantages and disadvantages as far as care planning and choice are concerned?
5 How can the take-up of Direct Payments be improved?

Ensuring choice

Direct Payments are a way of creating more choice for service users but they are not the only way. The practitioner guidance (1991) contains the following statements about creating choice in care planning:

1 **Consider alternatives**

In taking a fresh look at users' needs practitioners should not be constrained by the existing set of services. They should be equipped with the knowledge, or access to the knowledge, about the full range of services, not only in the statutory sector but also the independent sector.

Care planning should not be seen as matching needs with services 'off the shelf' but as an opportunity to rethink service provision for a particular individual. Within resource constraints, practitioners should give full rein to their creativity in devising new ways of meeting needs, picking up clues from users and carers about what might be most relevant and effective. Clearly, those who have some or all of the budget delegated to them will have greater scope to create alternatives or to press service providers into arranging different forms of service.

2 **Discuss options**

Once identified, these options should be fully discussed with the user and any relevant carers. This may involve service providers being invited to discuss the detail of their services directly with users, or users being taken on observation visits. For those users who have limited knowledge of what services provide or have difficulty with the concept of choice, for example, those with learning disabilities, this exploration of options has to be as practical as possible so that they can begin to understand what it will mean for them personally.

3 **Establish preferences**

Wherever possible, users should be offered a genuine choice of service options, appropriate to their ethnic and cultural background. This enables them to feel that they have some control over what is happening to them and reinforces their sense of independence.

(Department of Health, 1991, page 63)

Choice, alternatives, options, preferences

The message from government guidance could not have been clearer. The Department of Health emphasises that 'Services should be person-centred, seamless and proactive. They should support independence, not dependence and allow everyone to enjoy a good quality of life, including the ability to contribute fully to our communities.' (Department of Health, 2005). In reality, a key phrase has probably turned out to be 'wherever possible' because despite practitioners' best efforts, there are many constraints around providing genuine choice.

Clearly, it is an exaggeration to claim that no genuine choice is being offered. There are many examples of innovative and creative practice up and down the country. However, as we saw with the implementation of Direct Payments, there can often be a gap between what is meant to be happening and what happens in reality. We need to look at reasons why.

REFLECT

Reflect on your practice and the practice within your agency in general. Do you think that service users have a 'genuine choice of service options'? If they don't, what reasons are there for this?

Models of care planning

Community care

When community care was first introduced, various models of care management were discussed as being appropriate for local authorities to adopt (Clark and Lapsley, 1996). One model sees the practitioner holding a 'devolved budget', dealing with providers on an individual basis, negotiating service specification, agreeing contracts and so on. Here, an individual care manager has a relatively large amount of autonomy in how they dip into the mixed economy of care. In reality, the most common model adopted is one where the business of negotiating care provision and making contracts takes place centrally within a local authority. The individual practitioner in this case has much less autonomy because they mostly 'commission' from what has already been contracted. Most authorities operate a list of approved, contracted care providers who, in the first instance, their care managers are expected to use. Therefore, to a large degree, the amount of choice a service user has is bound to be linked to the range of provision their care manager is expected to commission from. In some areas, there will be more diversity than in others.

The degree of choice and diversity of provision will be shaped by wider social and economic factors such as budgets, the geography of the area – for example, rural or urban – the local labour market, the size and characteristics of the local voluntary sector, and so on. This is why the phrase 'wherever possible' is such an important one. This is also why it is important for practitioners to make sure that unmet needs are fed back to those responsible for planning service provision. It is no good for staff on the front line to complain about lack of options if they don't pass on to those higher up their specific comments about what should be available and what needs are not being met.

Costs

The issue of choice of provision cannot be raised without consideration of costs. All social care takes place within a financial context and care planning is bound to be constrained by budgetary factors. Practitioners are expected to produce care plans that are cost-effective and good value for money. Figure 8.1 below lists resources that can be accessed to help with costs.

The tradition of means testing in adult social care means that before a care plan is implemented the service user has to undergo a financial assessment. There is also the separate point that the cost of a care plan usually has to fall within certain 'benchmark figures' or else the practitioner is required to argue a special case with those who control the budgets. Several pieces of research indicate that practitioners are not always comfortable with the financial aspects of care planning. For some, this 'preoccupation' with costs and charging cuts across 'social work' principles such as need.

However, anyone responsible for producing a care plan is not doing anyone any favours (least of all the service user) by trying to ignore the financial dimension to care planning. It would be easy to produce an attractive care plan that will ultimately be unauthorised. All this is likely to do is unfairly raise expectations only to dash them later. It can also

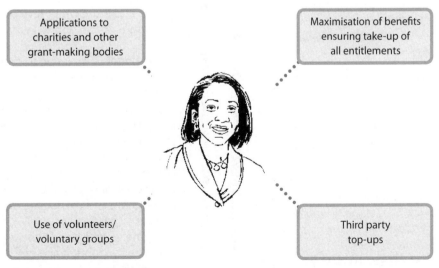

Figure 8.1 Resources that can be accessed to help with costs

create unnecessary equity issues within the agency. The budget constraints are usually there to ensure a fair allocation of resources as much as anything else. Skilful care planning exploits the system rather than simply fights or denies it. Issues of cost can be tackled in various ways.

Care planning

Graham Deakin is 52. He is a wheelchair user and has some cognitive impairment affecting memory and communication due to a motor vehicle accident about 16 years ago. He is on benefits and lives in a flat in a sheltered scheme. He receives domiciliary care every day. However, he gets bored and lonely, often complaining that he is 'fed up with the same four walls'. This can often lead him to get drunk as a way of dealing with his loneliness. This tendency has made it even more difficult for him to make relationships with other people. He has two sons but they both live quite a distance away and one has been in and out of prison several times, which upsets Graham. He blames himself and slips into self-pity.

You suspect that Graham is quite depressed but he won't accept help in this respect. For the last five years, his only annual holiday has been a week in a Welsh seaside resort. This is part of a scheme run by a charity for people with disabilities. This holiday is classified as 'respite' by the social services and is subsidised out of their younger persons' physical disability respite budget. Pressures on this budget mean that only one week a year can be afforded.

Questions

Having discussed it with Graham, you want to produce a care plan that enables him to have not only more holiday opportunities but also more chances to get out and meet people in general.

1 What ideas can you generate to enable him to meet this care objective?
2 Using a format suggested by official guidance, put together a care plan which addresses Graham's needs.

Strategies for care planning

Information

A major way of ensuring genuine choice is through the provision of information so that people know what is available and can then make an informed choice. In its original guidance on care planning, the Social Service Inspectorate outlined the following set of instructions.

Your information system should:
- ensure that people have information that is straightforward, relevant, accurate and sufficient so that they can make informed choices
- ensure that everyone has access to this information in a variety of forms appropriate to their needs
- be regularly reviewed and updated

and take special account of those people who:
- have different cultures and languages
- are sensorily impaired
- have restricted mobility
- are isolated within their communities
- have difficulty with reading or writing
- are not motivated to seek or use information.

You can do this by:
- consulting users, their carers, community groups and those who provide services about the content and style of the information
- giving better information to callers. You should consider the role of receptionists in relation to this
- building information networks on existing patterns of community life, e.g. libraries, religious and community centres, post offices and surgeries. Include key community leaders and spokespeople
- being open about what people can and cannot have and the constraints on their choices
- using the expertise and experience of others to define the content and presentation of information.

> Information in your guide about users whose needs make them eligible for services and the types of services available should be brief and clear.
>
> It should say:
> - for whom the service is intended
> - what it does
> - how available it is
> - what it costs
> - how to apply for it.
>   (Department of Health/Special Services Inspectorate (1991), pages 11–12)

ACTIVITY

Think about the range of people for whom your organisation produces care plans. Make a list of the various obstacles that they face in accessing information and then list the various ways in which information about services is available to them.

Assess how effective your agency is in providing sufficient information to service users so that they are aware of their options and can make a genuinely informed choice when it comes to care planning.

Time and effort

What we have seen so far indicates that if care planning is to involve service users fully and offer them genuine choice, this means that the practitioner has to be prepared to put in time and effort.

Firstly, they have to ensure that they themselves are up to date with as much relevant information as they can be. Strategies for this include the following.

- Collecting, reading and storing relevant leaflets, brochures, etc. on services – build up your own database. Ensure that you are familiar with the information stored in your office – or at least where to find it!
- Network both within your own organisation and in the wider community – locate and learn how to access the knowledge of others – other people's databases. There is more on working collaboratively in Chapter 6.
- Look out for open days, professional lunches, conferences, etc.

- Get your name on mailing and emailing lists of relevant information, e.g. Help the Aged, Mencap.
- Use the Internet – explore what's on the web and bookmark relevant sites.

The important thing with this is not to attempt to walk around with every last detail in your head but to know where to access information and to have a general idea of the range of information that's out there.

The second important point is for time and effort to be spent passing the correct information on to your client in a meaningful and helpful way. It is possible to run through various options relatively quickly on a verbal basis. However, have they all been heard, remembered and understood?

It is important to be aware of the language we use, and to check understanding.

When passing on information to service users it is important to use language that is unambiguous and to check understanding

An equally challenging task is enabling people to sample or try out different services so that they actually experience them before giving their agreement to a care plan. For example, it is good practice to give an older person the opportunity to see a choice of facilities (this could be day centres or residential homes), in order to help them find the provision that most suits their needs and preferences. However, this does raise some pertinent questions. Apart from the logistical questions of arranging transport and availability, an obvious one is how many should they see – all the ones on the list or just those with vacancies at the present time? Then there's the question of whether you should accompany them. Can they take a friend or relative? How long should they stay? Is it possible to get a realistic feel of a place just by visiting?

This throws up fundamental issues for the practitioner, particularly about their power to create or limit choice. It is very easy to manipulate choice. If someone never knows about an option, how are they able to choose it?

It is impossible to provide the perfect formula on exactly how to resolve all these issues. For one reason, if a practitioner is trying to manage a full caseload, there are limits to how much time and effort they can devote to one client at the expense of others. This can easily run into discriminatory practice. Clearly, practitioners need to work within their own agency's practice guidance, but the most effective way of promoting choice takes us back to the principle of user involvement. Much has been discussed on this topic in various sections of this book. As far as care planning is concerned, it is helpful to consider the four types of interaction set by Morris (1997, pages 52–53). These are:

1 **Consultation**: This means literally asking someone about what they want to happen in their lives and is the minimum form of involvement. Morris cautions that 'it can be all too easy to limit consultation to a friend/relative/neighbour identified as a "carer" who is probably easier to communicate with'.

2 **Participation**: This is a more active involvement in the decisions to be made about how to meet someone's needs. It requires professionals to recognise the expertise and experience of the person who needs support in their daily lives. This doesn't mean diminishing the expertise and experience of the practitioner but rather putting this at the disposal of the service user. Morris states that this 'requires a shift in culture'.

3 **Veto**: Giving someone a veto means giving them the right to say no. A care manager or a personal support worker could, for example, say to a service user, 'Let's try out this way of meeting your need but if you're not happy you can say no and we'll try something else.' Veto according to Morris 'is an important way of shifting the balance of power and a key method of enabling people to make choices'.

4 **Delegated control**: This means passing over responsibility for making decisions about how assessed needs are met to the person who needs the support. Direct Payments could be seen as a form of delegated control, but in practice some argue that local authorities attach too many strings to Direct Payments for them to be regarded as a pure example.

In choosing which type of interaction to pursue, Morris (1997, page 57) argues that 'It is not a question of picking just one form of user involvement but often using a combination, or using different forms at different times'.

As far as the question of offering choice in care planning is concerned, we have seen that there is a range of issues and constraints that practitioners and their agencies need to be aware of. These need to be confronted if the rhetoric of genuine choice is to become a meaningful reality for service users. Issues of cost need to be fully recognised. Good quality information has to be communicated and, finally, achieving 'genuine choice' for service users will inevitably involve time and effort for practitioners as they do their research, gather information and enable meaningful decision-making to take place. This requires that service users and carers have properly understood what is available.

KNOWLEDGE CHECK

1 What is the rationale for Direct Payments?
2 How is the procedure for Direct Payments supposed to work and what can sometimes prevent the smooth running of the procedure?
3 What are the three statements in practitioner guidance that refer to choice?
4 Why is it important to consider costs when care planning?
5 How can practitioners help with costs?
6 Identify six points that an agency needs to take note of in the way it provides information.
7 Explain three ways in which practitioners can gather the information they need to plan care effectively.
8 What are Morris' four types of interaction to ensure user involvement?

Care planning, care outcomes and care objectives

We saw that the Department of Health practitioner guidance talked about care planners setting objectives as well as the criteria for measuring how and whether they had been met. In recent years, there has been considerable discussion on how to successfully tighten up and focus this aspect of care planning by utilising a 'care outcomes' approach (Qureshi and Nicholas, 2001). This can be related to key messages from government. Much New Labour policy has been based on the concept of the 'Third Way'. This means that they are not committed to total public sector control of social care, neither are they committed to total privatisation. Instead they are happy to combine elements of each as long as certain key objectives are met. The government would say it is operating on the basis of 'what works'. We see evidence of this approach in *Modernising Social Services*:

> Our third way for social care moves the focus away from who provides the care, and places it firmly on the quality of services experienced by, and the outcomes achieved for, individuals and their carers and families.
>
> (Department of Health, 1998, Cm 4169, Para 1.7)

> At the individual level care planning needs to be thorough and outcome focused.
>
> (Social Care Group, 1998, para 3.4)

> It is rare to see the desired outcome of any service in the care plan or written in the case file.
>
> (Audit Commission/SSI, 2000, page 5)

The idea of using care outcomes in all areas of social work and social care is endorsed by recent shifts towards 'evidence-based practice'. It is an approach to care planning that emphasises transparency, accountability and, importantly, interventions based again on the principle of 'what works'. Risk assessment and risk management tools are examples of where evidence-based practice has become more established. Nevertheless, Qureshi and Nicholas argue that this shift towards focusing more on outcomes requires a 'culture change' in social services. Arguments for using an outcomes approach are that

it helps to clarify the rationale and purpose of any intervention and, if the desired outcomes are written in clear achievable objectives, not only are all parties clear about what's happening and why, the effectiveness of any intervention should be easier to measure – as the desired outcomes will be there as a clear point of reference together with the steps taken to achieve them. Evaluation of the effectiveness of social work interventions is another major, related theme of the late 1990s onwards.

What is an 'outcome'?

An 'outcome' is interpreted as the impact or effect on the lives of service users or carers (Qureshi and Nicholas, 2001). Specifically designed to inform the practice of those working with older people, the authors introduce three different types of outcome. These are concerned with: maintenance, change and process. The following extracts explain more about what is meant by these three outcomes.

Maintenance outcomes

These outcomes have to be maintained in a continuing way, although the level of service required to achieve this may vary over time. They may be maintained in the short term, during recovery or rehabilitation for example, or in the long term, perhaps where deterioration in a person's condition is expected.

An example of a maintenance outcome for the older person would be for that person to:

- be personally clean and comfortable
- be presentable in appearance
- have a nutritious and varied diet
- be in bed or up at appropriate times of day.

A maintenance outcome for the carer would be:

- to maintain health and well-being (physical, mental, emotional, spiritual)
- negative impacts of caring on health and well-being minimised; able to have sufficient sleep, exercise and some fulfilment/satisfaction within their life.

Change outcomes

Change outcomes are changes which result from tackling barriers to achieving quality of life, or reducing risks.

An end point to the intervention can be defined, at which the intended improvement can be said to have been achieved, or partly achieved, and the level of services required can be reduced, or the focus of continuing services becomes maintenance.

Qureshi and Nicholas (2001) give 'recovery or rehabilitation' as a general area for a change outcome. A specific example of such an outcome is:

● regaining skills and capacities (for independent living)

This is only an outcome of services if social care staff are explicitly working on specific activities which are designed to help people to re-acquire skills and capacities.

Other examples of change outcome are:

● reducing or eliminating risk of harm
● modifying the environment, averting homelessness, dealing with possible physical abuse or injury (if risks are being reduced and kept at lower levels by continuing service input then maintaining personal safety is perhaps more appropriate than this category).

Examples of family and carer related change outcomes would be:

● improving significant/close relationships
● enabling people to see each other's point of view, reducing tensions within relationships; mediating between conflicting interests.

Process outcomes

Process outcomes are the results or impacts of the way in which the package of services is provided.

A general area for a process outcome is that:

● services 'fit' with (or support) other sources of assistance and life choices.

A specific example of a 'process outcome' is:

● 'good fit' with cultural and religious preferences.

The person feels that services take account of preferences about relevant issues, such as the way in which domestic tasks are performed, expectations of family members, staff characteristics, language skills and the nature of appropriate food and activities.

Yet another general process outcome area would be that the older person has:

● influence over services, and impact of interactions with staff.

CASE STUDY

Care outcomes

Sidney Skinner is 58-years-old. He has two grown-up children – Roy, aged 30, and Maureen, aged 28 – who live nearby with their own families. Sidney is a foreman in a French polishing company. He has worked for the company for over 30 years. His main leisure activities are the occasional trip to the pub and going to football with his son Roy most weekends. His wife, Elsie, does a part-time job three mornings a week in the local newsagent. Sidney is a smoker, but despite having a bit of a cough in the mornings, has never had a day off work sick.

Three weeks ago Sidney had a serious stroke and was taken to hospital. The signs are that, while he may regain some functioning, he will stay mainly paralysed down his left side. The doctors are saying that his ability to speak will remain affected, as will his ability to eat the way he used to. His mobility is also likely to remain impaired and he will need physiotherapy. Incontinence will also be a factor in his life.

Sidney's employers are being understanding, but it is clear that unless his recovery exceeds expectations, he will not be able to return to his job. Sidney says he will be at a complete loss just being at home all day. Elsie has indicated that she will attend to Sidney's personal care needs as far as possible. She is in a dilemma about working. She could extend her hours at the newsagent's but that would mean leaving Sidney on his own at home for longer periods.

1 Imagine you need to draw up a care plan for Sidney. Using the outcomes described, try to write your care plan in terms of care objectives.

With the following being a specific process outcome:

- having a say over personal and domestic assistance.

The user or carer can, if they wish, influence tasks performed, timing or personnel involved, in order to achieve their desired outcomes.

How outcomes are useful

There is clearly a skill in being able to draw up meaningful, clear and measurable outcomes for care plans. It is easy to lapse into identifying a service and making this the outcome instead of specifying an outcome and then identifying a particular service or strategy as a means of attaining that outcome. Many agencies use the kinds of headings and examples given above, while others draw up their own. However generally applicable some of the outcomes might seem, they should not just be used in an 'off-the-peg' fashion, they still need to be individualised around a particular client. The 'outcomes' approach is meant to improve and clarify the links between the assessment stage and the care planning stage, particularly the activities of:

- setting priorities
- discussing options
- establishing preferences
- reconciling preferences and resources
- agreeing service objectives.

For most people you could say that the intended outcome was for them 'to remain living as independently as possible'. While completely understandable as an aim, it is nonetheless very vague and wouldn't tell anyone what to do next. It needs to be broken down. The care planning work between worker and client is about turning that broad aim into more specific outcomes. Importantly, the first task is gathering an understanding of what independence means for that person and then, in order for it to be realisable, looking at what should stay the same, what should change and how care should be arranged so that the broad aim is realised.

Subjective and objective dimensions to outcomes

A strength of using outcomes, together with agreed indicators of how you know when that outcome is

being met, is that it helps the process of monitoring the effectiveness of the care plan. Care planning becomes more focused. However, a possible weakness of this approach is that, if applied simplistically, it might over-emphasise what can be seen from 'the outside', concentrating simply on externally observable life conditions because they are the easiest to measure. As far as possible, both **objective** and **subjective** aspects should be considered. If, for example, we take the desired outcome for someone 'to be secure' then we should recognise that security is a subjective feeling as much as it is a set of objective circumstances, such as locks on doors and windows, safety systems fitted and so on. This underlines the prime importance of negotiating with the client themselves, establishing what 'feeling secure' actually means for them. Their own indicators might be the knowledge that someone was on the end of a phone, or that someone was going to call round at a particular time of day. These kinds of activities can then be built into a care plan and linked to that particular outcome.

Time objectives

Lastly, it is good practice to set a timescale for care planning. There are several good reasons for this, such as:

- so that needs can be met in a timely fashion and so prevent a situation deteriorating
- so that unnecessary risks are not allowed to develop
- all parties have some way of checking the progress of the implementation process. This enables people to have realistic expectations of what will happen and when
- relieving pressure on others – either informal networks or other services
- avoidance of drift.

The timescale set will be influenced by a range of factors, including:

- the complexity and seriousness of the case
- known availability of resources
- agency and government guidelines – for example, over discharges from hospital
- time available to the practitioner.

It is pointless and counterproductive to promise immediate results if, in reality, the plan is going to take time to come together. Similarly, to give no indication of timing leaves people anxious, uncertain, devalued and powerless.

User-defined outcomes

Most of what we have discussed so far has been about care outcomes that have been largely drawn up by professionals. In the spirit of 'user-involvement', there is no reason why service users should not be able to participate in drawing up their own outcomes. This practice is in its infancy but has been tried in various locations. The 'Shaping Our Lives' project has been working in this area since 1996. Together with other groups, it has conducted research into what a variety of service users (older people, mental health users, minority ethnic communities and disabled people) made of this idea and how it worked in practice.

The study found that:

- it was impossible to separate ideas of user-defined outcomes from action to define and achieve them
- involvement to support user-defined outcomes took more time and resources than usually envisaged
- users felt that services continued to show a lack of respect. The value of their own outcomes was not acknowledged nor valued
- users valued the ordinary things in life – cleaning, shopping, support at home; they found it very difficult to get services to prioritise support in these areas
- other services were very important to people beyond ideas of social care, in particular, housing and information
- although the initial research had highlighted the value of direct payments, the development projects showed that users were still not aware of this option
- it was important for users to meet together to strengthen their own voice in achieving the outcomes they valued.

There are several significant messages in these findings. One in particular showed that 'people in receipt of Direct Payments had very clear ideas about the outcomes that they had from the support that they arranged. This clearly showed the effectiveness and importance of Direct Payments in this regard – and pointed to possible lessons for other services to

provide a similar level of choice and empowerment.' Another important finding was that once service users grasped the idea of looking at services in terms of outcomes, they tended to view the outcomes they wanted for themselves from a 'holistic perspective'. This meant that they did not confine themselves to outcomes which could only be met by social care services; they included housing, transport, employment, income and benefits, and broader issues around discrimination and equality. This means that these broader outcomes – if they are to be met – imply at the very least, multi-disciplinary working and, more likely, new ways of working which require a degree of linking up and collaboration hitherto unprecedented in social care.

CASE STUDY

User-defined outcomes

Lucy Garner is 83-years-old. She has very restricted mobility and needs support to walk due to rheumatoid arthritis, osteoporosis and an ulcerated leg. Her husband, Harry, is physically fit but has dementia. Together, the couple have coped reasonably independently. They have a daughter who lives locally and keeps an eye on them; she works full-time. Because of a recent fall, Mr Garner is now in hospital for a least a month, maybe longer.

Questions

You have visited to assess and make a care plan for Mrs Garner. She has expressed a wish to stay in her own home.

1 How might your planning be expressed in terms of maintenance, change and process outcomes?
2 State how the time objectives for this care plan might be realistically assessed and set.
3 How might you ensure that at least some of your outcomes are 'user-defined'?

ACTIVITY

1 Explain the difference between subjective and objective aspects of outcomes.
2 Give five reasons to set time scale objectives.

Care planning as a holistic and culturally sensitive activity

We argued in Chapter 7 that a good assessment takes the whole person into consideration – their strengths and weaknesses, their existing networks, in short, their total situation. Care planning should be informed by exactly the same values. Terms like care plan and care package can often convey meanings that are clinical and businesslike, treating care as if it is a commodity, something 'cut and dried'. The person for whom the care plan has been drawn up runs the risk of being dehumanised or objectified by this way of thinking about care planning.

In order to achieve a care plan that is holistic and culturally sensitive we must take a person-centred approach. As already observed, many agencies and practitioners take it for granted that their practice is person-centred. Often we believe this without stopping to think whether this is actually the case.

REFLECT

Consider responses to the following two questions:

1 In care, what does 'person-centred' actually mean?
2 How would a 'person-centred care plan' differ from a 'non-person-centred care plan'?

The SSI report flags up the value of focusing on intended outcomes rather than fitting the person into an existing service. If, as a practitioner, you work for an agency that uses a lot of block-contracted provision, the temptation is to 'take the provision' to the client and the care plan boils down to basically linking the person to the services in the most appropriate way with very little other discussion. This probably happens quite frequently and probably many people make the most of it in a kind of 'fits where it touches' way – such are the low levels of many service users' expectations. However, this approach is unsatisfactory for all concerned and can be improved by at least starting with the person, not the service.

REFLECT

From your own experience how far would you say that the care plans produced by your agency are actually service plans? If they are, what are the reasons behind this? How can things change?

Cultural sensitivity

As we have seen elsewhere, all aspects of social care should be underpinned by anti-discriminatory practice. Most workers are aware of this but can interpret it in a way that is superficially well-intentioned but lacks cultural sensitivity.

CASE STUDY

A cultural issue

Pavel Szymczyk is a 78-year-old man who came from Poland after the Second World War. He is a widower with no children locally. He learned to speak English quite well. However, a few years ago he began to develop dementia. The effect of the dementia has been to make it more or less impossible for him to understand and communicate in English. Polish seems to be the only language he uses. The GP feels that Mr Szymczyk is in need of a care assessment because he is at risk of loneliness; he is forgetting to feed himself and failing to attend properly to his personal care.

Questions

1 What cultural issues does this case study raise?
2 What approach would you take to ensure that your care planning was culturally sensitive?

Language difficulties

If someone does not have English as their first language this raises many important issues about communication. For example, how do we ensure that we fully understand someone's situation? There are risks associated with using a relative as a translator because they may well give their own slant to what is being said – even without realising it. We need to seek the person's own views – unmediated. Serious consideration therefore needs to be given to finding a proper, trained interpreter.

An important point about language is that it is an essential part of what makes us who we are – it is our identity. If care services are given in a language that is not our own it is the same as living in a silent world. It cuts us off from social contact and an opportunity to express ourselves. Through language we establish who we are and what we are like. To take the opportunity to communicate away from somebody is to take away much of that person's individuality.

Diet

Diet is important in many religions and cultures. It is one of many cultural issues that can be problematic and can easily lend itself to stereotyping. The case study will illustrate one such difficulty.

CASE STUDY

An issue of diet

Ai Heng is an older Chinese woman who came to the attention of the social services. She came to Britain about 10 years ago when she joined her family. She has been in a sheltered scheme for the last three years. Her English is not particularly strong. The family are quite busy with their work and searched for help when Ai Heng became restricted in her mobility and quite low in mood. She was found a place in a day centre. The manager, in an attempt to be culturally sensitive, decided that they would order food especially for her from the local Chinese takeaway. They had great pleasure in serving up a meal of sweet and sour pork on a bed of rice. However, they were taken aback by Ai Heng's outraged response. Only with further investigation did it emerge that Ai Heng was Muslim and had never eaten pork in her life.

Questions

1 How easy is it for us to make assumptions about a person's cultural needs?
2 How do we balance cultural awareness without stereotyping?

There are many religious restrictions on diet. But religion need not be the only factor – vegetarians often feel that their lifestyle is ignored when care services are planned.

Religious practices

Residential homes or day centres that are predominantly geared up for white, Christian service users need to be sensitive to the desire of people from other cultures and religions to participate in religious worship. The response of one home, when they were told that a Muslim resident wanted to have a place where he could worship, was to partially clear the laundry. In Islam Friday is the holy day and it happened that Friday was the home's main laundry day, which simply added insult to injury. The resident was given the feeling that he was creating a fuss and disrupting the running of the home. This important part of his care plan had not been thought through, possibly because the care manager who placed him was not religiously minded.

In certain religions, there are particular ways of washing and dressing that need to be understood. There are also other issues to consider, such as whether it is permissible for a male member of staff to care for a female service user and vice versa. Helping a Muslim to eat using your left hand may cause offence. Different religions also take different stances on illness, dying and bereavement.

REFLECT

Given that few of us are expert on all the religions of the world, how can we ensure that we do not cause offence without realising it, nor formulate care plans that result in someone's basic needs not being met?

Culturally sensitive care planning requires that, as practitioners, we need to ensure maximum user involvement and participation. This requires an approach to care planning that is based on openness, good communication and creative thinking. Good practice encourages both the involvement of ethnic minority older people in their assessment and the development of their care plans. Such procedures should include ensuring that, where relevant, the service user and carer receive a copy of the care plan. In their report the SSI found that:

> The majority of care plans only provided a minimum of information about the arrangements for a service. The facility was available in most SSDs for care plans to be translated on request, but assessors were of the view that because the care plan contained limited information, it was therefore not worthwhile to be translated. After the assessment interview (sometimes assisted with an interpreter), the service user was given a copy of the care plan. This was usually in English regardless of the language spoken or literacy. Most of the black elders seen could not recall receiving a care plan and those who had did not understand it.
> (Department of Health/Social Services Inspectorate (1998), page 47)

Self-directed support

Person-centred and self-directed support (SDS) can face the following ideological obstacles.

The 'giving and doing' tradition: whereby social workers do as much as they can for service users and secure them the most support possible.

The loss of collectivism: where there is an apparent tension between the emphasis on the individual rather than on collective objectives.

The conflation of needs and wants: in all our authorities, but particularly in the one which has had least engagement with SDS, there is a view that personalisation addresses people's extravagant wants rather than their needs.

Mistrust of service users: both explicitly and implicitly there is widespread mistrust of service users and suspicion that people will seek to get as much out of the system as they can, while the professional has a responsibility to protect inappropriate demands on public funds.

> Professional staff often have concerns about whether service users – especially older people – can cope with the demands of SDS. Where these views were expressed there appeared to be a poor understanding of the different forms that personalisation could take, and a lack of appreciation of the contribution of support and brokerage for service users.
> (From *Here to Stay? Self-directed support: Aspiration and Implementation. A review for the Department of Health*, by Melanie Henwood and Bob Hudson (June 2007)

Care planning

Developing care plans or hospital discharge plans for ethnic minority service users may involve some additional work for the key worker in:

- researching the performance of existing providers (whether mainstream or ethnic minority) in attracting and keeping ethnic minority patients or users
- exploring other potential options which make use of the resources, including voluntary groups and informal care networks, of the relevant ethnic minority community
- introducing potential users to other existing ethnic minority users and support groups
- providing 'taster' experiences for users unfamiliar with the services available
- offering advocacy support for gaining access to other services or service providers
- facilitating complaints or concerns from users and carers about the racial or cultural appropriateness, or otherwise, of services.

For some users, care services tailored to their own cultural and linguistic backgrounds will be important; others may prefer referral to mainstream services. The key worker should seek to accommodate their wishes as far as available resources allow. However, users should not be expected to accept services in which the cultural dimension is a tokenistic 'bolt-on' extra (e.g. providing Asian meals in a mainstream day centre, with the remainder of the service unaltered). Cultural awareness must be integral to the service as a whole. Users and, where appropriate, their carers should be given copies of their care plan or discharge plan. For those unable to read English, it should be translated into a form they can understand.

CASE STUDY

A culturally sensitive care plan?

Mohamed Al Haq is a Pakistani man, aged 81 years, who lives with his son's family. He is a Muslim and has very limited English. He has severe shortness of breath and other problems related to heart disease. He is very immobile and needs a lot of help with personal care. There are incontinence problems, and he is also prone to ulcerated legs. Reluctantly the family have had to seriously consider residential care because the family set-up and the fairly crowded living conditions mean that caring for Mr Al Haq safely in the home is proving very difficult.

You have used a proper interpreter and establish that Mr Al Haq is willing to accept residential care for the good of the family, but he wants to go to a home where there are other Pakistani men. The problem is that your locality is mainly white and all of the homes in the immediate area do not have any other male Pakistani elders in them. The nearest home that would suit Mr Al Haq's wishes is a more multi-ethnic town in a different county about 40 miles away. However, not only is the family unhappy about the distance they would have to travel to see him, you also learn that the fees are above your local authority's benchmark figure.

Questions

1 What are the dilemmas for the practitioner in this scenario?
2 From the guidance you have read in this section, what approach would be constructive in achieving a culturally sensitive care plan?

There are aspects of implementing care or discharge plans for ethnic minority patients or users that call for particular attention, such as:

● checking the race equality policies and practices of possible providers
● influencing changes in provision, such as methods used to publicise provision, or the time and place of service delivery
● ensuring that interpreting and translation support services are available
● providing feedback to providers whose services are not found acceptable by potential ethnic minority patients or users
● initiating action through planning and service development sections to secure alternative services.

(Commission for Racial Equality, 1997, pages 60–1)

Achieving culturally sensitive care plans can be difficult. It can pose dilemmas to practitioners. Research shows that families from minority ethnic-cultural communities do not necessarily want separate services. They would be happy with mainstream provision if their needs were being met and if they did not feel that they were being patronised. Agencies need staff with a detailed knowledge of the communities they serve. Ethnic minority communities also need to know about the services that are available. Services need to meet the needs of different communities because a 'one-size-fits-all' approach does not work.

Monitoring care plans

Guidance tells us that the final task of the implementation phase consists in the establishment of monitoring arrangements to ensure that the care plan remains on course. Monitoring is one of the most important aspects of care planning but is also one of the most 'taken for granted' parts of the process. For many practitioners, the key activity of care planning is actually putting the package together; while for some care workers their role would be to implement the care plan. What happens in the period between implementation and review is often likely to be quite 'ad hoc' and reactive, as practitioners' attention necessarily switches to the more formal aspects of their job role – carrying out assessments, producing care plans and conducting reviews. To some extent, the feeling that monitoring is a kind of 'Cinderella' activity is reinforced both by a relative lack of coverage in official guidance and text books, and by institutional practices which tend to focus mainly on the quantifiable, for example, number of assessments, care plans and reviews undertaken. Monitoring is harder to quantify. A factor that can make monitoring harder to quantify is that practitioners are not always clear about what monitoring actually is. It can feel like quite a nebulous activity that somehow 'happens' in a variety of ways that are hard to pin down. In some cases, the assumption seems to be that the main responsibility for monitoring lies with service users and the care providers. This is a 'no news is good news' approach.

> ### REFLECT
>
> Note down the ways that you can monitor a care plan. Compare your list with another person's. Which is your most common method? Does it change depending on the type of care? Does it change depending on job role, for example, whether a care manager, or a care worker in a day or residential setting? Explain your answers.

The official practitioner guidance (1991) states:

The type and level of monitoring should relate to the scale of intervention and the complexity of the needs that are being addressed. Monitoring may be performed in a number of ways:

- home visits
- telephone calls
- letters
- questionnaires
- inter-staff/agency consultation
- observation.

All users who are in receipt of continuing services should have the benefit of some form of monitoring to ensure the appropriateness of that provision. However, the form of monitoring should be designed to cause as little disruption as possible to the users' daily pattern of living. (Department of Health, 1991, page 78)

CASE STUDY

Monitoring care plans

Liam

Liam Atkins is a 40-year-old former sergeant in the army. An accident 10 years ago has left him paralysed. He opted for Direct Payments three years ago, mainly out of exasperation. The domiciliary package that had been put together by social services was not to his liking. He did not like the attitude of some of his carers and thought they hadn't always been properly briefed. There was also a problem with the timings of the calls. He has made three official complaints to the highest level. He used his connections to hire a small team of personal assistants. He has said that social services have now effectively 'washed their hands' of him.

Mrs Godden

Beatrice Godden is 84. She lives on her own despite having advanced vascular dementia. She is adamant that she wants to stay in her home, where the GP has lived for the last 40 years. Her GP thinks residential care would be a safer option, as the GP is often having to attend to Mrs Godden, but respects Mrs Godden's wish to stay where she is. Mrs Godden is also known to CPNs and other mental health specialists. The neighbours in her street quite often find her wandering or distressed because she has locked herself out. They usually either contact one of Mrs Godden's two daughters or the social services. Mrs Godden has four domiciliary calls a day and attends a day centre three times a week.

Questions

1 From these two situations explain which methods you would use to monitor these two care plans.
2 Would you use the same methods for both cases? Give reasons.
3 Explain how you would agree and then record your monitoring arrangements.
4 Would you make any arrangements in either case for when you are absent from work for whatever reason? If so, what?

An important point to acknowledge is that monitoring arrangements must, as far as possible, be agreed with the service user and their carer(s). Over-monitoring is as intrusive as under-monitoring is neglectful. Many people would find being under constant surveillance oppressive, however well intentioned it was. Lightness of touch and subtlety are likely to be appreciated by all parties.

Why monitor?

The activities should have provoked you to reflect more on the purpose of monitoring a care plan. As we saw at the start of this section, it is 'to ensure that the care plan remains on course'. This becomes easier the more clear and specific the care outcomes are. Monitoring can also lead to care objectives being modified and the care plan 'tweaked' or even altered extensively.

As stated before, not only can some situations change rapidly, but you cannot always get it right first time. For example, someone who has attended a day centre once or twice might find that joining with a group of strangers is 'not their cup of tea' after all. Having tried the experience, they might express a wish to stay at home. This in turn, might lead to a discussion about how a solution might be found that lies somewhere between staying in all the time and going out to a day centre. It could possibly mean that the need is redefined. Instead of seeing it as a need for social contact, it could be that it is more about mental stimulation. Acquiring a computer and learning how to use it might meet this need; alternatively so might getting a cat and looking after it! It all depends on the individual concerned. Effective monitoring recognises the fluid and dynamic quality of care planning.

Monitoring, then, is a key part of the quality control process and, as such, is also about ensuring that the care provision is delivered as per service specifications. One of the reasons for creating the purchaser/provider split was to allow care planners to shop around more, and implicit in this was the desire to keep providers 'on their toes'. In reality, this has only partially happened. In areas where there are care shortages the providers are in a greater position of strength than was originally foreseen. For all kinds of reasons, an unhealthy collusion between purchaser and providers can sometimes exist. In such instances, the care planner has to ensure that meaningful

monitoring actually does take place even when there is a feeling that providers need to be kept on good terms.

Lastly, the official guidance (1991) states that an important purpose of monitoring is to 'support users, carers and service providers'. It continues:

> Support may take different forms:
> - counselling
> - progress-chasing
> - resolving conflicts or difficulties.
> (Department of Health, page 79)

Clearly, to carry out these important activities properly requires a full range of interpersonal, communication and caring skills on behalf of the practitioner. They often go unacknowledged by management or else are considered commonplace, straightforward activities. These are the 'behind the scenes' aspects of the care planning role that do not usually get quantified and recognised but without which care planning could not take place. They are in many ways the 'bread and butter' of the job.

REFLECT

How much of your role relates to planning, monitoring and reviewing care and support of individuals?

Who should monitor?

Monitoring is the responsibility of the practitioner responsible for implementing the care plan. In many instances this is the care manager but it might be a key worker. However, this does not mean that monitoring should be their sole responsibility. In the spirit of user involvement, the service user should be encouraged to monitor their own care plan. Often the day-to-day monitoring will be carried out by a key worker employed by the care providers. There is nothing wrong with providers monitoring care plans; after all, they are very close to the service user, have expertise, and on many matters are able to comment knowledgeably about how things are going. A report on services for older people with dementia published in 1997, however, found that:

> Monitoring was generally a well managed activity although there was some anxiety that it was

sometimes more about contract compliance than quality or continuing appropriateness of service. There was also concern that in some cases monitoring was carried out only by service providers and whilst this may be appropriate in some circumstances there must also be room for questioning whether service providers monitoring their own activities is the surest way to proceed with checking on quality of service.

(Department of Health/Social Services Inspectorate (1997), page 19)

A certain amount of caution also needs to be exercised when relying solely on carers for monitoring purposes. This is because the informal carer's agenda is not necessarily that of the service user. Service users who, for whatever reason, are unable to communicate their own views might end up with their carer expressing their views for them. There are, for example, cases where much-needed home care provision has been cancelled by carers because they feel the arrangements are having a negative impact on their own lives. Domiciliary care assistants can be seen as an intrusion, or somehow competitors, and the carer can also feel under surveillance in such situations. Giving and receiving care is a complex human activity and, while carers are rightly seen as an essential component of community care, this does not mean that their views about what is best for the one they care for should be left unchallenged.

There are different reasons why effective monitoring doesn't always happen and some of these are shown in the diagram below.

REFLECT

Reflect on the reasons why effective monitoring does not always happen. How many of these apply to your current caseload? Which are the most common? Could you add any others?

What types of cases are least likely to be monitored, in your opinion?

The last word

The monitoring of care should be taken seriously and therefore should have the appropriate amount of time allocated to it. To use an old adage 'a stitch in time saves nine', i.e. learning about and reacting quickly to care plan difficulties early on can prevent even bigger problems emerging later. The practitioner has to take a lead in this. It cannot simply be left on the basis of 'let me know if there are any problems'.

It is also apparent that, to monitor what is after all a complex set of human activities, a variety of methods will have to be used. Monitoring should usually be undertaken in a flexible, unobtrusive but focused fashion. It requires a range of different skills. If a rounded holistic view is to be achieved then more than one perspective must be sought. The ways in which the care plan is going to be monitored should be discussed with the relevant parties, especially the service user.

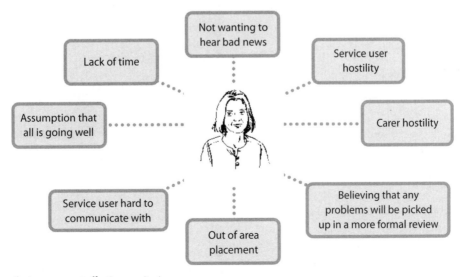

Figure 8.2 Factors that can prevent effective monitoring

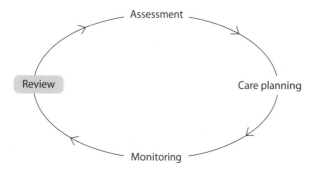

Reviewing care plans

Reviewing completes the assessment and care planning cycle. It is undertaken as a more formal activity than monitoring. As with other activities we have discussed, it should never be assumed that service users expect a review or even know what one is.

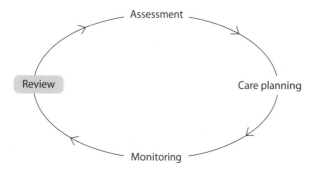

Figure 8.3   Reviewing is the final phase in the assessment and care cycle

What is a review?

This is a good question. In some agencies, a distinction is made between a review and a reassessment, but it is questionable whether there is a clear difference. The practice guidance (1991) regards one of the purposes of a review as being to 'reassess current needs' (page 84).

> A review of people's community care needs and services is not a concept to be found in legislation, except for a fleeting and general reference in relation to residential accommodation. Arguably, 'review', as the term is commonly used, amounts

to reassessment. Policy guidance states that the review process should look at whether services need to be increased, revised or withdrawn.
>
> (Mandelstam, 1998, page 172)

Different agencies tackle reviews differently. Care providers carry out reviews, and they would be guided by the National Minimum Standards Regulations. In community care arranged through statutory agencies, it is common for the review function to be separated out and given to dedicated 'Review Officers'. This has been for a variety of reasons – increasing the number of reviews to meet government targets is probably a key one. 'Clients receiving a review' is a Performance Assessment Framework Indicator for social services departments. The effects of this separation are hard to generalise. On the one hand, it could be regarded as elevating the importance of this activity by giving reviews a special status. On the other hand, especially where the status and pay of review officers is lower than that of other frontline workers, it is likely to somehow downgrade the activity. Reviews may also take place in residential and day care settings where the manager or another representative of the care provider conducts them. Reviews have specific meanings in specific contexts.

The following points are taken from the *Care Management and Assessment: Practitioner's Guide*.

● (A review is) ... the mechanism by which changing needs are identified and services adapted accordingly.
● Like assessment, reviewing should be needs-based.
● The scope of the review will depend upon the complexity of need and the level of invested

resources. The frequency will be governed by how much the needs are subject to change.

- The form and venue of the review should be substantially governed by what is judged to be the most effective way of involving users and carers.

(Department of Health (1991), page 83)

This guidance can be applied to any adult care review whatever the setting. Bearing in mind that the guidance is directed more specifically at care managers in statutory organisations, it goes on to state:

A review fulfils a number of different purposes which are to:
- review the achievement of care plan objectives
- examine the reasons for success or failure
- evaluate the quality and cost of the care provided
- reassess current needs
- reappraise eligibility for assistance
- revise the care plan objectives
- redefine the service requirements
- recalculate the cost
- notify quality assurance/service planning of any service deficiencies or unmet needs
- set the date for the next review
- record the findings of the review.

Discussion of the case study will have highlighted several issues. An important one is that in such cases a review needs to be based on a multi-disciplinary approach. This need not mean that each of the professionals involved should attend a review in person. Any attempt to do this would not only be difficult to arrange in practical terms – and therefore likely to cause unnecessary delay – but it would also be potentially overwhelming for the service user and their carer(s). Therefore, the reviewer needs to ensure that other professional opinion is sought by other means: reports, letters or pre-set review forms. Only with a full range of information from other disciplines, together with the service user's own input, can a meaningful interpretation be made of how effective the existing care plan is in meeting need and managing risk.

Confidentiality and recording issues

Reviews, like assessments, should be recorded in line with agency guidance, which in turn should reflect

good practice principles. Reviews are an opportunity to exchange case information between all relevant parties: service users, carers, providers and so on. Sometimes this can slip into a kind of competition about who knows the most about the service user. If the information is relevant to the care plan then this is obviously useful and can help the fine-tuning process. However, information about service users should remain confidential if there is no need for other parties to have it. Reviewers need to be clear with service users about what the rules of confidentiality are. In addition, their consent should be sought for what comments and details are to be passed to others, and in what form. For example, just because during a review a service user speaks of difficulties with their family, this should not mean that this information needs to go any further, or even be recorded. The service user should have some control over what is written.

Issues

As mentioned before, in drawing a distinction between a review and a reassessment some agencies imply that somehow a review is the lesser activity. Some authorities have allowed this distinction between assessments, reassessments and reviews to develop into a two-tier system.

The reviewing of care plans varied across SSDs, from those which adhered to procedural guidelines and were done at regular frequencies or were dictated by a change in the service user's circumstances, to those which were more on an ad hoc basis if done at all. In some cases, the assessors involved the service users and carers and, where necessary, an interpreter. However, the review was sometimes a paper exercise with some pressure on the worker and the service user as well to avoid change.

(Department of Health/Social Services Inspectorate, 1998, page 44)

People do not always understand the point of reviews because sometimes review officers indicate that if anything major needs changing the case will have to be 'reassessed'. This is not only a waste of time, it is a very confusing message to give. We make these points to underline the fact that a review is just that – a review. The reviewer should expect to reassess need and redefine care provision if appropriate. A review

Reviewing a care plan

Ahmed Rahman (58) was admitted to hospital after a stroke. This left him with right-side hemiplegia. After two weeks of medical investigation, treatment and rehabilitation, he was considered ready for discharge. He lives with his wife, an anxious and frail woman, and two teenage children aged 14 and 17.

The discharge care plan was based on medical opinion that he would gradually regain some use on his right side but that he would continue to experience spells of giddiness and dizziness. The family were advised that he shouldn't be left alone for long periods. Mr Rahman was offered physiotherapy as a day patient. He was also referred for an occupational therapy assessment. Mr Rahman's care assessment found that he could not wash, dress or get to the toilet without assistance; neither could he prepare and eat food. He agreed to have a care package of two domiciliary calls, one to help him get up and get dressed in the morning and the other to help with getting to bed.

The family were keen for him to return home and assured the assessor that they would take care of everything else. He was also issued a care call alarm in case of accidents.

After four weeks, the OT has assessed and issued on loan to Mr Rahman certain items of assistive technology, such as equipment for the bathroom. Information was given about where to purchase other smaller items. Suggestions were also made about how to adapt the house. These suggestions have not yet been taken up.

Several recent calls from the 17-year-old daughter make it clear that the family are under great stress. Mrs Rahman was said to have what appears like nervous exhaustion. The situation is not going well. Mr Rahman has not attended any physiotherapy, possibly because he is not ready in time for the hospital transport. The 14-year-old is now missing school to help out.

Questions

1. Refer back to the section on monitoring. How do you think this care plan should have been monitored? Give reasons.
2. You decide to call a review of the care plan. Explain how you would organise it. Whom would you involve? Where would it take place? What would be its scope?
3. What ideas might you have at this stage about how the care plan could be altered?

---

should not be a rubber-stamping exercise that enables agencies to meet performance targets. It is usually the only formal opportunity the service user has to raise any problems or highlight inadequacies they may be experiencing with their care provision.

Because of this, the use of advocates should be considered when reviewing the care of those without the ability to communicate meaningfully. In most areas voluntary agencies run advocacy services for different service user groups. If an appropriate independent advocate can be found, they will aim to ensure that the views of the service user are properly represented. Of course, advocates are not miracle workers or mind readers, so to function properly they need to have a chance to get to know the person on whose behalf they are advocating. When an advocate is simply brought in at the last minute, there is usually no way that they can gain any familiarity with the person's situation. However, even if an

advocate is limited because of lack of personal knowledge, this is better than relying on carers.

Power imbalances

Many service users are vulnerable and dependent people. They often worry that anything construed as dissatisfaction on their part may either cause their care provider to take offence or lead to the provision being taken away altogether. In such situations, service users will not 'rock the boat' for fear of being placed in a worse situation. It is a consequence of their powerlessness. The reviewer needs to be sensitive to this and do their best to empower their client.

Collusion between reviewer and care provider is easy to slip into for several reasons. In residential and day care settings, when the provider is on 'home territory', effort needs to be made by the reviewer to

Tips for ensuring reviews go smoothly

Preparation for the review:

- Look at the case file, in particular the initial assessment, subsequent assessments, care plans, records of past reviews and recent correspondence.
- Note down what the original issues were. What additional issues have emerged?
- Are there any recurrent themes, unmet needs or past issues unactioned?
- Who has been involved?
- Speak to staff in your agency who are familiar with the case. Is there anything in particular that needs to be raised? Any difficult or sensitive issues?
- Decide who the 'core group' should be – typically this is the client, relatives, care providers, any other regular worker such as a district nurse.
- Contact them and agree a convenient time, date and venue.
- Ask whether anyone else should be invited.
- Is an advocate or interpreter required? Has the advocate got enough time to ensure they are effective?
- Send out invitations to all relevant parties. Include the purpose of the review and what the review will cover – this will also need to conform to agency format.
- Ask to confirm attendance or not.
- For key parties unable to attend, send out paperwork/questionnaire seeking their input where appropriate. Enclose SAE and give time scale.
- Establish arrangements for chairing the meeting – normally the care manager, but it could be somebody else such as a key worker or home manager if in a residential setting.
- Establish an arrangement for recording the review. Think about whether the person chairing it should record it or whether it would be better if somebody else did this.

During the review:

- Ensure privacy and confidentiality.
- Give an idea of the time it will take.
- Clarify who is there, who they are – do people know each other?
- Repeat the purpose of the review.
- Explain the procedures for recording, disseminating the notes and so on.
- However limited their powers of comprehension and communication, always respect the service user by addressing them. Do not talk over them or talk about them as if they weren't there. This is very important.
- Don't use jargon.
- Try to ensure that the overall atmosphere of the review is relaxed but businesslike.
- Make sure that everyone has the opportunity to speak.
- Refer back to previous review.
- Use the prescribed format but not too mechanistically.
- Agree plan of action if necessary, assign responsibilities, set time scales, agree date of next review if possible or at least agree a time scale, e.g. in six months' time.

After the review:

- Send all relevant parties a written record.
- Follow up any recommendations or other actions.

Workers in different agencies will all have their own particular procedures but the watchwords are user and carer involvement, good recording, and to make the review purposeful it should not be simply a rubber-stamping ritual.

avoid becoming institutionalised. A service user's behaviour can easily be labelled 'awkward' or 'difficult' without challenge. Having two powerful figures ranged against them at 'their' review gives the service user little or no chance to express their opinion fully – particularly if it is critical. They are left with no 'voice' and no 'exit'. They must go along with what is decided for them.

Reviewers and providers can also easily lapse into jargon without realising it – this too excludes service users. As we stated earlier, service users often have little or no idea what a review is. Some people, especially those in institutions, believe that it is actually their *behaviour* under review. This creates unnecessary anxiety. Confusion about reviews can also emerge when a service user faces several different types of review from different workers. Research has shown that some service providers conduct reviews within the setting in which they provide the services. This happens a lot in residential homes, day centres and day hospitals; even domiciliary care providers do this. These 'partial reviews' focus primarily, but not entirely, on the service user in that particular setting or as a receiver of that particular service. They mean that people can go through several reviews by different workers, in different settings, and addressing different circumstances. Any changes arising from these 'partial reviews' will obviously impact on the remainder of the care plan. Therefore, the outcomes of these 'partial reviews' need to be carefully co-ordinated if the care plan is to remain viable and in line with the original objectives. Multiple small-scale 'partial reviews' can easily lead to the overall care plan unravelling as different service providers tinker with their bit of it.

REFLECT

You need to review the care of a woman who has been in residential care for over a year. She is mentally fine but hard of hearing. There is a range of health problems including diabetes, emphysema and heart problems. Her mobility is very impaired.

How would you arrange things so that (a) she could express her views as freely and frankly as possible and (b) you get a full picture of whether her needs are being met?

How regularly should reviews be held?

There is no 'correct' answer to this to cover all care situations. It depends on the case in question and the context. Official guidance does not determine what 'regular' means as far as statutorily arranged community care is concerned. However, National Minimum Standards regulations are more specific. The policy initiative Fair Access to Care Services stresses the need for local authorities to carry out regular reviews to ensure that services continue to meet objectives. Department of Health guidance (2001) stated:

Councils should review the circumstances of all individuals in receipt of social care services. Reviews should:

- establish how far the services provided have achieved the outcomes, set out in the care plan
- re-assess the problems and issues of individual service users
- help determine users' continued eligibility for support
- comment on how individuals are managing direct payments, where appropriate.

The last point is important, as we know the government wants to increase the take-up of Direct Payments. With this in mind, it should be remembered that someone on Direct Payments is still a service user but with more freedom to arrange their own services. As such, the approach to reviewing people on Direct Payments should be the same as that for those in receipt of care. Sometimes the feeling exists within practitioner groups that to be on Direct Payments is to want to be left completely alone, and this is what being 'independent' means. However, the situation still needs to be sensitively monitored and reviewed to ensure that the level of direct payment is correct for the level of need.

With respect to older people with dementia, the SSI (1997) argued:

... the particular vulnerability of older people with dementia, the potentiality for rapid changes in their circumstances and needs, and the likelihood that few will be able to report changes effectively or quickly, indicates the wisdom of more frequent reviews than for other, perhaps more articulate, service users.

(Department of Health/Social Services Inspectorate, 1997, page 19)

This guidance suggests that agencies and reviewers should avoid being bureaucratic in their approach to the timing of reviews. Just because operational guidelines might say that a review must take place within three weeks, six months or one year, this does not mean that it is a sign of efficiency to make sure that they take place on the *exact* day three weeks or six months later. The timing should be governed by factors such as need, risk and complexity. Some research by the SSI into how carers' needs were managed made this point:

Only a small number of cases will be actively care managed. Authorities need to be thinking about when and how to review the majority of cases. Evidence from this study indicates the need for a regular review:

- where the person being cared for has needs arising from a condition which is fluctuating or deteriorating
- where care packages rely heavily on the provision of informal care
- where there are no available alternatives to informal care
- where there is conflict between users and carers, or a history of poor family relationships
- where the health of the carer is uncertain.

(Department of Health/Social Services Inspectorate, 1995, page 25)

Reviews as part of the rationing process

In recent years reviews have become a means by which local authorities have been able (not without considerable challenge) to cut back on or withdraw services. Local authorities are not allowed under community care legislation to cut or withdraw services to a service user unless they change their criteria for service *and* review (or reassess) the case against these changed criteria. The Gloucestershire case in the 1990s was one of many which established that local authorities could respond to diminished resources by cutting back care, even if previous assessments had identified a need for that care.

Therefore before care can be reduced, an individual's care must be reassessed against changed criteria. These need to be applied to all service users in the cause of fairness. In effect, this has meant that, faced with budgetary pressures, some local authorities have asked reviewers to participate in what is basically a cost-cutting exercise. This is generally a demoralising process for all concerned. What is described as a review actually means the reviewer is going out and raising the threshold for services, almost inevitably meaning that for many, they lose provision. Reviewers can react to this situation in many ways; for example, resistance, cynicism or sometimes with a

'neutral'/bureaucratic 'just doing my job' approach. Some reviewers even become over-zealous in their role as money savers. In such cases, it is all the more important for reviewers to act in a professional manner. Fair distribution of resources is an important principle, so simply to falsify the review so that 'your' client doesn't lose out is not good practice. Neither is it good practice to go with the intention of cutting the service 'come what may'. It is always good practice to explain the context and purpose of the review as fully as possible, explain what rights of redress service users have, and then to conduct the review in the usual way – that is to say, on a needs-led basis.

ACTIVITY

Look up Local Authority Social Services Letter LASSL 97(13) and investigate the background into the Gloucestershire Judgment and the Sefton Case so that you develop an awareness of some of the complications in decision making about planning care.

KNOWLEDGE CHECK

1 Why does the meaning, nature and scope of a review need to be clarified with those involved?
2 Identify at least six different purposes a review can serve.
3 Explain the benefits of taking a multi-disciplinary approach to reviews.
4 Explain ways in which a reviewer can avoid a review becoming either a rubber-stamping exercise or one in which powerful professionals take over.
5 Explain factors that need to be taken into consideration when determining the timing of a review.
6 Identify possible circumstances when to call a particular process a 'review' is probably misleading because there is an ulterior motive.

References

Audit Commission/Social Services Inspectorate (2000) *Joint Review Team Fourth Annual Report 1999/2000*

British Institute for Learning Disabilities (2007) *Guidance on Person Centred Planning*, BILD

Clark, C., and Lapsley, I. (eds.) (1996) Planning & Costing Community Care in *Research Highlights in Social Work 27*, Jessica Kingsley Publishers

Commission for Racial Equality (1997) *Race, Culture and Community Care an agenda for action* vol 14,1, London

Department of Health (1991) *Care Management and Assessment: Practitioner's Guide*, London, HMSO

Department of Health/Social Services Inspectorate (1991) *Getting the Message Across*, London, HMSO

Department of Health/Social Services Inspectorate (1995) *What Next for Carers?* London, HMSO

Department of Health/Social Services Inspectorate (1997) *At Home with Dementia*, London, HMSO

Department of Health/Social Services Inspectorate (1998) *They Look After Their Own, Don't They?* London, HMSO

Department of Health/Social Services Inspectorate (2000) *New Directions for Independent Living*, London, HMSO

Department of Health (1998) *Modernising Social Services*, London, HMSO

Department of Health (2001) *Fair Access to Care Services*, London, HMSO

Department of Health (2005) *Independence, Well-being and Choice*, London, HMSO

Department of Health (2006) *Our health, our care, our say: a new direction in community services*, London, HMSO

Glasby, J. and Littlechild J. (2002) 'Independence pays? Barriers to the progress of direct payments', in *Practice*, vol 14 no 1

Hasler, F. (2003) 'Making choice a reality' in *Care and Health*, issue 34, 23 April–6 May

Henwood, M., and Hudson, B. (2007) *Here to Stay? Self-directed support: Aspiration and Implementation*, Department of Health/Melanie Herwood Associates

Mandelstam, M. (1998) *A–Z of Community Care Law*, London, JKP

Mandelstam, M. (1999) *Community Care Practice and the Law*, London, JKP

Morris J. (1997) *Community Care: Working in Partnership with Service Users*, Birmingham, Venture Press

Qureshi, H., and Nicholas, E. (2001) A new conception of social care outcomes and its practical use in assessment with older people, *Research, Policy and Planning*, 19, 2, 11-26

Social Care Group (1998) *Study of Care Management Arrangements: Summary para 3–4*

Waters, A. & Duffy, S. (19 July 2007) 'Individual Budget Integration: An exploration of the possible scope of Individual Budgets', for *In Control*, for the Department of Health

The following documents referred to on pages 291-92 are accessed through the Department of Health website:

Care Management and Assessment guidance (Department of Health in 1991)

Care Management and Assessment: Practitioners' Guide, Department of Health, 1991

Community Care in the Next Decade and Beyond, Department of Health, 1990

Improving the Life Chances of Disabled People (Cabinet Office, 2005)

Independence, Well-being and Choice (DH 2005).

Opportunity Age (DWP 2005)

Our health, our care, our say: a new direction in community services (DH 2006)

Useful websites

Joseph Rowntree Foundation: www.jrf.org.uk

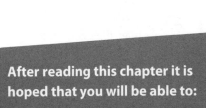

CHAPTER 9

Safeguarding vulnerable adults

Introduction

This chapter explores the sensitive subject of protecting adults from **abuse**, **neglect** and mistreatment. It covers all aspects of abuse and explores what is considered to be good **practice** in **safeguarding** adults from poor standards of care. Its aim is to increase your awareness of what abuse is in the context of care work, and to look at how health and social care workers should respond to such situations if they arise.

The chapter starts by looking at definitions of abuse and explores how abuse can affect individuals. We explore theories that provide some explanation of why abuse occurs, and how the anticipation of this may enable adults to be less exposed to vulnerable situations. We will also look at the policy context of safeguarding adults and what you can do as a care worker to protect the people that you work with.

This chapter addresses the following areas:

- Definitions of abuse
- Forms of abuse
- The context of abuse
- Signs and symptoms of abuse
- The experience of abuse
- Explanations of abuse
- The policy context of safeguarding adults
- Protection from other service users
- Procedures and good practice
- Support as a care worker

After reading this chapter it is hoped that you will be able to:

- understand definitions of abuse
- be able to recognise indicators of abuse
- know the relevant policy framework
- be aware of theories of abuse
- understand how abuse can affect individuals
- be able to apply principles of adult protection practice to your own care work.

Definitions of abuse

If we were to mention the word abuse to a room of people there would be various feelings, thoughts and reactions from the individuals in the group. Abuse is not an objective area of study in which facts and figures tell us what experiences people have, and exactly what we should do in such situations. Each of us will approach this area of study with different experiences and views.

There are different definitions of abuse and these can change over time. It is clear that abuse is a serious and complex area within care work. The protection of adults is a concern for all care providers, and therefore all individual care workers.

REFLECT

Think about the service user group that you work with and write down a definition of abuse relating to this group of people. Then compare it to the following descriptions:

> Abuse is a violation of an individual's human and civil rights by any other person or persons.
> (No Secrets, Department of Health, 2000)

> Abuse in any situation is a misuse of power. It can happen when people do something that they ought not to have done. This is sometimes referred to as committing abuse. Abuse can also occur when people fail to do something that they should have done. This can be referred to as abuse by omission.
> (Bradley, 2001, page 35)

Abuse can be viewed from different perspectives. A starting point may be to look at it from another point of view – focusing on the actions of the abuser.

These individual cases challenge us to consider what abuse is and to what extent we take into consideration the motivations of the person abusing or whether we just focus on the experience of the person being mistreated. They also show that abuse can occur as an isolated premeditated act, or it can occur when there is consistently poor practice in the delivery of health and social care.

REFLECT

Let us explore what your views on abuse might be. Order the following examples of abuse according to how severe you think they are.

1 A client being left in soiled clothing for an hour because the care worker got involved with another task.
2 A person being given a smaller portion of dinner because they are slow at eating and the care worker interprets this as a sign that they are not hungry.
3 An individual being punched by a stranger.
4 A person being given sedatives to calm them down and keep them quieter in the care home as their behaviour is very disruptive to others.
5 A person being told every day that they are worthless, a waste of space and a burden to the carer because the carer is worn down by the relentless care they have provided over the years at the expense of their own life.

ACTIVITY

Think about what is going on in all the examples above.

1 The first case was not an intentional act of abuse; the care worker was distracted by another task.
2 In the second case the care worker thinks they understand what the person needs and what is being communicated to them.
3 In the third, the abuse is a premeditated and calculated act with the intention of causing harm.
4 In the fourth, the well-being of other service users has been considered and this is seen as a sensible solution.
5 In the last case the carer may be struggling with their ability to continue coping emotionally.

careless unintentional neglect ➤ deliberate intentional abuse

Figure 9.1 Abuse can be seen as part of a continuum

Neglect means that actions are not being carried out, which then has a detrimental effect on the person being cared for.

Abuse here refers to the actions that are carried out and which have a negative effect on the person.

These definitions view the situation from the perspective of the abuser, what their motives are and how they have behaved.

Neglect may occur as a result of lack of attention to what the care task should involve and general poor care practice. An example of this may be a care worker holding a person's arms too tightly because they don't know how to assist the individual with their physical mobility. Neglect may also refer to deliberate and premeditated actions that cause harm; for example, a carer denying a service user their meal because that person has annoyed them.

It can be useful to consider abuse from the perspective of the abuser. It may help you to form a deeper understanding of situations where protection needs to be a particular focus. However, it must be remembered that the intention is not to provide excuses for the abuser and overlook the victim's experience of the abuse. The aim in this chapter is for you to develop a better understanding of all the issues relating to abuse so that you are able to become more effective in your role in adult protection; this should then provide a more positive outcome for all the individuals you support who are vulnerable to abuse.

Abusive situations

Let us return to the list of abusive situations that you were asked to put in order of severity. Having considered what might be going on with the abuser in each situation, let us look at what the experience of the individual service user/patient might be.

1 *An individual being left in soiled clothing for an hour.*
   This person may feel physical discomfort, embarrassment at the smell and a loss of their sense of dignity. They may also experience infections and ill-health.
2 *A person being given a smaller portion of dinner because they are slow at eating.*
   This person may experience gradual weight loss and lack of nutrition. They may also sense the inconvenience that they are causing and feel

anxious when eating, thereby developing low self-esteem.
3 *An individual being punched by a stranger.*
   They may be fearful of going out again, and therefore become socially isolated and depressed.
4 *A person being given sedatives to keep them quiet.*
   This person may not realise that the medication is having that effect on them and be unaware of the changes to their disposition.
5 *A person being told every day that they are worthless, a waste of space and a burden to the carer.*
   This person may believe what is being said to them and feel guilty about the trouble they are causing. They may think that everyone has this opinion of them.

Incidence of abuse

We are all individuals and this applies to those in support of care services, so it is impossible to predict the actual effect that abuse will have on individuals. Careless neglect can be as damaging an experience for the victim as an act of deliberate abuse. We may not be helping to address abuse if we just focus on deliberate actions; we also need to look at neglect as a significant area of adult protection.

Another way of looking at abuse is its *incidence*; the frequency and duration.

Figure 9.2 Abuse may be a one-off incident or an ongoing treatment

For instance, in the above left example of neglect:

- the long-term effects of mishandling the service user could be bruising and damage to joints
- in the short-term the person may fall to the floor
- the person may also experience a sense of being unworthy of better treatment.

The denying of one meal as an isolated incident may not have long-term damage to the individual, but ongoing lack of nutrition or drinks can cause dehydration and ill-health.

Again, our perception of this may be what we think of the abuser's reasons for the abuse. The following is what a son says about hitting his older mother, in a one-off incident.

I just flipped, I didn't mean to hit her; I feel terrible about it. I just can't listen to that moaning any more. I love her though and we need some help.

A one-off incident can affect individuals in a variety of ways. One person may be able to understand that a situation got out of hand and may want things to carry on as they did before. They may feel that the initial physical or emotional pain will go away, and there will be no long-term damage.

Another person who has experienced a one-off incident may feel very unsafe in that environment and wonder when the next physical assault will happen. They may also have had their sense of worth affected, wondering what they did to cause it, and believing that they deserved it. They may have physical damage, such as broken ribs, which are very painful and take a long time to heal. The person may have had to spend a very traumatic time in hospital, feeling very vulnerable and anxious about whether they should report the incident.

So, if abuse relates to such a diverse range of experiences, how are we meant to identify whether abuse is taking place, and if so, what our role is in responding to it?

The table below provides a useful way of looking at criteria for deciding if an action constitutes abuse. It separates out what the intentions of the person carrying out the actions are (potential abuser), and what the experience is of the person on the receiving end of the actions (potential victim of abuse).

Some of these categories are more straightforward than others. If someone intends to abuse another person, and then that individual experiences this as abuse, then it is easy to determine that abuse has taken place. Some of the other categories illustrate how complex this dimension of care work is. When we think about the status of individuals in society, and the power relationships that people have, we may need to recognise that abuse can take place even if it

is not intended as abuse, and not experienced as abuse:

- a carer: poor practice, but not intended as abuse
- a service user: not aware that things should be better for them, so not experienced as abuse.

So it is clear then that this is not abuse. Or is it? The following scenario explores this idea.

CASE STUDY

As a refugee from Algeria, Tahir Said-Guerni has low expectations of the treatment he will receive by those supporting him in Britain; he is just grateful that he is no longer in a situation where he is facing physical torture.

Josephine works with Tahir at the Resource Centre. His low expectations are confirmed by the care he is provided with by Josephine, who unintentionally lowers her standards when working with him.

Examples of her practice with him include:

- ignoring statements he makes which she is unable to understand
- not accessing interpretation services for him
- not encouraging him to engage in social contact outside the Resource Centre, and therefore limiting his development
- accepting his poor health as something attributable to the fact that he is a refugee and not accessing healthcare services for him.

Tahir seems content with the support that he receives (not experienced as abuse) and Josephine is just working in the same way as other care workers (not intended as abuse).

Question

1 What do you think? Is abuse, neglect or mistreatment taking place?

Categories of intent and experience	Intended as abusive	Not intended as abusive	Impossible to ascertain intent
Experienced as abusive	Clearly abuse	Probably abuse	Should be initially treated as abuse
Not experienced as abusive	Probably abuse	Clearly not abuse	Probably not abuse
Impossible to ascertain how experienced	Should be initially treated as abuse	Probably not abuse	Impossible to tell whether or not abuse

(McCarthy and Thompson (1994) in Carnaby (ed.) (2002), page 59)

Let us look at the facts of this case study:

Tahir gets:

- ignored
- denied access to appropriate services to which he is entitled
- limited and inaccurate assessment of his needs.

Josephine:

- ignores Tahir
- fails to access appropriate care services for him
- provides inadequate support compared to how she supports others at the Centre.

So how can it be that an abusive situation is not recognised as being abusive by both the victim (Tahir) and the **perpetrator** (Josephine)?

We now need to look at the **dynamics** of this situation.

Tahir has low self-esteem, partly due to degrading treatment he has previously received. This has lowered his expectations of how he should be treated; he does not feel as though he is deserving of a good-

quality experience. Therefore, Tahir does not recognise that he is being neglected.

Josephine has picked up on the low expectations that Tahir has, and is working in a way that reinforces them. She feels that Tahir would let her know or complain if he wanted to. She doesn't understand the complex nature of his situation and how she needs to be more aware of working in an anti-discriminatory way. Therefore, Josephine does not see that she is neglecting Tahir and certainly would not think of herself as an abuser.

As onlookers we can be more objective and identify that Josephine's poor practice does constitute neglect towards Tahir. She is not fulfilling her responsibilities to him and she is colluding with her colleagues in adopting a very poor practice when working with him. He is being discriminated against and neglected as an individual who should be in receipt of better service.

Just as the context of the relationship influenced Tahir and Josephine's perception of whether abuse was

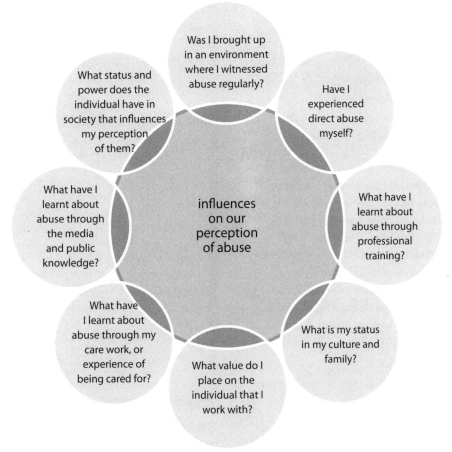

Figure 9.3 How our perceptions of abuse can be influenced

taking place, there are various factors that influence our understanding of what abuse is.

Eastman (1994) has researched the issue of dependency and how this influences a person's perception of whether a situation is abusive. He also explores the role of culture in setting expectations of behaviour, which may or may not be defined as abuse. People's perception of whether an individual incident is abusive is affected by further factors, including what they think of the individual abuser or the victim.

Identifying whether abuse is taking place is therefore made more complex by the subjective nature of it. In this next section we shall be focusing on the different forms of abuse that can be prevalent in the context of care work.

Forms of abuse

Just as there are a number of definitions of abuse, there are also different ways of categorising abusive behaviour. Some of these actions are not specific to the context of care; abuse takes place in society among people who are not involved in care services, either as professionals or as individuals using services; anyone can be punched, kicked or shouted at. Some individuals may experience some of these actions because they are vulnerable due to their age, mental capacity or physical mobility. Sometimes an incident of abuse may be the reason for the individual to access the support of care services; for example, a person arriving at accident and emergency having been physically assaulted, or a person needing mental health services following a prolonged period of emotional abuse that has resulted in the need for support with their mental illness. Other forms of abuse *are* specific to the care task, such as a person with limited physical mobility being left in soiled clothing or a person with mental health problems being befriended and supported in order to access their money.

Abuse may be categorised into the following forms:

● physical
● sexual
● material – finances, property, possessions
● psychological – emotional and intellectual.

For each of the following forms of abuse we will look at:

● examples of deliberate abuse
● examples of neglect
● examples of how this form of abuse relates to the care task.

Physical abuse

Examples of physical abuse are:

● hitting
● slapping
● pinching.

Such abuse relates to the care task in cases of:

● handling a person roughly
● placing them in a bath that is too hot
● leaving a person in soiled clothing
● not taking a person to the toilet to change their continence aids regularly.

Examples of *deliberate* physical abuse include tying someone to a chair to stop them from wandering around; and physical *neglect* includes failing to monitor a person's medication, or not ensuring that someone has sufficient drinks thereby allowing them to become dehydrated.

CASE STUDY

Physical abuse

Colin has cerebral palsy and uses a wheelchair for mobility. He has limited control over his gross motor skills and little manual dexterity; he requires physical support with all aspects of his personal care. Colin hates it when Sharon looks after him as she is very rough with him physically and he feels as though he is being yanked around. She never checks the bath temperature and he dreads being lowered in on the hoist as he has been scalded before.

Questions

1 Why might Sharon behave in this way?
2 Why might Colin feel he cannot say anything to her?

Individuals usually decide the type and amount of physical contact they have with people but not everyone has the luxury of such control over their lives. Physical contact can be more commonplace in the lives of people who need support than is usual with others. Manual dexterity and general mobility affect the amount and nature of physical contact that some people have with others, including care workers. Some abuse may happen to anyone, such as kicking or other kinds of physical assault. Other abuse originates from the care task and involves deliberate abuse of power or neglecting the responsibility to provide appropriate care. Individuals in care may have little control over the physical contact that they have with people or little control over their physical needs, which increases their dependency on people.

Sexual abuse

Examples of sexual abuse are:

- inappropriate touching
- teasing of a sexual nature
- unwanted physical contact of a sexual nature
- taking lewd photos
- rape.

Examples of such abuse as it relates to the care task include:

- unnecessary exposure of a person's body
- denying a person the freedom of expression in relation to their sexuality
- deliberately dressing someone provocatively
- not allowing someone choice in the expression of their sexuality.

Deliberate sexual abuse may involve an abuser getting an individual to touch their genitals. A case of *neglect* would be a care worker not responding to an obvious sexual risk with a person they are caring for.

Sexual abuse is not just a form of physical abuse; it also has a psychological dimension. People in care can be more vulnerable to sexual abuse when they have carers touching them as part of their personal care needs. The danger is that the boundary between care and sexual abuse may become less obvious and the person being cared for may at first be unclear about what is happening.

The people we care for may have a different sexual status in society than what is considered the norm. For example, older people are assumed not to have a sexual identity at all, let alone wanting to engage in healthy sexual relationships. This may prevent sexual abuse from being identified or acknowledged. An example of this is that, in the past, society has felt the need to protect people with learning disabilities from their own sexuality; women have been sterilised, and lives have been segregated according to gender to avoid the risk of sexual contact. This has been due to professional labelling of people as promiscuous. Today, people who form meaningful relationships may have them undermined as being meaningless and insignificant. If a person is not seen as a sexual being, the care provided may just focus on the physical actions, and any other aspects of their physicality are overlooked; this can then expose someone to sexual abuse.

An important area to consider in this respect is that of **consent**. The issues involve a person's:

- capacity to consent
- ability to articulate not consenting
- willingness to consent
- understanding of what is being consented to
- awareness of the implications of consenting.

Working with individuals at risk should not mean that they are denied opportunities for exploring or expressing their own sexuality.

Psychological abuse

Examples of psychological abuse include:

- shouting at the person being cared for
- frightening them
- threatening them
- humiliating them
- ignoring them.

Examples of such abuse relating to care work include:

- limiting a person's opportunity to develop their life skills
- not providing appropriate stimulation, causing a disruption in a person's development through the lifestages
- talking at a pace that the individual cannot understand
- making the person feel inadequate by emphasising what they cannot do.

Deliberate psychological abuse could be a case of telling someone how useless they are because of the time it takes them to get dressed. *Neglect* may be leaving someone alone for periods of time that are detrimental to them.

A person may experience abuse in terms of not being supported in their development appropriately. This may not be evident at first, and delay in development may be assumed as being part of the person's characteristics. Not reaching recognised milestones can provide a useful indicator of abuse in children, but these are less apparent in some adults. For example, a learning disabled individual may not be able to make themselves a hot drink and this may not be identified as being a feature of neglect. It could be because they have not developed such life skills even though they have the ability to learn these if they are supported.

Some carers may generate fear in a service user if their approach to working with that person is abrupt or rushed, provoking anxiety. If the care worker is always in a hurry and gets annoyed when the service user takes a long time to eat their meal, put on their clothes or get up the steps, then this may be communicated to the service user and it could cause pressure and distress.

Material abuse – possessions and finances

Examples of this kind of abuse include:

- theft of personal property
- persuading the individual to sign over property rights in the will.

Examples of this which relate to the care task are:

- lending personal items to another service user without the permission of the person who owns the items
- using an individual's personal finances to pay for a purchase that will be used by everyone in the care home.

Deliberate material abuse may involve an individual encouraging an older person to buy them gifts when they go out shopping. *Neglect* may be allowing a person with learning disabilities to spend all their money on buying other people drinks on the first day of a holiday when they needed support to make sure it lasted a week.

There are several reasons why a service user may need carers to be involved in looking after their possessions. They may depend on support for making purchases or in dealing with financial issues because

of their cognitive understanding of these matters. Abuse may arise from situations created by the abuser; for example, the behaviour of a stranger towards the service user may appear very friendly and beneficial, but then the stranger starts to steal money from that person. Older people are more vulnerable, particularly to strangers, because they live on their own, have set patterns of social contact and are socially isolated.

A care user with reduced physical mobility may require support from others, such as relatives, to handle and manage their possessions. However, you should not assume that such a care user can make sound judgements about their relatives' motives and abilities for taking responsibility for them.

There are two further forms of abuse that are identified in the government guidance *No Secrets*, which we look at in the section on policy, namely discrimination and neglect. We look at these separately as they can be discrete areas of abuse, even though they are also forms of physical, social, psychological and material abuse. The process and effects of discrimination on individuals is discussed in more depth in Chapter 3.

Discrimination

Examples of discrimination include:

- being excluded from activities
- being shouted at, called names
- being denied the opportunity to observe religious practices.

Discrimination may be the motive for abuse. An abuser may be motivated by racial hatred and intend to abuse individuals who are of a particular racial background. An example is a carer discriminating against a Muslim service user by not observing their wish to fast during Ramadan. There are different reasons why people abuse others, and it is not always easy to discern if discrimination is behind some of this. Discrimination is not just about a person being treated differently; it also occurs when an individual is treated the same as other people – but this leads them to have a negative experience. An example of this might be a group being told important information, but a person in the group who is deaf not being provided with an interpreter so that they can also access the information.

An example of *deliberate* abuse in this sense may include teasing someone about their use of English, or the clothes they choose to wear to reflect their culture. *Neglect* might be not supporting a person to access services because they are thought to be too old. Ageism may lead carers to make assumptions about an older person's needs, which could mean that some of that person's needs are not met.

Discrimination represents a violation of a person's identity. The actual method of discrimination may reflect any of the other forms of abuse. We will not be focusing on this a great deal in this chapter as it is dealt with substantially in Chapter 3.

There may be tensions over what constitutes abuse. Genital mutilation or female circumcision is widely practised in some countries, and highly valued by some cultures. In 2003 the government banned individuals in this country from taking children abroad in order to have this practice performed, as it is viewed as being an abuse of the child.

Neglect and acts of omission

Examples of neglect include:

- leaving someone alone for long periods without any stimulation
- leaving someone in the bath too long
- not providing basic care
- being careless and giving medication at the wrong time or in the wrong amounts
- letting someone have accidents regularly without obtaining professional support or advice, accepting that falls are inevitable.

Neglect is a significant issue of abuse as it acknowledges that abuse is broader than just deliberate, premeditated actions that are intended to harm. This also acknowledges that abuse can take place even if the perpetrator does not intend to do harm. They may not be motivated to abuse but what is important is that the individual victim has experienced a detrimental level of care. Pritchard distinguishes between active and passive neglect, and identifies the problems of defining, identifying and proving neglect as well as the issue of what to do about it once it has been identified (Pritchard, 2001, page 226).

- *Active neglect* is deliberately not carrying out appropriate care tasks, e.g. withholding items that are necessary for healthy daily living.
- *Passive neglect* is overlooking, not knowing what care a person needs, e.g. being careless, leaving them alone for too long.

REFLECT

Think about the potential for the different forms of abuse that the individuals you support may experience. Why are they more vulnerable to some forms of abuse?

- Physical
- Psychological
- Social
- Material
- Discriminatory
- Neglect

Statistics on occurrence of mistreatment of older people from the UK 'Study of Abuse and Neglect of Older People' in June 2007 (conducted by King's College, University of London, and the National Centre for Social Research, funded by Comic Relief and the Department of Health) revealed the following:

- three-quarters of those asked said that the effect of the mistreatment was either serious (43 per cent) or very serious (33 per cent)
- approximately one older person in 100 reported that they had been neglected in the past year. Of these, 85 per cent had not received help with a day-to-day activity (such as shopping, housework or meal preparation), 41 per cent had not received help with personal care
- overall, 2.6 per cent of people aged 66 and over living in private households (including sheltered housing) reported that they had experienced mistreatment involving a family member, friend or care worker during the past year. This equates to about 227,000 people aged 66 and over experiencing mistreatment, or around one in 40 of the older population. If mistreatment involving neighbours and acquaintances is included, the overall prevalence increases the numbers of older people who experience mistreatment to 342,400.

Mistreatment in the past year involving family, close friends and care workers: Respondents could mention more than one person. The predominant type of mistreatment reported was neglect (1.1 per cent), followed by financial abuse (0.7 per cent). The prevalence of psychological and physical abuse was similar (both 0.4 per cent), sexual abuse (reported cases were of harassment) was the least reported type (0.2 per cent). Women were more likely to say that they had experienced mistreatment than men: 3.8 per cent of women and 1.1 per cent of men.

Mistreatment in the past year varied significantly by marital status, and increased with declining health status, depression and loneliness:

- 51 per cent of mistreatment in the past year involved a spouse/partner
- 49 per cent another family member
- 13 per cent a care worker

- 5 per cent a close friend.
  (King's College and National Centre for Social Research)

The context of abuse

Having looked at definitions of abuse, and the different forms it may take, we will now explore how abuse happens and why.

The government has specified the following dynamics of abuse in the *No Secrets* guidelines. These illustrate the range of situations in which abuse might happen, and why those we work with are more vulnerable to abuse.

Dynamics of abuse

Scenarios of abuse	
Serial abusing	The perpetrator seeks out and grooms vulnerable adults in preparation for abuse. Learning-disabled adults may be vulnerable to this or people whose mental health does not equip them to be aware of those taking advantage of them. Use of the Internet for befriending people seems to have escalated incidences of this.
Long-term abuse	Ongoing abuse, sometimes in the context of a carer or relative relationship. Many people live in isolated circumstances without anyone being able to identify that abuse is taking place, let alone to free someone from the situation.
Opportunistic abuse	This happens as situations are presented to the perpetrator. A shopkeeper may not give a learning-disabled person their change and may tell them that there isn't any.
Situational abuse	This is due to pressures building up or a person challenging their carer's ability to manage their behaviour.
Neglect of needs	This is due to a carer not being able to support the individual appropriately.
Institutional abuse	This is due to poor care standards and routines that do not suit the needs of the service users.
Unacceptable treatments	Intervention which may be seen as part of a treatments programme but is actually abusing the individual, such as sanctions or punishment, restraining people or withholding food.
Staff not observing ADP (anti-discriminate practice)	The lack of responsiveness of staff to the needs of individuals due to their culture, religion, sexuality. Individuals discriminating against some groups.
Failure to access services	This involves not securing support or guidance for an individual from other agencies. Not accessing services for people perhaps because they are not valued enough and not seen as worth it.
Misappropriation of a person's money	This is misuse of benefits, usually by a family member. An individual claims money for the person but does not spend it on their care needs.
Fraud or intimidation, e.g. regarding wills and property	This involves altering a person's financial situation without them knowing or through coercion.

The following two scenarios illustrate the different contexts in which abuse can occur, to show just how broad is the range of situations that can lead to abuse, and that there is not one set of characteristics of abusers which will enable you to recognise them as they walk through the door!

Context of abuse

Victim of abuse	Cleo is an 86-year-old woman who lives in her own home	Daniel is 44, he lives with his older brother since his mum died
Abuser	Sophie is a home care worker who visits Cleo in the morning	Victim's brother
Form of abuse	Physical	Psychological Financial
What the abuser thinks	'I admit I might be a bit rough with her but it's nothing more than that – she's difficult to work with.'	'He was given more attention when we were children, and now he's a burden to me. It's his fault that Mum died, caring for him all the time. I only agreed to him moving in with me because that is what Mum wanted.'
What the person being abused thinks	'She scares me, I feel exhausted when she's gone and I ache all over.'	Daniel is not aware that he is being abused; he just doesn't like his brother, and knows his brother doesn't really like him.
Consequences of abuse	Physical pain Fear	Daniel is restricted in his social contact and does not develop skills which could facilitate independent living
Location of abuse	The victim's own home	Daniel's home
Duration of abuse	Regularly each week for years	Just started, since Daniel's mum died
Reasons why abuse may occur	Isolation of the care–victim relationship	Family values in society mean that the motivation of the abuser – carer stress – are seen as being OK

Risk and responsibility

One of the difficult aspects of supporting individuals who may be experiencing abuse is that of risk and responsibility. An adult may decide that they want to remain in the situation where abuse is taking place and it is not within the powers or responsibilities of the care worker to remove them from that situation without their consent.

REFLECT

With the service user group that you work with, what forms of abuse are they most vulnerable to?

'Harm' should be taken to include not only ill-treatment (including sexual abuse and forms of ill-treatment which are not physical), but also the impairment of, or an avoidable deterioration in, physical, intellectual, emotional, social or behavioural development.

(Law Commission, 1995)

Institutional abuse

Part of what we have discussed so far relates to the fact that abuse needs to be located in the same dialogue as that of care practice in order for it not to be sidelined as a rare issue, or abusers to be thought of as instantly recognisable. Institutional abuse is an example of where the care practice of individuals can go undetected and unreported for years as a culture of abuse prevents individuals, care workers or service users from identifying it. It is called institutional abuse because the abuse is related to the organisation, the culture and practices of the institution, whether this is a care home, day centre, home care agency, etc.

Institutional abuse may be a consequence of the following activities:

- poor practice in terms of reporting issues
- disrespect towards individuals' possessions
- secrecy in behaviour of staff
- lack of involvement of relatives and friends
- lack of written policies and guidelines
- no training structure
- weak leadership and poor management
- culture of blame means that staff are scared of speaking out
- limited access to external professionals
- organisation is set up around the needs of the staff not the service users
- individual callousness of care workers is not spoken about
- lack of structure in monitoring care plans.

- **Step 1: Listening to older people, their relatives and carers**
  Older people must be consulted about hospital menus, their meal requirements and preferences, and hospitals must repond to what they are told.

- **Step 2: All ward staff must become 'food aware'**
  Ward staff need to take responsibility for the food needs of older people in hospital.

- **Step 3: Hospital staff must follow professional codes**
  Hospital staff must follow their own professional codes and guidance from other bodies.

- **Step 4: Assessing signs of malnourishment**
  As 40 per cent of older people are malnourished on admission to hospital, all patients should be weighed and their height measured on admission.

- **Step 5: Introduce 'protected mealtimes'**
  Introduce protected mealtimes to ensure older patients are given appropriate assistance to eat meals when needed and sufficient time to eat their meals.

- **Step 6: Implement a 'red tray' system**
  Older people who need help with eating should be identified on admission and their meal placed on a red tray to signal the need for help.

- **Step 7: Use volunteers where appropriate**
  Where appropriate, hospital should use trained volunteers to provide additional help and support at mealtimes.

Figure 9.4 *Steps to help older people to maintain nutrition in hospital*

The NHS has been addressing concerns about the dehydration and malnourishment of people who enter hospital for medical reasons and then are unable to manage their own food and drink intake (see above diagram). In 2007/08 Age Concern promoted their 'Hungry to be Heard' campaign aimed at tackling these issues.

REFLECT

Why do you think institutional abuse can develop?

Why do individual care workers not identify, tackle or report abuse that takes place at work?

In care settings abuse may be a symptom of a poorly-run establishment. It can relate to organisational issues of inadequately trained staff who are poorly supervised and have little support from management or who work in isolation.

Punishments and sanctions have in the past been seen as a necessary aspect of developing an individual. For example, behaviour modification programmes that used to be considered as good practice with learning disabled people would be interpreted as abusive today. This illustrates how important it is that organisations do not become closed environments, so that those within or external to an organisation are allowed to comment on the practices of that organisation.

Some environments may develop practices that are not internally recognised as abusive by staff or service users because they are commonplace and sanctioned by management or colleagues. Organisational constraints or requirements may perpetuate incidences of abuse or promote a culture where abuse is not tackled effectively.

Signs and symptoms of abuse

So far we have been looking at what abuse is and its context in different situations. We will now look at how abuse can affect individuals and, importantly, at the signs of abuse we can all look out for. As mentioned earlier, it is not possible to state how abuse will affect an individual. It is, however, important to have some knowledge about the range of effects so that care workers:

- know how to recognise that someone is being abused
- know how to support an individual who has been abused.

Symptoms of abuse

A symptom of abuse is what happens to the person as a consequence of them being abused. Some types of abuse will harm a person in one particular way, while other abuses will produce more general effects.

To illustrate how one form of abuse can produce a range of effects, we will look at the examples of physical and psychological abuse.

The presence of these signs does *not* mean that abuse is necessarily taking place. There can be other reasons for any of these signs. A person with dementia may experience confusion about what they are doing on a daily basis and who other people are in their lives. A person who has recently experienced bereavement may become withdrawn and depressed. A person with changes to their physical mobility who has not had a review or reassessment may fall frequently and have bruising. (If an assessment is not made this may fall into the category of neglect.)

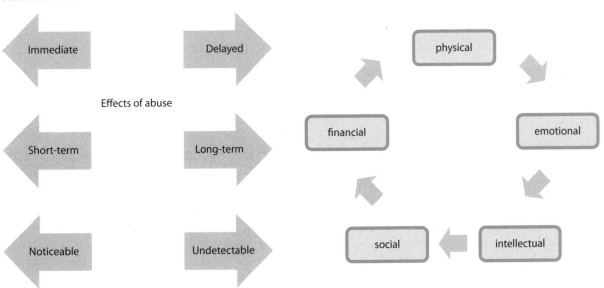

Figure 9.5 The effects of abuse

Effects of abuse

Physical abuse (e.g. being punched)	
Physical effects	Causes bruising and internal damage Temporary or more permanent loss of mobility depending on injuries
Psychological effects – emotions	Loss of ability to undertake daily living tasks will affect an individual's sense of independence and self-esteem Fear of abuse may preoccupy the person
Psychological effects – intellect	The pain experienced may affect an individual's ability to concentrate
Social effects	Withdrawal due to physical mobility Lack of motivation to socialise due to loss of self-esteem
Psychological abuse (e.g. being ignored and isolated for long periods of time)	
Physical effects	May affect a person's mobility or physical development. Withdrawal from social situations, communication affected
Psychological effects – emotions	Will affect the individual's self-esteem Anxiety about what is going on Depression
Psychological effects – intellect	Lack of stimulation means that the person is not engaging in activities that will stimulate them intellectually
Social effects	Lack of contact with others No opportunity for communication and development of relationships Lack of opportunity to develop social skills

Indicators of abuse

Signs	Indicators
Physical	Bruises
	Incontinence
	Broken limbs
	Scars
Emotional	Being distracted
	Anxiety
	Depression
	Lack of confidence
Intellectual	Delay in development
	Confusion
	Inability to concentrate
Social	Withdrawal from usual pattern of social interaction
	Difficulty in relating to other people or in general communication
	Not wanting to be in the company of the abuser or behaving in a particular way with the abuser (such as flinching when they approach)

Concern should be raised if changes are:

- sudden
- unexplained
- inconsistent with explanations provided by the person or others.

Safeguarding adults is about being more aware and alert to potential situations of abuse. Having a good knowledge of the signs of abuse can enable you to think about whether a situation of abuse may be occurring.

The experience of abuse

The Care Standards Act 2000 meant that there are national expectations of what good quality care should involve, and service users should be aware of the requirements of those who support them. They do not have to be accepting of poor-quality care that can result in neglect or abuse. This is important because people who experience abuse may not be in a good position, either physically or psychologically, to actually challenge the abuse and be instrumental in protecting themselves.

The diagram below shows the sort of feelings the service user might have about being abused.

Lack of expectation about Keith's life may lead to him being neglected socially and intellectually. His parents may not realise that they are neglecting him and others around the family may be very aware of the love that Keith's parents have for him, so do not want to comment on or intrude into the situation. It is more difficult to ascertain developmental neglect where the usual patterns of development may be less clear.

The low status of homeless people may make Dave more accepting of abusive behaviour towards him. He has got used to people swearing or spitting at him. His lack of esteem may expose him to further abusive behaviour, as he will not have the motivation to challenge it. He may feel that society is against him and therefore feel that there is not much point in complaining.

Some explanations of abuse tend to place a certain level of responsibility for the abuse on to the victim of abuse; they regard the individual service user as somehow contributing to the cause of the abuse. As care professionals it is important to identify your own understanding of abuse, and how this affects your practice. This can call for tough reflection and honesty about the way care is delivered.

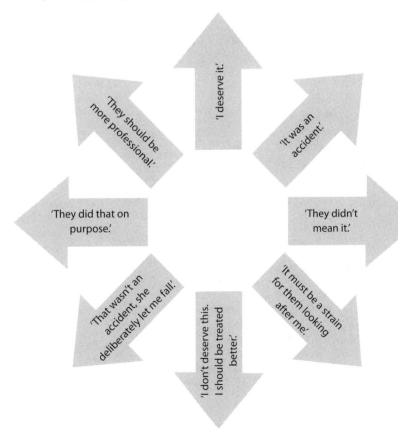

Figure 9.6 Service users might have responses like these to abuse

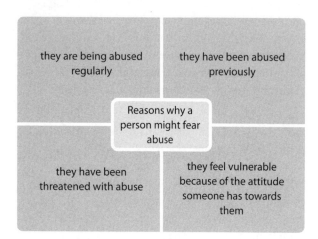

Figure 9.7 Why a person might fear abuse.

ACTIVITY

Look at the situations in Figure 9.8 where abuse is taking place. Think about the behaviour of the abuser and consider the following.

1 Why might the abuser be acting in this way?
2 Would the abuser recognise that they were abusing the person?
3 Would the victim of abuse see that they are being treated badly?

Fear of abuse

Most of us worry about different things in our lives and on occasions this can preoccupy us and affect our daily living; as an occasional occurrence this is part of normal life. Fear of abuse can be more than usual worry, it can be debilitating to an individual. They may not eat, or may eat excessively. They may not want to talk to anyone, not want to go out or not want to be at home alone, etc.

How fear of abuse can affect a person

You will notice that some of the effects of the fear of abuse are the same as those effects of actual abuse. This reinforces what we discussed earlier about focusing on the experience of the person being abused, rather than the intentions of the abuser.

A particular group of people who experience abuse are lesbians and gay men. As discussed in Chapter 3, prejudice against individuals can result in discrimination which may take the form of abuse. Negative feelings about a person or group may make someone feel justified in the abusive behaviour they display towards them. Individuals who are lesbian, gay men, bisexual, transsexual or a transvestite may

Figure 9.8 Examples of abuse

feel exposed to potential abuse owing to prejudiced ideas about them.

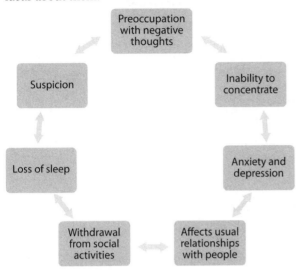

Figure 9.9 The effects of abuse.

Explanations of abuse

We mentioned earlier that it is important for care workers always to focus on the needs of the adult who is potentially vulnerable to mistreatment. It can, however, be useful for us to gain an insight into the reasons why abuse takes place. In this section we will be looking at possible explanations.

CASE STUDY

Being vulnerable to abuse

Mrs Petrokov is a 72-year-old Kosovan. She has difficulty in her physical mobility; she was attacked in her home town and did not receive appropriate medical care which has now left her with difficulty in walking. She moved here as a refugee with her son and his family. Her English is limited and she is not confident about learning a new language and new culture.

Mrs Petrokov experiences incontinence. This is explained away by reference to her age and the physical effects of her mobility. Her communication difficulties and confusion in her environment are attributed to dementia.

Question

1   Why is Mrs Petrokov vulnerable to abuse?

Negative images of refugees by the media create a low status of Mrs Petrokov. An abuser may think that she deserves it, or that it is not as serious as abusing someone who is English. Because Mrs Petrokov only has limited English, an abuser may think that she will be unable to tell anyone what they are doing.

Relationship between oppression and abuse

An understanding of what an individual needs will develop over time, and subsequent changes in practice mean that some previous care practices are now considered to have been very poor, or even abusive. This is an important consideration for care workers and reinforces the need to reflect on our own practices and the work practices of the organisations that we work for in order to ensure that potentially abusive practices are not condoned. Care workers do need to be aware of the potential for extreme examples of abuse, but it is equally important that we are conscious of the more subtle forms of abuse. Focusing on the experience of the service user enables care workers to consider whether any areas of practice may be experienced in a negative way by service users.

Theories of abuse

Theories can provide a framework for understanding why abuse might take place. They can be useful to care professionals when attempting to make sense of situations, when we are trying to understand what has happened, or for being aware of potential risks to individuals.

Phillips (1986) in Bytheway (1995) identified the following approaches.

1. The situational model

This explanation considers the situation surrounding the perpetrator–abused relationship. It explores whether the relationship is based on dependency. If one person is very reliant on the other for support, then the person doing the caring may experience exceptional stress. This stress may develop into an inability to cope or a need to manage the caring relationship in a way that leads to abusive behaviour.

'Carer stress' has provided an interpretation of abuse but it has also been criticised for making abuse sound simplistic. There are many family carers and care workers who are regularly placed under incredible physical and emotional strain when supporting people, who do not abuse and would not be able to comprehend any reason to abuse. There are also people who have no direct responsibility in supporting people and therefore are not subject to great strain who do nonetheless abuse individuals that they know.

2. Exchange theory

This **theory** identifies the importance of power in relationships. It looks at the dynamics of relationships and the importance of rewards and punishments as a feature of relationships. Relationships may be viewed as give and take, with a sharing in terms of needs. If a relationship changes and is no longer reciprocal this can create a change in the attitude of one person and create circumstances where abuse is more likely. Situations where spouses no longer feel important in a relationship, or the relationship has changed significantly and one person does not fulfil the role that they once did, could be explained by this theory.

There are some relationships where from the onset there is an apparent imbalance in what individuals gain from the relationship, and yet both parties are very content with the relationship. Some people feel very fulfilled from providing a caring role to others and would not perceive that they are gaining nothing from the relationship.

3. Symbolic interactionism

This idea places more emphasis on the expectations of certain groups than individual rewards and punishments. Assumptions as to how certain groups will respond with no understanding of the individual's history can set up circumstances for abuse.

Older people living in a care home may as a group be more predisposed to abuse than individual adults in their own homes as they have a different status in society, and the expectation that society has of how this group is treated may be lower than that of adults in their own homes.

Biggs and Phillipson (1992) in Bytheway (1995) added this fourth approach.

4. Social construction

While this theory was developed in relation to older people it can be applied to other groups. Society creates an understanding of groups and their expected behaviour by creating beliefs about individuals. People are then encouraged to conform in their behaviour which confirms those beliefs.

CASE STUDY

Applying theory to abuse

Robert has multiple sclerosis and is now using a wheelchair for his mobility. He requires support with all his care tasks. His communication skills are changing so that he has reduced speech, but has not yet acquired another form of visual communication. Robert is being abused by his wife; they still live together. She shouts at him when he can't do things and constantly tells him how useless he is and he is making her a prisoner because she has to care for him all the time and can't do other things.

Joni

Joni is the care worker for a home care agency. She visits the same individuals on a regular basis, some of them each morning; she works on her own. She rushes when she is with people, moving individuals in a very rough way. She once tied a woman to a chair with her own belt so that the woman would not fall off her chair while she was getting her ready.

Questions

1 Apply the theories of why people abuse to the situations of Robert and Joni.
2 What could be done to improve the situations? Think of how the situations could change in order either to:
   - prevent the abuse from happening in the first place, or
   - stop the abuse happening now and ensure it doesn't start again.

There are other dimensions to theories about why individuals abuse.

- *Attachments in early life*
  The ability of individuals to make emotional connections to people can be influenced by the attachments that they had in their own life, including those in early childhood.
- *Own experience of abuse*
  When we looked at what influences our own perception of whether abuse is taking place, one of the factors was whether we had experienced abuse ourselves. This could be as witnesses to regular abuse between parents or to other siblings, or it might be ourselves as the victims.
- *Social interaction*
  The place of individuals within society has an impact on how they are treated. The oppression of groups can reinforce any negative behaviour by an individual to a member of that group, or make a person think that it is acceptable.

Who are the perpetrators of abuse?

You will find that abusers can be:

- family members – mothers, fathers, aunts, uncles, brothers, sisters

- relatives by birth or marriage
- other family relations
- individual care workers
- groups of care workers
- neighbours
- friends
- strangers.

The statistics provided by Age Concern/Department of Health above (see page 000) are worth revisiting here.

The policy context of safeguarding adults

As discussed in Chapter 2, the way we work is influenced by our knowledge, understanding and experience. Part of this knowledge is provided by legislation and guidance from government and from organisational policies and procedures.

The history of the caring professions provides some startling examples where good practice of care delivery at one time is then viewed as poor or even abusive practice at a later date. One reason why this happens is due to changes in values and how these are reflected in policies that are introduced at different times. Adult protection has not featured strongly in policy historically, and some would say it has been completely neglected; more focus has been given to child protection. Spouse and partner violence and violence from strangers in the context of discrimination have been given more attention by the government. Research into abuse has also been limited, partly due to it not being on the mainstream political agenda and therefore not receiving funding.

All care workers have a role in safeguarding the adults that they support.

Local authorities are, however, now required to work with NHS organisations, trusts and primary care trusts, the police service and independent care providers in order to develop local joint strategies, policies and procedures for practice in relation to the protection of vulnerable adults (POVA), as the result of the government's *No Secrets* document published in 2000.

There is no specific legislation that provides a comprehensive framework for the care professional to work to, in relation to adult protection. A range of policies need to be considered depending on the vulnerable group that you work with, the care setting and your role with individuals.

Policies to protect adults

Policies that are historically linked to adult protection include those outlined in the table at the bottom of the page.

One of the aims of registering the care workforce is to prevent persons who have mistreated adults from continuing in different organisations.

Healthcare Commission Report January 2007

In January 2007 the Healthcare Commission published its findings into an investigation of learning disabilities services in the London Boroughs of Sutton and Merton.

The Healthcare Commission described 'outmoded, institutionalised care' that 'had led to the neglect of people with learning disabilities at Sutton and Merton Primary Care Trust'.

The Commission's Chief Executive stated that:

'The Trust was providing institutionalised care which sacrificed the needs of vulnerable individuals in favour of the needs of the service. It is simply not good enough.'

Their report highlighted the following.

- The overall model of care promoted dependency. People were cared for rather than supported to be as independent as possible. The views of people with learning disabilities were seldom heard and few staff had any specialist training in ways of communicating with people with learning disabilities.
- The environments in which people lived as impoverished and completely unsatisfactory; inadequate access for disabled people, poor decoration and furnishings and insufficient space for hoists in bedrooms and bathrooms. In some instances, limited space compromised the privacy and dignity of people with learning disabilities.
- Staff were not properly trained or supported to provide an acceptable level of care considered to be appropriate in the twenty-

The National Assistance Act 1948	Allows for local authorities to remove individuals with their consent from their homes to protect them for up to three months
National Assistance (Amendment) Act 1951	This allows for immediate removal with consent from the home
Court of Protection Rules 1948	The management of an individual's financial affairs
Domestic Violence and Matrimonial Proceedings Act 1976	Provides for injunctions against individuals
Domestic Proceedings and Magistrates Courts Act 1978	Introduced the idea of protecting the spouse from their partner
Mental Health Act 1983	Introduced the idea of capacity and ability of local authorities to remove an individual to safety
Matrimonial Homes Act 1983	This allowed for restricting, or reinforcing, the right of a spouse to live at home
NHS and Community Care Act 1990	Provides for the assessment of individual need
Enduring Powers of Attorney Act 1995	Allows for an individual to act on behalf of the vulnerable adult
Human Rights Act 1998	Ensures that the articles in the European Convention are not contravened in England
Disclosure of Public Interest Act 1998	Rights of (care) workers when reporting incidents
Care Standards Act 2000	Creation of National Minimum Standards
House of Commons Health Committee 2004	
Domestic Violence, Crimes and Victims Act 2004	
Crime and Disorder Reduction Partnerships	
Care Services Improvement Partnership	

first century. The report was not intended as condemnation of individual members of staff.

- Inadequate levels of staff meant that people were often left with little to occupy their time.
- Inappropriate use of restraint was identified as a serious matter of concern. In one case, a woman had routinely been restrained for many years through the use of an arm splint, which was applied to prevent her putting her hand in her mouth. Such practices have long been deemed inappropriate and harmful.
- Failures in management and leadership at all levels, from managers to the trust's board.

The Commission's report contains 25 recommendations and the Trust is required to prepare an action plan within nine weeks to address these. The Healthcare Commission will closely monitor the plan's implementation.

Office of the Public Guardian

The Office of the Public Guardian (OPG) was established in October 2007; it was set up to help protect people who lack the capacity to protect themselves by:

- setting up and managing a register of Lasting Powers of Attorney (LPA)
- setting up and managing a register of Enduring Powers of Attorney (EPA)
- setting up and managing a register of court orders that appoint Deputies
- supervising Deputies, working with other relevant organisations (for example, social services, if the person who lacks capacity is receiving social care)
- instructing Court of Protection Visitors to visit people who may lack mental capacity to make particular decisions and those who have formal powers to act on their behalf such as Deputies
- receiving reports from Attorneys acting under LPAs and from Deputies
- providing reports to the Court of Protection (COP), as requested, and dealing with cases where there are concerns raised about the way in which Attorneys or Deputies are carrying out their duties.

The OPG helps and supports Attorneys and Deputies in carrying out their duties and provides information on mental capacity to the public, legal and health professionals, and researchers. It can provide contacts with other organisations working in the field of mental capacity.

The OPG also has responsibility for policy issues relating to the Mental Capacity Act and in relation to mental capacity issues generally.

How do the OPG and COP work together?

The OPG works closely with the Court of Protection to make sure that the best interests of people who lack mental capacity are served.

If you have not made or registered an LPA for property and affairs or for personal welfare, and you lose capacity to make decisions on these areas for yourself, someone else may apply to the Court for the power to make these decisions for you.

Only the Court is able to decide who the best person to do this is and it will give that person whatever powers it believes are necessary for them to act in your best interests.

The Court may appoint a Deputy decision maker, who can be given a wide range of powers or it may make a single order, covering an individual decision.

In coming to its decision, the Court may ask the OPG to obtain a report on an individual case. This report can cover a wide range of issues and may involve the OPG sending a specialist visitor to gather the facts in the case.

Once the Court has made its order, it is up to the OPG to monitor and supervise any Deputies who are appointed. The OPG can decide on the level of supervision each case requires and this will depend on a wide range of factors.

Mental Capacity Act

The Mental Capacity Act 2005 for England and Wales provides a framework to empower and protect people who may lack capacity to make some decisions for themselves. It makes it clear who can take decisions in which situations, and how they should go about this. It also allows people to plan ahead for a time when they may lack capacity. It relates to major decisions about someone's property and affairs, healthcare treatment and where the person lives, as well as everyday decisions about personal care.

Key principles of the Act

There are five key principles in the Mental Capacity Act:

1 Every adult has the right to make his or her own decisions and must be assumed to have capacity to make them unless it is proved otherwise.
2 A person must be given all practicable help before anyone treats them as not being able to make their own decisions.
3 Just because an individual makes what might be seen as an unwise decision, they should not be treated as lacking capacity to make that decision.
4 Anything done or any decision made on behalf of a person who lacks capacity must be done in their best interests.
5 Anything done for or on behalf of a person who lacks capacity should be the least restrictive of their basic rights and freedoms.

Safeguarding Vulnerable Groups Act

This is aimed at strengthening safeguarding arrangements for individuals. Its purpose is to reduce the risk of individuals suffering harm at the hands of those employed (in either a paid or voluntary capacity) to work with them.

Independent Safeguarding Authority (ISA)

The introduction of the new Independent Safeguarding Authority (ISA) in 2008 is intended to support the implementation of the Safeguarding Vulnerable Groups Act and previously established Protection of Vulnerable Adults (POVA). The Authority will provide comprehensive protection across the whole of social care and the NHS. This will make it far more difficult for abusers to gain access to those who may be vulnerable to harm or exploitation.

From autumn 2008 it aims to cover the following areas.

- *Workforce coverage*
  Those who work with children or adults who may be vulnerable to abuse or exploitation in a wide

range of settings, in both paid and unpaid work, will be eligible for checks. This is a significant step forward from the existing Protection of Vulnerable Adults (PoVA) scheme, which has been implemented in regulated social care settings only.
- *Pre-employment vetting*
  The scheme will ensure that those who are known to present a risk of harm to others are prevented from entering the workforce in the first place.
- *Independent and consistent decision making*
  The new Independent Safeguarding Authority (ISA) will take all discretionary decisions on who should be placed on the barred lists both prior to an individual's employment and, if necessary, following a referral into the scheme.
- *Continuous monitoring*
  Where relevant new information becomes known about an individual who is already in the workforce and being monitored by the scheme, the ISA will if necessary review the original decision not to bar. Where they have registered with the scheme, the employer will be notified if a person's status has changed.

Dignity Guardians

These were announced in March 2007 as a measure to address poor quality services. Action on Elder Abuse is one such organisation that was awarded this responsibility.

Power of attorney

This is the process whereby someone is afforded responsibility for the management of an individual's finances. An individual, usually the next of kin, has to contact all other close relatives in the application of the power of attorney. There is, of course, the potential for this process to be abused. If a person is provided with powers of attorney and they start to abuse the power that they possess in making decisions about the individual's finances, then these can be reversed. An individual may require someone to be appointed with enduring power of attorney if they need the responsibility for decision-making to be taken on by someone else in the long term.

Human Rights Act

The 1998 Human Rights Act redresses the balance between the powers of the state and the citizen. It provides a framework of rights that can be used as a benchmark for reviewing the actions of social services and other public authorities. (Williams, 2001)

This legislation, which is discussed in more detail in Chapter 3, allows individuals to consider whether an organisation is acting appropriately in the way that it sets up care. Individuals can challenge situations; those most relevant to care and potential situations of abuse may be the Articles relating to privacy and right to family life.

Care Standards Act 2000

This comprehensive piece of legislation set up the current framework for the regulation of care services. One of the strategies that this legislation introduced was the National Minimum Standards for particular areas of care. These provide a benchmark of quality that can be referred to about how care should be provided.

> ## ACTIVITY
>
> 1 Locate the relevant National Minimum Standards for the sector that you work in. Think about how your organisation has responded to these standards, by finding and reading all the documents – policies and procedures – that mention abuse and adult protection.
> 2 What message does the current Mental Health Bill give to society in relation to the status of individuals with mental health problems? What protection do those individuals require from abuse?
> 3 Find out who is responsible for co-ordinating PoVA investigations, and what role you might have.

An illustration of their role in relation to addressing abuse is that if you provide home care for an adult with a physical disability there are now standards of service provision relating to domiciliary care:

- Standard 14 National Minimum Standards Domiciliary Care

- Robust procedures for responding to suspicion or evidence of abuse or neglect (including whistle-blowing) ensure the safety and protection of service users.

The translation of this policy into working practices involves the development of procedures within an organisation, staff training and education about vulnerability, and also the inclusion of service users in identifying issues of abuse and ensuring they are aware of their rights and the responsibility of the service.

No Secrets

This policy statement was produced by the Department of Health in 2000. It provides a detailed discussion of issues relating to the protection of adults from abuse and established expectations of how care services would work with other agencies.

Some key features of this document are that:

- it provides definitions of abuse (as stated earlier in this chapter)
- it is not service-specific and relates to all adults who experience vulnerability
- it recognises that abuse can take a number of forms and is prevalent in a range of situations with people
- it provides guidance and information about how agencies should work together.

No Secrets requires that agencies follow the principles of:

- working together
- actively promoting the empowerment of individuals
- supporting the rights of individuals
- recognising people who are unable to take their own decisions
- recognising that self-determination can involve risk
- ensuring the safety of vulnerable adults
- ensuring when independence and choice are at risk that the individual is supported
- ensuring that people know the law and can access the judicial process appropriately.

(Department of Health, 2000, page 21)

Other features are that:

- within organisations there should be one person responsible for managing responses to allegations of abuse
- the National Care Standards Commission should be informed of abuse in care settings
- the police should be involved more, and organisations should not attempt to deal with abuse as simply an issue of organisational discipline
- sexual relationships between staff members and service users are illegal.

These policies relate very specifically to adult protection. There are other types of policy that may have an impact on the experience of abuse, or provide an opportunity for preventing situations of abuse from arising.

Carers (Recognition and Services) Act 1995

1-(1) The carer may request a local authority ... to carry out an assessment of his ability to provide and to continue to provide care for the relevant person; and if he makes such a request, the local authority shall carry out such an assessment and shall take into account the result of that assessment when making their decision.

REFLECT

Think about the section on theoretical explanations of abuse and consider how the Carers (Recognition and Services) Act 1995 might contribute to the prevention of abuse.

Your response may include the comments that:

- a carer's stress can create a change in the relationship between individuals
- the government's recognition of the important role that carers play in supporting individuals can enable them to feel more valued
- a carer can receive support to reduce their stress and isolation.

Community Care (Direct Payments) Act 1995

REFLECT

A 42-year-old man with cerebral palsy who had experienced abuse from a carer previously has recently taken up the Direct Payments system.

How might this individual's experience of care and abuse change with the Direct Payments system?

Your response may include:

- being in control of the finances and organisation of his own care may empower him
- feeling more valued as someone who is not just a recipient of care
- having the power to stop a carer from providing his care.

The relationship between policy and abuse is not a clear one. It could be said that looking at the social construction theory as an explanation of abuse, Direct Payments could enable people with disabilities and older people to maintain a different status in society and have more power. It has been thought also that the reason why abuse is neglected as an area of study is because of the low value attributed to groups who are the most vulnerable.

ACTIVITY

When you have identified all the policies and procedures that are relevant to adult protection in your area of work, think about your awareness of each policy. Identify where you can obtain more information about these.

Protection from other service users

We identified earlier that perpetrators of abuse come in many forms and are not restricted to one type of person. It is therefore necessary to spend some time thinking about service users who are perpetrators of abuse themselves.

It is important not to dismiss the inappropriate or abusive behaviour of a service user as just being a part of the person's learning disability, mental health or age. This is not respectful of either the victim or the capacity of the individual who is abusing. Abuse from other service users has been acknowledged more recently due to the impact of the Human Rights Act 1998. Historically, much abuse has been ignored as a consequence of group care or dealt with in the confines of the organisation.

REFLECT

Why do tensions arise when the needs of individuals are addressed through the provision of group care?

In Chapter 3 we discussed the idea of labelling and grouping individuals together within false categories. Just because four people share the label of 'learning disabled' doesn't mean that they are best suited to live together. The needs or personalities of these four individuals may not necessarily match up. Trying to meet everybody's needs may result in compromises being made; individuals may be unable to exercise full choice or liberty when sharing an environment with others.

Even if usual daily living is fine, due to resource constraints, care provision often has to be prioritised; if an emergency situation arises with one service user, the provision of care to others is affected.

The earlier examples illustrate that group care has the potential to reduce the quality of experience of individuals. The immediate effect may be small, and not even noted in a care plan, but the ongoing persistent nature of it may prove very detrimental to an individual.

Another issue is where the actions of one person are directed at another service user and cause them harm. Individuals should not be exposed to more abuse by others because they share the same care needs. An experience of abuse is not lessened because that person has mental health needs themselves, or is physically or learning disabled. The importance of

addressing the abuse is not reduced because the abuser is also a service user. This is where identification of risk in care plans is so important and the significance of individuals being supported in advocacy or provided with advocates is important.

CASE STUDY

A source of abuse

Cliff is key worker to both Karen and Margaret, who are both learning disabled. Cliff had planned a trip with Margaret as part of her care plan to develop her independence in using public transport travelling to college. On the morning of the day, Karen has been destructive in the home and damaged some of Margaret's personal possessions. Karen is aggressive, and although she has never physically harmed anyone her behaviour has created an unpleasant atmosphere. The team decide that Karen needs some one-to-one input both to distract her from her current actions and to explore why she is feeling and behaving in the way that she is. This means that Margaret's one-to-one trip is postponed to another day.

Question

1 While the team may feel that they have managed the situation well and prevented further disruption, what do you think Margaret's experience of that day is? Her trip was cancelled and her potential for developing independence skills put on hold.

Self-harm

It is not possible in this chapter to explore all the issues relating to self-harm, but brief mention will be made of some points here.

Self-injury ranges from scalding a hand to overdosing and suicide. Cutting is considered to be the most common form of self-harm. The key feature is that the victim is also the abuser. This does not mean that others do not hold any responsibility. The injuries may be self-inflicted, but this does not mean that the cause of it is down to the individual.

Research has led to current thinking that self-injury is associated with deep emotional pain. An individual engages in self-injury as a way of responding to that emotional pain. It helps because cutting oneself or burning oneself releases feelings like self-hatred, anger or anxiety. This is a complex process and one that requires specialist support. As a care worker it would be important not to respond to an individual inappropriately and to acknowledge that you might not have the knowledge or skills to support this person without any guidance from others. The individual is entitled to the knowledge and skills of a professional trained in this area of work, and you would benefit from appropriate support.

An outcome of self-injury for the person is that of punishment or taking control of their own feelings.

It is easy to dismiss self-harm as just attention-seeking behaviour. This simplifies what psychological processes are involved in the behaviour and limits the potential for an appropriate response. There is a strong association between attempted suicide, deliberate self-harm and successful suicide.

It is important to know when the experience and expertise of other professionals is required to support you as a care worker in an area of care that you may feel inadequately trained or prepared for. Accessing other support is your right and demonstrates your awareness of your responsibilities.

Procedures and good practice

This section identifies some other areas of good practice involved in the protection of adults.

In following good practice you should:

- always make reference to national or local standards and procedures that state good practice
- keep up to date with new policies and procedures
- access advice from voluntary organisations which support the service user group that you work with
- ensure that service users are empowered and in control of the care that they are provided with, and are not just passive recipients of care
- ensure that individuals do not have a different or watered-down language used to explain their experience of abuse. For instance, do not report

that 'John was just being teased ...' if John was being tormented verbally.

Cambridge in Carnaby (2002) exposes the use of the word 'sedation' instead of 'poisoning' in relation to medication and people with learning disabilities.

Good practice starts with acknowledging that abuse does take place in care work, and sometimes the abusers are care workers, friends or relatives of the service user; abusers will not stand out from the crowd, they may look the same as you or me.

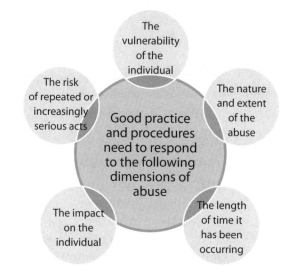

Figure 9.10 The importance of good practice and procedures

We investigated why abuse can take place in care settings when we looked at institutional abuse. Let us look at the dynamics of relationships with colleagues in order to anticipate possible scenarios, and for you to explore how you might handle situations if they arise.

Reacting to abuse

What might your feelings be if you saw a colleague physically abusing a service user?

- Disbelief?
- Worry?
- Making excuses for them?

Doing nothing is NOT an option, even if:

- *you are worried about the consequences*
  - Think about the consequences of the abuse continuing.

- *you dislike the person being abused*
  - We cannot like everyone who we meet in our lives. As professional carers we do not have to like everyone to be an effective source of support for care users, and to have professional responsibility for them.
- *you are a friend/close colleague of the abuser*
  - How long are you going to ignore the abuse – will you leave it too late?
- *it is a senior person or your manager doing the abusing*
  - Your loyalty and responsibilities lie clearly with the service user being abused. There is legal protection for you in disclosing abuse through the Public Interest Disclosure Act.

Doing nothing is NOT an option, even if you don't know what to do

Sometimes care workers can be guilty of misinterpreting situations and explaining away abuse (through disbelief, worry or making excuses). This is our way of having to deal with situations.

Figure 9.11 It is not an option to ignore the situation

Care workers need to review their own practice and to expose situations for what they are, when they have identified an issue of abuse. Chapter 4 emphasises the importance of not always relying on a professional's interpretation of the relationship. This is true also of perceptions of abuse; it would not be right only to acknowledge abuse when a professional had deemed it to be so.

You may think that:

- no one else has said anything
- the service user/patient has not said anything.

This does not mean that abuse is not taking place.

If you are in doubt:

- ask the care worker – let them know that you saw what happened and that you thought it was unacceptable
- ask the service user – their account of what is happening is important.

You may be in a position to manage the risk through the care plan.

Demonstrating good practice

Good practice also involves prompt and accurate recording procedures.

In making an accurate record of what happened you need to:

- make a written note of what happens in the appropriate document
- make this written record immediately after the event
- make sure your written record in the organisation's documentation is an accurate description of what you witnessed – not your opinions or thoughts
- make a written record of your thoughts and opinions separately, in case you need to refer to these at a later date
- inform your manager verbally as well
- follow up your reporting of an incident. If no one responds to let you know that they are managing the situation, ask why.

Good practice with regard to a person's material possessions would include:

- passing someone their handbag for them to get out their purse rather than getting it out for them
- handling personal possessions in full view of the person so that they have a sense of you doing it for and with, rather than instead of, them
- not allowing common access to people's possessions. Some people may need encouragement to retain their sense of personal space. Just because someone says 'Don't worry about me' doesn't mean it would be good practice always to accept this. Consider how you can help to empower people to assert themselves in situations which could lead to abuse
- encouraging the person to be proactive in their own protection by:
  - discussing his or her experience of care with people, to make it easier to raise concerns and not wait for more serious issues and complaints
  - not always being accepting and trusting of people; to be discerning and retain their control over situations.

You should consider what the service user's experience of any changes to their care might be. Challenge your own care practice and that of those around you. You need to make sure that incidents of abuse are not just seen as isolated events and that abuse is discussed in relation to a continuum of good/ bad practice. Good practice in relation to values and empowerment, for example, can limit the potential for abuse happening, whereas poor practice can create a situation where abuse might occur.

An atmosphere of openness allows care workers to discuss neglect and abuse in a practical way that does not make it a taboo area of discussion. It can be an emotive area of practice to discuss and while you do not want to develop a culture of blame and accusations, you also do not want to work in a culture of secrecy and fear. It will also help you as an individual to review your own professional practice in an open way that challenges preconceptions of abuse as being something that only happens in highly public 'tabloid-headline' ways.

The organisational constraints on good practice include:

- routines of the service users being dictated by the staff rota
- service users not being valued or given choice
- the needs of individuals not being set out in care plans for the staff to follow.

CASE STUDY

Organisational abuse

Highbury Lodge is a care home for older people. There is only one member of waking night staff on duty after 10 p.m. so clients have to be in bed by this time. Service users are sometimes rushed in their preparation for bed and 'encouraged' to put bed clothes on straight after dinner, as it makes things easier for the care staff. One service user who needs quite a lot of support goes to bed at 6.30 p.m. and doesn't have company in the evening.

Questions

1 What do you think of the practices of the care staff in this organisation?
2 Write a list of what could be done to address the situation at Highbury Lodge.

What to do if you …

In this section we offer some more opportunities to reflect on how you might handle situations that arise, and then offer some practical advice about what might be appropriate good practice.

What would you do in the following situations?

1 You suspect a person is being abused

This is **not** how to respond. Good practice would be to:

- ensure that the service user is supported and reassured
- report the reasons you suspect someone is being abused to a senior manager
- start by believing the service user, even if after investigation it is shown to be a false allegation.

2 You witness abuse

This is **not** how to respond. Good practice would involve:

- telling the service user what you have seen and that you are required to report it to your manager
- reporting what you observe
- reassuring the service user that your manager will support them and try to ensure their safety.

3 Someone tells you that they are being abused by a colleague

I'd think that they were exaggerating or misinterpreting something that had happened.

I'd tell them that it was probably just a one-off and I'm sure the person didn't mean it to be harmful.

This is **not** how to respond. Good practice would involve:

● telling the service user that they have done the right thing in reporting the abuse
● asking the service user what they would like to happen in terms of reporting the abuse
● asking the service user what support they feel that they would need in overcoming the abuse
● being clear with the service user about your responsibilities and issues of disclosure/confidentiality.

Support as a care worker

What do you need as a care worker when supporting an individual who is being abused? Being a care worker does not make you immune to the emotional experience of situations, or give you automatic skills to cope with new events. Your ability to handle situations of abuse may be affected by:

● your own experience of abuse
● the support you have or expect to be given by colleagues and/or your manager
● the identity of the abuser. It can be distressing to have to challenge the actions of respected colleagues or managers.

However, it may help to concentrate on the needs of the service user and to access support early on. Focusing on the fact that you have contributed to the abuse stopping may provide you with a means of coping with any emotions that arise. This can be important, especially where the service user may have not been aware of the abuse and they liked the abuser.

As a care worker you may also need support when dealing with difficult situations

Depending on the role you have, and on the nature of the organisation, you may be able to access support through formal supervision, team meetings or a mentor. Your manager should be able to support you, but you may need to ask for support if it is not offered to you.

If a situation at work raises issues you have not previously dealt with then you may need the support of professional help outside the organisation. This does not mean you are not fit to be a care worker; it is simply that you need appropriate support.

KNOWLEDGE CHECK

1. What is the most important aspect of definitions of abuse?
2. How would you describe 'neglect' and why is it considered to be a form of abuse?
3. Why does institutional abuse occur and how is it different from the actions of individuals?
4. Why do some family members abuse those that they care for, and how may this be experienced by the individual victim?
5. What behaviours may indicate that a person is experiencing abuse?
6. How can care workers be sure that they identify symptoms of abuse promptly?
7. How may a person respond if they are experiencing abuse?
8. What feelings may an individual have towards their abuser?
9. What are the current key policies that provide the framework for safeguarding adults?
10. What agencies are involved in policies relating to adult protection?
11. What are the responsibilities of care workers in issues regarding the safeguarding of adults?
12. What actions do managers need to take to ensure the effective management of adult protection in their organisations?

Glossary

Abuse: actions that are carried out and which have a negative effect on the person.

Assessment: a judgment about the care/support needs of an individual based on an understanding of the situation.

Criteria: a framework of statements against which a situation can be measured

Critical: a category of eligibility that relates to a person's circumstances. Critical implies that if intervention does not take place then the situation would deteriorate or may become life threatening.

Dilemma: situations in which somebody must choose one of two or more alternatives where there is no clear solution and all the options may be unsatisfactory.

Dynamics: the relationships of power between the people in a group.

Eligibility: the process whereby a person is considered to either meet or not meet the requirements to obtain services or equipment

Intersubjectivity: the idea that a situation is created because of our social interaction

Low: a category of eligibility that relates to a person's circumstances. Low implies that there is no immediate need and that the person's circumstances are unlikely to deteriorate if no intervention takes place.

Moderate: a category of eligibility that relates to a person's circumstances. Moderate implies that there is no immediate need for intervention but that lack of services or support would be detrimental to the person over time.

Monitoring: to check something at regular intervals in order to find out how it is progressing or developing.

Need: something that is an essential requirement in order for them to be able to function effectively or carry out daily living skills; may also relate to a desire or want for something.

Neglect: actions that are not being carried out, which then have a detrimental effect on the person being cared for.

Objective: free of any bias or prejudice caused by personal feelings, based on facts rather than thoughts or opinions.

Perpetrator: the individual or group who act inappropriately or carry out abuse.

Person-centred: an approach to working with people who need support that focuses on them at all stages and has them at the centre of all decisions and intervention.

Planning: a method of doing something that is worked out in advance. The activities relating to the decisions about services to a person and the arrangements of how they will be delivered.

Practice: an established way of doing something, especially one that has developed through experience and knowledge.

Rationing: the process whereby access to resources is restricted.

Reflection: careful thought, the process of reconsidering previous actions, events, or decisions.

Review: to examine provision of a service or a care plan to make sure that it is being delivered in relation to expectations or that the outcomes of the care plan are being met. The idea of review is that changes can be made.

Risk: the possibility of negative consequences occurring if an action is carried out.

Safeguarding: the policy and activities intended to prevent undesirable consequences from happening.

Subjective: an idea based on a person's opinions or feelings rather than on facts or evidence.

Substantial: a category of eligibility that relates to a person's circumstances.

Theory: the body of rules, ideas, principles, and techniques that applies to a subject, often used to inform actual practice.

Tools: care workers use different strategies or devices in their everyday work as a means of achieving something.

References

Bradley, A. (2001) *Understanding Abuse*, Worcestershire, British Institute of Learning Disabilities

Bytheway, B., Bacigalupo, V., Bornat, J., Johnson, J., Spurr, S. (1995) *Ageism*, Buckingham, Open University Press

Carnaby, S. (ed.) (2002) *Learning Disability Today: Key Issues for Providers, Managers, Practitioners and Users*, Brighton, Pavilion

Department of Health (2000) *Care Standards Act*, London, HMSO

Department of Health (2000) *No Secrets*, London, HMSO

Department of Health (2000) *National Minimum Standards for Care Homes*, London, HMSO

Eastman, M. (1994) *Old Age Abuse: A New Perspective*, London, Chapman and Hall/Age Concern

Humphries, S. and Gordon, P. (1992) *Out of Sight*, Plymouth, Northcote House

King's College London and National Centre for Social Research (2006) *UK Study of Abuse and Neglect of Older People*, (for Comic Relief / Department of Health, http://www.kcl.ac.uk

Law Commission (1995) *Mental Incapacity*, London, HMSO

Pritchard, J. (ed.) (2001) *Good Practice with Vulnerable Adults*, London, Jessica Kingsley

Sharkey, P. (2000) *The Essentials of Community Care*, Basingstoke, Macmillan

Williams, J. (2001) Critical Commentaries: Confidence *British Journal of Social Work* Vol. 31(4), pp. 631–32

Wilton, T. (2000) *Sexualities in Health and Social Care: A Textbook*, Buckingham, Open University Press

Useful websites

Action on Elder Abuse: www.elderabuse.org.uk

Ann Craft Trust: www.anncrafttrust.org.uk

British Institute of Human Rights: www.bihr.org

Mental Health Foundation: www.mentalhealth.org.uk

NHS overview of services and facilities across the UK: www.nhs.uk/servicedirectories

NHS: www.nhs.uk

The Equality and Human Rights Commission: www.equalityhumanrights.com

The Home Office (central government): www.homeoffice.gov.uk

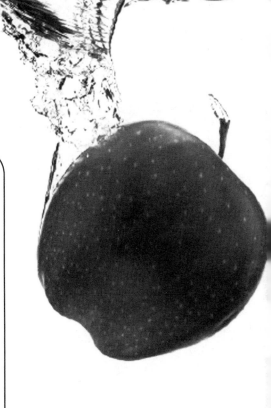

CHAPTER 10

Health education and promoting well-being

Introduction

The aim of this unit is to introduce the principles of **health education**, the approaches used, and to look at health education campaigns. Health education is a central component of health promotion, which in turn is a major part of public health.

Health education could be described as any activity that promotes health-related learning and therefore brings about some relatively permanent change in the thinking or behaviour of individuals. You will initially consider a range of different approaches to health education, including the role of the mass media and social marketing. You will then examine different models of behaviour change, relating these to the social and economic context.

Finally, you will gain understanding of health education campaigns, by actively planning, designing, implementing and evaluating a small-scale campaign.

This unit provides opportunities for you to participate in 'hands-on' planning, designing, implementing and evaluating health education campaigns.

Key learning outcomes for this section are that you will:

- understand different approaches to health education
- understand models of behaviour change
- know how to plan a health education campaign.

This chapter covers a broad range of issues which relate to the promotion of health. It opens by considering the various perspectives on health including the biomedical model and the social model, comparing these with your own understanding of health and other lay viewpoints. It explores the factors which underpin good health before moving on to consider differing types of health promotion activity including primary, secondary and tertiary prevention.

During the course of this chapter we will use case studies to illustrate how health promotion relates to them in practice. These case studies include:

Anne, a practice nurse, who works in a local GP practice with a practice list size of 2,500 people. She works within the Primary Health Care Team which is a mixture of people employed by different organisations but based together in the practice including GPs, health visitors, nursery nurses, treatment nurses, pharmacists, dieticians, administrative and reception staff and many others who are not based with the team but work alongside it, for example, the adult social care worker.

Anne is involved in almost every aspect of patient care and treatment, undertaking such tasks as:

- treating small injuries
- helping with minor operations carried out under local anaesthetic
- health screening
- family planning

- running **vaccination** programmes (e.g. against flu)
- running programmes to help people to stop smoking, reduce their alcohol consumption, lose weight, etc.

Margaret, a domiciliary care worker, who works with older people, and is employed by a private agency. The agency also employs other carers to work with children, people with learning disabilities, people with mental health problems or people with physical disabilities. Home care workers offer emotional and practical support in the home, to help people regain confidence and skills as they build up strength after hospital discharge, accidents or illness. Margaret's role involves the provision of flexible support services for family carers and service users including emotional and social support, listening and befriending, all of which help people achieve greater independence, enabling them to live at home as long as possible.

Sometimes Margaret helps with day-to-day activities, such as preparation of meals, going to the shops, paying bills, writing letters and keeping in touch with family and friends. Other times, she helps people to pursue leisure or educational activities that they would not normally be able to do.

Brian, an Occupational Therapist, who is employed by the local **Primary Care Trust** (PCT). He helps people who have permanent and substantial physical disabilities to be more independent in a range of activities, such as personal care (getting washed and dressed), and can advise on ways to improve mobility and help with improving capacity to carry out simple day-to-day tasks like preparing meals, getting in and out of bed and managing steps and stairs.

Brian works with service users with learning difficulties, trying to maximise their capacity to live independently. Other members of his team work with people with mental health problems or physical disabilities. Brian works across a range of age groups providing support to:

- reduce anxiety, helping people raise their confidence and help to manage their **disability**
- help to get appropriate support and assisting people to contact other relevant agencies or organisations
- provide information for people willing and able to fund their own adaptations or equipment

- assist carers to continue to maintain their caring responsibilities.

Occupational therapists (OTs) visit you at home to look at the practical difficulties you have and work with you to identify your needs through an assessment of needs.

Concepts of health and health promotion

Models of health

Lay models of health

The term 'lay' refers to a non-professional viewpoint; these are the models of health held by the public at large (as summarised in the table below by Stainton Rogers) as opposed to professionally or scientifically phrased perspectives. To the public, the term healthy is usually associated with not being ill; it is a negative perspective – one which is best summarised as not knowing what you had till you lost it. More positive perspectives might talk about 'building up your strength', 'being on good form' or 'having resistance to infections', aspects of physical health which emphasise the need for strength and robustness for everyday life.

So we can see that our notion of what being healthy means varies widely and is shaped by our experiences, knowledge, values and expectations as well as what others expect us to do.

Medical model of health

The biomedical model is probably the most widely known model of health. The **medical model** was first developed in the early part of the nineteenth century and has come to dominate all others in the Western

The body as a machine	Has strong links to the medical model of health in that it sees illness as a matter of biological fact and scientific medicine as the natural type of treatment for any illness.
Inequality of access	As above this perspective is rooted in a reliance on modern medicine to cure illness but is less accepting because of an awareness that there are great inequalities of access to treatment.
The health promotion account	This model emphasises the importance of a healthy lifestyle and personal responsibility; for example, if you are overweight it is simply a matter of your own choice of diet and lack of exercise which has led to this.
God's power	Health is viewed as part of spirituality – a feature of righteous living and spiritual wholeness. This might be seen as abstinence from alcohol consumption because it is an impure substance which is not only unholy but also can lead to immoral activity.
Body under siege	The person exists in a sea of challenges to their health, which might be communicable diseases, such as colds and flu, or stress at work.
Cultural critique of medicine	Science and the medical model on which healthcare is based can oppress certain groups (that is, they can take away their rights to self determination); this could be the way healthcare manages pregnancy as an example of oppressive practice against women or the treatment of minority ethnic groups.
Robust individualism	Best summarised as 'It's my life and I will do with it what I choose'.
Will power	Suggests that we all have a moral responsibility to remain healthy. This relies on strong will power to manage our health e.g. to eat the right things, take regular exercise and drink alcohol in moderation.

Lay models of health (after Stainton Rogers from L. Jones and M. Sidell, 1997, The Challenge of Promoting Health – Exploration and Action)

What does being healthy mean to you?

1 In Column 1, tick any statements which seem to you to be important aspects of your health.
2 In Column 2, tick the six statements which are the most important aspects of being healthy to you.
3 In Column 3, rank these six in order of importance - put '1' by the most important, '2' by the next most important and so on down to '6'.

	For me, being healthy involves:	1	2	3
1	Enjoying being with my family and friends			
2	Living to be a ripe old age			
3	Feeling happy most of the time			
4	Being able to run when I need to (e.g. for a bus) without being out of breath			
5	Having a job			
6	Being able to get down to making decisions			
7	Hardly ever taking tablets or medicines			
8	Being the ideal weight for my height			
9	Taking part in lots of sport			
10	Feeling at peace with myself			
11	Never smoking			
12	Having clear skin, bright eyes and shiny hair			
13	Never suffering from anything worse than a cold, flu or stomach upset			
14	Not getting things confused or out of proportion and assessing situations realistically			
15	Being able to adapt easily to changes in my life such as moving house, new job and so on			
16	Feeling glad to be alive			
17	Drinking moderate amounts of alcohol or none at all			
18	Enjoying my work without much stress or strain			
19	Having all the parts of my body in good working order			
20	Getting on well with other people most of the time			
21	Eating the 'right' foods			
22	Enjoying some form of relaxation/recreation			
23	Hardly ever going to the doctor			

When you have finished this exercise ask yourself ...

- Was this what I expected to find?
- Which of the lay perspectives from the previous table can I see in my own answers?
- How might the outcome vary if I were to complete this when I was 20 or 40 years older?
- How might someone with a physical disability have answered?
- How might someone living on benefits have answered?

world. Its history lies in the developing understanding of how the various parts of the body might work together to ensure good health. This scientific view of health and body functioning is summarised by Jones.

The medical model of health – Jones 1994

- Health is predominantly viewed as the absence of disease.
- Health services are geared towards the treating of the sick.
- A high value is placed on specialist medical services.

- Doctors and other qualified experts diagnose and sanction treatment.
- The main purpose of health services is curative – to get people back to work.
- Disease and illness are explained by biological science.
- It is based in the understanding of how diseases arise, emphasising risk factors.
- A high value is placed on scientific research methodology.
- Quantitative scientific evidence is generally given higher value than lay or qualitative evidence.

Social model of health

Although the biomedical model has contributed greatly to increases in life expectancy, public health measures based on the social model of health have contributed most to the decline in mortality during the twentieth century.

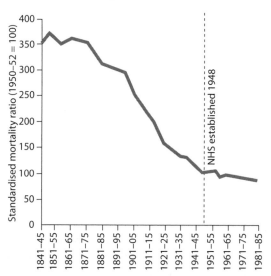

The standardised mortality ratio (SMR) is an index which allows for differences in age structure. Values above 100 indicate higher mortality than in 1950–52 and values below 100 indicate lower mortality.   (Source: OPCS)

Figure 10.1 Mortality trends, 1841–1985, England and Wales

REFLECT

Consider the information given to you in the graph above and think about the changing environmental impact over the last hundred years. Which model of health do you think this supports? Why do you think this?

A social model of health emphasises that to improve health it is necessary to address the origins of ill-health. These are the social conditions, which make ill-health more prevalent in some groups than others. The underlying philosophy is that the health differences between individuals and social groups are the result of a complex mixture of behavioural, structural, material and cultural factors which together impact on health. The social model has strong links to the different lay models of health because it recognises that people often have firmly-held views about their own health, which are sometimes at odds with those of professionals. For example, the need to address damp conditions in housing and its link to childhood asthma might be prioritised by people living in those conditions, as opposed to the need to tackle parental smoking prioritised by health services.

A holistic concept of health

One of the most widely known definitions of health is the 1948 **World Health Organization** (WHO) definition: 'A state of complete physical, mental and social well-being'. However, this illustrates the difficulty in attempting to define health when you consider two alternative definitions shown below and the range of broad dimensions to health:

- **physical health** – concerned with body mechanics
- **mental health** – the ability to think clearly and coherently, strongly allied to ...
- **emotional health** – the ability to recognise emotions and express them appropriately. The ability to cope with potentially damaging aspects of emotional health such as stress, depression, anxiety and tension
- **social health** – the ability to make and maintain relationships with others
- **spiritual health** – can be about personal creeds, principled behaviour, achieving peace of mind or religious beliefs and practices
- **societal health** – wider societal impact on our own individual health, for example, the impact of racism on people from a minority ethnic culture, the impact on women of living in a patriarchal society and the impact of living under political oppression.

It is important to recognise that these are not alternative models of health but different dimensions of one health; together they build a holistic concept of health which embraces all the various aspects discussed previously.

Definitions of health

With such a range of dimensions to health it is inevitable that there are many definitions of health.

> A satisfactory adjustment of the individual to the environment.
>
> (Royal College of General Practitioners, 1972)

> By health I mean the power to live a full adult, living, breathing life in close contact with what I love. I want to be all I am capable of becoming.
>
> (Katherine Mansfield)

> The extent to which an individual or group is able on the one hand, to realise aspirations and satisfy needs and on the other hand, to change or cope with the environment. Health is therefore seen as a resource for everyday life, not the objective of living: it is a positive concept emphasising social and personal resources as well as physical capabilities.
>
> (World Health Organization, 1984)

Factors affecting health

Margaret Whitehead mapped the influences on health in the following diagram, reflecting the range of influences which a social model will recognise:

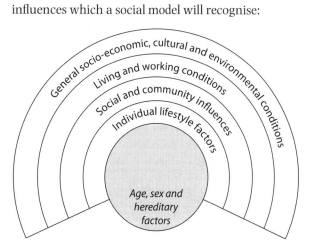

Figure 10.2 The Dahlgren/Whitehead model (1991) showing the underpinning influences of health inequalities

If we base our investigation of health promotion on this model of health, then it is necessary to consider the environmental influences on health. These factors would include social class, gender, race, unemployment, age, disability and lifestyle.

Socio-economic factors affecting health

By now you will have begun to recognise the range of factors which together impact on someone's health; in this section we explore some of these in more detail.

Social class

Social class has long been used as the method of measuring and monitoring health inequalities. Since the Black Report of 1988, it has been clearly identified and acknowledged that those from the lowest social groupings experience the poorest health in society. Current research suggests that the countries with the smallest income *differences* – rather than the richest countries – have the best health status. Where income differences remain great, as in the UK, health inequalities will persist. For example:

- children in the lowest social class are five times more likely to die from an accident than those in the top social class
- someone in the lowest social class is three times more likely to experience a stroke than someone in the highest class
- infant mortality rates are highest amongst the lowest social groups
- the difference in life expectancy between a man from one of the most affluent areas in this country and a man living in Manchester is six years.

Age

As might be expected, as people get older they are more likely to experience a wide range of illnesses. The health inequalities recorded above remain in the older generations but are often compounded by the loss of income that comes with retirement. This significantly increases the proportion of the population who are living on benefits as compared to other age groups in the population. Another factor is the longer lifespan of women, which means that because women make up a higher proportion of the older population there are often higher rates of illnesses specifically associated with women.

Culture

One of the most powerful influences on our health is the culture we are raised in. Culture can mean many things including our ethnicity, the region we live in, religious beliefs and so on, but probably the most important cultural influence is our family. The family can play a significant part in determining our health status through its key role in our socialisation, i.e. the types of behaviours we are raised to accept as normal. The health behaviours of adults in key positions in the family can have a major impact on the health of young people.

Gender

Men and women have widely differing patterns of ill-health. In the main this can be best summarised by saying that men suffer a higher rate of early mortality (deaths) while women experience higher rates of morbidity (illness). There are many specific examples which illustrate these points and they are linked to physiological, psychological and other aspects of gender characteristics influenced by the differing roles that the two genders are expected to adopt by society at large. Typically, men are less likely to access routine screening and other forms of health service, while women – who are seen as the main carers in the family – are more able to do so and therefore may be identifying potential health problems earlier. The results can be seen in the following patterns:

- under the age of 65 men are 3.5 times more likely to die of coronary heart disease
- suicide is twice as common in men as in women
- women experience more accidents in the home or garden while men experience more accidents in the workplace or sports activities.

Sexuality

Sexuality is a central aspect of being human. It encompasses sex, gender identities and roles, sexual orientation, eroticism, pleasure, intimacy and reproduction. Sexuality is experienced and expressed in thoughts, fantasies, desires, beliefs, attitudes, values, behaviours, roles and relationships. While sexuality can include all of these dimensions, not all of them are always experienced or expressed. A person's sexuality can be influenced by many factors, including biological, psychological, social, economic, political and religious factors and many other issues.

Encompassing such a range of facets it is inevitable that sexuality has a major part to play in influencing health. For example:

- young gay men have the highest rate of suicide of all groups, a situation which is directly related to the prejudice and discrimination about their sexuality
- some faith-based schools will not allow discussion of contraception and sex outside marriage because it breaches their faith-based guidelines

CASE STUDY

Challenging homophobia

John is employed by the local PCT as an outreach worker for the local gay community. His work specifically focuses on the needs of young gay men because of their high risk of suicide, but his work also encompasses other aspects of health such as substance use, smoking and sexual health. His work includes direct support for young gay men through a local community group, one-to-one client support and the creation of a local helpline which volunteers now help to staff.

Another aspect to John's role is to challenge organisational homophobia; for example, to encourage schools to challenge homophobic bullying through the development of appropriate policies coupled with training for staff on how to recognise homophobic bullying and how to challenge it appropriately. National research demonstrates that experience of homophobia and bullying at school is a significant contributor to the high rate of suicides in young gay men.

Questions

1 What examples of homophobia do you see in your college? These might be aimed at someone in particular or at gay people generally.
2 What negative comments or 'put downs' do people use that are about sexuality?
3 If a gay person hears these comments how do you think it might make them feel:
 – about themselves?
 – the people around them?
4 How might these comments contribute to clients feeling uneasy about accessing the service John provides?

- sexuality has strong political ties; for example, the introduction of section 28 of the Local Government Act 1988 that prohibits **local authorities** 'promoting homosexuality by publishing material, or by promoting the teaching in state schools of the acceptability of homosexuality as a "pretended family relationship". This prevents any discussion of the health needs of gay and lesbian young people in schools.

Income and expenditure

Disposable income has a clear link to health status. The poorest people in England are over 10 times more likely to die in their fifties than richer people – despite receiving similar healthcare. **Obesity** and smoking, two of the leading causes of preventable death, are more common in the lower economic groups. People are more likely to smoke if:

- they have no educational qualifications
- they live in rented accommodation
- they do not have a car and/or phone
- the adults in the household are traditionally involved in manual labour
- they live on means-tested benefits.

In a recent survey, two-thirds of respondents agreed that tackling poverty would be the most effective means of preventing disease and improving health. Not surprisingly, people in the lowest socio-economic groups (67 per cent) and the socially excluded (71 per cent) are more likely to agree than people in the higher socio-economic groups.

Employment status

For the vast majority of people, being unemployed leads to significantly poorer health. The unemployed have higher levels of depression, suicide and self-harm and a significantly increased risk of morbidity and mortality. Men unemployed at both census dates in 1971 and 1981 had mortality rates twice those of the rest of other men in that age range and those men who were unemployed at one census date had an excess mortality rate of 27 per cent.

Housing

Public health campaigners have been advocating for improvements in housing to better the public's health since the middle of the nineteenth century. For example, Edwin Chadwick's 'Report on an inquiry into the sanitary conditions of the labouring population of Great Britain' (1842) resulted in the first national Public Health Act (1848).

The link between housing and health remains true to this day. The Office for National Statistics Longitudinal Study shows that between 1971 and 1981 age-standardised mortality rates for social tenants (those in rented accommodation) were 25 per cent higher than for owner-occupiers. Although death rates have declined since that time the gap between these groups has widened, with owner-occupiers seeing greater reductions in death rates than those living in rented accommodation.

Diet and health

Nutrition has become a high-profile health issue, particularly in light of the way in which obesity has become so important on the health agenda (as illustrated by its prominence in 'Choosing health'). This is particularly because of startling recent trends in young children where among 3 to 4-year-olds there has been a 60 per cent increase in the prevalence of being overweight and a 70 per cent increase in rates of obesity. In addition to this, most adults in England are now overweight and one in five (around 8 million) are obese (Body Mass Index in excess of 30) with 30,000 deaths a year linked to

ACTIVITY

Tackling obesity is probably the single biggest public health challenge facing the country at the moment. As we saw earlier the 'will power' lay perspective would probably see this as simply a case of people not managing their own diet and level of activity effectively. But how real is that perception? To understand the broader societal issues which underpin the current obesity crisis, try to assess how each of the following might contribute to the current rising rates of obesity:

- fears about safety
- work and specifically the work–life balance
- income, or personal wealth
- transport and access to services
- planning and design of local community facilities/commercial sector
- English culture.

obesity at an estimated cost to the NHS of £500m a year.

Body Mass Index (BMI)

BMI is a reliable indicator of total body fat, which is related to the risk of disease and death. Body Mass Index can be calculated using weight and height with this equation.

$$BMI = \frac{\text{Weight in kilograms}}{\text{(Height in metres) x (Height in metres)}}$$

The score is valid for both men and women but it does have limits: it may *overestimate* body fat in athletes and others who have a muscular build and it may *underestimate* body fat in older persons and others who have lost muscle mass. Use this information to calculate your own body mass index (height in metres divided by height in metres squared).

Where does this place you in the ranges shown below?

	BMI
Underweight	Below 18.5
Normal	18.5 – 24.9
Overweight	25.0 – 29.9
Obese	30.0 and above

Obesity is a major public health concern today, contributing substantially to type 2 diabetes, coronary heart disease, hypertension, depression, cancers, high blood pressure and strokes

As well as its role in tackling obesity, diet also has a major part to play in managing the current trends in **cancer** where over the past 25 years the incidence of all cancers has risen by 8 per cent in men and 17 per cent in women. For example, up to 80 per cent of bowel and breast cancer may be preventable by dietary change.

Current recommendations are that everyone should eat at least five portions of a variety of fruit and vegetables each day, to reduce the risks of cancer and coronary heart disease and many other chronic diseases. Yet average fruit and vegetable consumption among the population in England is currently less than three portions a day.

The government-led '5 A DAY' programme aims to increase fruit and vegetable consumption by:

- raising awareness of the health benefits
- improving access to fruit and vegetables through targeted action.

The 5 A DAY programme has five strands which are underpinned by an evaluation and monitoring programme:

- National School Fruit Scheme
- local 5 A DAY initiatives
- national/local partners – government health consumer groups
- communications programme including 5 A DAY logo
- work with industry – producers, caterers, retailers.

Mass media

The mass media has an increasingly important role to play, both in informing people about current health issues but also in influencing attitudes to those issues. Broadsheet newspapers (like *The Times*, the *Independent* and the *Guardian*) tend to adopt a more factual approach to health issues, for example:

- *Organic food is healthier* – 29 Oct 2007
- *Male fertility at risk from chlamydia* – 15 Oct 2007
- *Confusion over advice on alcohol for pregnant women* – 11 Oct 2007
- *Methadone linked to big rise in Scottish drug deaths* – 8 Oct 2007

A selection of the news headlines from one newspaper alone (as above from the *Guardian*) shows the range of health issues they are routinely inviting the public to consider. This is a relatively factual approach to the reporting of health information which contrasts markedly with the style adopted by the so-called 'red tops' such as the *Sun*, *Star* and *Mirror*.

The *Sun*:

- *Health warning on all booze* – Tuesday, 29 May, 2007
- *Cig addicts 'health tax'* – Tuesday, 24 September, 2002

This type of reporting is more opinion forming or opinion driven, in that it attempts to shape public opinion as opposed to inform or reflect opinion which is already reasonably well formed. The tone of

headline may reflect the degree of agreement or disagreement with the health information/topic. This style of reporting can have a serious impact on health, as shown below in the box below left on the MMR vaccine.

REFLECT

What examples of health information/campaigning can you find in the printed media? Collect any examples in your own newspaper and magazines over a seven-day period. This exercise may be more effective if you work with others to maximise the number of different papers and magazines you can cover.

What examples did you find which were:

- paid-for advertising?
- unpaid coverage of new information?
- news coverage of new services/health-related projects?

What are the messages being conveyed in these pieces?

Did you find any examples of the same information presented differently in various papers and magazines?

What problems do you think this might present for the health promoter seeking media coverage?

MMR vaccine and the media

The role of the media in influencing health patterns has been most graphically illustrated through coverage of concerns about the safety of the measles, mumps and rubella (MMR) vaccine. A research paper by Andrew Wakefield, suggesting that MMR vaccination in young children might be linked to autism, sparked a media frenzy which gave considerable coverage to his viewpoint – despite findings from many other researchers providing no support for the MMR-associated form of autism. However, findings from a tracking survey of mothers with children aged 0-2 years found that 8 per cent considered the **MMR vaccine** a greater risk than the diseases it protects against and that 20 per cent considered the vaccine to have a moderate or high risk of side effects. Worryingly, the survey also showed that 67 per cent of people knew that some scientists had linked the MMR vaccine with autism – however, they also thought that the evidence in favour of such a link was evenly balanced, or that the evidence even favoured a link. The long-term media coverage of controversy over the vaccine appears to have led the public to associate MMR and autism, despite the overwhelming evidence to the contrary.

The impact of the media story continues today with MMR vaccinations still only at 86 per cent in June 2006 and as low as 73 per cent in London; this is some way short of the 95 per cent required to prevent an outbreak.

Race and discrimination

We have already seen how prejudice and discrimination can lead to higher rates of suicide in young gay men but Black and Minority Ethnic (BME) groups also experience poorer health due to prejudice and discrimination. BME groups experience higher mortality from a range of diseases such as diabetes, liver cancer, tuberculosis, stroke and heart disease. Establishing the cause of these variations has proved difficult; while interventions have tended to concentrate on cultural practices, this has ignored the compounding factors of poverty and low employment levels in these groups. So we discover that 67 per cent of people from ethnic minority backgrounds live in deprived areas which receive targeted neighbourhood renewal funding, compared with 40 per cent of the total population, i.e. people from ethnic minorities are more likely to live in poor/disadvantaged communities. The only possible explanation for this situation is one which acknowledges that racism must also play a part as a causative factor in leading to a higher-than-average experience of poverty and unemployment in these groups and hence contributing to their poorer health status.

Education

It is now well established that educational success is associated with better health. There are a number of possible explanations for this linkage.

- Educational success is linked to higher earnings, higher socio-economic status and lower rates of unemployment. Higher income tends to allow for a healthier lifestyle through being able to afford more nutritious but more expensive food, as well as better housing and holidays.
- Studies suggest that people with more years of education and higher level qualifications tend to exercise more, eat more nutritious and healthier diets, and smoke less.
- Education enables individuals to learn problem solving skills, a sense of purpose and future, and social competence, which instils in individuals a greater sense of belief in their ability to cope with adversity.

In general, children from low-income households go on to leave full-time education much earlier, and with fewer formal qualifications than their more affluent counterparts. Of all children born in 1970, for example, some 24 per cent failed to achieve any GCSEs or equivalent by the age of 30, while 23 per

cent went on to get a degree. Among children from low-income households, however, only 11 per cent went on to get a degree and 38 per cent achieved no formal qualifications.

Access to services

An understanding of the healthcare professional/ patient relationship can help explain the way in which people engage with local health services. It is suggested that this relationship is often at its least effective in the most disadvantaged communities. In 1994 Baldock and Ungerson attempted to summarise people's attitudes to community care services using a simple model which described four roles that people can adopt when services are made available to them in a free market format.

Consumers: People who expect nothing from the state and set out to arrange the necessary care by buying it themselves. They believe that using the market in this way gives them control and autonomy, much like buying a car or any other kind of consumer goods. These people know about services but prefer to purchase their own care for a variety of reasons including convenience, perceived quality, etc.

Privatists: These people have learned to manage alone. Adapting to being cared for in later life can mean leaving the family home and increased dependency, which they find hard to come to terms with because it means having to ask for help. They can become isolated and fail to access the necessary healthcare. Generally they do least well of the four in accessing services.

Welfarists: These people believe in the welfare state and their right to use it; they expect and demand their rights to the relevant services. They have both the understanding and the know-how to make sure they get the most from the system and use it effectively to access both public and voluntary provision.

Clientists: They accept passively what they are offered without demanding or expecting more. Neither do they expect services to be flexible and able to respond to their specific needs. This is commonly seen in older people and low-income groups, explaining how people in disadvantaged communities will often accept the poor state of their local health services and not challenge and demand better provision.

> ## REFLECT
>
> In recent years there has been a shift in attitude towards higher education, away from this being only available to an intellectual elite and towards it being an entitlement for all.
>
> Has your own family a history of accessing higher education or are you one of the first to do so?
>
> What advantages do you think accessing higher education might mean for you?
>
> How does your experience contrast with people who you know who haven't gone on to access higher education?

This model is just that – a model; it is a means of helping us understand how real world systems operate. It does not mean that people have to rigidly fit one role; they may move between roles dependent upon their circumstances. However, it will explain why people will have different experiences of using the same health services and how this can contribute to local health inequalities.

ACTIVITY

Margaret, the care worker, meets many different types of clients on a day-to-day basis. How might her relationship with her clients change, depending upon the way they present to services? Use Baldock and Ungerson's model to think about how each of the different roles might alter her relationship. For each in turn consider the main characteristics of the client's view of services and then describe how this might then appear in terms of a working relationship between Margaret and the client.

KNOWLEDGE CHECK

1 Using the lay models of health describe how each might apply to a person who smokes.
2 What are the main characteristics of the biomedical model of health?
3 Name five aspects of a holistic model of health.
4 List three facts which illustrate how social class is linked to health status.
5 How do smoking trends illustrate the link between income and health?
6 What are the main disorders linked to obesity?
7 List three facts which illustrate how educational attainment is linked to health status.
8 Summarise the main features of the Baldock and Ungerson model of service use in a free market economy.

Preventive measures and models

Just as there are many models of health so too there are many models of health promotion. One of the most widely accepted is that suggested by Tannahill (from Naidoo & Wills, 2000), who talks about three overlapping and related areas of activity.

- **Health education** – communication to improve health and prevent ill-health by improving people's knowledge about their health, and to change their attitudes to aspects of their health. The possibilities for health education to make a difference can be seen in the decline in smoking rates seen over the latter years of the last century.
- **Health protection** – population measures to safeguard health, for example, through legislation, financial or social means. This might include legislation to govern health and safety at work or food hygiene, and using taxation policy to reduce smoking levels or car use, by raising the price of cigarettes or petrol.
- **Prevention** – reducing or avoiding the risks of diseases and ill-health primarily through medical 'interventions'. There are several approaches and levels within which health promotion activity can take place; these are dealt with in more detail in the next section.

Tannahill's model emphasises the breadth of activities that can be included in the term health promotion, and the interconnectedness of the various spheres of activity.

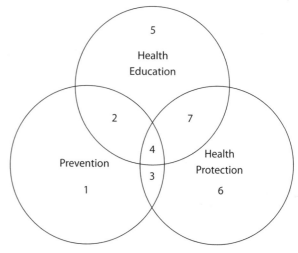

Figure 10.3 Tannahill's model of health promotion (Naidoo & Wills, 2000)

The following table illustrates the wide variety of activities that can be classed as health promoting, from those which operate at an individual level to those which depend upon national government action.

1	Preventive services	Immunisation, cervical screening, developmental surveillance
2	Preventive health education	Substance use education in schools
3	Preventive health protection	Fluoridation of water supplies
4	Health education for preventive health education	Lobbying for fluoridation or seat belt legislation
5	Positive health education	Work with young people to develop positive self-esteem
6	Positive health protection	Smoking bans in public places
7	Health education aimed at positive health protection	Lobbying for a ban on tobacco advertising or smoking bans in pubs

Different health-promoting activities

Health education

This is usually defined as the process of giving information and advice and of facilitating the development of knowledge and skills in order to change behaviour. Health educators will include a wide range of professionals, including teachers, social workers, practice nurses, health visitors, leisure centre staff and so on; some of these are dealt with in more detail later in this section. In some cases this is an acknowledged part of their role; for example, in health visiting and practice nursing it is accepted that part of the role is to work one-to-one with people to improve their knowledge and skills – to enable them to improve their own health. However, in some cases the potential for a health promotion role may not be so easily recognised. For example, a community beat officer walking the local streets will frequently come across groups of young people who might be smoking and/or intoxicated; this clearly presents a health promoting opportunity that they may not appreciate or be trained to deal with effectively.

There are also more developed models of health education, which see it as being about critical consciousness raising (among key policy makers and members of the community), testing values and attitudes of these people and empowering communities to address local health issues. In this model it also operates as a two-way process, informing policy makers as well (as members of the local community), raising their appreciation of the concerns of local people.

In this type of model the service user is not an empty vessel waiting to be filled with the right health knowledge – that is, someone who will simply change their behaviour once they are in receipt of the right knowledge or skill. Health education is fraught with ethical considerations. Two of the most important issues here would be the service user's right to self-determination and the need to remain non-judgemental. **Ethics** are important for health educators; as they draw out the service user's needs and work with them towards an informed choice, this may turn out to be a health-damaging choice for the service user. Can the professional now accept and respect that decision, and not coerce or persuade them to adopt a different choice, when that would be neither effective nor ethical? Clearly health education can present serious challenges to the educator.

The danger with health education activity is that health promoters become fixed on the goal of improved medical or physical health to the detriment of other aspects of holistic health. It can be too easy for professionals to adopt a judgemental approach, deciding what is best for the individual to the exclusion of that person's right to self-autonomy. It is important to remember that empowering people is an integral part of effective and ethical health promotion work.

In order to enable health promoters to make ethical judgements about the work they undertake, the following questions should be considered.

- Will the service user be able to choose freely for themselves?
- Will I be respecting their decision, whether or not I approve of it?
- Will I be non-discriminatory – respecting all people equally?
- Will I be serving the more basic needs before addressing other wants?
- Will I be doing good and preventing harm?
- Will I be telling the truth?
- Will I be minimising harm in the long term?
- Will I be able to honour promises and agreements I make?

These points are as applicable for a one-to-one service user/professional scenario as for a planner considering alterations to local roads in a housing estate. Here, for example, they might ask whether they have adequately involved the local people in the decision-making process and if they have respected their input, not valuing it differently from that of other professionals.

An occupational therapist works with clients in their own homes

Another example might be a midwife discussing smoking with a pregnant woman; here the midwife has considerable knowledge about the potential damage to the unborn child and the possibility of further health damage if the mother continues to smoke after the birth. However, to be an ethical health promoter the midwife must respect the service user's right to choose whether to continue smoking and not allow the service user's decision to continue smoking (should that be the case) to change the relationship.

CASE STUDY

Helping with rehabilitation

As an OT, Brian often has to work with clients who have suffered severely disabling accidents. He can see the challenges they face to rehabilitate their lives but observes that some make health choices which may be compromising their chance of achieving the best rehabilitation possible, for example, through excessive alcohol use or smoking. Imagine you are Brian working with a patient who has been severely disabled after a car crash and whom you have concerns about due to their alcohol consumption.

Questions

1 Think of three things you would most wish to convey to the person.
2 What things would you have to be mindful of when having this discussion?
3 Would having this conversation in the person's own home present any difficulties/opportunities for you?
4 How would you justify having this conversation with your patient?

This task is further complicated by the changing nature of health messages as the knowledge base for health education develops. This can lead to confusion within the general population, for example, the change in alcohol safe drinking limits recently moved from a weekly guidance to daily levels to reflect the shift towards binge drinking patterns.

The Department of Health advises that:

- men should not drink more than 3–4 units of alcohol per day

- women should drink no more than 2–3 units of alcohol per day.

Daily benchmarks apply whether you drink every day, once or twice a week, or occasionally.

However, research has suggested that the majority of health professionals are not clear what advice to give people and are not aware of the change.

Prevention

It is possible to see health promotion as solely focusing on preventing people from becoming ill in the first place. This is indeed an important part of the span of health promotion but it also includes two other categories of health promoting activity which deal with people who are already ill in some way. These three tiers of health promotion activity are outlined as follows.

Primary prevention

This is an attempt to eliminate the possibility of getting a disease; the childhood immunisation programme would be an example of a health protection activity under this heading. Other examples here would include smoking education as part of personal and social health education in schools, or leaflets and posters for use in promoting healthy eating.

Secondary prevention

This addresses those people identified as being in the early stages of a disease, usually through early detection of symptoms. Action here focuses on addressing the underlying causes to alleviate any further symptoms. Examples here might be action to address raised blood pressure taken by a doctor who identified those symptoms as part of a routine check-up for a patient. This action might be drug therapy but could also be a referral on to a physical activity scheme for promoting regular exercise, organised in collaboration with the local leisure services departments (usually referred to as an 'exercise on prescription' scheme).

What do people gain from support groups that they can't get from one-to-one counselling? What do one-to-one sessions provide that groups cannot? How do you think the two can complement each other?

This sort of scheme might also be used for people who are overweight or for people with mild depression. Therefore a range of secondary prevention issues can be addressed through one scheme. Alternatively, a 'stop smoking' group would be a secondary prevention initiative for someone who is already suffering from respiratory problems such as repeated chest infections, bronchitis and so on. Anne, in her role as a practice nurse, offers both one-to-one support and regularly runs a 'stop smoking' support group for patients within her practice.

The following are examples of tertiary prevention services:

- an exercise on prescription scheme
- a coronary rehabilitation scheme
- a stroke rehabilitation service
- a community drugs service.

1 Find out if you have any of these services operating in your area.
2 If you were a potential service user, how would you gain access to the service? What sources of information did you use to find about them?
3 What do they offer for the people using them?

Tertiary prevention

This refers to the control and reduction (as far as possible) of an already established disease. This is not easily distinguishable from medical care but it is possible to consider issues such as increasing the capacity of the individual to manage their condition and their own health. This might refer to supporting and enabling people with a history of heart attacks to regain their confidence to live a more fulfilling life, in control of their own destiny as far as is possible. It could also apply to someone suffering from Parkinson's disease being supported in learning about and managing their condition as independently as possible. A more common and less obvious example might be the provision of dentures to people who have had teeth extracted.

Approaches to health promotion

The term *health promotion* covers a wide range of different activities, all of which have a part to play in promoting health. None of these differing approaches is essentially the right way – they are simply different aspects which complement each other. The balance between them is very much a choice based on personal perspectives, influenced by our own life experience, personal beliefs and values, as illustrated in the wide range of differing lay perspectives on health. Ewles and Simnett (1999) characterise these differing approaches into broad headings which are summarised in the table below.

Model	Aim	Health promotion activity	Factors influencing choice of this model
Medical model (Interventionist)	Freedom from medically defined disease and disability To remain free from diseases associated with smoking, e.g. lung and heart diseases	Using a medical treatment to either prevent or reduce the effects of ill-health Encourage people to seek early detection and treatment of smoking-related disorders	Can be dependent upon the availability of an effective screening process and the necessary treatment Some screening processes remain imprecise and may register false negatives or positives Screening programmes can be very costly. If the condition is identified it doesn't necessarily mean it can be treated effectively
Behaviourist (Preventive/ Persuasive)	Promote individual behaviours in the population which keep people free from disease Changing people's smoking behaviour	Encourage adoption of 'healthier' lifestyle by changing attitude and therefore behaviour Persuade people either not to start smoking or, where they have started, to stop	Sounds sensible but evidence suggests this works best with educated middle and upper class social groups who respond to these health messages more readily. Lower socio-economic groups respond less well and as a result stop smoking messages have actually increased smoking-related health inequalities as they reduce smoking in middle classes but fail to do so in lower groups
Educationalist (Informative)	Provide people with the necessary knowledge and skills to enable them to make well-informed decisions To develop people's understanding of the effects of smoking on health and their decision making skills	Educational activity to disseminate information about health and maintenance of good health Development of skills required for healthy living Giving information to service users about the effects of smoking Developing their skills in quitting smoking or resisting enticement to start smoking	As above Skills development only works with those who have already committed to change; any attempt to engage people who have not decided to change their lifestyle is doomed to failure

Model	Aim	Health promotion activity	Factors influencing choice of this model
Service user-centred (empowerment)	Working on health issues on the service user's terms, not your own	Allowing the service user to identify health issues, choices and actions which they choose, thereby empowering the service user *Here the smoking issue would only arise if the service user selected it. Any further discussion would be led by the service user's willingness to address the topic*	Responding to the cues of the patient or client would be good practice in any educational approach. There is evidence that the public expect certain people (GPs, practice nurses, etc.) to question them about their health behaviours so people in key positions can raise the issue without it being challenging
Working to change society	Changing the physical and social environment to enable healthier lifestyles *To make smoking socially unacceptable, i.e. to change the way in which society as a whole views the behaviour – making it more difficult to smoke*	Working within the political or social system to change the physical/social environment *Increasing the number of public spaces covered by no smoking policies, making non-smoking the norm in society, making cigarette sales to children more difficult, banning tobacco advertising and sports' sponsorship*	This underpins the other approaches, enabling and supporting them. More people are motivated to quit as smoking becomes increasingly unacceptable and there are fewer places where they can smoke Most of this activity is only possible at an organisational, district or national level because it is about setting policy either for the organisation or the country
Fear	To frighten people into adopting a healthier lifestyle *To make the effects of smoking so frightening as to prevent people taking up smoking or to encourage those who do smoke to quit*	Educational activity to disseminate information about the effects of unhealthy lifestyles *For example, campaign using real life patients talking about their experiences of lung cancer brought on by smoking*	Although people were reluctant to use this approach at one time it increasingly has a place in current campaigning approaches, in this case bringing home to young people the message that smoking-related death can happen much earlier than they may think and emphasising the impact on family through the *testimonials* adverts. This usually requires campaigns only possible to organise at regional or national level

Approaches to health promotion

Understanding behaviour change

Understanding the complex processes which might influence a person to change their behaviour is essential for a health educator to be effective in their role. There are several models of behaviour change which we will now explore.

Health belief model

This was originally developed as a method to explain and predict preventive health behaviour. It originated around 1952 and is generally regarded as the beginning of systematic, theory-based research in health behaviour. The model suggests that an individual is most likely to undertake the recommended preventive health action if they believe:

- a threat to their health is real and serious

- that the benefits of taking the suggested action outweigh the barriers.

In many cases they might also need to be cued to take action.

Key concepts in the model include the following.

- **Perceived susceptibility** – their perception of how likely it is that they will get a particular condition that would adversely affect their health.
- **Perceived seriousness** – their beliefs about the effects a disease or condition would have on them, for example, the difficulties that a disease would create such as pain and discomfort, loss of work time, financial impact, difficulties with family, etc.
- **Perceived benefits of taking action** – once they have accepted their susceptibility to a disease and recognised it is serious, they may then feel motivated to act and attempt to prevent the disease. But this will also require them to feel there are real benefits from taking action.
- **Barriers to taking action** – action may not take place, even though they believe in the benefits of

taking action, because of perceived barriers relating to the nature of the treatment or preventive measures, which may be inconvenient, expensive, unpleasant, painful or upsetting.

- **Cues to action** – they may also require a 'cue to action' for the desired behaviour, for example, a call to participate in a screening programme.

Theory of reasoned action

This theory provides a framework to study the attitudes which underpin behaviours. It suggests that the most important determinant of a person's behaviour is behaviour *intent*, that is, the individual's intention to perform a particular behaviour. This is a combination of attitude towards performing the behaviour and the subjective norm.

If a person believes that the result of adopting a behaviour is positive, they will have a positive attitude towards that behaviour. If other people important to that person also view this action in a positive way then a positive subjective norm is created. Taken together, these two influences would strongly suggest the person would follow the health advice.

For example, if a person thinks that it is important to lose weight and this will make them healthier and happier, and their family and friends support this view, then it is more likely that they will adopt the

necessary lifestyle changes to reduce their body weight.

However, if this was a person considering quitting smoking who was concerned about the impact on their social life because all their friends smoked and those friends were not actively supportive, then it is less likely that this person would choose to quit.

Theory of social learning

Social learning theory (SLT) is a category of learning theories grounded in the belief that human behaviour is determined by interaction between three sets of factors: cognitive (knowledge and attitudes), behavioural (for example, personal skills), and environmental (services in the community, attitudes of peers). This three-way relationship can be seen in the diagram below.

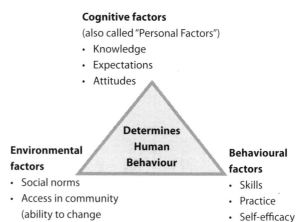

Figure 10.4 Factors determining human behaviour

There are three main aspects to social learning theory.

- The likelihood that a person will perform a particular behaviour again in a given situation is strongly influenced by their perception of the likely consequences, for example, the previous rewards or punishments which they experienced when performing the behaviour.
- People can learn by observing others (called *vicarious learning*), in addition to learning by participating in an act personally.
- Individuals are most likely to adopt behaviour observed by others they identify with (this has obvious links to peer education approaches).

Stages of change model

This model is now widely accepted and routinely used in substance use services, for smoking, alcohol and many illicit substances. It suggests there are five stages within the process of behaviour change:

- pre-contemplation – no intention to change behaviour in the foreseeable future; many individuals in this stage are unaware or under-aware of their problems
- contemplation – people are aware that a problem exists and are seriously thinking about overcoming it, but have not yet made a commitment to take action
- preparation – individuals in this stage are intending to take action in the next month and have unsuccessfully taken action in the past year
- action – individuals modify their behaviour, experiences or environment in order to overcome their problems; it requires considerable commitment of time and energy
- maintenance – people work to prevent relapse and consolidate the gains attained during action.

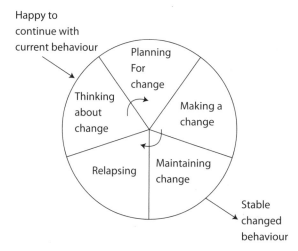

Figure 10.5 Prochaska and Di Clementes' model for behaviour change (from L. Jones and M. Sidell, 1997, The Challenge of Promoting Health – Exploration and Action)

While the model is frequently illustrated as a wheel, it is known that in many cases a person will have to repeat the process several times in order to successfully leave the cycle and achieve a stable changed behaviour. For example, think about the people you know who may have tried to quit smoking on several occasions; each of these attempts is part of the learning process which builds their chances of achieving the desired behaviour change. For this reason the process is often [...] the person gradually movin[...] desired change.

In her role as a practice [...] model of behaviour change every day when discussing health issues with a patient. If it is their first visit she will first attempt to assess where they are on the 'wheel'. If she is confident they will understand the concept, she may do this by simply showing them the model and asking them to identify where they see themselves on the wheel.

- It is unlikely that people will be outside the circle because at any one time a majority of people will be actively considering change – whether this is to do with their diet, smoking, physical activity and so on.
- However, if they are happy to continue with their behaviour she will simply provide some basic information about the health benefits of changing it and then invite them to come back when they feel their situation has changed.
- If they are thinking about change she will do exercises with them which help them evaluate the pros and cons of change versus sticking with the current behaviour, i.e. she uses the health belief model to help change their attitude to the behaviour.
- If they decide to change their behaviour, for example, to quit smoking, she will then help them plan effectively for the change. This might involve identifying situations which might lead to them having a cigarette and planning what they will do instead.
- Once they have changed the behaviour she will provide positive reinforcement, encouraging them to continue and discussing challenges they are experiencing and how to deal with them.

If they relapse she will work with them to draw out the learning they have gained from this attempt and how they can put it into practice next time, emphasising that relapse is an integral part of the process and that people frequently require several attempts to change their behaviour successfully.

Approaches, methods and materials

There are many ways in which you can communicate health promotion messages to your local community.

Interaction

It is hard to quantify the extent to which individual face-to-face interaction can contribute to health campaigning. However, it is clear that the general public hold certain groups within society in high regard and will therefore respect the information they obtain from such people as doctors, nurses, teachers and environmental health officers. This creates considerable potential for promoting key health messages simply through the day-to-day routine of work. It might mean a doctor suggesting to someone that they consider giving up smoking when they attend for a health check, or a district nurse suggesting that moderate activity is still possible and potentially beneficial for an older service user while visiting them at home. It is quite normal for health campaigns to engage these health promoters in the communication of a key message, for example, 'National No Smoking Day' when many health practitioners plan specific events to link with the national campaign and offer support to people wishing to quit smoking.

Leaflets

Leaflets are the backbone of health education activity. They can serve a wide variety of purposes, such as informing people about local services, providing information about specific health conditions, giving advice about specific health promotion issues or engaging people in thought about broader health considerations. In many cases leaflets are designed to support specific health campaigns, such as those for immunisation and National No Smoking Day. However, it is important to remember that for many people a leaflet will not be a useful means of communication. It was identified in a 2003 national research study for the DfES that:

● 5.2 million adults in England could be described as lacking basic literacy (that is, they were at entry level 3 or below according to National Standards for Literacy and Numeracy)
● more than one third of people with poor or very poor health had literacy skills of entry level 3 or below
● low levels of literacy and numeracy were found to be associated with socio-economic deprivation
● 53 per cent of all adults surveyed had entry or lower level practical skills in using information and communication technology (ICT).

Clearly many agencies still do little to take account of people's literacy levels because another survey of readability of patient information (produced by hospices and palliative care units) showed that 64 per cent of leaflets were readable only by an estimated 40 per cent of the population.

1 medium apple

2 broccoli florets

2 halves of canned peaches

1 handful of grapes

1 medium banana

3 heaped tablespoons of peas

1 medium glass of orange juice

7 strawberries

3 whole dried apricots

5 A DAY

3 heaped tablespoons of cooked kidney beans

16 okra

Just Eat More
(fruit & veg)

www.doh.gov.uk/fiveaday

© Crown copyright 2003

NHS

Figure 10.6   Sample materials from the 5 A Day initiative

Therefore a leaflet can be seen as a relatively simple tool, but it is important to consider a range of questions when designing or using one.

- Who is the leaflet for? A drugs leaflet appropriate for secondary school children will not be appropriate for primary schools.
- Who produced the leaflet and will they have an interest in the information? If it is a commercial organisation, such as a pharmaceuticals company, will this mean they have been selective in their reporting of the information?
- How long ago was it first produced – is the information still relevant or accurate? Information on drug-related harm changes very rapidly.
- Is the language level used appropriate to the *target audience* or is it too adult? Does it include abbreviations or technical terms?
- Is it well designed, i.e. will it grab the attention of the reader from amongst the other leaflets and posters? Will it connect specifically with the target audience?
- Are the key messages clearly identified or are there too many other distractions?
- In order to reach the target audience where is the best place to display this particular leaflet?

Posters

Posters provide an excellent tool for first catching the attention of the target audience and supporting the key broad messages which you might then develop in more detail within a leaflet. The factors which draw attention to a poster can be divided into two groups (see table below). Posters must be eye-catching and big enough to attract attention; they will need to be in colour, or if in black and white this should be for impact or dramatic effect. Wording should be minimal and very bold. Posters need to be placed carefully in places where the target audience will see them and should be routinely changed after a short period.

Physical characteristics	Motivational characteristics
Size – the whole of the poster as well as parts within it like key lettering	Novelty – unusual features or surprising objects
Intensity – bold headings	Interest – items of interest to the target audience
Colour – use of primary colours such as reds, greens and orange	Deeper motivations – e.g. fashion and sex
Pictures – using photographs and drawings	Entertainment or humour

Characteristics of posters

The role of the mass media

Many people would view the use of the **mass media** as the most effective means of reaching the population to promote health, probably assuming that because it reaches a large number of people its effect will be correspondingly great. However, there are other considerations to take into account.

The success of a health message conveyed by the mass media will be dependent upon the attitudes and viewpoint of the individual receiving the message. Therefore it is not surprising to find that many research studies have now shown that the direct persuasive power of mass media is very limited. Expectations that the mass media alone will produce dramatic long-term changes in health behaviour are doomed to disappointment.

What the mass media can do

So what success can realistically be expected when using the mass media in health promotion work? Appropriate aims here might include using it to:

- **raise awareness of health and health issues** (for example, to raise awareness about the link between over-exposure to the sun and the risk of skin cancer)
- **deliver a simple message** (for example, that babies should sleep on their backs not their tummies, or that there is a national advice line for young people wanting information about sexual health)
- **change behaviour if it is a simple one-off activity** (for example, phone for a leaflet) which people are already motivated to do and which it is easy to do. (Phoning for a leaflet is more likely if you are at home with a phone than if you're at a friend's house without your mobile or if the nearest phone is a broken public one two streets away.)

The use of mass media should be viewed as part of an overall strategy which includes face-to-face discussion, personal help and attention to social and environmental factors which help or hinder change. For example, mass media publicity is just one strand in a long-term programme to combat smoking.

What mass media cannot be expected to do

The mass media cannot:

- convey complex information (for example, about transmission routes of HIV)
- teach skills (for example, how to deal assertively with pressure to have sex without a condom or take drugs)
- shift people's attitudes or beliefs. If a message challenges a person's basic beliefs, he is more likely to dismiss the message than change his belief (for

example, 'My granddad smoked sixty a day till he died at 80, so saying I should stop smoking is rubbish')
- change behaviour unless it is a simple action, easy to do, and people are already motivated to do it (for example, it will only encourage those people who are already motivated to be more active to start walking because this is an easy and accessible form of exercise; it will not do this for those who are not motivated to be more active).

Using local media

While most people are familiar with national and regional media, i.e. the main national newspapers, local evening papers, national radio and television stations, it is far more likely that you will be dealing with local media. The local media can still be a very effective way of reaching people; the local free newspaper will most likely reach every house in your area – but how many people will actually read it?

Local media, both radio and print, often have a few key permanent staff members who may be with the paper or station for many years, but the reporters are usually juniors working their way up to the regional and national media. This means they may have little experience or understanding about the issues you are trying to highlight. The way to overcome this is to provide a press release where you give them the information you want to be included in the story. In the press release, make sure you provide:

- a title (if it is good enough they may use it directly)
- a brief summary of the main message you are trying to get across (usually three points maximum)
- details of what is happening where and when
- the names of any important people
- information on whether a picture might be possible (either for them to send a photographer or that you can provide one)
- a quote about the news item from someone they might be interested in
- some background facts
- the name of a person to contact to follow up the news release and their contact details.

If you write a good press release the paper may largely use it as it stands, or the radio station may read it directly. If they like your story they may wish to

...u. Should that happen, make sure you [...] questions they intend to ask before the [...]w. Tell them this will help you to prepare the necessary background information and improve the quality of your answers and therefore the interview.

Prepare for an interview beforehand

Planning a campaign

To plan a campaign effectively requires a clear understanding of what you are trying to achieve. A health promoter must define clear aims and objectives before starting any form of action. Planning should provide you with the answers to three questions.

- What am I trying to achieve?
- What am I going to do?
- How will I know whether I have succeeded?

Aims and objectives

A good start is to differentiate between an aim and an objective:

- **aim** – a broad goal
- **objective** – specific goal to be achieved.

Any one aim may have several supplementary objectives within it, while objectives are usually defined as being **SMART** (see below); those which are not, cannot be effective aids to planning. It is usually necessary to break down aims into specific objectives. Without this level of detail an objective becomes immeasurable and evaluation of the work is undermined.

Specific	defined in terms which are clear and not too vague
Measurable	when the work is finished we can see whether the objective has been achieved or not
Achievable	the target must be realistic, i.e. within our power to change
Relevant	is focused on addressing the issue within our broad aim
Timed	a timescale is agreed by which we expect to have delivered this objective.

For example, for a theatre in health education project one objective might be:

Engage young people in an accessible, fun but rigorous discussion about the legal, health, personal and social consequences of decisions made in relation to drugs, sex and crime. (See page 380.)

Identification of target audience

Identifying your target audience for a campaign starts with the question: 'What is the health need which I should be addressing?' The need for a campaign will usually come from one of four sources:

Normative need	Defined by an expert or professional according to their own standards; where something falls short of this standard then a need is identified; for example, percentage of people who are overweight or obese.
Felt need	Needs which people feel, i.e. things we want; for example, people might want their food to be free of genetically modified products.
Expressed need	A felt need which is voiced; for example, the felt need to have genetically modified free food becomes an issue of public debate with pressure groups focusing public debate on the issue.

Comparative need	Arises from comparisons between similar groups of people, where one group is in receipt of health promotion activity and the other is not; examples here might be one school having a well thought out and planned PSHE curriculum and another not.

REFLECT

If you were to undertake a piece of health promotion activity locally, how would you start to identify local needs which would frame the aims and objectives of your work?

- List possible sources of useful information.
- What information might they provide for you?
- How would you decide whether this information is a reliable basis for your decision making?

What felt or expressed needs are you aware of within the student body of your college?

Therefore as a health promoter the first action in undertaking any campaign is to identify the source of the need we are considering and this will identify whom we are targeting.

Liaison with other agencies

Health promotion is rarely effective when the activity is focused within one organisation. As we saw at the beginning of this chapter the causes of ill-health are so broad that it requires a wide-ranging response across agencies to influence health for the good. This is reflected in current government thinking through statutory duties to work in partnership on planning mechanisms such as the local community plan, community safety strategy, etc. When working with other agencies it is important to know whom you need at what stages of the work; this can help to ensure you do not miss them out of your planning and then find that they are either unable or unwilling to support the work or cannot fit in with your timescale.

Milestones

These are steps along the way to delivering the outcome or objective; they are useful for helping you plan the work effectively. For example, the milestones towards an objective which involved recruiting people from local voluntary agencies to participate in a focus group about support for carers might include:

- design publicity materials including leaflets, posters and press adverts
- order sufficient stationery to support the mailing of these materials
- compile a circulation list for the mail-out
- arrange for materials to be printed
- mail out to relevant people
- visit local community groups to raise awareness about the project.

Milestones can also contribute to the evaluation process for a piece of work; they can be documented as a series of process-related targets which can be easily measured in terms of achievement – 'that milestone was met on time'.

Evaluation and outcome measures

Evaluation is something which we actively engage in on a daily basis. If evaluation is basically about judging the worth of an activity, then this would include questions we ask ourselves such as:

Do I enjoy my job or should I apply for another one?

Will I use that restaurant again?

Or on a professional footing:

How did that session go?

Did I achieve what I set out to do?

Did that patient or service user really understand what I was explaining to her or was she just being polite when she said she did?

In the context of evaluating health promoting activity we are probably considering something of a more formal approach to evaluation, a type which is more public or open to scrutiny by an outsider and therefore capable of being made public. In this type of evaluation there are two key aspects.

- Defining what we hope to achieve – i.e. aims and objectives.
- Gathering information to assess whether we have met these.

The question of when to evaluate is closely bound up with the purpose of the evaluation. Is it to be a final *summative* assessment of what has happened? Evaluation of this type which seeks to establish the worth of work when it has reached its conclusion is termed an *outcome* evaluation. Or is it an ongoing appraisal of the progress made? Evaluation that involves feedback during the course of a project, when things are still taking shape, is termed *formative* or an evaluation of *process*.

As we have seen already, an **outcome measure** is the end point of the piece of work a health promoter undertakes. This can be a target as challenging as those seen in national policy, and require co-ordinated action at that level to deliver them. Conversely, it could be something quite small-scale, such as creating and improving the knowledge and skills of people from a specific geographical community about healthy cooking. There will be considerable overlap with objectives here but it is important not to confuse the two.

Objectives refer to the work required to deliver the outcome. In this example an objective might be to develop a model training programme for delivery with a group of women from the identified community. Outcomes refer to the product of the work. The health promoter will have to identify the desired outcomes in advance of the work to ensure that they design in to the process ways of measuring whether the product is delivered; for example, 'the knowledge and skills were successfully developed in the community and people then went on to alter their diet and eating behaviours'. It is not always possible to predict the outcome of a piece of work. It can create unintended or unexpected outcomes which are a by-product of the work. For example, in this situation the by-product might be better community relations due to the sustained programme of group activities during the cooking skills course, or the establishment of local community market gardening initiatives to grow local fresh produce.

Evaluation and outcome measures: Project Objectives

One objective from a Theatre in Education project with Y7–9 students.

Objective

State your objective here (use a separate sheet for each objective).

Engage young people in an accessible, fun but rigorous discussion about the legal, health, personal and social consequences of decisions made in relation to drugs, sex and crime.

Key Tasks/Activity

Briefly describe what service or activity you will be providing, and evaluating, that supports the achievement of this objective.

Interactive theatre performances by a team of actors with groups of 60–90 students, lasting 90 minutes.

Each Year group has a session on a different theme, watched by form tutors and other pastoral staff: Y7 Bullying, Y8 Drugs, Y9 Sex and Relationships.

Students will receive preparatory and follow-up work in the school.

Some preparatory and follow-up work will be done with school staff.

Results

What do you hope will change as a result of this activity?

- Students will show a greater repertoire of behaviours enabling them to make informed and safe decisions
- Students and staff will feel more confident and informed when discussing the issues raised in the performances
- Staff will feel able and confident to follow up this work
- Students and staff will feel that the interactive theatre experience can make this learning enjoyable and memorable

Measures

How will you measure if the described change is occurring/has occurred?

- Access student attitudes before and after the performances
- Access staff attitudes and confidence before and after the performances
- Observe and evaluate the performances
- Follow up after 6 months to review progress

Standard

Is it possible to define **levels of success**? It can be helpful to describe these at three levels (see below).

Start to think about what some of these mean in quantitative terms; for example, does high level of satisfaction mean 100 per cent were very satisfied, or 90 per cent, or less?

What will be the best you could hope for? (A great result!)

A highly enjoyable experience with high levels of satisfaction; students much more confident in discussion and feedback, staff very pleased, and happy to continue and develop the work; school uses some interactive techniques in its PSHE; we get to do more work with them!

What will you be happy with? (A satisfactory result)

The students and staff enjoy the day; there is evidence of some change in student knowledge and attitudes, and some staff express interest in continuing the work. Some follow-up takes place in school and there is evidence of links to the PSHE curriculum.

What will you be unhappy with? (A disappointing result)

Preparatory work is not done, or done badly; feedback from students and staff is only satisfactory; there is little evidence of increased knowledge or changed attitudes in the students. Staff don't attend the performances and show little interest in following up the work or using or developing the techniques as part of their curriculum.

Measuring the effectiveness of health promotion activity

Changing behaviour

Activities in the health education arena focus on the need to motivate individuals to change their health-related behaviours, most commonly in areas such as increasing physical activity, quitting smoking, adopting a healthier diet, adopting safe sex messages, etc. As you can imagine it is not easy to monitor the changing behaviour of a group of people, possibly over many months, to assess how successful a health promotion activity has been. This is exactly the problem faced by the smoking cessation services set up with the support of government funding in each health district in 1999/2000. The services must report how many people referred to them set a quit date, how many went on to quit smoking and how many were still not smoking after one month. To assess the effectiveness of the services in this way requires a considerable investment in administration to track the patients, collect the necessary information and collate it for return to the Department of Health.

In the case of behaviour change, outcome measures are often difficult to assess in a real-life situation as they are time-consuming and expensive to observe systematically. In the case of provision of a piece of fruit to every school child, the goal would be to increase their consumption of fruit and vegetables; this is clearly not an easy outcome to monitor systematically. Therefore, instead of trying to observe the eating patterns of the children directly, an indirect indicator using the children's self-reporting of changes to their own eating patterns might be used, or even changes in purchasing patterns in local shops as a 'proxy indicator'.

Therefore self-reported change (i.e. change people perceive they have made and are willing to report) is a very popular measure in health promotion evaluation, because it allows evaluation to take place without adding significantly to costs. Sometimes a project's aims and objectives are framed in terms of self-reported changes in knowledge, attitudes and behaviour. For instance, an HIV educational programme for young adults might aim to:

- increase knowledge
- generate positive attitudes towards condom use
- increase *self-reported* safer sexual practices involving condom use.

This illustrates a particular difficulty facing health promoters. It is difficult to see how information about sexual behaviour can be reported other than by those actually involved (routine observation of sexual activity is unlikely to be acceptable to subjects in the study!). Therefore the health promoter is reliant upon the subject's honesty in their self-reporting, an issue which is equally important in less private aspects of health promoting activity.

If self-reported behaviour change is not considered a robust enough measure then this must be externally verified in some way. In the Allied Dunbar Fitness survey of 1995, a large sample of the population were asked to self-assess their fitness. To gauge the accuracy of their assessment a smaller sub-sample were invited for a full fitness assessment and the results were compared against their self-reporting estimates. The results demonstrated that people routinely over-estimate both their level of activity and their level of fitness. This information became invaluable for informing the goals of future promotional activity.

An alternative to behaviour change is the use of knowledge and attitudes. However, it is not possible to bring about behaviour change directly through changes in knowledge or attitude change, since other factors can act to resist that change. A good example here is the fact that at any time over half the adult population who smoke would like to quit, but only a small proportion are ready to try at any one time. This reflects the fact that your health beliefs are also affected by other issues, for example, the stress involved in moving house, getting divorced or being

Routine observation of sexual activity is unlikely to be acceptable to subjects!

made unemployed would all act against a person's desire to quit smoking. However, changes in knowledge or attitude can mean that people are better informed and have the kinds of attitudes that predispose them towards a particular line of action. A success here might be moving someone from the pre-contemplative phase ('I am OK with my smoking') to contemplating quitting ('I'm thinking about quitting').

Cost-effectiveness

While much local health promotion activity may be viewed as being relatively cheap in relation to the illness it seeks to prevent, it is also hard to measure the precise outcome of the work. Therefore the investment of two or three hours' time by a practice nurse to help an individual quit smoking is considerably less expensive than the cost of extensive treatment for lung cancer. However, it is impossible to state categorically that the nurse's time led directly to that individual stopping smoking. Many other factors might have influenced the outcome, so it cannot be considered an **attributable outcome**.

In recent years, questions about the relation between costs and effectiveness in the field of health promotion have become important. In a world of limited resources costs clearly have to be taken into account. If, for instance, a health education programme is entirely effective in changing the health behaviour of a small group of people, but achieves this success through enormous financial and human resource investment, it is important to acknowledge that in the evaluation process. Without this information it is not possible to make comparisons between differing health promotion activities which achieve the same outcome, or health promoting activities and medical interventions.

Cost-effectiveness analysis (CEA) compares the costs of similar interventions that achieve a specific objective (for example, the cost of the new smoking cessation services compared with GPs providing routine advice on giving up smoking). If different interventions meet with similar success then it becomes important to know which is cheaper. This is useful if the success is the same in each case, but becomes difficult when there are differing degrees of success or costs are different. Therefore the ability to measure the cost-effectiveness in health promotion activity is fraught

with difficulties – particularly when you take into account the range of issues it has to address, and the local flexibility to design individual responses to health challenges. It is precisely this problem which the Health Development Agency (HDA) was set up to address by assessing the weight of evidence for specific interventions nationally and then informing local practitioners. This will be a work in progress because little investment has historically been made in the assessing the cost-effectiveness of health promotion activity.

Deciding what will be an appropriate and feasible measure of effectiveness or change is a crucial step in planning and carrying out an evaluation. Where it is difficult to gather information directly about the outcome of an activity, and where it is not possible to demonstrate a direct link between health promotion activities and the desired outcome, *intermediate and indirect indicators* are often used. For example, HIV/AIDS health promotion's ultimate aim is to reduce the incidence of infection, but trying to measure change along the way may be difficult so increasing condom use might be a suitable intermediate indicator.

Disease reduction

As we have already seen it is virtually impossible to attribute the most important outcome (reduction of a specific disease) specifically to a health promotion intervention. The range of other influences which impact on a person's life make this impossible. After all, if we are not able to state categorically that smoking causes lung cancer (the appropriate terminology is that there is a very strong association between the two), how can we say that the five minutes spent with this person counselling them on quitting smoking led to a reduction in lung cancer?

Therefore targets for disease reduction are usually set at national, regional or district level (as we have seen with the two national health strategies) but are rarely used as health promotion success indictors. Even national health promotion initiatives, such as the introduction of smoking cessation services, use short-term measures which are more easily attributable to the intervention – for example, the number of people setting a quit date, the numbers still stopped at one month, the numbers stopped at three and six months, and so on.

It must also be recognised that some disease patterns can take several years to change, even if the health promotion intervention succeeds. For example, the smoking cessation service can reduce the numbers of people smoking but for many people their cancer may already be established but undiagnosed; therefore it will take time for the impact of reducing smoking levels to take effect. Some health promotion interventions can actually lead to a rise in the incidence of disease; screening campaigns are a particularly good example of this. Whenever campaigns are undertaken to encourage uptake of screening it is inevitable that the numbers of additional patients seen will lead to an increased number of diagnoses.

ACTIVITY

As a practice nurse, Anne routinely gives people advice about smoking, alcohol consumption, diet and nutrition, and weight management. Considering what you have just read about evaluation, what measures would you suggest to her to help her measure and monitor her success as a health educator?

- What tests would you have to do to collect this information?
- How easy would it be for her to collect and record this information?
- How often would you need to collect it to monitor changes effectively?
- How practical is all of the above likely to be?
- What benefits other than changes to physical health might participants experience by being involved in the scheme?

What problems if any might this present to her interaction with her clients?

Evaluating personal practice

An essential part of being an effective health promoter is to be a reflective practitioner – that is, to review your practice, identify any areas of weakness or improvement, to identify what would improve your practice in the future and to build that into future work. This is an essential part of adult learning as described by Kolb in his model of experiential learning.

Model of experiential learning

This model has four elements: concrete experience, observation and reflection, the formation of abstract concepts and testing in new situations. Kolb represented these in the experiential learning circle – see page 61.

Kolb and Fry (1975) argue that the learning cycle can begin at any one of the four points – and that it should really be approached as a continuous spiral. However, it is suggested that the learning process often begins with a person *carrying out a particular action* – in this case your health promotion activity – and then seeing the effect of the action in this situation.

Following this, the second step is to *understand these effects in the particular instance* so that if the same action was taken in the same circumstances it would be possible to anticipate what would follow from the action.

In this pattern the third step would be to *understand the general principle* under which the particular instance falls. An educator who has learned in this way may well have various rules of thumb or generalisations about what to do in different situations. So you will begin to develop both confidence and competence to deal with managing health promotion activities (see section 2 for detail about health promotion competencies).

When the general principle is understood, the last step is its *application through action in a new circumstance* within the range of generalisation. In some representations of experiential learning, these steps (or ones like them) are sometimes represented as a circular movement. In reality, if learning has taken place the process could be seen as a spiral.

Reflective practice is about taking time out to carry out steps 2 and 3 and using other people to discuss how you are performing within a role so you can begin to generalise about your future practice to change and improve it. This could cover any aspect of the areas of competence in health promotion in section 2, whether this is acting ethically (for example, not using inappropriately sponsored materials), managing projects (for example, keeping to timescales in the milestone plan) or working in partnership (for instance, how well you maintain effective working relationships with your colleagues or other practitioners you are depending upon to get the job done).

KNOWLEDGE CHECK

1 State three facts which suggest that leaflets might not be an effective health education medium for some people.
2 Give three features to consider when designing a poster.
3 Give three examples of things the media can be used for in promoting health, and three it cannot be used for.
4 What is the difference between a felt need and an expressed need?
5 What is a SMART objective?
6 What is an outcome evaluation? How does it differ from a formative evaluation?
7 If health promotion activity is usually inexpensive, why is it hard to demonstrate its cost-effectiveness?
8 Why are disease reduction targets inappropriate measures for assessing the effectiveness of a health promotion programme?
9 What are the four steps of Kolb's experiential learning model?

Glossary

Aim: the 'aim', or outcome, is the broad goal for a piece of work. Usually a project has only one or two aims.

Attributable outcome: an outcome which can be directly related to a piece of health promotion activity; i.e. the cause and effect can be linked.

BMI: indicator of body fat, worked out by dividing body weight in kg by height in metres squared.

Cancer: a term which covers a wide variety of diseases caused by uncontrollable growth of a particular body tissue, e.g. lung, bone, etc.

Comparative need: identified from comparisons between similar groups of people, where one group is identified as having poorer health as a consequence of an identified difference.

Disability: disability is the consequence of impairment, or other individual difference. The disability a person experiences is determined by the way in which other people respond to that difference.

Equity: the principle of social justice – directing resources to those who need them most.

Ethics: to act ethically is to act in a principled manner.

Evaluation: to judge the worth of something.

Evidence-based practice: to base your practice on evidence of what works best.

Expressed need: a felt need which is voiced by a person or community.

Felt need: needs which people feel, i.e. things we *want*.

Health education: an aspect of health promotion which largely relates to educating people about good health and how to develop and support it.

Health promotion outcome: the result of a piece of health promotion work – a reduction in a particular disorder or an uptake in screening, for example.

Intervention: to intervene or take action in order to effect a change, e.g. to intervene by helping someone quit smoking.

Local authorities: the local organisation responsible for environmental health, building control, leisure facilities, refuse collection, street cleaning, etc.

Mass media: an umbrella term for a range of media which convey information to the general population including radio, television, newspapers and magazines.

Medical model: probably the most widely known model of health and the one that has come to dominate all others in the Western world; this adopts a scientific view of health and body functioning.

MMR vaccine: vaccination against measles, mumps and rubella.

Normative need: need identified by an expert or professional according to their own standards; where something falls short of this standard then a need is identified.

Obesity: a Body Mass Index in excess of 30.

Objectives: specific goals to be achieved in delivering a stated aim or outcome.

Outcome evaluation: this seeks to establish the worth of work when it has reached its conclusion.

Outcome measures: indicators of success for health promotion activity.

Prevention: reducing or avoiding the risks of diseases and ill-health primarily through medical interventions.

Primary Care Trust (PCT): new NHS organisations which have three key responsibilities: improve the health of their local population; develop local primary health care services; commission other local health services in line with local health needs.

Primary health care setting: usually a term used to refer to the GP surgery or health centre.

Sexually transmitted infection: diseases which can only be passed by sexual activity.

SMART: an acronym for effective objective setting. Objectives should be Specific, Measurable, Achievable, Realistic and Time-specific.

Societal change: attempts to elicit health improvement by changing society, e.g. by reducing tolerance to drink driving.

Summative evaluation: an assessment of what has happened.

Target audience: the group an activity is aimed at.

Vaccination: to challenge a person's immune system to produce antibodies by injecting a dead or weakened version of the disease organism.

Value judgements: to judge someone or something from a standpoint based on your own values; for example, 'because I don't smoke and believe it to be bad for the health, I think that a person who smokes is a bad person'.

World Health Organization: established on 7 April 1948, it was a response to an international desire for a world free from disease.

References

Acheson, Sir Donald, (1998) *The Independent Inquiry into Inequalities in Health*, The Stationery Office

Benzeval, M., Judge K. and Whitehead M. (1995) *Tackling Inequalities in Health, an Agenda for Action*, King's Fund Publishing

Davidson N., Townsend P. and Whitehead M. (1988) *Inequalities in Health: The Black Report and the Health Divide*, Penguin Social Sciences – Penguin Books

Department of Health (1992) *Immunisation against Infectious Disease*, The Stationery Office

Department of Health (2004) *At least five a week – evidence on the impact of physical activity and its relationship to health*, a report from the Chief Medical Officer

Downie, R.S., Tannahill, C. and Tannahill, A. (1996) *Health Promotion Models and Values*, Oxford University Press

Draper, P. (1991) *Health Through Public Policy*, Green Print

Ewles, L. and Simnett, I. (1999) *Promoting Health – A Practical Guide*, Bailliere Tindall

HM Government (1997) *Saving Lives: Our Healthier Nation*, The Stationery Office

HM Government (1992) *The Health of the Nation*, The Stationery Office

HM Government (2004) *Choosing Health – Making Healthy Choices Easier*, The Stationery Office

Hall, D. (1996) *Health for all Children*, Oxford University Press

Jones, L. and Sidell, M. (1997) *The Challenge of Promoting Health – Exploration and Action*, Open University

Katz, J. and Peberdy, A. (eds.) (1997) *Promoting Health: Knowledge and Practice*, Buckingham, Macmillan/OU Press

Kolb, D.A. and Fry, R. (1975) 'Toward an applied theory of experiential learning' in C. Cooper (ed.) *Theories of Group Process*, London, John Wiley

Naidoo, J. and Wills, J. (2000) *Health Promotion – Foundations for Practice*, Bailliere Tindall

Ungerson, C. and Baldock, J. (1994) *Becoming Consumers of Community Care*, York, Joseph Rowntree Foundation/Community Care

Useful websites

www.ohn.gov.uk Gateway for the *Our Healthier Nation* website – original document, technical data and regular progress updates

www.quick.org.uk Quality information checklist for young people to assess the quality of information they find on the Internet

www.wiredforhealth.gov.uk Provides teachers with access to relevant and appropriate health information

www.mindbodysoul.gov.uk Provides accurate and up-to-date health information for young people

www.bhf.org.uk/ Heart health information from the British Heart Foundation including information about activity and nutrition

www.homeoffice.gov.uk/drugs/index.html Information about the National Drugs Strategy and links to information about current drug use trends and patterns

www.doh.gov.uk Main Department of Health website – search here for links to *Choosing Health* Public Health White Paper and health statistics

www.nhs.uk/england/ This site connects you to local NHS services in England and provides national information about the NHS

www.givingupsmoking.co.uk The NHS quit smoking website, information about smoking, how to quit and where to access local services

www.cancerscreening.nhs.uk/ NHS screening programmes website, provides good-quality information about both cervical and breast cancer screening programmes

www.nhlbisupport.com/bmi/bmicalc.htm Calculate your own BMI using the information on this site

www.who.int/en/ The website of the World Health Organization

www.immunisation.org.uk/ Information about immunisation programmes

www.mmrthefacts.nhs.uk/ Government website specifically set up to provide quality information abut the MMR vaccine for parents, to counter the fall in public confidence in the vaccine

euro.who.int/observatory The European Observatory on Health Systems and Policies supports and promotes evidence-based health policy making through comprehensive and rigorous analysis of the dynamics of healthcare systems in Europe

www.dwi.gov.uk The Drinking Water Inspectorate (DWI) regulates public water supplies in England and Wales

www.hpa.org.uk/ The HPA is an independent body that protects the health and well-being of the population

CHAPTER 11

Research methods

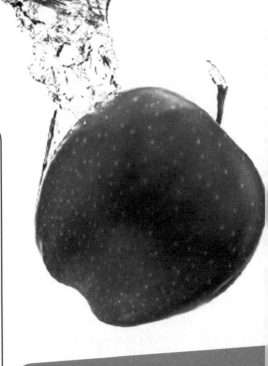

Introduction

This chapter is designed to provide a basic outline of key concepts and processes for those who are relatively new to research. As research claims to add to our knowledge, we begin by briefly exploring ideas about what knowledge is, the relationship between research and knowledge, and the ways in which research that is 'scientific' is said to construct knowledge. We then discuss more specifically why research is important for practitioners in health and social care. We examine some of the particular knowledge, questions and issues for research that we should be aware of in this field of study. Using a case study approach, we examine in more detail some important issues when it comes to reading and understanding research.

This chapter addresses the following areas:

- Research and knowledge
- Why research is important for practitioners
- Thinking about knowledge
- Reading research
- Doing your own 'primary' research
- The research process
- Access to research subjects
- Ethical considerations
- Outline of common primary research methods
- Action research
- The practitioner-researcher

Areas covered:

- Research and knowledge: some initial thoughts
- Why research is important for practitioners
- Thinking about knowledge
- Reading research
- Doing your own 'primary' research
- The research process
- Access to research subjects: sampling
- Ethical considerations
- An outline of common primary research methods
- Evidence-based practice
- Action research
- The practitioner-researcher
- Locating research on the web

Research and knowledge: some initial thoughts

Research is an activity that tries to discover answers to questions and to find knowledge. We all carry out research nearly every day to find out information at work and at home. Research is about questions of 'what?', 'how?', 'who?', 'where?' and 'why?' At home, for example, we might go on the Internet to find the cheapest plane tickets for a holiday; we might look for a plumber in the *Yellow Pages;* standing at the bus stop we will check the bus timetable to find out when the next bus is due. At work, we might need to look up some information about a client or check something in the organisational guidelines. We could look in the manual to find out why the computer is not working. Our information gathering might also involve asking someone's opinion or getting people to indicate their preference for a meeting.

We use research skills all the time and our lives are affected by the research of others. The media continually provide us with messages from the latest 'research', sometimes to educate us (for example, telling us about global warming), to inform and entertain us (for example, the country's sexual habits) or to advertise to us ('eight out of ten owners say that their cat prefers Whiskas'). Nowadays we are surrounded by more and more information but, increasingly, we are often unhappy with both the quantity of it and the quality. We might think that the 'experts' either often get it wrong or cannot agree among themselves; politicians are forever 'spinning' facts and doctoring the truth for their own ends. How do we judge what is trustworthy knowledge and what is not?

Scientific knowledge

Since the Enlightenment in the eighteenth century, priority has been given to 'scientific' knowledge over all other forms of knowledge – for example, folklore, religion, superstition, 'common sense' and so on. The word science is derived from the Latin *scire* meaning 'to know'. The knowledge derived from scientific research is considered to be more authoritative and trustworthy because it is based on systematic and rigorous methods. The scientific method is supposed to be both reliable and valid.

In research terms, concepts such as **reliability** and **validity** are very important. If a method of collecting data (information) is to be considered reliable, it means that another researcher using that method (or if the same person repeated the method later) they would come up with the same findings. Validity refers to the issue of whether the method used to collect data will actually answer the question you have asked, and not something else, and give a 'true' picture of what is being studied. So, for example, a valid test for depression should be able to confirm that a person actually was depressed rather than find they are depressed when, in fact, there was something else the matter with them.

We are desperate for scientists to find the solutions to important questions, for example, to find alternative sources of energy and cures for fatal diseases such as HIV/AIDS. Yet, ironically, nowadays we are increasingly sceptical about scientific research. For example, what is the truth about the safety of nuclear energy or genetically modified crops? Many of us don't know whether to trust science or not. It is apparent that there are some questions where the knowledge is highly contested and it may be impossible to determine the absolute truth of the matter. Questions of values must be taken into consideration. How, for example, can we ensure that we are looked after properly in old age? We need to have some way of deciding who and what to believe. We might, for instance, decide on the basis of how reliable the methods used were, how extensive the research was or maybe whose opinion you think is the most trustworthy.

Values

There are certain kinds of questions, for example, about people's rights, which are more questions of values and there is no possibility of finding the answer by conducting an experiment, carrying out an observation or a survey. Here we might make our decision more on the moral weight of the argument than on any factual evidence that might be available. As it happens, apart from questions where the answers are simple facts, most of the questions and issues in health and social care divide opinion about what exactly the 'correct' answers are. There are very few 'absolutes' or situations where there are no dissenting views. Values play a much more significant part in answering these questions than we might think. Research is about increasing our knowledge about questions and issues that we consider important. However, whether even scientific research can always get to the 'truth' is debatable. The truth is often messy and open to different interpretation, which is why it is important to be more aware of how research is carried out and how the knowledge that is presented to us is constructed.

Knowledge questions

Questions such as 'What is knowledge?', 'How do we know what we know?' and 'How do we know whether certain knowledge is true or valid?' are questions of **epistemology**. The word epistemology comes from the Greek word for knowledge, *episteme*. Basically, epistemology is the philosophy of knowledge or of how we come to know. Serious research must therefore concern itself with epistemological questions.

In thinking about these questions, you may have concluded that while some facts are relatively easy to ascertain (what time the next bus is due), other knowledge is a lot more complex to fully discover and comprehend. You might have also thought that some questions are quite hard to find answers to – especially if you are not entirely sure what it is you are trying to find out. Can we, for example, come up with a watertight definition of 'happiness' that everyone would agree with? In addition, people might *say* they are happy when they are not. Hairdressers are often told by their clients that the new style is 'great'. However, when they leave the salon the client might turn out to be thoroughly miserable with their new cut.

You might think that those who work in care should know whether their clients are satisfied with the service or not. However, such knowledge is not necessarily easy to find out and how someone can genuinely say they 'know' will require a more thoughtful approach and raises some difficult epistemological questions.

Consequently, what questions are asked and what methods are used to answer them are critical to

Fig Trees inspection

The Fig Trees residential care home for older people is being inspected by the Commission for Social Care Inspection (CSCI). CSCI sometimes use 'experts by experience' who accompany the CSCI inspector on inspections, talk to staff and service users, and help the inspector gain a rounded picture of the service. Their role is to look at the service, take notes, discuss with the inspector and write a report about what they have found. As part of the inspection, Donald, an 'expert by experience', has a chat with June, the deputy manager. Donald asks June, 'Are your residents happy?' June thinks for a while and answers, 'Yes, I think so.' Donald replies, 'You think so? You don't know for sure then? Isn't it your job to know whether your residents are happy or not?'

Donald makes a note to discuss with the inspector that he does not think June is much of a manager if she can't answer a basic question like that without hesitation. Meanwhile June is worried that she should have given a more definitive answer. June feels as if there was something she should know but she could not be absolutely sure about.

Questions

1 What are your thoughts about this exchange?
2 Is Donald being fair in his assessment of June?
3 What research could June carry out so as to be able to answer this question with more confidence and more authority?
4 What methods could be used to measure 'happiness'?
5 Can you see any problems or difficulties in researching this question in a way that that would enable you to be satisfied that you had got to the 'real truth of the matter'?

whether any research will be successful. There is a strong relationship between the quality of the knowledge gained and the quality of the research carried out to produce it. As we shall see, researchers use different methods according to the types of question to which they want answers. Research is both a lively and a relevant topic; we are all affected by research in our personal and working lives. There is therefore every reason for learning more about the various ways in which research can be carried out and some of the epistemological debates about how and what knowledge can be constructed as a result. Anybody – certainly any student – should be interested in where knowledge comes from.

Why research is important for practitioners

The phrase 'evidence-based practice' has found its way into common usage since the 1990s across a range of professional activity. For example, in a document commissioned by the Social Care Institute of Excellence (SCIE), Walter *et al* (2004) state that:

> Evidence-based policy and practice increasingly demands the use of research as a key tool to improve practice.

However, even before the term 'evidence-based practice' became so popular, research has always played an important part in health and social care policies and practices – and always will in some shape or form. It is one of the main reasons why policies and practices change over time. To provide an example, we can look at some specific policies and practices that have followed from the National Service Framework for Older People that was introduced in 2001. Each of the eight standards was informed, in some way, by research. As the authors of the National Service Framework (NSF) state:

> The proposals in this NSF are based on expert advice, the values underpinning care services and research evidence. In order for some weight to be attached to the supportive evidence, a typology was developed to distinguish between evidence stemming from, for instance, systematic reviews of existing information, the experience of patients or carers, and case studies of individual interventions.
> (Department of Health, 2001, page 10)

ACTIVITY

As we can see, the 'research' took various forms and came from different sources. Briefly explain what they were. What do you think are the benefits of using a range of sources? Do you think they all necessarily carry the same weight? Give your reasons.

Standard Six of the NSF was concerned with falls (and their prevention) in older people. Therefore this standard was not created on a whim, it was because a growing body of evidence constructed by medical, health and other researchers had found that falls were the most common cause of death in older people. However, the research showed that where falls were not fatal, older people were often still going to hospital. This not only disrupted the lives of older people' and had a negative impact on their general health and well-being, it also cost the NHS, and therefore the taxpayer, millions of pounds. As a consequence, a Falls Prevention Service has been set up in all localities. Falls Prevention Co-ordinator posts have been created and, through their work, new services have been set up and different practices have been adopted. This might include the use of hip protectors for older people at risk of falling in residential care; it might mean the provision of Tai Chi or other exercise classes in the community or educating health and social care workers about the 'risk factors' and what to do about them. Therefore, this policy, and the various practices that have been developed as a result, have been both driven and guided by research.

ACTIVITY

This is an opportunity to do some research of your own.
1 Go to the Department of Health website and find the National Service Framework for Older People.
2 Identify three pieces of research that informed the Standard on Falls.
3 Note the details of the research you have found. In which part of the NSF did you find the details listed?
4 Briefly explain how you carried out the research – how easy was it?

This exercise has required you to find out about research that has already been carried out by others. The name given to this form of research is **secondary research**. The research originally carried out by the various researchers is called **primary research**.

Thinking about knowledge

Research is a dynamic process. The knowledge constructed from research is constantly being updated and built upon. Sometimes new research findings challenge old research findings. When you visited the NSF web pages, you may have noticed that the findings from ongoing research are still being posted. This shows us that we can never say we have all the knowledge about a particular subject. We might not even be sure what questions we should be asking. Also, when we do learn some new knowledge – for example, about the value (or not) of hip protectors – we cannot necessarily say they work for everyone or in all circumstances. Therefore, new practices need to be evaluated, any lessons learned need to be published, and policies and practices need to be refined as knowledge about what does and doesn't work is updated.

The unknown

The former United States Defence Secretary Donald Rumsfeld famously once said:

> As we know,
> There are known knowns.
> There are things we know we know.
> We also know
> There are known unknowns.
> That is to say
> We know there are some things
> We do not know.
> But there are also unknown unknowns,
> The ones we don't know
> We don't know.
>
> (US Department of Defence news briefing, 12 February 2002)

Donald Rumsfeld was ridiculed for his 'unknown unknowns' statement

Rightly or wrongly, Rumsfeld was severely ridiculed for saying this. However, if you think about it, there must always be new knowledge which we don't know about yet – the 'unknown unknowns'. There are always new questions to be asked and new areas to find out about. However, we do not always know what they are!

Earlier we briefly discussed epistemological questions, such as 'how do we know what we know?' What we are discussing now touches on 'what there is to know'. We have talked about knowledge being 'constructed'. Some might suggest that knowledge is 'discovered' by the research rather than constructed. This makes it sound as if the researcher is making it up or 'manufacturing the truth'. This might raise doubts about how 'objective' or 'scientific' the research has been. These justifiable concerns bring us on to an important set of questions which researchers have to engage with. These are questions of **ontology**.

Ontology is a branch of philosophy concerned with the study of the nature of being and reality itself. We are not going to get overly philosophical at this point, but it is worth examining some basic ideas about what we mean by reality, if for no other reason than because researchers often claim to be finding out what is *really* happening.

The physical world and social world

Questions of ontology might ask, for example, whether there is a difference between the physical world (e.g. of plants, minerals and physical structures) and the social world (e.g. people, moods, relationships and social institutions such as families). Can these different 'worlds' be researched and known in the same way? In the physical sciences, for example, if a researcher wants to find out what happens when water is heated up, they would conduct an experiment. If the experiment repeatedly shows that at 100° centigrade the water is observed to boil, the researcher can formulate a 'law' or 'theory' that says whenever water is heated to 100° centigrade, in those conditions it will boil. This method is known as 'induction'. Other researchers can test out this theory and should find they get the same results. An inductive orientation to research is based on the idea that you can build knowledge by the accumulation of observational evidence. This method might be useful in the physical sciences, or even medical science, but is not always so helpful in the social sciences. Therefore other, more suitable, methods have had to be developed.

In this chapter, we are focusing on research that is primarily concerned with what happens with, between and to people (their health and well-being, sense of independence, security, quality of relationships and so on). Therefore, we are mainly focusing on questions of 'social reality'. Researching 'people' creates different challenges because, for one important reason at least, people are not just objects or substances and cannot be experimented on in the same way. People have feelings and attitudes; rocks don't! For that reason and others, those who carry out social research have to grapple with some important questions. For example, researchers live in the world they are researching. They have their own values and beliefs. How detached, objective and neutral can the social researcher be? Also, while it might be possible to observe behaviour from the outside, people also have a hidden, 'interior' mental world.

People therefore present much more complex subject matter. Questions of what someone is *really* feeling, or what is *really* happening among a group of people, are harder to determine. It can often be a matter of perspective.

ACTIVITY

Consider these questions.
1 Is the health of the British people getting better or worse?
2 What is the most effective cure for depression?
3 Are Direct Payments suitable for people with learning disabilities?

You might end up by saying it depends on how you define 'health', or what you call 'effective' or that 'it depends on the individual'. We could say that the knowledge we have in this area is *contingent* or *provisional* in that it depends on certain conditions, circumstances or events to be true.

Social researchers are therefore faced with ontological questions which they cannot avoid. For example, they must consider whether human or social behaviour is governed by generalised 'laws' in the same way as the physical elements or whether knowledge can only be considered specific to certain situations. Can human feelings and behaviour be predicted in the same way as, say, water can be when placed under certain conditions? Is it, for example, possible to predict whether attendance at an exercise class will bring about a certain decrease in the number of falls or whether going to a day centre will make an elderly person happy? 'Ontological questions' then are about the nature of reality. As you might imagine, this can lead into some interesting philosophical questions; but as this is an introductory chapter we cannot go too deeply into this area. However, Alan Bryman, renowned writer on social research, sets out two broad ontological positions: objectivism and constructionism. He states that:

> Objectivism is an ontological position that asserts that social phenomena and their meanings have an existence that is independent of social actors.
>
> (Bryman, 2001, page 17)

Constructionism is an ontological position (often also referred to as constructivism) that asserts that social phenomena and their meanings are continually being accomplished by social actors. It implies that social phenomena and categories are not only produced through social interaction but that they are in a constant state of revision.

(Bryman, 2001, page 18)

So, for example, an objectivist would believe that poverty (as an example of a social phenomenon) is a 'fact' in the world. They would believe that, as such, researchers can therefore go out into the world and measure it objectively to find out the extent of poverty, different trends in poverty and so on.

The constructionist believes that poverty does not exist 'independent of social actors' (e.g. people). Poverty therefore cannot be considered a fact in the same way that, say, Mount Everest is a fact in the world. The concept of poverty is not only therefore a human 'construction', but it is one where the definition is not fixed; it changes over time and according to changing social norms. People decide what poverty is. It can be measured, but first the meaning of poverty would need to be agreed. In this sense, poverty cannot be said to exist 'objectively' outside definitions devised by us as 'social actors'.

> **REFLECT**
>
> What approach best helps you understand other social phenomena such as disability or racial discrimination?

Do not worry too much about these distinctions at this point; just be aware that in the world of research – particularly social research – you cannot take what is 'real' for granted. Neither can it be assumed that we can always get at the 'truth'. Meanings and definitions differ. Mostly, finding the real 'truth' of the matter or the 'facts' is a lot more complex than many people think. Arguably, in many situations, the truth is relative rather than absolute.

Reading research

To avoid getting too abstract, we now turn to a specific case study in order to explore how evidence

from research has been used to inform a book designed to educate and guide practitioners in dealing with people with dementia. Remembering the different ideas about what is presented as fact, 'true' or 'correct', the reader should always be prepared to ask questions like 'how do they know that?', 'where did that information come from?' or 'how can I tell whether it's really true or not?' When somebody makes a 'knowledge claim', we need to have some evidence that it can be substantiated and that a scientific approach has been taken in producing the findings. We also need to be able to distinguish a knowledge claim from an argument. This means examining the evidence or research base. Reading research is therefore a critical act. You should be prepared to follow up sources and determine:

- who carried out the research
- what the study was about exactly
- what methods the researchers used
- what the findings are exactly.

Answering these questions will give you a sense of how reliable the findings are and how authoritative any conclusions drawn might be.

The following is an extract from a book called *Ethical Issues in Dementia Care* by Julian Hughes and Clive Baldwin. They are discussing the important topic of how to decide about treating patients who may not be able to give consent. They say:

Valid consent means that the person is not coerced. If we force you to take tablets, it cannot be said that you have consented to take them. The idea of coercion is, indeed, quite repulsive to most of us. However, it is not long since outright physical restraint was relatively common in hospitals and other institutions and it still is in many parts of the world. But even in more 'advanced' nations, some forms of coercion are still routine. Chairs that people cannot get out of are, in essence, a form of restraint. It cannot then be said that the person sits all day in the chair freely. Similarly, what about when the patient is given medication secretly in food or drink? It cannot be said that the person has consented to take this medication. It is not only covert medication, but also coerced medication

(Treloar, Beats and Philpot, 2000 quoted in Hughes and Baldwin, 2006, page 60)

This is an ethical discussion of some of the difficult dilemmas that health and social care practitioners face when dealing with people who have dementia. Like many texts, it is neither pure fact (what is), nor pure opinion (what should be); the discussion contains an argument and certain knowledge claims – often woven together. The authors are encouraging us to think about people's right to choice. They challenge us to think about how far practices that are meant to be in the person's best interests are, in some way, coercive, restrictive or a denial of choice and other rights. In order to back up what they are saying, the authors include a citation to some relevant research that has been carried out in this area – (Treloar, Beats and Philpot, 2000). The argument has therefore been made more powerful by the use of a published article to back it up. However, in the spirit of critical reading we should not simply take this for granted – we need to probe a bit more about what this evidence base is and how it is used.

ACTIVITY

Using an academic library, locate – either from the shelves or electronically – the following journal: *Journal of the Royal Society of Medicine*, 2000, Volume 93, Issue 8.

If you turn to pages 408–411, you will find the actual article that Hughes and Baldwin cite. It is called 'A pill in the sandwich: covert medication in food and drink'.

Read through the article, making notes and thinking about the following questions:

1 What was the study about?
2 What methods did the researchers use?
3 What are the findings exactly?
4 How 'authoritative' would you say the study was? Give reasons.
5 To what extent can you learn something new by reading about the research? How has it changed your thinking on the subject?

Compare notes with someone else if possible.

'A pill in the sandwich' at a glance

What was the study about?

The study was an investigation into the covert administration of medicines in food and drink in social and healthcare settings providing care for people with dementia.

What methods did the researchers use?

According to the article abstract (summary), the authors say:

> We used questionnaires to ascertain the views of people caring for patients with dementia in institutions and in the community ... In 24 (71 per cent) of 34 residential, nursing and inpatient units in south-east England.

What are the findings exactly?

Again, from the abstract:

> ... the respondent[s] said that medicines were sometimes given in this way [covertly]. It was often done secretly and without discussion, probably for fear of professional retribution. Few institutions had a formal policy on the matter. Of 50 people caring for demented patients in the community, 48 (96 per cent) thought the practice sometimes justifiable, but 47 believed that doctors should consult with carers before deciding. Even if, as most carers and some authorities believe, covert medication can be justified, the poor recording and secrecy surrounding the practice in institutions are cause for concern.

Authoritative?

The authors Treloar, Beats and Philpot are all medical doctors who work in geriatric psychiatry departments in various London hospitals. The *Journal of the Royal Society of Medicine* is a peer-reviewed, internationally read journal. This means that, before publication, any articles submitted are critically reviewed by at least two expert peer reviewers. Articles should not be published if the reviewers are not satisfied that the research has been carried out according to recognised academic and professional standards, nor if the findings or argument do not contribute anything new to the field. Therefore, this should lend some authority to what the authors are saying – certainly more so than an article published in a magazine or newspaper where the same rigorous standards do not apply. However, it need not mean that it cannot be challenged. The authors' own professional status and background might also suggest that they have some expertise on the matter; again this does not mean that all other doctors would agree with them. The research is based on a questionnaire survey of workers' views in 24 units in the south-east of England, so while this may not represent all such units nationally, at least some modest claims can be made for a section of the country. Whether you are convinced that the research is valuable is ultimately a personal choice; but the signs are that as long as huge claims are not made for what is a fairly small study, the authors make a useful and valid contribution to this area of care.

Often, research is not 'ground-breaking' or totally revolutionary or saying something completely new. It might add another dimension to an existing debate; it might take previous findings and slightly build on them; alternatively it might use other studies to construct an argument. Sometimes research takes exception to previous findings and invites another way of looking at things. Seldom does one piece of research or an article roll back the frontiers of knowledge completely or totally demolish the existing wisdom about a subject. For these reasons, when reading research it is useful to distinguish what kind of research it is, who the researchers are, where it has been published, what methods were used and what conclusions are being drawn. As indicated, research usually adds to rather than settles the debate about a particular subject. Therefore, read research with a 'scholarly scepticism' – do not blindly accept it; also, do not automatically reject research out of hand, but be prepared to probe it critically. It can be helpful to have an informed idea of the various uses, advantages and disadvantages of different research methods when trying to do this.

Doing your own 'primary' research

Who does primary research?

In theory, anyone can do research. However, to do it properly takes training, time, and, usually, some funding. Funds are needed for a variety of reasons – this might be to pay the researcher's salary, to cover costs of stationery, tapes and recording equipment, travel expenses, marketing, vouchers to participants

and so on. Research cannot be carried out for nothing.

Researchers are generally academics from universities or colleges, or they might be people who work in the research department of a health or social care organisation. For example, Age Concern England has a research department, most local authorities and PCTs have research departments and central government departments such as the Department of Health or Social Care Institute for Excellence (SCIE) also carry out research. Organisations in the 'third sector' such as the Joseph Rowntree Foundation carry out research. It is often the case that different organisations might work together. Alternatively, an organisation, for example, the Alzheimer's Society or the Parkinson's Disease Society, might commission and fund research from other organisations such as universities – see below.

Figure 11.1 The Alzheimer's Society funds research from other organisations (www.qrd.alzheimers.org.uk/grants.htm)

The research process

There are many ways in which research can be initiated and many ways of conducting research. However, in most cases research goes through a series of stages. Each will be discussed in more depth later in the chapter. However, briefly, these are usually:

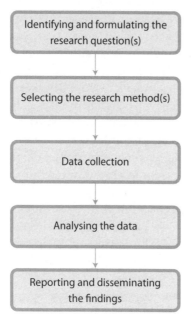

Figure 11.2 Stages of research

Identifying and formulating the research question(s)

The researcher(s) may, from their own practice or interests, identify an interesting problem or question to investigate. Alternatively, they may be directed to a

particular area of research because an organisation is offering money and facilities. A good example of such a research funder in health and social care is the Nuffield Foundation.

We can see that much research in health and social care is funded by large (often government-backed) organisations. However, there are also many smaller organisations (including universities) which are prepared to fund research. So, although the government often sets the research agenda, it does not mean that independent researchers cannot pursue projects of their own.

Remember, most research projects cannot provide definitive answers to big questions. The old adage in research is that it is best to be able to say a lot about a relatively narrow and focused area rather than a little about a huge area. So, for example, a project that set out to understand the causes of and solutions to adult abuse would be setting itself far too ambitious a goal. But a project that set out to understand whether the stress of carers for people with dementia was reduced by a sitting service might have a better chance of turning up some useful findings.

Selecting the research method(s)

This needs careful consideration and might involve the use of more than one type of method. The choice of research method will be greatly determined by the type of questions to which you want to find or explore the answers. The size of the population you want to study means that thought must be given to sampling (about which we will speak more later). Practical considerations, such as the time and funds available, also influence which methods are adopted. For example, if you are a lone researcher and you wanted to find out what people thought about NHS walk-in centres, it would be sensible to limit how many people you involved as it would be impossible to survey the whole country or even a town. Even then, if you decided that you wanted to get the views of 100 local residents, would you have the time to personally meet and interview them all for an hour each? If not, using a postal questionnaire might be a more appropriate method. To sort out these and other issues, the researcher will usually conduct a preliminary investigation called a **pilot study** to test out their ideas, iron out any snags and decide what will be the most appropriate methods to use. Often the pilot study can generate a whole new set of questions to investigate.

Data collection

This is the critical part and is usually one of the most time-consuming parts of research, mainly because it requires quite a lot of organisation. There are two broad categories of data: quantitative and qualitative. Different data collection methods are usually used in each case.

Quantitative data

Quantitative data is basically information that can be counted, measured, analysed and presented in statistical form. Statistics can then be compared and analysed for significant patterns and trends.

Qualitative data

Qualitative data, as the name implies, is less to do with measurement and more to do with meaning. So, for example, a researcher might collect quantitative data on the numbers of people who use a particular service – this might be broken down into different categories of user, for example, in terms of gender, age, ethnic group and so on. Qualitative data might be collected in order to find out how a particular

---

Tees Stroke Register

The Tees Stroke Register was set up to investigate the fact that, for many years, the populations of the adjacent health districts of Darlington and North Tees had different death rates for stroke. Also, after allowing for differences in age and sex of the population, both districts had Standardised Mortality Ratios (SMR) greater than that for England as a whole, but the SMR for Darlington was consistently higher than that for North Tees. The aim of this study was to explore possible reasons for the higher death rate in Darlington.

Methods used

The research team set up a survey of all the patients identified as having had a stroke. Care was taken to obtain details of all patients with a suspected stroke in hospital, at home, or in nursing or residential care. A computer register was established and a wide range of information about the patients was recorded at one week, one month and six months after the event.

Sample groups

There were 9,164 notifications about 3,890 possible stroke events (notifications about each patient came from a number of sources). From these, 1,894 patients with stroke were identified, where the history, examination and investigations fitted within a generally accepted definition of stroke.

Findings

The study established the largest population-based register of patients with stroke in the UK. Using statistical analysis, the higher death rate in Darlington was confirmed, but the incidence of stroke was lower than in North Tees. Thus more patients with stroke died in Darlington – a higher case fatality rate. There was some evidence that more patients in Darlington presented with a severe stroke, but on the other hand those in North Tees had a higher level of other health problems. Initial examination of information about patterns of care, including investigations and treatment, suggests that care in North Tees is more systematic, but this is only a tentative finding. Neither of these factors is enough to explain the differences in death rate and more detailed analysis of the large amount of data was said to be indicated.

More details of this study can be found at www.refer.nhs.uk, the website of the Department of Health's research findings register.

group felt about the service in depth. As you can see, there is the potential to use both quantitative and qualitative collection methods in order to gain a fuller picture of what you want to know.

University of Bath Community Stroke Project

The community stroke project was a Lottery-funded project set up to develop and evaluate a community scheme for stroke survivors, which consisted of both an exercise and interactive educational element. The aim of the scheme was to help stroke survivors with the adjustment to life after their stroke.

Methods

In partnership with the Stroke Association, the project team trained a number of dissemination volunteers – people who have participated in a scheme and are keen to help spread the word. Stroke survivors are invited to contribute to workshops where they discuss their experiences of community services and identify ways in which their needs could be met. The aim is that the results from the research and feedback from the participants will help further the debate on the level and types of support available to stroke survivors and their families after discharge from hospital.

More details about this project can be found at www.bath.ac.uk/health/research/rehabNet/projects.html

Both these studies are interested in stroke. The first wants to understand why the two areas had different survival rates and, in order to investigate this, a quantitative approach was required. In the second study, the research is more focused on finding out about people's experiences of using a particular service. Both types of research are useful to improve the overall health and well-being of stroke victims.

Other sources of data

Primary research need not directly involve people. Researchers can take a documentary approach. For example, they could look through case records, admission statistics or operational guidelines – it all depends on the research questions.

Analysing the data

Both types of data – qualitative and quantitative – require their own methods of analysis. Quantitative analysis requires a knowledge of statistics. For example, the research might want to know whether there is a statistically significant relationship (or correlation) between the incidence of mental ill-health and particular ethnic groups within a certain population. Computer programmes, such as SPSS for Windows, are now available to assist with quantitative data management and analysis. However, the researcher still needs to understand the tests for statistical significance. The analysis of qualitative data must be systematic and rigorous. It requires careful interpretation so that the researcher can understand the meanings contained in the data. Whichever way the analysis is undertaken, researchers need to show clearly what methods they used to analyse their data. It has to be a transparent process so that others can verify the validity of the findings and conclusions. Data analysis is strengthened through the process of methodological **triangulation**. This means that findings are confirmed by the use of different methods – for example, by using the findings from observation and interviews.

Reporting and disseminating the findings

There is no point in doing research without telling anyone about it. Once the analysis is complete, the findings have to be written up. The findings can be disseminated (broadcast) in many formats. However, usually the researcher writes a report. If the research has been funded then the funding body will certainly expect a report at least.

The final report will first set out the nature of the question investigated, then explain the choice of research method, how the data were analysed, explain the results and suggest conclusions that can be drawn from the findings. Academics might publish their findings in an academic journal or deliver a presentation at a conference. However, research findings are increasingly posted on the Internet.

Access to research subjects

Sampling

We have provided a brief overview of the research process. Research requires subjects to be studied and, as mentioned earlier, when it comes to research into health and social care, this means 'people'. Apart from the ten-yearly census carried out by the Office of National Statistics, which aims to include the whole population of the UK, just about all other studies settle for researching much smaller groups of people. This is for practical considerations as much as anything else. A sample is usually a small number of people who, in some way, could be said to represent the larger group under study.

Sampling is a critical part of most research projects and requires a little more discussion, as any conclusions drawn from research are only as good as the sample they are based on. Careful thought must therefore be given to how to select the research sample. This is especially the case with quantitative research where the researcher is going to use statistical analysis and wants to generalise their findings beyond the study group. However, even with qualitative research, where the researcher might want to focus on a small number of people, they must still decide which people to study. Also, a researcher may want to study a certain group, but this doesn't give the researcher the right to have information about or access to them. So, for example, if you wanted to find out if older people in your locality were clear about the availability and purpose of Direct Payments, you would need to make some critical decisions about whom exactly to involve in your study and how to gain access.

Choosing sampling methods

First, you would need to *operationalise* what you mean by 'older people' (i.e. turn the concept of older people into something that could be meaningfully studied). This might mean you decide to go for anyone who falls into the 65-plus age category. This would be your **target population**. However, potentially this means you could have a possible study group running into thousands. As discussed earlier, even if you wanted to involve everyone aged 65-plus, time and funding considerations would mean that this would be practically impossible – even if you decided on a telephone or postal survey. You therefore need to decide on a more manageable sample of older people.

There are different approaches you can take depending on the type of research you are going to undertake. There are formulae for determining sample size, but the important thing is to be practical. For a small target population, a sample of somewhere between 10–30 per cent is desirable; for a large target population (for example, over 100,000), it would be possible to proceed with a sample as low as one per cent. But, before you can choose a sample from a population, you need to have a sense of the overall population of people you want to study. The list of all those in the population who come into the category of person you want to study, and from which you will draw your sample, is called the **sampling frame**. So, for example, to ensure that your sample is taken from the greatest number of older people in your locality, you would need to obtain as complete a list as possible of the names of people aged 65-plus. As you can imagine, this is not always easy. Getting access to such information, assuming it existed, might require permission. Access to 'the field' always requires negotiation and inevitably some compromises. Organisations that possess data about people are usually bound by data protection legislation. The researcher might have to settle for a less than complete list. However, let us assume that you can gain access to a list of 2,000 names of older people over 65 in an area which a local council might hold (assuming one exists). This list can be used as a sampling frame. With a suitable sampling frame, you are ready to decide on your sample.

The most straightforward sample to obtain is **simple random sampling**, which is sampling on the basis of pure chance. Using a randomised approach comes under the heading of **probability sampling** as it cuts out the risk of **sampling bias** and gives a greater chance of being able to generalise from the findings. Sampling bias is where, either consciously or unconsciously, people are selected by the researcher who may not be a typical cross-section. To achieve randomness it can sometimes be as simple as picking names out of a hat. Researchers have also developed random number tables and computer programs to help them ensure that every person picked from the sampling frame had an equal chance of being chosen and the researcher could not bias it in any way. By using the 'hat' method you will end up with 200 possible participants. It should be random because every one of those 200 had an equal chance of being picked. Of course, having chosen 200, there is no guarantee that they will agree to participate, so to achieve the desired number you will have to dip back into the sampling frame.

Simple random sampling, as the name suggests, could and should turn up anybody. However, you might want to be more purposive. **Stratified sampling** is a particular form of random sampling. Here the researcher ensures that the characteristics of the group you want to study (its various strata) are proportionately represented before sampling takes place. For example, you might want to run a focus group of ten care home residents to find out about what they thought of the food. Let us say that the overall number of residents is 40 with 80 per cent females and 20 per cent males. You could well decide that you wanted to represent the 'stratum' of age proportionately in the sample i.e. 80 per cent females and 20 per cent males. You would therefore choose the 8 females at random from the 32 women and similarly the 2 males from the 8 men. The

participants would still be chosen at random but gender differences would be proportionately represented. The same formula could be used for other characteristics of stratification such as age or ethnic group.

There are two other useful forms of random sampling to consider here: **filter sampling** and **cluster sampling**.

Filter sampling

This method means that the researcher starts off with a larger sample of people who broadly fit the bill of whom they want to study. They then 'filter out' those people who are not specifically wanted. For example, because the researcher might be more interested in women in their middle age, from an initial sample of 500 women in an area who have been diagnosed with depression, 200 may be filtered out by age for people too young or old, leaving a group of 300 aged between 50 and 65. This subgroup of 300 may be further filtered to a group of 100 women who are unemployed. Finally, the researcher is left with an even smaller sub-group of unemployed 50- to 65-year-old women – exactly the group whom they particularly want to study.

Cluster sampling

This method is used by researchers who want to take a small sample from a large target population that may be spread over a wide geographical area. In a large town or city, a researcher might decide to sample from certain 'clusters' of streets, in selected areas of the town which have the characteristics in which the researcher is particularly interested, for example, where there is a high proportion of social housing.

Quota sampling

Quota sampling is quite common in market research. It is a relatively economical way of finding out people's views. Here, for example, the researcher decides that they might want to seek people's views about a new bus service. For their own reasons (typically to be able to say they have canvassed a variety of different user opinions), the researcher might want to ask 1,000 people using the following quotas: 300 car users – 50 of whom are disabled car users; 400 people who use the bus to commute; 300 pensioners who use the bus out of peak time. The researcher continues to ask people until they have met the required quota – it is obviously not fully random and therefore comes under the heading of **non-probability sampling**.

Other non-probability sampling methods include **opportunistic** or **convenience sampling**. Here the researcher is prepared to study whoever is available from their target population. If, for example, they wanted to find out what people's views were on day centre transport, they might arrange to meet up with the bus one day and start talking to whoever happened to be on the bus that particular day. In this type of situation, as in any social research, it is important to give people the opportunity not to participate. On such occasions the people involved should not be regarded as a 'captive audience'.

Snowball sampling

This method is useful to gain access to groups which are hard to reach, such as migrant workers, drug users or rough sleepers, where complete lists of the target population usually do not exist and it would be hard to get hold of any type of sampling frame. A researcher might want to find out about how much such groups were aware of local health services. Once one possible participant is identified – which might be through the help of a support organisation – and that person is asked if they know anyone else in a similar position who might be interested in being involved in the study. In this way, the sample 'snowballs' by word of mouth. As with all non-random and non-probability methods, the researcher cannot confidently generalise from their findings.

Gatekeepers

The discussion has not been exhaustive but has aimed to show a range of methods that researchers use in order to find subjects for their research. Where representation is important the researcher needs to consider probability sampling. However, a lot of research in health and social care uses non-probability sampling methods; this means that the researchers can generate interesting data but cannot confidently claim that their subjects are representative of a bigger target population.

It will have become obvious that finding subjects to participate in research is not necessarily easily. This becomes even more likely if the group you want to study is vulnerable, excluded or hard to reach. Researchers therefore usually need to identify a **gatekeeper** to help them. A gatekeeper is often someone in an official position whose job either brings them into contact with the type of people you want to study, such as a physiotherapist or drugs counsellor, or who has access to records from which a sampling frame can be generated, such as a senior manager in the local PCT. Finding the most appropriate gatekeeper and negotiating access with them can be quite time-consuming. They will usually require you to give certain safeguards (which we will cover in the next section on ethics).

Ethical considerations

Let us imagine that you were asked to participate in some research into some aspect of your life. It might be, for example, how often you see your GP and whether you were satisfied with the experience. Alternatively, it could be what your feelings were about caring for a sick relative. What concerns might you have about participating in such studies? Most 'would-be' participants would probably want certain assurances before they agreed to volunteer such personal information about themselves.

Most people would probably expect their personal details to be kept confidential in any research. They might want to know how much of their time it would take and, generally, what they were letting themselves in for. They might also want to know that the researcher was bona fide and was engaged in research that was responsible and had some purpose. They might also want to know what was going to happen with the information. When people are involved in research as subjects, there is a whole range of possible questions they might have.

We would probably all agree that such concerns are perfectly legitimate. However, for reasons such as communication or cognitive impairment, some research subjects may not be in a position to ask these and other questions. Therefore, for these and other reasons, research into health and social care is bound by certain ethical rules and principles which are designed to minimise risk and protect from harm not only the subject, but also the researcher, the researcher's funders and employing organisation.

What do we mean by harm?

Clearly, the harm a piece of research might cause is a matter of interpretation. However, it might be said to include:

● physical trauma or injury
● distress
● offence
● inconvenience
● coercion
● exploitation
● wasting time
● wasting resources
● doing something which will lead to disrepute of any of the parties involved or even litigation.

In general the practice of social research should be guided by the desire to maximise benefit and minimise risk, harm or inconvenience. For example, a study that required district nurses to wade through a 20-page questionnaire in order to find out their views on relatively trivial matters such as whether they wanted their diaries to be day- or week-to-view might produce some interesting findings, but not so interesting that the amount of time spent on it was justified.

CASE STUDY

When research goes wrong

The Stanford prison experiment

In 1971 a team of researchers led by Philip Zimbardo of Stanford University conducted a psychological study of people's behaviour in a 'mock prison'. The idea was to examine the subjects' behavioural responses to being in prison — both the guards and inmates. Zimbardo asked for undergraduate students to volunteer to 'play' the roles of both guards and prisoners and these roles were chosen at random. The 'prison' was actually a set of rooms in the basement of the Stanford psychology building. What happened was that the prisoners and, especially the guards, went far too much into their roles and the whole experiment got out of hand. The guards were being far more strict and even violent than was anticipated and several went well beyond what was necessary.

As a result, many prisoners became psychologically traumatised – one actually went on a genuine hunger strike to protest against the conditions. Two had to be removed from the experiment early. The role-play seemed to release sadistic tendencies in the guards. The level of emotional stress and the worrying behaviour on both the parts of the prisoners and the guards meant that the whole study had to be abandoned early. Follow-up work showed that the participants continued to have strong negative feelings towards each other for a long time after the experiment was over.

This was a real experiment carried out by a professor in a reputable university. However, the effects on the participants had not been thought through and even though the motives were said to be honourable, it was severely criticised on ethical grounds. Insufficient attention was given to protecting the interests of all those involved.

Questions

1 Supposing you wanted to conduct a similar investigation, how might you attend to the obvious ethical issues that such a study raises?
2 Write a set of guidelines for the a) researchers and b) participants that you think would minimise risk.

Key ethical principles

Informed consent

This means that potential participants should always be informed in advance and in understandable terms of any potential benefits, risks, inconvenience or obligations associated with the research that might reasonably be expected to influence their willingness to participate. Getting consent should normally involve the use of a participant information sheet which explains about the research and what participation will involve. The participant should be asked to sign to say that they understand what they have read and they are happy to give their consent and sign a consent form. Participants should be informed clearly that they have a right to withdraw their consent at any time and that any data that they have provided will be destroyed if they request it. Consent should also be ongoing. Therefore, if a person says 'yes' once at the start, it should not be assumed that, a while later, they are feeling the same way about participating.

Openness and honesty

Researchers should be open and honest about the purpose and content of their research and behave in a professional manner at all times. Participants should be given opportunities to access the outcomes of research in which they have participated. They should be offered a debrief, if appropriate, after they have provided data.

Protection from harm

As explained earlier, researchers must make every effort to minimise the risks of any harm, either physical or psychological, arising for any participant, researcher, institution, funding body or other person. Researchers need to carry out some form of a risk analysis. Where significant risks are identified, researchers should specify a risk management and harm alleviation strategy. For example, they should explain what they would do if a participant became very upset during an interview. Researchers in the UK also need to comply with the requirements of the UK Data Protection Act 1998, the Freedom of Information Act 2000 and any other relevant legal frameworks governing the management of personal information. Where research involves children or other vulnerable groups, an appropriate level of disclosure should be obtained from the Criminal Records Bureau for all researchers who may come into contact with participants. Participants should be given information about whom to contact if any issues that emerge during the research cannot be resolved by members of the project team.

Confidentiality

Researchers should respect and maintain the confidentiality of participants' identities and data at all times, unless explicit written consent has been given. In reality this means removing or changing participants' names and any other detail that may enable them to be identified such as circumstances or addresses. Typically, any tapes or other recordings made should be kept secure in locked cupboards or rooms and destroyed once they are no longer needed. Information held on computers should be password protected.

Professional and academic codes of practice and ethics

Researchers are usually bound by a published code of practice and ethical guidelines of a professional or governing body. Research which involves the NHS, for example, should always be conducted in compliance with an ethical protocol approved by the appropriate NHS Research Ethics Committee. University researchers have to gain approval from their own URECs (University Research Ethics Committees) and local authorities have LRECs (Local Research Ethics Committees). The Social Research Association has its own ethical guidelines which can be downloaded from its website.

Conclusion

Ethical matters and ethical protection have become increasingly debated in medical, health and social research in recent years. These days, researchers undertaking medical and social research are required to seek ethical approval for their projects. In order to obtain approval, they need to explain how informed consent to participate is sought, gained and recorded, how data is collected, stored and accessed, and how participants are informed of their rights within the

study. It is no longer acceptable, as it might have been in the 1960s and 1970s, for researchers to take a 'god-like' stance and go and do research 'to' people – justifying it because it is in the cause of scientific study. The needs, feelings and rights of all the participants must be properly taken into account.

Outline of common primary research methods

In an introductory chapter such as this it is not possible to cover all aspects of the various research methods used in health and social care research. Suggested reading is given at the end of the chapter for those who want to find out more. However, this section provides a brief overview of some of the main methods used, some of their strengths and weaknesses, and what kind of data they would generate.

Randomised Controlled Trials (RCTs)

Randomised controlled trials or studies are a quantitative research method used more often in medical research than social research. They are considered by many to be the 'gold standard' of research methods because of their close adherence to the traditional scientific model. Typically, they are studies in which participants are randomly put into two groups. There is a treatment (or intervention) group and a control group. The treatment group receives the new treatment under investigation (e.g. a new drug being trialled), and the control group receives either no treatment, the existing treatment or a placebo. The reason for assigning participants at random is to reduce the risk of bias and increase the probability that any differences between the groups can actually be attributed to whatever the treatment or intervention is.

Having a control group allows the researcher to compare the treatment with alternatives. For instance, the researchers might find that a particular new drug or treatment improves the symptoms or cures 70 per cent of cases. However, what happens in the control group is important. If perhaps 10 per cent improved, that could tell the researchers they are on to something with the new intervention. If the control group shows that 65 per cent improved anyway, then the efficacy of the new intervention looks less sure. RCTs are often conducted on a 'double-blind' basis. This means that not only do the participants not know which treatment they are having, but also neither do the experimenters. This removes all chance of bias. In general, large randomised trials tend to show results that are more clear-cut with a lower risk of error. Small randomised trials can often produce uncertain results and therefore have a moderate to high risk of error.

Ethical issues

With certain research questions, randomised controlled studies cannot be done for ethical reasons. For instance, it would be unethical to attempt to measure the effect of drinking on health by asking one group to drink half a bottle of whisky a day and another group to abstain, since the drinking group would be placed at risk and subject to unnecessary harm.

RCTs in practice

The following 'research recommendation' is taken from the National Institute for Health and Clinical Excellence (NICE) website (guidance.nice.org.uk/page.aspx?o=391164). In this case, it shows how research using RCTs is being sought to establish the efficacy (the capacity or power to produce a desired effect) of certain drugs for people with Alzheimer's disease. It states:

> **Individual research recommendation details**
>
> Research is required, preferably using [Randomised Controlled Trials] (RCTs), to investigate the effect of Memantine on subgroups

of people with Alzheimer's disease suggested to derive enhanced benefit from Memantine, such as those with behavioural disturbance.

If you want to find out more about Memantine and the clinical studies that have led to its development check the memantine website (www.memantine.com/en). From this, you will get a clearer idea of how clinical studies using RCTs have helped to test the efficacy of this drug. For example, look up the work of Reisberg *et al* (2003) published in the *New England Journal of Medicine*; it will show you how important statistical analysis is to this form of research.

RCTs are mostly suitable for research into medical interventions. However, even then they can have limitations. For example, a focus on the short-term may miss medium- and long-term side effects, or there may be conflict between results observed in a 'controlled' experiment versus use in 'real' life where other unforeseen factors can affect outcomes. They can have more limitations in other aspects of health and social care research. Apart from ethical considerations, they do not, for example, attempt to find out people's views or feelings.

Surveys

Surveys are a commonly used method in health and social research. Surveys are usually based on questionnaires (see page 408) and are a systematic way of collecting information about people's opinions or behaviour. They follow the same standard structure of questions for each respondent. The researcher is usually interested in a particular defined group, for example, young carers, home care users or maybe simply 'young people 16–25 years old'. Most surveys are snapshot surveys. The researcher conducts a 'one-off' study, gathering their data from the study group at one point in time (hence the phrase 'snapshot'). Surveys can be conducted by various methods; for example, face to face, telephone, postal or, nowadays, via email. Surveys can be analysed relatively quickly – these days often using computers. Findings from surveys are quantitative and the results can be shown in numerical form. For example, a survey result might be '43 per cent of boys thought it was important to use condoms and that 26 per cent of girls smoked to relieve stress' (BBC, 2005).

ACTIVITY

From the information you have been given about RCTs, how do you think this particular study might be organised?

The questionnaire

Questionnaires are almost always used in surveys. This is where the researcher designs a set of questions about a particular subject to be answered by respondents (the people being surveyed). It can be challenging to construct a good questionnaire. For example, if you want to establish someone's ethnic origins, what categories do you use for people to choose from? You must also avoid leading or emotionally charged questions. For example, giving someone a question such as, 'Do you think the monarchy should be: a) abolished within the next 2 years b) phased out over a longer period or c) at some other point?' rather assumes that getting rid of the monarchy is an option that most people would entertain. You would not be able to capture a full range of views on the subject – it could even be construed by some as offensive. It is often a good idea to 'pilot' a questionnaire to iron out the glitches. However, once the researcher has sorted out their questions, they can get a lot of useful information from respondents in one go.

With questionnaires the quality of the data is dependent on the quality of the questions. However, once the questionnaire has been successfully designed, the way it is used can vary. Sending it through the post to individuals is cheaper than paying for the travel and other costs of interviewers. However, this still leads to problems. The biggest problem is that people often do not return the questionnaire so the response rate can be very low. For example, a postal survey of users of mental health services carried out by the Healthcare Commission in 2006 had a response rate of 38 per cent. For full details of this survey visit the Healthcare Commission website.

Another problem with postal questionnaires is that if the participant has any problems completing the form there is no one there to help. Even when questionnaires are completed and returned satisfactorily, this does not necessarily guarantee a successful survey. The findings can be distorted because only those sufficiently motivated to respond actually reply. Therefore, only those participants who feel particularly strongly about a topic or who find it particularly interesting may respond. A personal visit by the researcher can minimise these risks, but this is obviously more expensive.

Closed and open questions

The most reliable and efficient way of using questionnaires is by direct interviewing. In this the researchers approach people and ask them if they would like to answer questions on the particular topic. 'Street' researchers have to be carefully briefed about whom to stop and interview. If the researcher is interested in questioning women between the ages of 35 and 50 there is inevitably an element of hit-and-miss about the operation. Misjudging people, for example, in terms of ages or job status, can be time-consuming and potentially embarrassing. Some questions are easier for the researcher to handle than others and this needs to be reflected in questionnaire design. For example, factual questions about whether someone is married, single, divorced, widowed or living with someone, or the person's occupation and age, might conceivably be sensitive but are fairly straightforward. Questionnaires usually start off with these relatively neutral questions. They are **closed questions** in that there is only one possible answer to them. 'Yes/no' questions are also closed questions, but these can be used to ask more potentially emotive questions such as:

- Do you agree with the government's current handling of asylum seekers?

It is normal to lead up to these types of emotive questions, giving the interviewer and interviewee a chance to build up some form of trust and relationship. The same would be true of 'revealing' personal questions such as:

- How often do you have sexual intercourse?

Just to have a 'yes/no' or a similar closed option on certain questions is quite limiting. The researcher may want to enquire about people's views, opinions or some aspect of their lifestyle in more detail. Such questions might be:

- What are your views on immigration?
- What should we do about anti-social behaviour among young people?
- What are your opinions about euthanasia?

These are called **open** or **open-ended questions** because there are many ways of answering them. Each response could be quite individual. In using more open questions, the researcher would be moving from a quantitative form of research to something more qualitative. The researcher therefore needs to employ different methods of analysis. These would be less statistical and more attentive to the language used and the themes and points raised in the answers. It would be harder to present the findings from such questions neatly in tabular or mathematical form (if at all).

A real-life survey

Under the National Health Service (Pharmaceutical Services) Regulations 2005, pharmacists must now undertake a patient satisfaction survey. The actual questionnaire is reproduced on the following page. Think about what sort of questions are being asked and the way the questions are structured. How might the findings be presented?

Details of the actual patient questionnaire can be found at:

www.dh.gov.uk/en/Publicationsandstatistics/
Publications/PublicationsPolicyAndGuidance/DH_073278

Likert scales

Likert scales are very common in quantitative research. Questionnaires, like the one mentioned above, often contain Likert scales (named after an American social scientist called Rensis Likert). Typically a statement is given and a set of responses provided to choose from. For example, 'The government is not doing enough to help older people with long-term care'. The respondent is asked to indicate his or her degree of agreement with the statement or some other kind of evaluation of the statement. Traditionally a five-point scale is used, although this can vary. This might be:

- strongly disagree
- disagree
- neither agree nor disagree
- agree
- strongly agree.

Likert scales use a **bipolar scaling method**, designed to measure either positive or negative responses to a statement on a scale of extremes. After the questionnaire is completed, each response may be analysed separately or responses may be totalled under headings in order to create a score for a group of responses.

Structured interviews

Advantages

- All respondents are asked the same questions so it is easy to replicate and can be standardised.
- They provide a reliable source of quantitative data.
- Large numbers can be used and it is an easy and quick method to administer.
- The relationship between researcher and respondent is clear and straightforward.

Disadvantages

- They can be time-consuming.
- Designing the right questions is crucial – failure to do so will lead to poor data.
- They can be limited in investigating complex issues.
- The questions are 'set in stone' and allow for no variation.

Longitudinal surveys

A more time-consuming and therefore expensive type of survey is the **longitudinal** or cohort survey. In this, a selected group (the cohort) is studied over a period of time (longitudinally), usually at predetermined intervals, for example, a year or six months after the previous survey. This enables the researcher to gain not only current information but also insights into the way the cohort's attitudes, status or behaviour change over a much longer time-span. So if the researcher wanted to find out the effect of closing a day centre, a longitudinal survey might be an effective method to use. You could investigate the

Community Pharmacy Patient Questionnaire

This section is about why you visited the pharmacy today

1. Why did you visit this pharmacy today?

To collect a prescription for: Yourself ☐ Someone else ☐   Both ☐   **OR**

For some other reason (please write in the reason for your visit):

If you did not collect a prescription, please go to Q3.

2. If you collected a prescription today, were you able to collect it straight away, did you have to wait in the pharmacy or did you come back later to collect it?

Straight away ☐   Waited in pharmacy ☐   Came back later ☐

3. How satisfied were you with the time it took to provide your prescription and/or any other NHS services you required?

Not at all satisfied ☐   Not very satisfied ☐   Fairly satisfied ☐   Very satisfied ☐

This section is about the pharmacy and the staff who work there more generally, not just for today's visit

4. Thinking about any previous visits as well as today's, how would you rate the pharmacy on the following factors? Please tick one box for each aspect of the pharmacy listed below, to show how good or poor you think it is.

ANSWERS:

	Very poor	Fairly poor	Fairly good	Very good	Don't know
a) The cleanliness of the pharmacy	☐	☐	☐	☐	☐
b) The comfort and convenience of the waiting areas (e.g. seating or standing room)	☐	☐	☐	☐	☐
c) Having in stock the medicines/appliances you need	☐	☐	☐	☐	☐
d) Offering a clear and well organised layout	☐	☐	☐	☐	☐
e) How long you have to wait to be served	☐	☐	☐	☐	☐
f) Having somewhere available where you could speak without being overheard, if you wanted to	☐	☐	☐	☐	☐

5. Again, including any previous visits to this pharmacy, how would you rate the pharmacist and the other staff who work there? Please tick one box for each aspect of the service listed below, to show how good or poor you think it is.

ANSWERS:

	Very poor	Fairly poor	Fairly good	Very good	Don't know
a) Being polite and taking the time to listen to what you want	☐	☐	☐	☐	☐
b) Answering any queries you may have	☐	☐	☐	☐	☐
c) The service you received from the pharmacist	☐	☐	☐	☐	☐
d) The service you received from the other pharmacy staff	☐	☐	☐	☐	☐
e) Providing an efficient service	☐	☐	☐	☐	☐
f) The staff overall	☐	☐	☐	☐	☐

6. Thinking about all the times you have used this pharmacy, how well do you think it provides each of the following services?

ANSWERS:

	Not at all well	Not very well	Fairly well	Very well	Never used
a) Providing advice on a current health problem or a longer-term health condition	☐	☐	☐	☐	☐
b) Providing general advice on leading a more healthy lifestyle	☐	☐	☐	☐	☐
c) Disposing of medicines you no longer need	☐	☐	☐	☐	☐
d) Providing advice on health services or information available elsewhere	☐	☐	☐	☐	☐

7. Have you ever been given advice about any of the following by the pharmacist or pharmacy staff?

Stopping smoking   ☐ Yes   ☐ No
Healthy eating   ☐ Yes   ☐ No
Physical exercise   ☐ Yes   ☐ No

8. Which of the following best describes how you use this pharmacy?

This is the pharmacy that you choose to visit if possible   ☐
This is one of several pharmacies that you use when you need to   ☐
This pharmacy was just convenient for you today   ☐

9. Finally, taking everything into account – the staff, the shop and the service provided – how would you rate the pharmacy where you received this questionnaire?

Poor ☐   Fair ☐   Good ☐   Very good ☐   Excellent ☐

10. If you have any comments about how the service from this pharmacy could be improved, please write them in here:

[Insert here, if required, additional questions relating to health care service provision]

These last few questions are just to help us categorise your answers

11. How old are you?

16-19 ☐   20-24 ☐   25-34 ☐   35-44 ☐   45-54 ☐   55-64 ☐   65+ ☐

12. Are you...   Male ☐   Female ☐

13. Which of the following apply to you:

You have, or care for, children under 16   ☐
You are a carer for someone with a longstanding illness or infirmity   ☐
Neither   ☐

Thank you for completing this questionnaire

Figure 11.3 Patient satisfaction survey

situation of the people just after the closure and follow up six months later.

Seven Up

While not a survey in the strictest sense, the famous 'Seven Up' TV documentaries made by the film director Michael Apted for Granada Television can be regarded as a form of longitudinal study. The Seven Up series consists of a series of documentary films that have followed the lives of 14 children since 1964, when they were 7 years old. Subsequently, every 7 years, Apted has attempted to film an update using as many of the original group as possible. Originally, the films set out to explore the link between socio-economic background and future outcomes. The children were selected from a range of socio-economic backgrounds. The latest episode, *49 Up*, was released in September 2005. It is clear that while it showed fascinating insights into how certain children's lives developed, the sheer length of the study (over 40 years) has led to many participants dropping out.

For those of you who are not aware of it, the series is available on DVD. If you are interested in people, relationships, personal and human development, these are a fascinating set of programmes.

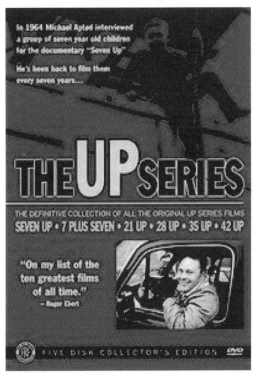

Figure 11.4   The Seven Up series has followed a group of children since 1964

Online surveys

In line with much of modern life, surveys are increasingly created and administered online. Different websites and software exist to enable people to design their own surveys quickly and effectively. Check out, for example, 'Survey Monkey' at www.surveymonkey.com.

Semi-structured interviews

Interviews using questionnaires are very structured; this method mainly produces data that can be quantified, tabulated (put into tables or charts) and analysed mathematically. The structured and predominately closed nature of the questions means that the respondents cannot go into much depth or bring in their own perspective. Researchers who are interested in collecting data that is more qualitative therefore tend to use interviews that have less structure and give the interviewee more time and space to develop their responses.

Semi-structured interviews are a way of combining a schedule of headings you want to cover while providing a certain amount of freedom to the participant to talk more about what they think is important. The researcher might have a set of six questions or themes that they want to cover. They would work through this structure with the participant, but there would be plenty of space for the person being interviewed to elaborate their answers on their own terms. So, for example, a semi-structured interview might start with the following two questions:

1   How did you come to find out about the drop-in centre?
2   What do you think you get out of it?

The interviewer is guiding the interviewee through a set of headings but they make their own individual response in each case in their own words.

Advantages

- A positive rapport can be generated between interviewer and interviewee.
- Complex issues can be discussed and clarified.
- The findings can be said to be more valid because the interviewee has used their own words more.
- They are easy to record.

Disadvantages

- They are more dependent on the skill of the interviewer.
- The interviewer has more chance of giving out unconscious signals and biasing the responses.
- They are time-consuming.
- They are not very reliable – in that you couldn't say you would get the same answers if the interview was repeated by another interviewer.
- The findings are more difficult to analyse and generalise from.

Open interviews

Open interviews are even less structured and require quite a high level of skill from the interviewer. An open interview might arise when a researcher wants to find out more about something they have little prior knowledge of themselves. They might, for example, want to find out how a patient is recovering from a new medical procedure. With no prior agenda, they give the respondent the opportunity to talk purely on their own terms. There clearly has to be some minimal structure but the researcher is prepared to be mainly guided by the interviewee as to what is important and what is not. Such interviews can produce very rich qualitative data and provide useful case studies, but it is not possible to generalise from such an open and fluid exchange. Also, with little or no structure, the potential for the interview to go wrong is quite high.

Focus groups

Focus groups have become increasingly popular both in market and social research in recent years. A focus group can be defined as a group of people selected and assembled by researchers because they come into a certain category – for example, carers of people with Alzheimer's disease or users of a particular mental health service. There is a difference between focus groups and more straightforward group interviewing.

Group interviewing involves interviewing a number of people at the same time, the emphasis being on questions and responses between the researcher and participants. However, with focus group research the researchers are looking to stimulate discussion among the group. Focus groups utilise the interaction among group members to discuss and draw out opinion on specific topics introduced by the researcher. For example, a researcher might want to gauge the focus group's reaction to a proposed change in a service.

The advantages of focus groups are that they enable researchers to gain insights into the common or shared understandings/reactions that people might have to a particular topic. They can be very effective at sparking lively discussion. However, it can also be difficult to identify different individual views from the group view, especially if 'strong' personalities start to dominate. Therefore, the role of the moderator is very important to be able to deal with conflict and facilitate as much free expression as possible. Recording and analysis can also be quite complex with many voices talking at once.

Focus groups in practice

Check out the SCIE website for more details of 'The Road Ahead', a project carried out by the Norah Fry Research Centre, University of Bristol, in partnership with North Somerset People First and the Home Farm Trust. Using focus groups, this project looked at the information needs of young learning disabled people, their parents and supporters in making the transition into adulthood.

Observation

Observation is one of the oldest methods in the medical and social sciences. As with all the methods there are different approaches that can be taken to observation. Two broad categories are *participant* and *non-participant observation*. A popular and straightforward form of non-participant observation is direct (reactive) observation.

Direct (reactive) observation

Examples of direct observation might be where psychologists directly observe children's behaviour when they play or physiotherapists study people recovering from a stroke performing some exercises. The observer will record their observations in notes, on a grid or chart with audio or videotape – sometimes more than one recording method is used. With direct observations, the subjects know that they are being observed. The researcher is obviously separate from those being observed. Direct/non-participant observers can use different techniques. A commonly used technique is *continuous monitoring*.

Continuous monitoring involves observing a subject or subjects and recording their behaviour over a period of time. With this method it does not take very long to accumulate a wealth of data. One of the difficulties with continuous monitoring is that while the observer is hoping to see what is naturally occurring, the effect of being observed can lead to people changing their behaviour. The most famous example of this was in the 1920s/30s when Professor Elton Mayo of the Harvard Business School conducted research into productivity and work conditions at the Western Electric Hawthorne Works in Chicago. The fact of Mayo doing research actually led to a marked increase on the normal levels of worker productivity. This change of people's behaviour when being observed is now often referred to as the *Hawthorne Effect*. Observers have to take this effect into account when planning their research.

Participant observation

Participant observation is where the researcher actually joins the group they wish to study, becoming as involved as possible in its activities. It is an approach to observation that has its roots in anthropology and ethnography. This form of observing blurs the distinction between the researcher and those being researched. When successful, it helps provide the researcher with an insider's view of that group's culture and what it is like to be in that group. It is claimed that one of the effects of observing while being a participant is that the people being observed act more 'naturally' and

the Hawthorne effect is diminished as the observer becomes accepted as 'one of them'.

There are two main approaches to participant observation. The researcher can be open and explain the nature of the research to the group they join – this would be following standard ethical principles. This is known as *overt participant observation*. A researcher might, for example, join an exercise class rather than just sit at the edge observing it.

> **REFLECT**
>
> Think about the advantages and disadvantages of observing in this way rather than just being a passive, external observer.

However, there are occasions when the researcher might decide not to reveal themselves or their true purpose. This is known as *covert participant observation*. As this involves deception on the part of the researcher, this can be criticised for its dubious ethics. However, sometimes it is justified when the benefits can be shown to outweigh the effect of the deception. An example might be in the past when researchers have passed themselves off as football hooligans to gain a better understanding about what motivates this form of behaviour. Such groups are hardly likely to give their consent to a researcher's presence.

Besides the ethical problems associated with participant observation, there are certain problems that researchers can face. For example, **observer bias** can occur when the researcher allows their own views and opinions to affect their judgement. Like all social researchers, observers usually write up their experiences in field notes. Good field notes should be honest and reflective – the researcher should examine their own views and behaviour critically. Nevertheless, on occasions, participant researchers can sometimes 'go native' – that is, they become so involved in the group they lose any sense of detachment and objectivity.

Conclusion

This section has briefly covered some of the various research methods used in medical, health and social care research. As will have become evident, different methods yield different types of data – no single method will fit all purposes. Researchers will often need to use different methods to learn more about a topic or issue. However, as discussed at the beginning of the chapter, even then they can seldom claim to have total and absolute knowledge of the subject. It should also be apparent that not only is the choice of method critical but the way in which the method is thought through and applied is important – for example, a badly constructed questionnaire will yield little of value; similarly a badly conducted observation or flawed experiment could quite easily create a false picture rather than adding to our knowledge. All research must be rigorous, open and ethical. So, while most people can learn to carry out research, proper training is definitely required if the findings are to be trusted to add anything new to our existing stock of knowledge.

Action research

Action research is based on the principle of researchers and practitioners working closely together, with the aim of bringing about a change in practice or policy within an organisation. It is becoming increasingly popular within health and social care particularly because it fits in with the philosophy of working in partnership with service users. The choice of methods depends on the aims of the specific project.

The practitioner-researcher

This chapter has explained how the work of practitioners in health and social care is informed and updated by research. As has been discussed, this is research which has been carried out by different researchers from different organisations – some governmental, some educational and some independent. Increasingly, practitioners are not only expected to be aware of the evidence base of research that is relevant to their particular area, it is also hoped that they will contribute to it in some ways. This might be through being a participant in research or, in certain circumstances, by being part of a research team. Walter *et al* (2004) in their work for SCIE, identified three key approaches to developing the use of research in social care. Stating that the three approaches need not be mutually exclusive, the three models are: the research-based practitioner model; the embedded research model; and the organisational excellence model.

The research-based practitioner model

- It is the role and responsibility of the individual practitioner to keep up to date with research and apply it to practice.
- The use of research is a linear process.
- Practitioners have high levels of professional autonomy to change practice based on research.

CASE STUDY

Berryhill Retirement Village

The Berryhill Retirement Village is in Stoke on Trent. It was developed by the ExtraCare Charitable Trust and Touchstone Housing Association. Between 2000 and 2003, a team from the School of Social Relations at Keele University explored what it was like to live and work in the new village. The team adopted a multi-method, participatory action research approach, a key feature of which was the close involvement of participants (the older residents). The study was funded by the Community Fund (now the Big Lottery Fund). The findings suggested that, for many, the Berryhill Village works well. However, it did highlight various ongoing challenges for all those involved. The study was subsequently written up and published. The reference is Bernard, M. et al (2004) *New Lifestyles in Old Age: Health, Identity and Well-being in Berryhill Retirement Village*, Bristol, The Policy Press.

- Professional education and training are important in enabling research use.

The embedded research model

- Research-informed practice is achieved by embedding research in the systems and processes of social care, such as standards, policies, procedures and tools.
- Responsibility for ensuring research-informed practice lies with policy makers and service delivery managers.
- The use of research is a linear and instrumental process.
- Funding restrictions, performance management, inspection and appraisal regimes are used to encourage research-informed practice.

The organisational excellence model

- The key to successful research use lies with social care delivery organisations: their leadership, management and organisation.
- Research use is supported by developing a research-minded culture.
- There is local adaptation of research findings and ongoing learning within organisations.
- Partnerships with local universities and intermediary organisations facilitate the creation and use of research.

(Walter *et al*, 2004, page xvii)

It would appear that there is some way to go in all of the approaches outlined. Their findings suggested that the successful development of the research-based practitioner model faced a number of barriers in terms of capacity both to access and interpret research. They also found that there is little evidence of how successful the embedded research model is currently and they say that it remains relatively undeveloped within the UK social care sector.

Conclusion

While many of the best ideas come from the front line, it is probably not feasible for individual practitioners to launch into their own health and social care research projects from a 'cold start', with little

expertise or resources. However, that does not mean that practitioners should not become involved in research in some way. People who are actually doing the job and working with service users and carers have a great deal to offer in terms of the knowledge and experience they bring and the ideas they can generate. If you are interested in research it is a good idea to build up experience by joining a bigger, more experienced team. You should contact those who are already involved in research and see what is going on and whether you could make a contribution. You can begin to acquire research skills and knowledge in this way. However, if you want to pursue a career as a researcher than you would need to go to college or university to undertake recognised research training. It is also a good idea to seek out pieces of research, either in journals or from the web, in which you are particularly interested and contact the researchers. Ask them more about the study – they may be planning further research in which case you might be asked to be involved in some way.

KNOWLEDGE CHECK

1. What is the study of *epistemology* concerned with?
2. What does it mean to say that a research method is *reliable*?
3. What does it mean to say that a research method is *valid*?
4. Briefly explain the difference between *primary* and *secondary* research.
5. How would you explain the difference between 'objectivist' and 'constructivist' perspectives on understanding the social world?
6. How do academic journals try to ensure that the articles they contain are scientifically credible and authoritative?
7. What are the five main stages of the research process?
8. Briefly explain the difference between a *quantitative* and a *qualitative* approach to social research. Give examples.
9. Why is it important for social researchers to know about *sampling*?
10. List five key ethical principles that social researchers should work to.
11. What is the purpose of *action research*?

Glossary

Bipolar scaling method: a way of measuring either positive or negative responses to a statement, often used in questionnaires. A Likert scale is a common bipolar scaling method.

Closed questions: questions where the possible answers are predetermined. For example, 'Have you been to your doctor in the last month: Yes or No?'

Cluster sampling: an approach to sampling using progressively smaller clusters or units sampling from a larger target population.

Convenience sampling: a non-probability sampling technique that involves using subjects who are the most convenient to get hold of.

Epistemology: the study of knowledge, of what constitutes valid knowledge and what does not, e.g. questions of how we come to know what we know.

Filter sampling: a form of random sampling that, from a large target population, progressively filters out unwanted groups in order to achieve a random sample of the particular group the researcher wants to study.

Gatekeeper: people, often in positions of power or authority, whom a researcher usually needs to go through in order to negotiate access to the field.

Longitudinal study: a form of study that investigates change in its subjects over a long period. The researcher usually returns to the group under study at regular intervals.

Non-probability sampling: an approach to sampling that is purposive and does not use random selection. The researcher is aware that the findings cannot be confidently generalised to the larger population.

Observer bias: this can occur when the researcher allows their preconceptions to influence their observations.

Ontology: the study of the nature of being; e.g. asks such questions as 'what is reality'?

Open questions: questions without predetermined categories of answers. For example, 'What are your views about how well your GP listens to what you are saying?'

Opportunistic sampling: *see* convenience sampling. A non-random approach to sampling where the researcher studies subjects that happen to be available to them.

Pilot study: a small-scale study that is carried out before a larger one. The researcher uses the pilot to evaluate areas such as the suitability of methods, ethical questions and the general feasibility of undertaking the research.

Primary research: original research that is derived from direct contact with the field. *See also* Secondary research.

Probability sampling: a form of sampling that uses some form of random selection. It is used to ensure that a sample is representative of the larger target population and therefore the results can be generalised.

Quota sampling: a non-probability sampling technique. Quotas of subjects are decided in advance by the researcher to represent the make-up of the wider target population. For example, a street interviewer interviewing ten members of the public might look for a quota of five men and five women, rather than interview the first ten people who come along.

Reliability: a method is considered reliable if similar results would be achieved by a different researcher using that method or if similar results would be found if the research was repeated.

Sampling: the process of selecting a smaller group of subjects from a larger population. The two main approaches are non-probability and probability sampling.

Sampling bias: this occurs when the sample is not representative of the larger population from which it has been drawn.

Sampling frame: the sampling frame is the complete list of subjects that the researcher is interested in studying. For example, if the researcher wants to interview a group of residents from a care home, the sampling frame will be a list of all those people resident in the home.

Secondary research: an approach that uses research findings which already exist. Secondary research uses sources such as reports, articles or books that have been produced by others. *See also* Primary research.

Simple random sampling: an approach to sampling that is based entirely on chance and each member of the population has an equal chance of being included in the sample. No form of filtering is used.

Stratified sampling: in a stratified sample the sampling frame is divided into different and distinct 'strata', for example, by age group, gender or ethnic group. Once 'stratified', a simple random sample is taken from each stratum.

Target population: the entire group of possible subjects that could be studied in an area of interest. The size of target populations means that researchers usually have to select a smaller subgroup or sample which is more manageable to study.

Triangulation: used to improve the reliability of the data, this involves using different methods to study the same area or issue. An example might be to use both observation and interviews to assess people's satisfaction with a day centre.

Validity: this refers to the accuracy and credibility of a piece of research. Research is considered valid if its design is such that it genuinely answers the research question(s) the researcher sets out to investigate.

References

Bernard, M., Bartlam, B., Biggs, S. and Sim, J. (2004) *New Lifestyles in Old Age: Health, Identity and Well-being in Berryhill Retirement Village*, Bristol, The Policy Press

Bryman, A. (2001) *Social Research Methods*, Oxford, Oxford University

Department of Health (2001) *National Service Framework for Older People*, London, Department of Health

Hughes, J. and Baldwin, C. (2006) *Ethical Issues in Dementia Care*, London, Jessica Kingsley

Treloar, A., Beats, B. and Philpot, M. (2000) 'A Pill in the Sandwich: Covert Medication in Food and Drink', *Journal of the Royal Society of Medicine*, 93(8) 408–411

Walter, I., Nutley, S., Percy-Smith, J., McNeish, D. and Frost, S. (2004) 'Improving the use of research in social care practice' in *Knowledge Review 07*,

June 2004, London, Social Care Institute for Excellence

Useful websites

Commission for Social Care Inspection (latest publications on all aspects of adult social care): www.csci.org.uk/default.aspx?page=2003

Department of Health Learning Disability Research Initiative (learning disability): www.bild.org.uk/05policyandresearch_dohinit.htm

Department of Health: Research Findings Register (a full range of health-related research): www.refer.nhs.uk/ViewWebPage.asp?Page=Home

Joseph Rowntree Foundation (Independent Living, carers, social inclusion, disability and care of older people): www.jrf.org.uk/research-and-policy/

Kings' Fund (health-related publications): www.kingsfund.org.uk/publications/briefings/index.html

National Institute for Health and Clinical Excellence (health and medically focused research): www.nice.org.uk

The Sainsbury Centre for Mental Health (mental ill-health): www.scmh.org.uk

Social Care Online (all aspects of social care): www.scie-socialcareonline.org.uk

Suggested further reading

Green, J. and Thorogood, N. (2004) *Qualitative Methods for Health Research*, London, Sage

Hek, G. and Moule, P. (2006) *Making Sense of Research: An Introduction for Health and Social Care Practitioners* (3rd edition), London, Sage

Kvale, S. (1996) *Interviews: An Introduction to Qualitative Research Interviewing*, London, Sage

Robson, C. (2002) *Real World Research: A Resource for Social Scientists and Practitioner-Researchers* (2nd edition), Oxford, Blackwell

Walter I., Nutley, S., Percy-Smith, J., McNeish, D. and Frost, S. (2004) *Improving the use of research in social care practice*, Knowledge Review 07: June 2004. London, Social Care Institute for Excellence

National Occupational Standards for NVQ Health and Social Care Level 4

The following grids are examples of where evidence generated for specific units/topics in this book may support the requirements of the National Occupational Standards and the dimensions therein.

Core units Group A

Candidates must achieve all **three** of the units listed.

Unit/ Element	Topic	Chapter
HSC41	**Use and develop methods and systems to communicate, Record and report**	
HSC41a	Identify methods and systems to promote effective communication and engagement with individuals and key people	Ch 5: Managing for quality Ch 4: Supporting individuals and their families
HSC41b	Develop and use communication methods and systems to promote effective communication	Ch 5: Managing for quality
HSC41c	Evaluate communication methods and systems	Ch 5: Managing for quality Ch 4: Supporting individuals and their families
HSC41d	Maintain and share records and reports	Ch 5: Managing for quality Ch 4: Supporting individuals and their families
HSC42	**Contribute to the development and maintenance of healthy and safe practices in the working environment**	
HSC42a	Contribute to monitoring compliance with health, safety and security regulations and requirements	Ch 5: Managing for quality Ch 4: Supporting individuals and their families
HSC42b	Contribute to the development of systems to manage risk to self, staff and others	Ch 5: Managing for quality Ch 4: Supporting individuals and their families
HSC42c	Contribute to the development of health, safety and security policies, procedures and practices	Ch 5: Managing for quality Ch 4: Supporting individuals and their families
HSC43	**Take responsibility for the continuing professional development of self and others**	
HSC43a	Take responsibility for own personal and professional development	Ch 2: Reflection in action Ch 5: Managing for quality Ch 11: Research methods
HSC43b	Contribute to the personal and professional development of others	Ch 2: Reflection in action Ch 5: Managing for quality

Core units group B

HSC45 is the required choice for the **Adults** endorsement.

Unit / Element		
HSC45	**Develop practices which promote choice, well-being and protection of all individuals**	
HSC45a	Develop and maintain effective relationships to promote the individual's choice about their care	Ch 4: Supporting individuals and their families Ch 7: Assessment Ch 8: Planning and reviewing services
HSC45b	Promote the individual's rights to expect and receive respect for their diversity, difference and preferences	
HSC45c	Promote the protection of all individuals	Ch 3: The value base of health and social care Ch 4: Supporting individuals and their families Ch 7: Assessment Ch 8: Planning and reviewing services

Adults optional units

Candidates taking the Adults pathway may select some or all of the four required optional units from the units listed below or from the Generic optional units.

Unit/Element		
HSC410	Advocate with, and on behalf of, individuals, families, carers, groups and communities	Ch 4: Supporting individuals and their families
HSC411	Manage a service which achieves the best possible outcomes for the individual	Ch 4: Supporting individuals and their families Ch 5: Managing for quality
HSC412	Ensure individuals and groups are supported appropriately when experiencing significant life events and transitions	Ch 4: Supporting individuals and their families Ch 7: Assessment Ch 8: Planning and reviewing services

Generic optional unit

HSC413	Manage requests for health and care services	Ch 1: The context of health and social care Ch 7: Assessment
HSC414	Assess individual needs and preferences	Ch 7: Assessment
HSC415	Produce, evaluate and amend service delivery plans to meet individual needs and references	Ch 8: Planning and reviewing services
HSC416	Develop, implement and review care plans with individuals	Ch 8: Planning and reviewing services
HSC417	Assess individuals' mental health and related needs	Ch 7: Assessment
HSC418	Work with individuals with mental health needs to negotiate and agree plans for addressing those needs	Ch 7: Assessment Ch 8: Planning and reviewing services
HSC419	Provide advice and information to those who enquire about mental health needs and related services	Ch 7: Assessment Ch 8: Planning and reviewing services
HSC420	Promote leisure opportunities and activities for individuals	Ch 4: Supporting individuals and their families Ch 8: Planning and reviewing services
HSC421	Promote employment, training and education opportunities for individuals	Ch 4: Supporting individuals and their families Ch 8: Planning and reviewing services
HSC422	Promote housing opportunities for individuals	Ch 4: Supporting individuals and their families Ch 8: Planning and reviewing services
HSC423	Assist individuals at formal hearings	Ch 4: Supporting individuals and their families
HSC424	Supervise methadone consumption	
HSC425	Support people who are providing homes for individuals and/or children and young people	
HSC426	Empower families, carers and others to support individuals	Ch 4: Supporting individuals and their families
HSC427:	Assess the needs of carers and families	Ch 4: Supporting individuals and their families Ch 8: Planning and reviewing services
HSC428	Develop, implement and review programmes of support for carers and families	Ch 4: Supporting individuals and their families Ch 7: Assessment Ch 8: Planning and reviewing services
HSC429	Work with groups to promote individual growth, development and independence	Ch 4: Supporting individuals and their families Ch 7: Assessment Ch 8: Planning and reviewing services
HSC430	Support the protection of individuals, key people and others	Ch 4: Supporting individuals and their families Ch 9: Safeguarding vulnerable adults
HSC431	Support individuals where abuse has been disclosed	Ch 9: Safeguarding vulnerable adults

HSC432	Enable families to address issues with individuals' behaviour	Ch 4: Supporting individuals and their families
HSC433	Develop joint working agreements and practices and review their effectiveness	
HSC434	Maintain and manage records and reports	Ch 5: Managing for quality Ch 4: Supporting individuals and their families
HSC435	Manage the development and direction of the provision	Ch 1: The context of health and social care Ch 5: Managing for quality
HSC436	Promote and manage a quality provision	Ch 5: Managing for quality
HSC437	Promote your organisation and its services to stakeholders	Ch 1: The context of health and social care Ch 5: Managing for quality
HSC438	Develop and disseminate information and advice about health and social well-being	Ch 10: Health education and promoting well-being
HSC439	Contribute to the development of organisational policy and practice	Ch 1: The context of health and social care Ch 5: Managing for quality
HSC440	Support effective governance	Ch 1: The context of health and social care Ch 5: Managing for quality
HSC441	Invite tenders and award contracts	Ch 1: The context of health and social care Ch 5: Managing for quality
HSC442	Monitor and evaluate the quality, outcomes and cost-effectiveness of substance misuse services	Ch 5: Managing for quality
HSC443	Procure services for individuals	Ch 5: Managing for quality
HSC444	Contribute to the selection, recruitment and retention of staff to develop a quality service	Ch 5: Managing for quality
HSC445	Recruit and place volunteers	Ch 5: Managing for quality
HSC446	Manage a dispersed workforce to meet the needs and preferences of individuals at home	Ch 5: Managing for quality
HSC447	Represent the agency in courts and formal hearings	
HSC448	Provide and obtain information at courts and formal hearings	
HSC449	Represent one's own agency at other agencies' meetings	
HSC450	Develop risk management plans to support individual's independence and daily living within their home	Ch 5: Managing for quality Ch 4: Supporting individuals and their families Ch 7: Assessment
HSC451	Lead teams to support a quality provision	Ch 5: Managing for quality

Additional unit

HSC452	Contribute to the development, maintenance and evaluation of systems to promote the rights, responsibilities, equality and diversity of individuals	Ch 3: The value base of health and social care Ch 5: Ch 5: Managing for quality

National Occupational Standards for Leadership and Management for Care Services

Four core units

Unit/Element	Topic	Chapter
LMC A1	**Manage and develop yourself and your workforce within care services**	
LMC A1.1	Manage and develop self in management and leadership roles	Ch 5: Managing for quality Ch 4: Supporting individuals and their families
LMC A1.2	Manage and develop workers through supervision and performance reviews	Ch 5: Managing for quality
LMC A1.3	Lead and manage continuous improvement in the provision	Ch 5: Managing for quality
LMC A1.4	Enhance the quality and safety of the provision of the workforce	Ch 4: Supporting individuals and their families
LMC B1	**Lead and manage provision of care services that respects, protects and promotes the rights and responsibilities of people**	
LMC B1.1	Lead and manage provision that complies with legislation, registration, regulation and inspection requirements	Ch 5: Managing for quality Ch1 : The context of health and social care Ch 4: Supporting individuals and their families
LMC B1.2	Lead and manage provision that promotes the rights and responsibilities	Ch 3: The value base of health and social care Ch 5: Managing for quality Ch 4: Supporting individuals and their families
LMC B1.3	Lead and manage provision that protects people	Ch 5: Managing for quality Ch 4: Supporting individuals and their families
LMC C1	**Develop and maintain systems, procedures and practice of care services to manage risks and comply with health and safety requirements**	
LMC C1.1	Implement and monitor compliance with health and safety requirements	Ch 4: Supporting individuals and their families Ch 5: Managing for quality Ch 7: Assessment
LMC C1.2	Promote a culture where needs and risks are balanced with healthy and safe practice	Ch 5: Managing for quality Ch 4: Supporting individuals and their families Ch 7: Assessment
LMC C1.3	Monitor and review systems, procedures and practice for the management of risk	Ch 5: Managing for quality Ch 7: Assessment
LMC E1	**Lead and manage effective communication that promotes positive outcomes for people within care services**	
LMC E1.1	Manage effective communication	Ch 2: Reflection in action Ch 5: Managing for quality Ch 4: Supporting individuals and their families
LMC E1.2	Ensure that management information systems support the delivery of positive outcomes for people and the provision	Ch 5: Managing for quality Ch 2: Reflection in action Ch 4: Supporting individuals and their families
LMC E1.3	Manage and maintain recording and reporting systems and procedures and use them effectively.	Ch 5: Managing for quality

Optional units (four to be selected)

LMC A2	**Facilitate and manage change within care services through reflective and flexible leadership**	
LMC A2.1	Develop and lead the implementation of a shared vision for your provision	Ch 5: Managing for quality Ch 2: Reflection in action
LMC A2.2	Develop a culture that is open and facilitates participation	Ch 2: Reflection in action Ch 5: Managing for quality
LMC A2.3	Promote a positive image of your provision and its contribution to the lives of people	Ch 1: The context of health and social care Ch 5: Managing for quality
LMC A3	**Actively engage in the safe selection and recruitment of workers and their retention**	
LMC A3.1	Review the requirements for the safe selection and recruitment of workers and their retention	Ch 5: Managing for quality
LMC A3.2	Actively engage in the safe selection and recruitment of workers	Ch 5: Managing for quality
LMC A3.3	Implement systems, procedures and practice to support retention	Ch 5: Managing for quality
LMC A4 (HSC446)	**Manage a dispersed workforce to meet the needs and preferences of individuals at home**	
LMC A4.1	Manage the work of staff in an individual's home	Ch 5: Managing for quality Ch 4: Supporting individuals and their families
LMC A4.2	Supervise and support staff to ensure that health and care services are meeting individual needs and preferences	Ch 5: Managing for quality Ch 4: Supporting individuals and their families Ch 8: Planning and reviewing services
LMC A4.3	Respond to day to day changes and emergencies	Ch 5: Managing for quality Ch 4: Supporting individuals and their families
LMC B2	**Lead and manage provision of care services that promotes the well-being of people**	
LMC B2.1	Lead and manage provision that involves people in decisions about the outcomes they wish to achieve	Ch 4: Supporting individuals and their families Ch 7: Assessment Ch 8: Planning and reviewing services Ch 5: Managing
LMC B2.2	Lead and manage provision that promotes people's social, emotional, cultural, spiritual and intellectual well-being	Ch 3: Values Ch 7: Assessment Ch 8: Plan & Review Ch 5: Managing for quality
LMC B2.3	Lead and manage provision that promotes people's health	Ch 5: Managing for quality
LMC B3	**Manage provision of care services that deals effectively with transitions and significant life events**	
LMC B3.1	Implement systems, procedures and practice to support people through transitions and significant life events	Ch 4: Supporting individuals and their families Ch 7: Assessment Ch 8: Planning and reviewing services
LMC B3.2	Lead and manage provision that supports people through transitions and significant life events	Ch 5: Managing for quality Ch 4: Supporting individuals and their families
LMC B3.3	Implement and review systems, procedures and practice for sharing information on transitions and significant life events	Ch 6: Collaboration Ch 8: Plan & Review
LMC B4	**Manage provision of care services that supports parents, families, carers and significant others to achieve positive outcomes**	
LMC B4.1	Manage effective working partnerships with parents, families, carers and significant others	Ch 6: Collaborative working Ch 4: Supporting individuals and their families
LMC B4.2	Manage systems and procedures to involve parents, families, carers and significant others	Ch 6: Collaborative working Ch 4: Supporting individuals and their families
LMC B4.3	Support workers to manage situations where there is conflict	Ch 5: Managing for quality Ch 4: Supporting individuals and their families

LMC B5	Manage and evaluate systems, procedures and practice for assessments, plans and reviews within care services	
LMC B5.1	Ensure that workers are competent to carry out assessments, plans and reviews	Ch 7: Assessment Ch 8: Planning and reviewing services Ch 5: Managing for quality
LMC B5.2	Manage the involvement of people in evaluating the effectiveness of assessments, plans and reviews	Ch 7: Assessment Ch 8: Planning and reviewing services Ch 5: Managing for quality
LMC B5.3	Evaluate systems, procedures and practices for reviewing the effectiveness of assessments, plans and reviews	Ch 7: Assessment Ch 8: Planning and reviewing services Ch 5: Managing for quality
LMC B7	Lead and manage group living provision within care services	
LMC B7.1	Develop the physical environment	Ch 5: Managing for quality Ch 4: Supporting individuals and their families
LMC B7.2	Plan, implement and review daily living programmes	Ch 7: Assessment Ch 8: Planning and reviewing services Ch 4: Supporting individuals and their families
LMC B7.3	Use group procedures to promote positive outcomes for people	Ch 4: Supporting individuals and their families Ch 8: Planning and reviewing services
LMC B7.4	Manage a provision that promotes group care as a positive experience	Ch 5: Managing for quality Ch 4: Supporting individuals and their families
LMC B8	Lead and manage provision of care services that promotes positive behaviour	
LMC B8.1	Implement and monitor behaviour policies, systems, procedures and practices	Ch 5: Managing for quality Ch 4: Supporting individuals and their families
LMC B8.2	Promote positive behaviour	Ch 5: Managing for quality Ch 4: Supporting individuals and their families
LMC B8.3	Support workers to promote positive behaviour	Ch 5: Managing for quality Ch 4: Supporting individuals and their families
LMC C2 (HSC450)	Develop risk management plans to support individual's independence and daily living skills within their home	
LMC C2.1	Prepare to carry out risk assessments	Ch 7: Assessment
LMC C2.2	Carry out risk assessments	Ch 7: Assessment
LMC C2.3	Develop, agree and regularly review risk management plans for individuals	Ch 7: Assessment Ch 8: Planning and reviewing services
LMC D1	Lead and manage work for care services with networks, communities, other professionals and organisations	
LMC D1.1	Manage effective working relationships with networks and communities	Ch 6: Collaborative working
LMC D1.2	Create and maintain effective working relationships and partnerships with other professionals and organisations	Ch 6: Collaborative working
LMC D1.3	Contribute to the development of local strategies and services	Ch 1: The context of health and social care Ch 6: Collaborative working
LMC D2	Manage workers within care services who are based in multi-disciplinary teams	
LMC D2.1	Establish and manage relationships to support workers based in external multi-disciplinary teams	Ch 5: Managing for quality Ch 6: Collaborative working
LMC D2.2	Promote effective procedures, protocols and practices for workers based in external multi-disciplinary teams	Ch 5: Managing for quality Ch 6: Collaborative working
LMC D2.3	Ensure workers based in external multi-disciplinary teams have opportunities for continuing professional development	Ch 5: Managing for quality Ch 6: Collaborative working

LMC D3	Lead and manage inter-professional teams within care services	
LMC D3.1	Promote effective inter-professional team working	Ch 6: Collaborative working Ch 5: Managing for quality
LMC D3.2	Ensure effective relationships with supervisors from other professions	Ch 6: Collaborative working Ch 5: Managing for quality
LMC D3.3	Promote effective team working	Ch 5: Managing for quality Ch 6: Collaborative working
LMC E2	**Identify, implement and evaluate systems, procedures and practice within care services that measure performance**	
LMC E2.1	Identify indicators and methods to measure the performance of the provision	Ch 5: Managing for quality Ch 1: The context of health and social care
LMC E2.2	Implement and monitor systems, procedures and practice to measure performance	Ch 5: Managing for quality Ch 1: The context of health and social care
LMC E2.3	Evaluate performance measurements systems, procedures and practice	Ch 5: Managing for quality Ch 1: The context of health and social care
LMC E3	**Monitor and manage the quality of the provision of care services**	
LMC E3.1	Implement systems, procedures and practice to meet quality standards	Ch 5: Managing for quality Ch 1: The context of health and social care
LMC E3.2	Develop a culture for promoting quality in which everyone participates	Ch 5: Managing for quality Ch 1: The context of health and social care
LMC E3.3	Implement, monitor and review quality systems, policies and procedures	Ch 5: Managing for quality Ch 1: The context of health and social care
LMC E4	**Lead and manage provision of care services that promotes opportunities, identifies constraints and manages risk**	
LMC E4.1	Identify and evaluate opportunities and constraints for the future development and viability of your provision	Ch 1: The context of health and social care Ch 5: Managing for quality Ch 4: Supporting individuals and their families
LMC E4.2	Evaluate the nature and significance of any risks to your provision	Ch 5: Managing for quality Ch 1: The context of health and social care
LMC E4.3	Assess and manage risk for the continuing development and viability of your provision	Ch 5: Managing for quality Ch 1: The context of health and social care
LMC E5	**Plan operations and manage resources to meet current and future demands on the provision of care services (Excluded Combination with E7)**	
LMC E5.1	Develop and review operational plans for the provision	Ch 5: Managing for quality Ch 1: The context of health and social care
LMC E5.2	Manage time and resources to deliver positive outcomes for people	Ch 5: Managing for quality Ch 4: Supporting individuals and their families
LMC E5.3	Evaluate whether and to what extent resources meet current and future demands	Ch 2: Reflection in action Ch 5: Managing for quality Ch 8: Planning and reviewing services
LMC E6	**Contribute to the strategic policies of care services**	
LMC E6.1	Evaluate the impact of strategic policies on the provision	Ch 2: Reflection in action Ch 5: Managing for quality Ch 1: The context of health and social care
LMC E6.2	Evaluate and implement strategic plans for the development of your provision	Ch 2: Reflection in action Ch 5: Managing for quality Ch 1: The context of health and social care
LMC E6.3	Provide feedback on strategic policies to influence the direction of the service	Ch 2: Reflection in action Ch 1: The context of health and social care Ch 5: Managing for quality

LMC E7	Develop, implement and review business plans and planning for the provision of care services (Excluded Combination with E5)	
LMC E7.1	Develop a business plan for your provision	Ch 5: Managing for quality
LMC E7.2	Implement, monitor and review the business plan	Ch 5: Managing for quality
LMC E7.3	Evaluate policies, procedures and practices for the business planning	Ch 5: Managing for quality Ch 1: The context of health and social care
LMC E8 (MSC E2)	Manage the finances in your area of responsibility	
LMC E9	Manage procedures within care services for making, responding to and learning from comments and complaints	
LMC E9.1	Implement and review systems, procedures and practice for the receipt of comments and complaints	Ch 5: Managing for quality Ch 4: Supporting individuals and their families Ch 1: The context of health and social care
LMC E9.2	Ensure that lessons are learned from comments and complaints	Ch 5: Managing for quality Ch 4: Supporting individuals and their families Ch 1: The context of health and social care
LMC E9.3	Evaluate the effectiveness of complaints systems, procedures and practice	Ch 5: Managing for quality Ch 4: Supporting individuals and their families Ch 1: The context of health and social care
LMC E10	Ensure policies, procedures and practice for the conduct of workers within care services are adhered to	
LMC E10.1	Ensure conduct within the provision complies with legislation, regulation, inspection and organisational requirements	Ch 5: Managing for quality Ch 1: The context of health and social care
LMC E10.2	Implement disciplinary and grievance procedures	Ch 5: Managing for quality
LMC E10.3	Arrange, conduct and report on disciplinary hearings	Ch 5: Managing for quality
LMC E11 (MSC F1)	Manage a project	
LMC E12 (MSC F2)	Manage a programme of complementary projects	
LMC E13	Market, costs and contract to ensure the viability of the provision of care services	
LMC E13.1	Identify potential markets and cost services	Ch 1: The context of health and social care Ch 5: Managing for quality
LMC E13.2	Negotiate contracts to ensure the continuing development and functioning of the provision	Ch 5: Managing for quality Ch 1: The context of health and social care Ch 4: Supporting individuals and their families
LMC E13.3	Monitor and evaluate marketing and contacting systems, procedures and practices for the provision	Ch 5: Managing for quality Ch 1: The context of health and social care

Appendix

Study skills

This appendix addresses the following areas;

- Time management
- Active learning
- Written skills
- Doing a literature search
- Internet searching

Time management

In higher education students are expected to study independently and take responsibility for their own learning. Time management is therefore one of the most important skills you need to develop. At the beginning of their studies, many students find it difficult to plan their work and use their time effectively and achieve the right balance between too little and too much. The main study activities – reading, searching the Internet, taking notes, writing assignments, for example – take everyone varying amounts of time. It is therefore important to:

- make a start! Get over the psychological hurdle by at least doing something. Avoid leaving things to 'later' and then finding that you do not have enough time to complete your work satisfactorily
- try not to do too much too early. You will become worn out and demotivated when you cannot keep it up
- make sure that you set yourself realistic goals – and keep to them
- achieve the right balance between the different activities. A classic mistake is to spend too much time on one study activity, for example, the background reading, and not enough time for the actual writing up.

How much time does studying take?

There is no easy answer to this question! You need to work out strategies depending on the task and time in hand. Inevitably, people work at different rates. Some find it easy to write clearly straight away. Others find this very difficult and need to write several drafts. Therefore, every time you carry out a task, try to develop a sense of how long it is taking you. You may find that you need to spend more time on certain activities to do them thoroughly, or that you are spending too long on others and need to try out new strategies for completing them faster. For example, the first time you write a 3,000-word essay, finding out how long it takes you will be a matter of trial and error. You will discover that if you begin writing too soon, you may not have allocated enough time for reading and research. This will probably mean that

you will have to keep changing the essay as you find out more. This wastes time in the long run. However, if you start too late, you may find that it is impossible even to complete the essay, let alone get a good mark.

Finding time

Everyone has other commitments, such as part-time work or family responsibilities. This means that it is important to ensure that you set aside enough time for study. It is useful to identify when you might have regular chunks of time free for study. You need to think about the activities you usually do in an average week and identify any gaps. For example, if you tend to have certain mornings or afternoons free, it can be useful to set them aside for study. Getting yourself into a routine makes it easier to plan your work and make it manageable.

> **ACTIVITY**
>
> Carry out a 'time audit' of a normal week. Where are the one-, two- and three-hour chunks of time you need to devote to study? If they are not obvious, where can they be 'created'?

Planning your time

When you have an overall strategy, you should then start to break down your work into more manageable sections. First you can decide what you are hoping to accomplish in a given week. Part of this will be determined by the timetable of the course you are studying. You will also need to set yourself tasks, such as reading a certain amount or searching for references on a specific topic. Once you have defined these smaller tasks, you will find it easier to manage your time. It also becomes easier to concentrate and see a task through to completion.

Compartmentalising

Studying can easily lead to people feeling overwhelmed. Compartmentalising your study (i.e. breaking the larger task down into smaller ones) makes your workload less threatening. Whatever level you reach in academic study, it is always possible to have a sense that you could do more. It will make you feel much more secure and confident if you draw boundaries around your work. This makes study achievable rather than never-ending. It is much better to accomplish a series of small, focused tasks than to fail to finish an ambitious but vague plan. For example, you might decide to track down and take notes from four relevant journal articles in the library in an afternoon session.

Active learning

You should not expect simply to *absorb* information and skills – you need to *acquire* them actively. It would be difficult to become a good driver just by going to lectures on driving. You need to get 'hands on', practice constantly, make mistakes and then improve. Similarly, it is hard to be a good student just through reading and listening. You need to participate and practise to get better. If your only real participation in an active process is writing your formal assignments, you will have had less practice – and therefore probably will do less well – than if you have been joining in throughout; for example, by asking questions, contributing to seminars, reading widely and taking notes.

Reading, listening and note-taking

Reading and note-taking, either from texts or lectures, are key study skills. However, you will get the most out of these activities if you take an *active* approach. This means using different strategies and techniques in order to engage with material more deeply. If you simply sit and read a textbook through from start to finish, it is unlikely that you will get very much out of the activity. You may feel as if you understand it, but until you test this out you cannot be sure. You will also probably remember little of the content afterwards. You need to read purposefully – identify what a section or chapter is about and make sure you understand what the author is saying and could express this in your own words. Always, for example, take notes, and annotate or highlight parts of the text

that you think are particularly interesting or relevant. If it's a library book you won't want to mark it – so take a photocopy. Make a point of looking up new or difficult words and write the meaning on your notes. If you gloss over them, not only will you not really understand what is being said, you will never feel confident enough to use them yourself. For example:

Reflexivity

This literally means a referring back to oneself. The reflexive self comes into prominence during late modern times. It mirrors the developmental phase of society because it involves a 'turning inwards' that entails tense confrontation. It is important to recognise that the human subject in possession of a self, free will and conscience is not a natural given, but is a result of historical and social evolution. 'The self' is a relatively recent invention. The reflexive self is quite different from the reflective self that is commonly referred to in the social work literature.

(Webb, 2006, page 19)

Reflective practice

Reflective practice can be linked to the writing of Donald Schon, who wrote *The Reflective Practitioner* in 1983. According to Schon, reflective practice involves continually reflecting on one's own practice experiences. At the same time, the reflective practitioner aims to apply professional knowledge to practice under supervision.

How much reading do I need to do?

It is tempting to say 'the more the better'. The more you read about a subject, the more you will understand it. The more you understand a subject, the more you can develop a critical perspective, which will enable you to appreciate the strengths and weaknesses of different authors and texts in the area. The more you can evaluate authors and texts, the more you can develop your own analysis and argument. Above all, the more you immerse yourself in a subject and engage with it, the more you will enjoy it. It is difficult to do well in a subject that you only pursue through duty. Although it may be a cliché, you will get more out of your studies if you put more in. However, you have to draw a line somewhere! It is impossible to read everything you would like to. Therefore, firstly you need to prioritise your reading, and secondly you need to get the most out of your reading.

Prioritising your reading: skim reading

Skim reading is a useful technique in making reading manageable and effective. This means getting an overview of a text quickly – the 'gist' basically. It is not a substitute for detailed reading. Instead, it is a useful way of establishing whether a text is relevant to your needs and should be read in more depth. It can also help you to get a sense of a subject that is unfamiliar to you, without necessarily going into great depth. If you are studying a new topic, it can take time to grasp what the important issues are, or who the foremost authors in the field are. Skim reading can help you acquire this sort of sense without getting bogged down in reading an outdated or irrelevant text.

Many students worry that they do not read quickly and will not be able to get through enough texts. In fact, reading slowly is often useful as it can mean you are someone who pays attention, concentrates and remembers what they are reading. Skim reading can be useful in deciding *what* needs reading slowly.

Skim reading is a way of sifting and sorting what is relevant and what is not.

When you have found a likely text, you can adopt the following strategies:

Read through the list of contents or the index (if a book) or the abstract (if an article) to see if the particular topics you are interested in are featured. Articles also use key words – look out for these.

It can be helpful if you want to get a sense of a specific chapter, for example, to see if you need to read it in detail. One way to do this is to read the introduction and conclusion of a chapter (or book). Even if they are not called 'introduction' and 'conclusion', you can still read the initial and closing paragraphs. These are the sections in which authors usually explain their main aims and arguments. If this looks promising, you may then try further reading.

Methods here include reading through subheadings, or the first and last sentences of paragraphs, or down the centre of a paragraph without reading each sentence fully. This will give you a sense of what the chapter is about and mean you have gained a bit more knowledge. However, if the chapter seems as if it is relevant to you, you will then need to go on to read it in more detail in order to get the most from it.

Reading and taking notes

When you do identify a text that needs to be read in detail, it is important that you take some form of notes. When you take notes it means you engage with the material, which will help you both to remember its content and to check that you understand it.

> **REFLECT**
>
> Avoid the photocopying trap. When you find a relevant source, it is often a good idea to photocopy it for future reference. Sometimes, however, people can fall into the trap of believing that simply by photocopying an article or chapter and filing it away in their folder, they are somehow learning its contents – if only it were that simple!

There are many ways of taking notes, ranging from an occasional underlining to something more extensive. The main challenges here are to develop a format of taking notes that makes sense to you and to strike the right balance regarding how much detail you record. If you make too few notes, they will mean nothing to you when you return to them later on. You will then have to do your reading all over again. On the other hand, if you make too many notes you may end up simply copying out the entire text, which defeats the object. People usually develop their own systems of shorthand and symbols that make sense to them. The main thing is to keep practising until you have an approach which enables you to look back at your notes weeks, months or even years later, and still be able to understand both them and what the original text was saying. So, although there is no one right way, here are some suggestions.

A key aspect of note-taking is to make sure you write down where your notes come from. Always start with the *full* reference before you make any notes at all.

Always use page numbers from the text so that you know where in a book material is located.

Find a system that you are comfortable with to help you break material down into the main points. For example, you can use headings or sometimes people use diagrams or maps rather than just words. It must make sense to *you*!

If you highlight or underline material, try to develop consistent criteria for doing so. If you just go through highlighting everything that looks important, you will probably find you have highlighted the whole text. It is better to have your own system so that, for example, if you have highlighted something it means something.

Whenever possible, it is better to put ideas into your own words. If you are able to express an idea in your own language it helps you to show you understand it. However, if you think someone has used a particularly good phrase which you would like to quote, then you must make it clear in your own notes that you are reproducing it *verbatim*.

ACTIVITY

Choose a section from another chapter in the book. Take notes so that in a month's time you will be able to remember what the main points were, where it came from exactly and whether there were any nice quotes you could use. In a month's time revisit your notes. Evaluate how useful they were.

Written skills

Features of a good piece of written work

Put yourself in the position of someone reading your work. It may be someone marking your essay or an interested reader going through a report you may have written. We are going to focus on essays in this section as they are one of the most common tasks students have to undertake. However, the characteristics of any good piece of written work are generally the same. You should ask yourself:

1 Have you actually got to the point or answered the question?
2 Have you presented a coherent and well-structured argument?
3 Is the essay clearly written?
4 Have you used your own words?
5 Is the essay clearly presented?
6 Is the essay written in an objective style, with relevant use of evidence?
7 Is the essay properly referenced?

We will take each point in turn.

Answering the question

In an essay you never simply write down all you know about a subject or just describe something. You are set a specific issue to think about in the light of what you have been studying. Your task is to argue a case focused on the question posed in the title. You need to be clear *how* your material relates to the question. *Everything* you discuss in the essay should be relevant to the task.

Structuring your essay

Your material should be presented in a clear and logical sequence, with one point following on from another. The basic essay structure is: introduction, main body and conclusion. The main body is where you focus on answering the title question or discuss statements made in the title. You back up your discussion using evidence you have found from your research. Usually there are two sides of an argument to be made, sometimes more. In order to present your argument clearly, you also need to make sure that you identify differences between perspectives. A well-structured essay means one that is sensibly organised and which the reader can understand. The usual format followed is:

Example One
Title: 'Discuss the success or otherwise of Direct Payments for people with disabilities'
Introduction:
Briefly outline what the essay is going to say.
Section 1:

Provide some background. Explain why Direct Payments were brought in, for whom, give examples, etc.

Section 2:
Outline reasons why they could be seen as a success.

Section 3:
Outline reasons why they could be seen as a failure.

Section 4:
Give overall evaluation based on comparing section 2 with section 3.

Conclusion:
Summarise and make a final response to question – do not introduce any new points in the conclusion.

Example Two
Title: 'Investigate ways of combating depression for older people in care homes'

Introduction:
Briefly outline what the essay is going to say.

Section 1:
Put the essay into some sort of context. Do a literature search on the incidence of depression in care homes and discuss your findings (it is important to aim for more than one source, preferably several). You could also provide some background data on the number of care homes for older people, how many people are in care homes and so on. Has this issue cropped up in official guidelines?

Section 2:
Explain why older people in care homes might be more at risk of depression (if, indeed, that's what the studies show). Discuss the various factors.

Section 3:
Write a section on strategies that are used to identify depression in such situations. Again, try to reference different sources of information for this.

Section 4:
From your research, discuss the various interventions that are being used to combat depression in older people in care homes.

Conclusion:
As before, summarise and make a final response to the question – do not introduce any new points as such but you could raise some issues for future consideration that might have emerged from the previous sections, e.g. it might be higher on care homes inspectors' agendas, etc.

Writing clearly

The most important aim of writing is to communicate your ideas. The best writing is accessible and free from errors. It is obviously important to pay attention to spelling, punctuation and grammar. These days, word processing programmes have spell and grammar checkers, so make sure you use them. They should pick up most errors. However, nothing can replace a human reader. Find someone to read through your work for sense, spelling and grammatical errors. There are reasons why you should try to improve your writing.

- Employers value people who can write clearly.
- Poor spelling and small mistakes, such as missing out full stops, make your work look sloppy (even if you have put a lot of effort in).
- Mistakes distract the reader from your ideas.
- Sometimes very poor grammar or punctuation can mean it is impossible for the reader to understand what you are trying to say. This means you are wasting your (and their) time.

Finally, one aspect of writing worth commenting on is language. You will, unfortunately, encounter many writers who use long, obscure and baffling terminology. Do not be tempted to follow their example! Keep difficult language and jargon to a minimum. Your aim is for the reader to engage with your ideas, not get bogged down in your prose style. Using obscure language will not make you sound more intelligent, particularly if you use some of the words wrongly!

Spot the difference:

As a result of the Care Standards Act 2000, many owners of residential and nursing homes have had to make further adaptations and improvements to their premises to meet the new standards. Faced with this additional burden, an increasing number of residential and nursing homes – especially the smaller private homes – have been forced to close. The knock-on effect of home closures and a shortage of places in residential care has been to worsen the 'bed-blocking' problem in hospitals, where chronically ill people cannot be discharged to their own homes because they are too frail or disabled to look after themselves. 102 words

As far as the owners of residential and nursing homes were concerned, the problems started, or at least got worse, when the Care Standards act 2000 was brought in, and by bringing this in, the Government introduced new standards which meant they (the owners of care homes) had to make adaptations and improvements to their premises so that the homes meet the new standards laid down in the act. In terms of the additional burdens that they faced, an increasing number of both residential and nursing homes of whatever size, but especially the smaller private homes, have been forced to face a closure situation or something similar. This has all contributed towards various 'knock-on effects'. Take 'bed-blocking' for example, which is the problem of hospitals of not being able to move people out of beds when there isn't a care home space available for people who have a long-term or chronic illness, who cannot be discharged to their own homes, because they are too frail or disabled to look after themselves, such closures do not help with this in the least. At the end of the day, this all adds to the problem. 193 words

The first piece reads well because it is better punctuated without long, rambling sentences. Importantly, it doesn't repeat itself and does not contain annoying errors such as a small 'a' for act, clichéd expressions such as 'at the end of the day' or phrases that are totally redundant. It also manages to be nearly half the number of words.

Using your own words

You must avoid paraphrasing and plagiarism at all times! The old quote goes:

> To steal ideas from one person is plagiarism, to steal ideas from many is research.

Plagiarising (passing someone else's work off as your own) is considered a cardinal sin. If detected, the culprit could get into serious trouble. These days colleges and universities even have software that can detect evidence of plagiarism, so heinous an act is it considered to be. If you feel uncertain about how well you write, it can be tempting to 'borrow' rather too heavily from books and journals. There are two ways in which students do this.

- *Paraphrasing*: this means sticking very closely to the original text and simply changing a few words.

- *Plagiarism*: this means using an author's words without any acknowledgement.

Both these practices must be avoided! In the case of paraphrasing, you will certainly lose marks. In the case of plagiarism, it is regarded as a form of cheating. Often students do not intend to be dishonest by using other writers' words and ideas. It is often more that students lack confidence in putting their ideas down on paper. However, whatever the motive, paraphrasing and plagiarism are both bad practice.

- If you simply reproduce other people's words, it is impossible for anybody (including you) to tell if you understand something.
- Plagiarised and badly paraphrased work is actually harder to read because it is made up of a mixture of other people's writing styles. It is better to have your own style running throughout – even if you think it could be more polished – than to have sudden changes.
- The whole essay can end up being very disjointed. It is difficult to put together a coherent structure from a collection of other people's points and prose styles.
- You will probably be detected – who wants the shame of being caught out?
- Your writing will get better if you keep practising your own style rather than borrowing from other people. As a result you will also gain confidence.

Essay presentation

The way in which your work is presented is very important. There are certain basic rules to follow when handing in an essay.

- Make sure that you write the title of the essay in full at the start. This is particularly important if you have more than one option, but is good practice in all cases.
- Number all pages.
- Leave a wide margin (at least 1 inch) on both sides of the page, and use double spaces between lines. This is to give lecturers room to write on your essay. It will be easier to make sense of comments if they are written next to the section in question.
- If you use a long direct quote (i.e. more than one sentence long or which takes up more than two lines of typing), you should indent the quote and use single spacing to distinguish it from the rest of

your writing. An indented quote looks like this. Remember to include the page number(s):

> If you have an indented quote, you do not need to use quotation marks. Use these only for short quotes that you incorporate within your writing. The fact that you have indented makes it clear you are quoting (Barton, (2003) page 134).

- Leave double spaces between paragraphs, to make it clear where they begin and end.
- Use a reasonable-sized font. It is best to use 12pt wherever possible. Any smaller than this is hard to read, and any larger can be annoying.
- Stick to black ink. Using other colours can look pretty, but can be tiring to read.

The main reason for using this form of presentation is that you make your work easier to read. Obviously this is better for the people who have to mark it! However, more than this, you want your ideas and words to come across clearly without your reader experiencing lots of distractions or struggling to decipher your work.

Using evidence effectively

Any opinions expressed need to be supported by – and developed on the basis of – evidence. For example, you may believe that families are less likely to look after older relatives in the same way as in the past. However, you cannot say this is 'true' unless you can find some supporting evidence. In this case, you would need to find data to show that there had been a significant change over time. It is not enough to base your views on your own experience alone, as this may not be representative. It is also important to remember that it is seldom possible to find one piece of evidence that conclusively proves or disproves a point. Often evidence is subject to criticism or discussion. You may need to consider more than one source.

Referencing

The need to back up your points with evidence has been stressed. However, it is unlikely that you will have the time to actually carry out primary research to do this. Therefore, it will mostly be on the basis of what you have found in the literature (secondary research). Proper referencing becomes [...] for the following reasons.

- It allows your reader to see where your information has come from.
- It provides evidence. You are referring to another authority to support your claim.
- It allows your reader to check up on your sources, either because they wish to see you have used them correctly, or because they wish to use them for your own research.
- It shows that you are not trying to pass off someone else's work as your own (see earlier section on plagiarism).

Referencing is therefore a very important academic convention. There are two elements to referencing: references that you include within the text of your essay (sometimes known as citations), and full references that you have in a list at the end.

References within the text

Every time you include information in an essay, you *must* say where it has come from. In the main body of your essay, you only need to provide the author, the date of publication and the page number (if you refer to a specific piece of information or use a direct quote). These can be incorporated in your writing in the following ways:

- Smith (2002) argues that the end is nigh.
- The end is nigh (Smith, 2002).
- The end is due to be nigh on a Tuesday (Smith, 2002:29).

In the above examples, the first two show different ways of fitting the reference into your writing. Either is acceptable. Which one you use depends on how your sentence is structured. The third example shows you how to incorporate a page number. In the other examples, this is not necessary because you are simply reporting Smith's overall idea. In the third example, it is necessary because you would need the page number to find such a specific piece of information in a book. You do not need to give full details of Smith's book here; these should be saved for the reference list at the end.

It is a good idea to check each paragraph of your work to make sure it is referenced. If all of the material in one paragraph is from the same source, you may need to include a reference both at the beginning and the

...nat you are clear
...s to. You should put
...r the reference to show
...ice.

...its about references within

S... ...re written by more than one
autho... ...re two authors, list them both, for
example: ...th & Franklin, 2001).

If there are more than two authors, do not write them all out in the text. Instead, use *et al* in place of the other names. This phrase means 'and others'; it is used to save space. For example, a book written by Smith, Franklin and Webber would be referred to as Smith *et al* (2001). However, you should make sure you name all the authors in your bibliography at the end; authors like their credits!

If you use a reference from a website (see below for Internet references), you should insert 'online' into the citation. For example, you could say Smith (2000, online).

If you refer to a chapter that has been written by a named author in an edited volume, you should use the chapter author's name (not the editor's). Always cite the person who has actually done the writing. For example, you might read a book called *New Directions for Social Care*, published in 2004, which has been edited by Paterson. Inside the book, you find a useful chapter entitled 'Homelessness', which has been written by Berthoud. In your text, you should therefore refer to Berthoud (2004). The section on the reference list on the next page shows you how to reference the book at the end.

If you want to cite two different works by the same author from the same year, call one 'a' and the other 'b' and list them alphabetically in your bibliography. For example,

Department of Health (2001a) *Better Prevention, Better Services, Better Sexual Health – The National Strategy for Sexual Health and HIV*.

Department of Health (2001b) *Medicines and Older People – Implementing medicines-related aspects of the NSF for older people*.

Sometimes you read a book in which the author refers to another text. Although this text sounds very interesting, and you would like to refer to it, you have not read it personally. You need to make this clear. You do not want to make it appear that you have read the work firsthand if this is not the case. So, for example, you may have read a book written by Burton in 2001. Burton refers to a book written by Hibbert in 1963. In *your* essay, you record this in one of the following ways:

- Hibbert (1963, in Burton, 2001) argued that depression is caused by loneliness.
- Arguably depression is caused by loneliness (Hibbert, 1963 in Burton, 2001).

When you get to your reference list, you should only give the full reference for Burton, as this is the book which you have both read and referred to. If your reader wishes to check up on Hibbert's work, they know to look for its reference in Burton's book.

List of references

This refers to the full list of all references you have used at the end of your essay. Under the Harvard system, you should only have one list and it should include only those texts which you have both read and referred to in your essay. Do not include general background reading or make separate a reference list and bibliography. There are different kinds of sources, but all should be laid out in a similar way. The format is as follows:

Author, (date), *Title (note italics)*. Place of publishing, Publisher.

There are small variations on this theme, depending on whether you are using an edited volume, a journal, a newspaper article, etc., but the basic aim is to stick to this layout as far as possible. Below are some examples:

A book written by a single author:
Lymbery, M. (2005) *Social Work with Older People*. London, Sage.

A chapter from an edited volume:
Monk, J. (2006) 'Do Direct Payments offer people with learning disabilities greater choice and control?' in Brown, K. (ed.), *Vulnerable Adults and Community Care*, Exeter, Learning Matters, 56–68.

An article from a journal:
Sayce, L. (1998). 'Stigma, discrimination and social exclusion: what's in a word?', *Journal of Mental Health*, 7 (4): 331–343.

An article from a newspaper:
Hanley, L. (2007). 'Don't assume family care is always best for our elderly', *The Guardian*, 13 July.

Another important area of referencing is how to list Internet sources. The best approach is to follow the above layout as closely as possible. The significant difference is that, unlike books or journals, Internet material changes. Therefore you also need to give the date you found the material. You also need to check the date that the material was originally posted and include this as the main date of the source. You must reference the *exact* address of the web page you were looking at. An example of an Internet reference could be:

Department of Health (2000) *Carers and Disabled Children Act 2000*
www.opsi.gov.uk/acts/acts2000/pdf/ukpga_20000016_en.pdf (accessed 27/08/07).

In the above example, it would have been too vague simply to cite the Department of Health address. Indeed, although the Act concerned was published by the Department of Health, at the time of writing, the website where many Acts are now available is that of the Office of Public Sector Information. That is why the exact page address (URL) has been given. It allows the curious reader to track down the original source.

You will encounter numerous small variations in uses of the Harvard system. For example, different publishers use slightly different forms of punctuation. The important thing is that you include the right information in the right order.

Summary

The essay writing process – at a glance:

- Identify the key issues in the essay question.
- Collect material and information which you could include in your essay.
- Begin making notes on material which you will include.
- Draw up an essay plan which organises your material.
- Write your first draft.
- Read through and amend your first draft.
- Write your final draft.
- Proofread your final draft.
- Hand it in – on time!

Doing a literature search

Most librarians are only too willing to help if you are in a library. Alternatively, these days much can be done online. Many libraries have online search tutorials. However, whether in a library or searching electronically you need to take certain initial steps. Even the best librarian cannot read your mind. You must start by defining your topic precisely. Clarify the words, terms and phrases to describe the exact subject in which you are interested. Be as specific as possible. For example, 'adult care' is far too vague; it needs to be narrowed down to something like 'palliative care for older people in England'. You can then start by looking for relevant material by searching on the library catalogue.

A literature search involves using a range of resources to find books, journals, databases and websites that are concerned with the subject you are researching, in order to produce a list of references for you to consult. It is unlikely that the literature required will all be located in just one library. Always keep a list of all the references you find as you go along and then list them at the end of your piece of work in the bibliography.

Suggested further reading

Ely, C. and Scott, I. (2007) *Essential Study Skills for Nursing*, Edinburgh, Mosby
Hart, C. (2001) *Doing a Literature Search: A Comprehensive Guide for the Social Sciences*, London, Sage
Payne, E. (2006) *Developing essential study skills* (2nd ed.), Harlow, FT Prentice Hall

Internet searching

Search engines

Search engines help you to search for web pages by keywords or phrases. They are useful for searching for specific rather than general information. There are many search engines available for finding information on the Internet. They vary in how they search for and organise information. For a truly comprehensive search you may need to use several search engines and use multi-search engines. Multi-search engines (also called metasearch engines and metacrawlers) send your search query to several search engines at the same time and compile the results for you. However, they are restricted to quite simple searches. To find other types of information or formats (e.g. images) use speciality search engines.

Search engines for finding scholarly literature

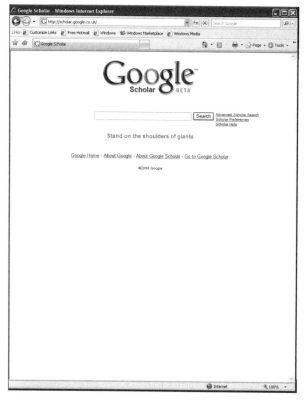

Google Scholar

Windows Live Search Academic Toolbar

Subject gateways

Subject gateways allow you to browse subject lists of good quality and evaluated subject resources. Intute (www.intute.ac.uk/socialsciences) is a reliable, expert subject gateway for Social Welfare. It is a free online service providing access a very good range of web resources for education and research.

Databases

The amount of medical, health and social science literature currently available to students and researchers is massive, and is increasing rapidly. Getting access to research that has been undertaken on a topic or question is made considerably easier by the development of databases that can be searched using free text (i.e. ordinary language). Most of the medical, health and social science databases record and retrieve published literature. Some good examples are as follows.

ASSIA (Applied Social Sciences Index and Abstracts)

ASSIA is updated monthly and provides a comprehensive source of social science and health information for the practical and academic professional.

ESRC Society Today

ESRC Society Today is a free online database dating back to the mid-1980s and updated daily. It includes the most current social science research funded by the Economic and Social Research Council (ESRC) which is the leading research funding and training agency addressing economic and social concerns in the UK.

PubMed

PubMed is a free service of the National Library of Medicine. It includes over 14 million citations for biomedical articles back to the 1950s. These citations are from MEDLINE and additional life science journals. PubMed includes links to many sites providing full text articles and other related resources.

Social Care Online

Content for Social Care Online is drawn from a range of resources including journal articles, websites, research reviews, legislation and government documents, audio/visual material and service user knowledge. It claims that:

'It is the UK's most extensive free database of social care information. With everything from research briefings to reports, government documents, journal articles and websites, and you find it all with the click of a button. Updated daily by SCIE's experienced information managers, Social Care Online offers unrivalled free access and ease of use.'

Social Services Abstracts

Social Services Abstracts is a database that covers social work, human services and related areas, including social welfare, social policy, and community development. It provides abstracts from journals and dissertations, and citations to book reviews, from 1980 and is updated monthly.

References

BBC (2005) http://news.bbc.co.uk/1/hi/england/4692373.stm

Schön, D. (1983) *The Reflective Practitioner. How professionals think in action*, London, Temple Smith

Webb, S. (2006) *Social Work in a Risk Society: Social and Political Perspectives*, Basingstoke, Palgrave

Index

This index is in word by word order. Page numbers in italics indicate figures and diagrams. See also glossary sections at the end of chapters for terms.